WESTMAR COLLEGE LIBRARY

W9-BQZ-164

# An Introduction to Mathematical Models in the Social and Life Sciences

MICHAEL OLINICK
Middlebury College

**ADDISON-WESLEY PUBLISHING COMPANY**

Reading, Massachusetts
Menlo Park, California
London • Amsterdam • Don Mills, Ontario • Sydney

H
61
.O48

*To My Parents*
Frank and Freeda Olinick

Copyright © 1978 by Addison-Wesley Publishing
Company, Inc. Philippines copyright 1978 by Addison-Wesley Publishing Company, Inc.

All rights reserved. No part of this publication may
be reproduced, stored in a retrieval system, or trans-
mitted, in any form or by any means, electronic,
mechanical, photocopying, recording, or otherwise,
without the prior written permission of the publisher.
Printed in the United States of America. Published
simultaneously in Canada. Library of Congress Catalog Card No. 77-77758.

ISBN 0-201-05448-5
ABCDEFGHIJ-MA-798        96337

The aim of this book is to encourage the teaching of mathematical model building relatively early in the undergraduate program. The text introduces the student to a number of important mathematical topics and to a variety of models in the social and life sciences.

# Preface

Particular problems in political science, ecology, psychology, sociology, economics, anthropology, epidemiology, business management, and hospital planning provide the motivation for the development of tools and techniques employed throughout applied mathematics: differential equations, axiomatics, probability theory, matrix algebra, simulation, and linear programming.

I selected models primarily from the behavioral sciences for a number of reasons:

1. They show the rich variety of disciplines to which mathematics is making important contributions;

2. Because such models require less technical background knowledge than classical models in physics, chemistry, and engineering, students can examine in depth many different applications in a one-semester course;

3. Students feel more familiar with social phenomena than with physical ones and thus are more eager to challenge the assumptions of models and to develop alternative ones on their own;

4. These models provide a unique opportunity for a student with a minimal background in calculus to learn about some mathematical developments of the twentieth century.

## STRUCTURE OF THE BOOK

The first chapter introduces the idea of a mathematical model by reexamining a familiar physical example: what happens when an object falls toward the earth. There is a discussion of the classification of models into deterministic, probabilistic, and axiomatic categories.

Chapters 2 through 5 concentrate on deterministic models. "Stable and Unstable Arms Races" (Chapter 2) presents L. F. Richardson's theories about the outbreak of war. The model is a system of two linear differential equations with constant coefficients. The mathematical analysis is kept to an elementary level; it exploits the idea that a derivative gives a good approximation to the behavior of a function near a point of tangency. I have presented this material several times to students during their first calculus course.

As in subsequent units, Chapter 2 begins with a verbal description of a real-world problem and then proceeds to show how a mathematical model can be built that reflects the important assumptions. A good portion of each chapter is devoted to a mathematical analysis of the model, in which new mathematical tools are developed. After the analysis, we proceed to discuss how the model can be tested against real-world data and indicate how it can be refined and improved.

Chapters 3 and 4 on ecological models go more deeply into the use of differential equations as modeling tools. First, models of population growth for a single species are introduced. These use the standard types of first-order differential equations. In Chapter 4, nonlinear systems of differential equations provide the language for examining simple models of the fluctuations of populations of interacting species. These two chapters, together with Chapter 13 on epidemics, are the only ones in the text which demand technical mastery of a year's study of calculus. The background material on differential equations and functions of two variables is presented in appendices.

Chapter 5 presents linear programming as a model for solving many important planning and production problems. Topics include convexity, polygonal convex sets in the plane, the simplex method, and an introduction to duality. To permit flexibility in using the text, the extensive use of linear algebra in presenting the simplex algorithm is omitted. We restrict ourselves to stating some of the results in matrix notation.

Chapters 6 through 8 focus on axiomatic models. In the sixth chapter, "Social Choice and Voting Procedures," we discuss some of the injustices associated with commonly used voting mechanisms. The problem of interest becomes: "Can one construct a voting procedure which avoids these shortcomings?" We state and prove Arrow's Theorem that a seemingly plausible list of properties such a mechanism should satisfy turns out to be inconsistent. Chapters 7 and 8 present axiomatic treatments of some basic questions of contemporary measurement and utility theory. Beyond the usual demand for "mathematical maturity," there are no specific mathematical prerequisites for understanding these three chapters.

Chapters 9 through 13 develop an extensive treatment of probabilistic models. There is particular emphasis on Markov processes because of their widespread use as models in the mathematical social sciences. The treatment is self-contained; no prior knowledge of probability or linear algebra is assumed. It has been my experience that much of the material in Chapters 9 and 10 can be assigned for self-study by the students. Outlines of proofs for the main results about regular and absorbing Markov chains are presented. The results are easily understood and applied by students with three years of high-school mathematics. I would reserve discussion of the proofs for a class which had already completed two or more years of college mathematics.

Once the background in probability theory is presented, there are a number of recent applications: population growth models, paired-associate learning, sports competition, cultural stability, and the spread of epidemics. The stochastic version of a simple deterministic model of population growth discussed in Chapter 3 is presented along with a comparison of the results obtained by the two approaches. Chapter 13 on epidemics also compares and contrasts deterministic and probabilistic models of the same problem.

Chapter 14 concludes the text. Here computer simulation is introduced by examining the way in which a St. Louis hospital staff decided how many additional surgical and recovery rooms would be needed if it added a fixed number of new beds.

Five appendices provide background information on sets, matrices, systems of linear equations, functions of several variables, and differential equations.

A chart at the end of the preface shows the dependencies of each chapter on the earlier ones. There is more material in the text than can be covered in a one-semester course, so the chart will enable instructors to create a variety of different courses to emphasize their students' interests and mathematical preparation. To make a modeling course accessible to students at the earliest point in their undergraduate curriculum, experience in computer programming was not made a prerequisite for the book. I believe the text is sufficiently flexible in its structure, however, to permit an instructor to emphasize programming if he wishes.

## CONCLUDING REMARKS

In writing this book, I followed my belief that the student can learn more about building mathematical models by studying critically, and in some depth, a relatively few models than he can by learning, in isolation, a large assortment of techniques. All the models presented are simple ones, in the sense that researchers have constructed more sophisticated and more re-

Chart of Chapter Dependencies

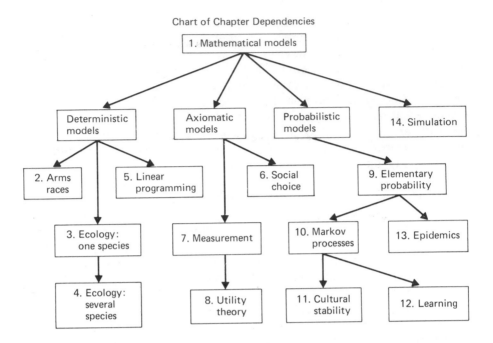

alistic ones to model the same phenomena. Thus, the reader will not find the latest developments in mathematical learning theory, for example, in this text, nor will he see a survey of the models commonly used by ecologists today in their study of interacting populations. The models which are analyzed here have been for the most part, however, significant in the development of a mathematical approach to one or more disciplines.

The text hopefully encourages the reader to go beyond the stage of examining the works of others and to begin to function as a model builder on his own. At the end of each chapter there are suggested projects that demand the creation of new models or involve extensions of old ones. There is also a list of relevant journals and a bibliography to aid further exploration.

The reader will also note that extensive space has been set aside for historical and biographical notes on the development of the mathematical models and the men who invented them. My hope is that these will dispel any lingering notions that mathematics is the creation of colorless automata. As in every other creative activity, mathematics and mathematical applications come from the minds of active individuals responding to the crucial social and cultural issues of their day.

*Middlebury, Vermont*                                                                 M.O.
*January 1978*

I am very pleased to express my appreciation and gratitude to the many people who motivated the writing of this book and assisted in its production.

My interest in mathematical model building traces back to undergraduate years at the University of Michigan. There I was fortunate to be able to study mathematical psychology with Clyde Coombs and general systems with Kenneth Boulding. Another strong Ann Arbor influence was Anatol Rapoport whose book *Fights, Games and Debates* first led me to attempt a classroom presentation of Richardson's arms race model. Professor Rapoport carefully reviewed the entire manuscript of a first draft of this book. His many valuable comments, criticisms, and suggestions resulted in a number of important revisions.

Acknowledgments for many other helpful remarks are due to the individuals who reviewed part or all of the text. They include Kenneth J. Arrow (Harvard University), Gordon H. Bower and George B. Dantzig (Stanford University), Gerard Debreu (University of California, Berkeley), Hans Hoffmann (State University of New York, Binghamton), N. K. Kwak (St. Louis University), William F. Lucas (Cornell University), the late Oskar Morgenstern, Irwin W. Sandberg (Bell Laboratories), Homer H. Schmitz (Deaconess Hospital, St. Louis), and Harvey A. Smith (Oakland University).

I wish also to thank several reviewers who have suggested improvements in the book: James O. Friel (California State University, Fullerton), S. E. Goodman (University of Virginia), Jack Macki (University of Alberta), and Carl D. Meyer, Jr. (North Carolina State University).

Several colleagues have used various chapters in this book as texts in their

# Acknowledgments

courses. They are Grace Bates (Mount Holyoke College), John D. Emerson and James A. Krupp (Middlebury College), Sherwood D. Silliman (Cleveland State University), and Brian J. Winkel (Albion College). Their classroom testing has resulted in many substantial improvements and the correction of innumerable errors.

To the many Middlebury students who struggled with heaps of unbound and mimeographed drafts of these chapters I also owe a debt of gratitude. Their enthusiastic response to the material was a continuing stimulus to me to revise and improve my presentations.

I am very grateful to Jane Owen for her excellent work in cheerfully typing and retyping drafts of the text. My thanks also extend to Elizabeth L. Hacking, Stephen H. Quigley, and Ruth W. Page of the staff of Addison-Wesley Publishing Company for their constant cooperation and help.

A special note of acknowledgment is due my wife, Judy. In addition to her never faltering encouragement and moral support, she overcame a life-long abhorrence of mathematics long enough to read the galley proofs of the book carefully and suggest many improvements in style, language, and punctuation.

# Contents

# 1 Mathematical Models

The status of a science is commonly measured by the degree to which it makes use of mathematics.

S. S. Stevens

It is still an unending source of surprise for me to see how a few scribbles on a blackboard or on a sheet of paper could change the course of human affairs.

Stanislaw Ulam

1

## I. MATHEMATICAL SYSTEMS AND MODELS

### A. Mathematical Systems

Science studies the real world. In their role as scientists, human beings are interested in discovering the laws that govern observed phenomena. When the phenomena are better understood, then we may make valid predictions about future behavior. In a more active capacity, such understanding can lead to intelligent efforts to control the phenomena or at least to influence them.

In this book, we will examine how *mathematical systems* can be used as tools to help achieve some of these aims. Although you will see some examples from the physical sciences, most of our attention will be on problems of primary interest to social and life scientists.

A *mathematical system* consists of a collection of assertions from which consequences are derived by logical argument. The assertions are commonly called the *axioms* or *postulates* of the system. They always contain one or more primitive terms which are undefined and hence have no meaning inside the mathematical system.

A familiar mathematical system is that of plane geometry. Two of the primitive terms in this system are "point" and "line." As examples of axioms in this system, we have

**AXIOM 1   Given two distinct points, there is a unique line containing the points,**

and

**AXIOM 2   Given a line $L$ and a point $p$ not belonging to $L$, there is a unique line which contains $p$ and is parallel to $L$.**

Not all of the terms in an axiom are necessarily primitive. The concept "parallel" which occurs in the statement of Axiom 2 is not itself primitive, but may be defined using primitive terms. Two distinct lines are said to be *parallel* if there is no point which belongs to both of them. In a similar fashion, every axiom of plane geometry can be written in terms of the primitive concepts of the system.

To be *mathematically interesting*, it is necessary only that the set of axioms of the system be consistent and be "rich" enough to imply a number of non-trivial consequences. It has been known for hundreds of years that the standard axioms of plane geometry form a consistent collection. Nowhere in the large number of theorems that are implied by this set of axioms will you find two results that contradict each other.

The usual axioms of plane geometry may be modified without losing consistency. If Axiom 2 is replaced by

**AXIOM 2'   Given a line $L$ and a point $p$ not belonging to $L$, there is no line containing $p$ which is parallel to $L$,**

then the resulting system is still consistent. This remarkable result was the surprising conclusion of many attempts to show that Axiom 2 (known as

Euclid's Fifth Postulate) was itself a consequence of the other axioms of plane geometry.

We are not primarily going to focus on systems which are only mathematically interesting. Our concern is with *scientifically interesting* systems. The criteria to be met for this label are that the primitive terms should correspond to, or at least be idealizations of, objects that exist in the real world and that the axioms should reflect our experiences of how these objects relate to each other.

The mathematical system of plane geometry is also a scientifically interesting one. In fact, the system was evolved over a long period of time to put together in an organized and coherent fashion the observations that people had made about certain features of the world in which they lived.

One product of this mathematical system has been a collection of highly useful theorems about the measurement of the areas of many different regions of the plane. Applications of these results are too numerous and familiar to be mentioned here.

Quite often a system which was developed primarily, or solely, because of its mathematical interest has turned out also to be of fundamental scientific interest. The physical theory of relativity created by Albert Einstein (1879–1955) makes use of a geometry (called Riemannian geometry) in which Axiom 2' rather than Axiom 2 is true. (Further discussion of this point is contained in Chapter 14).

The axioms of a mathematical system will usually consist of statements about the existence or uniqueness of certain sets of elements, existence of various relations on these sets, properties of these relations, and so forth. Logical argument, or *deduction*, is applied to the mathematical system to obtain a set of mathematical conclusions. These conclusions are theorems about the primitive terms which were not immediately evident from the statements of the axioms.

## B.  Mathematical Models

When a mathematical system is constructed in an attempt to study some phenomenon or situation in the real world, it is usually called a *mathematical model*. There are many ways to model parts of the real world, and mathematics is only one of them. A road map of Los Angeles is an example of another kind of model. The map is a model of the city. If a motorist understands the symbols that are used in the map, then much information about the city becomes available in a package small enough to carry around in one's pocket. The motorist can use the map, for example, to plan a route from the La Brea tar pits to the corner of Westholme and Wilshire Boulevards.

The road map is one representation of many important features of the city. But it omits many other features that may be crucial. Most road maps do not contain sufficient information to tell a motorist what is the speediest route to take between two points in the city during the morning rush hour, for example.

The map is also almost useless to a door-to-door encyclopedia salesperson who wishes to find neighborhoods whose social and economic characteristics indicate good selling opportunities. For this purpose, a different kind of model of the city is needed. (For other kinds of models, see the discussion in Chapter 14.)

A mathematical model of a complex phenomenon or situation has many of the advantages and limitations of other types of models. Some factors in the situation will be omitted while others are stressed. In constructing a mathematical system, the modeler must keep in mind the type of information he wishes to obtain from it.

The role that mathematical models play in science is illustrated by the relatively simple schematic diagram of Fig. 1.1.

The scientist begins with some observations about the real world. He wishes to make some conclusions or predictions about the situation he has observed. One way to proceed, (E), is to conduct some experiments and record the results. The model builder follows a different path. First, he abstracts, or translates, some of the essential features of the real world into a mathematical system. Then by logical argument, (L), he derives some mathematical conclusions. These conclusions are then interpreted, (I), as predictions about the real world.

To be useful, the mathematical system should predict conclusions about the world that are actually observed when appropriate experiments are carried out. If the predictions from the model bear little resemblance to what actually occurs in the real world, then the model is not a good one. The modeler has not isolated the critical features of the situation being studied or the axioms misrepresent the relations among these features. On the other hand, if there is good agreement between what is observed and what the model predicts, then there is some reason to believe that the mathematical system does indeed capture correctly important aspects of the real-world situation.

What happens quite frequently is that some of the predictions of a mathematical model agree quite closely with observed events, while other predictions do not. In such a case, we might hope to modify the model so as to improve its accuracy. The incorrect predictions may suggest ways of rethinking the assumptions of the mathematical system. One hopes that the revised model

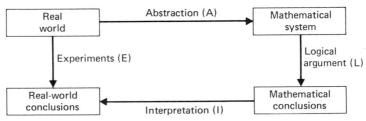

**Fig. 1.1**   Schematic diagram of the modeling process.

will not only preserve the correct predictions of the original one, but that it will also make further correct predictions. The incorrect inferences of the revised model will lead, in turn, to yet another version, more sophisticated than the earlier one. Thus, by stages, we develop a sequence of models each more accurate than the previous ones.

We shall return to the general discussion of mathematical models and their advantages and limitations later in this chapter. To clarify some of the points that have already been made, it is useful to examine now a familiar mathematical model in some detail.

## II. AN EXAMPLE: MODELING FREE FALL

### A. Formulation of the Model

Consider the fable that tells of Isaac Newton (1642–1727) sitting beneath the branches of an apple tree directly in the path of a descending apple. Whether or not Newton was ever actually struck by a plummeting piece of fruit, we do know that he was interested in the analysis of the motion of falling bodies. The real-world situation we wish to model here is described simply: an object, initially at some distance from the surface of the earth, is released; some time later, it strikes the earth.

This qualitative phenomenon is observed every day. If we are careful, we can measure the height of the object above the ground when it is released and we can also record the number of seconds that elapse before it strikes the ground. We wish to find a quantitative relationship between these observed values.

Our mathematical analysis of this situation begins by isolating the important concepts. Since we can measure distance and time, it is reasonable to develop a model in terms of these quantities. We will let $t$ represent time measured in seconds and $y$ represent distance above the ground, measured in feet. As time varies, so does this distance. Thus $y$ is some function, $y = y(t)$, whose exact nature is as yet not known. We may start our stopwatch at $t = 0$ when the object is at distance $y_0$ feet above the ground.

Newton also realized that the mass $m$ of the object was an important consideration in such a problem. One of the general laws of motion that Newton had formulated was that the product of the mass and acceleration of a moving body is equal to the sum of the forces acting on it.

For our first model, we will assume that there is only one force acting on the object, the gravitational attraction of the earth. Then Newton's law of motion has the familiar form

$$F = ma, \tag{1}$$

where $a$ is the acceleration of the body and $F$ is the gravitational force.

Recall from elementary calculus that acceleration is the second derivative with respect to time of the position function $y(t)$, so that $ma = my''$. We also assume that the gravitational attraction is proportional to the mass of the object with proportionality constant $g = -32$ ft/sec/sec. Substituting these assumptions into Eq. (1) produces

$$mg = my'' \tag{2}$$

or

$$y'' = -32. \tag{3}$$

## B. Analysis of the Model

Equation (3) is our mathematical model for a falling object. It is a simple second-order differential equation. We apply the tools of mathematical analysis (logical argument) to derive some mathematical conclusions. In this case, this means we should solve the differential equation. Integrate each side of Eq. (3) with respect to the variable $t$ twice to obtain first

$$y' = -32t + C \tag{4}$$

and then

$$y = -16t^2 + Ct + D \tag{5}$$

where $C$ and $D$ are constants of integration. If we set $t = 0$ in (4), we find that $C$ is equal to the value $y'(0)$, which we will denote by $v_0$. Setting $t = 0$ in Eq. (5) gives a value of $D$ equal to $y(0) = y_0$. Thus we have

$$y' = -32t + v_0, \tag{6}$$

$$y = -16t^2 + v_0 t + y_0. \tag{7}$$

## C. Interpretation of the Model

We may now interpret these mathematical conclusions as statements about the falling object. Since the derivative of the position function gives velocity, Eq. (6) is a prediction of the velocity of the object at every instant, if $v_0$ is its initial velocity. In particular, if the object is simply released from a rest position, then $v_0 = 0$ and

$$y' = -32t, \tag{8}$$

while

$$y = -16t^2 + y_0. \tag{9}$$

Equation (9) can be used to answer our original question about the relation between the initial height of the object and the time it takes to reach the ground. When the object strikes the earth, we have $y = 0$. Substituting this into Eq. (9) gives the corresponding elapsed time, $t_F$, for the fall:

$$0 = -16t_F^2 + y_0, \tag{10}$$

or

$$t_F = \frac{\sqrt{y_0}}{4}. \tag{11}$$

Our analysis thus gives a prediction for how long an object takes to fall a distance $y_0$ feet to the ground if it is released from rest. The analysis also yields a number of other predictions:

1. The velocity and position of the object at any time are independent of the object's mass. This follows because $m$ is missing from Eqs. (3)–(11).

2. Using Eqs. (6) and (7), the velocity and position can be predicted for situations in which the object is given any initial velocity. If $v_0$ is positive, then the model can be used to discuss what happens when the object is thrown upward, away from the earth, at the start of its motion.

3. If the object is released ($v_0 = 0$) at height $y_0$, then the velocity of the object when it strikes the earth is $y'(t_F) = -32 t_F = -32(\sqrt{y_0/4}) = -8\sqrt{y_0}$ ft/sec.

## D. Tests and Refinements of the Model

Let us concentrate, for a moment at least, on the predictions of Eq. (11). We can test the validity of our model by dropping objects from various heights, recording the time of fall, and comparing this number to the predicted value. We record some typical values in Table 1.1.

The first few values in the table seem reasonable and consistent with everyday experience, but can we say the same for the final entries? The last entry in Table 1.1 indicates that the predictions of a model can sometimes be shown incorrect without actually performing any physical or social experiments. The number 240,000 represents the approximate distance (in miles) between the earth and the moon. According to the model, an object leaving the surface of the moon should fall to the earth in about two and one-half hours. In particular, if whoever is holding the moon in place should suddenly let go, the moon — asserts this model— would crash into the earth about 150 minutes later. Since no one is really holding on to the moon, why hasn't it fallen?

This "thought experiment" indicates that the model cannot be accurate for all values of $y_0$. Where does the model go astray? We know, as did Newton, that, in the first place, the force of the earth's gravitational attraction on an object varies with the distance between the object and the *center* of the earth. The farther away the object is, the smaller is the attraction. It is only when the object's distance from the surface of the earth is small in comparison to the earth's radius (about 4,000 miles) that it is reasonable to treat the gravitational

**Table 1.1**

| Initial height ($y_0$) | Predicted time of fall ($t_F = \sqrt{y_0/4}$) |
|:---:|:---:|
| 16 ft | 1 sec |
| 100 ft | 2.5 sec |
| 625 ft | 6.25 sec |
| 25,600 ft | 40 sec |
| 240,000 mi | $2\frac{1}{2}$ hr |

force as constant. To refine the model, the first correction is to replace the simple constant $g$ by an appropriate decreasing function of $y$.

This refined model would still predict that the moon will eventually crash into the earth, although it will take somewhat longer than 2 or 3 hours. The fact that the moon has not done this indicates yet another difficulty with our model. The moon, or any object moving in three-dimensional space, has components of motion in three mutually perpendicular directions. The model considers only motion in one direction. Even though the force acts along that line of direction, it turns out that the object itself need not move exactly along that line.

For a simplified example, consider motion in the plane. Construct a normal Cartesian coordinate system with $x$- and $y$-axes and origin $O$. The position of an object at any time $t$ is given by a pair of numbers $(x(t), y(t))$ representing the coordinates of its location as functions of time. Imagine a circular disk of radius $R$ with center at $(0, -R)$ and suppose that the moving object under consideration is at the point $(0, 16)$ at time $t = 0$; see Fig. 1.2. Assume that the only force acting on the object is a constant force of $-32$ in the vertical direction.

If the vertical component of velocity at time $t = 0$ is zero, then the $y$-coordinate is given, according to Eq. (9), by

$$y(t) = -16t^2 + 16. \tag{12}$$

If the horizontal component of velocity at time 0 is $c$ ft/sec, then the $x$-coordinate of motion is

$$x(t) = ct, \tag{13}$$

since there is no force acting in a horizontal direction.

Should the value of $c$ be zero, then the object will slide directly down the $y$-axis and will hit the disk at the origin at time $t = 1$. If $c$ is nonzero, then the

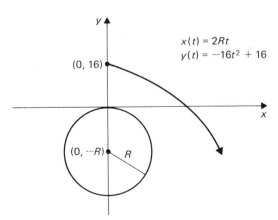

**Fig. 1.2**   Motion in the plane. Whether the object hits or misses the disk depends on its initial position and velocity.

motion is more complicated. From Eq. (13), we have $t = x/c$ so that Eq. (12) may be rewritten as

$$y = \frac{-16x^2}{c^2} + 16. \tag{14}$$

Equation (14) indicates that the path of motion in the $(x,y)$-plane will be a parabola.

In particular, if $c$ should be equal to $2R$, then the object will never hit the disk! For during the first second of motion, $0 < t < 1$, the object is moving in the first quadrant, since both $x$- and $y$-coordinates are positive. At time $t = 1$, the object is at the point $(2R, 0)$. For $t > 1$, the $y$-coordinate is negative, while the $x$-coordinate is larger than $2R$. Since no point on the disk has an $x$-coordinate greater than $R$, the parabola will not intersect the disk.

As we have just seen, the initial horizontal speed of the moving object must be considered before determining whether or not the object will hit the disk. The initial position of the object also must be examined. For if $c = 2R$, but the object is at $(0, 4 - R)$ at time 0, it may hit the disk. For example, when $t = \frac{1}{2}$, we would have $x = 2R(\frac{1}{2}) = R$, while $y = -16(\frac{1}{2})^2 + (4 - R) = -R$. The point $(R, -R)$ lies both on the disk and on the parabolic path of the object.

A similar but more complicated analysis is possible for an object moving in three-dimensional space under the influence of the earth's gravitational attraction. Here the force is directed along a line between the object and the center of the earth. Depending on the object's initial distance from the earth and the various components of its initial velocity, it will either crash into the earth or orbit about it in an elliptical path. [See Chapter 3 of Simmons, 1972, for a detailed derivation.]*

This more complex mathematical model may be forced upon us if we are planning a trip to the moon or if we must solve some other serious astronomical problem. The simple model of Eq. (3) breaks down for objects relatively far from the earth and for objects moving with great speed. If our concern is for apples falling from trees, or for other situations in which a relatively small object begins its fall from rest from a position fairly close to the surface of the earth, is the simple model still good?

Equation (11) was the main prediction of the simple model. We have already indicated how the validity of this equation can be tested by dropping objects from various heights and timing the duration of their fall. There is an even simpler experiment to test the prediction that the elapsed time $t_F$ is independent of mass: simultaneously release two objects of moderate but different masses from the same height and observe whether or not they reach the ground together.

This is the type of experiment allegedly conducted by Galileo (1564–1642) who was the first person to derive the equations leading to Eq. (11). Legend has it that Galileo dropped balls of different weights from the top of the Tower

---

\*     References in brackets are to be found at the end of the chapter.

of Pisa and timed their descent. There appears to be as much truth in this tale as in the story of Newton and the apple (it has been conjectured that Newton made up this tale in response to repeated inquiries from those seeking a simple explanation for his deep discoveries). Galileo did conduct many experiments with objects rolling down inclined planes; interesting new discoveries about his experimental and theoretical work have recently been made [see Drake, 1973 and 1975].

In any case, the experiment we have described works out fairly well in practice and is a standard laboratory assignment in many introductory physics courses. The experiment does not always produce the desired results, however. Once, I dropped a crumpled sheet of paper out the window of my ninth-floor office at the same time my two-year-old son released a sheet of paper that had been folded into the shape of a glider. The two sheets of paper came from the same pad, so their masses were essentially the same. According to our model, they certainly should have reached the ground at about the same time. My crumpled wad plummeted straight to the ground in a matter of seconds while the glider actually rose several feet before gradually floating to the earth a few minutes later. Why has our model failed us again?

The answer is easy. We have neglected in the model some important forces that act on our falling object: air resistance and wind currents. Recall that Newton's law really asserts that the *sum* of the forces acting on an object equals the product of mass and acceleration:

$$\sum_i F_i = ma. \tag{15}$$

To refine our model to make it more realistic, we have to account for these other forces in our differential equations. There are some relatively easy ways to include air resistance in this model (see Exercise 26), but the representation of wind currents can be a very tricky mathematical problem.

The moral of this story is that if you want a model which gives realistic predictions over a broad range of relevant variables (in this case, distance, mass, density, initial velocity, and so on), you must be willing to deal with complex mathematical systems. If you seek a simple and elegant model, you must be careful to describe its somewhat limited applicability. Thus, if Eq. (3) is to be an accurate model of a falling object, we must restrict ourselves to situations in which the object is of moderate mass, is dropped relatively close to the earth's surface, and falls through a vacuum. If we design an experiment by building a tube and then pumping out the air before dropping the object inside it, the observed data will be quite close to those predicted by Eq. (11).

## III. CLASSIFICATION OF MATHEMATICAL MODELS

The simple mathematical model of a falling object given by the equation $y'' = -32$ and the possible refinements of it that have been discussed in the preceding sections are examples of what are called *deterministic models*. The assumption behind a deterministic model is that the entire future behavior of a system is exactly and explicitly determined by the present status of the system and the forces acting on it. In other words, if we know everything about the system at a particular moment (the state of each of its component variables and the forces impinging on them), then we can predict its behavior at every future instant. This was the belief that led to the very fruitful development of the physical sciences. Much of our understanding of the behavior of physical systems comes from deterministic models employing the tools of calculus. Powerful analytic techniques were developed to analyze more and more complicated models. The availability of these techniques and the predictive successes of these models in the physical sciences motivated many thinkers to employ similar models in the study of social and biological systems. Chapters 2–4 of this text explore some of these deterministic models in detail.

There are several important objections to the use of such deterministic models in the social and life sciences. In the first place, some philosophers have argued that deterministic models of social systems must necessarily assume that human beings have no free will; few people are willing to accept this view of humans.

A second objection arises from the discovery of Werner Heisenberg (1901–1976) in the early part of this century that purely deterministic models are insufficient even to study physical processes. Heisenberg showed that it is impossible, even in theory, to know the exact state of a physical system: the act of observation itself changes the system. We can conclude from deterministic models only the *average* behavior of a group of atoms, but we cannot assert with certainty anything about the future course of an individual atom. This observation has fundamentally affected the physical sciences (see the discussion at the beginning of Chapter 9) and led to the introduction of *probabilistic models.*

Probabilistic models are also predictive models. The basic assumption of such models is that the system under investigation can occupy one of several different possible states at each moment, with different probabilities. If we know the probability distribution governing the system at the present moment and the forces acting upon the system, then we can predict the probability distribution at subsequent times. Thus, a probabilistic model of an object falling to the surface of the earth will predict for each time $t_0$ after the object is released the probability, or likelihood, that the object has reached the ground by time $t_0$. A substantial part of this text, centered around Chapters 9–12, discusses probabilistic models.

Since deterministic models often provide good approximate predictions and since they usually employ the familiar tools of calculus and differential equations, they are still widely used in the physical as well as social and life sciences. In Chapter 9 and again in Chapters 11 and 13, you will see the differences between a deterministic and a probabilistic model of the same situation.

A third objection to the calculus-oriented deterministic model centers on the use of the calculus. Since calculus was largely invented to help solve physical problems, there is no intrinsic reason why it should be the appropriate tool for the formulation and investigation of all social and biological systems, even if a deterministic approach is assumed. Indeed, new mathematical tools such as the theory of games, linear programming, and graph theory have been forged in recent decades to analyze such systems. Linear programming is the subject of Chapter 5.

The deterministic and probabilistic approaches we have been discussing share the property of being *predictive* in nature; they both aim at saying something about the future (or perhaps the past) of a system whose present state is fairly well described. These can be contrasted with models that are primarily *descriptive* in nature. Descriptive, or *axiomatic models*, as they are sometimes called, are highlighted in this text in Chapters 6, 7, and 8.

The model in Chapter 6 is concerned with the possible existence of a voting mechanism that is constrained to satisfy certain "fairness" restrictions. Chapters 7 and 8 also present descriptive models; these describe different types of measurement and when each can be used.

The development of such axiomatic models hopefully will broaden your view of mathematics. Many people still believe that "mathematics is the study of numerical and geometrical concepts." Such definitions were common in texts and dictionaries even in recent years. Mathematicians today have a much wider view of their discipline. As John Kemeny and J. Laurie Snell [1962] phrase it,

> Mathematics is best viewed as the study of abstract relations in the broadest sense of that word. From this point of view it is not surprising that mathematics is applicable to any well-defined field. Whatever the nature of the phenomena studied in a given social science, their various components do bear certain relations to each other, and once one succeeds in formulating these abstractly and precisely, one is in a position to apply the full machinery of mathematical analysis.

## IV. USES AND LIMITATIONS OF MATHEMATICAL MODELS

The continuing development of a useful co-ordinated science of social, biological, and physical behavior is an important challenge for us. In what ways can we expect mathematics to help?

If we begin to analyze even a simple situation involving interpersonal relations, for example, the first thing we observe is how complex the situation really is and just how many different variables are present. It is difficult to cope with so many factors adequately in an intuitive and discursive way. As long as our formulation remains vague and imprecise, our observations are likely to be muddled, unclear, and not well understood by others.

Casting our thoughts into a mathematical model will have immediate advantages. Mathematics is a precise and unambiguous language. In order to use it, we must first clarify to ourselves just what are the underlying assumptions we are making. The mathematical model forces us to organize our thoughts in a more systematic way and this should contribute to the clarity of our thinking.

Once the model has been formulated, it is possible to use mathematical tools to derive new observations or conclusions from the model that may have escaped us if we proceeded with a more intuitive approach. These conclusions will not only shed light on the assumptions we have originally made about the system under study, but they will also suggest further experiments and observations which will lead to more complete knowledge of the system.

Quite often, the modeler discovers that a mathematical formulation of a problem turns out to be the same as someone else's formulation of what appears to be a totally different situation. The logistic equation—presented in detail in Chapter 3—has been used, for example, to model the growth of populations, the spread of infectious diseases, rates of chemical reactions, and consumer demands for commercial goods. Thus, the use of mathematical models can reveal unsuspected relations among superficially disparate systems which have the same basic underlying structure.

As we have seen in the discussion of falling objects, a simple mathematical model cannot precisely mimic the behavior of a real-world phenomenon. Some aspects of the real world are highlighted and others are neglected or perhaps ignored. Mathematics is but one tool to be used in gaining an understanding of the real world and it must be supplemented by other approaches.

As you study the models presented in this text, you may wish to consult Fig. 1.1 of this chapter from time to time. Our emphasis will be on the steps of abstraction, logical argument, and interpretation. It has often been written that it is difficult, perhaps impossible, to write down rules for the abstraction process. Many model builders believe that it is an art, rather than a science, and that it is best learned through the careful study of selected examples and repeated practice on the part of the apprentice in constructing models. The text material, exercises, and projects in this book have been designed to provide you with such practice.

The step we have labeled "logical argument" is the one that is most familiar to mathematics teachers and their students, while the process of "interpretation" follows fairly easily from the original formulation of the model.

The final critical step in mathematical modeling is a comparison with the interpreted results of the model with the observations obtained from direct interaction with the real world. I have tried to show in this text a number of places where an originally simple model is refined in the light of these comparisons. The measurement of how closely the model fits the real world is, in general, a complicated problem which involves the full use of statistical techniques. We do not have space in this book to delve deeply into this field.

---

**EXERCISES**

---

## I. MATHEMATICAL SYSTEMS AND MODELS

1. Is "angle" a primitive term in geometry? What about "belonging to"? What are the other primitive terms?

2. To what extent are the axioms of geometry "self-evident truths" rather than expressions of cumulative experience?

3. A *realization* of a mathematical system is a physical representation of the set of axioms in the sense that real-world quantities can be found to take the place of the primitive terms in such a way that the statements of the axioms can be seen to be true relations among the real-world quantities. Is there such a real-world representation of the axioms of plane geometry? Show that a mathematical system which has a realization must have a consistent set of axioms.

4. A *projective plane P* is a mathematical system consisting of primitive terms called "points" and "lines" and a relation of "containment" satisfying the three axioms:

    A) Any two distinct points are contained in a unique line;

    B) Any two distinct lines contain a unique point;

    C) There are four points such that no three are contained in the same line.

a) Show that there are four lines in $P$, no three of which contain the same point.

b) Show that every line in $P$ contains at least two points.

c) Show that every line in $P$ contains at least three points.

5. Find a realization of the projective plane with exactly 7 points. Is there a realization with fewer points?

6. Find a realization of the projective plane with an infinite number of points. Is the projective plane a mathematically interesting system?

7. Consider the mathematical system $S$ consisting of primitive terms "point" and "line" and a relation of "containment" satisfying these four axioms:

    A) Each line contains a nonempty collection of points;

    B) Any two distinct lines contain a point;

    C) Each point is contained in exactly two lines;

    D) There are precisely four distinct lines.

a) Find a realization of $S$.

b) Prove that each line in $S$ contains precisely three points.

c) Show that there are precisely six distinct points in $S$.

d) Is this a mathematically interesting system?

8. A set of axioms is *independent* if no axiom in the set can be derived logically from the others.

a) Show that axiom $A_1$ is independent of Axioms $A_2, A_3, \ldots, A_n$ if the system consisting of $A_2, \ldots, A_n$ has a realization in which $A_1$ is false.

b) Use (a) to formulate a criterion for the independence of a set of axioms.

9. In what sense is a "model airplane" a model of an airplane?

10. How do the literary concepts of "simile" and "metaphor" function as models?

11. List some other types of models you have encountered.

## II. AN EXAMPLE: MODELING FREE FALL

12. Suppose the model of free fall is $y'' = g$ where $g$ is an unknown constant.

a) Analyze mathematically this model. What is the analogue of Eq. (11)?

b) Describe an experiment which would determine the value of $g$.

13. Assuming that $v_0$ is nonzero, use Eq. (7) to find $t_F$. Comment on the fact that you obtain two different values for $t_F$. Show that one of these can be discarded if $v_0$ is negative. What happens if $v_0$ is positive?

14. If $v_0$ is nonzero, what is the velocity of the object when it hits the ground?

15. Suppose a ball is thrown upward from a height of 3 feet with an initial velocity of 8 ft/sec. Use the model of Eq. (3) to analyze its motion. In particular, find

a) the maximum height the ball reaches;

b) the time at which the ball is again 3 feet from the ground;

c) the number of seconds the ball is in the air;

d) the speed with which the ball strikes the ground; and

e) the maximum speed the ball ever achieves.

16. A man falls off the top of a building 1024 ft high. Three seconds later, Wonder Woman (who can fly) arrives at the point from which the man fell. She dives down in an effort to save him. If she is capable of an initial velocity of 50 ft/sec, will she reach him before he hits the ground?

17. A more correct version of Newton's law than (1) is that force is equal to the derivative, with respect to time, of mass times velocity.

a) Show that if the mass is constant, then this law reduces to (1).

b) Analyze the motion of a falling bucket of sand with a hole in it. The bucket originally weighs 10 pounds but loses sand at a constant rate of $\frac{1}{2}$ pound each second.

Problems 18–21 concern the mathematical model developed in connection with Fig. 1.2.

18. For what range of values of $c$ will an object initially at $(0, 16)$ eventually strike the disk?

19. If $c = 2R$, for what values of $y_0$ will an object initially at $(0, y_0)$ eventually strike the disk?

20. A motorcycle leaves the edge of a tall cliff with a velocity of 60 mph in a horizontal direction. Develop a mathematical model for the subsequent motion.

21. An airplane releases a nuclear bomb from a height of 40,000 feet. If the plane has a top speed of 600 mph, how far from the center of impact can the plane be when the bomb hits the ground? Can the plane's crew survive the shock of the bomb's explosion? What information do you need to answer these questions?

22. Suppose the gravitational attraction of the earth on an object varies inversely with the square of the distance between the object and the center of the earth.

  a) Show that an object $M$ miles from the surface of the earth experiences an acceleration of $a = 32(4000)^2/(M - 4000)^2$ ft/sec/sec.

  b) Develop and analyze the model for free fall if acceleration is given as in part (a).

  c) According to the model of (b), how long should it take the moon to fall to the earth?

  d) Is the result of (c) relevant to an astronaut's trip home from a lunar exploration?

23. Using the inverse square law of Exercise 22, analyze the motion of a rocket fired from the earth's surface with a vertical velocity of $v_0$ ft/sec. Compute the maximum height that the rocket can reach. How large must $v_0$ be so that this height is greater than the distance from the earth to the moon? (Neglect the gravitational attraction of the moon on the rocket.)

24. Can a mathematical model of free fall be developed using position ($y$) and velocity ($v$) as the basic variables? Is it reasonable to adopt such an approach?

25. The main force producing the acceleration of an object in a vacuum is the force of gravity which causes the object to fall toward the earth. Archimedes (287–212 B.C.) discovered a force in the opposite direction: an object immersed in a medium (such as air or water or a gas) is buoyed up by a force equal to the weight of the medium displaced by the object.

  a) If $m$ is the mass of the object and $M$ is the mass of the medium displaced, show that the net force of gravity on the object is $32(m - M)$.

  b) Use the result of (a) to explain why a stone does not float in a lake of water, but a canoe does.

  c) Why does a balloon filled with helium rise in the air?

  d) Can buoyancy be ignored for a stone falling through the air? A snowflake?

26. From experimental observations, scientists have determined that air resistance of an object varies with the velocity of the object. Suppose that air resistance varies in direct proportion to velocity and is directed in the direction opposite to that of the velocity vector. Develop a mathematical model for the motion of an object hurled downward toward the earth from a height of $y_0$ feet through the atmosphere with an initial velocity of $v_0$ ft/sec. Take into account the forces of gravity and air resistance. Show that the motion may be modeled by the differential equation $dv/dt = 32 - kv$ where $k$ is some constant.

27. Without solving the differential equation of Exercise 26, show that the velocity of a falling object subject to air resistance will "eventually" reach $32/k$ ft/sec regardless of the initial velocity $v_0$.

28. Develop a model for a freely falling object if the air resistance is proportional to the square of the velocity.

### III. CLASSIFICATION OF MODELS

29. A mathematical model's predictions need not be forecasts of *future* events. They may be about phenomena that have occurred but for which observations have either not yet been made or are unknown to the modeler. Find examples of such models. Consider

instances in which it may not be possible to construct experiments; e.g., a mathematical model for the frequency and intensity of political revolutions.

30. What kind of mathematical model is the usual set of axioms of plane geometry? What is being modeled?

## IV. USES AND LIMITATIONS OF MATHEMATICAL MODELS

31. In what ways would you guess that high-speed electronic computers have affected the formulation of mathematical models of complicated phenomena? What benefits does the ability to do thousands of numerical calculations quickly confer? Are there any drawbacks?

---

## REFERENCES

Drake, Stillman, "Galileo's discovery of the Law of Free Fall." *Scientific American* **228**, Number 5 (May 1973), 84–92.

Drake, Stillman, "The role of music in Galileo's experiments." *Scientific American* **232**, Number 6 (June, 1975), 98–104.

Kemeny, John G., and J. Laurie Snell, "On the methodology of mathematical models," in *Mathematical Models in the Social Sciences* (Boston: Ginn, 1962).

Kline, Morris, *Mathematics and the Physical World* (New York: Crowell, 1959).

Maki, Daniel P., and Maynard Thompson, Chapter 1 of *Mathematical Models and Applications* (Englewood Cliffs, N.J.: Prentice-Hall, 1973).

Simmons, George F., *Differential Equations with Applications and Historical Notes* (New York: McGraw-Hill, 1972).

# 2
# Stable and Unstable Arms Races

There is scarce truth enough alive to make societies secure, but security enough to make fellowships accurs'd. Much upon this riddle runs the wisdom of the world. This news is old enough, yet it is every day's news.

William Shakespeare, *Measure for Measure*

## I. THE REAL-WORLD SETTING

Under my term of leadership . . . I am certain we will remain strong.  A strong defense is the surest way to peace.  Strength makes detente attainable.  Weakness invites war, as my generation knows from four bitter experiences.  Just as America's will for peace is second to none, so will America's strength be second to none.  We cannot rely on the forbearance of others to protect this nation.  The power and diversity of the armed forces . . . are essential to our security.

> President Gerald R. Ford
> Address to Congress
> August, 12, 1974

We must maintain a military force that is capable of deterring any threat to this nation's security, whatever the mode of aggression . . . I wish—with all of my heart—that the expenditures that are necessary to build and to protect our power could all be devoted to the programs of peace.  But until world conditions permit, and until peace is assured, America's might—and America's bravest sons who wear our Nation's uniform—must continue to stand guard for all of us.

> President Lyndon B. Johnson
> State of the Union Message
> January 17, 1968

These quotations, from two recent American Presidents of different political parties, exemplify the attitudes underlying the models to be studied in this chapter.

Imagine a nation, called Blue, whose people believe themselves desirous of a peaceful world.  The leaders of this country share the people's fervent desire to achieve peace and avoid war.  This is, of course, the public position of the vast majority of the world's governments; we assume that it is a sincerely held one.

The president of Blue and the other leaders of the government are not pacifists, however.  They will not go out of their way to launch aggression, but they will not sit idly by if their country is attacked.  The citizens of Blue share this attitude.  They believe in self-defense and will fight to protect their nation and way of life.  For this reason, they must be prepared to fight if necessity demands it.

The people of Blue feel that the maintenance of a large army and the stockpiling and improvement of weapons systems are purely defensive gestures.  They have peaceful intentions and believe that if every nation were similarly solely concerned with self-defense, there would be no occasion for war.  Aggressive acts are the cause of war; self-defense is not an aggressive act.

There is another large nation in this world, called Red.  The people and leaders of Red share these same ideals, intentions, and ethical beliefs.  They do not have hostile designs against anyone, but they are willing to fight to protect their homeland.  The actions of the government of Blue to build and maintain armaments do not go unnoticed by the people of Red.  Although the leaders of Blue continually proclaim peaceful intent, the weapons they have could be used to attack and destroy Red.  The people of Red would consider their government derelict in its duty if it did not build up its armed forces for a secure defense. And so, the leaders of Red act accordingly.

The ensuing increase in arms expenditures by Red is noted by Blue.  We know enough about the sensibilities of the people of Blue to determine that these increases will be seen as threatening to Blue's security and they will cry out for strengthening Blue's defensive forces.

In these past few paragraphs, we have sketched a highly simplified outline of an all-too-familiar international political problem.  We wish to analyze the consequences of this situation to see what would happen if nations did behave in this manner.

The basic assumption is that of "mutual fear."  The more that one nation arms, the more the other nation is spurred to arm.  The more arms Blue accumulates, the more incentive is provided for Red to build up arms, and the more arms Red has, the more Blue is stimulated to arm.  If the incentives to arm derive entirely from mutual fear and if neither side had any arms to start with, then an arms race would not start.  But the slightest move on the part of one nation to build an army would initiate the whole vicious spiraling arms race.

This "mutual fear" model would predict that the armaments of both nations would continue to increase indefinitely as time went on.  This cannot actually happen in the real world.  No country has infinite resources.  There is a limit to the amount of arms any nation can accumulate.  When armament expenditures begin to absorb too large a portion of a nation's budget, there are protests within the country against raising the burden of arms costs still higher.  Perhaps these limits force a leveling off of the arms race to some point of stability. Perhaps they do not.

The verbal analysis of this "mutual fear" situation is the sort we regularly see in newspaper and magazine articles and hear in the public speeches of our politicians.  The verbal analysis cannot be carried much further.  If we formulate a mathematical model of the situation, however, we can carry the analysis a good way and develop some consequences that may help us construct a more sophisticated theory of international politics.

In this chapter we will first present a very simple deterministic model of a "mutual fear" arms race.  Examination of the consequences of this model will lead to the development of a more complex model that reflects more of the real-world situation.  Mathematical analysis of this second model will yield new predictions about the course of arms races.  We will then try to compare these predictions to an actual arms race.

## II.  CONSTRUCTING A DETERMINISTIC MODEL

There are five major steps in the construction of a deterministic model of a situation which evolves over time:

1. The critical variables are isolated and defined.  In the models of arms

races, the variables studied will be armament expenditures, their rates of change, and time.

2. Assumptions about relationships among the critical variables are made and formulated as equations or inequalities. In a "mutual fear" situation, we are supposing that the rate of change of arms expenditures with respect to time of one country will depend on the armament expenditures of the other country.

3. Mathematical analysis is applied to the equations and inequalities. We hope to solve them or at least to discover information about the nature of the solutions. The analysis hopefully will give us new relations among the variables which are consequences of the assumed relations, but which were not immediately evident.

4. The results of the mathematical analysis are interpreted as statements about the real world and compared with what actually happens in the real world.

5. The model is accepted, discarded, or improved. If the predicted relations are found to coincide closely with what we observe in the real-world situation, we may accept the model as a correct formulation. If the observations are in strong disagreement with the results of the mathematical analysis, discard the model and try a new approach. If some of the observations confirm the model and others do not, modify the assumptions about the relationships among the variables and formulate more accurate equations.

We will carry out these steps for a simple arms race model in the next section.

## III. A SIMPLE MODEL FOR AN ARMS RACE

### A. The Assumptions

Let $x$ and $y$ represent the yearly rates of armament expenditures of the two nations in some standardized monetary unit. These numbers are nonnegative and change with time. Let $t$ stand for time in years; assume that $t \geqslant 0$ and that observation of the arms race begins at $t = 0$. The rates of change of $x$ and $y$ with respect to time are the derivatives $dx/dt = x'(t)$ and $dy/dt = y'(t)$.

Other important variables may occur to the reader. To keep this model simple, we will ignore, at least temporarily, other relevant quantities.

We wish to develop a simple model which reflects in some fashion the assumption of mutual fear: the more one nation arms, the more the other is spurred to arm. There are a variety of ways in which this assumption could be formulated mathematically. It could be translated to mean that each country adjusts the level of its armaments to the level of the other country's. A more general approach would be that each country adjusts the rate of increase or decrease of its armaments in response to the level of the other's. In order to obtain a simple model, we will interpret this assumption to mean that each nation changes its expenditures at a rate which is directly proportional to the existing expenditures of the other nation.

Mathematically, the equations which state this assumption are

$$\frac{dx}{dt} = ay \tag{1}$$

$$(a, b > 0)$$

$$\frac{dy}{dt} = bx \tag{2}$$

where $a$ and $b$ are positive constants. We do not claim, at this point, to know what numerical values $a$ and $b$ have. We do not need this knowledge to continue the mathematical analysis. The final results will show how the conclusions depend on the values of these parameters.

## B. Mathematical Analysis

Equations (1) and (2) form what is called a *system* of first-order differential equations. A *solution* of the system is a pair of differentiable functions, $x = f(t)$ and $y = g(t)$, so that

$$f'(t) = ag(t) \quad \text{and} \quad g'(t) = bf(t) \quad \text{for all} \quad t \geq 0. \tag{3}$$

If the armament expenditures at time $t = 0$ of the two nations are $x_0$ and $y_0$, respectively, then we also insist that our solution satisfy these *initial conditions*; that is, $f$ and $g$ satisfy Eq. (3) and

$$f(0) = x_0, \quad g(0) = y_0 \tag{4}$$

It can be shown that there is a unique pair of functions which satisfy the conditions of Eqs. (3) and (4). The proof is outlined in the Exercises. We want to derive some information about the nature of the solution functions $f$ and $g$.

In the first place, the fact that the parameters $a$ and $b$ are positive implies that the derivatives $dx/dt$ and $dy/dt$ are nonnegative. Thus $f'(t) \geq 0$ and $g'(t) \geq 0$. From elementary calculus, we may conclude that $f$ and $g$ are nondecreasing functions of $t$.

Secondly, differentiate each side of Eq. (1) with respect to $t$ and obtain

$$\frac{d^2 x}{dt^2} = a\left(\frac{dy}{dt}\right); \quad \text{that is,} \quad f''(t) = ag'(t). \tag{5}$$

In other words, the second derivative of $f$ is also nonnegative. The geometric conclusion of this is that the graph of $f$ is concave up. By differentiating Eq. (2) we may conclude by a similar argument that the graph of $g$ is also concave up.

We can obtain more information about the relationship between the solution functions by making use of the chain rule to write

$$\frac{dy}{dx} = \frac{dy/dt}{dx/dt} = \frac{b}{a}\frac{x}{y}. \tag{6}$$

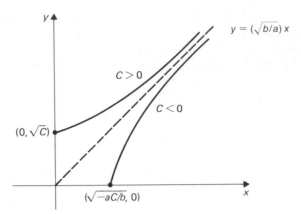

**Fig. 2.1**   $C = y_0^2 - (b/a)x_0^2$. The two curves illustrate the possibilities for the simple arms race model.

Rewriting Eq. (6) in differential form and integrating, we obtain

$$\int y \, dy = \int \left(\frac{b}{a}\right) x \, dx \tag{7}$$

or $y^2/2 = (b/a)(x^2/2) + K$ which gives

$$y^2 = \left(\frac{b}{a}\right) x^2 + C \tag{8}$$

where $C = 2K$ is the constant of integration. The value of $C$ is obtained by substituting $t = 0$ into Eq. (8) and using the fact that $y(0) = g(0) = y_0$, while $x(0) = f(0) = x_0$. What is more important for our understanding of this simple arms race model is that Eq. (8) is the equation of a hyperbola in the plane with straight-line asymptote $y = \sqrt{b/a}\,x$. The graph of the hyperbola in the plane is sketched in Fig. 2.1.

Suppose that at some time the $x$ and $y$ values determine a point in the interior of the first quadrant on the upper branch of the hyperbola. Then as time continues, the points $(x(t), y(t))$ remain on this branch, moving in a northeasterly direction since (by Eq. 6) the slope of the tangent line is positive. This branch lies above the asymptote line, so that $y > \sqrt{b/a}\,x$. Equation (1) then gives

$$\frac{dx}{dt} = ay > a\sqrt{\frac{b}{a}}\,x = \sqrt{ab}\,x$$

or

$$\frac{dx}{dt} > \sqrt{ab}\,x.$$

Thus, as the $x$-coordinate increases, so does the velocity of the horizontal motion. The motion along the hyperbola is speeding up and the values of $x$ and $y$ will increase without bound as time increases; that is,

$$\lim_{t \to \infty} x(t) = \lim_{t \to \infty} y(t) = \infty.$$

The same result can be established for motion along the lower branch of the hyperbola.

## C.  The Conclusions

It is possible, for those who know a little more about differential equations, to find explicit formulas for the solution $f$ and $g$ as functions of $t$ (see Exercise 3). Even without doing this, we have enough information to analyze the qualitative consequences of this simple arms race model: both nations will spend more and more money on armaments as time proceeds, with no limit on the expenditures.

Note that this mathematical prediction is consistent with part of the verbal analysis of this "mutual fear" model. The mathematical prediction of indefinitely large expenditures, however, violates common sense observations that there must be a finite limit to the expenditures. The model must be modified to reflect this observation. Such a model will be explored in the next section.

## IV.  THE RICHARDSON MODEL

## A.  The Assumptions

For the refined model, begin with the premise of mutual fear expressed by the assumption that the rate of change of armament expenditures of each country is directly proportional to the expenditures of the other country. We will also attempt to include the "limiting factors" discussed above. This can be done by assuming that excessive armament expenditures present a drag on the nation's economy so that the actual level of expenditures depresses the rate of expenditure changes. A mathematical way of expressing this is to assume that the rate of change for a nation is directly and negatively proportional to its own expenditures. More precisely, a simple refinement of the original model would be the system of differential equations:

$$\frac{dx}{dt} = x'(t) = ay - mx, \tag{9}$$

$$a, b, m, n > 0;$$

$$\frac{dy}{dt} = y'(t) = bx - ny, \tag{10}$$

where $a, b, m,$ and $n$ are all positive constants.

Rather than proceed to a mathematical analysis of this model, we will consider a model which is a further refinement of this one. The idea of the second refinement is that some people argue that the cause of increasing arms expenditures is not mutual stimulation but permanent underlying grievances of each country against the other. To satisfy these analysts, Lewis F. Richardson (1881–1953) proposed the following model:

$$\frac{dx}{dt} = x'(t) = ay - mx + r, \tag{11}$$

$$\frac{dy}{dt} = y'(t) = bx - ny + s, \tag{12}$$

where $a, b, m,$ and $n$ are positive constants while $r$ and $s$ are constants which may have any sign.

Assignment of a positive value to $r$ or to $s$ indicates that there is a grievance by one country against the other which spurs it to accumulate arms. If we assign a negative value to one of these parameters, however, then we are asserting that there are underlying feelings of goodwill which tend to diminish perceptions of threat and hence to decrease dependence on arms.

The differential equations of the Richardson model then assert that the rates of arms expenditure increase of one nation depend positively on the expenditure level of the other country, negatively on the country's own expenditures, and positively on underlying grievances. The values assigned to the six parameters measure the extent of these effects.

The Richardson model is quite a flexible one. Analysts who differ in their beliefs as to the relative importance of the three determinants of rate of change may choose values for the parameters to reflect their preferences. If one of the three factors is believed irrelevant to changes in expenditures, then the corresponding parameter can simply be set equal to zero. If, for example, all the constants except $r$ and $s$ are zero, then only the grievances are considered as contributing to changes in armaments.

Thus you can use the Richardson model if you believe that an arms race is a self-stimulating process or if you believe that self-stimulation has nothing to do with accumulation of arms. Assigning nonzero values to all the constants gives a model which contains the essential assumptions of our verbal description:

1. Arms accumulate because of mutual fear;
2. There is resistance within society to ever-increasing arms expenditures;
3. There are considerations independent of expenditure levels which contribute to the buildup of armaments.

We shall see that the nature of solutions to the system of differential equations of the Richardson model depends, not on the precise values of the parameters, but on their relative magnitudes and the signs of the "grievance" terms, $r$ and $s$.

## B. Elementary Analysis of the Model

Let us suppose that the arms race begins at time $t = 0$ and the differential Eqs. (11) and (12) are valid for all time $t \geqslant 0$. Suppose also that at $t = 0$, Blue and Red are respectively spending at annual rates of $x_0$ and $y_0$ monetary units on armaments. It can be shown there is a unique pair of differentiable functions of $t$, $x = f(t)$, and $y = g(t)$ such that

$$f'(t) = a\,g(t) - m\,f(t) + r, \tag{13}$$

$$g'(t) = b\,f(t) - n\,g(t) + s, \tag{14}$$

$$f(0) = x_0, \qquad g(0) = y_0. \tag{15}$$

It is possible to solve the system of differential equations to obtain $f$ and $g$ explicitly as functions of $t$, the six parameters, and the initial expenditures. The necessary mathematical procedures require a good background in linear algebra and are beyond the scope of this text. The interested reader may wish to consult the book by Sanchez or the one by Brauer, Nohel, and Schneider listed in the References. In this chapter, we will analyze the system with the tools the student has learned in elementary calculus.

The techniques and concepts of calculus shed light on an important aspect of arms races: stability. Some of the terms in the Richardson equations act to increase expenditures, while others put a brake on spiraling costs. Is it possible that the combined effect of all the terms will force arms expenditures ultimately to become "stabilized"? Will the level of expenses approach or remain at some fixed, constant amount?

The mathematical requirement that a nation's expenditures stay constant is that the rate of change be zero. We say that the arms race *stabilizes* when both nations reach a level of constant expenditures. For stablization to occur, then, both rates of change must become zero; that is,

$$\frac{dx}{dt} = 0 = \frac{dy}{dt}. \tag{16}$$

From the Richardson equations, this is the same as demanding that

$$ay - mx + r = 0 \tag{17}$$

and

$$bx - by + s = 0. \tag{18}$$

In our analysis, we will assume that the parameters are all nonzero. The exploration of the special cases in which some of the parameters are assigned values of zero will be left for the Exercises.

Accordingly, we may rewrite Eq. (17) as

$$y = \frac{m}{a}\,x - \frac{r}{a}. \tag{17a}$$

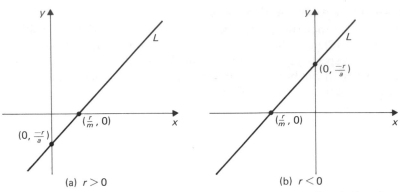

Fig. 2.2    The line $L: y = (m/a)x - (r/a)$. At points along this line, $dx/dt = 0$.

This is the equation of a straight line $L$ with slope $m/a$, $y$-intercept $(0, -r/a)$ and $x$-intercept $(r/m, 0)$; see Fig. 2.2.

It is useful to think of the Richardson system of differential equations as the equations of motion of a particle in the $(x,y)$-plane. The first equation gives the horizontal component of velocity and the second equation gives the vertical component of velocity. The equations assert that the velocity components are functions purely of the $x$- and $y$-coordinates of a point and of certain constants. All that we really require here is to recall simple facts such as: if $dx/dt$ at some point is positive, then $x(t)$ is increasing at this point so that the particle will tend to move to the right; if $dx/dt$ is negative, the particle tends to the left. If $dy/dt$ is positive (negative), then the particle will move up (down).

If at some instant of time, the levels of expenditures $(x_1, y_1)$ of Blue and Red happen to coincide with a point on $L$, that is, $ay_1 - mx_1 + r = 0$, then $dx/dt$ at $(x_1, y_1)$ will be zero. The expenditures of Blue at that moment will not be changing. Of course, $dy/dt$ at this point is likely to be nonzero, so the level of expenditures may move up or down at that instant toward a point not on $L$.

The line $L$ is called the *optimal line* for Blue. We shall see that the Richardson model implies that Blue is continuously changing its expenditures levels so as to bring them closer to the optimal line.

We wish to explore the limiting behavior of the Richardson arms race model as $t$ gets large. Three cases can be distinguished:

1. a runaway arms race in which $x \to \infty$ and $y \to \infty$,
2. mutual disarmament in which $x \to 0$ and $y \to 0$, and
3. a stable arms race in which $x \to x^*$ and $y \to y^*$ for some positive numbers $x^*$ and $y^*$.

If there is a stable arms race, it is easy to determine the values of $x^*$ and $y^*$. We consider the lines $L$ and $L'$ where $dx/dt = 0$ and $dy/dt = 0$, respectively. The line $L'$ is Red's optimal line. The two lines intersect in a point $(x^*, y^*)$; see Fig. 2.3. At this level of armament expenditures, the rates of increase for

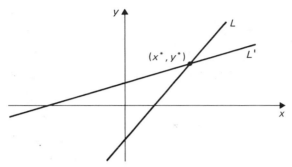

**Fig. 2.3** The intersection of optimal lines at $(x^*, y^*)$, the point of stability. At this point, both derivatives $dx/dt$ and $dy/dt$ are zero.

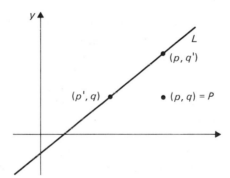

**Fig. 2.4** The point $(p, q)$ lies below and to the right of the line $L$.

both nations are 0 and they will maintain this level, $(x^*, y^*)$, which will be called the *point of stability*.

The optimal line $L$ divides the plane into two open half-planes; see Fig. 2.4. One half-plane consists of all the points to the "right" of $L$ and the other is made up of all points to the "left" of $L$. More formally, a point $P$ *lies to the right* of a line $L$ if the horizontal line through $P$ hits $L$ at a point with smaller $x$-coordinate while $P$ lies *above* $L$ if the vertical line through $P$ hits $L$ at a point with smaller $y$-coordinate.

Suppose that $(x_1, y_1)$ is any point not on the optimal line $L$ and let $(x_2, y_1)$ be the corresponding point on $L$. Then $ay_1 - mx_2 + r = 0$ while the derivative $dx/dt$ at $(x_1, y_1)$ has value

$$
\begin{aligned}
x'(x_1, y_1) &= ay_1 - mx_1 + r \\
&= ay_1 - mx_1 + r - 0 \\
&= ay_1 - mx_1 + r - ay_1 + mx_2 - r \\
&= m(x_2 - x_1).
\end{aligned}
\tag{19}
$$

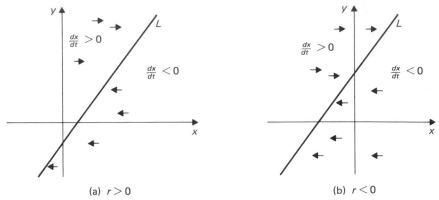

(a) $r > 0$                                      (b) $r < 0$

**Fig. 2.5**   Blue adjusts expenditures toward the line $L$.  On $L$, $dx/dt = 0$.

Now we see that $dx/dt$ at $(x_1, y_1)$ is positive exactly when $x_2 > x_1$ and this occurs exactly when $(x_1, y_1)$ lies to the left of $L$.  The derivative is negative similarly exactly when $(x_1, y_1)$ lies to the right of $L$.  Thus, if $(x_1, y_1)$ lies to the left of $L$, then the horizontal motion at that moment is toward $L$, while if $(x_1, y_1)$ lies to the right of $L$, the horizontal motion is also toward $L$.  In either case, the Richardson model implies that Blue is always adjusting its expenditures to move them toward the optimal line; that is, Blue is trying to stabilize its arms expenses.  See Fig. 2.5.

Similar analysis yields corresponding results for Red's optimal line $L'$ along which $dy/dt = 0$.  The derivative is negative at any point above $L'$ and is positive at any point below $L'$.  Thus, the vertical motion is always toward $L'$; the nation of Red always adjusts its expenditures toward its optimal line.

### C.  Does Stability Occur?

We have just seen that the Richardson model predicts horizontal movement toward $L$ and vertical movement toward $L'$.  In other words, if the initial level of armament expenditures is $(x_0, y_0)$, then Blue will change its expenditures to bring them closer to its optimal line and so will Red.  In this section, we will investigate what effects these motions have on the possibility of stabilizing the arms race.

If $x$ and $y$ represent armament expenditures, then we attach no meaning, for the present, to these variables being negative.  We consider, then, only the behavior of solutions of the Richardson model when $x$ and $y$ are nonnegative.  We examine only the portion of the graph relating $y$ and $x$ which lies in the first quadrant.

**Mutual grievances**   Let us first investigate the arms race in which each side has a permanent underlying grievance against the other side.  Mathematically, this means we will assume that the parameters $r$ and $s$ are both positive.

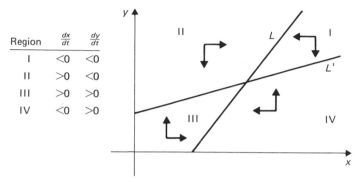

| Region | $\frac{dx}{dt}$ | $\frac{dy}{dt}$ |
|--------|------|------|
| I   | <0 | <0 |
| II  | >0 | <0 |
| III | >0 | >0 |
| IV  | <0 | >0 |

**Fig. 2.6** The optimal lines split up the first quadrant into four regions. The arrows indicate the horizontal and vertical directions of motion in each region.

In this situation suppose that Blue and Red are completely disarmed, so that the initial expenditure level is $(0, 0)$. According to the Richardson model, the rates of change of expenditures at this instant would be

$$\frac{dx}{dt} = a0 - m0 + r = r > 0 \tag{20}$$

and

$$\frac{dy}{dt} = b0 - n0 + s = s > 0, \tag{21}$$

so that each nation would start arming itself.

Can this system be stable? In the case where $r$ and $s$ are both positive, the point of stability $(x^*, y^*)$ will lie in either the first quadrant or the third quadrant (see Exercise 15). We will start with the case that $(x^*, y^*)$ lies in the first quadrant. Then the lines $L$ and $L'$ will be as pictured in Fig. 2.6. These lines split the first quadrant into four regions. Label them counterclockwise I, II, III, IV so that the origin is in region III.

If the initial armament expenditures are at $(0, 0)$, then, as we have seen, both $x$ and $y$ will increase. The net result will be to move the expenditures toward a point $(x_1, y_1)$ deeper in region III, closer to the stability point $(x^*, y^*)$ a short time later. If $(x_1, y_1)$ is any point in region III, then again $dx/dt$ and $dy/dt$ will be positive and the motion will still be in a "northeasterly" direction toward $(x^*, y^*)$. If at some instant, the motion carries the particles to the piece of the line $L$ separating regions III and IV, then at such a point $dx/dt = 0$ while $dy/dt$ is positive; the resulting motion is vertical and returns to region III. Similarly, at every point on the part of $L'$ separating regions II and III, $dy/dt = 0$ while $dx/dt$ is positive; again motion is back into region III. No matter where in region III the initial level of expenditures $(x_0, y_0)$ is, the long-term behavior of the arms race is movement toward $(x^*, y^*)$ and stability results. See Fig. 2.7.

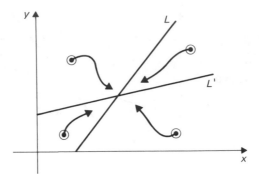

**Fig. 2.7**  The stable case.  Possible initial
levels $(x_0, y_0)$ are circled.

The initial expenditure levels $(x_0, y_0)$ could, of course, be at a point in one
of the other three regions of the first quadrant.  It is easy to check that in any
of these cases, the movement is again toward the stable point $(x^*, y^*)$.  In
Fig. 2.7, this is shown for several different initial levels.  Thus, whenever the
optimal lines intersect in the first quadrant and the grievance terms $r$ and $s$ are
positive, we have a stabilizing arms race.  Any deviation from the "Balance of
Power" point $(x^*, y^*)$ will tend to be corrected.

**Stable point in third quadrant**  To continue the analysis for the case when
the parameters $r$ and $s$ are positive, consider what happens if $(x^*, y^*)$ is in the
third quadrant.  Then the relationship of the optimal lines $L$ and $L'$ is the one
pictured in Fig. 2.8.

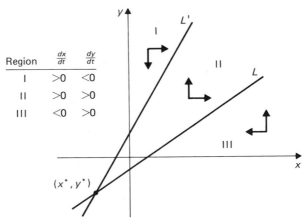

| Region | $\frac{dx}{dt}$ | $\frac{dy}{dt}$ |
|--------|-----------------|-----------------|
| I      | $>0$            | $<0$            |
| II     | $>0$            | $>0$            |
| III    | $<0$            | $>0$            |

**Fig. 2.8**  Runaway arms race.  Grievance terms $r$ and $s$
are both positive.

Since the stable point is unobtainable through any positive levels of armament expenditures, a stabilizing arms race is not possible. The first quadrant is
split into three regions as indicated in Fig. 2.8. Investigation of the signs of
$dx/dt$ and $dy/dt$ in these regions show that no matter what the initial level of
expenditures is, the motion of the system eventually carries expenditures into
the second region. Once the expenditures reach a point in this second region,
both $x$ and $y$ values continue to increase and the expenditures reach indefinitely
high levels; there is a runaway arms race no matter what the initial expenditures
were.

In the Exercises, you will prove that the situation just discussed can only
occur if $mn < ab$; that is, the "combined" effect of the braking terms is not
enough to offset the terms which measure mutual stimulation to increase arms
expenditures.

**The bad effect of good will**    In this section we will show that there are some
cases in which the nature of the ultimate behavior of the Richardson model
depends upon the initial level of expenditures. Look at the situation pictured
in Fig. 2.9. This can occur only if at least one of the "grievance" terms, $r$ or $s$,
is negative; that is, only if at least one of the nations has feelings of "good will"
toward the other.

Suppose the initial level of expenditures is at the point $(x_0, y_0)$ in Fig. 2.9.
Expenditures will not remain at this point, because it is not the point of stability.
Since $(x_0, y_0)$ is to the left of $L$ and below $L'$, the $x$-coordinate and $y$-coordinate
will both increase and the expenditures will move to a new point in region I
farther from the stable point. The arms expenditures for both nations will increase indefinitely as time goes on. There is a runaway arms race.

On the other hand, suppose that the initial level is at $(x_1, y_1)$ in region III
of Fig. 2.9. Now we are to the right of $L$ and above $L'$ so both coordinates will
decrease and we will move to another point in region III farther from the stable
point. We are headed toward mutual disarmament.

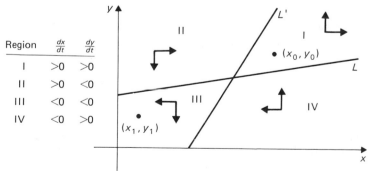

| Region | $\frac{dx}{dt}$ | $\frac{dy}{dt}$ |
|--------|------|------|
| I | >0 | >0 |
| II | >0 | <0 |
| III | <0 | <0 |
| IV | <0 | >0 |

**Fig. 2.9**  An ambiguous case. Both grievance terms $r$ and $s$ are
negative.

If the initial point is in region II or IV, then the analysis is more complicated. These cases will be discussed in some detail in later sections. The basic result, however, is easy to state. The ultimate behavior is either a runaway arms race or total disarmament, depending on whether we move first into region I or region III. This is determined by the location of the initial expenditure levels.

There is a rather ironic situation here. If underlying grievances exist (both $r$ and $s$ positive), then a stable arms race may result, independent of how high the initial level of expenditures is or how great the disparity in expenditures of the nations is at the start. When the underlying feelings are of goodwill (negative values for $r$ and $s$), then a runaway arms race is an alternative to disarmament, and the eventual outcome very much depends on where you start.

This ambiguous case arises when the lines $L$ and $L'$ intersect in the first quadrant. If the point of intersection happens to lie in the third quadrant, and $r$ and $s$ are both negative, then the arms race becomes a march to mutual disarmament regardless of the location of the initial point (see Exercise 19).

**Summary of results**    The eventual outcome of an arms race which follows the Richardson model depends upon the relative sizes of the parameters $a, b, m,$ and $n$ and the signs of $r$ and $s$. We have noted the following typical cases:

*Case 1*    If $mn - ab$ is positive, $r$ and $s$ are positive, then there will be a stabilized arms race.

*Case 2*    If $mn - ab$ is negative, $r$ and $s$ are positive, there will be a runaway arms race.

*Case 3*    If $mn - ab$ is positive, $r$ and $s$ are negative, then there will be total disarmament.

*Case 4*    If $mn - ab$ is negative, $r$ and $s$ are negative, then the situation is ambiguous. There will either be disarmament or a runaway arms race, depending on the initial level of expenditures.

### D.  Further Analysis of the Richardson Model

Suppose that you wish to study the Richardson model in a situation where investigation indicates that the values of the various parameters should be

$$a = 1, \qquad m = 2, \qquad r = -5, \qquad b = 6, \qquad n = 2, \qquad s = -12.$$

The optimal lines are $L$: $y - 2x - 5 = 0$ and $L'$: $6x - 2y - 12 = 0$. The two lines intersect at the stable point $(x^*, y^*) = (11, 27)$.

Since the grievance terms $r$ and $s$ are negative and $mn - ab = 4 - 6$ is negative, you have the ambiguous case in which ultimate behavior of the system depends on the location of the initial level of expenditures.

Observation of this particular system at time $t = 0$ shows that the initial level is $(x_0, y_0) = (15, 15)$. At this point, the derivatives are given by

$$x'(x_0, y_0) = x'(15, 15) = 15 - 2(15) - 5 = -20$$

and
$$y'(x_0, y_0) = y'(15, 15) = 6(15) - 2(15) - 12 = 48.$$
The signs of these derivatives indicate that the initial point is in region IV of Fig. 2.9. You cannot tell, from any of the mathematical analysis yet presented, what the ultimate behavior of this particular arms race will be. In this section, we will present two techniques—of general application in the solution of systems of differential equations—which will help determine the outcome.

**The Euler method**   This method, introduced by the great Swiss mathematician Leonhard Euler (1707–1783), is based on a simple geometric interpretation of the derivative.

Suppose that $u = f(t)$ is a differentiable function of $t$ and that the value of the function and its first derivative are known at a number $t_0$. We wish to approximate the value of the function at a nearby number $t_0 + \Delta t$. Direct computation may be quite difficult. Note, however, that the graph of the tangent line to the curve $u = f(t)$ stays close to the curve near point of tangency $(t_0, f(t_0)) = (t_0, u_0)$. The slope of the tangent line is given as $f'(t_0) = u'(t_0, u_0)$. It is a simple matter to use the equation of the tangent line to find the point on the line with first coordinate equal to $t_0 + \Delta t$. If $\Delta t$ is small, then the second coordinate of this point is a good approximation to the value $f(t_0 + \Delta t)$ since the tangent line will not wander far from the curve (see Fig. 2.10). The smaller $\Delta t$ is, of course, the better the approximation will be. Analytically, the actual change in the function from $t_0$ to $t_0 + \Delta t$ is
$$\Delta u = f(t_0 + \Delta t) - f(t_0) = f(t_0 + \Delta t) - u_0.$$
The approximation is that $\Delta u$ is roughly equal to $f'(t_0)\Delta t$ so that
$$f(t_0 + \Delta t) \approx u_0 + f'(t_0)\Delta t,$$

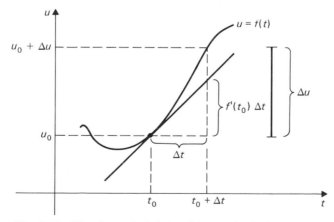

**Fig. 2.10**   The change in height of the graph of a function near the point of tangency is approximated by the change in height of the tangent line.

which may also be written as

$$f(t_0 + \Delta t) \approx u_0 + u'(t_0, u_0)\Delta t,$$

where $\approx$ is a symbol representing "approximately equal to."

---

**EXAMPLE**   Suppose $u = f(t) = \sqrt{t}$ and $t_0 = 4$. Then $u_0 = \sqrt{4} = 2$ and $f'(t) = 1/(2\sqrt{t})$ so that $f'(t_0) = f'(4) = u'(4, 2) = 1/(2\sqrt{4}) = \frac{1}{4}$. The approximation that is made here is

$$\sqrt{(4 + \Delta t)} \approx 2 + \frac{1}{4}\Delta t.$$

If we wish to compute $\sqrt{4.41}$, for example, then we take $\Delta t = .41$. The approximate value is $2 + \frac{1}{4}(.41) = 2.1025$. The actual value of $\sqrt{4.41}$ is 2.100. The approximation here is quite good.

---

   Many calculus texts contain detailed discussion of this method of "increments" for approximations. See, for example, Section 2.4, "The increment of a function" in George Thomas' *Calculus with Analytic Geometry*, Third Edition (Reading, Mass.: Addison-Wesley, 1960).

   The method of increments is the basis for Euler's technique of approximating solutions to differential equations. In the context of the Richardson arms race model, suppose the initial level of expenditures is $(x_0, y_0)$. Then the rate of change for Blue is $x'(x_0, y_0) = ay_0 - mx_0 + r$ and for Red it is $y'(x_0, y_0) = bx_0 - ny_0 + s$. In a short time interval $\Delta t$, the amount $\Delta x$ that the arms expenditures for Blue will change is approximately $x'(x_0, y_0)\Delta t$. The change of expenditures for Red during this same time interval is denoted $\Delta y$ and is approximately equal to $y'(x_0, y_0)\Delta t$.

   Thus at time $t_0 + \Delta t = 0 + \Delta t = \Delta t$, the new expenditure levels will be at the point $P_1 = (x_1, y_1)$. The coordinates of these points are estimated by the method of increments to be

$$x_1 \approx x_0 + x'(x_0, y_0)\Delta t$$

and

$$y_1 \approx y_0 + y'(x_0, y_0)\Delta t.$$

If we choose $\Delta t$ to be small, then the estimated coordinates will be quite close to the actual coordinates at time $\Delta t$.

   Once a new point $P_1$ has been estimated, it may be treated as the initial point of the system and the method of increments can be applied again. This may be done as often as you like. The general formula for estimating successive points would be

$$P_{i+1} = (x_{i+1}, y_{i+1}) \qquad \text{where} \qquad \begin{cases} x_{i+1} = x_i + x'(x_i, y_i)\Delta t \\ y_{i+1} = y_i + y'(x_i, y_i)\Delta t \end{cases} \tag{22}$$

This formula for $P_{i+1}$ can be applied to any system of differential equations, in which $dx/dt$ and $dy/dt$ are given as explicit functions of $x$ and $y$. For the Richardson arms race model the formula becomes

$$P_{i+1} = (x_{i+1}, y_{i+1}) \qquad \text{where} \qquad \begin{cases} x_{i+1} = x_i + (ay_i - mx_i + r)\Delta t \\ y_{i+1} = y_i + (bx_i - ny_i + s)\Delta t \end{cases}. \qquad (23)$$

For the particular Richardson model we have been discussing in this section, the formula reduces to

$$P_{i+1} = (x_i + (y_i - 2x_i - 5)\Delta t, \; y_i + (6x_i - 2y_i - 12)\Delta t),$$
$$P_0 = (15, 15). \qquad (24)$$

If $\Delta t$ is chosen to be .01, then repeated use of Eq. (24) yields the following data:

| $i$ | $x_i$ | $y_i$ | $x'(x_i, y_i)$ | $y'(x_i, y_i)$ |
|---|---|---|---|---|
| 0 | 15 | 15 | $-20$ | 48 |
| 1 | 14.8 | 15.48 | $-19.12$ | 45.84 |
| 2 | 14.6088 | 15.9384 | $-18.2792$ | 43.776 |
| 3 | 14.426 | 16.3762 | $-17.4759$ | 41.8037 |
| 4 | 14.2512 | 16.7942 | $-16.7083$ | 39.9191 |
| 5 | 14.0842 | 17.1934 | $-15.9749$ | 38.1182 |
| ... | | | | |
| 10 | 13.3524 | 18.9347 | $-12.7702$ | 30.2452 |
| 20 | 12.2988 | 21.4099 | $-8.18774$ | 18.9731 |
| 30 | 11.6216 | 22.9583 | $-5.28485$ | 11.8129 |
| ... | | | | |
| 90 | 10.401 | 25.1702 | $-.631807$ | .006562 |
| 91 | 10.3947 | 25.1709 | $-.618515$ | .002640 |
| 92 | 10.3885 | 25.1711 | $-.60588$ | $-.001123$ |

Since both derivatives at $P_{92}$ are negative, the point $P_{92}$ is in region III and, by our previous analysis, we may conjecture that the ultimate result of this particular arms race will be total disarmament.

This incremental method yields a definite and believable result. It is difficult to ascertain the ultimate behavior of an arms race in this way, however, unless we are willing to make a great many computations. In these computations, moreover, there is a slight error at each step because the incremental method yields only approximations. This error may build up over the many steps necessary in the computation so that the actual position of the expenditure levels may be quite far away from the estimated one. The trick is to make $\Delta t$ small enough so that the accumulated error is small, but large enough so that the number of calculations before reaching region I or III is reasonable.

Rather than pursue this method any further at this stage—or examine the many refinements mathematicians have developed for the numerical solution of systems of differential equations—we will describe another method of answering the stability question. This method will accurately predict the outcome of the arms race, will not involve extensive calculations, and is mathematically defensible.

**The point-slope method**   The motivation behind this method derives from trying to answer the question, "Is it possible that the movement of arms expenditures levels could be motion *along a straight line* toward the stable point?"

Let $P_0 = (x_0, y_0)$ be the initial point and consider the straight line $L^*$ through $P_0$ and the stable point $S = (x^*, y^*)$. The slope of this line is

$$\frac{y^* - y_0}{x^* - x_0}.$$

If the motion of the point representing armament expenditures is given by the Richardson model, then the chain rule gives:

$$\frac{dy}{dx} = \frac{dy/dt}{dx/dt} = \frac{bx - ny + s}{ay - mx + r}. \tag{25}$$

This measures the slope of the line tangent to the curve along which the point is moving at the instant when the point is at $(x, y)$. See Fig. 2.11.

Suppose that this direction of motion happens to be along $L^*$ and furthermore assume that every point on $L^*$ has this property; namely, the slope of the line $L^*$ through $S$ and the point is equal to the derivative $dy/dx$ evaluated at the point. Then, if the initial point is on $L^*$, all subsequent points (hence all subsequent levels of arms expenditures) will be on $L^*$. This is true because at $t = 0$, the point is on $L^*$ and is moving along $L^*$ and any instant later it has reached another point on $L^*$ where $dy/dx$ determines the new direction of motion and this direction is again along $L^*$.

We can find the equation of such a line $L^*$ by using this property that we have assumed for it: a point $(x, y)$ is on $L^*$ if and only if $dy/dx$ at that point is equal to the slope of the line from $S$ to the point; that is,

$$\frac{bx - ny + s}{ay - mx + r} = \frac{y^* - y}{x^* - x}. \tag{26}$$

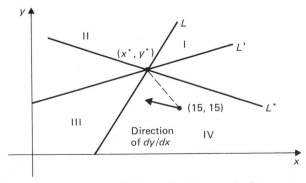

**Fig. 2.11**   Illustration of the point-slope method.

This equation may be solved for $y$ as a function of $x$. In the example under consideration, a point $(x, y)$ is on $L^*$ if and only if

$$\frac{6x - 2y - 12}{y - 2x - 5} = \frac{27 - y}{11 - x}. \tag{27}$$

This is equivalent to

$$(6x - 2y - 12)(11 - x) = (27 - y)(y - 2x - 5).$$

Perform the indicated multiplication and rearrange terms to obtain

$$y^2 - 54y - (6x^2 - 132x - 3) = 0. \tag{28}$$

Equation (28) may be treated as a quadratic equation in $y$ with constant term $6x^2 - 132x - 3$. The two solutions are

$$y = 27 + \sqrt{6}(x - 11) \quad \text{and} \quad y = 27 - \sqrt{6}(x - 11). \tag{29}$$

The equations in Eq. (29) are equations of straight lines. Both lines pass through the stable point $(11, 27)$. The first equation represents a line of positive slope that runs through regions I and III and is not of interest to us. The second line has negative slope and lies in regions II and IV. This is the equation of the desired line $L^*$.

Consider any point on $L^*$ in region IV. Here $dx/dt$ is negative and $dy/dt$ is positive, so that the direction of motion is "northwesterly." Since the point is on the special line $L^*$, the motion is along $L^*$. Starting at any such point, the motion will be toward the stable point as time progresses. A similar consideration of the signs of $dx/dt$ and $dy/dt$ shows that if motion starts at a point of $L^*$ in region II, subsequent motion is along $L^*$ toward the stable point.

Now a point $(x, y)$ will be on $L^*$ exactly when $y + \sqrt{6}(x - 11) - 27 = 0$. This line divides the plane into two regions, one below the line and one above it, for which $y + \sqrt{6}(x - 11) - 27$ is negative and positive, respectively. These correspond to the inequalities

$$\frac{6x - 2y - 12}{y - 2x - 5} > \frac{27 - y}{11 - x} \tag{30}$$

for points below $L^*$, and

$$\frac{6x - 2y - 12}{y - 2x - 5} < \frac{27 - y}{11 - x} \tag{31}$$

for points above $L^*$ in regions II and IV.

If $(x, y)$ is a point in the plane above $L^*$, and we connect that point to the stable point with a straight line, then the direction of motion from this point will be above this line, and closer to region I. The ultimate motion will carry arms expenditures levels into region I and the arms race will escalate without limit.

If, on the other hand, the initial point of the arms race is below $L^*$, then the direction of motion away from the point is below the line connecting that point to the stable point. The motion is toward region III, which the system will eventually enter. Total disarmament will result.

For the particular example under consideration with initial point $(15, 15)$, the direction of motion at this point is

$$\frac{6(15) - 2(15) - 12}{15 - 2(15) - 5} = \frac{48}{-20} = -2.4,$$

while the slope of the line from $(15, 15)$ to the stable point $(11, 27)$ is

$$\frac{27 - 15}{11 - 15} = -3.$$

Since $-2.4$ is greater than $-3$, the direction of motion is below the line from $(15, 15)$ to $(11, 27)$, so the movement is away from the stable point and toward region III. The result is eventual disarmament.

If we consider a particular case of the Richardson arms race model, with assigned values for the parameters and the initial expenditures, then the set of all later expenditures traces out a curve in the plane. This curve may move toward the stable point, or toward the origin, or it may simply assume larger and larger values of both coordinates without limit as time goes on. Equipped with the point-slope method and the analysis of earlier sections, we can determine quickly which of these three outcomes will occur.

## V.  INTERPRETING AND TESTING THE RICHARDSON MODEL

### A.  Interpretation

The Richardson model is simple and limited. It assumes that the rate of growth of armaments is influenced by only three factors and that these influences are additive in their effect. When a person considers that many other forces operating in the real world may have an effect on arms races and that the interrelationships among these forces are undoubtedly quite complex, he might easily conclude that the Richardson model is too simplified to be of any real interest.

On the other hand, we have seen that the model does include—in mathematical language—some of the most common arguments about arms races that have been made by political analysts. Moreover, when we examine the mathematical implications of the model, we see that some of them are in accord with common sense. The conclusions of our mathematical analysis in Section IV can be interpreted to give us these qualitative statements:

1.  The presence of permanent underlying grievances will prevent total disarmament. As long as such grievances exist, countries will continue to arm even if their "rivals" have no weapons.

2.  A stabilization of the arms race is achievable if the amount of mutual fear (measured by $ab$) is sufficiently tempered by the constraints ($m$ and $n$) on the sizes of armament budgets.

3. Total disarmament is possible if there are underlying feelings of goodwill, but this will not occur if the level of armament expenditures is already above a certain critical amount or if mutual fear is too strong.

In addition to this qualitative information, the Richardson model also predicts how the arms race will develop quantitatively over time. In the case of a stabilized arms race, for example, the model tells what path will be taken toward the stable point.

If we wish to test this theoretical model against a real arms race, our first task is to consider more carefully how to measure the variables $x$ and $y$. Next we would need to determine how to assign weights to the six parameters, or at least how to assess the signs of $r$ and $s$ and the relative magnitudes of $mn$ and $ab$.

It should be useful at this point to discuss the history of the Richardson model and how it came to be derived in order to explain the cause of a World War.

## B. Lewis Fry Richardson

The mathematical model of an arms race that we have been studying was the creation of a man named Lewis Fry Richardson. Richardson was born on

Lewis F. Richardson.
Photograph reproduced by
permission of Stephen
A. Richardson.

October 11, 1881 at Newcastle-upon-Tyne in the county of Durham, England. His father had a tanning business and his mother came from a family of corn merchants. Richardson attended Cambridge University where he studied under the famous Cavendish Professor of Physics, Sir J. J. Thompson, discoverer of the electron. Richardson worked variously as a chemist, physicist, meteorologist, teacher of physics, and president of a technical college.

His scientific work in the field of meteorology was highly regarded. His book, *Weather Prediction by Numerical Process*, was published in 1923 and is considered a classic work in the field. The excellence of Richardson's contributions to meteorology and physics journals led to his receiving a Doctor of Science degree from London University in 1926 and his election to the Fellowship of the Royal Society the next year.

Richardson's family had a strong attachment to the Quaker religious community and the Society of Friends was a persistent influence in his life. He once wrote, "Its solemn emphasis on public and private duty . . . its condemnation of war pulled me away from the many warlike applications of physics." Richardson served with an ambulance convoy attached to the 16th infantry division of the French army during World War I. It was during this period that he began to write about the causes and avoidance of war.

Richardson developed his model of a two-nation arms race during the middle 1930's. He later extended the model to describe an arms race among *n* nations and tried to apply this refined model to the situation in Europe. He submitted a paper on this to an American journal urging immediate acceptance because he thought its publication might avert an impending war. The editors saw fit to reject the paper.

Not long after the outbreak of World War II, Richardson resigned his principalship of the Technical College and School of Art in Paisley, Scotland. In his retirement he continued to pursue his researches into the causes of war. In the last few years of his life, he returned to his earlier interests in meteorology. Richardson died on September 30, 1953.

## C.  Background of Richardson's Model

Manifestations of hostility among nations are often apparent in the invectives that appear in speeches and in the press. The difficulty of incorporating hostility as a variable in a mathematical model is in finding a suitable, objectively measurable quantity to represent the amount of hostility.

Richardson saw armament expenditures in monetary units as a good index of hostility. He proposed that indices of international trade be used as measures of the amount of cooperation between nations. Accordingly, the net amount of hostility would be the difference between arms expenditures and international trade. If this quantity is negative, then the magnitude of difference could be interpreted as net cooperation. Note that this would enable us to attach meaning to negative values of $x$ and $y$ in the model.

In developing his model, Richardson was attempting to discover the causes of World War I. He assumed that when armaments can reach constant equilibrium values, then no war occurs. If the armaments increase indefinitely, he concluded that war would eventually start.

Richardson [1960b, p. 15] defended his inclusion of what we have called the "mutual fear" factor in his model by quoting Sir Edward Grey, who was the British Foreign Secretary at the outbreak of World War I:

> The increase of armaments that is intended in each nation to produce consciousness of strength, and a sense of security, does not produce these effects. On the contrary, it produces a consciousness of the strength of other nations and a sense of fear . . . . The enormous growth of armaments in Europe, the sense of insecurity and fear caused by them—it was these that made war inevitable . . . . This is the real and final account of the origin of the Great War.

As to the presence of terms involving the burdens of arms expenditures, Richardson notes the remarks of Winston Churchill and Prince von Bülow. Churchill records that on November 3, 1909 when he was President of the Board of Trade, he began a memo to the British cabinet with these words:

> Believing that there are practically no checks upon German naval expansion except those imposed by the increasing difficulties of getting money, I have had the enclosed report prepared with a view to showing how far those limitations are becoming effective. It is clear that they are becoming terribly effective.

Prince von Bülow, who was the German Chancellor, wrote in 1914 [Richardson, 1960b, p. 15]:

> It is just possible that the effect of convulsively straining her military resources to the uttermost may, by reacting on the economic and social conditions of France, hasten the return of pacific feelings . . . Should the three-year military service entail an income tax, this would also probably have a sobering effect.

In 1935, when Grey's statement that the enormous growth of armaments was the real cause of the war was quoted in a Parliamentary debate, L. S. Amery, said in reply [Richardson, 1960b, p. 15–16]:

> With all respect to the memory of an eminent statesman, I believe that statement to be entirely mistaken. The armaments were only the symptoms of the conflict of ambition and ideals, of those nationalist forces, which created the war . . . It was insoluble conflicts of ambitions and not in the armaments themselves that the cause of the war lay.

It was statements like Amery's that impelled Richardson to include the terms $r$ and $s$ measuring underlying grievances into his system of differential equations.

Thus we see how Richardson was led to include the three causes of armament expenditure increases and decreases into his model, and how he arrived at armament expenditures as an indication of hostility. Is there some way to test this model? What predictions can we make from it that can be compared to reality?

## D.  Testing the Model

In this section, we will test the Richardson model against the actual arms race that took place in Europe in the years prior to the outbreak of World War I.

In the first decade of this century, it was apparent to many observers that there was a great likelihood of a war arising. The principal foes in the war would be France and Germany. It was clear that France would be allied with Russia and Germany with Austria-Hungary. It was thought that Great Britain would most likely support France and Russia, but the role of some other important European nations (Italy, Turkey) was in doubt.

Richardson attempted to test his model as an arms race between two blocs: France and Russia on one side, Germany and Austria-Hungary on the other.

He began with assumptions that the degree of "mutual fear" and the braking effects of high armament budgets were the same on both sides; that is, he set $a = b$ and $m = n$ in Eqs. (11) and (12) to obtain:

$$\frac{dx}{dt} = ay - mx + r \tag{32}$$

$$\frac{dy}{dt} = ax - my + s. \tag{33}$$

If we add these equations, we obtain

$$\frac{d(x + y)}{dt} = (a - m)(x + y) + (r + s). \tag{34}$$

Finally, if we set $z = x + y$, we obtain the differential equation

$$\frac{dz}{dt} = (a - m)\left(z + \frac{r + s}{a - m}\right). \tag{35}$$

The variable $z$ represents the total armament expenditures for both sides. Equation (35) then makes a prediction which can be checked: Total armament expenditures will increase at a rate which is proportional to total expenditures. Mathematically, this asserts that if we plot $dz/dt$ against $z$ we should obtain a straight line.

Richardson tabulated the armament budgets in millions of pounds sterling of the four powers in the years immediately before World War I. He estimated $dz/dt$ for each two-year period by simply taking the differences in total budgets

**Table 2.1**

|               | 1909  | 1910  | 1911  | 1912  | 1913  |
|---------------|-------|-------|-------|-------|-------|
| France        | 48.6  | 50.9  | 57.1  | 63.2  | 74.7  |
| Russia        | 66.7  | 68.5  | 70.7  | 81.8  | 92.9  |
| Germany       | 63.1  | 62.0  | 62.0  | 68.2  | 95.4  |
| Austria-Hungary | 20.8 | 23.4 | 23.4  | 25.5  | 26.9  |
| Totals        | 199.2 | 204.8 | 214.9 | 238.7 | 289.0 |
| Increases     |       | 5.6   | 10.1  | 23.8  | 50.3  |
| 2-year average |      | 202.0 | 209.8 | 226.8 | 263.8 |

Adapted from Richardson, *Arms and Insecurity*, 1960, p. 32.

for the years and then plotted this difference against the average total for the two years. The data is presented in Table 2.1 and the graph of his results in Fig. 2.12.

The four points do lie close to a straight line. Richardson [1960b, p. 33] himself wrote:

> Since I first drew this diagram . . . I have been incredulous about the marvelously good fit. Yet there is certainly no simple mistake . . . The regularity of these phenomena shows that foreign politics had then a rather machine-like quality, intermediate between the predictability of the moon and the freedom of an unmarried young man.

The slope of the line in Fig. 2.12 is about 0.73. The slope predicted by the model is $a - m$. Richardson gives some data to indicate that a reasonable figure for $m$ is .2 so that $a$ is roughly .9. Since $a = b$ and $m = n$ in this situation, we have $ab = .81$ and $mn = .04$. Since $ab > mn$, we have the ambiguous case.

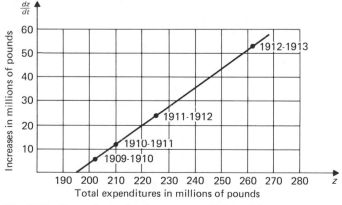

**Fig. 2.12**  Rate of growth of $z$ versus $z$. (Adapted from Richardson, 1960b, p. 33.)

If we extrapolate the observations in Fig. 2.12 along the straight line to the point where $dz/dt = 0$, we find that there $z = 194$ million pounds sterling. At this level of expenditures, the total expenditures would remain constant. Richardson [1960b, pp. 33–34] concludes,

> As love covereth a multitude of sins, so the good will between opposing alliances would just have covered 194 million pounds of defense expenditure on the part of the four nations concerned. Their actual expenditure in 1909 was 199 million; and so began an arms race which led to World War I.

The critical reader may not be so quick to accept this argument as evidence that the Richardson model is an accurate description of the dynamics of arms races. We have already pointed out that a number of simplifying assumptions were made in the original formulation of the model. More simplifying suppositions were necessary to make the prediction Richardson claims is verified by the facts. You might well consider, for example, why Richardson left out the armaments of Great Britain in his calculations when it was evident that this nation was an ally of France and Russia. Does the model justify the statement that a stabilized arms race implies that there will be no wars?

We have presented Richardson's model not because we believe in all its assumptions or in its universal applicability to all arms races, but rather to illustrate model building, improving, interpreting, and testing procedures. In commenting on the importance of Richardson's work, Rashevsky and Trucco [Richardson, 1960b, Preface p. ix] state quite well the case for studying such a model:

> The value of this work is not in the particular formulation of his theory but in the fact that Richardson shows *how* the problems of the causes of war can be subject to mathematical treatment and to rigorous mathematical thought. Even in physics, no matter how good a mathematical theory of a given set of phenomena is, it is eventually improved almost to a point beyond recognition. But the *basic* ideas of a good theory remain through all those changes. Look at the difference between Planck's original formulation of discontinuous emission of radiation and the present-day formulation of quantum mechanics. Yet the latter would not have been possible without the former. Richardson's equations will be changed by future investigators, some of his conclusions will be abandoned, but his work will remain forever as the first study of war on a rigorous basis of mathematical reasoning. Whatever the shortcomings of this model, it will have to be studied by every investigator who delves into the causes and origins of war. This work is a starting point for the development of a new branch of sociology.
>
> The practical aspects of any theory seldom come at once. Radio, which was made possible by Maxwell's theory, came long after his death. Einstein's theoretical prediction of the equivalence of mass and energy remained for 40 years without any applications. When they came, they came with a vengeance. Richardson may have over-emphasized the immediate applicability of his work. Its long range usefulness cannot be doubted.

## EXERCISES

### I. THE REAL-WORLD SETTING

1. What evidence can you find that a "mutual fear" situation exists today in the Middle East, Northern Ireland, or between the United States and the Soviet Union?

### II. CONSTRUCTING A DETERMINISTIC MODEL

2. Comment on the importance of the assumption that the variables in a deterministic model must represent observable and measurable quantities.

### III. A SIMPLE MODEL FOR AN ARMS RACE

3. Let $a = b = 1$ in Eqs. (1) and (2).

a) Verify that $f(t) = Ce^t + De^{-t}$ and $g(t) = Ce^t - De^{-t}$ give a solution to the system of differential equations, where $C$ and $D$ are arbitrary constants.

b) Find the appropriate values of $C$ and $D$ if $x_0 = 3$ and $y_0 = 1$.

c) Sketch the graphs of $f$ and $g$.

d) Determine $\lim_{t \to \infty} f(t)$ and $\lim_{t \to \infty} g(t)$.

4. Show that the constant $C$ of Eq. (8) is equal to $y_0^2 - (b/a)x_0^2$.

5. What happens in the simple arms race model in each of the following cases?

a) $x_0 = y_0 = 0$;

b) $x_0 = 0$ and $y_0$ is positive;

c) $x_0$ is positive and $y_0 = 0$.

6. Analyze the simple arms race model if $a$ and $b$ are both negative. What assumptions does this model reflect? Can these assumptions be defended?

7. Analyze the simple arms race model if $a$ and $b$ have opposite signs. What assumptions does this model reflect? Can these assumptions be defended?

8. Is it possible that $(x(t), y(t))$ asymptotically approaches some point $(x^*, y^*)$ in the first quadrant as time goes on? Why?

9. This problem develops a closed form solution for the function $x = f(t)$ of the simple arms race model.

a) Show that differentiation of Eq. (1) gives $x''(t) = ay'(t) = abx(t)$.

b) By substituting $x = e^{mt}$ into the equation of part (a), show that there are two values for the constant $m$, $m_1$, and $m_2$, which make the equation valid.

c) Let $f_1(t) = e^{m_1 t}$ and $f_2(t) = e^{m_2 t}$. Show that if $x(t) = Cf_1(t) + Df_2(t)$ where $C$ and $D$ are any constants, then $x''(t) = abx(t)$.

d) If $x = f(t)$ and $y = g(t)$ are solutions satisfying Eqs. (3) and (4), show that $f(0) = x_0$ and $f'(0) = ay_0$ while $g(0) = y_0$ and $g'(0) = bx_0$.

e) If the function $f$ satisfies Eqs. (3) and (4) where $f(t) = Cf_1(t) + Df_2(t)$, show that $C + D = x_0$ and $Am_1 + Bm_2 = ay_0$.

f) Solve the equations of (e) for $C$ and $D$ in terms of $x_0, y_0, m_1$, and $m_2$.

g) Show that if $f(t)$ satisfies Eqs. (3) and (4) and is given by (e), then

$$f(t) = \frac{(\sqrt{ab}\,x + ay)e^{\sqrt{ab}\,t} + (\sqrt{ab}\,x - ay)e^{-\sqrt{ab}\,t}}{2\sqrt{ab}}.$$

h) Let $f(t)$ be the function of part (g). Find $\lim_{t \to \infty} f(t)$.

i) Sketch a graph of $f$.

10. Find $g(t)$ explicitly as a function of $t$ so that $g$ satisfies Eqs. (3) and (4). Carry out the steps analagous to parts (a)–(g) of Exercise 9.

## IV. THE RICHARDSON MODEL

11. Show that $x = Ae^t + 4Be^{-6t} - (\frac{5}{3})$, $y = Ae^t - 3Be^{-6t} + (\frac{3}{2})$ is a solution of

$$\frac{dx}{dt} = 4y - 3x + 1$$

$$\frac{dy}{dt} = 3x - 2y + 2$$

for any choice of constants $A$ and $B$. What is the ultimate behavior of an arms race with these equations? Sketch the graphs of $x$ and $y$ as functions of $t$. If the expenditures at $t = 0$ are $x_0$ and $y_0$, find $A$ and $B$ in terms of $x_0$ and $y_0$.

12. Discuss the effect of setting $r$ and $s$ both equal to 0 on the question of stability; that is, investigate the consequences of the model given by Eqs. (9) and (10).

13. Discuss the stability question for the Richardson model in the cases

a) $a = 0$,

b) $n = 0$.

Begin by determining the equations of the optimal lines.

14. Can the lines $L$ and $L'$ be parallel? What happens to the arms race in this case?

15. a) Show that if $mn - ab \neq 0$, then the lines $L$ and $L'$ intersect at the point $(x^*, y^*)$ where

$$x^* = \frac{rn + as}{mn - ab} \quad \text{and} \quad y^* = \frac{br + ms}{mn - ab}.$$

b) If the grievance terms $r$ and $s$ are positive, show that the stable point $(x^*, y^*)$ lies in the first or third quadrant of the plane, depending on the sign of $mn - ab$.

16. Prove that $dy/dt$ is negative at every point above $L'$ and positive at every point below $L'$. Show that this implies that Red always adjusts its expenditures toward its optimal line.

17. Verify the details of the argument that if $r$ and $s$ are positive and $mn - ab$ is negative, then the arms race always leads to runaway expenditures regardless of the location of the initial point.

18. Show that the lines $L$ and $L'$ can assume the configuration of Fig. 2.9 only when at least one of the "grievance" terms is negative.

19. Show that if $r$ and $s$ are negative and $(x^*, y^*)$ is in the third quadrant, then the lines $L$ and $L'$ split the first quadrant into three regions and that the arms race tends to total disarmament for an initial point in any of the three regions.

20. a)  Carry out the Euler procedure for the example in IV. D. with initial level (15, 24). What is the outcome in this case?

b)  Verify the result in (a) by using the "point-slope method."

21.  Consider the differential equation $dx/dt = 2 - (x/t)$ with $x(1) = 2$.

a)  Verify that $x = t + (1/t)$ is a solution. What is $x(2)$?

b)  Use the Euler method to solve the differential equation. With $\Delta t = .1$, what value does this assign to $x(2)$?

22.  Apply Euler's method to the example of Section IV.D. with $\Delta t = .1$ and $\Delta t = 1$. What conclusions can you draw about the outcome of the arms race?

23.  Does Eq. (26) always determine two straight lines? If so, find the equations of these lines.

24.  In the Richardson model, is it possible that arms expenditure levels will tend to approach some point $(\hat{x}, \hat{y})$ in the first quadrant which is not the stable point? Why?

25.  The system $dx/dt = y - 2x - 5$, $dy/dt = 6x - 2y - 12$, first introduced at the beginning of Section IV.D, has solution

$$x(t) = Ae^{(-2+\sqrt{6})t} + Be^{(-2-\sqrt{6})t} + 11$$
$$y(t) = \sqrt{6}Ae^{(-2+\sqrt{6})t} - \sqrt{6}Be^{(-2-\sqrt{6})t} + 27$$

for any constants $A$ and $B$.

a)  Verify this by substitution into the system of differential equations.

b)  Evaluate $A$ and $B$ if at $t = 0$, we have $x_0 = y_0 = 15$.

c)  For the values of $A$ and $B$ obtained in part (b), determine the limiting behavior of this arms race using the explicit formulas of (a). Is the answer consistent with that obtained in Section IV.D?

## V.  INTERPRETING AND TESTING THE RICHARDSON MODEL

26.  Richardson's model predicts that the rate of change of total expenditures, $z = x + y$, is a linear function of total expenditures. Can you construct a different model of an arms race which leads to the same conclusion?

---

## SUGGESTED PROJECTS

---

1.  One can argue that in the real world, a runaway arms race is impossible since there is an absolute limit to the amount any country can spend on arms; the gross national product minus some amount for survival. How can this idea be incorporated into the Richardson model?

2.  Extend the Richardson model to the situation of three nations. Derive a set of differential equations if the three are mutually fearful so that each one is spurred to arm by the expenditures of the other two; examine the stability question for this example. Also derive equations if two of the nations are close allies who are not threatened by the arms buildup of each other but are threatened by the expenditures of the third; discuss the possibilities for stability in this case.

3. The basic assumptions of our model require that $a, b, m$, and $n$ be positive numbers. If negative values are assigned to these, the model would go in reverse: the armaments of the rival would act as a brake and one's own armaments as a spur. Investigate the stability of such an arms race. Can such a model be defended on the basis of real-world observations?

4. Suppose the underlying differential equations have the form

$$\frac{dx}{dt} = ay^2 - mx + r$$

$$\frac{dy}{dt} = bx^2 - ny + s,$$

where $a, b, m$, and $n$ are positive. Sketch the stability curves $dx/dt = 0$ and $dy/dt = 0$. How many stable points are there? Discuss the outcomes of such an arms race for various intersections of the stability curves.

5. During his research work in Bali with Margaret Mead, the anthropologist Gregory Bateson became interested in the factors that keep cultures together or drive them apart. Bateson described two basic forms of relationship between groups in a culture, "symmetrical" and "complementary." In a symmetrical relation the same behavior is exchanged: more of it in Red is answered by more of it in Blue. In complementary relations, opposite and mutually dependent behaviors are exchanged. Bateson was influenced by Richardson's arms race model. Investigate Bateson's theory and explore how the Richardson model can be adapted to formulate the theory in mathematical terms. This provides another good example of how essentially similar mathematical models can be used to investigate real-world problems that, at first sight, appear to have little to do with each other.

## REFERENCES

The development of the model of an arms race discussed in this chapter is due to L. F. Richardson, "Generalized foreign policy," *British Journal of Psychology Monographs Supplements*, **23** (1939). Richardson's more extended writings on the causes of war may be found in his two books: *Statistics of Deadly Quarrels* (Chicago: Quadrangle Books, 1960a) and *Arms and Insecurity: A Mathematical Study of the Causes and Origins of War* (Pittsburgh: Boxwood Press, 1960b). Preface to *Arms and Insecurity* was written by Nicolas Rashevsky and Ernesto Trucco.

The treatment of the Richardson model presented here derives from, and was inspired by, Chapters 1 and 2 of Anatol Rapoport's *Fights, Games and Debates* (Ann Arbor: University of Michigan Press, 1960).

For further reading in this area, see Thomas L. Saaty, *Mathematical Models of Arms Control and Disarmament* (New York: Wiley, 1968).

General mathematical discussions of systems of linear differential equations with constant coefficients may be found in Fred Brauer, John A. Nohel, and Hans Schneider, *Linear Mathematics* (New York: Benjamin, 1970) and David A. Sanchez, *Ordinary*

*Differential Equations and Stability Theory* (San Francisco: Freeman, 1968), especially Chapter 4.

The use of derivatives to approximate function values is discussed in George B. Thomas, *Calculus with Analytic Geometry*, 3rd Edition (Reading, Mass: Addison-Wesley, 1960). Numerical solution of differential equations is discussed at length in S. D. Conte and Carl de Boor, *Elementary Numerical Analysis*, 2nd edition (New York: McGraw-Hill, 1972).

Bateson's writings are found in Gregory Bateson, *Steps To An Ecology of Mind* (Scranton: Chandler Publishing Company, 1972).

# 3 Ecological Models: Single Species

The fact that ecology is
essentially a mathematical
subject is becoming ever more
widely accepted. Ecologists
everywhere are attempting
to formulate and solve their
problems by mathematical
reasoning.

E. C. Pielou

## I. INTRODUCTION

This chapter initiates the study of simple deterministic models for population growth. As Pielou notes in her book, *An Introduction to Mathematical Ecology*, "The investigation of the growth and decline of population is, historically, the oldest branch of mathematical ecology." Chapter 3 examines models for the changes in single-species population. The mathematical tool employed is the first-order differential equation. In Chapter 4, some models for population growth are examined which present important features of interaction between two species occupying the same territory. In particular, we will study the oscillation of population sizes of two competing species and the dynamics of predator-prey populations. Here the mathematical tool is the autonomous system of first-order differential equations. The mathematical analysis is self-contained.

## II. THE PURE BIRTH PROCESS

Imagine a population made up entirely of identical organisms which reproduce at a rate that is the same for every individual and which does not vary with time. If we assume that each individual lives forever, that the organisms do not interfere with one another, and that there is sufficient space and resources to sustain all the individuals, then we are dealing with what ecologists term a "pure birth process." This process has been used to study yeast cells growing by fission, the propagation of new ideas, the increase in the number of scientists over time, as well as many other types of population growth. The mathematical model for this process is a first-order differential equation

$$\frac{dP}{dt} = bP,$$

where $P = P(t)$ is the population at time $t$ and $b$ is the positive constant *birth rate* for each individual.

The opposite of the pure birth process—the *pure death process*—is described by essentially the same mathematical model. In the pure death process, it is assumed that no births occur and that each individual has the same positive probability $d$ of death at every moment, a probability that does not change with time or with the age of the individual. The constant $d$ is called the death rate. The differential equation describing these assumptions has the form

$$\frac{dP}{dt} = -dP.$$

The original model can also be employed to describe a population in which both births and deaths occur. Assume again that the birth rate $b$ and the death rate $d$ are positive constants, independent of time, size of population, and age of individual. The model is the differential equation

$$\frac{dP}{dt} = (b - d)P.$$

Setting $a = b - d$, we see that the same equation

$$\frac{dP}{dt} = aP$$

describes all three situations.

**Analysis of the model**    What are the mathematical consequences of this model and what are the corresponding interpretations? First, separate the variables $P$ and $t$ to obtain

$$\int \left(\frac{1}{P}\right) dP = \int a\, dt.$$

(Students who have not worked with differential equations before may wish to consult Appendix V.) Carry out the indicated integration to arrive at the relation

$$\log P = at + C$$

where $C$ is an arbitrary constant and "log" denotes the natural logarithm; we may write $\log P$ rather than $\log |P|$ because we know population will always be nonnegative. If the population is known at some particular instant, then the value of $C$ is easily computed. If, for example, $P = P_0$ at time $t = 0$, then $\log P_0 = a0 + C = C$. Thus

$$\log P = at + \log P_0.$$

Exponentiating each side of this equation yields an explicit relation between population $P$ and time $t$:

$$P = P_0 e^{at}.$$

The behavior of this function depends on the sign of $a$. If $a$ is positive, $P$ is a steadily increasing, unbounded function of $t$. If $a$ is zero, $P$ is the constant function whose value is $P_0$ for all $t$. If $a$ is negative, then $P$ is a steadily decreasing function of $t$ that approaches zero as $t$ grows large. See Fig. 3.1 for graphs of these three possibilities.

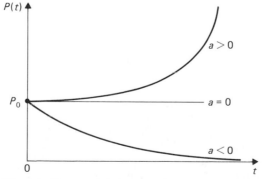

**Fig. 3.1**    The graph $P(t) = P_0 e^{at}$. The shape of the curve depends on the sign of $a$.

**Exponential growth**    The constant $a$ would be positive in the case of a pure birth process or if the birth rate $b$ exceeded the death rate $d$. The model would predict that the population will steadily increase and become indefinitely large. Ecologists would say that the population is undergoing *exponential growth*. Since the model asserts that there is no limit to the number of individuals in this population, it is clear that the model is not a completely realistic picture.

Before this model is scrapped, however, let us note that it may be a realistic one for the growth of some populations over relatively short time intervals. As an example of this, the population of the United States during the period from 1790 to 1860 grew at such an exponential pace. See Fig. 3.2. To get an idea of what the growth rate $a$ was during this period, let $t = 0$ correspond to 1790 and $P_0 = 3.929$ million, the population counted in the 1790 census. If the population growth actually followed an exponential curve, then the number of people in the United States in the year 1830 ($t = 40$), for example, would satisfy

$$P_{40} = P_0 e^{40a}.$$

This equation may be solved for $a$ by taking logarithms:

$$\log P_{40} = \log P_0 + 40a,$$

or

$$a = \frac{\log P_{40} - \log P_0}{40}.$$

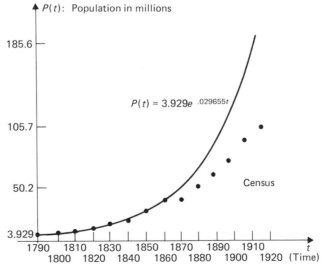

**Fig. 3.2**   A comparison of population growth in the United States from 1790 to 1920 with the exponential curve $P(t) = 3.929e^{.029655t}$. The "fit" is extremely close for the period 1790–1860.

The census data give $P_{40} = 12.866$ million. The value of $a$ would then be $a = .029655$ and the equation for United States population growth would be

$$P(t) = 3.929e^{.029655t}.$$

By the choice of constants, this model exactly predicts the population levels in the years 1790 and 1830. To test how well the model works as a predictor in other years, examine Table 3.1. Observe from this table that the predicted values of population are very close to the observed ones for the years 1790 to 1860. The largest error is less than 2 percent of the population. Since the census data, especially in the early years of the republic, was itself subject to many errors, this is as good a "fit" as we might reasonably expect.

As a long-term model of United States population growth, the model is not a very good one, as the data from 1870 through 1970 show. Important factors such as wars, immigration, variations in the birth and death rates, and changes in the age structure of the population are missing from the model. Nevertheless, simple exponential growth is an accurate way of portraying the change in population in the United States during the early and middle nineteenth century. We may also conclude that if the pattern of growth established during that period continued until the present day, the population of the United States today would be well in excess of 800 million!

**Table 3.1** A comparison between actual population based on census data in the United States and that predicted by exponential growth with rate .029655. The "error" term is found by subtracting the actual population from the predicted one. The "percent error" is the error divided by the actual population.

| Year | Predicted population (in millions) | Actual population (in millions) | Error | Percent error |
|------|-----------------------------------|--------------------------------|-------|---------------|
| 1790 | 3.929 | 3.929 | 0 | 0 |
| 1800 | 5.285 | 5.308 | −.0227 | −.42 |
| 1810 | 7.11 | 7.24 | −.1301 | −1.8 |
| 1820 | 9.564 | 9.638 | −.0737 | −.76 |
| 1830 | 12.866 | 12.866 | 0 | 0 |
| 1840 | 17.307 | 17.069 | .2385 | 1.4 |
| 1850 | 23.282 | 23.192 | .0902 | .39 |
| 1860 | 31.319 | 31.443 | −.1235 | −.39 |
| 1870 | 42.131 | 38.558 | 3.5733 | 9.3 |
| 1880 | 56.676 | 50.156 | 6.5195 | 13 |
| 1890 | 76.241 | 62.948 | 13.293 | 21 |
| 1900 | 102.56 | 75.995 | 26.5646 | 35 |
| 1910 | 137.964 | 91.972 | 45.9923 | 50 |
| 1920 | 185.591 | 105.711 | 79.88 | 76 |
| 1930 | 249.659 | 122.775 | 126.884 | 103 |
| 1940 | 335.844 | 131.669 | 204.175 | 155 |
| 1950 | 451.781 | 150.697 | 301.084 | 200 |
| 1960 | 607.741 | 179.323 | 428.418 | 239 |
| 1970 | 817.54 | 203.185 | 614.355 | 302 |

Scientists have obtained similar conclusions about exponential growth models for other living organisms. The simple model $dP/dt = aP$ is often very accurate when the environmental conditions are close to ideal: no natural enemies of the species are present, resources are unlimited, and there is sufficient space for the organisms to develop without interfering with each other.


## III. EXPONENTIAL DECAY

If the sign of $a$ is negative, then the function $P(t) = P_0 e^{at}$ remains positive for all values of $t$, but steadily decreases toward zero as $t$ increases. If the population under consideration consists of all individuals belonging to a particular species, then the model predicts that the species will become extinct as all the individuals will eventually die off. As noted above, the constant $a$ would be negative if the death rate exceeds the birth rate or if the assumptions of the pure death process are valid.

Unfortunately, there are conditions in our environment today which make a pure death process quite likely for the future growth of some species. The extensive use of pesticides, particularly DDT, in the mid-twentieth century has had the unexpected consequence of drastically reducing the live birth rate of certain species of birds. One of the best-documented studies concerns the plight of the peregrine falcon, a bird of prey that once bred on cliffsides across the United States. The extensive use of DDT began in 1946 and the first signs of decrease in the peregrine population were noted within a year. In the 23 breeding seasons between 1947 and 1970—during which time DDT and similar persistent pesticides were abundantly used—the peregrine has become all but extinct as a breeding bird in the continental United States. Research has now shown that DDT absorbed by the birds inhibited an enzyme that facilitates the transporting of calcium from the blood to the site of eggshell production in the oviduct. As a result, the falcons lay thinner eggs, which crack under their weight when they brood them. Since the number of live births dropped dramatically while the death rate among adults remained essentially unchanged, it is not surprising that in some areas of the country less than ten percent of the pre-pesticide breeding population remains.

The decay of radioactive material is another example of pure exponential decay, since the number of atoms that decompose in a given unit of time is proportional to the total number present. The rate of decay of a radioactive element is often expressed in terms of its *half-life*. This is the time required for a quantity of the element to decrease by a factor of one-half. In terms of the function $P(t) = P_0 e^{at}$, this number is given by $(-\log 2)/a$, which is independent of $P_0$.

In the late 1940's, Willard F. Libby discovered radiocarbon, a radioactive isotope of carbon with a half-life of approximately 5600 years. The ratio of radioactive to nonradioactive carbon present in all living organisms has remained essentially constant over many centuries. When the organism dies, it stops absorbing new radiocarbon, so that the ratio decreases exponentially over the years. If an old bit of charcoal has half the radioactivity of a living tree, then it came from a tree that died about 5600 years ago.

Libby and his co-workers developed the technique of radiocarbon dating to determine the ages of many objects dating back as much as 50,000 years. This technique has been of great significance to archeologists and anthropologists whose use of radiocarbon dating and other observations indicate, for example, that man arrived in the Western Hemisphere only about 11,500 years ago.

The common isotope of uranium has a half-life of 4.5 billion years while rubidium decays into strontium with a half-life of 50 billion years. Using a dating technique based on the exponential decay of these radioactive elements, geologists have determined the ages of rocks found on the earth and on the surface of the moon. From these, they are obtaining a better picture of the development of our planet.

## IV. LOGISTIC POPULATION GROWTH

### A. The Logistic Model

The basic assumption of the pure exponential model is that the rate of increase of population is proportional to the size of the population; that is, the rate is a constant, independent of the size of the population. The model assumes that sufficient resources are available to sustain any level of population so that there is no interference between individuals in the population. These assumptions are not very realistic. Every species of organism inhabits some restricted environment, with a finite amount of space and a limited supply of resources. The environment has a "carrying capacity," an upper limit on the number of individual organisms that can exist on the available resources. As the size of the population gets closer to this carrying capacity, its rate of growth must slow down. Any realistic model of population dynamics should reflect this feature. This section examines a mathematical model that attempts to do this.

Briefly stated, the argument in the paragraph above is that the rate of growth is not constant, but is dependent on the size of the population. The mathematical model should then assert that the rate of population is in fact a function of the population; mathematically, the statement looks like

$$\frac{dP}{dt} = f(P)$$

where $f$ is some function of population size $P$. How should $f$ be selected?

If the population ever reaches a zero level, then of course it will always remain at zero. Hence the function $f$ should have the property that $f(0) = 0$. Suppose we write the function $f$ as $f(P) = Pg(P)$ where $g$ is also a function of $P$.

Then $f(0) = 0g(0) = 0$ regardless of the form of the function $g$. How then should $g$ be selected?

The idea that rate of growth will slow down as population gets larger and larger can be captured by the condition that $g'(P)$ be negative. The simplest model is then obtained by making the function $g$ as simple as possible; namely, assume that $g$ is a linear function

$$g(P) = a - bP$$

where $a$ and $b$ are positive constants. Then the model assumes the form

$$\frac{dP}{dt} = P(a - bP).$$

This is called the *logistic equation* or the *Verhulst-Pearl equation*.

Note that this derivation of the logistic model does not make explicit use of the carrying capacity of the environment. There are several other ways of arriving at this model. We will outline one path: suppose that $aP$ is the rate at which the population would increase if the environment possessed unlimited space and resources. Then we might assume that the actual growth rate is the potential rate multiplied by a factor measuring the proportion of the maximum attainable size of the population which is still unrealized. If $M$ is the maximum possible population size in the environment, then $M - P$ is the amount of growth still available and $(M - P)/M$ would be the fraction of maximum attainable size still possible. The assumption is then that the actual rate of growth is $aP(M - P)/M$. The differential equation expressing the model would be

$$\frac{dP}{dt} = aP\frac{M - P}{M} = aP - \left(\frac{a}{M}\right)P^2,$$

which is easily recognized as the Verhulst-Pearl equation.

### B. Mathematical Analysis

The logistic equation may be solved by a nice application of the technique of partial fraction decomposition. The differential equation

$$\frac{dP}{dt} = P(a - bP)$$

may be written in the equivalent form

$$\int \frac{dP}{P(a - bP)} = \int dt$$

after separating variables and integrating.

Now the fraction $1/(P(a - bP))$ may be decomposed as

$$\frac{1}{P(a - bP)} = \frac{1/a}{P} + \frac{b/a}{a - bP}$$

so that we have the equivalent integration problem

$$\int \frac{1}{P} + \frac{b}{a - bP}\, dP = \int a\, dt.$$

Simple integration then yields

$$\log P - \log(a - bP) = at + C$$

where $C$ is a constant of integration.

This last equation may be rewritten as

$$\log \frac{P}{a - bP} = at + C.$$

Exponentiation of each side gives

$$\frac{P}{a - bP} - Ke^{at}$$

where $K$ is the constant $e^C$. It is useful to rewrite this equation as

$$P - \frac{aKe^{at}}{1 + bKe^{at}} = \frac{a}{b + (1/K)e^{-at}} - \frac{a/b}{1 + (1/bK)e^{-at}} = \frac{k}{1 + e^{d-at}}$$

where $d = -\log(bK)$ and $k = a/b$.

Since $a$ is positive, $e^{-at}$ tends to 0 as $t$ increases. Thus $\lim_{t \to \infty} P = k = a/b$. The logistic model then predicts that population will increase and asymptotically approach the carrying capacity $a/b$. Note that at the capacity level of $P = a/b$, the logistic equation gives $dP/dt = 0$. See Fig. 3.3 for a graph of the population

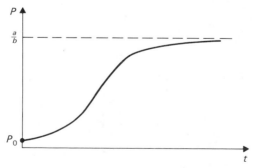

**Fig. 3.3**   The logistic curve $P = k/(1 + e^{d-at})$.

as a function of time. This curve is called the *logistic curve*, and resembles an elongated letter *S*.

## C. Testing the Logistic Model

Laboratory experiments with a variety of species have shown that the growth of many populations, under appropriate conditions, follows the logistic curve. As a second model of growth of the United States population, consider the logistic equation. We shall show that this model gives an accurate portrait of the changes in the nation's population for much of its history.

In each of its forms, the logistic model of population as an explicit function of time contains three constants. To test the equation as a model of population growth in the United States, we must assign numerical values to these constants. It is possible to do this if the populations $P_0$, $P_1$, and $P_2$ are known at the three times $t_0$, $t_1$, and $t_2$. To this end, rewrite the equation of the logistic curve as

$$d - at = \log\left(\frac{k - P}{P}\right)$$

where $a$, $d$, and $k$ are the constants to be determined. With the equation in this form, we have

$$d - at_0 = \log\left(\frac{k - P_0}{P_0}\right) = A,$$

$$d - at_1 = \log\left(\frac{k - P_1}{P_1}\right) = B,$$

and

$$d - at_2 = \log\left(\frac{k - P_2}{P_2}\right) = C.$$

These equations yield the relationships

$$B - A = a(t_0 - t_1), \qquad C - A = a(t_0 - t_2),$$
$$a = (B - A)/(t_0 - t_1), \qquad \text{and} \qquad d = at_0 + A.$$

From the first pair of equations, we have

$$(t_0 - t_2)(B - A) = (t_0 - t_1)(C - A).$$

For simplicity, suppose that the dates chosen are equally spaced so that $t_1 - t_2 = t_1 - t_0$. Then $2(B - A) = C - A$ or $2B = A + C$. This equation gives

$$\log\left(\frac{k - P_1}{P_1}\right)^2 = \log\left(\frac{k - P_0}{P_0}\right) + \log\left(\frac{k - P_2}{P_2}\right)$$

or

$$\left(\frac{k - P_1}{P_1}\right)^2 = \left(\frac{k - P_0}{P_0}\right)\left(\frac{k - P_2}{P_2}\right).$$

Since $P_0$, $P_1$, and $P_2$ are known, we have a quadratic equation in $k$. This has two roots, $k = 0$, and

$$k = \frac{P_1(2P_0P_2 - P_0P_1 - P_1P_2)}{P_0P_2 - P_1^2}.$$

The root $k = 0$ corresponds to the fact that if the population ever reaches zero, it will remain there forever. The nonzero root for $k$ gives the carrying capacity. Once $k$ is computed from the known values $P_0, P_1$, and $P_2$, then $A$, $B$, and $C$ are easily calculated. From these the values of $a$ and $d$ can then be found. As an example, suppose the population figures of the censuses in 1790, 1850, and 1910 are used to determine the constants. The value of $k$ turns out to be 197.274 and the predicted equation for population growth in the United States looks like:

$$P(t) = \frac{197.274}{1 + e^{(3.896 - .031t)}} \text{ millions.}$$

Comparisons between the predictions of this model and the actual population figures are given in Fig. 3.4 and in Table 3.2. The table shows that the model gives an excellent portrayal of the changes in United States population from 1790 through 1950, the largest deviation being less than 4 percent. The model fails, however, after the middle of the twentieth century. It does not predict the increase in the birth rate that led to the unexpected and unprecedented increase of 30 million Americans between 1950 and 1960. The model clearly has failed to include some factors that critically affected population changes in the last 30 years.

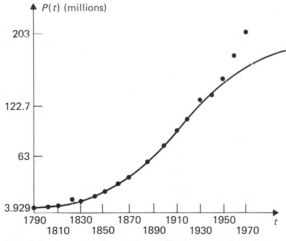

**Fig. 3.4**   A comparison of population growth in the United States from 1790 to 1970 and the logistic curve $P(t) = 197.274/(1 + e^{3.896 - .031t})$. As in Fig. 3.3, the heavy dots represent actual population levels.

**Table 3.2**  A comparison between actual population in the United States and that predicted by a logistic equation. The "error" term is found by subtracting the actual population from the predicted one. The "percent error" is the error divided by the actual population.

| Year | Predicted population (in millions) | Actual population (in millions) | Error | Percent error |
|------|------|------|------|------|
| 1790 | 3.929 | 3.929 | 0 | 0 |
| 1800 | 5.336 | 5.308 | .028 | .53 |
| 1810 | 7.228 | 7.24 | −.0120 | −.16 |
| 1820 | 9.757 | 9.638 | .1188 | 1.23 |
| 1830 | 13.109 | 12.866 | .2433 | 1.89 |
| 1840 | 17.506 | 17.069 | .4371 | 2.56 |
| 1850 | 23.192 | 23.192 | 0 | 0 |
| 1860 | 30.412 | 31.443 | −1.0308 | −3.28 |
| 1870 | 39.372 | 38.558 | .8137 | 2.11 |
| 1880 | 50.177 | 50.156 | .0211 | .042 |
| 1890 | 62.769 | 62.948 | −.1789 | −.28 |
| 1900 | 76.870 | 75.996 | .874 | 1.15 |
| 1910 | 91.972 | 91.972 | 0 | 0 |
| 1920 | 107.395 | 105.711 | 1.6839 | 1.59 |
| 1930 | 122.398 | 122.775 | −.3772 | −.31 |
| 1940 | 136.318 | 131.669 | 4.649 | 3.53 |
| 1950 | 148.678 | 150.697 | −2.019 | −1.34 |
| 1960 | 159.230 | 179.323 | −20.0925 | −11.2047 |
| 1970 | 167.944 | 203.185 | −35.2411 | −17.34 |

The dates chosen above that were used to determine the constants in the logistic equation were the ones selected by Raymond Pearl and Lowell J. Reed in a 1924 study of the United States population growth curve. Impressed by the closeness of the fit of the logistic equation to the census data from 1790 through 1920 (the only numbers available to them), they wrote [Pearl and Reed, 1920], "so far as we may rely upon present numerical values, the United States has already passed its period of most rapid population growth, unless there comes into play some factor not now known and which has never operated during the past history of the country to make the rate of growth more rapid. This latter contingency is improbable."

Pearl and Reed's estimate of an eventual population in the nation of slightly under 200 million was wrong, but not because they made a poor choice of sample years. Almost any triple of years selected for $t_0$, $t_1$, and $t_2$ which roughly coincide with early, middle, and contemporary dates will yield a particular form of the logistic curve with a similar property—the jump in population from 1950 to 1960 just does not parallel the climb of the logistic curve.

A more accurate model of the growth of United States population can be obtained by refining the model in several different ways. The function $g(P)$—chosen to be linear in the logistic model—might be taken to be a polynomial of higher degree so that higher-order effects of the size of population on the growth rate could be included. Additional factors might be attached to the differential equation to incorporate the concept that the rate of change of population is not only a function of population but of time as well. We might also try to include such factors as immigration, the medical and public health discoveries that have increased life expectancy by 15 years in the last half-century, changes in the age structure of the population, and the effects of depressions and periods of economic prosperity. The population might be divided into ethnically or religiously determined groups which display different patterns of birth rates. Some of these approaches are outlined in the exercises.

Demographers are using increasingly complex and sophisticated mathematical models of both deterministic and probabilistic character to study changes in population growth in the past and to make projections about the future. An elementary probabilistic model of population growth is presented in Chapter 9.

## V. HISTORICAL AND BIOGRAPHICAL NOTES

### A. Thomas Robert Malthus

"Explanations of population changes have been advanced by writers of many nationalities, religions, occupational specialties, and educational attainments," wrote Ralph Thomlinson in a [1965] study of population dynamics:

> Independent and dependent variables which have been used for this purpose include total population, density, fertility, mortality, migration, climate, food, topography, energy sources, standard of living, level of aspiration, urbanization, degree of world liness, transport facilities, technological development, balance of trade, genetic deterioration, age-sex distribution, socioeconomic class, religious belief, type of government, alcohol consumption, state of knowledge, and various combinations thereof. Most of these generalizations are over-simplified or obsolete; some are generally viewed as ludicrous; and a few are brilliant contributions to man's understanding of his own propagation, wandering, and demise.

Prior to the eighteenth century, most of the writing on population was marred by superficial observations, strong doses of moral pronouncements, and a general failure to distinguish between folklore and factual evidence. It was believed by many, for example, that intellectual pursuits tended to diminish the power of procreation, that prostitutes could not conceive, while "idiots bred like rabbits."

The central figure in the history of population theory is the Reverend Thomas Robert Malthus (1766–1834). Malthus, the second of eight children of an English country gentleman, won honors as a mathematics graduate of Cambridge University. He was ordained as a minister in the Church of England in 1788. A year after his marriage in 1804, Malthus accepted an appointment as professor of history and political economy in the East-Indian College, Hailebury, England. In addition to his teaching duties, Malthus published

Thomas Malthus. From
a portrait by John Linnell.
Reproduced by permission
of Jesus College,
Cambridge University.

three important books on political economy, many pamphlets and tracts, and
six editions of his famous essay on population.

Malthus' work on economics included a general theory of rent and the
distribution of wealth, which has been cited as one of the foundation stones of
modern economic thought.  In biology, Charles Darwin wrote of his debt to
Malthus for the phrase "struggle for survival" and for the concept that species
may alter through selection.  "In October 1838, I happened to read for amuse-
ment 'Malthus on Population'," wrote Darwin, "and being very well prepared
to appreciate the struggle for existence which everywhere goes on, from long
continued observation of the habits of animals and plants, it at once struck me
that under these circumstances favorable variations would tend to be preserved,
and unfavorable ones to be destroyed.  The result would be the formation of a
new species.  Here then I had a theory by which to work."*

The first edition of his essay on population was published in 1798 under the
title, "An Essay on the Principle of Population as It Affects The Future Improvement of Society, with Remarks on the Speculations of Mr. Godwin,
M. Condorcet, and Other Writers."  Condorcet and Godwin had each published works in 1793 emphasizing their optimistic beliefs in the perfectibility of

---

* *The Autobiography of Charles Darwin*, New York: Harcourt, Brace, 1959, p. 120.

man and society. They foresaw a day when inequality would be eliminated along with crime, disease, and war, a period in which reason would hold sway over emotion and base instincts.

Malthus had a contrary view. Social progress was illusory: "The structure of society, in its great features, will probably always remain unchanged." He thought man to be a lazy creature by nature, impelled to productive work only by a wife and children who needed food and shelter.

The essay on population sought to develop the consequences of two fundamental observations:

> First, that food is necessary to the existence of man. Secondly, that the passion between the sexes is necessary and will remain in its present state. These two laws ever since we have had any knowledge of mankind appear to have been fixed laws of our nature; and as we have not hitherto seen any alteration in them, we have no right to conclude that they will ever cease to be what they now are.

In 1826, a sixth edition of the essay appeared. It was titled, "An Essay on the Principle of Population, or A View of Its Past and Present Effects on Human Happiness, with an Inquiry into Our Prospects Respecting the Future Removal or Mitigation of the Evils which It Occasions." Here Malthus summarizes three important conclusions:

> (1) Population is necessarily limited by the means of subsistence. (2) Population invariably increases where the means of subsistence increase, unless prevented by some very powerful and obvious checks. (3) These checks, and the checks which repress the superior power of population, and keep its effects on a level with the means of subsistence, are all resolvable into moral restraint, vice, and misery.

During his lifetime and in subsequent generations, Malthus' essay provoked considerable controversy and debate. In tracing the development of a mathematical modeling approach to population, the next important contributor was one of the participants in this debate, Adolphe Quetelet.

## B. Lambert Adolphe Jacques Quetelet

Mathematician, astronomer, sociologist, poet, statistician, physicist, man of letters, meteorologist—it is difficult to fit Quetelet into a single category. "Nature had endowed him not only with a vivid imagination and a mind of power, but also with the precious gift of indomitable perseverance," wrote Edouard Mailly [1875, p. 169].

Quetelet was born in Ghent, Belgium on February 22, 1796 and educated in the local schools. In 1819 he received the first Doctor of Science degree awarded by the University of Ghent and shortly thereafter he assumed a professorship of mathematics at the Brussels Athenaeum. In Brussels, he quickly established many associations with the artists and writers of the area, became a member of the reading committee for the royal theater, and published many poems in the annual almanac of the local literary society.

Lambert A. J. Quetelet.
From a portrait by
J. Demannez. Copyright
Bibliothèque royale
Albert Ier, Brussels
(Cabinet des Estampes).
Reproduced by
permission.

His academic lectures, whether on elementary mathematics, calculus, experimental physics, or astronomy were well received. "He was very highly esteemed by his pupils," Mailly [1875, p. 172] noted. "There was something about him at once imposing and amiable, while there was a complete absence of anything like pedantry or haughtiness. Although marked with smallpox, his physiognomy was refined and impressive; it was only necessary to fix his large dark eyes, surmounted with heavy black brows, upon the refractory, to insure at once silence and submission."

Although much of his early research was devoted to questions of primarily mathematical interest, Quetelet soon turned to applications. He superintended the construction of the Royal Astronomical Observatory and served as its first director from 1828 until his death in 1874, five days short of his seventy-eighth birthday. Work at the observatory included cataloging of stars, a careful study of atmospheric waves for the purposes of improving meteorology, and measurements of terrestrial magnetism.

Quetelet's contribution to the development of the social sciences derive from his efforts to apply probability and statistics to the study of man. He created the concept of the "average man" as the central value about which measurements of a human trait are grouped according to the normal probability curve. In addition to the normal distribution of heights and weights, Quetelet observed that there were relative propensities of specific age groups to commit crimes. He wrote [Mailly, 1875, p. 179],

> What is very remarkable is the frightful regularity with which crimes are repeated. Year after year are recorded the same crimes, in the same order, with the same punishments; in the same proportions.... The number condemned to the prison, irons, and the scaffold is as certain as the revenue of the state. We can tell in advance how many individuals will poison their fellows, how many will stain their hands with human blood, how many will be forgers, as surely as we can predict the number of births and of deaths.

Quetelet's use of the terms and concepts of physics in the study of man and his social systems provoked wide argument and discussion on the issue of "free will versus determinism." He was strongly convinced that there were discoverable principles dictating man's behavior [Mailly, 1875, pp. 179–180]:

> Man, without knowing it, and supposing that he acts of his own free will, is governed by certain laws from which he cannot escape. We may say that the human species, considered as a whole, belongs to the order of physical phenomena.... Although his will is restrained within very narrow limits, man contains within him moral forces which distinguish him from the animal, and by which he can, to some extent, modify the laws of nature. These perturbing forces act ... slowly ... they are analogous to those astronomical variations in the systems of the world which require centuries for their investigation. The study of the natural and perturbing forces of man, in other words, social mechanics, would develop laws as admirable as those which govern celestial and inanimate bodies.... If science has advanced thus in the study of worlds, may we not look for equal progress in the study of man? Is it not absurd to suppose that, while all else is controlled by admirable laws, the human race alone is abandoned to blind chance?

In his 1835 book *On Man and the Development of his Faculties: An Essay in Social Physics*, Quetelet criticizes Malthus and the economists who came after him for not clearly establishing the necessary foundation for bringing the theory of population within the domain of the mathematical sciences. He proposes two principles to fill this "important gap" [Quetelet, 1969, p. 49]. First, population tends to grow according to a geometric progression. Second, "the resistance, or the sum of the obstacles opposed to the unlimited growth of population, increases in proportion to the square of the velocity with which the population tends to increase."

Later Quetelet draws an analogy between the growth of population and the motion of a body through a resisting medium. His writing is somewhat obscure on these points. No mathematical treatment is given and, although he claims to have made "numerous researches" on this subject, none are presented. Quetelet's comments, however, were the probable source that stimulated the first detailed presentation study and presentation of logistic growth. This was the work of Quetelet's Belgian colleague Pierre-François Verhulst.

Pierre-François Verhulst.
From a portrait by
L. Flameng.  Copyright
Bibliothèque royale
Albert Ier, Brussels
(Cabinet des Estampes).
Reproduced by permission.

## C.  Pierre-François Verhulst

Verhulst, born in Brussels October 28, 1804, was a brilliant student who received his Doctor of Science degree from the University of Ghent after only three years of study.  His mathematical research included contributions in the calculus of variations, the study of maxima and minima of functions, and number theory, as well as in the applications of probability.

Plagued by poor health, Verhulst traveled to Italy in 1830.  While in Rome, he worked for reforms in the government of the pontifical states.  Hoping to persuade the Pope to grant a constitution to the residents, Verhulst drew up a proposed pact.  It was well received by several foreign ministers but the confidential document fell out of the hands of the diplomats and into the clutches of the police.  Fearing physical attack, Verhulst prepared to barricade himself in his lodgings to withstand a possible siege.  He was ordered to leave Rome and return to Belgium.

Back home, he made an unsuccessful attempt to enter politics and tried his hand at writing historical essays.  Finally, he returned to the academic life, accepting appointment at the free university of Brussels in 1835.  There he taught mathematical subjects from geometry and trigonometry to calculus and probability as well as astronomy and celestial mechanics.  Under the influence of Quetelet, under whom he had studied at Ghent, he investigated the applications of statistical tools to social problems.

Verhulst developed a model of population growth which he called "logistic growth"; it is the one studied in Section IV.  His memoirs on the subject were published in 1838, 1845, and 1847.  Although he attempted to test his model on actual population data, he was frustrated by the inaccurate census information then available.  He noted, for example, that the figures on the population of England were obtained from a consideration only of the number of births.  These, in turn, were counted by examining the number of babies baptized into the Church of England.  Thus religious dissenters, infant deaths, and immigrants were overlooked.  "Probably owing to the fact that Verhulst was greatly in advance of his time, and that the then existing data were quite inadequate to form any effective test of his views, his memoirs fell into oblivion," wrote G. Udney Yule in a presidential address to the British Royal Statistical Society in 1925, "but they are classics on their subject."

Verhulst's discovery of the logistic curve and its application to population growth was forgotten for 80 years.  It was rediscovered independently by two American scientists working at Johns Hopkins University, Raymond Pearl and Lowell J. Reed.

## D.  Raymond Pearl

It is likely that biology will eventually be as full-panoplied with mathematically expressed theory as physics now is.  The process is already started, and the history of the old natural sciences like astronomy, physics and chemistry admits of no doubt as to the final outcome.  There is no substitute for mathematics to state in rational shorthand the relations between natural phenomena or generalizations about them.

This was the prediction of the American biologist, geneticist, and statistician Raymond Pearl [1939].  A prolific and articulate writer on many subjects, Pearl was widely respected by his colleagues for his applications of statistics to biology and he was well known to the public of his day as a provocative commentator on human behavior.

The Pearl family traced its ancestry back to Pearls who entered England at the time of the Norman conquest in 1066.  The first to settle in the United States was John Pearl who came to this country about 1670.  His descendents for the next two hundred years remained in the region of New England comprising northeastern Massachusetts, southwestern Maine, and southern New Hampshire.  It was in Farmington, New Hampshire that Raymond Pearl was born on June 3, 1879.

He attended the local elementary and secondary schools and entered Dartmouth College at the age of 16 to pursue—or so his parents and grandparents intended—the study of Greek and Latin.  Like many college students today, Pearl was intoxicated at first by the relative freedom and extracurricular activities of the campus.  His interests were reflected by low grades in his freshman year.  It was in that year, however, that he discovered his true intellectual interest.

Raymond Pearl.
Photograph reproduced
by permission of
Johns Hopkins University.

Biology was one of the required courses for first-year students at Dartmouth at that time and it appealed to Pearl. By the end of the first week of classes, he was asking the instructor to help him switch from a classics major to the natural sciences. "The subject obsessed him," according to one commentator. "He talked, thought, studied, and dreamed in terms of biology." Although he was the youngest student in his class at Dartmouth, by his senior year Pearl was serving as assistant in the general biology course.

Upon receiving his bachelor's degree in 1899, Pearl began work in the doctoral program in zoology at the University of Michigan, which he completed in three years. After a short period as a zoology instructor at Michigan, he embarked on a two-year study period at the University of Leipzig, the Marine Biological Station in Naples, and the University of London. In London, he studied biometrics under Karl Pearson, whose influence led Pearl to his life's work on the use of statistics to study populations.

The remainder of Pearl's professional life was spent at the Johns Hopkins University in Baltimore. He served there as professor of biometry and vital statistics in the School of Hygiene and Public Health, professor of biology in the School of Medicine, research professor and director of the Institute of Biological Research, and statistician at Johns Hopkins Hospital. He died of a coronary thrombosis on a weekend trip to Hershey, Pennsylvania on November 17, 1940.

In a biographical memoir, H. S. Jennings [1943], once Pearl's teacher, wrote of his former student, "He was a man of unusual height and weight, physically an impressive figure. His was a masterful personality, of extraordinary resourcefulness and initiative, of wide knowledge, astonishing power of work, remarkable versatility and scope, and strong ambitions. His interest in biology was encyclopedic. In his contributions he touched upon most aspects of the subject. . . . The breadth of Pearl's interests did not mean that his interest in particular subjects was weak. On the contrary, his interest in any subject to which he gave his attention was so intense that at any given moment he might seem a partisan and propogandist of a particular field or method of biological science."

During his 40-year professional career, Pearl wrote nearly 700 technical articles and essays and 17 books. His work appeared in journals of research in zoology, genetics, physiology, medicine, and statistics, agricultural publications, encyclopedias, newspapers, popular science magazines, literary and political journals. "This is a remarkable record of publication," wrote Jennings. "It may be questioned whether in America it has ever been equaled by a man of science, in extent and variety."

The range of Pearl's work can be seen by comparing his first paper, "On preparing earthworms for section" which appeared in the *Journal of Applied Microscopy* in 1900 and his last, "Some biological considerations about war," written for the *American Journal of Sociology* in 1940.

A glance through the 37-page list of his publications shows works on animal behavior, genetics, care and breeding of poultry, laboratory and field techniques in biology, theoretical and practical results in statistics, disease, longevity and mortality, contraception, eugenics, world overpopulation, business cycles, food prices, religion and Darwinism, and philosophical pragmatism.

It was the biology of man, however, which attracted more of Pearl's activity than any other subject. Many of his research results in this area prompted controversy and were widely discussed. An extensive statistical study in 1926, for example, of the effects of the use of alcohol on longevity and mortality persuaded Pearl that moderate consumption of alcohol is not harmful. A similar study in 1938 convinced him that tobacco is harmful to human life even in small quantities. Other research led Pearl to conclude that length of life varied inversely with the pace of living, that intellectuals had a better chance than manual workers of living longer, and that heredity dominated over environment in influencing many important parameters of life.

Socially prominent and popular, Pearl was famous for his excellent dinner parties. He was a connoisseur of good food and wine and possessed, according to one witness, "an almost boyish delight in playing at times the role par excellence himself of amateur cook and salad mixer."

One of Pearl's strongest recreational interests was music.  He led for some years an evening amateur music ensemble.  When a report on the Dartmouth class of 1899 was written 35 years after its graduation, Pearl's devotion to music was recalled [Dartmouth College, 1941]:

> He might be the first American to deliver the Heath Clark lectures at the University
> of London, or the most skillful juggler of the logistic curves of Verhulst; to us he
> was still the boy cornetist and the fellow who single-handed conjured the first Dart-
> mouth band into existence out of rustic young neophytes and rusty and discarded
> tubas.  He was our full-fledged impressario before we even knew there was such a
> word, and no crowd of urchins ever followed the Pied Piper of Hamelin so devotedly
> and gaily as we of '99 and all our Dartmouth contemporaries followed the imperious
> form of Pearl, as in corduroy or white duck trousers and with much "windy suspira-
> tion of forced breath" he poured strange harmonies on the campus air.

Pearl served as president of several important scientific organizations including the American Society of Zoologists, American Society of Naturalists, American Statistical Association, American Association of Physical Anthropologists, and the International Union for Scientific Investigation of Population Problems.  He received many honorary degrees and other awards, including membership in the National Academy of Sciences.

Pearl's own views towards the future of man may be gleaned from the final sentences of his last published work.  "The standard pattern of national behavior, to which there are no exceptions, is to combat evil with evil," he wrote [Pearl, 1941].  "But real and enduring peace will never be achieved by such techniques.  For a true evolution of new patterns of sociality that will be lasting and embrace all mankind there must first evolve among men more decency and dignity, more tolerance and forbearance, and more capacity of co-operation for the common good in the conduct of human life.  The prime condition necessary for the meek to inherit the earth is that they shall *abound* in the qualities of meekness."

### E.  Lowell Jacob Reed

Raymond Pearl was perhaps best known to the public for the projections of United States populations size that were the product of research completed with his colleague Lowell J. Reed.  Like Pearl, Reed's family roots were in New England.  Born in Berlin, New Hampshire on January 8, 1886, he received his bachelor's and master's degrees from the University of Maine.  After completing his Ph.D. in mathematics at the University of Pennsylvania, he returned to Maine to teach physics and mathematics.

His academic career was interrupted for a period of service during World War I in Washington as chief of the Bureau of Tabulations and Statistics for the War Trade Board.  His ties with the government continued in later years as he served as a consultant for the Army, Navy, Air Force, Selective Service, and the Veterans Administration.

Lowell Reed at his
New Hampshire farm.
Photograph reproduced by
permission of Johns
Hopkins University.

Reed's long association with Johns Hopkins began in 1918 when he was appointed an associate professor of biostatistics in the School of Hygiene and Public Health. Several years later, he succeeded Pearl as chairman of the department. An effective administrator, Reed served as dean of the public health school, vice-president of Johns Hopkins Hospital, and vice-president of the university.

His principal research interests were in the fields of mathematical methods in biology and medicine, mathematical statistics, and demography. He was internationally known for contributions to biostatistics and public health administration. His work included many important advances in the study of epidemics.

In the early 1920's, Pearl and Reed worked on interpolation formulas for population curves, with special reference to the United States. After trying various purely empirical curve-fitting equations, they realized that no such formula could be regarded as a general law of population growth, however good it might prove for practical purposes over a limited period. Consideration of the general principles underlying population changes led them to the mathematical model of logistic growth. Pearl and Reed's discovery of the logistic curve was quite independent of Verhulst; they learned of the Belgian's work months after deriving all the mathematical details for themselves.

At a 1925 conference, Reed predicted that it would take a century for the United States to reach a population of 200 million and, that when it did, there would be such pressure on the country's food resources that new sources of sustenance would have to be found in the tropics.

Although this prediction turned out to be wrong, others that he made, such as forecasting the rapid growth of the metropolitan New York region, were both accurate and useful to planners.

At the age of 67, Reed retired from Johns Hopkins after 35 years of service. He hoped to return to his 300-acre farm in Shelburne, New Hamsphire to enjoy the quiet life of its rugged woodlands. Barely three weeks after his retirement began, Reed was called back to Johns Hopkins and asked to accept the presidency of the university. He served well in this position for three years and finally found permanent retirement at 70.

Happily turning over his office to Milton Eisenhower, younger brother of President Dwight Eisenhower, Reed moved back to his native New Hampshire. He died in the town of his birth on April 29, 1966.


### F.  A Final Note of Caution

In discussing the difficulties and limitations of the logistic model for the growth of human populations, the sociologist Donald Olen Cogwill wrote [Bose *et al.*, 1970],

> Initially the theory was based upon experiments with yeast, fruit flies, and chickens and the conditions of these experiments should be carefully noted:
>
> 1.  The initial population was very small in relation to the space which was provided for it;
>
> 2.  Ample food was provided throughout the experiments;
>
> 3.  The food was introduced into the experimental environment by the experimenter and it was not generated by the species which was the subject of the experiment; and
>
> 4.  The spatial limits of the environment were held constant.

The reader should consider carefully whether such conditions are reasonable to assume operative for human populations.


### EXERCISES


### II.  THE PURE BIRTH PROCESS

1.  The rate of growth of a certain population of bacteria in a culture is directly proportional to the size of the population. If an experiment begins with 1000 bacteria and if one hour later the count is 1500 bacteria, then how many bacteria are present at the end of 24 hours?

2. Suppose that the population of a town was 2000 twenty years ago and that it increased continuously at a rate proportional to the existing population. If the population of the town is now 6000, find a formula relating population and time. What has been the rate of growth?

3. Suppose the population of a city doubles its original size in 50 years and triples it in 100 years. Can the population be increasing at a rate propotional to the number present? Why?

4. Suppose the population of a yeast colony is given by $P(t) = P_0 e^{at}$ and the population at time $t_1$ is $P_1$. Find a formula for $a$ in terms of $t_1$, $P_1$, and $P_0$.

5. If population $P(t)$ is growing exponentially, prove that the changes in $P$ in successive time intervals of equal duration form the terms of a geometric progression. This is the source of Thomas Malthus' famous dictum, "Population, when unchecked, increases in a geometrical ratio. Subsistence increases only in an arithmetic ratio. A slight acquaintance with numbers will shew the immensity of the first power in comparison of the second."

6. If a certain population increases at a rate proportional to the number in the population and it doubles in 45 years, in how many years is it multiplied by a factor of 3?

7. A population of bacteria grows exponentially. When initially observed, there were 100,000 bacteria. Another observation $t_1$ minutes later showed 200,000 bacteria. A third observation was taken 10 minutes after the second one; this time 1,000,000 bacteria were present.

a)  Find the equation of growth of the bacteria.

b)  How many bacteria were there after 20 minutes?

c)  What is the value of $t_1$?

8. If the population of a country is undergoing exponential growth at a rate of $r$ percent per year, show that the population doubles every $r/\log 2$ years. This number is called the "doubling time." Compute the doubling time if $r = 2$.

9. (*Emmell*) A human birth rate of 50 live births annually per 1000 population is considered very high. In 1971, several countries in Africa had birth rates of 52 per 1000. A low birth rate today is about 15 per 1000; in 1971, Sweden and Luxembourg had the world's lowest birth rates of 13.5 per 1000. Current death rates range from 5 deaths per 1000 to 30 per 1000. On a world-wide basis, the annual birth rate in 1971 was 34 per 1000 and annual death rate was 14 per 1000. What is the annual rate of increase of the world's population? Complete the following table, using the result of Exercise 8:

| Country | Growth rate (per 1000) | Doubling time |
|---|---|---|
| East Germany | .1 | |
| Denmark | .5 | |
| United States, Japan | 1.1 | |
| Argentina | 1.5 | |
| World | | |
| Afghanistan | 2.5 | |
| Ghana | 3 | |
| Costa Rica | 4 | |
| Kuwait | 8.2 | |

10. What happened in the United States between 1860 and 1870 that could have accounted for a halt in exponential growth?

11. Assume that United States population has grown exponentially. Estimate the growth rate using each of the following years in place of the year 1830 as done in the text. Compare each set of predictions with the actual data.

 a) 1800    b) 1850    c) 1900    d) 1970

12. In the pure birth process, suppose the birth rate is not constant, but instead is proportional to $P^k$ for some small positive constant $k$. Find the differential equation for growth of a population fitting this description. Solve the equation and interpret the result. This model gives a good picture of the population growth in some developing countries (Watt, K. E. F., *Ecology and Resource Management: A Quantitative Approach*, New York: McGraw-Hill, 1968).

## III. EXPONENTIAL DECAY

13. A certain radioactive substance has a half-life of 10 years. What fraction of an amount of this substance decays in 15 years?

14. Verify the claim made in the text that the half-life of a radioactive substance is independent of $P_0$.

15. A carved wooden stick found at an archaeological site near Madison, Wisconsin had 40 per cent of the radioactivity of a living tree. When was the stick carved?

16. A population, initially of 10,000 individuals, has an annual decay rate of .1. In how many years will the population decrease to 1 person?

## IV. LOGISTIC POPULATION GROWTH

17. A third derivation of the Verhulst-Pearl equation is based on the notion that a term involving the square of the population is a reasonable measure of "crowdedness." It would represent the frequency with which members of the population encounter each other. Is it reasonable that this frequency would have an inhibitory effect on the rate of population growth? Why? How does this lead to the logistic equation?

18. Models of population growth may be derived from the differential equation $dP/dt = f(P)$ by various choices of simple functions for $f$. For each of the following types of functions, determine reasonable choices for the signs of the coefficients, solve the resulting equations and interpret the results:

 a) $f(P) = a$                    b) $f(P) = a + bP$
 c) $f(P) = a + bP + cP^2$        d) $f(P) = a \sin(bt + c)$

19. At some point in the solution of the logistic differential equation, we implicitly assumed that population $P$ was always below the carrying capacity $a/b$. Where? How valid is this assumption?

20. Suppose a forest fire destroys a large portion of the resources on which a population feeds. The carrying capacity of the environment is then below the initial population $P_0$. Analyze the logistic model in this situation to the point where you can sketch the graph of population as a function of time. (Compare with Exercise 19.)

21. Show that the logistic curve has a single point of inflection. At what value of $t$ does it occur? What is the corresponding population? How does it compare to the limiting population? Is the logistic curve symmetric about the point of inflection?

22. Show that some of the answers for Exercise 21 can be obtained from the Verhulst-Pearl equation without solving for $P$ in terms of $t$.

23. In Pearl and Reed's model of United States population growth, find the year when the rate of population growth first began to slow down (see Exercise 21).

24. How can you determine the constants in the logistic equation if the populations at three different times are known, but the times are not equally spaced?

25. Assume that the growth of population in the United States from 1790 to 1860 is adequately explained by a pure-birth process. How closely does the logistic model explain growth in population from 1860 to 1970? Take 1870, 1920, and 1970 as the years to use in computing the constants in the logistic equation. What does this model predict as the "carrying capacity" of the United States?

26. Find the value of the constants in the equation of the logistic curve using the census data for the years 1790, 1880, and 1970. What is the predicted carrying capacity? How well does the resulting curve fit actual census data?

27. An initial population of 100 inhabits an area with a carrying capacity of 100,000. In the first year, the population increases to 120. Assume that the population follows logistic growth.

  a) Determine the population as an explicit function of time.

  b) How many years will it take the population to reach 95,000?

28. Find census data for the population of a Western European nation and determine how valid the logistic model is for that population. Take $t_0$, $t_1$, and $t_2$ to be spaced 100 years apart.

29. Repeat Exercise 28 for world population. How accurate do you think the available census data are?

30. Sociologists recognize a phenomena called "social diffusion," the spreading of a piece of information, technological innovation, or cultural fad among a population. The individuals in the population can be divided into those who have the information and those who do not. In a fixed population whose size is known, it is reasonable to assume that the rate of diffusion is proportional to the number who have the information and the number yet to receive it.

  a) If $x$ denotes the number of individuals in a population of $N$ people who have the information, then show that a mathematical model for social diffusion is $dx/dt = kx(N - x)$ where $t$ represents time and $k$ is a proportionality constant.

  b) Solve the equation in (a) and show that it leads to a logistic curve.

  c) At what time is the information spreading fastest?

  d) How many people will eventually receive the information?

  e) Discuss how this model might be modified to analyze an epidemic of a communicable disease.

---

## SUGGESTED PROJECTS

---

1. Consider a model for the population of scientists alive at any given time. It has been reported that 90 per cent of all scientists who have ever lived are alive today. What sort of model is consistent with this fact?

2. A simple generalization of the logistic equation is the differential equation $dP/dt = aP + bP^2 + cP^3$. Analyze the consequences of this model. Discuss how to evaluate the constants $a, b$, and $c$. Does this model give a good picture of population growth in the United States from 1790 to the present?

3. Some animal populations are periodically reduced by hunters or trappers for commercial gain. Consider the problem of determining the optimal rate of removal by a hunter who wishes to maximize *long range* economic gain; killing the entire population in one year means great profits that year but no income in subsequent years. Determine effective strategies for the hunter if the population is growing (a) exponentially and (b) logistically. See the papers of Colin W. Clark (References) for some suggested approaches.

4. The *average growth rate* of a population is given by $(1/P)(dP/dt)$. In the logistic model this average growth rate is largest when the population is smallest. (Why?) This is an unrealistic model for some species which may face extinction if the population becomes too small. Suppose that $m$ is the minimum viable population for such a species. Consider the modified logistic equation $dP/dt = (a - bP)(P - m)$. Solve this equation and interpret the results. In particular, show that the population eventually becomes extinct if $P$ is ever less than $m$.

5. (*Grossman and Turner*) Biologists have discovered that the growth, survival, and reproduction of cells is determined by nutrients flowing across the cell walls. During the early stages of a cell's growth, the rate of increase of the weight $W$ of the cell will then be proportional to its surface area. If the shape and density of the cell do not change during growth, the weight will be proportional to the cube of a radius while the surface area is proportional to the square of a radius. Show that a reasonable model for the growth of the weight of the cell as a function of time is given by the solution of the differential equation $dW/dt = cW^{2/3}$ where $c$ is a positive constant. Investigate the consequences of this model. What are the limitations of this model of cell growth? Develop a differential equation model which takes into account the fact that there may be a maximum weight which the cell cannot exceed.

6. In recent experiments at Columbia University's Institute of Cancer Research, Fred R. Kramer and his associates have been studying the growth of an RNA population in the presence of a fixed concentration of replicase molecules. Kramer has observed that the early stage of growth is nearly exponential ($dP/dt = aP$) but that after a certain period of time, population approaches linear growth ($dP/dt = b$). Develop a differential equation model for population growth consistent with these observations. Solve the equation and interpret the results. Derive some predictions from the model that Kramer can test against his other experimental data.

---

## REFERENCES

---

Population models for human and nonhuman organisms are developed in detail in each of the following books:

Emmell, Thomas C., *An Introduction to Ecology and Population Biology* (New York: Norton, 1973).

Grossman, Stanley I., and James E. Turner, *Mathematics for the Biological Sciences* (New York: Macmillan, 1974).

Pielou, E. C., *An Introduction to Mathematical Ecology* (New York: Wiley, 1969).

Poole, Robert W., *An Introduction to Quantitative Ecology* (New York: McGraw-Hill, 1974).

More sophisticated models of human population growth can be found in:

Harrison, G. A., and A. J. Boyce (eds.), *The Structure of Human Populations* (Oxford: Clarendon Press, 1972) and

Pollard, J. H., *Mathematical Models for the Growth of Human Populations* (Cambridge: Cambridge University Press, 1973).

Ralph Thomlinson presents a survey of world population trends and population theories in his book *Population Dynamics: Causes and Consequences of World Demographic Change* (New York: Random House, 1965).

The use of exponential decay models to date ancient objects is presented in W. F. Libby, *Radiocarbon Dating* (Chicago: University of Chicago Press, 1955) and Henry Faull, *Ages of Rocks, Planets and Stars* (New York: McGraw-Hill, 1966).

The sad fate of the peregrine falcon is reported in the papers of a research conference which have been edited by Joseph J. Hickey, *Peregrine Falcon Populations; Their Biology and Decline* (Madison: University of Wisconsin Press, 1969).

Pearl and Reed's original paper on a logistic model for United States population is "On the rate of growth of the United States population since 1790 and its mathematical representation," *Proceedings of the National Academy of Sciences* **6** (1920), 275–288. Pearl gives an extended discussion of this work in his book *Studies in Human Biology* (Baltimore: William and Wilkins, 1924). A critical history of the logistic model which contains complete references to the works of Quetelet and Verhulst is G. Udny Yule's paper, "The growth of population and the factors which control it," *Journal of the Royal Statistical Society* **88** (1925), 1–58. The more recent cited paper by D. O. Cogwill is "The use of the logistic curve and the transition model in developing nations," in Bose, Desai and Hain (eds.), *Studies in Demography* (Chapel Hill: University of North Carolina Press, 1970).

The works of Colin W. Clark mentioned in Suggested Project 3 include "Economically optimal policies for the utilization of biologically renewable resources," *Mathematical Biosciences* **12** (1971), 245–260 and "The dynamics of commercially exploited natural animal populations," *Mathematical Biosciences* **13** (1972), 149–164.

## BIOGRAPHICAL REFERENCES

### T. R. Malthus

Malthus, Thomas R., *An Essay on the Principle of Population and A Summary View of the Principle of Population*, edited with an introduction by Antony Flew (Baltimore: Penguin, 1970).

**R. Pearl**

"A Thirty-Fifth Report of the Class of 1899 of Dartmouth College," (Hanover, N.H.: Dartmouth College, 1941).

Jennings, H. S., "Biographical memoir of Raymond Pearl," *National Academy of Sciences Biographical Memoirs* **22** (1943), 295–347.

Pearl, Raymond, "Review of *Mathematical Biophysics* by N. Rashevsky," *Bulletin of the American Mathematical Society* (1939), 223–224.

Pearl, Raymond, "Some biological considerations about war," *American Journal of Sociology* **46** (1941), 487–503.

**L. A. J. Quetelet**

Mailly, Edouard, "Eulogy on Quetelet," *Annual Report of the Board of Regents of the Smithsonian Institution for the Year 1874* (Washington: Government Printing Office, 1875), 169–183.

Quetelet, Lambert A. J., *A Treatise on Man and the Development of his Faculties* (Gainesville, Fla.: Scholars' Facsimiles and Reprints, 1969).

**P. F. Verhulst**

De Seyn, E. (ed.), *Dictionnaire Biographique des Sciences, des Lettres et des Arts en Belgique*, Tome Second, (Brussels: Editions L'Avenir, 1936), p. 1128.

Miner, John R., "Pierre-François Verhulst, the discoverer of the logistic curve," *Human Biology* **5**, (1933), 673–685.

# 4
# Ecological Models: Interacting Species

There are craft standards in both mathematics and ecology and the ideal interdisciplinary study simultaneously enhances our understanding of the empirical world and constitutes an example of elegant craftmanship by both ecological and mathematical standards. That is a difficult set of criteria, but there is no reason to believe that science at its best is easy.

Lawrence B. Slobodkin

## I. INTRODUCTION

The previous chapter developed some models for population growth of a single species inhabiting an environment in which the amount of resources never changed and the numbers of other species also remained fixed. Although such a situation may sometimes be approached in laboratory experiments, an effective mathematical model should not ignore the fluctuations of the other important variables in an ecosystem.

In this chapter several models will be presented which attempt to represent the population dynamics which can occur in a system when two or more species interact with each other in the same environment. As is the case with most of the material in this book, only relatively simple models will be considered. We will look in detail at two particular models which were the classic beginnings of mathematical ecology. They form the bases on which more sophisticated models have been constructed.

Those readers unfamiliar with partial derivatives and the other basic ideas of the calculus of several variables should read Appendix IV before tackling Section III.

## II. TWO REAL-WORLD SITUATIONS

### A. Predator and Prey

Consider first the effects of interdependence of two species, one of which serves as food for the other. A classic formulation of this situation is that of a population of rabbits, who feed on clover, and a population of foxes, who feed on rabbits. The assumptions usually made about the situation are these:

1. In isolation, the rate of change of population of one species is proportional to the population of that species. In the absence of foxes, it is assumed that the rabbits population will exhibit exponential growth. If there are no rabbits, the fox population will undergo a pure death process.

2. There is always so much clover that the rabbits have an ample supply of food. The only food available to the predatory foxes are the rabbits.

3. The number of kills of rabbits by foxes is proportional to the frequency of encounters between the two species. This, in turn, is proportional to the product of the populations of rabbits and foxes. Thus there will be few kills if there are few rabbits or few foxes and many kills only when both populations are relatively large.

If $R$ denotes the population of rabbits at time $t$ and $F$ is the number of foxes, then the predator-prey model asserts that $R$ and $F$ are functions of time which satisfy the pair of first order differential equations,

$$\frac{dR}{dt} = aR - bRF$$

$$\frac{dF}{dt} = mRF - nF,$$

where $a, b, m$, and $n$ are positive constants.

Although this model was initially developed to study actual animal populations, it has been used to consider other interactions as well. In a series of research papers, George Bell has attempted to apply the concepts of this model to analyze the immune response to infections. When a living being is infected by a replicating organism, such as bacteria or a virus, an immune response may be produced. The response is characterized by the production of antibodies which bind to the infecting material and hasten its destruction. Antigen plays the role of prey (rabbits) and antibody the role of predator (fox). [Bell, 1973]

## B. Competitive Hunters

A different situation involving interacting populations is one in which two species have a common prey or food source. Here the predators are in competition with each other. Each removes from the environment a resource that would stimulate the growth of the population of the other. We shall refer to this situation as one involving competitive hunters.

The assumptions about this situation are somewhat similar to the ones set down in the predator-prey case:

1. In the absence of one of the predators, the other predator's population increases at a rate proportional to its size.

2. There is a sufficient number of prey to sustain any level of predator population.

3. The competition between the predators is proportional to the product of the population of these two species.

If $U$ and $V$ denote the populations of the two predators, then the model asserts that $U$ and $V$ are functions of time $t$ satisfying the pair of differential equations,

$$\frac{dU}{dt} = aU - bUV$$

$$\frac{dV}{dt} = mV - nUV,$$

where $a, b, m$, and $n$ again are positive constants.

## III. AUTONOMOUS SYSTEMS

### A. Three Autonomous Systems

In the discussion of mathematical models in this text, three different pairs of differential equations have been presented: one for Richardson's arms race between two nations, one for a predator-prey relationship, and one for a competitive hunters situation. There are certain similarities in these systems which should be explored.

In each of the three systems of differential equations, there are two variables, call them $x$ and $y$, which are functions of a third variable, say $t$. In each case, the model is an assertion that a certain pair of differential equations involving these variables is true. The models look like this:

$$\text{Arms race:} \qquad \frac{dx}{dt} = ay - mx + r, \qquad \frac{dy}{dt} = bx - ny + s;$$

$$\text{Predator-prey:} \qquad \frac{dx}{dt} = ax - bxy, \qquad \frac{dy}{dt} = mxy - ny;$$

$$\text{Hunters:} \qquad \frac{dx}{dt} = ax - bxy, \qquad \frac{dy}{dt} = my - nxy.$$

In all three models, the differential equations are of the type

$$\frac{dx}{dt} = x'(t) = F(x, y)$$

$$\frac{dy}{dt} = y'(t) = G(x, y).$$

The rates of change of $x$ and $y$ are given as explicit functions of $x$ and $y$ alone and do not include the third variable $t$.

Such systems of differential equations are called *autonomous systems*. A solution of such a system is a pair of scalar functions $x = x(t)$ and $y = y(t)$ such that

$$x'(t) = F(x(t), y(t)) \qquad \text{and} \qquad y'(t) = G(x(t), y(t))$$

for all $t$ in some interval.

A nonautonomous system would have the form

$$\frac{dx}{dt} = H(x, y, t)$$

$$\frac{dy}{dt} = I(x, y, t),$$

where $H$ and $I$ are functions of the three variables. One such example would be the system

$$\frac{dx}{dt} = xy - 2x + \sin t$$

$$\frac{dy}{dt} = \frac{x}{t} + y^3.$$

## B.  Some Mathematical Facts

If the functions $F$ and $G$ of an autonomous system and their first order partial derivatives are continuous in some domain $D$ of the $xy$-plane, then the system always has a solution.  Furthermore, if $(x_0, y_0)$ is any point in $D$ and $t_0$ is any number, then there is a *unique* solution defined on some interval about $t_0$ satisfying the initial conditions $x(t_0) = x_0$, $y(t_0) = y_0$. (Any standard differential equations text will contain a precise formulation and proof of this existence-uniqueness result; in particular, see the books by Sanchez or Bear listed in the References.)

It is a simple matter to check that in our three models the functions $F$, $G$, $F_x$, $F_y$, $G_x$, and $G_y$ are continuous over the entire $xy$-plane.  This is left as an exercise.

Autonomous systems of differential equations have been extensively studied and there is a rich literature about the nature of solutions to such systems.  Only a few basic properties will be considered here.

As time $t$ varies, a solution $x = x(t)$, $y = y(t)$ of the system describes parametrically a curve lying in the $xy$-plane.  This curve is called an *orbit*, or *trajectory*, of the system.  Figure 1 of Chapter 2 shows two possible orbits for the elementary spiraling arms race model $dx/dt = ay$, $dy/dt = bx$.

In ecological models the concern is primarily with the possible values attained by $x$ and $y$ and only secondarily with the times at which these values are achieved.  What is wanted, then, is information about the geometric nature of the possible orbits.  The first theorem we have asserts that the orbit is independent of the starting time.

■ *THEOREM 1*    If $x = x(t)$, $y = y(t)$ is a solution of the autonomous system,

$$x'(t) = F(x, y)$$
$$y'(t) = G(x, y),$$

and $t_0$ is any constant, then the functions $x_1(t) = x(t + t_0)$, $y_1(t) = y(t + t_0)$ also give a solution to the system.

*Proof of Theorem 1*    We must show that

$$x_1'(t) = F(x_1, y_1) \qquad \text{and} \qquad y_1'(t) = G(x_1, y_1).$$

This is easily done by making use of the chain rule for differentiation. According to the chain rule,

$$x_1'(t) = x'(t + t_0)(t + t_0)' = x'(t + t_0)(1) = x'(t + t_0),$$

and similarly,

$$y_1'(t) = y'(t + t_0).$$

Since $x'(t) = F(x(t), y(t))$ and $y'(t) = G(x(t), y(t))$, replacing $t$ by $t + t_0$ gives

$$x_1'(t) = x'(t + t_0) = F(x(t + t_0), y(t + t_0)) = F(x_1(t), y_1(t))$$

and

$$y_1'(t) = y'(t + t_0) = G(x(t + t_0), y(t + t_0)) = G(x_1(t), y_1(t)),$$

which was to be shown. This concludes the proof. $\square$

It is very important to notice the basic distinction between a *solution* of the system and an *orbit* of the system. An orbit is a curve that may be represented parametrically by more than one solution. The pairs of functions $x(t), y(t)$ and $x(t + t_0), y(t + t_0)$, for $t_0 \neq 0$, represent distinct solutions, but they represent the same curve parametrically; that is, both solutions give rise to the same orbit.

---

**EXAMPLE**    The pairs $x(t) = \cos t$, $y(t) = \sin t$, and $x(t) = \cos(t + \pi/3)$, $y(t) = \sin(t + \pi/3)$ are different solutions to the system $x'(t) = -y(t)$, $y'(t) = x(t)$. Both, however, represent the same orbit, the familiar unit circle with equation $x^2 + y^2 = 1$.

---

Our second theorem guarantees that two distinct orbits for an autonomous system cannot cross anywhere; otherwise there would be two different orbits through the same point.

■ **THEOREM 2**    Through any point there passes at most one orbit.

**Proof of Theorem 2**    Suppose, to the contrary, that $C_1$ and $C_2$ are distinct orbits which both pass through the same point $(x_0, y_0)$. Let $x_1(t), y_1(t)$ be a solution which represents $C_1$ parametrically and let $x_2(t), y_2(t)$ be a solution representing the orbit $C_2$.

The two orbits must reach the common point $(x_0, y_0)$ at different times, since otherwise the uniqueness of the solutions would be violated. Thus there are distinct numbers $t_1$ and $t_2$ such that

$$(x_1(t_1), y_1(t_1)) = (x_2(t_2), y_2(t_2)) = (x_0, y_0).$$

By Theorem 1, the pair of functions

$$x(t) = x_1(t + t_1 - t_2), \qquad y(t) = y_1(t + t_1 - t_2)$$

also serve as a solution to the autonomous system of differential equations.

Note now that $x(t_2) = x_1(t_2 + t_1 - t_2) = x_1(t_1) = x_0$ and similarly, $y(t_2) = y_0$. By the uniqueness of solutions of the system with prescribed initial values, the pair $x(t), y(t)$ is identical to the pair $x_2(t), y_2(t)$. Thus the orbit associated with $x(t), y(t)$ must be $C_2$. On the other hand, from the definition of $x(t), y(t)$, we see that this pair is a reparametrization of the orbit given by $x_1(t), y_1(t)$. Hence the orbit associated with $x(t), y(t)$ must be $C_1$. The conclusion is that $C_1$ and $C_2$ coincide and are not distinct. This contradiction to the initial assumption that the orbits were distinct establishes the truth of the theorem. $\square$

Armed with these two theorems and the existence-uniqueness result, we will be able to show that the orbits of an autonomous system must either be single points or "simple" curves.

## C. Types of Orbits
Consider the autonomous system of differential equations,

$$\frac{dx}{dt} = 7y - 4x - 13$$

$$\frac{dy}{dt} = 2x - 5y + 11.$$

One simple solution to this system is the pair of constant functions,

$$\begin{aligned} x(t) &= 2 \\ y(t) &= 3 \end{aligned} \quad \text{for all } t.$$

The orbit of this solution is the single point $(2, 3)$ in the $xy$-plane. A quick calculation shows that $dx/dt = dy/dt = 0$ at this point. This is consistent with the fact that the derivatives of constant functions are zero.

More generally, suppose there is a constant solution $x(t) = x_0$, $y(t) = y_0$, for $-\infty < t < \infty$, to an autonomous system. By the uniqueness of solution, no other orbit could pass through the point $(x_0, y_0)$. Since these are constant functions, it is true that

$$x'(t) = 0, \; y'(t) = 0, \; -\infty < t < \infty$$

and since the functions are solutions to the system, we have

$$x'(t) = F(x(t), y(t)) = F(x_0, y_0),$$
$$y'(t) = G(x(t), y(t)) = G(x_0, y_0).$$

Thus, if there is such a constant solution, it must be the case that

$$F(x_0, y_0) = G(x_0, y_0) = 0.$$

Conversely, if there is a point $(x_0, y_0)$ in the plane at which both $F(x_0, y_0)$ and $G(x_0, y_0)$ equal zero, then certainly the constant functions $x(t) = x_0$, $y(t) = y_0$, $-\infty < t < \infty$, form a solution of the system.

The first step in the analysis of an autonomous system of differential equations is to locate these special points.

**DEFINITION**   Any point $(x_0, y_0)$ in the plane at which the functions $F$ and $G$ are both zero is called a *critical point* of the system. Any other point in the plane is called a *regular point*.

---

**EXAMPLE**   The autonomous system

$$\frac{dx}{dt} = x^2 + y^2 - 100 = F(x, y)$$

$$\frac{dy}{dt} = x - 2y + 10 = G(x, y)$$

has two critical points, $(-10, 0)$ and $(6, 8)$. The point $(-8, 6)$ is a regular point since $G(-8, 6) = -10 \neq 0$ even though $F(-8, 6) = 0$. The point $(0, 0)$ is also a regular point because $F(0, 0) = -100$ while $G(0, 0) = 10$.

The critical points for this example can be found by graphing the curves $F(x, y) = 0$ and $G(x, y) = 0$ and determining their points of intersection. Here we have the intersection of a circle and a straight line (see Fig. 4.1).

---

Other names for critical points are singular points, stable points, points of equilibrium, and equilibrium states. A critical point may be thought of as a point where the motion described by the pair of differential equations of the

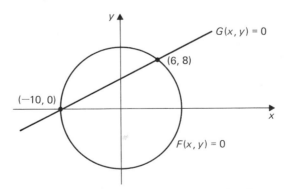

**Fig. 4.1**   The stable curves and critical points for the autonomous system $dx/dt = x^2 + y^2 - 100$, $dy/dt = x - 2y + 10$.

system is in a state of rest; both horizontal velocity ($dx/dt$) and vertical velocity ($dy/dt$) are zero. At a critical point, both rates of change are zero so that if the orbit starts at such a point, it remains there forever. The critical points can be found by determining the intersections of the two "stable curves" $F(x, y) = 0$ and $G(x, y) = 0$.

**Simple curve orbits**    If an orbit begins at a position which is not a critical point, then at least one of the rates of change, $dx/dt$ or $dy/dt$ will be nonzero and the orbit will move away from the point. In an autonomous system, only two things are possible:

1. The orbit will never return to the starting point. This is illustrated in Fig. 2.1 where the orbit is a piece of one branch of an hyperbola.

2. If the orbit ever returns to the starting point, it will simply retrace the same closed curve over and over again. As an example of this, consider again the solution $x(t) = \sin t$, $y(t) = \cos t$ of the system $dx/dt = -y$, $dy/dt = x$ whose orbit is the unit circle.

The orbit for an autonomous system can never cross itself to produce a path, for example, like that traced out by a figure eight (see Fig. 4.2). This is true because the velocities at any point, $x'(t_1), y'(t_1)$, are completely determined by the coordinates of the point $x(t_1), y(t_1)$. If we come back to this point at a later time $t_2$, then the velocities are the same: $x'(t_2) = x'(t_1) = F(x(t_1), y(t_1))$ and $y'(t_2) = y'(t_1) = G(x(t_1), y(t_1))$. In particular, the slopes of the tangent lines

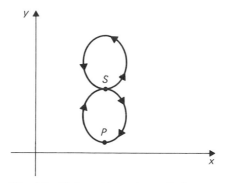

**Fig. 4.2**    If the orbit begins at $P$, then the first time it reaches the point $S$, the tangent line will have positive slope; the second time it has negative slope. This curve cannot be the orbit of an autonomous system of differential equations.

to the curve are the same at the two times and so the direction of motion is exactly the same both times.

In an autonomous system, the orbit is traversed in a fixed direction determined by the system of equations. The direction could only be reversed if a critical point is reached or if the curve crosses itself. We have seen that neither of these is possible if the orbit contains a regular point.

Although the orbit can never actually reach a critical point if it does not begin at one, it is possible to approach a critical point asymptotically. As an example, consider the system

$$\frac{dx}{dt} = -x,$$

$$\frac{dy}{dt} = -y.$$

This system has one critical point, the origin $(0,0)$. This corresponds to the constant solution $x(t) = y(t) = 0$, $-\infty < t < \infty$. Another solution to the system is the pair $x(t) = y(t) = e^{-t}$, $-\infty < t < \infty$. This solution describes parametrically an orbit which is the subset of the line $y = x$ lying in the positive first quadrant. Since $\lim_{t \to \infty} e^{-t} = 0$, the points of this orbit asymptotically approach the origin as time increases.

## D. Behavior Near a Critical Point

It is of some interest to discover how an orbit behaves in the neighborhood of a critical point. In the ecological models, a critical point corresponds to a "steady state" of zero population growth or decline for both species. What happens if population levels are near a critical point, but not exactly at it?

We will be looking at three different kinds of behavior that may occur:

1. Stable equilibrium—every orbit near a critical point always approaches it asymptotically;
2. Unstable equilibrium—orbits starting near the critical point always proceed away from it;
3. Cyclical behavior—the orbits move around the critical point in tracing out simple closed curves.

Examples of (1) and (2) occurred in the analysis of Richardson's arms race model. Cyclical behavior appears in the system $dx/dt = -y$, $dy/dt = x$ which has the origin as its only critical point. The other orbits are circles centered at the origin. See also Fig. 4.3–4.5.

The basic properties of autonomous systems that have been developed here make possible fruitful analysis of the ecological models presented at the beginning of this chapter.

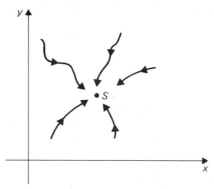

**Fig. 4.3** Stable equilibrium. Orbits which pass through regular points near the critical point $S$ asymptotically approach $S$.

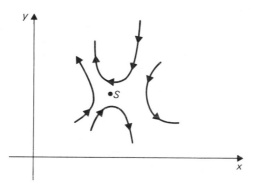

**Fig. 4.4** Unstable equilibrium. Orbits which pass through regular points near the critical point tend to move away from the critical point.

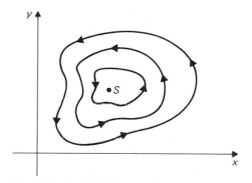

**Fig. 4.5** Cyclical behavior. The orbits passing near the critical point form simple closed curves moving around the critical point.

## IV. THE COMPETITIVE HUNTERS MODEL

### A. Initial Analysis

As in the study of the Richardson arms race model, analysis begins by locating the critical points, the points where both time derivatives are zero. Since $dx/dt = x(a - by)$, note that $dx/dt = 0$ along the lines $x = 0$ and $y = a/b$. Similarly, $dy/dt = 0$ along the lines $y = 0$ and $x = m/n$, since $dy/dt = y(m - nx)$. There are two critical points: $(0,0)$ and $(m/n, a/b)$. Each of these single points represents a possible orbit. If initially there are no members of either species, then obviously there can be no gain or loss of any individuals. If there are exactly $m/n$ members of one species and $a/b$ of the other at the start, then the populations will remain at these levels indefinitely.

Several other orbits for the competitive hunters system can also be readily identified. If $x = 0$ and $y$ is positive at some instant, then at that moment, $dx/dt = 0$ while $dy/dt = my > 0$. The population of the first species will remain at zero while the population of the second is increasing. Geometrically, this means that the positive $y$-axis is a possible orbit. By a similar argument, the positive $x$-axis is shown to be an orbit.

The one-point and open ray orbits just found are, of course, quite special and do not indicate the shape of a more typical orbit. They give information, however, that helps determine what those other orbits look like. For example, the fact that orbits cannot intersect each other implies that an orbit which begins in the interior of the first quadrant must always remain there; the boundaries of the first quadrant are made up of other orbits. Thus if initially there are positive numbers of each species present, then there will always be positive numbers.

Continuing the analysis in the spirit of the Richardson model, note that the lines $y = a/b$ and $x = m/n$ divide the first quadrant into four rectangular regions. The derivative $dx/dt$ is positive whenever $y < a/b$ and is negative when $y > a/b$. The derivative $dy/dt$ is positive if $x < m/n$ and negative if $x > m/n$. These facts help establish the general drift of the various orbits. These are indicated in Fig. 4.6.

Figure 4.6 indicates that if initial population levels are in region IV where $x > m/n$ and $y < a/b$, then the population of the $x$ species will increase while the population of the $y$ species will decrease. The orbit would remain in region IV.

On the other hand, if initially the population of the $y$ species is above its critical level of $a/b$ while the numbers of the $x$ species are below the critical level $m/n$, then the former species will flourish and the latter will decline. An orbit beginning in region II remains in this region.

If both species are initially below their critical level, the orbit will begin in region III. Analysis of the signs of $dx/dt$ and $dy/dt$ show that both species will increase in numbers for a while, but the ultimate behavior is unclear. The orbit might enter region IV, region II, or asymptotically approach the critical point.

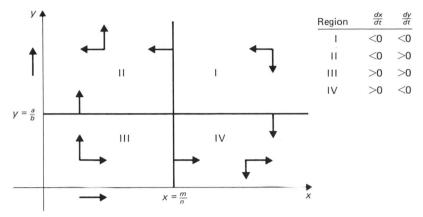

| Region | $\frac{dx}{dt}$ | $\frac{dy}{dt}$ |
|--------|------|------|
| I   | <0 | <0 |
| II  | <0 | >0 |
| III | >0 | >0 |
| IV  | >0 | <0 |

**Fig. 4.6**  Signs of $dx/dt$ and $dy/dt$ for the competitive hunters model.

Analogous remarks may be made if the initial populations of both species are above the critical levels, although in that case, both populations will decrease at the start.

## B. Further Analysis

There is a powerful technique that sheds further light on the qualitative behavior of an orbit of an autonomous system of differential equations. It is based on a theorem that asserts that the nature of an orbit near a critical point $S$ of the system $dx/dt = F(x, y)$, $dy/dt = G(x, y)$ may be determined by expanding $F$ and $G$ in a Taylor series about the point $S$ and retaining only the linear terms. The solutions of these linear equations near the critical point will often have the same general qualitative nature as the exact solutions.

Some explanations are necessary here. Suppose that $z = f(x, y)$ is a function of $x$ and $y$ that behaves nicely near the point $(p, q) = S$. Let $h$ and $k$ be small numbers. A *Taylor series* expansion of $f$ about $S$ is an infinite series of the form

$$f(p, q) + a_1 h + a_2 k + a_3 h^2 + a_4 k^2 + a_5 hk + a_6 h^3 + a_7 h^2 k + \cdots$$

where each term is a constant multiple of a product of a power of $h$ and a power of $k$. The coefficients $a_i$ are found by evaluating partial derivatives of $f$ of various orders at the point $S = (p, q)$. The first two coefficients are $a_1 = f_x(p, q)$ and $a_2 = f_y(p, q)$.

If the function $f$ is "nice" near $(p, q)$, then the series converges to the value $f(p + h, q + k)$. More exactly, if there is some circle centered at $(p, q)$ inside of which all of the partial derivatives of $f$ of all orders are continuous, then the series converges to $f(p + h, q + k)$ whenever $(p + h, q + k)$ lies inside that circle.

Terminating the Taylor series at a finite number of terms would then give an approximation to the value of $f(p + h, q + k)$. In particular, a crude approximation may be obtained by using only the first three terms; that is,

$$f(p + h, q + k) \approx f(p, q) + f_x(p, q)h + f_y(p, q)k.$$

This approximation is a good one provided $h$ and $k$ are both small in absolute value; the error, in fact, is bounded by $Ah^2 + Bhk + Gk^2$ for fixed constants $A$, $B$, $C$. In this approximation, we have neglected all powers of $h$ and $k$ beyond the linear terms. (A fuller treatment of the Taylor series expansion is given in most textbooks on several variable calculus; one reference is Section 3.7 of Robert Seeley, *Calculus of Several Variables*, Glenview, Illinois: Scott, Foresman, 1970.)

In the competitive hunters model, the function $F(x, y)$ has the form $F(x, y) = ax - bxy$ so that $F_x(x, y) = a - by$ while $F_y(x, y) = -bx$. At the critical point $S = (m/n, a/b)$, both functions $F$ and $F_x$ are zero, while $F_y(m/n, a/b) = -bm/n$. Applying the linearized Taylor series approximation with $f = F$, $p = m/n$ and $q = a/b$, we conclude that

$$F\left(\frac{m}{n} + h, \frac{a}{b} + k\right) \approx \frac{-bm}{n}\, k.$$

A similar analysis for $G(x, y) = my - nxy$ shows that

$$G\left(\frac{m}{n} + h, \frac{a}{b} + k\right) \approx -\frac{an}{b}\, h.$$

Define, next, two new variables $u$ and $v$ by $u = x - (m/n)$ and $v = y - (a/b)$. This gives $du/dt = dx/dt$ and $dv/dt = dy/dt$. Furthermore $x = (m/n) + u$ and $y = (a/b) + v$. The Taylor series approximation can be rewritten as

$$F(x, y) \approx -\left(\frac{bm}{n}\right)v,$$

$$G(x, y) \approx -\left(\frac{an}{b}\right)u.$$

Thus we have

$$\frac{du}{dt} = \frac{dx}{dt} = F(x, y) \approx -\left(\frac{bm}{n}\right)v,$$

$$\frac{dv}{dt} = \frac{dy}{dt} = G(x, y) \approx -\left(\frac{an}{b}\right)u.$$

By the theorem on the general nature of the orbit, we conclude that the orbits near the critical point of the original system behave like the orbits of the simpler system

$$\frac{du}{dt} = -\left(\frac{bm}{n}\right)v,$$

$$\frac{dv}{dt} = -\left(\frac{an}{b}\right)u.$$

The orbits of this simpler system are obtained by first noting that the chain rule gives

$$\frac{du}{dv} = \left(\frac{b^2 m}{an^2}\right)\left(\frac{v}{u}\right)$$

and separation of variables yields

$$\int an^2 u \, du = \int b^2 mv \, dv.$$

Integrate and rewrite to obtain

$$an^2 u^2 - b^2 mv^2 = K,$$

where $K$ is an integration constant.

Rewrite this last equation in terms of the original variables:

$$an^2 \left( x - \frac{m}{n} \right)^2 - b^2 m \left( y - \frac{a}{b} \right)^2 = K,$$

which is the equation of an hyperbola in the $xy$-plane with center at $(m/n, a/b)$. The value of the constant $K$ depends on the initial population levels of the two species. Once these are known, $K$ may be determined and with it, which of the two branches of the hyperbola represents the actual orbit. One branch of the hyperbola asymptotically approaches the $x$-axis, the other asymptotically approaches the $y$-axis.

The qualitative behavior of the orbits of the original competitive hunters model which pass close to the critical point must be like the qualitative behavior of these hyperbolas; that is, either the $x$ values increase indefinitely as the $y$ values tend to zero or the $y$ values increase indefinitely as the $x$ values tend to zero.

## C. Exact Orbits

To obtain the exact orbits for the competitive hunters model, note that the equations of the system

$$\frac{dx}{dt} = ax - bxy, \qquad \frac{dy}{dt} = my \quad nxy$$

may be combined into a single first order differential equation

$$\frac{dy}{dx} = \frac{my - nxy}{ax - bxy} = \frac{y(m - nx)}{x(a - by)}.$$

Separating the variables and integrating gives

$$\int \frac{a - by}{y} \, dy = \int \frac{m - nx}{x} \, dx$$

and when the antiderivatives are found,

$$a \log y - by = m \log x - nx + C,$$

where $C$ is an integration constant.

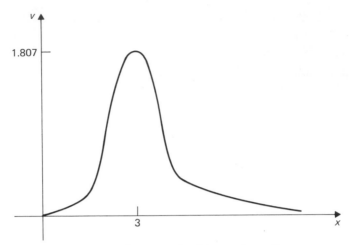

**Fig. 4.7**   The graph of $v = x^m e^{-nx}$ with $m = 6$, $n = 2$.

Exponentiate each side to obtain

$$y^a e^{-by} = K x^m e^{-nx}$$

where $K$ is the constant $e^C$.

It is not possible to solve this last equation to obtain $y$ as an explicit function of $x$. It is possible, thanks to a technique invented by Vito Volterra, to obtain a graph of this relationship in the $xy$-plane.

Volterra began by noticing that he could graph the functions $v = x^m e^{-nx}$ and $u = y^a e^{-by}$ in the $(x, v)$ and $(y, u)$ planes, respectively, and that these graphs are similar in form. Figure 4.7 shows this curve for a particular choice of constants $m$ and $n$.

The initial analysis showed that the orbit will remain the first quadrant of the $(x,y)$-plane. The other three quadrants will be used to represent the first quadrants of the $(y,u)$-, $(u,v)$-, and $(v,x)$-planes, respectively. Figure 4.8 indicates how to do this:

To find a point on the orbit of the solution to the system, use Volterra's procedure:

1. Select a positive value for $x$, say $x_0$.

2. Determine the value $v_0$ corresponding to $x_0$ from the equation $v = x^m e^{-nx}$.

3. Determine the value $u_0$ corresponding to $v_0$ from the relationship $u = Kv$.

4. Determine the $y$ values (in general, there will be two) corresponding to $u_0$ by finding where the vertical line through $(u_0, v_0)$ intersects the curve $u = y^a e^{-by}$.

5. Extend horizontal lines through these $y$ values until they intersect the vertical line through $(x_0, 0)$ in the $(x,y)$-quadrant. These intersections determine points on the orbit.

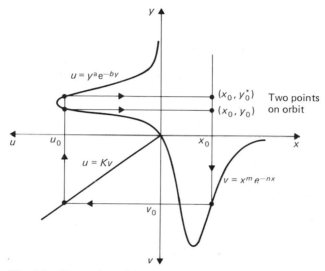

**Fig. 4.8**  Illustration of the Volterra mapping technique.

If this procedure is followed for a large number of choices for $x_0$, an accurate picture of the orbit in the $(x,y)$-plane emerges (see Fig. 4.9). Note again that each orbit asymptotically approaches one of the coordinate axes, even if the initial point of the orbit is chosen to be relatively far from the critical point. Although the Volterra mapping technique requires careful graphing, it has greater applicability than the analytic technique of using the linearized Taylor series expansion.

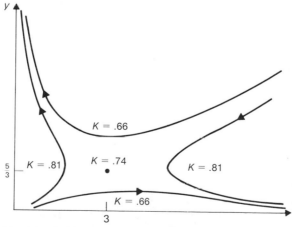

**Fig. 4.9**  Orbits of the competitive hunters model. Here $a = .5$, $b = .3$, $m = .6$, $n = .2$. The critical points are $(0,0)$ and $(3, 5/3)$.

### D.  Interpretation of Results

The mathematical analysis of the competitive hunters model yields several conclusions:

Equilibrium is possible.  There is a critical positive population for each species.  If each maintains that level, they can coexist in the same environment.

The equilibrium is highly unstable.  If, at any instant, the population levels are not at the critical sizes, then the effects of competition will be for one species to flourish, while the other dies out.  If one species exceeds its critical size, while the other fails to achieve its, then the first one emerges triumphant.  If both species are either above or below the critical sizes, then more detailed knowledge of the size of the parameters $a, b, m,$ and $n$ and exact numbers of initial population levels must be known to predict which species will win out.

The prediction emerging from the model that only one species is likely to survive is consistent with known biological laws.  It is called the *principle of competitive exclusion.*  The noted zoologist Ernst Mayr comments in his book *Populations, Species and Evolution* [1970],

> The result of competition between two ecologically similar species in the same
> locality is either (1) the two species are so similar in their needs and their ability to
> fulfill these needs that one of the two species becomes extinct, either (1a) because
> it is "competitively inferior," that is, it has a smaller capacity to increase or
> (1b) because even though competitively equivalent it had an initial numerical dis-
> advantage; or (2) there is a sufficiently large zone of ecological nonoverlap (area
> of reduced or absent competition) to permit the two species to coexist indefinitely.
> In sum: two species cannot indefinitely coexist in the same locality if they have
> identical ecological requirements.  This theorem is sometimes referred to as the
> Gause principle, after the Russian biologist Gause who was the first to substantiate
> it experimentally.  Yet . . . the principle was known long before Gause.  Darwin dis-
> cussed it at length in his *Origin of Species.* . . . The validity of this exclusion prin-
> ciple has been tested in numerous laboratory experiments in which mixed popula-
> tions of two species were established in a uniform environment.  In virtually every
> case, one of the two species was eliminated sooner or later.

### E.  Modifying the Model

The competitive hunters model makes two major predictions:

1.  One species will die out.
2.  The other species will grow indefinitely numerous.

The first prediction, as just noted, is consistent with many observations and experiments.  The second is not.  The source of this second prediction is one of the assumptions made in building the model: in the absence of one of the species of hunters, the other species increases at a rate proportional to its population size; that is, it would experience exponential growth.

To improve the model, this assumption should be replaced by a more realistic one. Perhaps the assumption should be: in the absence of one species, the other species experiences logistic growth. The reader is invited to formulate a model built on this assumption and to derive the appropriate mathematical conclusions and real-world interpretations from it.

## V. THE PREDATOR-PREY MODEL

### A. Analysis

Turn now to an examination of the predator-prey model, the system

$$\frac{dx}{dt} = ax - bxy = x(a - by),$$

$$\frac{dy}{dt} = mxy - ny = y(mx - n),$$

where $a, b, m, n$ are positive constants, $x$ is the population of prey (rabbits), and $y$ the population of predators (foxes). As in the case of the competitive hunters model, $dx/dt = 0$ along the lines $x = 0$ and $y = a/b$, while $dy/dt = 0$ on the lines $y = 0$ and $x = n/m$. The critical points are $(0,0)$ and $(n/m, a/b)$. The positive $x$-axis and the positive $y$-axis are also orbits. All other orbits of interest are contained entirely in the first quadrant of the $xy$-plane.

The lines $y = a/b$ and $x = n/m$ divide the first quadrant into four rectangularly shaped regions. The differences between the predator-prey model and the competitive hunters model become evident when the signs of the derivatives $dx/dt$ and $dy/dt$ are determined in each of these four regions. See Fig. 4.10. Note that $dx/dt$ is positive if $y < a/b$ and negative if $y > a/b$, while $dy/dt$ is positive whenever $x > n/m$, but negative if $x < n/m$. The general drift of the orbits of the system is evident from Fig. 4.10.

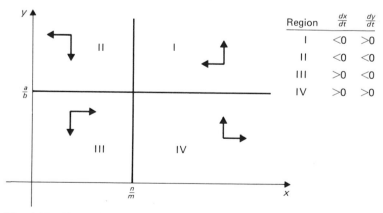

| Region | $\frac{dx}{dt}$ | $\frac{dy}{dt}$ |
|--------|-----|-----|
| I | $<0$ | $>0$ |
| II | $<0$ | $<0$ |
| III | $>0$ | $<0$ |
| IV | $>0$ | $>0$ |

**Fig. 4.10**  Signs of $dx/dt$ and $dy/dt$ for the predator-prey model.

No matter where the initial population levels are located, the orbit will follow a counterclockwise direction about the critical point. For example, if there are a small number of rabbits and foxes at the start (initial level in region III), then the rabbit population will increase at first while the fox population decreases. The small number of foxes poses little threat to the rabbits, while the scarcity of rabbits means that the foxes have a difficult time finding ample food.

When the rabbit population reaches a critical level of $n/m$, then the fox population also begins to increase. For a time, while the orbit is in region IV, both species experience a growth in numbers. Eventually the fox population exceeds its critical level of $a/b$. Now the foxes are sufficiently plentiful to endanger the rabbit population whose numbers begin to decline while the fox population increases; the orbit is in region I. When the rabbit population declines below $n/m$, as the orbit enters region II, then there is not a sufficient supply of prey to sustain a large fox population. Both species lose numbers until the orbit reaches region IV again.

The fluctuations of the populations then seem to be following a cyclical pattern of some sort. What is not clear from this initial analysis is whether the orbits are spiraling toward the critical point, spiraling away from it, or possibly exhibiting some other type of oscillation. To answer this question, consider the linearized Taylor series expansion.

The functions to be approximated are $F(x, y) = ax - bxy$ and $G(x, y) = mxy - ny$. The calculations yield

$$F\left(\frac{n}{m} + h, \frac{a}{b} + k\right) \approx \left(\frac{-bn}{m}\right)k$$

and

$$G\left(\frac{n}{m} + h, \frac{a}{b} + k\right) \approx \left(\frac{am}{b}\right)h.$$

Make the change of variables $u = x - (n/m)$, $v = y - (a/b)$ so that

$$\frac{du}{dt} = \frac{dx}{dt} = F(x, y) \approx -\left(\frac{bn}{m}\right)v,$$

$$\frac{dv}{dt} = \frac{dy}{dt} = G(x, y) \approx \left(\frac{am}{b}\right)u.$$

The orbits near the critical point of the predator-prey system will have the same general behavior as the orbits of the simpler system

$$\frac{du}{dt} = -\left(\frac{nb}{m}\right)v,$$

$$\frac{dv}{dt} = \left(\frac{am}{b}\right)u.$$

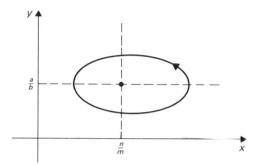

**Fig. 4.11**  Elliptical orbit of the linearized
version of the predator-prey model.

(For a rigorous proof of this claim, see Chapter 6 of Otto Platt, *Ordinary
Differential Equations*, San Francisco: Holden-Day, 1971.) Using the fact that
$du/dv = -(b^2 n/am^2)(u/v)$, separate variables, integrate and conclude that the
simpler system has a solution satisfying

$$am^2 u^2 + b^2 n v^2 = K$$

where $K$ is a constant of integration. Rewriting this equation in terms of the
original variables gives

$$am^2 \left( x - \frac{n}{m} \right)^2 + b^2 n \left( y - \frac{a}{b} \right)^2 = K.$$

This is the equation of an ellipse with center at $(n/m, a/b)$ and with axes parallel
to the coordinate axes of the $xy$-plane. Near the critical point, the orbits are
elliptical trajectories centered at the critical point. The orbits do not spiral
toward the point or away from it (see Fig. 4.11).

It is possible to solve the simpler system for $u$ and $v$ explicitly as functions
of $t$. This is done by computing second derivatives with respect to $t$:

$$u'' = \frac{-bn}{m} v' = \frac{-bn}{m} \left( \frac{am}{b} \right) u = -anu$$

$$v'' = \frac{am}{b} u' = \frac{am}{b} \left( \frac{-bn}{m} \right) v = -anv.$$

Note that both these equations are of the form $z'' - -pz$ where $p$ is a positive constant. The general solution of such a second order differential equation
is $z = A \sin \sqrt{p} t + B \cos \sqrt{p} t$, where $A$ and $B$ are constants. Thus $z$ is a periodic
function with period $2\pi/\sqrt{p}$.

The solution of the simpler system is a pair of functions of $t$, $u$ and $v$, with the
same period $2\pi/\sqrt{an}$. Recalling that the average value of a continuous func-
tion $f$ on an interval $[\alpha, \beta]$ is defined as $(1/\beta - \alpha) \int_\alpha^\beta f(t)\,dt$, it is easy to check

that $u$ and $v$ have average values of 0. Since $u = x - (n/m)$ and $v = y - (a/b)$, this means $x$ and $y$ would have average values of $n/m$ and $a/b$, respectively. The conclusion is that near the critical point the trajectories display periodic movement and are approximated by ellipses with period $2\pi/\sqrt{an}$.

The Volterra mapping technique can be used to find a more exact orbit to the original predator-prey model. Note that

$$\frac{dy}{dx} = \frac{G(x, y)}{F(x, y)} = \frac{y(mx - n)}{x(a - by)}$$

in the original system. After the variables are separated in this differential equation and integration is completed, the solution looks like

$$a \log y - by = mx - n \log x + C$$

which may be written as

$$(y^a e^{-by})(x^m e^{-nx}) = K.$$

For any particular choice of constants $a$, $b$, $m$, $n$, $K$, Volterra's method gives a graph of the set of all points $(x, y)$ satisfying the equation. The only modification required in the procedure of Section IV.C is in Step 3 where the relationship $uv = K$ must now be used in place of $u = Kv$. Figure 4.12 shows a typical result.

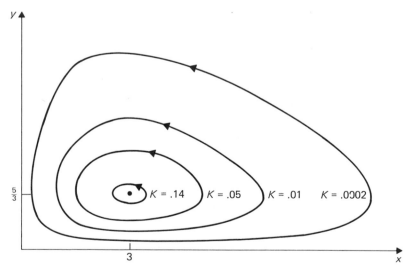

**Fig. 4.12**   Orbits for the predator-prey system $dx/dt = ax - bxy$, $dy/dt = mxy - ny$ obtained from the Volterra mapping technique. Here $a = 5$, $b = 3$, $m = 2$, and $n = 6$. Critical points are $(0, 0)$ and $(3, 5/3)$. All orbits move in a counterclockwise direction. The constant $K$ is determined by initial conditions $(x_0, y_0)$ and is equal to $x_0^n y_0^a / e^{by_0 + mx_0}$. At $(3, 5/3)$, $K = .156$.

## B.  Interpretation and Testing of Results

A. J. Lotka was the first person to formulate and study closely mathematical models of interacting populations.  In his 1925 book, *Elements of Physical Biology*, Lotka considered a wide variety of relationships which can occur between two species, including the models presented in this chapter.  V. Volterra began to consider such models at the request of a zoologist, Umberto D'Ancona, who was studying the variations in numbers of fishes caught in the Adriatic during the period of World War I.  Beginning in 1926, Volterra developed a mathematical analysis for interactions among any number of species.

The early work of Lotka and Volterra has been revised and generalized by many mathematicians and mathematical biologists and many experiments have tested the conclusions of their models in laboratory situations.  The simple predator-prey model devised by Lotka and Volterra predicts oscillations in the numbers of the two species.  Such oscillations have been observed in experiments, but only in fairly complex ones.  A common outcome of simpler (and thus less natural) experiments is that the predators devour all the prey and then die out themselves.  In a carefully designed experiment, C. B. Huffaker in 1957 created a predator-prey oscillation using as prey a mite that feeds on oranges and another species of mite as its predator.  The Lotka-Volterra model compares reasonably well with the observed data.

Population oscillations in the world have also been observed.  E. R. Leigh, in a 1969 study, concluded that the fluctuations in the numbers of Canadian lynx and its primary food, the hare, trapped by the Hudson's Bay Company between 1847 and 1903 were periodic.  The observed period is not in good agreement with that predicted by the Lotka Volterra model.  This may be due to the fact that the numbers of animals trapped were not a fair representative sampling of the actual populations.  More likely, there are other environmental factors affecting the lynx and the hare that are not included in the model.

An interesting property of the predator-prey model is revealed by considering the effect of removing both species from the community in quantities proportional to their numbers.  This commonly happens when the environment is subject to pesticide sprays inimical to both species.  The effect is reflected by a decrease in the coefficient $a$ and an increase in the coefficient $n$ in the differential equations defining the model.  Since the average number of predators is about $a/b$ and of prey is about $n/m$, the long-term consequences are to decrease the average predator population while *increasing* the average number of prey.  One moral is clear: it can be self-defeating for man to use an insecticide against a species whose population is already being controlled by a natural predator.

An example reinforces this observation.  The accidental introduction in the United States of the cottony cushion insect *icerya purchasi* from Australia in 1868 threatened to destroy the American citrus industry.  To counteract this, a natural Australian predator, a ladybird beetle (*novius cardinalis*) was imported.  The beetles kept the scale insects down to a relatively low level.  When

DDT was discovered to kill scale insects, farmers applied it in the hopes of reducing further the scale insect population. DDT, however, was also fatal to the beetle; the overall effect of using insecticide was to increase the numbers of the scale insect.

### C. Modifying the Model

Several variations of the Lotka-Volterra predator-prey model have been proposed that offer more realistic descriptions of the interactions of the populations.

1. If the population of rabbits is always much larger than the number of foxes, then the considerations that entered into the development of the logistic equation may come into play. If the number of rabbits becomes sufficiently great, then the rabbits may be interfering with each other in their quest for food and space. One way to describe this effect mathematically is to replace the original model by the more complicated system,

$$\frac{dx}{dt} = ax - bx^2 - cxy$$

$$\frac{dy}{dt} = mxy - ny$$

where $a, b, c, m, n$ are positive constants.

2. Most predators feed on more than one type of food. If the foxes can survive on an alternative resource, although the presence of their natural prey (rabbits) favors growth, a possible alternative model is the system

$$\frac{dx}{dt} = ax - bx^2 - cxy,$$

$$\frac{dy}{dt} = mxy + ny - py^2$$

where $a, b, c, m, n, p$ are positive constants.

3. P. H. Leslie and J. C. Gower studied a third variation, the system of equations

$$\frac{dx}{dt} = ax - bxy$$

$$\frac{dy}{dt} = \left(c - e\frac{y}{x}\right)y,$$

where the parameters $a, b, c, e$ are again positive constants.

Here the term $y/x$ arises from the fact that this ratio ought to affect the growth of the predator. When foxes are numerous and rabbits are scarce, $y/x$

is large and the growth of fox population will be small. Conversely, when the supply of rabbits is ample for the foxes, $y/x$ is small and there is slight restriction on the increase of the predators.

The orbits associated with the Leslie–Gower model are curves that spiral in toward the critical point. Figure 4.13 illustrates a typical situation of this stable equilibrium.

The detailed development and analyses of these variations and the creation of new ones are left as suggested modeling projects for the reader.

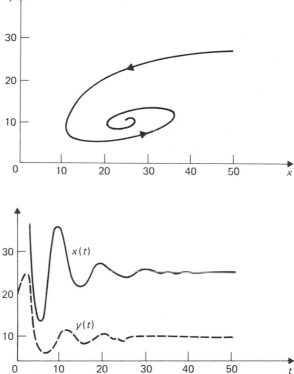

**Fig. 4.13**  Results of the Leslie-Gower model for a predator-prey system. Here $dx/dt = ax - bxy$, $dy/dt = (c - e(y/x))y$. The curves illustrated are for $a = 1$, $b = .1$, $c = 1$, $e = 2.5$ and initial populations $x_0 = 80$, $y_0 = 20$. The critical point is (25, 10). The top graph shows the orbit of a solution of the system of differential equations; it spirals in toward the critical point. The bottom graph shows $x$ and $y$ as functions of $t$. From E. Pielou, *An Introduction to Mathematical Ecology*, New York: John Wiley, 1969. Reprinted by permission of the publisher and author.

## VI. CONCLUDING REMARKS ON SIMPLE MODELS IN POPULATION DYNAMICS

It is easy to list many ecological factors that have been omitted from the simple models considered here:

1.  Nonuniformity of the environmental conditions. The ecological system under investigation will not be uniform in either space or in time. The simple models will then have their best validity only over small geographical areas and short periods of time.

2.  Individual differences in organisms constituting the population. The growth rate for a population of rabbits, for example, is only an average for the entire population and may differ markedly among individuals, especially those of differing ages.

3.  Immigration and emigration. Except in carefully controlled laboratory experiments, the ecosystem is not isolated from the rest of the world. Animals may enter or leave at any time.

4.  Spatial clumping of the organisms so that the effects of density dependence will not be the same everywhere.

5.  Effects of time lag in the response of organisms to environmental change. The simple differential equations models assert that growth rates adjust instantaneously to changes in population levels.

6.  Effects of other species which interact with the system. Rabbits have other enemies than foxes, for example, while foxes do not limit their diet to rabbits.

7.  Random disturbances. An unexpected fire, flood, or epidemic affects population levels immediately and often with catastrophic results.

In spite of the fact that we have not taken into account these and many other factors, it sometimes is found that actual populations behave in a manner very similar to that predicted by the simple models. There are several possible explanations for this:

- The factors neglected may indeed be of negligible importance.

- Some of the neglected factors may be important, but may cancel each other out.

- The resemblance of a model to the real-life process it is intended to represent may not be as close as it seems. Closer investigation of the predictions of the model and the actual situation may reveal crucial differences.

These three explanations should always be considered in the evaluation of any mathematical model of a real world phenomenon.

Alfred J. Lotka.  Photograph
reproduced by permission of
Metropolitan Life Insurance
Company.

## VII.  THE MEN BEHIND THE MODELS

### A.  Alfred James Lotka

The father of demographic analysis, Alfred James Lotka (1880–1949) made
many important early contributions to the development of a mathematical
approach to the study of social phenomena.  Besides his own considerable
research on population theory, evolutionary processes, and self-renewing aggre-
gates, Lotka wrote books and articles informing social scientists and the general
public of new developments in science and suggesting ways that mathematics
might be used to study behavior.

Lotka was born in Lemberg, Austria on March 2, 1880 to American parents.
He received his early education in France, but obtained his professional training
in England (Birmingham University), Germany (University of Leipzig), and the
United States (Cornell, Johns Hopkins).  This variety of educational background
produced in his works, according to one critic, "a happy alliance of the deductive

turn of the French spirit, the pragmatic tendency of the English character, and the Germanic concern for precision and erudition."

After his arrival in the United States in 1902, Lotka worked as a chemist for a commercial chemical company, an assistant in physics at a major university, an editor for *Scientific American* publications, and an examiner for the U.S. Patent Office. In 1924, he joined the statistical bureau of the Metropolitan Life Insurance Company in New York City. During the quarter century he worked for Metropolitan, Lotka developed systematically and in collaboration with others the demographic analysis he had initiated as a young man.

His 95 technical papers and six books comprise "permanent contributions of high scholarly standing" according to Frank W. Notestein. He wrote, "To Dr. Lotka's work, the field of demography owes virtually its entire central core of analytical development." Among his major discoveries was a demonstration of how a closed population (no immigration or emigration) develops a stable age distribution and a characteristic rate of increase. Lotka showed how the intrinsic growth rate should be computed and revealed how misleading is the more naïve approach that uses only the crude difference between birth and death rates.

Lotka's most significant impact on the progress of mathematical modeling has been through his book *Elements of Physical Biology*. Originally published more than fifty years ago, it was reissued in 1956 under the more descriptive title *Elements of Mathematical Biology*. In reviewing the book, Herbert A. Simon [1959] discussed its contribution:

> A sect—and by any reasonable definition, mathematical social scientists formed one—needs arcana, as source both of its special wisdom and of passwords by which its members can recognize each other. In the Thirties, a person who had read Lotka's *Elements of Physical Biology* and Richardson's *Generalized Foreign Policy*, and who was acquainted with the peculiar empirical regularities compiled by Zipf was almost certainly a fellow-sectarian. These works represented a large fraction of the literature, outside of economics, in mathematical social science. . . . It is easy to show that much that has happened in mathematical social science in the thirty years since the publication of the first edition of *Elements of Physical Biology* lies in the direction along which the book points.

Simon [1959] describes Lotka as a "forerunner whose imagination creates plans of exploration that he can only partly execute, but who exerts great influence on the work of his successors—posing for them the crucial questions they must answer, and disclosing more or less clearly the directions in which the answers lie."

Lotka was widely respected by his colleagues who elected him to the presidencies of the American Statistical Association and the Population Association of America. "Dr. Lotka was a scientist of the first rank, but he was much more," wrote Notestein [1950]. "His popular writings . . . reveal a delicate sense of humor and a deep consideration of the arts. A quiet, learned, modest, and gently humorous man, a wise counselor, . . . Dr. Lotka will always be held in highest esteem by his colleagues of the demographic profession among whom his is the greatest name, and by his friends, who valued the man above his knowledge."

Lotka's attitude toward the role of scientific models can be seen in some excerpts of an article on Einstein's theory of relativity that he wrote for a general audience in 1920 [Lotka, 1920]:

> One of the foremost aims of science is to build up a conception of the world which shall correspond more and more closely with our experience. As the scope of our experience, our observation, enlarges we shall naturally be forced, from time to time, to modify the world-picture we have already formed. . . .

> We must seek to overcome mental inertia, to liberate ourselves from preconceived ideas. History has taught us that men are apt to fail to distinguish the *absurd*, the illogical, from the merely *unfamiliar*. Profiting by former experience of the race, we may reasonably expect to cut short our term of apprenticeship. . . .

> We are so constituted that of the world in which we live we perceive at any instant only one aspect, a snapshot, as it were, taken from the point of space and time at which we happen to be stationed. . . .

> The thing of paramount importance to us humans, living in a real world, is not what relations *ought to exist* among our observations, but what relations *actually do exist*. If there is disagreement, we shall do well to change our conceptions to fit the facts, for facts are stubborn things which refuse to adapt themselves to fit our conceptions. . . .

> It is not for us to shape the external world in accordance with our concepts; we must build up our conceptual world-picture in accordance with observation. *If a new observation cannot by any manner of means be made to fit into our conception of the world, we may be forced to change that conception.*

## B. Vito Volterra

Born in Ancona, Italy on May 3, 1860, Vito Volterra was an only child, whose father died when Volterra was barely two years old. He began the serious study of arithmetic and geometry at age 11 and was pursuing the calculus by the time he was 14. Resisting his family's wishes that he enter a commercial profession, Volterra opted for a scientific career. He was awarded his doctorate in physics from the University of Pisa in 1882. He served first as a professor of mechanics and of mathematics at Pisa and later spent thirty years on the faculty of the University of Rome.

Volterra's major contributions to pure mathematics lay in the development of functional analysis and the theory of integral equations. By means of the functional calculus, Volterra was able to show that the Hamilton-Jacobi theory of the integration of the differential equations of dynamics could be extended to more general problems of mathematical physics. His research work on problems of elasticity is also quite well known and led to his creation of a fairly general theory of "dislocations."

Vito Volterra.
Reproduced from
Dizionario Enciclopedico
Italiano. Vol. XII, Rome
1961, with permission
from Istituto della
Enciclopedia Italiana
fondata da Giovanni
Treccani.

At the outbreak of World War I, Volterra and others organized meetings and distributed propaganda urging Italy to enter the war on the side of the Allies. When she did, Volterra enlisted in the armed forces, joining the air force at the age of 55! He established the Office of War Inventions in Italy and traveled frequently to England and France in order to help promote technical and scientific cooperation among the Allies.

After the war, Volterra resumed his position at the university in Rome. His most important work after 1918 was in the field of mathematical biology. Volterra investigated in great detail complex models for the interaction of species. We have seen that the Lotka-Volterra model predicts the existence of periodic fluctuations in the predator and prey species. Ecologists had previously observed such fluctuations, but had generally believed them to be explained only by external causes.

Volterra rebelled against the Fascist government of Mussolini that held power in Italy during the 1930's and the early years of World War II. When Volterra refused to take an oath of allegiance to the government, he was stripped of his university position in 1931 and forced the next year to resign from all

Italian scientific academies. He continued his mathematical research nonetheless and published continuously until shortly before his death on October 11, 1940. His published papers, numbering nearly 300, have been collected in five large volumes.

## EXERCISES

### II. TWO REAL-WORLD SITUATIONS

1. Is the relation between a parasite and its host the same as that between predator and prey?

2. What assumptions underlie the conclusion that frequency of encounters between two species is proportional to the product of the two populations? Are these assumptions reasonable?

3. Show that the system $dR/dt = aR - bRF$, $dF/dt = mRF - nF$ reflects the three verbal assumptions made about the predator-prey situations.

4. Formulate another model which is consistent with the verbal assumptions about predator-prey situations.

5. Show that the system $dU/dt = aU - bUV$, $dV/dt = mV - nUV$ reflects the verbal assumptions made about the competitive hunters situation. Formulate a different model consistent with these assumptions.

### III. AUTONOMOUS SYSTEMS

6. Show that $y = 0$, $x = e^{at}$ is a solution of both predator-prey and competitive hunters models. What do the orbits look like? In which direction are they traced out? Answer the same questions if it is specified that $x = 0$ is one of the functions in a solution.

7. Show that the functions $F$, $G$, $F_x$, $F_y$, $G_x$, $G_y$ are continuous over the entire $xy$-plane in the cases where $F$ and $G$ come from

a) Richardson arms race model,

b) Predator-prey model,

c) Competitive hunters model.

8. Verify the details of the claims related to the example presented immediately before Theorem 2.

9. Show that, in general, the Richardson arms race system has only a single one-point orbit.

10. Can the predator-prey or competitive hunters models fail to have two distinct one-point orbits? Why?

11. A critical point $S$ of an autonomous system is called an *isolated critical point* if there is a circle of positive radius centered at $S$ inside of which there are no other critical points.

a) Show that the critical points of the predator-prey and competitive hunters models are isolated.

b) Find an autonomous system with a nonisolated critical point.

12. An isolated critical point $S$ of an autonomous system is *stable* if, given any positive number $e$, there is a positive number $d$ such that (i) every orbit in the $d$-neighborhood of $S$ for some $t = t_1$ is defined for all $t \geq t_1$, and (ii) if a trajectory satisfies (i), it remains in the $e$-neighborhood of $S$ for $t > t_1$.

Are the critical points of the ecological models presented in this chapter stable?

13. A stable critical point is called *asymptotically stable* if every orbit satisfying (i) and (ii) of Exercise 12 also satisfies $\lim_{t \to \infty} (x(t), y(t)) = S$.

Are the critical points of the ecological models presented in this chapter asymptotically stable?

14. Which cases of the Richardson arms race model exhibit stable equilibrium? unstable equilibrium?

15. Check that $x = y = e^{-t}$ is a solution of the system $x' = -x$, $y' = -y$. Can you find any other solutions?

## IV. THE COMPETITIVE HUNTERS MODEL

16. Can Euler's method be applied to analyze this model? What are the results?

17. Find a linearized Taylor series expansion for each of the following functions about the indicated point:

a) $F(x, y) = y/x$ about $(1, 2)$,

b) $F(x, y) = \sin(xy)$ about $(0, 0)$,

c) $F(x, y) = y^{1/2} + \log x$, about $(4, 1)$.

18. If $G(x, y) = my - nxy$, show that the Taylor series approximation gives

$$G\left(\frac{m}{n} + h, \frac{a}{b} + k\right) \approx -(an/b)h.$$

19. Use linearized Taylor series to study the nature of orbits of the competitive hunters model near the critical point $(0, 0)$.

20. Consider the function $f(x) = x^m e^{-nx}$ where $m$ and $n$ are positive constants and suppose the domain of $f$ is the set of all nonnegative numbers.

a) Show that $f(x) \geq 0$ for all $x \geq 0$.

b) Show that $f(x) = 0$ if and only if $x = 0$.

c) Use L'Hôpital's rule to determine $\lim_{x \to \infty} f(x)$.

d) By consideration of the first derivative, show that $f$ has a maximum value when $x = m/n$. What is the maximum value?

e) Find the points of inflection and regions of positive and negative concavity in the graph of $f$.

f) Sketch a careful graph of $f$.

21. Choose numerical values for the parameters in the competitive hunters model and use the Volterra mapping technique to locate at least a dozen points on an orbit of a solution.

22. The competitive hunters model is approximated, near the critical point $(m/n, a/b)$ by the simpler system $u'(t) = -(bm/n)v$, $v' = (am/b)u$. Compute $u''(t)$ and $v''(t)$ and solve the resulting second-order differential equations to find exact solutions for $u$ and $v$ as functions

of $t$. (This problem requires knowledge of differential equations beyond that demanded in the text.)

23. The equation $an^2(x - (m/n))^2 - b^2m(y - (a/b))^2 = K$ does not represent an hyperbola if $K = 0$.

a) What does it represent?

b) Are there initial levels of population $(x_0, y_0)$ that would make $K = 0$?

c) If $K = 0$, show that the orbit asymptotically may approach the critical point? Does this contradict the principle of competitive exclusion?

## V. THE PREDATOR-PREY MODEL

24. Verify the details of the linearized Taylor series expansion for the predator-prey model.

25. Check that $z = A \sin \sqrt{p}t + B \cos \sqrt{p}t$ does satisfy $z'' = -pz$.

26. What can you say about the nature of the orbits for the predator-prey model if initial population levels make the constant $K = 0$ (p. 103 and p. 104)?

27. Carry out the indicated integration to verify that the average values of $u$ and $v$ are 0.

28. Use the Volterra mapping technique to graph some orbits of the predator-prey model if $a = 4$, $b = 2$, $m = 3$, and $n = 1$.

29. The orbits of the competitive hunters model are the graphs of solutions to the first order differential equation

$$\frac{dy}{dx} = \frac{my - nxy}{ax - bxy},$$

while orbits of the predator-prey model are graphs of solutions to the equation

$$\frac{dy}{dx} = \frac{mxy - ny}{ax - bxy},$$

By consideration of $d^2y/dx^2$ discuss whether the orbits have inflection points.

30. (*Kemeny and Snell*) The predator-prey and competitive hunters models are special cases of the more general model

$$\frac{dx}{dt} = xG(y)$$

$$\frac{dy}{dt} = yH(x),$$

where $G(0)$ and $H(0)$ are non-zero.

a) Find the critical points of such a system.

b) Are there any one-point orbits? straight-line orbits?

c) Prove that if $x_0 > 0$ and $y_0 > 0$, then $x(t) > 0$ and $y(t) > 0$ for all $t$, where $x_0 = x(0)$ and $y_0 = y(0)$.

d) By consideration of $dy/dx$, find an equation whose graph is the orbit of such a system.

e) Prove that if the solution is periodic, of period $T$, then $\int_0^T H(x)\, dt = \int_0^T G(y)\, dt = 0$.

f) Let $(p, q)$ be a critical point in the first quadrant other than the origin. Prove that the approximate orbits near this point are hyperbolic if $G'(q)H'(p) > 0$ and are elliptic if $G'(q)H'(p) < 0$.

g) Show that the behavior of the solutions on the axes and near the origin depends only on $G(0)$ and $H(0)$.

h) Show that these results are consistent with the information obtained about the predator-prey and competitive hunters models.

---

## SUGGESTED PROJECTS

1. Re-examine the analysis of the arms race model of Chapter 2 in the light of the mathematical techniques presented in this chapter. Now that you know more about autonomous systems, you ought to be able to say more. Can you?

2. How does Bell modify the predator-prey model to study the immune response to infections? What are his conclusions? (See References.)

3. Generalize the competitive hunters model to reflect the assumption that one species experiences logistic population growth in the absence of the other. Formulate the model as a system of differential equations. Analyze the model using the techniques of this chapter. What are the conclusions? Are they consistent with observed behavior?

4. Analyze mathematically one or more of the three suggested variations of the predator-prey model. How do the conclusions differ from those of the simpler model?

5. Consider an ecological system with three interacting species that contains both predator-prey and competition as features. Formulate a system of differential equations to model this situation. Analyze the mathematical system and interpret the conclusions.

6. If the constants $b$ and $n$ are taken to be negative in the competitive hunters model, the resulting model represents what ecologists label "mutualism" or "symbiosis." This is a relationship in which both species gain from their association with each other. It is a relationship favored by natural selection and is very common in nature. Find some instances of mutualism. Analyze the mathematical model. Interpret the results.

---

## REFERENCES

### MATHEMATICAL ECOLOGY

The texts by Evelyn Pielou and Robert Poole cited in the References of Chapter 3 are excellent introductions to the broad area of mathematical ecology. Lotka's pioneering work is available in his book *Elements of Mathematical Biology* (New York: Dover, 1956). A recent survey of nonlinear models of population growth is given by Narendra Goel, Samaresh Maitra, and Elliott Montroll in *On The Volterra and Other Nonlinear Models of Interacting Populations* (New York: Academic Press, 1971).

Lawrence B. Slobodkin is an ecologist who has warned against the uncritical acceptance of mathematical models by biologists. See his book *Growth and Regulation in Animal Populations* (New York: Holt, Rinehart and Winston, 1961) and a more recent paper, "Comments from a biologist to a mathematician," in Simon A. Levin, ed., *Ecosystem Analysis and Prediction* (Philadelphia: Society for Industrial and Applied Mathematics, 1975), pp. 318–329. He begins the paper with a list of "ten things I very much wish mathematicians would stop doing in population biology."

George Bell's work is described in his paper, "Predator-prey equations simulating an immune response," *Mathematical Biosciences* **16** (1973), 291–314.

Exercise 30 is adapted from John G. Kemeny and J. Laurie Snell, *Mathematical Models in the Social Sciences* (Boston: Ginn, 1962), p.33.

## COMPETITION

Mayr's comments on competition may be found in his book *Populations, Species and Evolution* (Cambridge: Harvard University Press, 1970). For an earlier approach see G. F. Gause, *The Struggle for Existence* (New York: Hafner, 1934). Pielou and Poole both describe some of the experimental tests of the model.

## PREDATION

In his *Animal Ecology* (New York: McGraw-Hill, 1931), Royal N. Chapman presents an English translation of some of Volterra's work under the title "Variations and fluctuations of the number of individuals in animal species living together." Also of interest are Volterra, *Leçons sur la theorie de lutte pour la vie* (Paris: Gauthier-Villars, 1931) and D'Ancona, U., *The Struggle for Existence* (Leiden: Brill, 1954).

Huffaker's study, "Experimental studies on predation: dispersion factors and predator-prey oscillations," has been reprinted in *Readings in Population and Community Biology*, edited by W. E. Hazen (Philadelphia: Saunders, 1970).

Leigh's paper, "The ecological role of Volterra's equations," appears in *Lectures on Mathematics in the Life Sciences: Some Mathematical Problems in Biology*, edited by M. Gerstenhaber (Providence, R. I.: American Mathematical Society, 1968).

The graphical results of the Leslie–Gower model have been reprinted from Pielou's book, which contains a more complete discussion. See also P. H. Leslie and J. C. Gower, "The properties of a stochastic model for the predator-prey type of interaction between two species," *Biometrika*, **46** (1960), 219 234.

## MATHEMATICAL BACKGROUND

In addition to the texts on differential equations cited earlier and Seeley's book, see David A. Sanchez, *Ordinary Differential Equations and Stability Theory: An Introduction* (San Francisco: Freeman, 1968), Chapter 4.

Note also H. S. Bear, Jr., *Differential Equations* (Reading, Mass.: Addison-Wesley, 1962).

## BIOGRAPHICAL REFERENCES

Lotka, Alfred J., "A new conception of the universe," *Harpers Monthly Magazine*, March 1920, 477–487.

Notestein, Frank W., "Alfred James Lotka, 1880–1949," *Population Index* **16** (1950), 22–29.

Simon, Herbert A., "Review of 'Elements of Mathematical Biology,'" *Econometrica* **27** (1959), 493–495.

# 5 Linear Programming

Industrial production, the flow of resources in the economy, the exertion of military effort in a war theater—all are complexes of numerous interrelated activities. Differences may exist in the goals to be achieved, the particular processes involved, and the magnitude of effort. Nevertheless, it is possible to abstract the underlying essential similarities in the management of these seemingly disparate systems.

George B. Dantzig

## I.  WHAT IS LINEAR PROGRAMMING?

### A.  Introduction

Many problems that arise in the real world have to do with finding the optimal values of some variables. A businessperson is usually concerned with maximizing profits, although in some situations he or she may want to minimize costs. The dietician for a large high school has the responsibility for providing a nutritionally adequate hot-lunch program that puts the smallest burden on the school budget. Transportation engineers may wish to design a mass transit system that will carry the largest number of workers from their jobs to their homes during the rush hours. Forest rangers are interested in picking locations to station fire-fighting equipment to minimize the time needed to reach any blaze that may erupt in the forest. Countless other examples of this nature may be given.

   A large class of these problems can be successfully modeled as problems of optimizing a linear function of several variables subject to a finite number of linear constraints. The subject of *linear programming* (often abbreviated as LP) deals with the formulation and solution of such problems.

   The formal theory of linear programming was not developed until shortly after World War II, although various special linear programming problems had been solved earlier. At first glance, the standard methods of calculus to locate maxima and minima of functions might seem to be all that is needed to solve such problems. Unfortunately, calculus is rarely of much help as the extreme values of a linear function almost always occur on the boundary of its domain. New techniques were required. Fortunately, in 1947 an American mathematician, George B. Dantzig, discovered an efficient algorithm for solving linear programming problems. Dantzig's algorithm and the availability of high-speed computers has made possible the application of linear programming models to many important real-world decision-making situations. In the next section, we will present a fairly simple LP problem and a detailed discussion of its solution. Although the example is not a very sophisticated one, it does evidence many of the important concepts that arise in linear programming.

### B.  A Detailed Example: Maximizing Revenue with Limited Resources

Each year the Fromage Cheese Company has a sale to celebrate the anniversary of the opening of its first store. This year, company president Henry Brewster decided to offer two gift packages of cheese at a special price.

   The Fancy Assortment will contain 30 ounces of Cheddar cheese, 10 ounces of Swiss cheese, and 4 ounces of Brie. The Deluxe Assortment will be a package with 12 ounces of Cheddar, 8 ounces of Swiss, and 8 ounces of Brie. In the past, these two assortments have been very popular and Brewster is certain that he can sell out his entire stock if he prices the Fancy Assortment at $4.50 a box and charges $4 for the Deluxe combination.

Brewster has in his storage rooms 6000 ounces of Cheddar, 2600 ounces of Swiss, and 2000 ounces of Brie. He must decide how many packages of each assortment to prepare. Being a prudent businessman, he would like to find the numbers that will maximize his revenue.

We may begin to develop a mathematical formulation of Brewster's problem by letting $x$ denote the number of packages of the Fancy Assortment and $y$ the number of packages of the Deluxe Assortment that will be prepared. Brewster's job is to determine the values of $x$ and $y$ for which the quantity $M = 4.5x + 4y$ is maximized.

The total amount of Cheddar cheese that would be used in $x$ packages of the Fancy Assortment and $y$ packages of the Deluxe would be $30x + 12y$. Of course, he cannot sell more Cheddar cheese than he has in stock. This implies that there is a constraint on the number of packages he may prepare; namely, $x$ and $y$ must be restricted so the inequality

$$30x + 12y \leqslant 6000 \tag{1}$$

holds.

There are similar constraints on the Swiss and Brie cheeses. These are, respectively,

$$10x + 8y \leqslant 2600 \tag{2}$$

and

$$4x + 8y \leqslant 2000. \tag{3}$$

Brewster's choice for the number of packages of the two assortments he can sell is governed by these three inequalities together with the trivial observation that $x$ and $y$ must be nonnegative numbers. Mathematically, he is restricted to the choice of a point in the *constraint* (or *feasibility*) *set*

$$C = \{(x, y): x \geqslant 0, y \geqslant 0, x \text{ and } y \text{ satisfy (1), (2) and (3)}\}.$$

The constraint set $C$ can be described nicely in a geometric way. Consider the inequality (1). The points in the plane whose coordinates satisfy this inequality are the points which lie on or below the line $L_1$ whose equation is

$$30x + 12y = 6000. \tag{4}$$

Since $x$ and $y$ cannot be negative, Brewster is only concerned with points in the first quadrant of the $(x,y)$-plane which lie on or below $L_1$. This set is the shaded triangle shown in Fig. 5.1.

Now we may consider the effect of the second inequality. This forces Brewster to choose only those points which lie on or below the line $L_2$ whose equation is

$$10x + 8y = 2600. \tag{5}$$

The combined effect of inequalities (1) and (2) is to restrict Brewster's choice to the region of the first quadrant consisting of those points which lie on or below both the lines $L_1$ and $L_2$. This region is shown in Fig. 5.2.

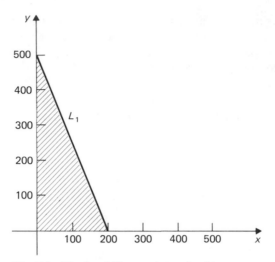

**Fig. 5.1**    The feasibility set determined by inequality (1).

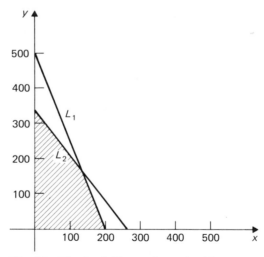

**Fig. 5.2**    The feasibility set determined by inequalities (1) and (2).

The third inequality (3) imposes one final restriction. The points not only must lie in the first quadrant below the lines $L_1$ and $L_2$, they must also lie on or below the line $L_3$ with equation

$$4x + 8y = 2000. \qquad (6)$$

This set of points is shown in Fig. 5.3.

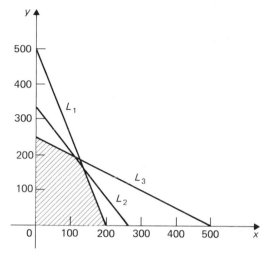

**Fig. 5.3**  The feasibility set determined by
inequalities (1), (2), and (3).

We have a geometric representation of the constraint set of Brewster's problem. It is a polygonal region in the plane with five vertices: $(0, 250)$, $(0, 0)$, $(200, 0)$, $(140, 150)$, $(100, 200)$. The coordinates of the last two vertices listed here are found by determining the points of intersection of $L_1$ with $L_2$, and $L_2$ with $L_3$. This involves solving pairs of linear equations, a straightforward algebraic procedure.

The coordinates of any point in this polygonal region give a feasible mixture of the two assortments. There are, of course, still an infinite number of points in the constraint set so there are infinitely many different combinations of Deluxe and Fancy Assortments that can be packaged with the cheese that is available.

Let's see how we can narrow Brewster's choices even more. Suppose he is considering for the moment a mixture $P_0 = (x_0, y_0)$ which corresponds to a point in the interior of the constraint set. (See Fig. 5.4.)

If $P_0$ lies in the interior of $C$, then we can find a point, like $P_1 = (x_1, y_1)$, which also lies in $C$ but both of whose coordinates are greater than the corresponding coordinates of $P_0$. In other words, it is possible to squeeze out a few more packages of each cheese assortment with the available inventories. But the more packages Brewster can prepare, the more revenue he takes in. Thus, no point in the interior of the constraint set is an optimal choice for Brewster. The optimal choice will be one of the points on the boundary of $C$. We have helped Brewster narrow his choices to a smaller set, but there are still infinitely many different combinations from which to pick. We need some further restrictions.

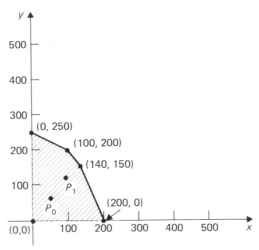

**Fig. 5.4**   The constraint set for the Fromage
Cheese Company example.

The number Brewster is trying to maximize is his total revenue, $M = 4.50x + 4y$. Let's examine how this quantity behaves along one of the edges of the boundary of the constraint set, say the straight line segment from $(0, 250)$ to $(100, 200)$. This is a piece of the line $L_3$, so the coordinates of any point on this edge must satisfy equation (6). The edge can be described analytically as

$$\{(x, y): 4x + 8y = 2000, 0 \leqslant x \leqslant 100\}.$$

For points on this edge, we have $8y = 2000 - 4x$ so that $4y = 1000 - 2x$. Thus the revenue obtained from a point $(x, y)$ on this edge can be written as

$$M = 4.50x + 4y = 4.50x + 1000 - 2x = 2.50x + 1000.$$

Clearly the larger we can make $x$, the larger we will make the revenue. But we have seen that $x$ can be no larger than 100 if we are to remain on this edge. If Brewster is going to choose a point on this edge, then he should choose the vertex $(100, 200)$.

We can argue similarly for the other edges of the boundary. For any edge, the revenue is maximized at one of the endpoints of the edge; that is, at one of the vertices of the constraint set.

Hence, Brewster needs only to consider the five vertices of $C$ to find his optimal mixture. His problem is reduced to deciding among a finite set of alternatives. One way he can do this is to list all the vertices and compute the revenue associated with each one. This is done in Table 5.1.

The table shows that the optimal choice for Brewster is to prepare 100 packages of the Fancy Assortment and 200 packages of the Deluxe Assortment. This will produce a revenue of \$1250. This particular mixture uses up all of

**Table 5.1**

| Vertex $(x, y)$ | Revenue $= 4.5x + 4y$ |
|---|---|
| $(0, 0)$ | $0 |
| $(0, 250)$ | $1000 |
| $(100, 200)$ | $1250 |
| $(140, 150)$ | $1230 |
| $(200, 0)$ | $900 |

the Swiss and Brie cheese he has, but only 5400 of the 6000 available ounces of Cheddar.

The constraint set, and hence its vertices, are determined without consideration of the particular prices that will be charged for the two cheese assortments. If Brewster decides to charge amounts other than $4.50 and $4 for the two assortments, his optimal mixture will still be given by one of the five vertices we have found. To find the best mixture, he need only retest the vertices with the new revenue function. If his stock should change, or if he should decide to alter the relative proportions of the three cheeses in the assortments, then the constraint set would change. In such a case, he would have to find the vertices of the new constraint set and test the revenue function at each of these points.

What can we learn from this example that will be useful for the general linear programming problem? In the next section, we will formulate the general problem and see that its solution is qualitatively much like that of the Fromage Cheese Company example.

## C. The Linear Programming Problem

The mathematical problem of the previous section—stripped of its cheesy crust—is simply this:

Maximize the quantity $M = 4.5x + 4y$

subject to the constraints:

$$30x + 12y \leqslant 6000,$$
$$10x + 8y \leqslant 2600,$$
$$4x + 8y \leqslant 2000,$$
$$x \geqslant 0, \qquad y \geqslant 0.$$

The important feature of the expressions occurring in this problem is that all of the variable terms are of degree one; that is, $x$ and $y$ occur alone and only to the first power. There are no terms of type $xy, x^2, xy^3, x^{1/2}, \ldots$. Expressions of the form $ax + by$ ($a, b$ constants) are called *linear combinations of $x$ and $y$*. More generally, if $x_1, x_2, \ldots, x_n$ are variables and $a_1, a_2, \ldots, a_n$ are constants, then the expression

$$a_1 x_1 + a_2 x_2 + \cdots + a_n x_n$$

is called a *linear combination of the $x_i$'s.* Linear programming is concerned with problems involving such linear combinations.

The general linear programming problem has the following precise mathematical form:

Maximize the linear combination

$$M = c_1 x_1 + c_2 x_2 + \cdots + c_n x_n \tag{7}$$

subjects to the linear constraints:

$$a_{11} x_1 + a_{12} x_2 + \cdots + a_{1n} x_n \leqslant b_1$$
$$a_{21} x_1 + a_{22} x_2 + \cdots + a_{2n} x_n \leqslant b_2$$
$$\cdots \tag{8}$$
$$a_{m1} x_1 + a_{m2} x_2 + \cdots + a_{mn} x_n \leqslant b_m$$
$$x_1 \geqslant 0, \quad x_2 \geqslant 0, \quad \ldots, \quad x_n \geqslant 0$$

where the $c_i$'s, $b_i$'s and $a_{ij}$'s are given constants.

Any set of values for the $x_i$'s that satisfies all the inequalities of (8) is called a *feasible solution* of the problem. A set of values for the $x_i$'s that maximizes $M$ is called an *optimal solution*. The linear programming problem asks for an optimal, feasible solution.

We will briefly summarize here the basic results about solutions of linear programming problems. Each inequality of (8) determines a closed half-space of Euclidean $n$-dimensional space $R^n$. The intersection of the $m + n$ half-spaces of (8) gives the set of all feasible values for the $x_i$'s. This set, called the *feasibility set* or *constraint set*, has a very special form. It turns out to be what mathematicians call a *polygonal convex set.*

If some of the constraints are mutually inconsistent, then the feasibility set turns out to be empty. In this case, the linear programming problem has no solution. Even if the constraint set is nonempty, the problem may still have no solution; see Exercise 12 for an example. For this to happen, it is necessary, but not sufficient, that the feasibility set be unbounded.

If the linear programming problem has a solution, however, then it always has one that occurs at one of the vertex points of the constraint set. Since there are a finite number of constraints, there will be only a finite number of vertices.

In theory, one could solve any linear programming problem by finding all of the vertices and then computing the value of $M$ at each vertex. In practice, this is not a reasonable way to proceed. Even for a moderate number of constraints, the feasibility set may have a very large number of vertices. It would be a formidable task, even for a computer, to determine all the coordinates of all the vertices.

The algorithm devised by Dantzig and refined by others finds the solution in a much more economical fashion. The strategy behind Dantzig's approach is simple. Start with any feasible solution that is a vertex of the constraint set. Then move to a "nearby" vertex at which $M$ has a greater value. Repeat this process until you arrive at an optimal solution.

Dantzig's algorithm, called the *simplex method*, not only tells how to move from one vertex to another, it also helps find a feasible solution at which to start and it gives a method for determining when we have arrived at an optimal, feasible solution.

We will devote the major part of this chapter to an elaboration of the ideas of the past few paragraphs. Before we do this, however, we will describe some problems that can be formulated using linear programming models.

## D. More Examples of LP Problems

1. *The Breakfast Problem.* Jennifer and Jordan will only eat cereal for breakfast. In fact, they will eat only Brand $X$ or Yukkies. Their mother Janet is concerned about the children receiving adequate nourishment in the morning. According to the box tops of the cereals, one ounce of Brand $X$ provides $\frac{1}{3}$ milligram of iron and 3.8 grams of protein, while the same amount of Yukkies offers 1 mg of iron and 2.4 gm of protein. Janet wants her children to obtain at least 1 mg of iron and 5 gm of protein from their breakfast cereals, but she wants to provide these levels of nutrients at the lowest possible cost. If one ounce of Brand $X$ costs 4¢ while one ounce of Yukkies sells for 6.5¢, how should she mix the cereals to accomplish her goals?

We will let $x$ represent the number of ounces of Brand $X$ to be served and $y$ the number of ounces of Yukkies. Then Janet has the following problem:

Minimize $m = 4x + 6.5y$

subject to the constraints:

$$\begin{aligned}
(\tfrac{1}{3})x + \quad y &\geq 1, \quad \text{(iron)} \\
3.8x + 2.4y &\geq 5, \quad \text{(protein)} \\
x \geq 0, \quad y &\geq 0.
\end{aligned}$$

This type of problem occurs quite frequently in applications. It does not precisely fit the format of a linear programming problem as we defined it, but we can quickly change that. We need only note that an inequality of the form $ax + by \geq c$ is equivalent to the inequality $-ax - by \leq -c$, and that the minimum value of a quantity $m$ is equal to the negative of the maximum value of $-m$. Thus we can write Janet's problem as:

Maximize $M = -m = -4x - 6.5y$

subject to the constraints:

$$\begin{aligned}
-\tfrac{1}{3}x - \quad 1y &\leq -1, \\
-3.8x - 2.4y &\leq -5, \\
x \geq 0, \quad y &\geq 0
\end{aligned}$$

so that it fits the definition of an LP problem.

For numerical computations, it is sometimes convenient if the coefficients of the constraints are integers. In this problem, we may multiply the first constraint by 3 and the second by 10 to obtain the equivalent problem:

Maximize $M = -4x - 6.5y$

subject to the constraints:

$$x + \quad 3y \geqslant 3,$$
$$38x + 24y \geqslant 50, \tag{9}$$
$$x \geqslant 0, \quad y \geqslant 0.$$

2. *A Smuggling Problem.* The Turkish Poppy Company imports heroin into the United States to 20 different dealers through 5 different ports. Let $x_{ij}$ denote the number of pounds to be shipped from port $i$ to dealer $j$. Since the dealers are located in different parts of the country, there is an associated cost, $c_{ij}$, of sending 1 pound of heroin from port $i$ to dealer $j$. The total shipping cost $m$ is given by a double sum:

$$m = \sum_{j=1}^{20} \sum_{i=1}^{5} c_{ij} x_{ij}$$

and the company would like to minimize this cost.

There are two important constraints operating here. First, each dealer has ordered a particular amount of heroin that he believes he can sell in his area of the market. Thus the company must satisfy the order of each dealer. If the $j$th dealer has ordered $d_j$ pounds, then we have a constraint of the form

$$\sum_{i=1}^{5} x_{ij} = d_j.$$

We have one such constraint for each of the 20 dealers.

The second type of constraint arises because the heroin must be smuggled into the United States. There are different security measures at each of the five ports of entry, so that different amounts of heroin can be smuggled through different places. Suppose that the smuggling capacity of the $i$th port is $s_i$ pounds of heroin. Then the total number of pounds shipped from each port cannot exceed the smuggling capacity of that port. We formulate this restriction as

$$\sum_{j=1}^{20} x_{ij} \leqslant s_i, \, i = 1, 2, 3, 4, 5.$$

This description of the smuggling problem requires two transformations to convert it into a standard LP problem. First, we need to change the minimizing requirement to a maximizing one; we saw how to do this when we discussed the breakfast problem. Second, we notice that some of the constraints are equations rather than inequalities. This difficulty is also easily remedied. We simply note that the equation

$$ax + by = c$$

is equivalent to insisting that the inequalities

$$ax + by \geqslant c \qquad \text{and} \qquad ax + by \leqslant c$$

both hold. Thus we replace each constraint of the form $\sum_{i=1}^{5} x_{ij} = d_j$ by the pair:

$$\sum_{i=1}^{5} x_{ij} \leqslant d_{ij} \qquad \text{and} \qquad \sum_{i=1}^{5} -x_{ij} \leqslant -d_j.$$

The smuggling problem is an example of what is called a "transportation problem." Many of the earliest applications of linear programming were to transportation problems and these still provide a fair share of LP work. It is not unusual today to solve transportation problems involving as many as 3,000 constraints and 15,000 variables.

3. *An Assignment Problem.* Mary Muttoni is the chairperson of the history department at a small university. One of her duties is to make up the teaching schedule. The catalog of the university promises that the department will offer four large lecture courses for freshmen next term. These are:

> History A: A Survey of American History,
>
> History B: Revolutions and Counterrevolutions,
>
> History C: European Intellectual History,
>
> History D: China and Japan.

There are four professors in the department who can teach any of the four courses. Because of their different backgrounds, expertise, and enthusiasms, they will attract different numbers of students in each course. Muttoni estimates the student appeal of each instructor in each course and derives a set of enrollment estimates. These are displayed in Table 5.2.

Each professor will be assigned to only one course and each course is to be taught by only one faculty member. The chairperson wishes to maximize the total enrollment in the four courses by assigning the available professors to the different courses.

**Table 5.2**

| Professor \ Course | A | B | C | D |
|---|---|---|---|---|
| Doggoff | 310 | 260 | 270 | 290 |
| Josephs | 270 | 330 | 250 | 210 |
| Reapingwillst | 210 | 230 | 190 | 280 |
| Cragdodge | 240 | 210 | 220 | 200 |

We can formulate this problem using linear programming. Let $x_{ij}$ be the variable which is equal to 1 if the $i$th professor is assigned to the $j$th course and 0 otherwise. Thus there are 16 variables in the problem. Let $e_{ij}$ be the number of students the $i$th professor will attract if he teaches the $j$th course.

The chairman's problem is:

Maximize $M = \sum_{i=1}^{4} \sum_{j=1}^{4} e_{ij}x_{ij}$

subject to the constraints:

$$\sum_{i=1}^{4} x_{ij} = 1 \ (j = 1, 2, 3, 4), \quad \begin{array}{l}\text{(Each course is assigned} \\ \text{one professor.)}\end{array}$$

$$\sum_{j=1}^{4} x_{ij} = 1 \ (i = 1, 2, 3, 4), \quad \begin{array}{l}\text{(Each professor is} \\ \text{assigned one course.)}\end{array}$$

and each $x_{ij} \geqslant 0$.

### E. Vector Formulation of the LP Problem

We wish to give a compact statement of the linear programming problem using vector notation. We will denote vectors in this chapter by boldface type.

**DEFINITION   (See Appendix II.)   If $A$ is an $m \times n$ matrix and x is an $n \times 1$ vector, then $A$x is the $m \times 1$ vector whose $i$th component is the product of the $i$th row of $A$ and the vector x; that is,**

$$A\mathbf{x} = \mathbf{y} = \begin{pmatrix} y_1 \\ y_2 \\ \vdots \\ y_m \end{pmatrix}$$

**where $y_i = a_{i1}x_1 + a_{i2}x_2 + \cdots + a_{in}x_n$.**

**DEFINITION   If $A$ and $B$ are matrices of the same size, then $A \leqslant B$ means that $a_{ij} \leqslant b_{ij}$ for all entries of the two matrices. In particular, if x and y are $k \times 1$ vectors, then x $\leqslant$ y if and only if**

$$x_1 \leqslant y_1, \qquad x_2 \leqslant y_2, \qquad \ldots, \qquad \textbf{and} \qquad x_k \leqslant y_k.$$

The following theorem is easily proved and shows that the notion of inequality for matrices has the same features as inequalities for numbers.

■ *THEOREM 1*   Suppose $A, B, C$, and $D$ are matrices of the same size. Then

a) If $A \leqslant B$ and $B \leqslant C$, then $A \leqslant C$;

b) If $A \leqslant B$ and $C \leqslant D$, then $A + C \leqslant B + D$;

c) If $A \leqslant B$, then $cA \leqslant cB$ for any positive constant $c$ and $cA \geqslant cB$ for any negative constant $c$.

With these properties in mind, we can restate the general linear programming problem:

Find an $n \times 1$ vector $\mathbf{x}$ such that

$$M = \mathbf{c} \cdot \mathbf{x} \quad \text{is maximized} \tag{7'}$$

subject to the constraints:

$$A\mathbf{x} \leqslant \mathbf{b}, \tag{8'}$$
$$\mathbf{x} \geqslant \mathbf{0},$$

where $\mathbf{c}$ is a given $1 \times n$ vector, $\mathbf{b}$ is a given $m \times 1$ vector, $A$ is a given $m \times n$ matrix and $\mathbf{0}$ is the zero vector, all of whose components are 0.

## II. CONVEX SETS

### A. Definitions, Examples, Basic Properties

In Part II, we will discuss in more detail the nature of the feasibility set of a linear programming problem. We will concentrate on feasibility sets arising from problems involving two variables. In such cases, the feasibility set lies in the plane and we can make use of geometric intuition. Our aim is to outline a proof that optimal feasible solutions of LP problems can be found at the vertices of the feasibility sets.

**DEFINITION**   **If** $\mathbf{x} = (x_1, x_2, \ldots, x_n)$ **and** $\mathbf{y} = (y_1, y_2, \ldots, y_n)$ **are points in Euclidean $n$ dimensional space, then the *line segment* between $\mathbf{x}$ and $\mathbf{y}$ is the set of vectors of the form**

$$\mathbf{w} = t\mathbf{x} + (1 - t)\mathbf{y} \qquad \text{where} \qquad 0 \leqslant t \leqslant 1. \tag{10}$$

You may think of the parameter $t$ in Eq. (10) as a time variable and consider that the line segment is traced out by moving from $\mathbf{y}$ at $t = 0$ to $\mathbf{x}$ at $t = 1$. The set of all vectors satisfying Eq. (10) where $t$ can be any real number is the set of points of the entire line through $\mathbf{x}$ and $\mathbf{y}$.

**DEFINITION**   **A subset $K$ of Euclidean $n$-dimensional space is said to be *convex* if, whenever $\mathbf{x}$ and $\mathbf{y}$ belong to $K$, then so does every point of the line segment between $\mathbf{x}$ and $\mathbf{y}$.**

The following are all examples of convex figures in the plane (see Fig. 5.5):

a) The entire plane,
b) A straight line in the plane,
c) The region between two parallel lines,
d) The interior of a square, triangle, or circle,
e) The first quadrant of the plane.

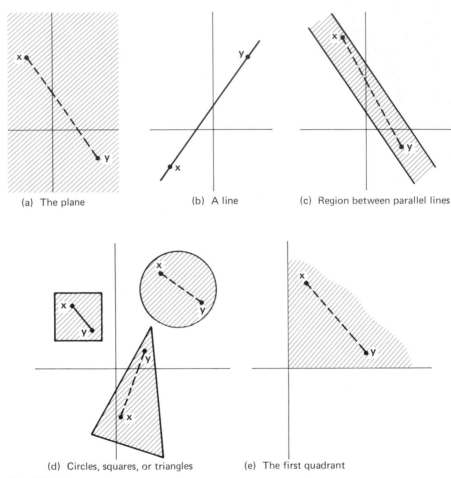

(a)  The plane

(b)  A line

(c)  Region between parallel lines

(d)  Circles, squares, or triangles

(e)  The first quadrant

**Fig. 5.5**    Convex sets.

The idea of a convex set can be further clarified by examining some sets in the plane which are not convex (see Fig. 5.6):

a)  The region between two concentric circles,

b)  The interior of a star,

c)  The plane with the origin deleted,

d)  Two disjoint disks,

e)  The letter $U$.

The pictures of Fig. 5.6 indicate that it is often easy to prove that a particular set is not convex. We just have to locate two points in the figure so that the straight line segment between them does not lie entirely in the figure. To

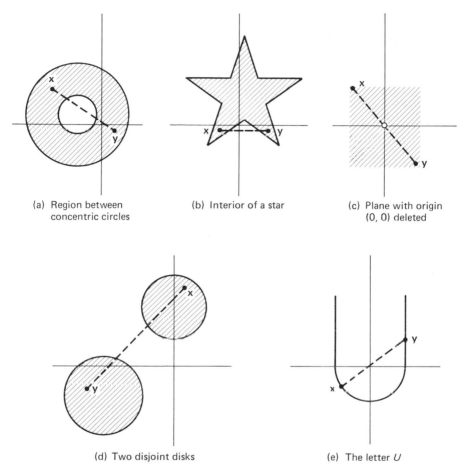

(a) Region between concentric circles

(b) Interior of a star

(c) Plane with origin (0, 0) deleted

(d) Two disjoint disks

(e) The letter *U*

**Fig. 5.6**  Nonconvex sets.  In each case, the segment between *x* and *y* does not lie entirely inside the set.

establish the convexity of a figure usually requires more work.  We shall see how this is done for a particular set in Theorem 2.  First, we give an important definition.

**DEFINITION**   **If a is a given $1 \times n$ vector and $b$ a given constant, then the set of all vectors x in Euclidean *n*-dimensional space satisfying $a \cdot x \leqslant b$ is called a *closed half-space*.  The set of vectors for which $a \cdot x = b$ is called the *boundary* of the closed half-space.**

In the special case $n = 2$, the inequality $a_1 x_1 + a_2 x_2 \leqslant b$ is satisfied by exactly those points which lie on one side of the boundary line $a_1 x_1 + a_2 x_2 = b$.

■ *THEOREM 2*    Every closed half-space is a convex set.

***Proof***   Suppose **y** and **z** lie in the closed half-space consisting of vectors which satisfy $\mathbf{a} \cdot \mathbf{x} \leqslant b$. Let **w** be any point on the line segment between **y** and **z**. Then we have

$$\mathbf{a} \cdot \mathbf{y} \leqslant b, \quad \mathbf{a} \cdot \mathbf{z} \leqslant b, \quad \text{and} \quad \mathbf{w} = t\mathbf{y} + (1 - t)\mathbf{z} \quad \text{for some } t \text{ in } [0, 1].$$

We must show that $\mathbf{a} \cdot \mathbf{w} \leqslant b$.

Now

$$
\begin{aligned}
\mathbf{a} \cdot \mathbf{w} &= \mathbf{a} \cdot (t\mathbf{y} + (1 - t)\mathbf{z}) \\
&= t(\mathbf{a} \cdot \mathbf{y}) + (1 - t)(\mathbf{a} \cdot \mathbf{z}) \\
&\leqslant tb + (1 - t)b \quad \text{since } t \text{ and } 1 - t \text{ are nonnegative} \\
&= b. \ \square
\end{aligned}
$$

The next theorem gives a very general and very important property of convex sets.

■ ***THEOREM 3***   The intersection of any collection of convex sets is convex.

***Proof***   Let $P$ and $Q$ be any two points in the intersection. Then $P$ and $Q$ belong to each convex set of the collection. But each convex set contains the segment between $P$ and $Q$. Thus the segment belongs to every set in the collection so that it belongs to the intersection. $\square$

Theorems 2 and 3 provide the first essential fact about feasibility sets. Each feasibility set of a linear programming problem consists of all vectors that simultaneously satisfy a finite number of linear constraints. Each constraint defines a closed half-space. Thus the feasibility set is the intersection of a finite number of closed half-spaces, each of which is convex by Theorem 2. Theorem 3 then gives us

■ ***THEOREM 4***   The feasibility set of a linear programming problem is a convex set.

**DEFINITION**   A *polygonal convex set* **is the intersection of a finite number of closed half-spaces.**

### B. Polygonal Convex Sets in the Plane
Now let us focus attention on polygonal convex sets in the plane. An *edge* of a polygonal convex set $K$ is defined to be the intersection of $K$ with the boundary line of a closed half-plane determining $K$. Since an edge is the intersection of two convex sets, it must also be convex. In fact, it is a convex subset of a line. There are only a few possibilities for the geometric character of an edge.

■ *THEOREM 5*    A subset $K$ of a line is convex if and only if $K$ is one of the following:

a)  $K$ is the entire line;
b)  $K$ is the empty set;
c)  $K$ is an open or closed ray;
d)  $K$ is a segment of the line, with or without either endpoint; or
e)  $K$ is a single point.

*Proof*    It is easy to verify that each of these sets of type (a)–(e) is convex. We shall show how to prove the converse. Suppose $K$ is a convex subset of the line. If $K$ is nonempty, then there is at least one point $p$ of the line that belongs to $K$. If $K$ is not the entire line, then there is at least one point $q$ of the line which does not belong to $K$.

Now we can parameterize the line so that it consists of all points of the form

$$w_t = tp + (1 - t)q \qquad \text{where} \quad t \quad \text{can be any real number.}$$

The *positive side* of the line consisting of all points $w_t$ for which $t$ is positive and the *negative side* is similarly defined. We are given that $p$ is on the positive side of $q$. Since $K$ is convex, and $q$ does not belong to $K$, there can be no points of $K$ on the negative side of $q$. All points of $K$ lie on the positive side of $q$.

Thus the set of parameter values $t$ corresponding to points of $K$ is bounded below by 0. Since this is a set of real numbers, it has a greatest lower bound $t_r$ with $t_r \geqslant 0$. Let $r$ be the corresponding point of the line; that is $r = w_{t_r}$. (It is possible that $r = q$.) By the definition of greatest lower bound and the fact that $K$ is convex, we have that no point to the left of $r$ belongs to $K$ and all points between $r$ and $p$ belong to $K$.

Now if all the points to the right of $r$ (that is, all points $w_t$ with $t > t_r$) belong to $K$, then $K$ is either a closed or open ray, depending on whether or not $r$ belongs to $K$. Suppose then that some point $s$ to the right of $r$ does not belong to $K$. Let the corresponding parameter value be $t_s$.

Consider again the set of parameter values $t$ corresponding to points of $K$. This set is bounded above by $t_s$ and so it must have a least upper bound $t_u$. Let $u$ be the corresponding point of the line, $u = w_{t_u}$. Then $K$ consists of all points between $r$ and $u$, including or excluding the points $r$ and $u$. Thus if $K$ is a convex subset of a line and is not of type (a), (b), (c), or (e), then it must be of type (d). See Fig. 5.7. □

**Fig. 5.7**    Location of points along $K$ as given in proof of Theorem 5.

Not all of the cases mentioned above can occur for the feasibility set of an LP problem. Recall that an edge of a polygonal convex set in the plane is the intersection of a boundary line of a closed half-space with the set. Because of this, it can be shown, by reasoning similar to that in the proof of Theorem 5, that an edge containing more than one point must be either a closed segment or a closed ray; that is, an edge always contains its endpoints.

By a *vertex* of a polygonal convex set $K$ in the plane we will mean a point of $K$ which is contained in at least two distinct boundary lines. A vertex will be an endpoint of the edge of the polygonal convex set. We want to prove the fundamental theorem that a linear function defined on $K$ assumes its largest and smallest values at vertex points.

First, consider a linear function $f(x, y) = \alpha x + \beta y$ defined along some line $L$ with equation $y = mx + b$. Then we have

$$f(x, y) = \alpha x + \beta(mx + b) = (\alpha + \beta m)x + b.$$

If the quantity $\alpha + \beta m$ is zero, then the function is constant along $L$. If $\alpha + \beta m$ is positive, then $f$ is a strictly increasing function of $x$, while if $\alpha + \beta m$ is negative, $f$ is a strictly decreasing function of $x$ (see Fig. 5.8).

In any case, if we examine the function along some closed segment of the line $L$, then the minimum value of $f$ will occur at one endpoint and the maximum values at the other. If we examine $f$ along a closed ray, then there are two possibilities:

1. The minimum value occurs at the endpoint of the ray and there is no maximum value for $f$, or

2. The maximum value of $f$ occurs at the endpoint and there is no minimum.

We are now ready to outline the proof of the basic theorem on the location of extreme values of a linear function at the vertices of a polygonal convex set.

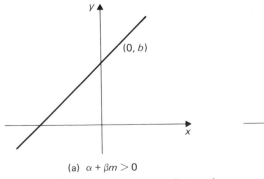

(a)  $\alpha + \beta m > 0$

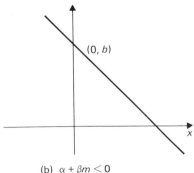

(b)  $\alpha + \beta m < 0$

**Fig. 5.8**   The graph of $y = (\alpha + \beta m)x + b$.

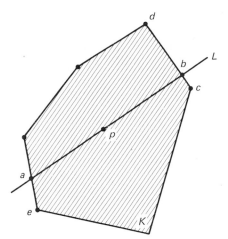

**Fig. 5.9**   Intersection of a line and a bounded polygonal convex set in the plane.

Suppose $K$ is a polygonal convex set in the plane and that $p$ is an interior point of $K$; that is, $p$ is not on any edge. See Fig. 5.9. Let $L$ be any line containing $p$ and suppose $L$ intersects the boundary of $K$ in two points. Then the value of $f$ at $p$ must lie between the values of $f$ at these two points. We may label the two points $a$ and $b$ in such a way that

$$f(a) \leqslant f(p) \leqslant f(b). \qquad (11)$$

Now the point $b$ lies on an edge of $K$ with vertices $c$ and $d$. On this edge, the function $f$ takes on its extreme values at the vertices. Label the vertices so that

$$f(c) \leqslant f(b) \leqslant f(d). \qquad (12)$$

Combining inequalities (11) and (12) gives us $f(p) \leqslant f(d)$. In other words, associated with each interior point of the convex set $K$, there is a vertex at which the value of $f$ is at least as large.

Similarly, we can find a vertex $e$ of the edge containing $a$ with $f(e) \leqslant f(a) \leqslant f(p)$, so that given an interior point $p$ of $K$, there is a vertex at which $f$ is at least as small.

Since a polygonal convex set has a finite number of vertices, there are vertices at which the function $f$ assumes its greatest and smallest values. This completes an outline of the proof of the desired result. This is only an outline, because we have not considered all possibilities. We assumed, for example, that the line $L$ through $p$ intersected the boundary of the convex set in exactly 2 points. It may happen that the line does not intersect the boundary at all or that it intersects the boundary in only one point. Figure 5.10 illustrates these possibilities.

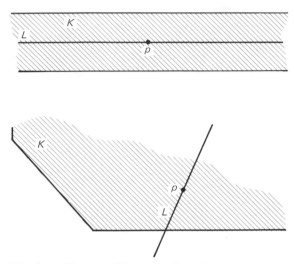

**Fig. 5.10**   Two possible ways a line might intersect an unbounded polygonal convex set in the plane.

In the case where the line and the boundary do not intersect, there is no problem. Either the function $f$ is constant on the line or it takes on all real values. If the latter occurs, there is no optimal solution to the LP problem.

Suppose the line intersects the boundary at one point. If $f$ has no maximum on the line, the LP problem again has no optimal solution. On the other hand, if $f$ has a maximum, it must occur at the point on the boundary. That boundary point lies on an edge of $K$. If the edge is a closed segment, then $f$ assumes a value at one of the two vertices of that edge which is greater than the value $f(p)$. If the edge is a closed ray, then again there is either no maximum for $f$ or the value of $f$ at the endpoint of the ray exceeds the value $f(p)$.

In every case, then, if $f$ takes on a maximum value on the polygonal set $K$, it takes that value at one of the vertices.

To make use of simple geometric figures in the plane, we have restricted our considerations to LP problems involving only two variables.

Even in this case, we have presented only an outline of the proof that the optimal feasible solution occurs at a vertex point. Furthermore, our proof involved checking a fair number of special cases.

If the reasoning discussed here is generalized to LP problems involving more than two variables, it is reasonable to suspect that the number of special cases that can arise will be outrageously large. Surely, I hope you are thinking, there is a way to generalize the ideas of this proof which handles all the cases at the same time. There is indeed such a proof for the general LP problem with $n$ variables, but it requires some mathematical tools we do not have space to develop in this book. The reader with a stronger background in linear algebra or functions of several variables may wish to consult the proofs in the following References: George B. Dantzig, *Linear Programming and Extensions* and George Hadley, *Linear Programming*.

## III. THE SIMPLEX METHOD

### A. Basic Solutions

**1. Changing inequalities to equations**    The feasibility set of a linear programming problem is given by a set of inequalities. It is usually easier to work with equations than with inequalities, and so the first step in the simplex method is to convert the system of inequalities into a system of equations.

This is accomplished by introducing new variables into the problem. We can illustrate this procedure with the Fromage Cheese Company example of Section I. For each feasible mixture $(x, y)$ of the two assortments, we define *slack variables* $u, v$, and $w$ to represent, respectively, the amount of Cheddar, Swiss and Brie cheeses that will remain in stock after the packages have been prepared. The problem we want to solve then becomes:

Find nonnegative numbers $x, y, u, v, w$ such that

$$M = 4.5x + 4y \quad \text{is maximized}$$

subject to the constraints:

$$30x + 12y + u = 6000,$$
$$10x + 8y + v = 2600, \tag{13}$$
$$4x + 8y + w = 2000.$$

**2. Solving systems of equations**    Before reading this section, you should review the Gauss-Jordan method for solving systems of linear algebraic equations; this method is described in Appendix III.

Consider then the following problem: Given the three equations:

$$8x - 8y + 2u + 4v + 2w = -14,$$
$$4x + 2y - 2u - v + 7w = 29, \tag{14}$$
$$1x + 4y + 3u + 5v + 7w = 2,$$

solve for $u, v, w$ in terms of $x$ and $y$.

This problem can be solved in a very systematic way. For notational convenience, we deal only with the matrix of coefficients:

$$
\begin{array}{ccccc}
x & y & u & v & w \\
\end{array}
$$
$$
\left(
\begin{array}{ccccc|c}
8 & -8 & ② & 4 & 2 & -14 \\
4 & 2 & -2 & -1 & 7 & 29 \\
1 & 4 & 3 & 5 & 7 & 2 \\
\end{array}
\right) \tag{15}
$$

**Step 1**    Eliminate $u$ from each row (equation) except the first row, where $u$ will be made equal to 1.

This requires two operations:

a)  Divide every entry of the first row by the coefficient of $u$; this number is called the *pivot element* and it is circled in (15).

This operation yields the matrix:

$$
\begin{matrix}
x & y & u & v & w & \\
\begin{pmatrix}
4 & -4 & 1 & 2 & 1 & -7 \\
4 & 2 & -2 & -1 & 7 & 29 \\
1 & 4 & 3 & 5 & 7 & 2
\end{pmatrix}
\end{matrix}
\tag{16}
$$

b)  Eliminate $u$ from the second row by replacing the second row with the sum of the second row and twice the first row.  Similarly, eliminate $u$ from the third row by replacing the third row with the sum of the third row and $-3$ times the first row.  By the "first row," we mean the first row of (16). This yields:

$$
\begin{matrix}
x & y & u & v & w & \\
\begin{pmatrix}
4 & -4 & 1 & 2 & 1 & -7 \\
12 & -6 & 0 & ③ & 9 & 15 \\
-11 & 16 & 0 & -1 & 4 & 23
\end{pmatrix}
\end{matrix}
\tag{17}
$$

**Step 2**    Eliminate $v$ from all rows of (17) except the second.  Again, there are two operations:

a)  Divide the second row by the pivot, that is, the coefficient of $v$, and

b)  Add $-2$ times new row 2 to row 1 and add new row 2 to row 3.  The result of these two operations is:

$$
\begin{matrix}
x & y & u & v & w & \\
\begin{pmatrix}
-4 & 0 & 1 & 0 & -5 & -17 \\
4 & -2 & 0 & 1 & 3 & 5 \\
-7 & 14 & 0 & 0 & ⑦ & 28
\end{pmatrix}
\end{matrix}
\tag{18}
$$

**Step 3**    Eliminate $w$ from all rows except the third.  Our operations for this step will be performed on the matrix of (18):

a)  Divide the third row by the pivot 7, the coefficient of $w$ in the third row;
b)  Add 5 times row 3 to row 1 and add $-3$ times row 3 to row 2.  The final matrix is:

$$
\begin{matrix}
x & y & u & v & w & \\
\begin{pmatrix}
-9 & 10 & 1 & 0 & 0 & 3 \\
7 & -8 & 0 & 1 & 0 & -7 \\
-1 & 2 & 0 & 0 & 1 & 4
\end{pmatrix}
\end{matrix}
\tag{19}
$$

This matrix corresponds to a system of equations equivalent to the original one, but with a simpler structure:

$$-9x + 10y + u = \quad 3,$$
$$7x - 8y + v = -7, \qquad (20)$$
$$-x + 2y + w = \quad 4,$$

from which we may read off

$$u = \quad 3 + 9x - 10y,$$
$$v = -7 - 7x + \ 8y, \qquad (21)$$
$$w = \quad 4 + \ x - \ 2y.$$

Now there are infinitely many particular solutions to this system. They are produced by assigning arbitrary numerical values to $x$ and $y$ and using Eq. (21) to calculate the corresponding values of $u, v,$ and $w$. For example, setting $x = 1$ and $y = -2$ gives $u = 32, v = -30, w = 9$.

One particular solution is singled out. This is the one obtained when $x$ and $y$ are both zero. In this case, we have

$$x = y = 0, \qquad u = 3, \qquad v = -7, \qquad w = 4.$$

This is called a *basic solution* and $u, v, w$ are called *basic variables* while $x$ and $y$ are the *nonbasic variables*.

For the original system of equations, we could have designated any two variables as nonbasic and asked for the other three in terms of these. The solution procedure would have been essentially the same, although the matrices at each stage would not have looked the same. In the final matrix of the problem, a basic variable will be represented with exactly one entry equal to 1 and all other entries in that column equal to 0. Each basic variable has the "1" in a different row from all the other basic variables. The values of the basic variables in the basic solution appear in the righthand-most column of the matrix.

The Gauss-Jordan procedure described in Appendix III will always yield a matrix from which the basic and nonbasic variables can be identified readily.

**3. Basic solutions and the LP problem**   We have rewritten the linear programming problem about the Fromage Cheese Company in the form: Find nonnegative values of $x, y, u, v$ and $w$ so that $M = 4.5x + 4y$ is maximized and such that the equations (13) are all satisfied. Any solution of the system (13) for which all variables are nonnegative is called a *feasible solution*. Any solution of Eq. (13) for which $M$ is maximized is called an *optimal* solution. The linear programming problem is to find a feasible solution which is also optimal. The Fundamental Existence Theorem of Linear Programming states that if there exists an optimal, feasible solution, then there exists one which is also basic. Stated geometrically, this is just the result that linear functions on polygonal convex sets achieve their extreme values at the vertices.

For the cheese example, the solution

$$x = 0, \qquad y = 0, \qquad u = 6000, \qquad v = 2600, \qquad w = 2000.$$

is both feasible and basic. The basic variables are $u, v$, and $w$. Geometrically, this solution is located at the vertex where the two edges $x = 0$ and $y = 0$ intersect.

This particular solution gives $M = 0$, which is clearly not optimal. We can increase $M = 4.5x + 4y$ by increasing either $x$ or $y$. One way to go about this is to concentrate on increasing one of the variables. Since a unit increase in $x$ boosts $M$ more than a unit increase in $y$, it is reasonable to begin by making $x$ as large as possible, while keeping $y = 0$. When $y = 0$, Eq. (13) can be written

$$
\begin{aligned}
u &= 6000 - 30x, \\
v &= 2600 - 10x, \\
w &= 2000 - 4x.
\end{aligned}
\tag{22}
$$

From these equations, it is apparent that increases in $x$ have the effect of decreasing $u, v$, and $w$. To retain a feasible solution, we must insure that these variables remain nonnegative. From the equation for $u$ in (22), we see that $x$ can be increased to 200 before $u$ becomes negative. Similarly, $v$ does not become negative until $x$ exceeds 260 and $w$ does not become negative until $x$ exceeds 500.

Thus we can increase $x$ up to 200 without driving the other variables below zero, but we cannot increase $x$ beyond 200. If we let $x = 200$, we obtain (using Eq. 22) a new basic feasible solution:

$$x = 200, \qquad y = 0, \qquad u = 0, \qquad v = 600, \qquad w = 1600$$

for which the revenue has increased: $M = (4.5)(200) = 900$.

Geometrically, we have moved from the vertex $(0,0)$ to the vertex $(200,0)$ which is the intersection of the two edges $y = 0, u = 0$.

The step we have just described is the heart of the simplex method of solving linear programming problems. In the next section, we will describe the simplex method in more detail by carrying out all the steps necessary to solve the Fromage Cheese Company example. We can describe the general outline a little more carefully here, however.

First, we need to start with a basic feasible solution. We begin by adding a slack variable to each constraint. This gives us a total of $n + m$ variables in the problem. The solution in which each of the original $n$ variables is set equal to 0 will be a basic, feasible solution. The basic variables will be the $m$ slack variables. Geometrically, we have located ourselves at the vertex where the edges $x_1 = 0, x_2 = 0, \ldots, x_n = 0$ intersect. Generally, this will be a highly nonoptimal solution.

Second, we seek a new solution in which one of the $x_i$ becomes basic and one of the slack variables, say $u_j$, becomes nonbasic. The simplex method advises us on how to choose $x_i$ and $u_j$ so that the new solution remains feasible and increases $M$. The new solution is obtained from the old one by using the Gauss-Jordan technique. Geometrically, we move from the initial vertex to the vertex where the edges $x_1 = 0, \ldots, x_{i-1} = 0,\ u_j = 0,\ x_{i+1} = 0, \ldots, x_n = 0$ intersect. This step is repeated a sufficient number of times until $M$ is made as large as it can be.

## B. The Simplex Method

The first step in the simplex algorithm to solve the problem of maximizing $M = \mathbf{cx}$ subject to $A\mathbf{x} \leqslant \mathbf{b}$ and $\mathbf{x} \geqslant 0$ is to replace the system of inequalities by equations. This can be done by the addition of slack variables.

The Fromage Cheese Company problem can be formulated as:   Find non-negative values of $x, y, u, v, w$ such that:

$$
\begin{aligned}
30x + 12y + \ \ u &= 6000, \\
10x + \ 8y + \ \ v &= 2600, \\
4x + \ 8y + \ w &= 2000, \\
-4.5x - \ 4y \ + \ M &= 0,
\end{aligned}
\tag{23}
$$

and so that $M$ is as large as possible.

We write the matrix of coefficients of Eqs. (23) in a special form, called the *extended simplex tableau* (Tableau 5.1)

**Tableau 5.1**

| $x$ | $y$ | $u$ | $v$ | $w$ | $M$ | | |
|---|---|---|---|---|---|---|---|
| 30 | 12 | 1 | 0 | 0 | 0 | 6000 | $u$ |
| 10 | 8 | 0 | 1 | 0 | 0 | 2600 | $v$ |
| 4 | 8 | 0 | 0 | 1 | 0 | 2000 | $w$ |
| $-4.5$ | $-4$ | 0 | 0 | 0 | 1 | 0 | $M$ |

$\uparrow$

The first three rows of the tableau indicate that we have a basic feasible solution with basic variables $u, v$, and $w$. (The basic variables at each stage appear again to the right of the last column). The value of these basic variables when the nonbasic ones ($x$ and $y$ at this stage) are zero are indicated in the final column. The entry in the lower right-hand corner of the tableau gives the current value of $M$.

The bottom row of the tableau represents the equation $-4.5x - 4y + M = 0$. This equation remains valid for all $x$ and $y$, by the definition of $M$.

The fact that $x$ and $y$ appear with negative coefficients in this row means that if either $x$ or $y$ is increased, the value of $M$ must also be increased for the equation to hold.

We want to increase $M$, but at the same time retain a basic feasible solution. To do this, we need to select one nonbasic variable and make it basic while we pick a basic variable and change it to a nonbasic one. This process is described more succinctly by saying we pick one variable to *enter the basis* and one to *leave the basis*.

Any variable which appears with a negative coefficient in the bottom row of the tableau can be selected to enter the basis. In practice, the variable whose coefficient has the largest absolute value is chosen, because this gives the largest immediate increase in $M$. There is no guarantee, however, that this practice will lead to the optimal solution in the smallest number of steps.

Suppose we decide to pick the variable in the $j$th column to enter the basis. This is often indicated by drawing a short arrow under the coefficient of this variable in the bottom row; we have done this in Tableau 5.1.

When a variable enters the basis, its value is going to increase. This is going to affect the other variables in each of the other equations represented in the tableau. The other nonbasic variables are going to remain equal to 0. Thus the variables which are now basic are going to change to preserve the equations. But each basic variable occurs with nonzero coefficient in exactly one row of the tableau, so it is affected by only one equation.

We really don't care how a currently basic variable will change as long as it remains nonnegative. We lose feasibility, however, if it should become negative. Now a basic variable starts out as positive, so we have only to worry about its decreasing. It will decrease only if the coefficient of the $j$th variable (the one that is entering the basis) in the row containing the basic variable is *positive*. If that coefficient is zero or negative, the basic variable will not decrease. To illustrate this point, suppose we have the equation

$$2x + 0y - 5z + u = 375$$

and $u$ is a basic variable. If the variable $z$ or the variable $y$ is picked to enter the basis, there is no problem: increasing $z$ or $y$ by any positive amount can only cause an increase of $u$. But if $x$ is chosen to enter the basis, then $x$ can only be increased to $\frac{375}{2}$ before $u$ becomes negative.

This sets the stage for explaining how to select a variable to leave the basis if the $j$th variable is going to enter the basis. We compute the ratio of the entries in the last column of the tableau to the *positive* entries of the $j$th column. The row which gives the smallest ratio contains the variable which will leave the basis.

Let's illustrate this for Tableau 5.1. The negative coefficient with greatest absolute value in the bottom row is $-4.5$. Thus we will let $x$ enter the basis. The other entries in the $x$-column are all positive so compute all the ratios of the entries in the last column to the corresponding elements in the first column.

This is indicated in Tableau 5.2:

**Tableau 5.2**

|  | $x$ | $y$ | $u$ | $v$ | $w$ | $M$ |  |  |
|---|---|---|---|---|---|---|---|---|
| $\dfrac{6000}{30} = 200$ | ㉚ | 12 | 1 | 0 | 0 | 0 | 6000 | $u$ |
| $\dfrac{2600}{10} = 260$ | 10 | 8 | 0 | 1 | 0 | 0 | 2600 | $v$ |
| $\dfrac{2000}{4} = 500$ | 4 | 8 | 0 | 0 | 1 | 0 | 2000 | $w$ |
| | $-4.5$ | $-4$ | 0 | 0 | 0 | 1 | 0 | $M$ |

↑

The smallest ratio is 200. It occurs in the first row and the basic variable of that row is $u$. Thus, $u$ will leave the basis when $x$ enters. The *pivot entry* is the coefficient of the variable which is entering the basis which appears in the row of the lowest ratio.

The critical next step in the simplex algorithm is to use the Gauss-Jordan procedure to make the pivot element 1 and to make all the other entries in that column zero, including the entry in the bottom row of the tableau. This is necessary if the variable of that column is to satisfy the definition of being basic. The Gauss-Jordan procedure is used because it guarantees that the system of equations represented by the new tableau will be equivalent to the original system of equations.

When we apply the Gauss-Jordan procedure to Tableau 5.2, we obtain Tableau 5.3.

**Tableau 5.3**

| $x$ | $y$ | $u$ | $v$ | $w$ | $M$ |  |  |
|---|---|---|---|---|---|---|---|
| 1 | $\frac{2}{5}$ | $\frac{1}{30}$ | 0 | 0 | 0 | 200 | $x$ |
| 0 | 4 | $-\frac{1}{3}$ | 1 | 0 | 0 | 600 | $v$ |
| 0 | $\frac{32}{5}$ | $-\frac{2}{15}$ | 0 | 1 | 0 | 1200 | $w$ |
| 0 | $-\frac{11}{5}$ | $\frac{3}{20}$ | 0 | 0 | 1 | 900 | $M$ |

↑

As before, we can read off a basic feasible solution from the tableau. The basic variables are $x, v, w$. Their values appear in the final column. The non-basic variables are $y$ and $u$ and their value is 0. The current value of $M$ is 900.

The bottom row of Tableau 5.3 contains a negative number. This tells us that we have not yet reached an optimal solution. There is only one negative entry and that appears in the $y$-column. This means that in the next step, the variable $y$ is going to enter the basis. To find the variable that will leave the basis, compute the ratios of the last column to the positive entries in the $y$-column; see Tableau 5.4.

**Tableau 5.4**

|  | $x$ | $y$ | $u$ | $v$ | $w$ | $M$ |  |  |
|---|---|---|---|---|---|---|---|---|
| $\dfrac{200}{2/5}=500$ | 1 | $\frac{2}{5}$ | $\frac{1}{30}$ | 0 | 0 | 0 | 200 | $x$ |
| $\dfrac{600}{4}=150$ | 0 | ④ | $-\frac{1}{3}$ | 1 | 0 | 0 | 600 | $v$ |
| $\dfrac{1200}{32/5}=187\frac{1}{2}$ | 0 | $\frac{32}{5}$ | $-\frac{2}{15}$ | 0 | 1 | 0 | 1200 | $w$ |
|  | 0 | $-\frac{11}{5}$ | $\frac{3}{20}$ | 0 | 0 | 1 | 900 | $M$ |

$\uparrow$

The smallest ratio (150) occurs in the second row. The basic variable of that row is $v$. Hence $v$ will leave the basis when $y$ enters. The pivot entry is 4. The Gauss-Jordan procedure is used as before. We obtain a new tableau:

**Tableau 5.5**

|  | $x$ | $y$ | $u$ | $v$ | $w$ | $M$ |  |  |
|---|---|---|---|---|---|---|---|---|
| $\dfrac{140}{1/15}=2100$ | 1 | 0 | $\frac{1}{15}$ | $-\frac{1}{10}$ | 0 | 0 | 140 | $x$ |
|  | 0 | 1 | $-\frac{1}{12}$ | $\frac{1}{4}$ | 0 | 0 | 150 | $y$ |
| $\dfrac{240}{2/5}=600$ | 0 | 0 | ②⁄₅ | $-\frac{8}{5}$ | 1 | 0 | 240 | $w$ |
|  | 0 | 0 | $-\frac{1}{30}$ | $\frac{11}{20}$ | 0 | 1 | 1230 | $M$ |

$\uparrow$

In this feasible solution, $x = 140$, $y = 150$, $w = 240$, $u = v = 0$ and $M = 1230$. This is still not the best we can do because there remains a negative entry in the bottom row. The variable $u$ should be brought back into the basis. To find the variable which should leave, we need to compare the two ratios

$140/(\frac{1}{15}) = 2100$ and $240/(\frac{2}{5}) = 600$. We do not compute a ratio for the second row because the coefficient of $u$ in this row is negative. Since $600 < 2100$, the basic variable of the third row—which is $w$—will leave the basis. The result of applying the Gauss-Jordan procedure with pivot entry $\frac{2}{5}$ is:

**Tableau 5.6**

| $x$ | $y$ | $u$ | $v$ | $w$ | $M$ | | |
|---|---|---|---|---|---|---|---|
| 1 | 0 | 0 | $\frac{1}{6}$ | $-\frac{1}{6}$ | 0 | 100 | $x$ |
| 0 | 1 | 0 | $-\frac{1}{12}$ | $\frac{5}{24}$ | 0 | 200 | $y$ |
| 0 | 0 | 1 | $-4$ | $\frac{5}{2}$ | 0 | 600 | $u$ |
| 0 | 0 | 0 | $\frac{5}{12}$ | $\frac{1}{12}$ | 1 | 1250 | $M$ |

The new basic feasible solution is

$$x = 100, \quad y = 200, \quad u = 600, \quad v = w = 0, \quad \text{and} \quad M = 1250.$$

Since none of the entries of the bottom row of Tableau 5.6 is negative, it is not possible to increase $M$ any more. We have arrived at a basic, feasible, optimal solution of the problem. We see again that the best mixture is 100 packages of the Fancy assortment and 200 packages of the Deluxe. We also read off from this solution that $v = z = 0$ means that all of the Swiss and Brie cheeses will be used up, but since $u = 600$, there will be 600 ounces of Cheddar remaining.

If you re-examine Fig. 5.4, you will see that the effect of the simplex method applied to the cheese example is to start at the vertex $(0,0)$ of the feasibility set and then to move in a counterclockwise manner around the boundary until the vertex $(100, 200)$ is reached.

Note how the iterative step of the simplex method replaces one equality constraint by an inequality constraint and one inequality by an equality. This corresponds geometrically to a move from one vertex of the feasibility set to an adjacent vertex.

Dantzig's simplex method provides a systematic way of moving from one basic feasible solution to another basic feasible solution which increases the value of $M$. The simplex method is an iterative algorithm; that is, it calls for the repetition of the same sequence of basic steps. We have seen that the iteration stops when all entries in the bottom row of the extended tableau are positive. When this happens, we have found an optimal, feasible solution. The iteration may stop for another reason, however. Suppose some entry in the bottom row of the tableau is negative, so that at the next step the associated variable is to become basic. Now suppose that *every* entry in that column is negative or zero. This means that there is no limit on how much we may increase that variable. No matter how large we make it, the other variables will remain nonnegative and we will retain feasibility. On the other hand, the larger we can make that variable, the larger we can make $M$. Thus, there is no limit to the size of $M$. In this case, the linear programming problem has *no* optimal solution. The simplex method not only delivers the solution when the problem has one, it also tells you when no solution exists.

## C. The Use of Artificial Variables

We have seen that it may be useful to introduce slack variables into linear programming problems. They help convert inequalities into equations and often provide an initial basic solution. In this section I will show that it is sometimes useful to introduce yet another set of new variables.

Let's start by considering the breakfast problem of Section I.D. We may write this problem as:

Find nonnegative numbers $x$ and $y$ such that

$$\begin{aligned} x + 3y &\geqslant 3, \\ 38x + 24y &\geqslant 50, \end{aligned}$$

and for which $M = -4x - 6.5y$ is maximized.

To convert the inequalities to equations, we add slack variables $u$ and $v$ so the problem becomes

Find nonnegative numbers $x, y, u$, and $v$ so that

$$\begin{aligned} x + 3y - u \qquad\qquad &= 3, \\ 38x + 24y \qquad - v \qquad &= 50, \\ 4x + 6.5y \qquad\quad + M &= 0, \end{aligned} \tag{24}$$

and $M$ is as large as possible.

The variables $u$ and $v$ measure the amount of iron and protein, respectively, that is in excess of the daily requirement. Rather than "slack" variables, they might more appropriately be called *surplus* variables in this problem.

Because the coefficients of $u$ and $v$ are $-1$ instead of $+1$ in Eq. (24), the system of equations does not give a basic solution. This is not a happy state of affairs, because the simplex method must start off with a basic feasible solution. If we multiply the first two equations of Eq. (24) by $-1$ we do obtain an equivalent system which is basic:

$$\begin{aligned} -x - 3y + u \qquad\qquad &= -3, \\ -38x - 24y \qquad + v \qquad &= -50, \\ 4x + 6.5y \qquad\quad + M &= 0. \end{aligned} \tag{25}$$

The basic solution here is $x = y = 0$, $u = -3$, $v = -50$. Unfortunately, this solution is not *feasible*, because $u$ and $v$ are negative. Again, we cannot make use of the simplex method.

One way out of these difficulties lies in the introduction of *artificial variables* for each constraint equation having no basic variable. These are "artificial" variables because they do not represent any real quantity in the process being modeled, in contrast to the slack variables which do correspond to real features.

The new artificial problem has the form:  Find nonnegative numbers $x, y, u, v, a, b$ such that

$$
\begin{aligned}
x + \quad 3y - u \quad + \; a \qquad\qquad &= \; 3 \\
38x + 24y \quad\; - v \quad\;\; + \; b \qquad &= \; 50 \\
4x + 6.5y \qquad\qquad + \; pa + pb + M' &= \; 0
\end{aligned}
\tag{26}
$$

for $M'$ as large as possible.

In this statement, $p$ is an unspecified but very large positive number and $M' = M - pa - pb$. It is important to note two things at this point:

1. If a basic feasible solution exists for the original problem, then it will constitute a basic feasible solution for the artificial problem (with $a = b = 0$ being nonbasic variables);

2. The simplex method can be applied to the artificial problem.

The result of applying the simplex method will be an optimal, basic feasible solution of the artificial problem. I claim that in this basic feasible solution, the variables $a$ and $b$ will both be 0. For, if either one were positive, then the quantity $M' = M - pa - pb$ could be increased even more by decreasing $a$ or $b$. This would contradict the fact that we are at an *optimal* solution of the artificial problem. This verifies the claim. Since $a = b = 0$, the optimal value for $M'$ is the optimal value for $M$ and we have an optimal, basic feasible solution for the original problem.

The extended tableau for the artificial problem Eq. (26) has the form

**Tableau 5.7**

| $x$ | $y$ | $u$ | $v$ | $a$ | $b$ | $M'$ | |
|---|---|---|---|---|---|---|---|
| 1 | 3 | $-1$ | 0 | 1 | 0 | 0 | 3 |
| 38 | 24 | 0 | $-1$ | 0 | 1 | 0 | 50 |
| 4 | 6.5 | 0 | 0 | 0 | 0 | 1 | 0 |
| | | | | $p$ | $p$ | | |

In this tableau, the variables $a$ and $b$ are not quite basic because of the presence of the $p$'s in the bottom row. We can make them basic by replacing the last row by the last row minus $p$ times the sum of row 1 and row 2. This yields a tableau (Tableau 5.8) in which $a$ and $b$ are basic.

**Tableau 5.8**

| $x$ | $y$ | $u$ | $v$ | $a$ | $b$ | $M'$ | | |
|---|---|---|---|---|---|---|---|---|
| 1 | 3 | $-1$ | 0 | 1 | 0 | 0 | 3 | $a$ |
| ㊳ | 24 | 0 | $-1$ | 0 | 1 | 0 | 50 | $b$ |
| 4 | 6.5 | 0 | 0 | 0 | 0 | 1 | 0 | $M$ |
| $-39p$ | $-27p$ | $p$ | $p$ | 0 | 0 | 0 | $-53p$ | |

↑

We now apply the simplex algorithm as described in Section III.B. Since $p$ is a large positive number, the negative entry with the largest absolute value in the bottom row is $4 - 39p$. Thus in the first step of the simplex method, the variable $x$ will enter the basis. The standard computation of ratios gives $\frac{3}{1} = 3$ in the first row and $\frac{50}{38} = 1\frac{6}{19}$ in the second row. Thus $b$ will leave the basis. The pivot element is 38 and the Gauss-Jordan procedure produces a new tableau (Tableau 5.9).

**Tableau 5.9**

| $x$ | $y$ | $u$ | $v$ | $a$ | $b$ | $M'$ | | |
|---|---|---|---|---|---|---|---|---|
| 0 | $\left(\frac{45}{19}\right)$ | $-1$ | $\frac{1}{38}$ | 1 | $-\frac{1}{38}$ | 0 | $\frac{32}{19}$ | $a$ |
| 1 | $\frac{12}{19}$ | 0 | $-\frac{1}{38}$ | 0 | $\frac{1}{38}$ | 0 | $\frac{25}{19}$ | $x$ |
| 0 | $\frac{151}{38}$ | 0 | $\frac{2}{19}$ | 0 | $-\frac{2}{19}$ | 1 | $-\frac{100}{19}$ | $M'$ |
| 0 | $-\dfrac{45p}{19}$ | $p$ | $-\dfrac{p}{38}$ | 0 | $\dfrac{39p}{38}$ | 0 | $-\dfrac{32p}{19}$ | |

↑

Since there are negative numbers in the bottom row of this tableau, the simplex method continues through another iteration. This time the variable $y$ will enter the basis and $a$ will leave. The pivot element is $\frac{45}{19}$. The Gauss-Jordan procedure yields Tableau 5.10.

**Tableau 5.10**

| $x$ | $y$ | $u$ | $v$ | $a$ | $b$ | $M'$ | | |
|---|---|---|---|---|---|---|---|---|
| 0 | 1 | $-\frac{19}{45}$ | $\frac{1}{90}$ | $\frac{19}{45}$ | $-\frac{1}{90}$ | 0 | $\frac{32}{45}$ | $y$ |
| 1 | 0 | $\frac{4}{15}$ | $-\frac{1}{30}$ | $-\frac{4}{15}$ | $\frac{1}{30}$ | 0 | $\frac{13}{15}$ | $x$ |
| 0 | 0 | $\frac{151}{90}$ | $\frac{209}{3420}$ | $-\frac{151}{90}$ | $-\frac{209}{3420}$ | 1 | $-\frac{364}{45}$ | $M'$ |
| 0 | 0 | 0 | 0 | $p$ | $p$ | 0 | | |

Now none of the entries in the bottom row of the tableau are negative (remember that $p$ is a very large positive number). Hence we have arrived at an optimal, feasible solution for the breakfast problem. We can read off the solution from Tableau 5.10:

$$x = \frac{13}{15}, \qquad y = \frac{32}{45}, \qquad M = -m = -\frac{364}{45}.$$

Thus Janet should mix $\frac{13}{15}$ ounces of Brand X cereal with $\frac{32}{45}$ ounces of Yukkies. This mixture will provide $(\frac{13}{15}) + 3(\frac{32}{45}) = 3$ mg of iron and $3.8(\frac{13}{15}) + 2.4(\frac{32}{45}) = 5$ g of protein so that both minimal nutritional requirements are exactly met. The cost of this mixture is $\frac{364}{45}$ or about 8.1 cents.

### D.  The Condensed Tableau

In this section we will present a slightly streamlined representation of the simplex method. Instead of working with the extended tableau, we perform the necessary calculations on a smaller tableau. This *condensed* tableau is especially useful for small scale LP problems that are going to be solved by paper-and-pencil calculations. It was introduced by E. M. L. Beale and Steven Vajda in the 1950's and extensively used by Albert W. Tucker. It is sometimes referred to as the *Tucker Tableau*.

We begin by examining more closely the effect on the extended tableau of a single iteration of the simplex method. Suppose we are about to perform the step which puts the variable $y$ into the basis and removes the variable $w$. We represent the tableau before iteration schematically:

| | $y$ | | Any other column | | $w$ | |
|---|---|---|---|---|---|---|
| Pivot row $\cdots$ | $p$ | $\cdots$ | $q$ | $\cdots$ | 1 | $\cdots$ |
| | $\vdots$ | | $\vdots$ | | $\vdots$ | |
| Any other row $\cdots$ | $r$ | $\cdots$ | $s$ | $\cdots$ | 0 | $\cdots$ |
| | $\vdots$ | | $\vdots$ | | $\vdots$ | |

In performing the iteration, the first step is to divide each element of the pivot row by the pivot element, which in this case is denoted by $p$. The effect of this step on the tableau is to change its form to:

| | $y$ | | Any other column | | $w$ | |
|---|---|---|---|---|---|---|
| | $\vdots$ | | $\vdots$ | | $\vdots$ | |
| Pivot row $\cdots$ | 1 | $\cdots$ | $q/p$ | $\cdots$ | $1/p$ | $\cdots$ |
| | $\vdots$ | | $\vdots$ | | $\vdots$ | |
| Any other row $\cdots$ | $r$ | $\cdots$ | $s$ | $\cdots$ | 0 | $\cdots$ |
| | $\vdots$ | | $\vdots$ | | $\vdots$ | |

Next, the new pivot row is used to make all other entries in the $y$-column (or pivot column) equal to 0. If the entry in some row in the pivot column is $r$, then that row is replaced by that row minus $r$ times the pivot row. Performing this step produces the after-iteration tableau:

|  | $y$ | | Any other column | | $w$ | |
|---|---|---|---|---|---|---|
|  | $\vdots$ | | $\vdots$ | | $\vdots$ | |
| Pivot row $\cdots$ | 1 | $\cdots$ | $q/p$ | $\cdots$ | $1/p$ | $\cdots$ |
|  | $\vdots$ | | $\vdots$ | | $\vdots$ | |
| Any other row $\cdots$ | 0 | $\cdots$ | $s - \dfrac{rq}{p}$ | $\cdots$ | $-r/p$ | $\cdots$ |
|  | $\vdots$ | | $\vdots$ | | $\vdots$ | |

The idea behind the condensed tableau presentation is to eliminate from the extended tableau as many columns as there are basic variables. If a variable $u$ is basic at some step, then the column corresponding to it is omitted. Thus the $w$ column would not appear in the before-iteration tableau of our example.

What happens after the iteration? Since $w$ is no longer basic, it will be represented by a column. Since $y$ has become basic, no $y$ column will appear. A simple way to take care of this is to move the $w$ column into the slot previously occupied by the $y$ column.

We will illustrate the condensed tableau in a particular example. Consider the Fromage Cheese Company example once again. Before the first interation in which $x$ enters and $u$ leaves the basis, the tableaux are:

**Tableaux 5.11**   Before iteration

| $x$ | $y$ | $u$ | $v$ | $w$ | $M$ | |
|---|---|---|---|---|---|---|
| 30 | 12 | 1 | 0 | 0 | 0 | 6000 |
| 10 | 8 | 0 | 1 | 0 | 0 | 2600 |
| 4 | 8 | 0 | 0 | 1 | 0 | 2000 |
| $-4.5$ | $-4$ | 0 | 0 | 0 | 1 | 0 |

| $x$ | $y$ | | |
|---|---|---|---|
| 30 | 12 | 6000 | $u$ |
| 10 | 8 | 2600 | $v$ |
| 4 | 8 | 2000 | $w$ |
| $-4.5$ | $-4$ | 0 | $M$ |

(a)  Extended tableau                 (b)  Condensed tableau

After the first iteration, they look like:

**Tableaux 5.12**   After iteration

| $x$ | $y$ | $u$ | $v$ | $w$ | $M$ | |
|---|---|---|---|---|---|---|
| 1 | $\frac{2}{5}$ | $\frac{1}{30}$ | 0 | 0 | 0 | 200 |
| 0 | 4 | $-\frac{1}{3}$ | 1 | 0 | 0 | 600 |
| 0 | $\frac{32}{5}$ | $-\frac{2}{15}$ | 0 | 1 | 0 | 1200 |
| 0 | $-\frac{11}{5}$ | $\frac{3}{20}$ | 0 | 0 | 1 | 900 |

| $u$ | $y$ | | |
|---|---|---|---|
| $\frac{1}{30}$ | $\frac{2}{5}$ | 200 | $x$ |
| $-\frac{1}{3}$ | 4 | 600 | $v$ |
| $-\frac{2}{15}$ | $\frac{32}{5}$ | 1200 | $w$ |
| $\frac{3}{20}$ | $-\frac{11}{5}$ | 900 | $M$ |

(a)  Extended tableau                 (b)  Condensed tableau

The condensed tableau has the advantage of keeping track of the essential information, while discarding the inessential. In this example, the extended tableau requires the linear programmer, or his computer, to perform computations and keep track of 28 numbers at each step. For the condensed tableau, this is reduced to 12 numbers.

Noting that the entry $s - (rq)/p$ can be written as $s + q(-r/p)$, we can write the transformation rules for changing a pre-iteration condensed tableau to its post-iteration format:

1. Pivot Entries

    a) In the pivot row, the pivot element is replaced by its reciprocal; each remaining entry is the old entry divided by the pivot element.

    b) In the pivot column, each old entry (except the pivot) is divided by the negative of the pivot to obtain the new entry.

2. Entries not changed in step 1.

    a) Add to each entry $s$: the product of the old entry in the same column to the right or left of the pivot and the new entry in the same row above or below the pivot. These changes are exhibited in the following scheme:

| $p$ | $\cdots$ | $q$ |
|---|---|---|
| $\vdots$ | | $\vdots$ |
| $r$ | $\cdots$ | $s$ |

| $1/p$ | $\cdots$ | $q/p$ |
|---|---|---|
| $\vdots$ | | $\vdots$ |
| $-r/p$ | $\cdots$ | $s + q(-r/p)$ |

Before iteration    After iteration

To make sure these rules are well understood, let us carry out the operations on the condensed Tableau 5.11(b):

1. Pivot Entry. The pivot entry is 30, the pivot row is the first row and the pivot column is the first column.

    a) $(p \to 1/p)$:   $30 \to \frac{1}{30}$

       $(q \to q/p)$:   $12 \to \frac{12}{30} = \frac{2}{5}$

                 $6000 \to \frac{6000}{30} = 200$

    b) $(r \to -r/p)$:   $10 \to -\frac{10}{30} = -\frac{1}{3}$

                  $4 \to -\frac{4}{30} = -\frac{2}{15}$

              $-4.5 \to 4.5/30 = \frac{3}{20}$

At this point, the new condensed tableau has the form

| $\frac{1}{30}$ | $\frac{2}{5}$ | 200 |
|---|---|---|
| $-\frac{1}{3}$ | ———— | ———— |
| $-\frac{2}{15}$ | ———— | ———— |
| $\frac{3}{20}$ | ———— | ———— |

2. The remaining entries: $s \rightarrow s + q(-r/p)$

| $s$ | $s + (q(-r/p))$ | | |
|---|---|---|---|
| 8 (row 2, column 2) | $8 + [12 \quad (-\frac{1}{3})]$ | $=$ | 4 |
| 2600 | $2600 + [6000 \, (-\frac{1}{3})]$ | $=$ | 600 |
| 8 (row 3, column 2) | $8 + [12 \quad (-\frac{2}{15})]$ | $=$ | $\frac{32}{5}$ |
| 2000 | $2000 + [6000 \, (-\frac{2}{15})]$ | $=$ | 1200 |
| $-4$ | $-4 + [12 \quad (\frac{3}{20})]$ | $=$ | $-\frac{11}{5}$ |
| 0 | $0 + [6000 \, (\frac{3}{20})]$ | $=$ | 900 |

Check that these computations produce Tableau 5.12(b).

Once mastered, these transformations greatly reduce the time and space necessary to use the simplex method to solve LP problems. In addition to its computational advantages, the condensed tableau also sheds light on another important topic in linear programming, *duality*. This is the subject of the next section.

## E. Duality

In our continuing saga of Henry Brewster and his cheese company, I must tell you now that Henry ages all the cheeses himself from milk produced by cows on his uncle's farm. Instead of packaging his cheeses into gift assortments, Henry has the option of selling his stock to a wholesale distributor.

Suppose the distributor is willing to pay $u, v$, and $w$ dollars per ounce for Cheddar, Swiss, and Brie cheeses, respectively. Then the distributor would have to offer a total of

$$m = 6000u + 2600v + 2000w$$

dollars to buy Brewster's entire stock. The distributor would like to keep the number $m$ as small as possible.

Now Henry is not going to sell his stock if the prices offered by the distributor are too low. He quickly calculates that the distributor would pay him

$$30u + 10v + 4w$$

dollars for exactly the combination of cheeses that go into one package of the Fancy Assortment. Since Henry can receive $4.50 for such a package if he sells it himself, he will not give up the ingredients for less than $4.50. Thus the distributor, in his quest to minimize $m$, is faced with the constraint

$$30u + 10v + 4w \geqslant 4.5.$$

Similarly, the distributor must offer at least $4 for the packet of ingredients that go into one box of the Deluxe Assortment; that is,

$$12u + 8v + 8w \geqslant 4.$$

The Distributor's Problem can then be stated as:    Find nonnegative numbers $u, v,$ and $w$ such that

$$m = 6000u + 2600v + 2000w \text{ is minimized}$$

subject to the constraints:

$$30u + \quad 10v + \quad 4w \geqslant 4.5,$$
$$12u + \quad 8v + \quad 8w \geqslant 4.$$

Henry's problem and the distributor's problem are closely related.  One is a maximization problem and the other is a minimization one.  The coefficients of the function to be optimized in one problem are the constant terms in the constraints of the other problem.  In fact, every coefficient appearing in Henry's problem also appears in the distributor's problem and vice-versa (see Section I.C.).  These two problems are examples of what are called *dual* problems. Note that Henry's problem has two variables and three constraints, while the distributor's problem features three variables and two constraints.

We will now give the general definition of a *primal* LP problem and its *dual*.

**DEFINITION**   **Given a linear programming problem in the form: Find an $n \times 1$ vector $\mathbf{x} \geqslant 0$ such that**

$$M = \mathbf{cx} \text{ is maximized} \tag{P}$$

**subject to the constraints:**

$$A\mathbf{x} \leqslant \mathbf{b},$$

**where $A$ is an $m \times n$ matrix, b is an $m \times 1$ vector and c is a $1 \times n$ vector, the problem:**
   **Find a $1 \times m$ vector $\mathbf{y} \geqslant 0$ such that**

$$m = \mathbf{yb} \text{ is minimized} \tag{D}$$

**subject to the constraints**

$$\mathbf{y}A \geqslant \mathbf{c}$$

**is called the *dual* of (P) and (P) is called the *primal* problem.**

In expanded form, the primal problem has the familiar form:

Maximize $M = c_1 x_1 + \quad c_2 x_2 + \cdots + \quad c_n x_n$

subject to:

$$a_{11}x_1 + a_{12}x_2 + \cdots + a_{1n}x_n \leqslant b_1$$
$$a_{21}x_1 + a_{22}x_2 + \cdots + a_{2n}x_n \leqslant b_2$$
$$\cdots$$
$$a_{m1}x_1 + a_{m2}x_2 + \cdots + a_{mn}x_n \leqslant b_m$$

while the dual problem has the form:

Minimize $m = b_1 y_1 + b_2 y_2 + \cdots + b_m y_m$

subject to:

$$a_{11} y_1 + a_{21} y_2 + \cdots + a_{m1} y_m \geqslant c_1$$
$$a_{12} y_1 + a_{22} y_2 + \cdots + a_{m2} y_m \geqslant c_2$$
$$\cdots$$
$$a_{1n} y_1 + a_{2n} y_2 + \cdots + a_{mn} y_m \geqslant c_n.$$

The expanded form of the primal and dual problems makes clear some of the relations between them:

a) The coefficients of the function to be maximized in the primal problem are the constants in the constraints of the dual problem;

b) The coefficients of the function to be minimized in the dual problem are the constants in the constraints of the primal problem;

c) A variable of the dual problem is assigned to each constraint of the primal problem;

d) A variable of the primal problem is assigned to each constraint of the dual problem.

The dual problem is not in the standard form of a Linear Programming problem as given in Section I. It is, however, equivalent to the problem:

Maximize $-m = -b_1 y_1 - b_2 y_2 - \cdots - b_m y_m$

subject to:

$$-a_{11} y_1 - a_{21} y_2 - \cdots - a_{m1} y_m \leqslant -c_1$$
$$\cdots$$
$$-a_{1n} y_1 - a_{2n} y_2 - \cdots - a_{mn} y_m \leqslant -c_n$$

which is in the standard form.

A more compact form of the dual problem can be given by introducing the idea of the *transpose* of a matrix. If $A$ is any $m \times n$ matrix, then the transpose of $A$, written $A^T$, is the $n \times m$ matrix whose $ij$th entry is the $ji$th entry of $A$; that is, $(A^T)_{ij} = A_{ji}$.

As an example, if

$$A = \begin{bmatrix} 30 & 12 \\ 10 & 8 \\ 4 & 8 \end{bmatrix}, \text{ then } A^T = \begin{bmatrix} 30 & 10 & 4 \\ 12 & 8 & 8 \end{bmatrix},$$

while the transpose of $\mathbf{b} = [b_1 \; b_2 \; b_3]$ is

$$(\mathbf{b})^T = \begin{bmatrix} b_1 \\ b_2 \\ b_3 \end{bmatrix}.$$

There are several important properties of the transpose which are easily proved. They are collected in the following theorem.

■ **THEOREM 6**    Let $A$ be any $m \times n$ matrix. Then:

a) $(-A)^T = -(A^T)$

b) $(A^T)^T = A$

c) $(AB)^T = B^T A^T$.

d) If $A$ and $B$ are of the same size, then $A \leqslant B$ if and only if $A^T \leqslant B^T$.

The proof of this theorem is left as an exercise.

Using the transpose, we may write the dual of Eq. (P) in the form:    Find $\mathbf{y} \geqslant 0$ such that

$$M = (-\mathbf{b})^T(\mathbf{y})^T \text{ is maximized} \tag{D'}$$

subject to

$$-A^T(\mathbf{y})^T \leqslant (-\mathbf{c})^T.$$

This formulation is helpful in establishing the important result of the next theorem.

■ **THEOREM 7**    The dual of the dual is the primal.

**Proof**    The primal problem is given by Eq. (P). Let the dual problem be described by Eq. (D'). Then by our first definition, the dual of Eq. (D') is:

Find a $1 \times n$ vector $\mathbf{z} \geqslant 0$ such that

$$m = \mathbf{z}(-\mathbf{c})^T \text{ is minimized}$$

subject to:

$$\mathbf{z}(-A^T) \geqslant (-\mathbf{b})^T.$$

This is equivalent to the problem:

Find $\mathbf{z} \geqslant 0$ such that

$$M = -m = \mathbf{z}(\mathbf{c})^T \text{ is maximized} \tag{27}$$

subject to

$$\mathbf{z}A^T \leqslant (\mathbf{b})^T.$$

Now let $\mathbf{x} = (\mathbf{z})^T$ so that $(\mathbf{x})^T = ((\mathbf{z})^T)^T = \mathbf{z}$. This gives $\mathbf{z}(\mathbf{c})^T = (\mathbf{x})^T(\mathbf{c})^T = (\mathbf{cx})^T = (\mathbf{cx})$ since $\mathbf{cx}$ is a real number. We also have $\mathbf{z}A^T = (\mathbf{x})^T(A^T) = (A\mathbf{x})^T$ so that the constraints $\mathbf{z}A^T \leqslant (\mathbf{b})^T$ can be written as $(A\mathbf{x})^T \leqslant (\mathbf{b})^T$. By Parts (b) and (d) of Theorem 6, this inequality is the same as $A\mathbf{x} \leqslant \mathbf{b}$. Substituting in (27), we find that the dual of the dual is:

Find $\mathbf{x} \geqslant 0$ such that

$$M = \mathbf{cx} \text{ is maximized}$$

subject to:

$$A\mathbf{x} \leqslant \mathbf{b},$$

which is the primal problem. □

Eventually, we wish to establish the Fundamental Duality Theorem which asserts, in part, that if the primal and dual problems both have feasible solutions, then they both have optimal solutions with $M = m$. As a step in that direction, we first prove the following Theorem.

■ **THEOREM 8**    Let $\mathbf{x}$ be a feasible solution to the primal problem and $\mathbf{y}$ a feasible solution to the dual. Then $\mathbf{cx} \leqslant \mathbf{yb}$.

**Proof**  Since $\mathbf{x}$ is feasible for the primal problem, we must have $A\mathbf{x} \leqslant \mathbf{b}$. We know that $\mathbf{y} \geqslant 0$, so that $\mathbf{y}(A\mathbf{x}) \leqslant \mathbf{yb}$. On the other hand, $\mathbf{y}$ is feasible for the dual problem so that $\mathbf{y}A \geqslant \mathbf{c}$, and multiplication of each side by the non-negative vector $\mathbf{x}$ gives $(\mathbf{y}A)\mathbf{x} \geqslant \mathbf{cx}$. We combine the inequalities with the associative rule for matrix multiplication to obtain:

$$\mathbf{cx} \leqslant (\mathbf{y}A)\mathbf{x} = \mathbf{y}(A\mathbf{x}) \leqslant \mathbf{yb}$$

which is the desired result.  □

**Corollary 1**   If the primal and dual problems both have feasible solutions, then both have optimal feasible solutions.

**Proof**  Let $\mathbf{y}$ be any feasible solution to the dual problem. The primal problem fails to have an optimal solution exactly when the function $M = \mathbf{cx}$ is unbounded. But for any feasible solution $\mathbf{x}$ of the primal problem, Theorem 8 asserts that $M$ is no larger than the fixed number $\mathbf{yb}$. Thus $M$ is bounded and the primal problem must have an optimal, feasible solution. The proof that the dual problem also has an optimal, feasible solution is similar.  □

**Corollary 2**   Suppose $\mathbf{x}$ is a feasible solution to the primal problem and $\mathbf{y}$ is a feasible solution of the dual problem. If $\mathbf{cx} = \mathbf{yb}$, then $\mathbf{x}$ and $\mathbf{y}$ are optimal solutions of the primal and dual problems, respectively.

**Proof**  Suppose, to the contrary, that $\bar{\mathbf{x}}$ is a feasible solution to the primal problem with $\mathbf{c}\bar{\mathbf{x}} > \mathbf{cx}$. Since $\mathbf{cx} = \mathbf{yb}$, we have $\mathbf{c}\bar{\mathbf{x}} > \mathbf{yb}$, contradicting Theorem 8.  □

Suppose, then, that we have feasible solutions to the primal and dual problems. According to Theorem 8 and its corollaries, both problems have optimal, feasible solutions. Suppose $M^*$ is the largest feasible value for $M$ in the primal problem and $m^*$ is the smallest feasible value for $m$ in the dual problem. From Theorem 8, we have $M^* \leqslant m^*$. In fact, it turns out that $M^* = m^*$. This statement is part of the Fundamental Duality Theorem. We will show how the simplex method can be used to prove this statement.

We may begin by examining the condensed initial tableaux for the primal and dual problems. These will have the form of Tableaux 5.13 and 5.14.

**Tableau 5.13**    Initial condensed tableau
for primal

| $x_1$ | $x_2$ | $\cdots$ | $x_n$ | |
|---|---|---|---|---|
| $a_{11}$ | $a_{12}$ | $\cdots$ | $a_{1n}$ | $b_1$ |
| $a_{21}$ | $a_{22}$ | $\cdots$ | $a_{2n}$ | $b_2$ |
| $\cdots$ | | | | |
| $a_{m1}$ | $a_{m2}$ | $\cdots$ | $a_{mn}$ | $b_m$ |
| $-c_1$ | $-c_2$ | $\cdots$ | $-c_n$ | $0$ |

**Tableau 5.14**    Initial condensed tableau
for dual

| $y_1$ | $y_2$ | $\cdots$ | $y_m$ | |
|---|---|---|---|---|
| $-a_{11}$ | $-a_{21}$ | $\cdots$ | $-a_{m1}$ | $-c_1$ |
| $-a_{12}$ | $-a_{22}$ | $\cdots$ | $-a_{m2}$ | $-c_2$ |
| $\cdots$ | | | | |
| $-a_{1n}$ | $-a_{2n}$ | $\cdots$ | $-a_{mn}$ | $-c_n$ |
| $b_1$ | $h_2$ | $\cdots$ | $b_m$ | $0$ |

The simplex method proceeds by selecting a sequence of pivot elements and using them to perform Gauss-Jordan eliminations. We wish to show that if corresponding pivot entries are chosen in the tableaux for the primal and dual problems at every stage, then the pattern of relations among the coefficients evidenced in Tableaux 5.13 and 5.14 is retained after the Gauss-Jordan process has been completed. To see why this is true, suppose at some stage, the primal and dual tableaux look like Tableaux 5.15 and 5.16.

**Tableau 5.15**    Primal problem
before iteration

| | | | |
|---|---|---|---|
| $\cdots$ ⓟ $\cdots$ | $q$ $\cdots$ | | $x$ |
| $\cdots$ $r$ $\cdots$ | $s$ $\cdots$ | | $x'$ |
| $\cdots$ $y$ $\cdots$ | $y'$ $\cdots$ | | $M$ |

**Tableau 5.16**    Dual problem
before iteration

| | | | |
|---|---|---|---|
| $\cdots$ Ⓝ $\cdots$ | $-r$ $\cdots$ | | $y$ |
| $\cdots$ $-q$ $\cdots$ | $-s$ $\cdots$ | | $y'$ |
| $\cdots$ $x$ $\cdots$ | $x'$ $\cdots$ | | $+m$ |

We now perform the basic iteration step of the simplex method using $p$ for the pivot element in the primal problem and $-p$ in the dual problem. Using the rules of Section III.D, we obtain the post-iteration condensed tableaux: Tableaux 5.17 and 5.18.

**Tableau 5.17**    Primal problem after iteration

| | | | |
|---|---|---|---|
| $\cdots$ $1/p$ $\cdots$ | $q/p$ | $\cdots$ | $x/p$ |
| $\cdots$ $-r/p$ $\cdots$ | $s - (qr/p)$ | $\cdots$ | $x' - (xr/p)$ |
| $\cdots$ $-y/p$ $\cdots$ | $y' - (qy/p)$ | $\cdots$ | $M - (xy/p)$ |

**Tableau 5.18**    Dual problem after iteration

| | | | |
|---|---|---|---|
| $\cdots$ $-1/p$ $\cdots$ | $r/p$ | $\cdots$ | $-y/p$ |
| $\cdots$ $-q/p$ $\cdots$ | $-s + (rq/p)$ | $\cdots$ | $y' - (qy/p)$ |
| $\cdots$ $x/p$ $\cdots$ | $x' + (-xr/p)$ | $\cdots$ | $+ m + (xy/p)$ |

A comparison of the tableaux shows that the duality pattern which existed before iteration continues to hold after iteration. Note also that the sum of the numbers in the lower right-hand corner of the primal and dual tableaux has been retained; it is equal to $M + m$ both before and after the iteration. In particular, if both $M$ and $m$ start at 0, so that $M = -m$, this inequality will be maintained at each and every step.

What happens when we reach the optimal, feasible solution? In the primal tableau, the entries in the last row will be nonnegative. The entries in the last column will also be nonnegative because they represent values of the basic variables. But the entries in the last column $(x/p, \ldots, x' - (xr/p), \ldots)$ of the primal tableau are exactly the entries in the last row of the dual tableau. (See Tableaux 5.17 and 5.18.) Since all these entries are nonnegative, we have reached an optimal solution of the dual problem also. The optimal values of both problems are given by the numbers in the lower right-hand corner of the tableaux. But we have just shown that their absolute values are equal! Thus, the maximum value of $M$ in the primal problem is exactly the same as the minimum value of $m$ in the dual problem. This is the result we promised.

We actually can deliver more than we promised. The solution of the dual problem would appear in the last column of the final tableau for the dual problem. But the entries in this column $(-y/p, \ldots, y' - (qy/p), \ldots)$ also appear in the last row of the final tableau for the primal problem. (See Tableaux 5.17

and 5.18.) Thus, the solution of the dual problem can be read off from the solution tableau of the primal problem. By duality, we can turn things around; that is, the solution of the primal problem can be read off the final tableau for the dual. In summary, the solution to both the primal and dual problems is contained in the final tableau of either problem.

Let us illustrate some of these results with the Fromage Cheese Company example. The variables $x$ and $y$ represented the number of packages of the two assortments to be prepared. The variables $u, v$, and $w$ were slack variables in the original primal problem corresponding to excess amounts of Cheddar, Swiss, and Brie cheeses. In the dual problem, they represented the prices to be offered by the distributor for an ounce of each of these cheeses. The final tableau for the primal problem is shown in Tableau 5.6.

**Tableau 5.6**

| $x$ | $y$ | $u$ | $v$ | $w$ | | |
|---|---|---|---|---|---|---|
| 1 | 0 | 0 | $\frac{1}{6}$ | $-\frac{1}{6}$ | 100 | $x$ |
| 0 | 1 | 0 | $-\frac{1}{12}$ | $\frac{5}{24}$ | 200 | $y$ |
| 0 | 0 | 1 | $-4$ | $\frac{5}{2}$ | 600 | $u$ |
| 0 | 0 | 0 | $\frac{5}{12}$ | $\frac{1}{12}$ | 1250 | $M$ |

We read off the solution of the distributor's problem from the bottom row:

$$u = 0, \qquad v - \frac{5}{12}, \qquad w - \frac{1}{12}, \qquad M - 1250.$$

The distributor's best offer to Brewster is that he will buy all the cheese at $0 per ounce of Cheddar, $\frac{5}{12}$ per ounce of Swiss, and $\frac{1}{12}$ per ounce of Brie. This will cost the distributor $1250, exactly the same amount that Henry would earn if he sold all the cheese in gift packages. The role of $x$ and $y$ in the distributor's problem is to measure slack, the amount that the distributor's offer exceeds the constraints, $30u + 10v + 4w \geqslant 4.5$ and $12u + 8v + 8w \geqslant 4$. Since $x = y = 0$ in the solution of the dual problem, there is no slack. The distributor's offer exactly meets the constraints.

We may summarize what we have proved in this section by stating the central theorem about duality.

■ **THEOREM 9 (FUNDAMENTAL THEOREM OF DUALITY)**    Let Eq. (P) be a primal linear programming problem and Eq. (D) its dual.

a) If both problems have feasible solutions, then both have optimal, feasible solutions and the maximum value of $M$ is the same as the minimum value of $m$.

b) If one of the problems has feasible solutions, but the objective function ($M$ or $m$) is unbounded, then the other problem has no feasible solutions.

c) If one of the problems has a feasible solution, but the other problem does not, then the problem with feasible solutions has no optimal feasible solution.

d) It is possible that neither problem has a feasible solution.

***Proof***  a) We have already indicated how the simplex method may be used to prove this result;

b) The proof is by contradiction and use of Corollary 1 of Theorem 8;

c) The proof is left as an exercise for the reader;

d) Consider the primal problem of maximizing $x_1 + x_2$ subject to the constraints $x_1 - x_2 \leqslant -1$ and $-x_1 + x_2 \leqslant 0$. It is easy to show that the feasibility set of this problem and of its dual are both empty. $\square$

There are many other interesting aspects of duality theory. You may find extended discussions of these in any of the more advanced texts on linear programming listed in the References at the end of this chapter. I do want to indicate here, however, several applications of duality.

In the first place, the natural formulation of a particular question may be a linear programming problem in dual form; for example, the problem of the distributor buying cheese from Henry Brewster. To solve this problem directly, using the simplex method, requires the addition of both slack variables and artificial variables before an initial basic feasible solution can be found. If we switch to the primal problem, less work is required as a basic feasible solution is produced as soon as slack variables are introduced.

As another example, suppose that an optimal feasible solution of a primal LP problem has been found. It is then discovered that an additional constraint should have been used but was omitted from the original formulation of the problem. When this constraint is added, the feasibility set may be significantly affected. The optimal feasible solution of the original problem may not even be feasible for the new problem. If we restrict ourselves to using only primal problems, then we would have to start all over again. The addition of a constraint in the primal problem, however, corresponds to the addition of a new variable in the dual problem. The basic feasible optimal solution of the original problem gives a basic feasible solution to the dual problem even with the new variable added (simply let the new variable be nonbasic) and the simplex method can continue from this step; instead of going back to $M = 0$, we are beginning from a relatively large value of $M$.

As a final example, duality theory has a very close connection to the theory of two-person games. The Fundamental Duality Theorem and the simplex method of linear programming provide a constructive proof of the best known result in two-person zero-sum game theory, the Von Neumann Minimax Theorem.

## F.  Some Wrinkles in the Simplex Method

In the basic iteration step of the simplex method of solving linear programming problems, the first task is to select the pivot element. The pivot column is determined by choosing a column whose entry in the bottom row of the tableau is negative. Any such column will do, although in practice we usually select the column by finding the negative entry in the bottom row with greatest absolute value.

Once the pivot column is chosen, the pivot row is selected by examining the ratios of the entries in the last column of the tableau to the corresponding positive entries in the pivot column. The pivot row is the row for which these ratios is smallest.

We have already discussed what happens if all the entries in the pivot column are nonpositive (Section III.B). In such a case, the function $M$ is unbounded and the LP problem has no optimal, feasible solution.

Suppose that some of the entries in the pivot column are positive, but that there is a "tie" between two or more of the ratios for the minimum value. In this case, we can choose any of the associated rows as the pivot row. After applying the Gauss-Jordan procedure, two (or more) of the variables that were in the basis will have become zero. However, only one of them has left the basis (the one determined by the pivot row); the others remain in the basis. In such a case, it is possible that the iteration does not increase the value of $M$; it may remain unchanged.

There is another situation in which the iteration does not improve the value of $M$. Suppose that a particular entry in the pivot column is positive, but the entry in the last column of the tableau in the associated row is 0. This will happen only if one of the basic variables has value 0 at this stage. Then the minimum ratio will be 0 so that this variable will be picked to leave the basis. The variable that enters the basis will remain equal to 0 and the value of $M$ will not change when the Gauss-Jordan procedure is implemented. Geometrically, we will not have moved to a new vertex by this iteration, but have only changed our minds about which variables to call "basic."

The term *degeneracy* is used to indicate a situation when we have a basic feasible solution in which at least one of the basic variables has value 0. Degeneracy occurs fairly frequently in the solution of linear programming problems, but it commonly causes no difficulty. The simplex algorithm may be continued and after several more steps, the value of $M$ will begin to increase again.

It is theoretically possible, however, that the value of $M$ will never increase, but that we will cycle repeatedly through a set of nonoptimal basic feasible solutions. The simplex method, as we have described it, cannot prevent this from happening. Imagine for a moment a feasibility set in which vertices $v_3, v_7$, and $v_2$ are all adjacent to each other, but the optimal value of $M$ occurs at vertex $v_1$. It is possible that the simplex algorithm will take us from $v_3$ to $v_7$ to $v_2$

and then back to $v_3$ again. If this occurs, we will repeat these steps over and over and never reach the optimal vertex $v_1$.

Artificially constructed examples of cycling under the simplex method have been discovered, so the theoretical possibility is really an actual one. Oddly enough, cycling has never occurred in any of the thousands of linear programming problems arising from real-world situations that have been solved by the simplex method. It is comforting to know, however, that the simplex method can be modified to avoid the possibility of cycling.

## IV. HISTORICAL REMARKS

Although its roots extend back at least 150 years, linear programming is definitely a twentieth-century development.

Before World War II (1939–1945), there was a vast literature on the subject of linear algebraic equations, but comparatively little work done on systems of linear inequalities. The procedure for finding the general solution for systems of equations is due to Carl Friedrich Gauss (1826) and Camille Jordan (1904), and its basic elements are taught in high-school algebra courses. The problem of optimizing a linear-function subject to a system of linear inequalities, on the other hand, was not perceived as one with many important applications until the 1940's.

The early years of that decade brought a number of large-scale planning tasks associated with the war and with related civilian activity. It also saw the development of Von Neumann and Morgenstern's theory of games as a tool for economic analysis. It was gradually discovered that there were many common features in the planning tasks and that these features were at the heart of an important part of game theory.

Many of these connections between hitherto unrelated topics were brought together in 1947 by an American mathematician, George Bernard Dantzig, who formulated the standard linear programming problem and discovered the simplex method for solving it. Dantzig's discoveries and his efforts to popularize the use of linear programming earned him the title of "the father of linear programming."

George Dantzig is the son of Tobias Dantzig, the author of the well known book *Number: The Language of Science*. George Dantzig was born in Portland, Oregon on November 8, 1914. After receiving his A.B. degree from the University of Maryland (1936) and M.A. at the University of Michigan (1938), Dantzig worked as a statistician for the United States Bureau of Labor Statistics for two years. He resumed his graduate studies at the University of California in Berkeley in 1939, but left in 1941 for an 11-year stint with the United States Air Force. He was a statistician during the war years and served as chief mathematician on the staff of the Air Force Comptroller from 1945 to 1952. He received his doctorate from Berkeley in 1946 for a thesis written under the

Then President Gerald Ford (right) presents the National Medal of Science to George B. Dantzig, October 1976. Reproduced by permission of the Office of President Ford.

supervision of Jerzy Neyman, one of the prime builders of the modern theory of mathematical statistics.

Dantzig was a research mathematician for the Rand Corporation during the 1950's and joined the Berkeley faculty in 1960. Six years later, he took up a professorship in operations research and computer sciences at Stanford University, where he now teaches. In 1976, President Gerald Ford awarded Dantzig the National Medal of Science, the nation's highest science award. In the White House ceremony, Dantzig was cited "for inventing linear programming and discovering methods that led to wide-scale scientific and technical applications to important problems in logistics, scheduling, and network optimization, and to the use of computers in making efficient use of mathematical theory."

The practical importance of linear programming depends on an efficient algorithm for solving problems that involve hundreds of variables and constraints. The simplex method has proved, through thousands of applications, to be such an algorithm. It was Dantzig who developed the method which is now recognized as the forte of linear programming methodology.

Dantzig points out that the famous French mathematician Jean Baptiste Joseph Fourier (1768–1830) was perhaps the first person to study systematically linear inequalities. Fourier was interested in a problem which reduced to determining the lowest point of a polygonal convex set. He suggested in a paper written in 1826 that the solution be found by a vertex-to-vertex descent to a minimum value, a basic idea in the present simplex method.

In addition to his formulation of the LP problem and the development of the simplex method, Dantzig is also credited with the introduction of the use of slack and artificial variables. He was also one of the first persons to suggest an efficient modification of the simplex method to prevent cycling.

John Von Neumann (see Chapter 8) introduced the concept of duality and emphasized its importance in discussions with Dantzig in 1947, and conjectured the equivalence of two-person zero-sum game theory and linear programming. This conjecture was extended and proved by Dantzig and by David Gale, Harold Kuhn, and Albert W. Tucker, who developed much of the important theory of duality. This equivalence provides the most elementary proof of Von Neumann's Minimax Theorem. Other early important contributions to the theory of linear programming and its industrial applications were made by Abraham Charnes and William W. Cooper.

The first conference on linear programming was organized by Tjalling C. Koopmans for the Cowles Commission for Research in Economics. The conference, held in Chicago in June 1949, brought together mathematicians, statisticians, and economists from universities and government agencies to present the first papers on the theory of linear programming and a broad range of applications. The papers of this conference [Koopmans, 1951] are the pioneering works in this field.

Dantzig's book on linear programming and its extensions [Dantzig, 1963] contains much interesting material on the origins of linear programming and how it was influenced by military, economic, and theoretical problems. Dantzig and his colleagues developed linear programming against an intellectual background that featured Von Neumann's theoretical model of general economic equilibrium and Wassily Leontief's empirical input-output model of the U.S. economy, while in the foreground stood a host of important real-world planning and production problems that demanded solution.

The development of linear programming took place alongside the development of high-speed electronic computers. The simple, iterative nature of the simplex method meant that it was easily programmable. As the capacity and speed of computers has increased dramatically in the last twenty years, so has the range of applications of linear programming. As an effective instrument for planning, linear programming is used successfully today by many businesses, industries, and agricultural firms. The mathematical theory is also a rich one, employing many of the elegant ideas of linear algebra. Although the theory of the simplex method is largely understood, there remain a number of intriguing unsolved questions for the research mathematician.

---

## EXERCISES

---

### I. WHAT IS LINEAR PROGRAMMING?

#### B. A Detailed Example: Fromage Cheese Company

1. a) Show that the edge from $(100, 200)$ to $(140, 150)$ can be described analytically as $\{(x, y): 10x + 8y = 2600, 100 \leqslant x \leqslant 140\}$.

   b) Along this edge, show that $M = 4.5x + 4y$ has the form $M = 1300 - .5x$.

   c) At which vertex of this edge does $M$ achieve its largest value?

2. a) Find an analytic expression for the edge between $(140, 150)$ and $(200, 0)$.

   b) Show that along this edge $M$ can be written as a function of $x$ only.

   c) At which vertex of this edge does $M$ take on the largest value?

3. Carry out the program of Exercise 2 for the remaining edges of the feasibility set.

4. Find the optimal mixture for each of the following revenue functions:

   a) $M = 3x + 1y$,     b) $M = 3x + 2y$,

   c) $M = 2x + 3y$,     d) $M = 2x + 5y$.

5. Find the optimal mixture if Brewster wishes to maximize the total number of packages he can prepare.

6. Show that any point on the edge between $(100, 200)$ and $(140, 150)$ is an optimal mixture for the revenue function $M = 5x + 4y$. Thus optimal, feasible solutions of LP problems need not be unique.

7. Suppose the price of a Fancy Assortment is fixed at \$4.50, but the price, $\$b$, for the Deluxe Assortment is allowed to vary. Show that the optimal mixture is

   a) $(200, 0)$ if $0 \leqslant b < \$1.80$,

   b) $(140, 150)$ if $\$1.80 < b < \$3.60$,

   c) $(100, 200)$ if $\$3.60 < b < \$9$,

   d) $(0, 250)$ if $b > \$9$.

What happens in the cases that $b = \$1.80$ or \$3.60 or \$9?

8. Brewster also has in stock 2240 ounces of Mozarella cheese. He decides to include 7 ounces of Mozarella in the Fancy Assortment and 8 ounces in the Deluxe. He will charge \$5.30 for the new Fancy Assortment and \$4.50 for the Deluxe. Determine the new feasibility set for this problem (it will have 6 vertices) and find the mixture of packages that maximizes revenue.

9. Instead of putting his stock into Fancy and Deluxe Assortments, Brewster might have chosen to offer the Aristocrat and Regency Assortments. The Aristocrat contains 25 ounces of Cheddar, 5 ounces of Swiss, and 10 ounces of Brie; it sells for \$4.10. The Regency

Assortment consists of 10 ounces of Cheddar, 16 ounces of Swiss, and $5\frac{1}{3}$ ounces of Brie; it sells for \$4.90. Find the optimal mixture of these two assortments.

10. Formulate the problem of maximizing revenue with the original stock of cheeses if Brewster wants to package some number of all four assortments. How far can you go toward solving this problem?

### C. The Linear Programming Problem

11. Show that the linear programming problem: Maximize $x + y$ subject to the constraints: $x \geqslant 0$, $y \geqslant 0$, $x - y \leqslant -1$, $-x + y \leqslant 0$ has no feasible solutions.

12. Let $C$ be the set of all points $(x, y)$ in the plane satisfying $x \geqslant 0$, $y \geqslant 0$, $-x - 2y \leqslant -8$.

a) Show that $C$ is nonempty and unbounded.

b) Prove that the LP problem: Maximize $M = 2x + 3y$ subject to the constraint that $(x, y)$ lie in $C$ has no feasible, optimal solution.

c) Show that the LP problem: Maximize $M' = -3x - 6y$ subject to the constraint that $(x, y)$ lie in $C$ does have an optimal, feasible solution.

13. Choose any two points in the feasibility set of the Fromage Cheese Company example. Prove that any point on the line segment between these two points also lies in the feasibility set.

14 Consider a linear programming problem of the form: Maximize $c_1 x + c_2 y$ subject to the constraints:

$$x \geqslant 0, y \geqslant 0$$
$$a_i x + b_i y \leqslant d_i \ (i = 1, 2, \ldots, N).$$

The set of points satisfying $a_i x + b_i y = d_i$ for some $i$ form a *boundary* line of the feasibility set. A *vertex* of the feasibility set is a point in the feasibility set which lies on at least two distinct boundary lines. Prove that the number of vertices of the feasibility set is at most $N + 2$.

15. a) Construct a linear programming problem whose feasibility set has the vertices $(1, 2)$, $(3, 5)$, and $(2, 9)$.

b) Construct a linear programming problem whose feasibility set has vertices $(0, 0)$, $(4, 0)$, $(4, 5)$, $(2, 7)$, and $(0, 5)$.

### D. More Examples of LP Problems

16. Solve the breakfast problem geometrically by determining the feasibility set and its vertices and then testing the cost function at each vertex.

17. How many variables are involved in the smuggling problem? What is the total number of constraints if the problem is written in the standard form of a linear programming problem?

18. Solve, by trial-and-error, or any other method, the assignment problem described in the text.

19. Consider a linear programming problem in standard form. Show that it is equivalent to the problem: Find nonnegative numbers $x_1, \ldots, x_n, u_1, \ldots, u_m$ such that $M = c_1 x_1 + \cdots + c_n x_n$ is maximized subject to the constraints $a_{i1} x_1 + a_{i2} x_2 + \cdots + a_{in} x_n + u_i = b_i \ (i = 1, 2, \ldots, m)$.

20. In making change, a cashier wishes to minimize the number of coins he hands over to the customer. Formulate this situation as a linear program. Show that this problem has a simple solution if United States coins only are used.

21. The mathematics editor for Addison-Wesley wishes to visit prospective authors who are located in 20 different cities in the United States. She wishes to plan her route so that her total distance traveled is kept to a minimum. Formulate this as a linear programming problem. How does the problem change if she insists on never visiting the same city twice?

22. The admissions director of a small college is faced with the task of admitting a freshman class of at most 500 students. The typical male applicant can be expected to have a combined SAT score of 1200, contribute $8000 to the college as an alumnus, cause $200 damage to dormitory buildings and classrooms, and cost $2400 per year to teach. The typical female applicant can be expected to have combined SAT scores of 1300, contribute $3000 as an alumna and cause $100 in damages. Because of different course selections, she can be educated at a cost of $2000 per year.

   The college president demands a freshman class that will eventually contribute at least $2.5 million to the college, the faculty insists that the average SAT score be 1250 or higher, and the maintenance department can handle up to $85,000 in damages. The college treasurer wants to educate the class at the lowest possible cost.

   Set up a linear programming problem whose solution will tell the admissions director how many men and how many women to admit. Identify the variables, write down the constraints and the function to be optimized. Solve the problem geometrically.

23. (*The knapsack problem*). A person is planning a backpacking camping trip and has decided to carry no more than 70 pounds. Let $w_j$ be the weight of the $j$th object on the list of possible items to be carried and let $v_j$ be its relative value compared to the values of other items the hiker would like to have on the trip. Set up a linear programming problem whose solution will tell the hiker which items to select so that the total value will be maximized while the total weight is kept under 70 pounds.

24. (*The marriage problem*). Suppose each of $m$ women rate on a numerical scale the happiness they would expect to have if they married each of a list of $n$ men. Consider the problem of arranging a set of marriages that would maximize the total happiness. Formulate this problem as one of a linear programming type if:

   a) $m = n$ and each person must marry exactly one spouse;

   b) monogamy is required but not everyone needs to wed;

   c) polygamy is permitted;

   d) the women are allowed to rate some of the men as "unacceptable."

25. A Chicago newspaper reporter, Lawrence Green, is editing a book on the war in Indo-China. The book will contain photographs, reprints of articles previously published, and some original essays. There will be 40 items in all in the book. The author would like to have at least 12 photographs in the book and at least as many original articles as reprints. The book reviewers will criticize the project severely if more than 10 of the items are reprints. Green does not have time to write more than 20 original essays for the book. The publisher estimates that each photograph will sell 1000 copies of the book and each original essay will attract another 1500 buyers, but that each reprinted article will cause 200 potential readers to purchase something else. Under the author's contract, he is to receive $250 for each photograph, $100 for each reprinted article, and $900 for each original

essay that appears in the book. Taking all these factors into consideration, find the mixture of photos, reprints, and original essays that will

a)  maximize the number of books sold;

b)  maximize the author's payoff;

c)  maximize his payoff if he is also given 25¢ for each each copy of the book sold.

Set up this problem in standard linear programming format using three variables. Then show that it can be stated as a problem involving only two variables and hence can be solved geometrically.

### E.  Vector Formulation of the LP Problem

26.  Prove Theorem 1.

27.  Determine $A$, $\mathbf{b}$, and $\mathbf{c}$ for the linear programming problem:
Maximize $M = 3x + 4y$ subject to the constraints:

$$x \geqslant 0, \qquad y \geqslant 0$$
$$x + 2y \leqslant 3, \qquad x + y \leqslant 2, \qquad y \leqslant 8.$$

28.  Determine $A, \mathbf{b}$, and $\mathbf{c}$ for the problem:
Minimize $2x + 5y$ subject to the constraints:

$$x \geqslant 0, \quad y \geqslant 0, \quad x + y \geqslant 3, \quad x + 3y \geqslant 3, \quad 3x + 4y \leqslant 7.$$

29.  Let $A = \begin{bmatrix} 2 & 3 \\ 1 & 4 \end{bmatrix}$, $\mathbf{b} = \begin{bmatrix} 6 \\ 4 \end{bmatrix}$, and $\mathbf{c} = [2, 3]$.

Solve geometrically the linear programming problem: Maximize $\mathbf{c}X$ subject to the constraints: $\mathbf{x} \geqslant 0$ and $A\mathbf{x} \leqslant \mathbf{b}$.

30.  Solve the linear programming problem: Find $\mathbf{x} \geqslant 0$ so that $\mathbf{c}\mathbf{x}$ is as large as possible, subject to $A\mathbf{x} \leqslant \mathbf{b}$, if

$$A = \begin{bmatrix} -1 & -3 \\ -1 & -2 \end{bmatrix}, \mathbf{b} = \begin{bmatrix} -3 \\ -2 \end{bmatrix}, \text{ and } \mathbf{c} = [3, 5].$$

31.  Find the matrix form for the Fromage Cheese Company problem.

32.  Find the matrix form of the breakfast problem.

33.  Find the matrix form of the smuggling problem.

34.  Find the matrix form of the assignment problem.

35.  Find the matrix form of the problem of Exercise 22.

### II.  CONVEX SETS

### A.  Definitions, Examples, Basic Properties

36.  Show that the point $\frac{1}{2}\mathbf{x} + \frac{1}{2}\mathbf{y}$ is the midpoint of the line segment between $\mathbf{x}$ and $\mathbf{y}$; that is, it divides the segment into two pieces of equal length.

37.  Show that each of the sets of Fig. 5.5 (except for the interior of the circle) is the feasibility set of some linear programming problem and hence is convex.

38. Prove that a circle, together with its interior, is a convex set.

39. Let $S$ be an arbitrary set in Euclidean $n$-dimensional space. The *convex hull of $S$* is the intersection of all convex sets containing $S$. It is denoted by co $S$.

 a) Prove that co $S$ is convex.

 b) In what sense is co $S$ the "smallest" convex set containing $S$.

 c) Prove that $S$ is convex if and only if co $S = S$.

40. Sketch the convex hull of the set of points in the plane,

$$S = \{(0,0), (4,5), (5,4), (11, -3), (-1, -2)\}.$$

41. Determine the convex hull of each of the nonconvex sets of Fig. 5.6.

42. If $A$ and $B$ are subsets of euclidean $n$-dimensional space, then the *sum of $A$ and $B$* is the set $A + B = \{\mathbf{a} + \mathbf{b} : \mathbf{a}$ belongs to $A, \mathbf{b}$ belongs to $B\}$.

 a) If $A$ and $B$ are convex, prove that $A + B$ is convex.

 b) If $A + B$ is convex, does it follow that $A$ and $B$ are both convex? Give a proof or a counterexample.

 c) Define the sum of a finite collection of sets and prove that the sum of a finite number of convex sets is always convex.

43. Let $\mathbf{x}_1, \mathbf{x}_2, \ldots, \mathbf{x}_k$ be a finite collection of vectors. Then a *convex combination* of these vectors is any vector of the form $a_1\mathbf{x}_1 + a_2\mathbf{x}_2 + a_2\mathbf{x}_2 + \cdots + a_k\mathbf{x}_k$ where the $a_i$ are non-negative real numbers with $a_1 + \cdots + a_k = 1$. Prove that the convex hull of an arbitrary set $S$ is equal to the set of all convex combinations of finite sets of points belonging to $S$.

44. If $S_1$ and $S_2$ are convex sets, show that any point of co$(S_1 \cup S_2)$ can be written as a $\mathbf{s}_1 + (1 - a)\mathbf{s}_2$ where $\mathbf{s}_1$ belongs to $S_1, \mathbf{s}_2$ belongs to $S_2$ and $a$ is a number between 0 and 1.

45. Generalize the result of Exercise 44 to the convex hull of the union of a finite number of convex sets.

46. a) Is the empty set convex?

 b) Is a set with exactly one point convex?

 c) Is a set with exactly two points convex?

 d) Can a set with a finite number of points be convex?

### B. Polygonal Convex Sets in the Plane

47. Show that each of the sets (a)–(e) in the statement of Theorem 5 is convex.

48. If $(x, y)$ is a boundary point of a polygonal convex set $K$ in the plane, but is not a vertex point, then the coordinates of the point exactly satisfy the equation of one of the closed half-planes determining $K$ but yield a strict inequality when substituted into any of the other half-plane equations. Prove this.

49. Give examples, if possible, of polygonal convex sets in the plane for which some edge is a a) closed segment, b) closed ray, c) single point.

50. Prove that if an edge of a polygonal convex set contains more than one point, then the edge is either a closed segment or a closed ray.

51. In Section II.B, we discussed the behavior of a linear function along a nonvertical line $L$. What can you say about the values of a linear function along a vertical line?

52. Prove that if $p$ is an interior point of a polygonal convex set in the plane, then the intersection of any line through $p$ with the boundary of the convex set is either empty, a single point, or two points.

53. A point $p$ of a convex set $K$ is called an *extreme point* of $K$ if it is impossible to write $p$ as $p = \alpha x + (1 - \alpha)y$, where $0 < \alpha < 1$, and $x, y$ are distinct points of $K$.

    a)  Show that every extreme point of a convex set $K$ in the plane lies in the boundary of $K$; that is, the interior of every circle centered at the point contains points in $K$ and points not belonging to $K$.

    b)  Give an example of a boundary point which is not an extreme point.

    c)  Can a convex set in the plane have every boundary point also be an extreme point? What if the set is a polygonal convex set?

    d)  Show that a point of a polygonal convex set in the plane is an extreme point if and only if it is a vertex.

54. The *interior* of a convex set is the set of all points not on the boundary. Show that the interior of a polygonal convex set in the plane is the intersection of a finite number of open half-planes.

55. If $f$ is a linear function of two variables, show that

    a)  $f(\alpha x, \alpha y) = \alpha f(x, y)$ for all real numbers $\alpha$.

    b)  $f(x + x', y + y') = f(x, y) + f(x', y')$.

56. A real-valued function $f$ defined on a convex set $K$ is a *convex function* if $f(\alpha \mathbf{p} + (1 - \alpha)\mathbf{q}) \leqslant \alpha f(\mathbf{p}) + (1 - \alpha)f(\mathbf{q})$ for all $\alpha$ between 0 and 1 and all $\mathbf{p}$ and $\mathbf{q}$ in $K$.

    a)  Prove that every linear function is convex.

    b)  Let $K$ be the closed interval $[0, 1]$ and consider the function $f(x) = x^2$. Is $f$ convex? Is $f$ linear?

    c)  Find some examples of nonconvex functions.

## III.  THE SIMPLEX METHOD

### A.  Basic Solutions

57. Solve Exercises 1–10 of Appendix II.

58. Show that when slack variables are added to the standard linear programming problem, the matrix of coefficients contains the $m \times m$ identity matrix. What can you say about the presence of an identity matrix after an iteration?

59. Solve the system of Eqs. (14) for $x, y, w$ in terms of $u$ and $v$.

60. Begin with the basic feasible solution of the Fromage Cheese Company example,

$$x = y = 0, \qquad u = 6000, \qquad v = 2600, \qquad w = 2000$$

and discuss what happens to $M$ if you try to increase $y$ as much as possible, keeping $x = 0$.

### B.  The Simplex Method

61. Solve the problem of the Fromage Cheese Company using the simplex method, but let $y$ enter the basis at the first step. How many iterations are necessary?

62. Show that the entries of the $M$-column never change at any step of the simplex method; thus it is not necessary to include this column in the tableau.

63. Solve, by the simplex method, the Fromage Cheese Company problem with revenue function $M = 5x + 4y$. See Exercise 6.

64. Use the simplex method to solve the linear programming problem of Exercise 10.

65. What happens when the simplex method is applied to the problem: Maximize $2x + 2y$, subject to the constraints: $x \geqslant 0$, $y \geqslant 0$, $-x - 2y \leqslant -8$?

66. Solve the linear programming problem of Exercise 25.

67. Solve the linear programming problem of Exercise 27.

68. Solve the linear programming problem of Exercise 29.

69. Solve the linear programming problem of Exercise 30.

70. The Masters Company produces three different lines of bowling pins. Each pin is processed by three different kinds of machines for different lengths of time and is sold for a different level of profit. The time, in minutes, for each type of pin in each machine is given by the matrix:

|  | I | II | III |
|---|---|---|---|
| Atlantic | 2 | 1 | 3 |
| Vegas | 4 | 9 | 6 |
| Dutch-Boy | 3 | 4 | 5 |

In each week, 90 hours of machine time are available for machine I, 200 hours on machine II, 600 hours on machine III. Each set of Atlantic pins earns the company a profit of $6, each set of Vegas pins earns a profit of $5, and each set of Dutch-Boy pins earns a profit of $4. Use the simplex method to find the optimal production mixture for the company.

### C. The Use of Artificial Variables

71. Resolve the breakfast problem of this section if the price of Brand X is reduced to 3¢ per ounce.

72. Show that once an artificial variable leaves the basis in the simplex method, it will never return to the basis at a later iteration.

73. Solve the linear programming problem: Finding nonnegative numbers $x_1, x_2$, and $x_3$ such that
$$m = 4x_1 + 8x_2 + 3x_3 \text{ is minimized}$$
subject to:
$$x_1 + x_2 \geqslant 2,$$
$$2x_2 + x_3 \geqslant 5.$$

74. Solve the linear programming problem of minimizing $-2x_1 - 2x_2$ for nonnegative values of $x_1$ and $x_2$ such that $2 \leqslant x_1 + x_2 \leqslant 4$.

75. Find nonnegative numbers $x_1, x_2, x_3, x_4$, and $x_5$ such that $M = x_1 + x_2 + x_3 - x_5$ is as large as possible, subject to the constraints:
$$2x_1 + x_2 + \qquad + 2x_4 - 2x_5 \leqslant 1$$
$$x_1 \qquad + 2x_3 - x_4 \qquad \geqslant 3$$
$$x_2 - x_3 \qquad \geqslant 0$$
$$-x_1 \qquad + 3x_5 \geqslant 2.$$

### D. The Condensed Tableau

Use a condensed tableau to solve each of the following linear programming problems.

76. Maximize $7x - y$ subject to the restrictions: $x \geqslant 0$, $y \geqslant 0$, $x + y \leqslant 10$, $x + 10y \leqslant 20$, $2x + 3y \geqslant 5$.

77. Maximize $3x_1 + 5x_2 + x_3 + 2x_4$ subject to the constraints:

$$3x_1 + 6x_2 + 5x_3 + 4x_4 \leqslant 5$$
$$2x_1 + 5x_2 + x_3 + 6x_4 \leqslant 6$$
$$x_1 + x_2 + 5x_3 + x_4 \leqslant 7,$$
$$x_i \geqslant 0 \ (i = 1, 2, 3, 4).$$

78. Find $\mathbf{x} \geqslant 0$ such that $\mathbf{cx}$ is maximized, subject to $A\mathbf{x} \leqslant \mathbf{b}$, if

$$\mathbf{c} = (5, 3, 1), \ \mathbf{b} = \begin{bmatrix} 15 \\ 10 \\ 5 \end{bmatrix}, \text{ and } A = \begin{bmatrix} 3 & 5 & 1 \\ 5 & 2 & 0 \\ 4 & 0 & 1 \end{bmatrix}.$$

79. Minimize $-3x_1 + 2x_2 - 5x_3 - 6x_4$ subject to the constraints:

$$2x_1 + 16x_2 + x_3 + x_4 \geqslant 4$$
$$x_1 + 3x_2 + 2x_3 + 5x_4 \leqslant 20$$
$$3x_1 - x_2 - 5x_3 + 10x_4 \leqslant -10,$$
$$x_i \geqslant 0, \ i = 1, 2, 3, 4.$$

80. The assignment problem of Section I.D.

### E. Duality

81. Show that the dual of the breakfast problem has a natural statement of the job of a pill salesman trying to convince Janet to give up on the cereals and buy his iron and protein capsules.

82. Solve the breakfast problem by applying the simplex method to the dual problem.

83. Prove Theorem 6.

84. Solve the distributor's problem directly using the simplex method. How many iterations are required?

85. What is the dual of the assignment problem of Section I.D?

86. What is the dual of the smuggling problem of Section I.D?

87. Prove (c) of Theorem 9.

88. Verify the claims made about the example given for the proof of part (d) of Theorem 9.

89. Recently passed federal legislation requires the Masters Company to test the safety of each of its bowling pins (see Exercise 70). The company estimates that an Atlantic pin will require 3 minutes of safety testing, the Vegas pin will need 4 minutes, and the Dutch-Boy will take 5 minutes. If the company can afford up to 1000 hours of testing each week, what is the optimum mixture for production? Use your solution to Exercise 70 together with duality.

90. Let $\mathbf{x}$ be a feasible solution to a primal problem and $\mathbf{y}$ a feasible solution to the dual problem. Prove that $\mathbf{x}$ and $\mathbf{y}$ are optimal solutions if and only if whenever a variable

of one of the problems is positive, then the corresponding constraint of the other is *tight*; that is, the weak inequality is an equality. What can you say about the constraint of one of the problems if the corresponding variable in the dual problem is zero?

### F. Some Wrinkles in the Simplex Method

91. Prove that in the case of a tie for the minimum ratio, the Gauss-Jordan procedure makes at least two of the variables that were in the basis equal to 0 when the iteration is completed.

92. Show that the value of $M$ does not improve if a tie for the minimum ratio occurs.

93. Show that if the minimum ratio is 0, then no entry in the final column of the tableau changes when the iteration is completed.

94. Show that cycling cannot occur if at each step, the minimum ratio is unique and positive.

95. (*Beale*). Show that cycling can occur for the problem: Maximize $.75x_1 - 20x_2 + .5x_3 - 6x_4$ subject to the restrictions that each variable remain nonnegative and

$$.25x_1 - 8x_2 - x_3 + 9x_4 \leqslant 0$$
$$.5x_1 - 12x_2 - .5x_3 + 3x_4 \leqslant 0$$
$$x_3 \qquad \leqslant 1.$$

96. Use the convexity of the feasibility set to prove that if the value of $M$ is greater at some vertex $v_0$ than at all vertices *adjacent* to $v_0$, then it is greater at $v_0$ than it is at any other vertex of the feasibility set. Show that this implies that the simplex algorithm terminates at a global maximum and not a local maximum.

---

## SUGGESTED PROJECTS

---

1. Investigate more carefully the proof that the simplex method converges after a finite number of iterations. What is a realistic bound on the number of required iterations? What effects the length of time the simplex method uses more, the number of variables or the number of constraints?

2. How can the simplex method be modified so that cycling will not occur? The first example of cycling in the unmodified simplex method was given by Hoffman in 1951; a simpler example (Exercise 95) was discovered by Beale in 1955. Charnes, "Optimality and degeneracy in linear programming," [1952] and the article by Dantzig, Orden, and Wolfe [1955] present two different ways of avoiding cycling. Which is more efficient? Is it possible to construct an example simpler than Beale's in which cycling occurs? Suppose a linear programming problem is chosen "at random." What is the probability that degeneracy will occur? What is the probability that cycling will happen under the ordinary simplex method?

3. Many real-world problems require answers which are integers. Consider, for example, Exercises 22 and 25 as well as the Fromage Cheese Company problem. It often turns out, however, that even if all the coefficients in a linear programming problem are integral, the simplex method may yield an optimal feasible solution in which some of the variables are nonintegral. If these values are rounded off to the nearest integer, the resulting numbers may not give a feasible solution. Even though feasible, the rounded off

solution is not necessarily the optimal *integral* solution. Find examples in which these possibilities occur. The field of *integer programming* is devoted to the study of finding optimal, feasible integral solutions. What are the major solution algorithms that have been developed? How do they compare to the simplex method? See Reference of Garfinkle and Nemhauser [1972].

4. In the assignment problem (Section I.D) each variable can take on only two possible values, 0 or 1. Furthermore, the coefficients of the constraints (which are all equations) are also 0 or 1. How can these special features be exploited in finding a simpler solution scheme than the simplex algorithm?

5. The linearity assumptions of the standard LP problem are not always realistic. The basic assumption is what economists call "constant returns to scale"; for example, the linearity assumption says that if all resources are exactly doubled, then final production and profit are also exactly doubled. Often, however, there are situations of increasing returns per unit increase of resource (convexity) or decreasing returns (concavity) or some more complicated relationship. The general problem of *mathematical programming* is to optimize a function $g(\mathbf{x})$ where $\mathbf{x}$ is restricted to lie in some set $S$ in Euclidean $n$-dimensional space and so that each of the inequalities $f_i(\mathbf{x}) \leqslant 0$ ($i = 1, 2, \ldots, m$) is satisfied. Investigate extensions of the simplex method to solve such a problem if $S$ is a convex set and the functions $g$ and $f_i$ ($i = 1, \ldots, m$) are convex. See Exercise 56 and Reference Kuhn and Tucker [1951] or Chapter 7 of Karlin [1959].

---

## REFERENCES

---

The notation and basic outline of this chapter follow the treatment of Glicksman [1963] but at a less elementary level. Readers with a moderate background in linear algebra will find understandable and comprehensive treatments of linear programming in Dantzig [1963] or Hadley [1962]. Dorfman, Samuelson, and Solow [1958] emphasize applications to economic theory. Sakarovich [1971] gives a rapid, linear algebra approach that contains proofs of the major results.

Beale, E. M. L., "Cycling in the dual simplex algorithm," *Naval Research Logistics Quarterly* **2** (1955), 269–276.

Charnes, Abraham, "Optimality and degeneracy in linear programming," *Econometrica* **20** (1952), 160–170.

Charnes, Abraham, William W. Cooper, and A. Henderson, *An Introduction to Linear Programming* (New York: Wiley, 1953).

Dantzig, George, B., "The programming of interdependent activities: mathematical model" in Tjalling C. Koopmans, *Activity Analysis of Production and Allocation* (New York: Wiley, 1951), pp. 19–32.

Dantzig, George, B., "A proof of the equivalence of the programming problem and the game problem," in Tjalling C. Koopmans, *Activity Analysis of Production and Allocation* (New York: Wiley, 1951), pp. 330–335.

Dantzig, George, B., "Maximization of linear function of variables subject to linear inequalities," in Tjalling C. Koopmans, *Activity Analysis of Production and Allocation* New York: Wiley, 1951), pp. 339–347.

Dantzig, George, B., *Linear Programming and Extensions* (Princeton: Princeton University Press, 1963).

Dantzig, George B., Alex Orden, and Philip Wolfe, "The generalized simplex method for minimizing a linear form under linear inequality restraints," *Pacific Journal of Mathematics* **5** (1955), 183–195.

Dorfman, Robert, Paul A. Samuelson, and Robert M. Solow, *Linear Programming and Economic Analysis* (New York: McGraw-Hill, 1958).

Gale, David, *The Theory of Linear Economic Models* (New York: McGraw-Hill, 1960).

Gale, David, Harold W. Kuhn, and Albert W. Tucker, "Linear programming and the theory of games," in Tjalling C. Koopmans, *Activity Analysis of Production and Allocation* (New York, Wiley, 1951). pp. 317–329.

Garfinkle, Robert and George L. Nemhauser, *Integer Programming* (New York: Wiley, 1972).

Glicksman, Abraham, *An Introduction to Linear Programing and the Theory of Games* (New York: Wiley, 1963).

Hadley, George, *Linear Programming* (Reading, Mass: Addison-Wesley, 1962).

Hoffman, Alan J., "Cycling in the simplex algorithm," National Bureau of Standards Report No. 2974, December 16, 1953.

Karlin, Samuel, *Mathematical Methods and Theory in Games, Programming and Economics*, Vol. I (Reading, Mass: Addison-Wesley, 1959).

Koopmans, Tjalling C., *Activity Analysis of Production and Allocation* (New York: Wiley, 1951).

Kuhn, Harold W. and Albert W. Tucker, "Non-linear programming," *Proceedings of the Second Berkeley Symposium on Mathematical Statistics and Probability* (Berkeley and Los Angeles: University of California Press, 1951), pp. 481–492.

Sakarovitch, Michel, *Notes on Linear Programming* (New York: Van Nostrand Reinhold, 1971).

Vajda, S. *Theory of Games and Linear Programming* (New York: Wiley, 1956).

A recently discovered simple rule for choosing the pivot element in the simplex method so as to avoid cycling is discussed in Robert G. Bland, "New finite pivoting rules for the simplex method," *Mathematics of Operations Research* **2** (1977), 103–107.

# 6
# Social Choice and Voting Procedures

The general will is always right and tends to the public advantage; but it does not follow that the deliberations of the people are always equally correct. Our will is always for our own good, but we do not always see what that is; the people is never corrupted, but it is often deceived.

Jean-Jacques Rousseau

## I. THREE VOTING SITUATIONS

This chapter illustrates the use of axiomatic models by investigating some of the procedures used by groups of voters to determine collective judgments from individual preferences. These procedures characteristically have certain injustices associated with them. An axiomatic approach reveals that attempts to redesign the procedures or invent new ones to avoid these inequities are doomed to frustration.

An illustrative real-world example is the United States Senate and its attempts to reach agreement on certain types of important issues. The model to be developed concerns certain kinds of collective judgments, which are exemplified by the following three illustrations.

**EXAMPLE 1**    The President nominates a South Carolina lawyer for a position on the United States Supreme Court. The Senate must decide whether to confirm the nomination or not.

**EXAMPLE 2**    Three proposals for dealing with the dependents' deduction feature of the federal income tax have been offered. Proposal A calls for a substantial increase in the amount of the deduction so that it will more accurately reflect the costs of rearing children in today's economy. Proposal B seeks the abolition of the dependents' allowance; its advocates wish to discourage parents from planning large families. Proposal C is simply that the present level of the deduction be retained. The Senate must adopt one of these mutually exclusive proposals.

**EXAMPLE 3**    A commission on national goals asks the Senate for its evaluation of the order of importance of three current problems: the economy, the plight of urban areas, and the protection of the environment. In this situation, the Senate must indicate an ordering of three alternatives.

There are 100 senators, two from each state. Assume that there has been sufficient discussion and debate on the matters before the Senate so that each member has already his or her own personal preference among the alternatives open. What procedure should be used in passing from this set of 100 individual preferences to a collective preference?

## II. TWO VOTING MECHANISMS

### A. Simple Majority Voting

The first situation, that of confirming a nomination to the Supreme Court, poses little difficulty. Each senator announces a vote for or against the nominee. If a simple majority of those voting favors the nominee, the nominee is confirmed. Otherwise, the nominee is rejected. (Should the Senate split evenly, then the ballot of the Vice-President is counted to determine the majority position.)

Decision making by simple majority voting is, of course, the most familiar scheme for determining the collective judgment of a group of individual voters. Together with the concept that each individual has but a single vote, it forms the heart of what many would define as "democracy." "The very essence of democratic government," wrote Alexis De Tocqueville in *Democracy in America*, (1835) "consists in the absolute sovereignty of the majority; for there is nothing in democratic states which is capable of resisting it." In his first inaugural address, Abraham Lincoln observed, "Unanimity is impossible; the rule of a minority, as a permanent arrangement, is wholly inadmissible; so that, rejecting the majority principle, anarchy or despotism in some form is all that is left."

As you will see, simple majority voting is a fair and effective procedure to adopt when a group is asked to decide between *two* alternatives or candidates. What happens, however, when the group must choose among three or more alternatives? How does the Senate actually reach a decision when faced with a situation like that described in Example 2? It adopts a procedure used by many legislative bodies: change the format of the problem from one involving a choice among three alternatives to a series of choices between two alternatives.

To illustrate this process with the income tax example, the Senate might first decide between proposals A and B on a simple majority vote. The winning proposal would then be pitted against C and the eventual winner then decided by a simple majority vote between these two alternatives.

The idea is to use the simple majority principle—because of a strong belief in its fairness—even when it may not be immediately applicable. Is there anything wrong here?

Re-examine for a moment the individual preferences of the senators. Assume that a certain amount of reasonableness and consistency exists in each senator's personal ordering of the desirability of the three proposals. In particular, assume that each senator's ordering is *transitive*. This means that if $x, y$, and $z$ are any three alternatives and a senator prefers $x$ over $y$ and he prefers $y$ over $z$, then he must prefer $x$ over $z$.

If an individual's preferences are transitive, then his preference list can be denoted in a convenient way. Suppose a senator finds proposal C most attractive, proposal B least attractive, and proposal A intermediate to the other two. Denote the preference list by (C A B). Then transitivity implies that one proposal is favored over another exactly if it appears to the left of the other in the list.

We now make our first demand on the decision making process: the collective preference must also be transitive. We want to guarantee that whenever the group prefers $x$ to $y$ and prefers $y$ to $z$, then it must also prefer $x$ to $z$. It is on this imminently reasonable and apparently innocent demand that simple majority voting stumbles badly. At least since the time of Condorcet (1743–1794), those concerned about just voting procedures and mechanisms noted the possibility that intransitive social preferences could result when the variation of simple majority voting described above is applied to a list of individual transitive preferences.

To be specific, there are six possible ways an individual can rank-order the three proposals: (A B C), (A C B), (B C A), (B A C), (C A B), and (C B A). Suppose that the preferences of the senators on the dependents' allowance proposals break down as follows:

$$
\begin{array}{lr}
\text{(A B C)} & \text{31 votes,} \\
\text{(B C A)} & \text{34 votes,} \\
\text{(C A B)} & \text{35 votes.}
\end{array}
$$

To simplify this example, assume that none of the other three orderings are represented.

Which proposal will be adopted? If the originally outlined procedure is followed, the Senate will first choose between A and B. Since 66 senators prefer A over B, B will be eliminated from consideration. A second vote will be taken between A and C. Now 69 senators will opt for C and only 31 for A. Thus, Proposal C will be the one adopted by the Senate.

A loud objection can be expected from the advocates of proposal A. It has already been established, they would argue, that the Senate prefers A to B. It is also clear that in a direct vote between B and C, B would receive 65 votes so that the Senate certainly prefers B to C. But if the Senate prefers A to B and B to C, then it must prefer A over C to maintain transitivity.

The Senate's normal procedures do not necessarily lead to transitive group preferences, as you have just seen. But is transitivity always so important? In any legislative situation, it might be argued, the body always has at any moment only the option between two proposals. Only after one of the original two proposals is voted down in favor of the other may a third proposal be introduced.

If group transitivity is not guaranteed, however, more serious problems arise. The result of the legislative deliberation may depend, not on the individual wishes of the members or the inherent worth of the proposals, but on the *order* in which the proposals are offered for consideration. To illustrate with this same example, suppose the agenda is arranged so that A and C are the two original proposals discussed. When a vote is taken, C triumphs over A. When proposal B is finally introduced it competes against C and wins, 65 to 35.

The author of each of the three proposals then has a legitimate argument that his or her proposal is the one which is "most favored" by the Senate as a whole. The modification of simple majority voting discussed here, although almost universally employed by legislative bodies, is seen then not to be a just one. The procedure yields nontransitive group preferences. It does not always produce the same collective preference given the same set of individual preferences. It is subject to manipulations by those who control the ordering of items on the agenda.

What procedure should be used if the group wishes to guarantee transitivity and to guarantee that the group decision is purely a function of the individual preferences? How is the "will" of the group to be determined? One possibility often suggested is to adopt a weighted voting scheme.

## B. Weighted Voting

Weighted voting mechanisms are often used to score athletic, artistic, and beauty contests. The individual ratings of a collection of judges are pooled to determine the final over-all rankings of the contestants. Preassigned numerical weights are attached to each first-place rating, each second-place rating, and so on. A contestant receives a score that is the sum of the weights of the opinions of the individual judges. The group ranking of the contestants is then determined by their total scores. The person with the highest number of points is the winner, the individual with the next highest number is the first runner-up, and so on down the list. Notice that this procedure can be employed in either a situation like Example 2 or Example 3.

Consider a typical example of this procedure in which there are four contestants, labelled $w, x, y$, and $z$ and three judges. Judges 1 and 2 each rank the contestants in the order $(x \ y \ z \ w)$ while judge 3 ranks them $(z \ w \ x \ y)$. If 5 points are assigned for a first-placed ranking by a judge, 4 points for second, 2 for third and 1 for fourth, then $x$ earns 12 points, $y$ and $z$ each earn 9, and $w$ earns 6. The winner is contestant $x$, while $y$ and $z$ tie for second, and $w$ is last.

What are the weaknesses of such a voting mechanism? Suppose that between the time the judges' ratings are submitted and the winner is announced, it is discovered that $y$ has broken the rules of the contest. He is disqualified. The scoring system is now applied to the remaining contestants. It should yield the same results, we believe, especially since $y$ is inferior to $x$, according to the tastes of each individual judge.

Yet if $y$ is deleted, the rankings become $(x \ z \ w)$ for judges 1 and 2 and $(z \ w \ x)$ for judge 3. Now when the weights are tabulated, $x$ still has 12 points, but $z$ has 13 and $w$ has 8. The master of ceremonies dutifully declares $z$ the winner of the contest. Needless to say, $x$ is furious and his attorney sues the contest committee, claiming his client has been treated unjustly.

This weighted voting scoring mechanism violates an ethical value and poses a practical political problem. Whether a group believes $x$ is better than $z$ or not should be a judgment independent of the group's feelings about a third contestant $y$. Weighted voting does not preserve this independence.

Here is the practical political problem: In the example, judges 1 and 2 have given their true preferences in their ratings. They think $x$ is best and would like to see $x$ emerge as the eventual winner. Suppose that they have heard rumors that $y$ has not been completely rigorous in following the rules. If Judges 1 and 2 were to switch their ratings to $(x \ y \ w \ z)$, they would make it more likely for $x$ to win over $z$ in the event that $y$ is disqualified. This would involve the two judges in falsifying their own preferences.

A fair and equitable voting mechanism should not encourage such falsification. Each voter should feel secure in casting a personal ballot that lists the alternatives exactly in the order in which he would like to see the outcome. Weighted voting schemes remove this security.

The procedure of weighing places in individual preference orderings with numbers and using these numbers to find the societal ordering of proposals or candidates is attributed to Jean-Charles de Borda (1733–1799). Borda served as both a cavalry officer and a naval captain, made several contributions to the progress of mathematical physics, and was elected to the French Academy of Sciences. His "Memoire sur les Elections au Scrutin," published in 1781, was the first mathematical theory of electrons. When confronted with the possibility that voters might mask their true preferences in order to help their favorite candidate emerge on top, Borda is reported to have replied "My scheme is only intended for honest men."

Various other schemes have been proposed for determining a group-preference ranking from lists of individual preferences, and some of them are widely used. Each seems to suffer from one or another defect. The injustices of these voting mechanisms raises the question of whether it is possible to design one which everyone will agree is just and democratic. If it is possible, what would the rules of such a voting procedure look like?

## III.  AN AXIOMATIC APPROACH

What is a *just* voting mechanism? To answer this question, we begin by listing some conditions or axioms that a voting system might reasonably be required to satisfy if it is to be labeled a "fair" one. Once the set of axioms is set, mathematical questions can be asked. Is the set of axioms consistent? If so, how many different structures satisfy them? If the axioms are inconsistent, which ones should be eliminated or modified?

In the first place, the mechanism will be translating a list of individual voter preferences into a group-preference list. The voters may differ greatly in their likes and dislikes of candidates or proposals, and we do not wish to restrict the freedom of any voter to state his true preferences. Accordingly, the first axiom looks like this:

**AXIOM 1 (INDIVIDUAL SOVEREIGNTY)   Each voter may order the candidates (or alternative proposals) in any way he or she chooses and may even indicate indifference between pairs of candidates.**

The second axiom demands that the system always produce a societal judgment that is transitive and which depends only on the individual ballots cast by the voters.

**AXIOM 2 (EXISTENCE OF SOCIAL WELFARE FUNCTION)   For every collection of lists of individual preferences, the mechanism produces a unique list of society's preferences. The society's preferences are transitive.**

Note that Axiom 2 removes the inequities associated with simple majority voting when more than two alternatives are being considered. It also rules out some schemes which do guarantee transitivity. For example, one mechanism might be to put all the individual lists into a hat and draw out at random one of these which will be designated society's preference list. Since the societal choice corresponds to some particular individual's, it will be transitive. This scheme would not satisfy Axiom 2, because a second implementation of the mechanism (drawing again from the hat) might result in a different outcome. The *uniqueness* feature of the societal list would be violated.

The third axiom is a weak constraint that has generated no controversy among voting-theory experts. It simply asks that in those cases where everyone prefers $x$ to $y$, so does the society.

**AXIOM 3 (UNANIMITY)    If every individual prefers one alternative to another, so does the society.**

It would certainly be unreasonable to claim that the society's ranking reflected that of its members if no one agreed with it.

The weighted voting schemes discussed in Section II satisfy Axioms 1, 2, and 3; the proof is left to the reader. The fourth axiom is designed to eliminate the difficulties associated with such systems.

**AXIOM 4 (INDEPENDENCE OF IRRELEVANT ALTERNATIVES)    The social ordering of any pair of alternatives depends only on the preferences of the individuals between the members of that pair.**

This axiom implies that if we want to know whether the society prefers $x$ to $y$ or $y$ to $x$, we need only examine the rankings of $x$ and $y$ on each voter's preference list; we need not look at the rankings of any other candidates.

To understand this axiom better, return for a moment to the beauty contest example. If the rankings as originally turned in by the judges give a group judgment of $x$ higher than $z$, then any other set of ballots in which judges 1 and 2 rank $x$ higher than $z$ and in which judge 3 ranks $z$ higher than $x$ will result in a group judgment of $x$ higher than $z$ if Axiom 4 holds. In other words, any two elections in which all voters preserve their preference between two particular candidates will yield the same group preference between *those* two candidates.

A voting mechanism which satisfied Axiom 4 would insure that voters gain nothing by disguising their true preferences.

It is very easy to design a voting mechanism which satisfies the first four axioms. Simply designate some particular voter as a dictator and decree that society's preference list will just be a copy of that one person's list. The reader should verify that this dictatorial mechanism is consistent with Axioms 1–4. Although it is certainly an extremely efficient voting mechanism, it is not what most people would call a "democratic" institution. The final axiom rules out such systems.

**AXIOM 5 (NONDICTATORSHIP)   There is no voter with the power that for all choices $x$ and $y$, if he prefers $x$ to $y$, then so does the society regardless of how other voters feel about $x$ and $y$.**

To make the axiomatic model realistic, assume that there are a finite number of individual preference lists. To make it interesting, assume that there are at least three different alternatives to be ranked. (The reader is asked to show that simple majority voting satisfies Axioms 1–5 if there are exactly two candidates or proposals being considered.)

These five axioms describe conditions all of which seem natural and desirable to demand of a voting mechanism. You may, in fact, believe that the axioms demand too little for the mechanism to deserve the adjective "democratic." The axioms do not demand, for example, that each voter's preference list be treated equally; some individuals might be given more "votes" than others. The axioms do not require that society prefer $x$ to $y$ if a simple majority prefers $x$ to $y$. The axioms also do not insist that the same procedures be used on all pairs of alternatives. Conceivably, a mechanism that used a dictator to decide between Todd and Millner while using simple majority voting on Emerson vs. Peterson might be allowed.

The surprising fact is that even this "reasonable" set of axioms is inconsistent. The five demands are incompatible with each other. It is impossible to devise any voting mechanism which will simultaneously satisfy all of them.

This result is known as the General Impossibility Theorem. It was first stated by Kenneth J. Arrow in 1951 in a pioneering essay that sought to place voting theory on an axiomatic basis. Arrow's original proof contained an error and a correct proof was first supplied by Julian Blau in 1957. Arrow's theorem has provoked a considerable amount of discussion by social scientists, philosophers, political theorists, and economists.

## IV. ARROW'S IMPOSSIBILITY THEOREM

We state the theorem in a manner which is both provocative and which indicates the direction of its proof:

**THEOREM (ARROW'S GENERAL IMPOSSIBILITY THEOREM)**    Axioms 1–4 imply the existence of a dictator.

The remainder of this section is concerned with a proof of the theorem. Assume then that there is a voting mechanism satisfying Axioms 1–4. One additional definition is necessary.

**DEFINITION   A set $V$ of individual voters is *decisive for alternative $x$ against alternative $y$* if $x$ is socially chosen by the voting mechanism whenever every individual in $V$ prefers $x$ to $y$ and every individual not in $V$ prefers $y$ to $x$.**

This concept is somewhat subtle and requires some explanatory remarks:

a) If the mechanism is a dictatorial one, then the dictator is a one person set who is decisive for every pair of alternatives.

b) Axiom 3 on Unanimity asserts that the set of all voters is decisive for every pair of alternatives. Should every voter prefer $x$ to $y$, then so would society. Of course, not every voter might share this preference for $x$ and $y$. If some of the voters prefer $x$ to $y$ and others prefer $y$ to $x$, we need to know more about the details of the voting mechanism to determine the societal ranking.

c) Decisiveness is really a *potential* power. If $V$ is a set which is decisive for $x$ against $y$, then one of the conditions that must be present in order to predict that society prefers $x$ to $y$ is that everyone in the set $V$ prefers $x$ to $y$. If a particular individual belongs to $V$ and he prefers $y$ to $x$, then the fact that $V$ is decisive for $x$ against $y$ does not really give $V$ much influence on the outcome.

d) The other condition that must be met if decisiveness is to be used to predict a societal ranking is that all the individuals not in $V$ must prefer $y$ to $x$. If $V$ is decisive for $x$ against $y$, if everyone in $V$ prefers $x$ to $y$, and if someone not in $V$ prefers $x$ to $y$, then we can make no accurate prediction about the societal ranking of $x$ against $y$ unless we have more detailed knowledge about the voting mechanism.

To clarify this point, suppose we have a society with five members: Mike, Judy, Eli, Abby, and Sasha. The voting mechanism is simple, but rather peculiar. The societal ranking is always exactly the opposite of Mike's preference ranking. Let $x$ and $y$ be any two alternatives. Then the set whose members are Eli, Abby, and Sasha is decisive for $x$ against $y$. If these three prefer $x$ to $y$ and the other two members prefer $y$ to $x$, then in particular, Mike prefers $y$ to $x$. Since Mike prefers $y$ to $x$, the society prefers $x$ to $y$. Consider, however, what happens if Eli, Abby, Sasha, and Mike all prefer $x$ to $y$. Then society will prefer $y$ to $x$, even though Mike has voted the same way as all the members of a decisive set.

e) A set $V$ may be decisive for $x$ against $y$ but not necessarily decisive for $y$ against $x$ or decisive for any other pair of alternatives. This is due to the fact that Axioms 1–4 do not require the voting mechanism to operate the same way for all pairs of alteratives.

With these warnings about the notion of a decisive set in mind, we proceed to the main part of the proof of the theorem. The proof proceeds by verifying two claims:

*Claim I*    There is some pair of alternatives and some individual who is decisive for that pair.

*Claim II*    If an individual is decisive for some pair of alternatives, then he or she is decisive for every pair of alternatives; that is, the individual is a dictator.

*Proof of Claim I.* For any pair of alternatives $x$ and $y$, there is at least one nonempty decisive set; namely, the set of all individuals. Among all sets of individuals which are decisive for some pair of alternatives, pick a minimal set. This is a set $V$ of voters and a pair of alternatives $x, y$ so that $V$ is decisive for $x$ against $y$ and no proper subset of $V$ is decisive for *any* pair of alternatives.

If such a minimal decisive set contains exactly one voter, then we are done with Claim I. Hence, assume that $V$ contains at least two voters. Let $V^*$ be the set consisting of exactly one voter from $V$, $\hat{V}$ the subset of $V$ consisting of all voters in $V$ not in $V^*$, and let $V'$ be the set of all voters in the society not in $V$. Now $V^*$ is a proper subset of $V$. We shall show that $V^*$ is decisive for some pair of alternatives, thus contradicting the minimality of $V$.

Suppose that $V$ is decisive for $x$ against $y$ and let $z$ be any other alternative. Suppose that the voter in $V^*$ ranks the alternatives $(x\ y\ z)$, all the voters in $\hat{V}$ rank them $(z\ x\ y)$, and all the voters in $V'$ rank them $(y\ z\ x)$.

Note first that all voters in $V = V^* \cup \hat{V}$ prefer $x$ to $y$ and all voters not in $V$ prefer $y$ to $x$. Since $V$ is decisive for $x$ against $y$, society prefers $x$ to $y$.

Next note that $\hat{V}$ is smaller in size than $V$, so it is not decisive for any pair. In particular $\hat{V}$ is not decisive for $z$ against $y$. This implies that society prefers $y$ to $z$, for, otherwise, we would have society preferring $z$ to $y$ when everyone in $\hat{V}$ does and no one outside $\hat{V}$ does.

Finally, use the transitivity of the societal preference. Society prefers $x$ to $y$ and $y$ to $z$. Thus society prefers $x$ to $z$.

We then have one election in which $V^*$ prefers $x$ to $z$, everyone outside $V^*$ prefers $z$ to $x$, and the society prefers $x$ to $z$. By Axiom 4 on Independence of Irrelevant Alternatives, society will prefer $x$ to $z$ *whenever* all individuals maintain these preferences between $x$ and $z$. Hence $V^*$ is decisive for $x$ against $z$. This contradicts the assumption that $V$ is a minimal decisive set. The conclusion, then, is that minimal decisive sets contain precisely one voter. Claim I is verified.

*Proof of Claim II.* Let $J$ be some individual member of the society and write:

1. "$a\,\bar{D}\,b$" to mean that $a$ is socially preferred to $b$ whenever $J$ prefers $a$ to $b$ regardless of the orderings of other individuals, and
2. "$a\,D\,b$" to mean that $a$ is socially preferred to $b$ if $J$ prefers $a$ to $b$ and all other voters prefer $b$ to $a$.

These notations are useful since the condition of dictatorship is that $a\,\bar{D}\,b$ for all pairs of alternatives $a$ and $b$, while $a\,D\,b$ is true if and only if $J$ is a decisive set for $a$ against $b$.

To complete the proof of Claim II, the following lemma is useful.

**LEMMA**    Suppose there are three alternatives $a, b, c$. Then

1. $a\,D\,b$ implies $a\,\bar{D}\,c$, and
2. $a\,D\,b$ implies $c\,\bar{D}\,b$.

***Proof of Lemma***    Let $J$ rank the alternatives $(a\ b\ c)$ and suppose everyone else ranks $b$ higher than $a$ and $c$. Since $a\,D\,b$, we conclude that society prefers $a$ to $b$. Since all individuals prefer $b$ to $c$, so does society. By transitivity, society prefers $a$ to $c$. The axiom on Independence of Irrelevant Alternatives asserts that whenever $J$ prefers $a$ to $c$, so does society regardless of how the other voters rank $c$ and $a$. In other terms, $a\,\bar{D}\,c$.

To prove that $a\,D\,b$ implies $c\,\bar{D}\,b$, suppose first that $J$ ranks the alternatives in the order $(c\ a\ b)$ and all other voters rank them $(c\ b\ a)$ or $(b\ c\ a)$. Since $a\,D\,b$, society prefers $a$ to $b$. By unanimity, society prefers $c$ to $a$. Transitivity then gives a society preference of $c$ over $b$. Applying Axiom 4 again, we have $c\,\bar{D}\,b$.

This completes the proof of the lemma.

We can now finish the proof of Claim II. Suppose $x\,D\,y$ for some pair of alternatives $x$ and $y$.

***Case 1***    There are exactly three alternatives: $x, y, z$.

We must show that $a\,\bar{D}\,b$ for all pairs of alternatives; that is,

1. $x\,\bar{D}\,z$     2. $z\,\bar{D}\,y$
3. $x\,\bar{D}\,y$     4. $y\,\bar{D}\,z$
5. $z\,\bar{D}\,x$     6. $y\,\bar{D}\,x$

The proof of (1) follows directly from the lemma with $a = x$, $b = y$, and $c = z$. Similarly, (2) follows from a direct application of the lemma. Now that we know that $x\,D\,z$, we also have $x\,D\,z$. Now apply the lemma with $a = x, b = z$, and $c = y$. The conclusions are that $x\,\bar{D}\,y$ and $y\,\bar{D}\,z$, giving (3) and (4). The proofs of (5) and (6) are left to the reader.

***Case 2***    There are more than three alternatives.

Suppose $x\,D\,y$ holds and let $a$ and $b$ be any alternatives.

i) If $x$ and $y$ are the same as $a$ and $b$, add a third alternative $z$ to $x$ and $y$ and apply the result of Case 1 to show that $x\,D\,y$ implies $x\,\bar{D}\,y$ and $y\,\bar{D}\,x$. Hence both $a\,\bar{D}\,b$ and $b\,\bar{D}\,a$ hold.

ii) If exactly one of $a$ and $b$ is distinct from $x$ and $y$, add it to $x$ and $y$ to form a triple and apply Case 1.

iii) If both $a$ and $b$ are distinct from $x$ and $y$, two steps are needed: First, add $a$ to $x$ and $y$; obtain $x\,\bar{D}\,a$ so that $x\,D\,a$. Second, consider the triple $x, a, b$; obtain $a\,\bar{D}\,b$.

Thus $x\,D\,y$ for *some* $x$ and $y$ implies $a\,\bar{D}\,b$ for *all* alternatives $a$ and $b$. This completes the proof of Claim II and hence the proof of the theorem.  $\square$

Since Axioms 1–5 are inconsistent as they stand, any attempt to strengthen them—such as demanding that all voters be treated equally—will not remove inconsistency. A voting system which satisfies some of the axioms must violate some of the others. We will not enter here the heated argument as to which is the "best" axiom to modify or discard. The interested reader may follow the debate by consulting the References.

## V.  KENNETH JOSEPH ARROW

The most prestigious and coveted international honors are the annual Nobel Memorial Prizes. These awards are given for outstanding achievements in medicine, literature, peace, chemistry, physics, and—since 1969—economics. The announcements of these awards each autumn are front-page news.

The Swedish Academy of Science selected Harvard University professor Kenneth J. Arrow as a co-winner of the 1972 Nobel Prize in Economics. The academy cited Arrow's pioneering contributions to general economic equilibrium theory and welfare theory. Although Arrow has made several key breakthroughs in economic theory, many of his colleagues rate the Impossibility Theorem of this chapter as his major achievement. According to the well-known economist Paul Samuelson, himself a Nobel Laureate in 1970, this theorem "is not only a stellar contribution to economics, it is as well a breakthrough for political science, and I would dare assert, for philosophy itself."

Arrow was born, reared, and educated in New York City, graduating from the City College of New York in 1940 at the age of 18. His advanced degrees

Kenneth J. Arrow

were taken at another Manhattan institution, Columbia University. After a four-year stint in the United States Army Air Force during World War II, Arrow was a research associate with the Cowles Commission at the University of Chicago from 1947 to 1949. The Impossibility Theorem was part of his PhD thesis and in finished form was published as a book, *Social Choice and Individual Values*, in 1951.

In 1949, Arrow joined the faculty of Stanford University where he taught for almost 20 years and was a major force in developing at Stanford an outstanding group of economic theorists and mathematical model builders. He also worked briefly with the Council of Economic Advisers during the administration of President John F. Kennedy. Since 1968, Arrow has been at Harvard, where he is now actively working on a study of efficiency of decision making in economic systems.

Arrow has written or edited eight different books whose topics include the mathematical theory of inventory and production, time series analysis of inter-industry demands, linear and nonlinear programming, public investment and optimal fiscal policy, the theory of risk bearing, and general competitive analysis.

"Despite the deep abstraction of his econometric theories, friends consider Professor Arrow basically a humanist, a scholar who has always tried to apply fundamental theory to such social problems as medical care, education, race discrimination and water resources," wrote Robert Reinhold [1972] in a *New York Times* profile.

In appraising the work for which Arrow received a Nobel Prize, Samuelson [1972] wrote, "Men have always sought ideal democracy—the perfect voting system. ... What Kenneth Arrow proved once and for all is that there cannot possibly be found such an ideal voting scheme. The search of the great minds of recorded history for the perfect democracy, it turns out, is the search for a chimera, for a logical self-contradiction. ... Aristotle must be turning over in his grave. The theory of democracy can never be the same ... since Arrow."

Despite his many honors and the demands of his research, Arrow has been remarkably available to undergraduate students and younger colleagues. He was the only senior faculty member at Harvard, for example, who volunteered to take on an assignment to lead discussion sections of an introductory economics course, a task usually delegated to graduate student teaching assistants.

## EXERCISES

### I. THREE VOTING SITUATIONS

1. Show that a voting mechanism which gives a satisfactory resolution of situations in which a single best alternative must be chosen (as in Example 1) can be modified to handle situations when a full ranking of various alternatives is required (as in Example 2).

2. Are there any voting situations essentially different from those described in Examples 1–3? How are the outcomes determined in such situations?

## II.  TWO VOTING MECHANISMS

3.  What safeguards protect minority rights in systems using simple majority voting?

4.  Suppose the senators are split in the following manner:

$$\text{(A B C) 49 votes}$$
$$\text{(B C A) 49 votes}$$
$$\text{(C A B)  2 votes}$$

If modified simple majority voting is used here, will the judgments of the Senate be transitive?

5.  If 51 senators share the preference ranking (A B C), show that the Senate will have transitive preferences.

6.  Is it necessary for a majority of senators to share a common preference ranking to guarantee that the Senate judgments will be transitive?  Why?

7.  Consider a legislative body that only passes resolutions if they are supported by more than two-thirds of the members.  How would such a body settle questions like those proposed by Examples 2 and 3?  What inequities does such a system possess?

8.  In order to correct past discrimination, it has been proposed that for a limited period, the votes of women be given twice the consideration of the votes of men; that is, each woman receives two votes on every proposal while each man receives one.  Proposals are adopted or rejected on a simple majority count.  Can intransitive results emerge?  What other injustices are associated with such a system?

9.  There are 1,000,000 shares of stock in Shores Construction Company.  Two shares are owned by Mrs. Shores, and the remaining shares are split evenly between her two sons. In deciding company policies, each share holder has a number of votes equal to the number of shares he controls.  How much relative power does Mrs. Shores have?

10.  The outcome of a weighted voting mechanism depends not only on the rankings of the individual judges, but on the points assigned to each place in the rankings.  For the example described in the text, determine the rankings of the contestants if a second place is worth only 3 points.

11.  In Olympic gymnastics competition, four judges individually assign a number between 0 and 10 to each contestant.  The highest and lowest scores are discarded and the contestant receives the average of the two intermediate scores.  What injustices would be associated with such a voting mechanism?

12.  In many voting situations, the individual voter is permitted to designate more than one contestant as his preference, but is not allowed to rank-order his preferences.  For example, 10 candidates may be running for three positions on a local school board.  Each voter may place X's besides the names of three candidates.  The candidates who receive the largest number of X's are the winners.  How fair is such a voting mechanism?

## III.  AN AXIOMATIC APPROACH

13.  Show that simple majority voting satisfies Axioms 1–5 if there are exactly two alternatives.

14.  Which of the five axioms are satisfied by weighted voting mechanisms?

15.  Construct voting mechanisms that satisfy all the axioms except

a)  Axiom 1,      b)  Axiom 2,      c)  Axiom 3,      d)  Axiom 4,      e)  Axiom 5.

16.  Weaken Axiom 2 by eliminating transitivity of societal preferences, and construct various mechanisms that satisfy the new set of axioms.

17.  Weaken Axiom 2 by eliminating the demand for a unique societal preference and construct a mechanism which satisfies the new set of axioms.

18.  In what way does Axiom 4 eliminate the possibility of voters manipulating the system by disguising their true preferences?

## IV.  ARROW'S THEOREM

19.  Construct a voting mechanism for which there is a set $V$ of voters and a pair of alternatives $x$ and $y$ so that $V$ is decisive for $x$ against $y$, but $V$ is not decisive for $y$ against $x$.

20.  The five-person society discussed under remark (d) has a mechanism which does not satisfy the Unanimity Axiom.  Why?  Suppose the mechanism is modified so that $x$ is socially preferred to $y$ whenever everyone prefers $x$ to $y$; otherwise, the societal preference is the opposite of Mike's.  What axioms does this system satisfy?

21.  Prove that a minimal decisive set will always exist if there is a finite number of voters.  Construct a voting mechanism for a society with an infinite number of voters in which minimal decisive sets do not exist; that is, show that if $V$ is any set of voters decisive for some pair of alternatives, then there is a proper subset of $V$ which is also decisive for some pair of alternatives.

22.  What happens in the proof of Claim I if the minimal decisive set is the set of all voters?  Can this happen in a system satisfying Axioms 1–4?

23.  In the proof of Claim I, it is tacitly assumed that $V'$ is nonempty.  Can you prove that $V'$ always contains at least one voter?

24.  a)  Prove that $a\bar{D}b$ implies $aDb$.

b)  Find an example in which $aDb$ is true, but $a\bar{D}b$ is not.

25.  Prove that $xDy$ implies $z\bar{D}x$ and $y\bar{D}x$ if there are exactly three alternatives $x, y$, and $z$; that is, verify (5) and (6) of Case 1.

26.  Verify the details of the argument of Case 2.

## SUGGESTED PROJECTS

1.  Instead of discarding some axioms or weakening them to obtain a consistent set, you might think about strengthening the first axiom.  Axiom 1 allows voters to list the alternatives in order of preference, but does not allow for expression of intensity of differences between alternatives.  Two voters may both list $x$ and $y$ at the top of their lists, although the first voter's feelings are almost indifferent toward the two, while the second voter much prefers $x$ to $y$.  Investigate methods of incorporating intensities into individual preference lists.  Discuss the consistency of sets of axioms allowing for such measures.

2.  Peter Fishburn has shown that the Axioms 1–5 are consistent if there are an *infinite* number of voters.  Investigate his proof.  What is the real-world relevance of this result?

3. Some voting theorists have argued that the modified simple majority vote system is satisfactory because intransitivity rarely occurs. Is there some way of measuring the likelihood of intransitivity? Can you find instances in Senate voting where proponents have used intransitivity to their advantage by adjusting the agenda?

4. A voting mechanism is called *manipulable* if there is an individual who may, by mis-representing his or her preferences, secure an outcome preferred to the choice that would have been made if he or she expressed a true preference. Under certain "reasonable" sets of axioms, it can be shown every voting mechanism is either dictatorial or manipulable. How do these axioms compare with Axioms 1–4? See the paper by Allan Gibbard for one approach.

5. Can the standard voting systems (simple majority, weighted voting, and so on) be characterized axiomatically? H. P. Young isolated three characteristics of voting systems, which he termed "consistency," "the cancellation property," and "faithfulness." He was able to prove that any mechanism which is consistent, faithful, and has the cancellation property must be a weighted voting system. Are these three properties reasonable ones? Check the details of Young's proof. Derive, if possible, an axiomatic characterization of simple majority voting.

6. Develop a proof of Arrow's Theorem which shows that Axioms 1, 2, 4, and 5 imply that Unanimity is violated.

---

## REFERENCES

---

For a fuller treatment of Arrow's approach, see his book *Social Choice and Individual Values*, Second edition (New York: Wiley, 1963). The first correct proof of Arrow's Theorem may be found in J. H. Blau, "The existence of social welfare functions," *Econometrica* **25** (1957), 302–313. For an alternative proof and insight into Suggested Project 2, read P. C. Fishburn, "Arrow's impossibility theorem: concise proof and infinite voters," *Journal of Economic Theory* **2** (1970), 103–106.

For a critical view of the importance of Arrow's result to social theory, see Gordon Tullock, "The general irrelevance of the general impossibility theorem," *Quarterly Journal of Economics* (1967), 256–270.

Three recent books discuss at length the axiomatic development of the theory of social choice and voting mechanisms. They are Peter C. Fishburn, *The Theory of Social Choice* (Princeton: Princeton University Press, 1973), Prasanta K. Paatanaik, *Voting and Collective Choice* (Cambridge: Cambridge University Press, 1971), and Amartya K. Sen, *Collective Choice and Social Welfare* (San Francisco: Holden-Day, 1970).

Allan Gibbard's paper is "Manipulation of voting schemes: a general result," *Econometrica* **41** (1973), 587–601 and H. P. Young's is "An axiomatization of Borda's rule," *Journal of Economic Theory* **9** (1974), 43–52.

Some of the discussion of the significance of Arrow's work may be found in Robert Reinhold, "Equilibrium theorists: Kenneth J. Arrow," *The New York Times*, October 26, 1972, p. 71, and in two articles by Paul A. Samuelson: "Pioneers of economic thought," *The New York Times*, October 26, 1972, p. 71 and "The 1972 Nobel Prize for Economic Science," *Science*, November 3, 1972, pp. 487–489.

# 7 Foundations of Measurement Theory

It is a scientific platitude that there can be neither precise control nor prediction of phenomena without measurement. Disciplines as diverse as cosmology and social psychology provide evidence that it is nearly useless to have an exactly formulated quantitative theory if empirically feasible methods of measurement cannot be developed for substantial portions of the quantitative concepts of the theory.

Dana Scott and Patrick Suppes

## I. THE REGISTRAR'S PROBLEM

The academic year at Middlebury College is divided into three major components: two 12-week semesters sandwiching a five-week "Winter Term." During the Winter Term each faculty member offers, and each student enrolls in, one course. Because of the experimental nature of many of the courses offered, enrollment is often restricted to 20 or 25 students in each class. Since a typical Winter Term will find 1500 students on campus and only 70 courses, it is clear that not every student will be able to take the course she most desires.

When a student registers for Winter Term, then, she lists five courses in descending order of preference. The registrar assigns each student to a course, using these preferences as a guide. At the present time, the registrar uses a procedure based on the desire to maximize the number of students who receive their first choice. There has been considerable discussion lately about the fairness and desirability of this particular priority scheme. An alternative method of assigning students to courses has been devised which has gained some support. The philosophy behind this scheme is not to maximize the number of first choices, but to maximize the total amount of happiness among the students towards the courses they are assigned. This assignment procedure can be given a rather tidy mathematical formulation.

Denote the students by $i = 1, 2, \ldots, n$ and the courses by $j = 1, 2, \ldots, m$. Let $r_{ij}$ denote how happy student $i$ would be if she is assigned course $j$. Define the variable $x_{ij}$ to be equal to 1 if student $i$ is placed in course $j$ and 0 otherwise. The total amount of happiness would then be represented by

$$r_{11}x_{11} + r_{21}x_{21} + \cdots + r_{n1}x_{n1} + r_{12}x_{12} + \cdots + r_{nm}x_{nm}$$

or, in more compact form,

$$\sum_{j=1}^{m} \sum_{i=1}^{n} r_{ij}x_{ij}.$$

There are several restrictions on the registrar which must be taken into account. First of all, every student must be assigned to some course and only to one course. Second, no course should be assigned more students than the instructor is willing to admit. Denoting the enrollment limit on the $j$th course by $C_j$, the Registrar's Problem is formulated as follows:

$$\text{Maximize} \sum_{j=1}^{m} \sum_{i=1}^{n} r_{ij}x_{ij}$$

subject to the restrictions:

(1)  Each $x_{ij} \geqslant 0$,

(2)  $\displaystyle\sum_{j=1}^{m} x_{ij} = 1$ for all $i$, and

(3)  $\displaystyle\sum_{i=1}^{n} x_{ij} \leqslant C_j$ for all $j$.

The Registrar's Problem is an example of what mathematicians call a "linear programming" problem (see Chapter 5). Algorithms exist for the solution of such linear-programming problems, although when $n$ and $m$ are as large as 1500 and 70, respectively, high-speed electronic computers must be used to execute them.

In this chapter and the succeeding one, we want to focus more sharply on the aspect of the Registrar's Problem which remains somewhat vague in this presentation: what precisely is $r_{ij}$ and how is it determined?

## II. WHAT IS MEASUREMENT?

### A. A Physical Analogy

We let $r_{ij}$ denote "how happy student $i$ would be if she is assigned course $j$." In the mathematical formulation of the Registrar's Problem, it is clear that we are presuming that each $r_{ij}$ is a real number which measures this happiness. Is it clear, however, that it is always possible to measure such psychological attributes by numbers? What is meant by "measuring" an attribute? Is there more than one way to do it? What inferences, if any, can be made from a measurement scale? How can you construct such a scale?

These questions form the basic problems of *measurement theory*. In the mid-1960's four distinguished social scientists [David Krantz, R. Duncan Luce, Patrick Suppes, and Amos Tversky, 1972] began a collaborative study of the foundations of measurement theory that resulted in two large volumes. Early in their first book, the authors discuss the roles of theories of measurement in sciences:

> "... The measurability of the variables of interest in physics is taken for granted and the actual measurements are reduced, via the elaborate superstructure of physical theory, to comparatively indirect observations. Other sciences, especially those having to do with human beings, approach measurement with considerably less confidence. In the behavioral and social sciences we are not entirely certain which variables can be measured nor which theories really apply to those we believe to be measurable; and we do not have a superstructure of well-established theory that can be used to devise practical schemes of measurement. ... A recurrent temptation when we need to measure an attribute of interest is to try to avoid the difficult theoretical and empirical issues posed by fundamental measurement by substituting some easily measured physical quantity that is believed to be strongly correlated with the attribute in question: hours of deprivation in lieu of hunger; skin resistance in lieu of anxiety; milliamperes of current in lieu of aversiveness, etc."

It should not be surprising then that our first insights into measurement will come from considerations of measurement in the physical sciences. The question of what is meant by "measuring an attribute" may perhaps best be answered by examining first a physical attribute, weight. A provisional definition of *measuring an object's weight* might be "assign some number to that object." This is a very poor definition, since the same number might be assigned to every object.

A careful analysis of a physical attribute is not possible unless there is some means of deciding which of two objects possesses more of the attribute than the other. A refinement of the first definition might be the following: to measure an object's weight means to assign a number to that object in such a way that one object is at least as heavy as a second object if and only if it is assigned a number at least as large as the second.

This added restriction rules out the possibility of assigning all objects the same number. It relies on the fact that the concept of the "weight" of an object is intimately connected with a relation between objects, the relation "at least as heavy as." This relation can be established empirically by placing any pair of objects on the separate pans of a balance and observing which pan descends.

Write $A * B$ if object $A$ is at least as heavy as object $B$. To measure weight is to find a function $w$ from the set of objects to the set of real numbers such that $w(A) \geqslant w(B)$ if and only if $A * B$.

It is natural to define "$A$ has the same weight as $B$" to mean that $A * B$ and $B * A$. As an easy exercise, the reader should show that $w(A) = w(B)$ if and only if $A$ has the same weight as $B$.

It is now easy to describe a procedure for assigning weights to a finite set of objects $A_1, A_2, \ldots, A_n$. By testing $A_1$ against each of the other objects on the pan balance, then $A_2$ against all of the other objects, and so on, find a lightest element $A_j$. This is an object $A_j$ such that $A_i * A_j$ for all $i \neq j$. Assign weight 0 to object $A_j$. If there is any $A_i$ such that $A_j * A_i$, then $A_j$ and $A_i$ have the same weight, so also assign weight 0 to $A_i$.

Next consider the set of remaining objects which have yet to be assigned a weight. Find a lightest element in this set. Assign weight 1 to this object and to any object of the same weight. Repeat the process on the set of remaining objects (assigning weight 2 to its lightest element) and continue in this manner until all objects have been assigned a weight.

## B.  Relations

With this relatively simple example as background, we can discuss the general problem of defining what it means to measure attributes. The formulation of the problem uses the concept of a "relation" from elementary set theory. See Appendix I for the necessary background on sets.

**DEFINITION**    A *relation* on a set $S$ **is a subset** $R$ **of the Cartesian product** $S \times S$. **If** $x$ **and** $y$ **are elements of** $S$, **we say that** $x$ *is R-related to* $y$ **or** $x R y$ **whenever** $(x, y)$ **is an element of** $R$.

A number of examples will be given to illustrate this idea.

**EXAMPLE 1**    Let $S$ be a set with four elements, $S = \{a, b, c, d\}$. The Cartesian product $S \times S$ consists of 16 ordered pairs,

$$S \times S = \{(a, a), \ldots, (a, d), (b, a), \ldots, (b, d), \ldots, (d, a), \ldots, (d, d)\}.$$

A relation on $S$ consists of some subset of these sixteen ordered pairs. One such example is a relation with three elements, $R = \{(a, c), (a, d), (b, d)\}$. We have $a\,R\,c$, $a\,R\,d$, and $b\,R\,d$ and for no other pair $i$ and $j$ is it true that $i\,R\,j$.

**EXAMPLE 2**    Let $S$ be the set of all positive integers and consider the relation $R$ defined by $x\,R\,y$ if and only if the difference $x - y$ is even. Thus $(2, 4)$ is an element of $R$, while $(3, 2)$ is not. The relation $R$ consists of all pairs $(x, y)$ such that either both $x$ and $y$ are even or both $x$ and $y$ are odd.

**EXAMPLE 3**    Let $S$ be the set of all real numbers and let $R$ be the set of all ordered pairs $(x, y)$ such that $x \geqslant y$. Note that $(5, 3)$ is an element of $R$, but $(3, 5)$ is not. Since the Cartesian product $S \times S$ consists of all ordered pairs of real numbers, it can be represented geometrically by the points in the plane. Any relation on $S$ then corresponds to some subset of the plane. The relation $R$ defined here is shown graphically in Fig. 7.1.

**EXAMPLE 4**    Let $S$ be the set of all people in Georgia and let $R$ be the relation defined by $x\,R\,y$ if and only if $x$ knows $y$.

**EXAMPLE 5**    Let $S$ be the set of all men in the United States Navy and let $R$ be the relation defined by $x\,R\,y$ if and only if $y$ must obey an order given by $x$.

**EXAMPLE 6**    Let $S$ be the set of all automobiles in Honest Harry's Used Car Lot. Define a relation $x\,R\,y$ if and only if $x$ costs more than $y$.

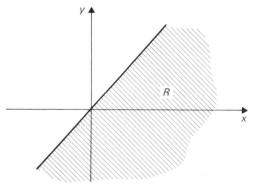

**Fig. 7.1**    The shaded region $R$ consists of all pairs $(x, y)$ of real numbers such that $x \geqslant y$.

**EXAMPLE 7**    Let $S$ be the set of all objects in your attic and let $R$ be the relation defined by $x\,R\,y$ if and only if $x$ is at least as old as $y$.

**EXAMPLE 8**    Let $S$ be the set of all words in the English language and let $R$ be the relation defined by $x\,R\,y$ if and only if $x$ precedes $y$ in the dictionary.

**EXAMPLE 9**    Let $S$ be the set of all ordered pairs of real numbers. Define a relation $(x, y)\,R\,(x', y')$ if and only if $x < x'$ or $x = x'$ and $y < y'$. For example, we have $(3, 20)\,R\,(5, 11)$ and $(3, 20)\,R\,(3, 21)$. This relation is called the *lexicographic* or *dictionary order*.

**EXAMPLE 10**    Let $S$ be the set of all courses offered by your college and let $R$ be the relation $x\,R\,y$ if and only if you like course $x$ at least as much as course $y$.

---

Relations may be classified by the presence or absence of certain properties. A few of the more important properties will be considered here.

**DEFINITION   If $S$ is a set and $R$ is a relation on $S$, then**

1.  $R$ **is** *reflexive* **if** $x\,R\,x$ **for all** $x$ **in** $S$,
2.  $R$ **is** *symmetric* **if** $x\,R\,y$ **always implies** $y\,R\,x$,
3.  $R$ **is** *transitive* **if** $x\,R\,y$ **and** $y\,R\,z$ **always implies** $x\,R\,z$, **and**
4.  $R$ **is** *connected* **or** *total* **if for every pair of elements** $x$ **and** $y$ **in** $S$, **either** $x\,R\,y$ **or** $y\,R\,x$ **or both.**

Example 3 is reflexive, transitive, but not symmetric. Example 2 is symmetric. Example 6 is transitive, but neither reflexive or symmetric. Example 4 is probably not transitive. Examples 3 and 7 are connected, while Examples 1 and 2 are not.

## C. Definition of Measurement

This section provides a careful definition of measurement and explores some of its elementary consequences. By a *relational system*, we mean a pair $\alpha = \langle S, R \rangle$ where $S$ is a set and $R$ is a relation on $S$. A *measure* for a relational system $\alpha$ is a function $m$ from $S$ to the real numbers such that for all $x$ and $y$ in $S$,

$$x\,R\,y \text{ if and only if } m(x) \geqslant m(y).$$

To measure an attribute possessed by a set of objects, people, or events means to find a measure $m$ which preserves the relation determined by the attribute. The "Basic Representation Problem" then is: which relational systems have measures?

Note first that it is not always possible to find a measure for a given relational system.

**EXAMPLE 11**   Let $S$ be the set of three elements $\{x, y, z\}$ and let $R$ be the relation $\{(x, y), (y, z), (z, x)\}$. The relational system $\langle S, R \rangle$ has no measure. Suppose, to the contrary, that there is a measure $m$. Since $x R y$ and $y R z$, we must have $m(x) \geqslant m(y)$ and $m(y) \geqslant m(z)$. But $m(x), m(y)$, and $m(z)$ are real numbers so it follows that $m(x) \geqslant m(z)$. Since $m$ is a measure, the definition implies that $x R z$ or $(x, z)$ is an element of $R$. This, however, is not the case.

The relational system described in Example 11 failed to have a measure essentially because the relation was not transitive. The reasoning given in the discussion of this example extends to a more general situation, stated in Theorem 1. The proof is left as an exercise.

■ **THEOREM 1**   If a relational system $\alpha = \langle S, R \rangle$ has a measure, then $R$ is a transitive relation.

Theorem 1 says that one necessary condition for a relational system to have a measure is that the relation be transitive. It is easy to establish a second necessary condition; namely, the relation must be connected.

■ **THEOREM 2**   If the relational system $\alpha = \langle S, R \rangle$ has a measure, then $R$ is a connected relation.

**Proof**   If $x$ and $y$ are any two elements of $S$, then $m(x)$ and $m(y)$ are defined and are real numbers. It must be true that either $m(x) \geqslant m(y)$ or $m(y) \leqslant m(x)$. In the former case, $x R y$ and in the latter, $y R x$. Thus either $(x, y) \in R$ or $(y, x) \in R$. □

Theorems 1 and 2 indicate that the relational systems of Examples 1 and 2 have no measures associated with them.

## III.  SIMPLE MEASURES ON FINITE SETS

One of the major goals of measurement theory is to establish necessary and sufficient conditions on relational systems under which various numerical representations can be constructed. The relation must be connected and transitive if there is to be any hope of constructing a measure. If the set $S$ is finite, then these two conditions are also sufficient.

■ **THEOREM 3 (FIRST REPRESENTATION THEOREM)**   Let $R$ be a relation on a finite set $S$. There exists a measure on the relational system $\langle S, R \rangle$ if and only if $R$ is connected and transitive.

**Proof**   Theorems 1 and 2 establish the "only if" part of the conclusion. It remains to show that if $R$ is connected and transitive, then it is always possible to find a measure. The idea behind the proof is essentially the same as the one used in describing how to assign numerical weights to a set of objects.

Denote the elements of the set $S$ by $x_1, x_2, \ldots, x_n$. Since the relation $R$ is connected and transitive, we can find, by checking all possible pairs of elements, an element $x_j$ such that $x_i R x_j$ for all $i \neq j$. Define $m(x_j)$ to be 0. If there is any element $x_i$ so that $x_j R x_i$ as well as $x_i R x_j$, then define $m(x_i)$ to be 0 also.

At this point, at least one and possibly more elements of $S$ have been assigned measure 0. Consider the subset $S'$ of remaining elements. Find an element $x_k$ of $S'$ so that $x_m R x_k$ for all $x_m \neq x_k$ in $S'$. Define $m(x_k) = 1$. If there is any other element $x_m$ of $S'$ with $x_k R x_m$ as well as $x_m R x_k$, then also define $m(x_m) = 1$.

Repeat the entire process on the set $S''$ of elements which have not yet been assigned measures, using a measure of 2 to distinguish one or more special members of $S''$. Continue in the indicated manner until each element of $S$ has been assigned a measure. This will take at most $n$ steps.

It should be clear from the method of construction that $m$ satisfies the definition of a measure; that is, $x R y$ if and only if $m(x) \geqslant m(y)$. This completes an outline of a proof of Theorem 3. $\square$

The finiteness of the set $S$ was used at several crucial steps in the proof of Theorem 3. The theorem remains true if $S$ is a countably infinite set, but may fail if $S$ is uncountable; see the Exercises for the relevant definitions and examples.

Note that the proof of Theorem 3 not only establishes the existence of a measure, but provides an effective method of constructing one.

The numerical values of a measure function $m$ are sometimes called *scale values*. In the proof of Theorem 3, the numbers 0, 1, 2 and so on were suggested for scale values. There is nothing sacred about this set. Any increasing sequence of real numbers could have been used. The next example amplifies this point.

---

**EXAMPLE 12**  Let $S$ be the set of three elements $\{x, y, z\}$ and $R$ the relation $\{(x, y), (y, z), (x, z)\}$. Since this relation is connected and transitive, the elements can be represented numerically by a measure, according to Theorem 3. If the procedure outlined in the proof of that theorem is followed, the result is

$$m(z) = 0, \qquad m(y) = 1, \qquad \text{and} \qquad m(x) = 2.$$

These values are not determined by the measurement model. We could set

$$m(z) = -17, \qquad m(y) = \sqrt{23}, \qquad \text{and} \qquad m(x) = 10$$

and still satisfy the definition of a measure. In fact, any three numbers $m(x)$, $m(y), m(z)$ satisfying the inequalities $m(z) < m(y) < m(x)$ would be an admissible set of scale values.

---

Such scales are called *ordinal scales*. Any transformation of the scale numbers that preserves their original order yields another admissible scale. A transformation that changes the order in any way would give a set of scale values which is not admissible. The resulting numbers, $m(x_i)$, would define a function which is not a measure.

If $\alpha = \langle S, R \rangle$ is a relational system where $S$ is finite and $R$ is connected and transitive, the elements of $S$ can be labelled $x_1, x_2, \ldots, x_n$ in such a way that if $m$ is any measure, then $m(x_1) \leqslant m(x_2) \leqslant \cdots \leqslant m(x_n)$. This is called the *standard ordering* on $S$.

The mathematical model just developed gives a partial solution to the question posed by the Registrar's Problem. It is possible to assign numbers to a given student which measure her happiness about being enrolled in the available courses exactly when the student can state her relative preference for each pair of courses, provided these preference judgments are transitive.

By asking the student a series of questions requiring her always to indicate which one of two courses she prefers to the other, we can construct her preference ordering among all 70 courses.

The reason this model gives only a partial solution to the question originally asked will become apparent in the next section of this chapter.

## IV. PERCEPTION OF DIFFERENCES

Suppose the measure guaranteed by Theorem 3 is used to determine numerical values $r_{ij}$ measuring the relative happiness of students toward courses. We soon encounter a student who complains, "I would be almost equally happy with my first- as with my second-choice course, but quite a bit less happy with the third choice. If you assign measures of 3, 2, and 1 to these choices, you are not really representing my feelings in a completely accurate way."

This type of objection forces us to ask if it is possible to choose a scale of numbers that will accurately reflect the differences perceived by the student between different *pairs* of courses. Let's consider a mathematical formulation of this question.

Write $(x, y) R^* (z, w)$ to denote the student's judgment that the difference in happiness between courses $z$ and $w$ does not exceed the difference in happiness between courses $x$ and $y$. Note that $R^*$ defines a relation on the set $S \times S$. This type of relation, which is a subset of the set $(S \times S) \times (S \times S)$, is called a *quaternary relation* on $S$ as opposed to a *binary relation*, which is a subset of $S \times S$.

The problem is to find a measure which preserves both $R$ and $R^*$. More precisely, does there exist a real-valued function $u$ defined on the set $S$ such that for all $x, y, z, w$ in $S$,

1.  $u(x) \geqslant u(y)$ if and only if $x R y$, and
2.  $u(x) - u(y) \geqslant u(z) - u(w)$ if and only if $(x, y) R^* (z, w)$?

If $u$ is any real-valued function defined on $S$, then $u$ induces a connected, transitive relation on $S$. Simply define a relation $R'$ by $x R' y$ if and only if $u(x) \geqslant u(y)$. The question can then be posed this way: Is there a real valued function $u$ on $S$ which preserves $R^*$ such that the induced relation $R'$ is identical to the relation $R$?

Consider first the simpler question: Is there a real-valued function on $S$ which preserves the relation $R^*$? Using reasoning similar to that in the proofs of Theorems 1 and 2, one concludes that an affirmative answer can be expected only when $R^*$ is connected and transitive. The exact result is stated in the next theorem.

■ **THEOREM 4**    Suppose $S$ is a set and $R^*$ is a quaternary relation on $S$. If there is a real-valued function $u$ defined on $S$ such that

$$u(x) - u(y) \geqslant u(z) - u(w) \text{ if and only if } (x, y) R^* (z, w),$$

then the relation $R^*$ satisfies four properties:

1.  $R^*$ is connected.
2.  $R^*$ is transitive.
3.  If $(x, y) R^* (z, w)$, then $(x, z) R^* (y, w)$.
4.  If $(x, y) R^* (z, w)$, then $(w, z) R^* (y, x)$.

**Proof**    If $x, y, z$, and $w$ are any elements of $S$, then the real numbers $u(x) - u(y) = A$ and $u(z) - u(w) = B$ must satisfy the inequality $A \geqslant B$ or the inequality $B \leqslant A$. In the former case, $(x, y) R^* (z, w)$, and in the latter, $(z, w) R^* (x, y)$. Thus $R^*$ is connected.

Next, suppose $(x, y) R^* (z, w)$ and $(z, w) R^* (a, b)$, where $x, y, z, w, a, b$ are arbitrary elements of $S$. We have the inequalities

$$u(x) - u(y) \geqslant u(z) - u(w)$$

and

$$u(z) - u(w) \geqslant u(a) - u(b),$$

which imply

$$u(x) - u(y) \geqslant u(a) - u(b),$$

so that $(x, y) R^* (a, b)$. This shows that $R^*$ is transitive.

Condition (3) is satisfied, since if $(x, y) R^* (z, w)$, then

$$u(x) - u(y) \geqslant u(z) - u(w),$$

which implies (by adding like terms to each side of the inequality)

$$u(x) - u(z) \geqslant u(y) - u(w).$$

This inequality, in turn, gives $(x, z) R^* (y, w)$ by the hypothesis on $u$.

The proof that condition (4) holds is left to the reader. □

The four conditions of Theorem 4 are necessary for the existence of the required measure $u$, but unlike the case for binary relations, they turn out not to be sufficient. There exists a finite set and a quaternary relation $R^*$ on it that satisfies the four conditions but for which it is not possible to construct a numerical scale preserving $R^*$.

In a 1958 paper in the *Journal of Symbolic Logic*, Dana Scott and Patrick Suppes prove an even stronger result: If $S$ is a finite set and $R^*$ a quaternary relation on $S$, then there is no finite list of axioms that provides necessary and sufficient conditions for the existence of a real-valued function $u$ preserving $R^*$.

Scott and Suppes cite an example, essentially due to Herman Rubin, that indicates the kind of difficulty that arises in trying to construct a set of necessary and sufficient conditions.

---

**EXAMPLE 13**  A student is presented a list of 10 possible courses. By comparing each of the courses with every other one, her order of preference is determined to be $x_1, x_2, \ldots, x_{10}$. Eleven pairs of courses are given special designations: Denote

$(x_1, x_2)$ by $A$,  $(x_7, x_8)$ by $E$,  $(x_5, x_6)$ by $I$,

$(x_2, x_3)$ by $B$,  $(x_9, x_{10})$ by $F$,  $(x_1, x_5)$ by $J$,

$(x_3, x_4)$ by $C$,  $(x_6, x_7)$ by $G$,  $(x_6, x_{10})$ by $K$.

$(x_4, x_5)$ by $D$,  $(x_8, x_9)$ by $H$,

In each pair, the first course is preferred to the second. Suppose the student perceives $A, B, C, D$ as equal in difference to $E, F, G, H$, respectively, that the difference between courses in $K$ is greater than the difference in courses in $J$ and that the difference in $I$ is greater than the difference in $K$. Then the relations between the remaining pairs may be chosen so that any subset of nine courses can be represented by a measure $u$ which preserves $R^*$, but the full set of 10 courses cannot! The interested reader may wish to work out the details of this example.

---

## V. AN ALTERNATIVE APPROACH

Since it is not possible to discover or prove a Representation Theorem for arbitrary finite sets and quaternary relations, we need to try some alternative approaches to the problem of measurement that will satisfy our complaining student of Section IV. One alternative will be presented in this section and another, called *Utility Theory*, will be discussed in Chapter 8.

The relation $R$ was obtained by asking a subject to compare each pair of elements in a set and to give her judgment on which possesses more of the relevant attribute than the other. The relation $R^*$ was then obtained by asking the subject to compare each pair of elements with every other pair. We can obtain a measure $u$ if we restrict ourselves to asking for comparisons only between pairs when the pairs represent elements that the subject perceives as being consecutive elements in the ordering. If the student has ranked the courses in the order $x_1, x_2, x_3, \ldots, x_n$, then we ask for comparisons when the pairs are $(x_1, x_2), (x_2, x_3), (x_3, x_4), \ldots, (x_{n-1}, x_n)$. The alternative approach based on this idea is stated more carefully in Theorem 5.

■ **THEOREM 5 (SECOND REPRESENTATION THEOREM)**    Let $\alpha = \langle S, R \rangle$ be an ordered relational system where $S = \{x_1, x_2, \ldots, x_n\}$ is the standard ordering on $S$. Let $T$ be the set of all ordered pairs $(x_i, x_j)$ where $j = i + 1$ and let $R^\S$ be a relation on $T$. Then there is a measure $u$ on $\alpha$ satisfying the two conditions:

1. $u(x_i) \geqslant u(x_j)$ if and only if $x_i \, R \, x_j$, and
2. $u(x_{i+1}) - u(x_i) \geqslant u(x_{j+1}) - u(x_j)$ if and only if $(x_i, x_{i+1}) \, R^\S \, (x_j, x_{j+1})$ exactly when $R^\S$ is connected and transitive.

**Proof of Theorem 5**    We outline the proof of sufficiency. Since $T$ is finite and $R^\S$ is connected and transitive, there is a positive-valued measure $m^\S$ for the system $\langle T, R^\S \rangle$. More precisely, $m^\S$ is a function from $T$ to the positive real numbers such that

$$m^\S(x_i, x_{i+1}) \geqslant m^\S(x_j, x_{j+1}) \text{ if and only if } (x_i, x_{i+1}) \, R^\S \, (x_j, x_{j+1}).$$

We can then define a measure $u$ as follows:
Let $u(x_1) = 0$,

$$u(x_2) = u(x_1) + m^\S(x_1, x_2) = m^\S(x_1, x_2),$$
$$u(x_3) = u(x_2) + m^\S(x_2, x_3) = m^\S(x_1, x_2) + m^\S(x_2, x_3),$$
$$u(x_4) = u(x_3) + m^\S(x_3, x_4) = m^\S(x_1, x_2) + m^\S(x_2, x_3) + m^\S(x_3, x_4),$$

$$\cdots$$

$$u(x_k) = u(x_{k-1}) + m^\S(x_{k-1}, x_k) = \sum_{j=1}^{k-1} m^\S(x_j, x_{j+1}),$$

$$\cdots$$

$$u(x_n) = u(x_{n-1}) + m^\S(x_{n-1}, x_n) = \sum_{j=1}^{n-1} m^\S(x_j, x_{j+1}).$$

Since $m^\S(x_j, x_{j+1})$ is nonnegative, it follows that

$$u(x_1) \leqslant u(x_2) \leqslant u(x_3) \leqslant \cdots \leqslant u(x_n)$$

so that $u$ preserves the order on $S$; that is, $u$ preserves the relation $R$. Furthermore, we have

$$u(x_k) - u(x_{k-1}) = m^\S(x_{k-1}, x_k).$$

Thus

$$(x_i, x_{i+1})\, R^\S\, (x_j, x_{j+1})$$

if and only if

$$m^\S(x_i, x_{i+1}) \geqslant m^\S(x_j, x_{j+1}),$$

if and only if

$$u(x_{i+1}) - u(x_i) \geqslant u(x_{j+1}) - u(x_j).$$

Hence the measure $u$ also preserves $R^\S$. This completes the proof of sufficiency. For necessity, see Exercise 29. $\square$

To illustrate the procedure outlined in the proof, suppose we have a set of five elements with standard order $x_1, x_2, x_3, x_4, x_5$. Then the set $T$ consists of four pairs,

$$T = \{(x_1, x_2), (x_2, x_3), (x_3, x_4), (x_4, x_5)\}$$

(see Fig. 7.2). Suppose that examination of the relation $R^\S$ indicates that the standard ordering on $T$ is

$$(x_3, x_4), \quad (x_2, x_3), \quad (x_4, x_5), \quad (x_1, x_2),$$

so that $m^\S(x_3, x_4) \leqslant m^\S(x_2, x_3) \leqslant m^\S(x_4, x_5) \leqslant m^\S(x_1, x_2)$ for every measure $m^\S$ on the system $\langle T, R^\S \rangle$. If scale values of $3, 5, 6, 7$ are chosen for $m^\S$, then the proof of Theorem 5 defines a measure $u$ by

$$u(x_1) = 0,\ u(x_2) = 7,\ u(x_3) = 12,\ u(x_4) = 15,\ u(x_5) = 21.$$

Now the measure $u$ can be used to define a relation $R^u$ on the full set $S \times S$. Define $(x, y)\, R^u (z, w)$ if and only if $u(y) - u(x) \geqslant u(w) - u(z)$. Note that $R^\S$ is a

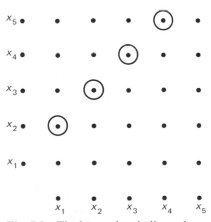

**Fig. 7.2**  The heavy dots indicate the elements of $S \otimes S$. The members of $T$ are circled.

subset of $R^u$, so we might say that $R^u$ extends $R^\S$. As an example, note that since

$$u(x_4) - u(x_2) = 15 - 7 = 8$$

while

$$u(x_5) - u(x_4) = 21 - 5 = 6,$$

we have

$$(x_2, x_4)\, R^u\, (x_4, x_5).$$

The choice of scale values for $m^\S$ is, as we have seen earlier, unique only up to an order-preserving transformation. We might have chosen, with equal validity, scale values of $1, 2, 4, 8$. With these values for $m^\S$, we obtain a measure $v$ on $S$ with

$$v(x_1) = 0, \quad v(x_2) = 8, \quad v(x_3) = 10, \quad v(x_4) = 11, \quad v(x_5) = 15.$$

As in the previous paragraph, we may use $v$ to define a relation $R^v$ on $S \times S$. Again, $R^\S$ will be a subset of $R^v$ so that $R^v$ also extends $R^\S$. Now, however, we will have $v(x_4) - v(x_2) = 11 - 8$ while $v(x_5) - v(x_4) = 15 - 11 = 4$ so that in this extension $(x_4, x_5)\, R^v\, (x_2, x_4)$.

One set of scale values for $m^\S$ is consistent with the student's judgment that there is a greater difference between $x_2$ and $x_4$ than between $x_4$ and $x_5$, while a different set of scale values is not. In this alternative approach, we have agreed not to ask the subject to make comparisons between pairs $(x_2, x_4)$ and $(x_4, x_5)$. This example shows that we cannot determine what judgment the student would make on these pairs solely on the information we have concerning the pairs in the set $T$. The Second Representation Theorem (Theorem 5) then gives a measure $u$ which is a better reflection of the student's attitude toward the courses in the winter term than the ordinal measure $m$, but it does not completely answer the objections raised by the student complaint of Section IV.


## VI.  SOME HISTORICAL NOTES

Although it has been recognized since ancient times that measurement is essential to any scientific theory attempting to explain real-world phenomena, no attempt to study the foundations of measurement theory was made until this century. The German mathematician Otto Ludwig Hölder (1859–1937) published an axiomatization for the measurement of mass in 1901. The general theory of measurement in physics was studied quite extensively by the British physicist Norman Robert Campbell (1880–1949). Campbell noted that the basic quantities measured by physicists all shared two common properties:

1.  Given any two objects, it is always possible to decide which one "possesses" more of the quantity than the other;

2.  There is an operation of combining any two objects that corresponds to the arithmetical operation of addition.

To cite one example, think of the process of determining lengths of a set of straight, rigid rods. If we place two rods side by side so that they coincide at one end, we determine which one is longer by examining the other end and observing which one extends farther. Thus Property (1) is satisfied. For Property (2), note that two or more rods can be combined or *concatenated* by placing them end-to-end in a straight line. The concept of length dictates that the length of such a concatenated rod be the sum of the lengths of the component rods.

In the discussion of ordinal scales in this chapter, we saw how to axiomatize Property (1). Property (2) demands the extra condition that the measure of the concatenation of any two objects be equal to the sum of the measures of the subjects.

Campbell distinguished between two kinds of measurement, which he called "intensive" and "extensive." A measurement is *extensive* if the underlying quantity satisfies Properties (1) and (2) and *intensive* if it satisfies only Property (1). Most psychological and sociological attributes are intensive while most physical properties are extensive in nature.

Measurement theory is now an active branch of all the mathematical social sciences. Much of the current work in this area was stimulated by axiomatic studies undertaken by R. Duncan Luce and Patrick Suppes, beginning in the 1950's.

---

## EXERCISES

---

### II.  WHAT IS MEASUREMENT?

Exercises 1–4 refer to the example of Section II.A.

1.  Prove that $w(A) - w(B)$ if and only if $A * B$ and $B * A$.

2.  How would you describe, using the "$*$" notation, the fact that $A$ is heavier than $B$?

3.  Let $A, B$, and $C$ be any three objects. Show that the following statements are all true:

a)  $A * A$

b)  If $A * B$ and $B * C$, then $A * C$.

c)  Either $A * B$ or $B * A$ or both.

4.  If $w(A) = 1$ and two copies of object $A$ exactly balance one copy of $B$ in a pan balance, does it follow from the procedure outlined in II.A that $w(B) = 2w(A)$? Why? How would you modify the procedure to insure this?

5.  Determine which of the Examples 1–12 are reflexive, symmetric, transitive, and connected.

6.  Let $C$ be the set of all ordered pairs $(a, b)$ of real numbers. Define $(a, b) R(c, d)$ if and only if $a > c$ and $b > d$. Is this relation transitive? Is it connected?

7.  Find an example of a relation that is symmetric and transitive, but is not reflexive. (Consider the relation "$x$ is a sibling of $y$.")

8. Write $x P y$ if $(x, y)$ is an element of the relation $P$ and $x P y$ if $(x, y)$ is not an element. A connected, transitive relation is sometimes referred to as a *weak order*. A *strong order* is a relation $P$ which is transitive and satisfies an "asymmetry" condition: $x P y$ implies $y P x$. Show that any weak order is the union of two disjoint sets, one of which is a strong order and the other is an equivalence relation. An *equivalence relation* is a relation which is reflexive, symmetric, and transitive.

9. Is a strong order always connected? Can it be reflexive?

10. Consider the relations on the set of real numbers determined by the concepts of $>$, $\geqslant$, $=$, $\leqslant$, $<$, $\neq$. Which are weak orders? strong orders? equivalence relations?

11. Let $S$ be the set of integers. Define a relation $R$ by $x R y$ if and only if $x - y$ is a multiple of 5. Show that $R$ is an equivalence relation.

12. Let $S$ be the set of all adults in New England. Define a relation $R$ by $x R y$ if and only if $x$ lives with $y$. Is $R$ an equivalence relation?

13. Let $R$ be an equivalence relation on a set $S$. Split $S$ into subsets by agreeing to put $x$ and $y$ into the same set exactly when $x R y$. Show that this procedure partitions $S$ into a collection of pairwise disjoint subsets. These subsets are called *equivalence classes*. Carry out this process with the relation of Exercise 17; how many equivalence classes are there?

14. Can the process of creating equivalence classes defined in Exercise 13 be carried out if $R$ is not an equivalence relation? Why?

15. A *semi-order* is a relation $P$ on a set $S$ satisfying the following three axioms for all $x, y, z, w$ in $S$:

i) $x P x$

ii) If $x P y$ and $z P w$, then either $x P w$ or $z P y$.

iii) If $x P y$ and $y P z$, then either $x P w$ or $w P z$.

Prove that every semi-order is transitive.

16. Write out a proof for Theorem 1.

### III. SIMPLE MEASURES ON FINITE SETS

17. At what steps in the proof of Theorem 3 is the finiteness of the set $S$ used?

18. Show that procedure of the proof of Theorem 3 leads to $m(z) = 0$, $m(y) = 1$, $m(x) = 2$ for the relation of Example 12.

19. For Example 12, show that the function with scale values $m(x) = -17$, $m(y) = \sqrt{23}$, $m(x) = 10$ also satisfies the definition of a measure.

20. Let $S$ be the set $\{w, x, y, z\}$ and $R$ the relation $\{(w, x), (x, y), (w, y), (w, z), (z, y), (x, z)\}$.

a) Show that $R$ is connected and transitive.

b) Find a measure for this relational system.

21. Suppose that $m$ and $u$ are measures on the relational system $\langle S, R \rangle$ where $S$ is finite. Show that there is an order-preserving function $f: M \to M$ where $M = \{m(x_i)\}$ such that $u(x_i) = f(m(x_i))$ for all $i$.

22. How many different questions of the type "Do you prefer course $i$ to course $j$?" must you ask a student to construct a preference ordering for a set of 70 courses?

23. Show that the relation of Example 9 is connected and transitive, but the system $\langle S, R \rangle$ has no measure in the sense of Theorem 3.

24. A set $S$ is said to be *countably infinite* if there is a one-to-one correspondence between the elements of $S$ and the set of all positive integers. Show that Theorem 3 is true if $S$ is a countably infinite set.

25. a) Let $S$ be the set of all ordered pairs $(a, b)$ of real numbers such that $a = 0$ or 1 and $0 \leqslant b \leqslant 1$. Let $R$ be the lexicographic order on $S$. Does the system $\langle S, R \rangle$ have a measure?

b) Let $T$ be the set of all ordered pairs $(a, b)$ of real numbers such that $a = 0$ and $b$ is either between 0 and 1 or between 2 and 3. Let $R$ be the lexicographic order on $T$. Does the system $\langle T, R \rangle$ have a measure?

## IV. PERCEPTION OF DIFFERENCES

26. Let $u$ be a real-valued function defined on a set $S$. Define a relation $R'$ on $S$ by $x R' y$ if and only if $u(x) \geqslant u(y)$. Show that $R'$ is necessarily reflexive, transitive, and connected. Will $R'$ be symmetric?

27. Prove that condition (4) of Theorem 4 holds.

28. Verify the claims made about Example 13.

## V. AN ALTERNATIVE APPROACH

29. Prove that the conditions in the statement of Theorem 5 are necessary.

30. Show that scale values of $3, 5, 6, 7$ for $m^\S(x_3, x_4), m^\S(x_2, x_3), m^\S(x_4, x_5), m^\S(x_1, x_2)$ yield the measure $u(x_1) = 0$, $u(x_2) = 7$, $u(x_3) = 12$, $u(x_4) = 15$, $u(x_5) = 21$.

31. Show that $R^\S$ is a subset of both $R^u$ and $R^v$.

32. List the members of $R^u$ and $R^v$ explicitly.

33. Use scale values of $2, 3, 5, 10$ instead of $3, 5, 6, 7$ for the function $m^\S$ to determine a measure $w$. Show that in the extension $R^w$ you have $(x_2, x_4) R^w(x_4, x_5)$ and $(x_4, x_5) R^w(x_2, x_4)$.

34. Concatenation on a set $S$ may be defined formally as a function $f$ from $S \times S$ to $S$. We denote $f(x, y)$ by $x \triangle y$.

a) Give an example of a concatenation such that $x \triangle y \neq y \triangle x$.

b) A concatenation is said to be *associative* if $x \triangle (y \triangle w) = (x \triangle y) \triangle w$ for all $x, y, w$ in $S$. If $\triangle$ is an associative concatenation, show that the following definition is unambiguous: "If $n$ is a positive integer, then $nx$ is defined to be $x$ concatenated with itself $n$ times; e.g., $2x = x \triangle x$."

35. An *extensive measurement system* is axiomatically defined as a triple $\langle S, R, \triangle \rangle$ where $S$ is a set, $R$ is a connected and transitive relation on $S$, and $\triangle$ is an associative concatenation on $S$ satisfying the following four properties:

i) If $x R y$, then $(x \triangle z) R (y \triangle z)$.

ii) If $x R y$, then there exists a $w$ in $S$ such that $x R (y \triangle w)$ and $(y \triangle w) R x$.

iii) $(x \triangle y) R x$

iv) If $x R y$, then there is a positive integer $n$ such that $y R nx$ for all $x, y, z$ in $S$.

Prove the following Representation Theorem: If $\langle S, R, \triangle \rangle$ is an extensive measurement system, then there is a real-valued function $m$ defined on $S$ such that:

$$m(x) \leqslant m(y) \text{ if and only if } x\,R\,y$$

and

$$m(x \triangle y) = m(x) + m(y)$$

for all $x$ and $y$ in $S$.

36. Show that the function $m$ guaranteed by the theorem in Exercise 35 is unique up to multiplication by a positive constant.

37. Show that the ordinary conceptions of length and weight satisfy the axioms of an extensive measurement system.

## SUGGESTED PROJECTS

1. A *quasi-measure* on a relational system $\langle S, R \rangle$ is a real-valued function $m$ defined on $S$ such that $m(x) \geqslant m(y)$ if $x\,R\,y$. We do not require that $x\,R\,y$ whenever $m(x) \geqslant m(y)$. What are necessary and sufficient conditions for the existence of quasi-measures? What are the analogues of the Representation Theorems presented in this chapter for quasi-measures? Identify some real-world quasi-measures.

2. Find necessary and sufficient conditions on a relation defined on an infinite set that will guarantee the existence of a measure in the sense of Theorem 3. Keep in mind Exercises 23–25.

3. It has been argued that in many situations, observed equality relations may not be transitive. A person may judge rod $x$ as long as rod $y$ which in turn is judged as long as rod $z$; yet $x$ may be judged longer than $z$. Such judgments arise whenever the differences between $x$ and $y$ and between $y$ and $z$ are too small to be noticed. The combined difference, however, may be sufficiently large to make a difference between $x$ and $z$ noticeable. The classic example is a sequence of cups of coffee each containing one more grain of sugar than the previous cup. An observer could probably detect no difference in sweetness between two adjacent cups. If "equally sweet" is a transitive relation, then we would have to conclude that a cup with no sugar in it is as sweet as one in which 10 teaspoons of sugar have been dissolved!

To handle such situations, R. Duncan Luce introduced the idea of a semi-order as the type of relation to capture the notion of strict preference (See Exercise 15). If $P$ is a semi-order, then an indifference relation $I$ can be defined by $x\,I\,y$ if and only if neither $x\,P\,y$ nor $y\,P\,x$. Show that $I$ is reflexive and symmetric, but not necessarily transitive. Prove the following Representation Theorem: If $P$ is a semi-order on a finite set $S$, then there is a real-valued function $f$ defined on $S$ and a positive number $\delta$ such that for all $x$ and $y$ in $S$,

$$f(x) > g(y) + \delta \text{ if and only if } x\,P\,y.$$

The constant $\delta$ may be interpreted as a single "just noticeable difference" unit. Is this Representation Theorem true for infinite sets?

4. Some mathematical psychologists have investigated attributes which appear to have a property somewhat analogous to a physical concatenation operation. This is the property that for each pair of objects $x$ and $y$, there is a third object which lies "halfway"

between $x$ and $y$ in terms of possession of the attribute under study. For example, a subject may be presented with two tones of different loudness and asked to adjust a variable tone until its subjective intensity "bisects" the loudness of the given pair.

A *bisection system* is a triple $\langle S, R, B \rangle$ where $R$ is a connected, transitive relation on a set $S$, and $B$, the bisection operation, is a function from $S \times S$ to $S$. The element $B(x, y)$ is interpreted as the subject "midpoint" between $x$ and $y$.

Find a reasonable set of axioms on the function $B$ which guarantees the existence of a real-valued scale $f$ defined on $S$ which preserves the relation $R$ and such that the scale value assigned to the "midpoint" is a weighted average of the scale values of the "endpoints."

## REFERENCES

The most comprehensive recent work on measurement theory is the two-volume study of David Krantz, R. Duncan Luce, Patrick Suppes, and Amos Tversky, *Foundations of Measurement* (New York: Academic Press, 1972). See also L. Pfanzagl, *Theory of Measurement* (New York: Wiley, 1968)—especially for a treatment of bisection systems; Chapter 2; "Psychological measurement theory" of Clyde H. Coombs, Robyn M. Dawes, and Amos Tversky, *Mathematical Psychology: An Elementary Introduction* (Englewood Cliffs: Prentice-Hall, 1970); and Patrick Suppes and Joseph L. Zinnes, "Basic measurement theory" in R. Duncan Luce, Robert R. Bush, and Eugene Galanter, *Handbook of Mathematical Psychology* (New York: Wiley, 1963), Vol. I, pp. 1–76.

For measurement theory aimed toward applications in sociology, consult P. Abell, "Measurement in sociology," *Sociology* 2 (1968), 1–20 and 3 (1969), 397–411; Chapter 2 of James S. Coleman, *Introduction to Mathematical Sociology* (Glencoe: Free Press, 1964); and Chapter 7 of Thomas J. Fararo, *Mathematical Sociology: An Introduction to Fundamentals* (New York: Wiley, 1973).

Significant earlier works are:

Campbell, N. R., *Physics: The Elements* (London: Cambridge University Press, 1920), republished as *Foundations of Science* (New York: Dover, 1957) and *An Account of the Principles of Measurements and Calculations* (London: Longmans, Green, 1928).

Hölder, Otto, "Die axiome der quantität und die lehre von mass," *Berichte Über Die Berhandlungen Der Könglich Sächsischen Gesellschaft Der Wissenschaften Zu Leipzig, Mathematisch-Physische Classe* 53 (1901), 1–64.

Luce, R. Duncan, "Semi-orders and a theory of utility discrimination," *Econometrica* 24 (1956), 178–191 and *Individual Choice Behavior* (New York: Wiley, 1959).

Scott, Dana, and Patrick Suppes, "Foundational aspects of theories of measurement," *Journal of Symbolic Logic* 23 (1958), 113–128.

Suppes, Patrick, "A set of independent axioms for extensive quantities," *Portugaliae Mathematica* 10 (1951), 163–172.

# 8

# Introduction to Utility Theory

Some reckon time by stars,
And some by hours;
Some measure days by Dreams,
And some by flowers;
My heart alone records
My days and hours.

Madison Cawein

## I. INTRODUCTION

This chapter continues the axiomatic discussion, begun in Chapter 7, of certain aspects of measurement theory. The problem that motivated the development of the material in the preceding chapter is considered again, from a new point of view. The problem is to construct a numerical measurement of "happiness"; in particular, to assign numbers that measure how happy a particular student would be if she were assigned various different courses by the college's registrar.

The point of view of this chapter is called *utility theory*. The theory dates back at least two hundred years to a time when nobles of the French court asked mathematicians for advice on how to gamble. Quite a rich theory has been developed and various aspects of it have been tested experimentally in situations requiring decision making with incomplete knowledge.

Consider the set $S$ of possible choices of courses to which the student might be assigned. Using the mechanisms of Chapter 7, or some other scheme, it is determined that the student prefers course $x$ over course $y$ and course $y$ over course $z$. Utility theory aims to assign numerical weights to these preferences.

Suppose we offer the student a choice: she may have course $y$, her intermediate choice, or she may flip a coin. If the coin comes up heads, she gets course $x$, while if it comes up tails, she gets course $z$. Which option does she prefer: the certainty of $y$ or the gamble between $x$ and $z$?

If the coin is weighted so that it always comes up heads, then she will certainly always prefer the gamble: there is a certainty that she will receive her first choice. If the coin is weighted so that it always lands with tails showing, then she will forego the gamble and take course $y$.

Suppose the coin is an honest one so that the likelihood of winning $x$ on the flip is the same as winning $z$. What can we say if the student prefers course $y$ to a gamble with an honest coin? We should be able to deduce that she perceives the difference in happiness between $x$ and $y$ to be less than the difference between $y$ and $z$. (Why?)

The theory of utility is based on the assumption that there is a way of weighting the coin so that the student has no preference between the gamble and the certainty. This ideal weight can then be translated into a measure of happiness about the course $y$.

The remainder of this chapter develops a mathematical model reflecting the ideas of this previous paragraph.

## II. GAMBLES

In developing utility theory, it is convenient to introduce two binary relations on the set $S$, one based on strict preference ($P$) and one on indifference ($I$).

**DEFINITION**   **If $S$ is a set and $P$ is a binary relation on $S$, define the *indifference relation* $x\,I\,y$ for any pair of elements $x$ and $y$ of $S$ if and only if neither $x\,P\,y$ or $y\,P\,x$.**

The first theorem indicates why this is an important relation.

■ **THEOREM 1**    Suppose $u$ is a real-valued function defined on $S$ such that $u(x) > u(y)$ if and only if $x\,P\,y$. Then the following conditions hold:

1. Given any two elements $x$ and $y$ of $S$, exactly one of three possibilities is true: $x\,P\,y$, $y\,P\,x$, or $x\,I\,y$;
2. $P$ is transitive;
3. $I$ is reflexive, symmetric, and transitive;
4. If $x\,P\,y$ and $y\,I\,z$, then $x\,P\,z$; and
5. If $x\,I\,y$ and $y\,P\,z$, then $x\,P\,z$.

*Proof of Theorem 1*    The proof depends upon the elementary-order properties of the real numbers and is similar in spirit to the proofs studied in Chapter 7. Condition (4) will be proved here; the other properties are left as an exercise for the reader.

Suppose then that $x\,P\,y$ and $y\,I\,z$. Consider the numbers $u(y)$ and $u(z)$. If $u(y) > u(z)$, then we would have $y\,P\,z$, while if $u(z) > u(y)$, we must have $z\,P\,y$. Since neither $y\,P\,z$ nor $z\,P\,y$, we must have $u(y) = u(z)$. But $x\,P\,y$ gives $u(x) > u(y)$ and, hence, $u(x) > u(z)$. Thus $x\,P\,z$. □

We come now to the crucial definition for utility theory.

**DEFINITION**    Let $x$ and $y$ be any two elements of a set $S$ and let $p$ be a number, $0 \leqslant p \leqslant 1$. Then the symbol $px + (1 - p)y$ represents the *gamble*, or *lottery*, that has two possible outcomes, $x$ and $y$, with probabilities $p$ and $1 - p$, respectively.

The phrase "probability" $p$ may be interpreted as meaning roughly that if the gamble is repeated a very large number of times, we may expect outcome $x$ to occur about $100p$ percent of the time. For example, think of the symbol $.25x + .75y$ as representing the gamble of flipping a coin that has been weighted so that it turns up heads (outcome $x$), on the average, 25 percent of the time. Alternatively, imagine a coin that comes up tails three times as often as heads, but has no predictable pattern.

The gamble $1x + 0y$ is simply denoted as $x$.

Gambles with three or more possible outcomes may also be defined. The symbol $px + qy + (1 - p - q)z$ would represent a gamble with three possible outcomes, $x, y$, and $z$, having probabilities $p, q, 1 - p - q$, respectively, where $p$ and $q$ are nonnegative numbers whose sum is at most 1.

It is also possible to consider gambles in which one of the possible outcomes is itself a gamble. Suppose, for example, you are offered this proposition:

Flip a coin. If it comes up heads, you receive a new automobile (outcome $x$). If it comes up tails, then you roll a die. If the die shows a "3" you win a radio (outcome $y$); otherwise you lose \$10,000 (outcome $z$).

Assuming that the coin and the die are "honest," this compound gamble can be represented as

$$\frac{1}{2}x + \frac{1}{2}\left(\frac{1}{6}y + \frac{5}{6}z\right).$$

If this particular gamble were repeated a large number of times, say 12,000, what should happen? The coin should turn up heads about 6000 times and tails 6000 times. For the 6000 rolls of the die, we should see a "3" about 1000 times and one of the other five numbers about 5000 times. Thus we should expect $x$ to be the outcome about $\frac{1}{2}$ of the time, $y$ about $\frac{1}{12}$ of the time and $z$ about $\frac{5}{12}$ of the time. This means that the gamble should be equivalent to a gamble with three outcomes $x, y, z$, having respective probabilities of $\frac{1}{2}$, $\frac{1}{12}$ and $\frac{5}{12}$; that is, the gamble

$$\frac{1}{2}x + \frac{1}{2}\left(\frac{1}{6}y + \frac{5}{6}z\right)$$

is equivalent to the gamble

$$\frac{1}{2}x + \frac{1}{12}y + \frac{5}{12}z.$$

Since the two gambles are equivalent, any reasonable person should be indifferent if offered a choice between them. There is no reason to prefer one of the gambles over the other.

## III. AXIOMS OF UTILITY THEORY

A utility measure on a set $S$ is determined by establishing preferences among the elements of the set of all gambles with outcomes in $S$. Some of these preferences will necessarily be dictated by the preference and indifference relations, $P$ and $I$, which hold among the elements of $S$. For example, if the student prefers course $x$ to $y$, then she should prefer the gamble $.7x + .3y$ to the gamble $.7y + .3x$, since the preferred outcome is more likely in the first gamble than in the second.

Utility theory assumes that there are binary relations $P$ and $I$ on the set of gambles with outcomes in $S$ that are consistent with the already established preference and indifference relations on $S$, satisfy the conditions (1)–(5) of Theorem 1, and also satisfy some additional reasonable axioms.

The first three axioms simply assert that the student should be indifferent if offered a choice between essentially equivalent gambles. Formally, these axioms look like this:

For all $x, y, z$ in $S$ and all real numbers $p, 0 \leqslant p \leqslant 1$,

**AXIOM 1**    $[px + (1 - p)y] I [(1 - p)y + px]$.

**AXIOM 2**  $[px + (1 - p)\{qy + (1 - q)z\}] I [px + (1 - p)qy + (1 - p)(1 - q)z]$
**where $q$ is any number, $0 \leqslant q \leqslant 1$.**

**AXIOM 3**  $[px + (1 - p)x] I x.$

Consider now two gambles: $.3x + .7z$ and $.3y + .7z$. In both gambles, outcome $z$ has probability $\frac{7}{10}$ and the other outcome has probability $\frac{3}{10}$. Which gamble would the student prefer? Clearly it should depend on her preference between outcomes $x$ and $y$. If she prefers $x$ to $y$, then she should prefer the first gamble to the second and if she is indifferent between $x$ and $y$, then there is no reason for her to prefer one gamble over the other. This example indicates that two additional axioms are reasonable.

**AXIOM 4    If $x P y$, then for any $p > 0$, $[px + (1 - p)z] P [py + (1 - p)z].$**

**AXIOM 5    If $x I y$, then for any $p$, $[px + (1 - p)z] I [py + (1 - p)z].$**

To see how these axioms fit together, suppose that the student prefers course $x$ to course $z$. Then if she is offered two different gambles with $x$ and $z$ as the outcomes, she should prefer the gamble in which there is a greater likelihood of outcome $x$. Axioms 1–5 enable us to prove this result.

■ **THEOREM 2**    If $x P y$ and $p$ and $q$ are numbers with $0 < q < p < 1$, then

$$[px + (1 - p)y] P [qx + (1 - q)y].$$

***Proof of Theorem 2***    Since $0 < q < p < 1$, we have $0 < p - q < 1 - q$, and by Axiom 3,

$$y I \left[ \frac{p - q}{1 - q} y + \frac{1 - p}{1 - q} y \right].$$

Axiom 4 gives

$$\left[ \frac{p - q}{1 - q} x + \frac{1 - p}{1 - q} y \right] P \left[ \frac{p - q}{1 - q} y + \frac{1 - p}{1 - q} y \right] I y.$$

Let $z$ denote the gamble

$$z = \frac{p - q}{1 - q} x + \frac{1 - p}{1 - q} y$$

so that we have, using condition (4) of Theorem 1, $z P y$. The gamble $px + (1 - p)y$ is equivalent to the gamble $qx + (1 - q)z$ so that

$$[px + (1 - p)y] I [qx + (1 - q)z].$$

Using Axiom 4 again, we have $[qx + (1 - q)z] P [qx + (1 - q)y]$. Transitivity of $P$ completes the proof. □

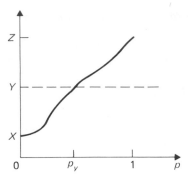

**Fig. 8.1**  Graph of the measure
of the gamble $px + (1 - p)z$ as a
function of $p$.  The letters $X$, $Y$, $Z$
indicate the measures of the
gambles $x$, $y$, $z$, respectively.  If
the measure is a continuous
function of $p$ and if $Y$ lies
between $X$ and $Z$, then for some
$p_y$ between 0 and 1, the measure
of $p_y x + (1 - p_y)z$ should be $Y$.

A utility measure will be defined on the set of all gambles with outcomes in
$S$ in such a way that the measure of one gamble will be greater than the measure
of another exactly when the first gamble is preferred to the second.  The measures
will be identical if there is indifference between the gambles.

To establish the existence of such a measure, we require one additional
axiom.  Consider the gamble $px + (1 - p)z$.  If $p = 0$, then this gamble is equivalent to the certainty of outcome $z$, while if $p = 1$, then the gamble is identified
with the outcome $x$.  It seems reasonable that a slight change in the value of $p$
should result only in a small change in the utility measure of the gamble.  Thus
as $p$ varies continuously from 0 to 1, the utility measure of $px + (1 - p)z$ should
vary continuously from the measure of $z$ to the measure of $x$.  If $y$ is some outcome whose measure lies between the measure of $z$ and the measure of $x$, then
the intermediate value theorem of elementary calculus would assert that there
is at least one value of $p$ for which the measure of $y$ is equal to the measure of
$px + (1 - p)z$.  (See Fig. 8.1.)

The final axiom captures this idea in terms of the preference and indifference
relations:

**AXIOM 6**   **If $x, y$ and $z$ are elements of $S$ with $x P y$ and $y P z$, there is at least
one number $p$, $0 \leqslant p \leqslant 1$, such that $[px + (1 - p)z] I y$.**

Axiom 6 asserts that there is always some gamble which is indifferent to
the certainty of $y$ and whose prescribed outcomes are two events, one preferred
to $y$ and one preferred less than $y$.  In fact, there is exactly one such gamble.

■ *THEOREM 3*    If $x P y$, $y P z$ and $[px + (1 - p)z] I y$, then $p$ is unique.  Furthermore, $p$ is strictly between 0 and 1; that is, $0 < p < 1$.

*Proof of Theorem 3*    If $p = 0$, then the gamble $px + (1 - p)z$ is equivalent to the outcome $z$ and we would have $z I y$, which violates the assumption that $y P z$.  A similar argument shows that $p$ cannot be equal to 1.

Now let $q$ be any number between 0 and 1 which is not equal to $p$, but such that $[qx + (1 - q)z] I y$.  The transitivity of $I$ implies that

$$[qx + (1 - q)z] I [px + (1 - p)z].$$

This, however, contradicts Theorem 2.  □

## IV. EXISTENCE AND UNIQUENESS OF UTILITY

### A. Existence

The axioms and theorems of Section III provide the ammunition to state and prove a representation theorem for utility functions.  Compare Theorem 4 below with Theorems 3 and 5 of Chapter 7.

■ *THEOREM 4 (THIRD REPRESENTATION THEOREM)*    There is a real-valued function $u$ defined on $S$ such that

1. $u(x) > u(y)$ if and only if $x P y$,

and

2. $u(px + (1 - p)y) = pu(x) + (1 - p)u(y)$

for every pair of elements $x$ and $y$ of $S$ and every real number $p$, $0 \leqslant p \leqslant 1$.

*Proof of Theorem 4*    Suppose first that $x I y$ for all $x$ and $y$ in $S$.  In this case, let $u(x) = 0$ for all elements $x$ of $S$.  It is a triviality that (1) and (2) are satisfied.  If there is not complete indifference, then find some pair of elements $x_1$ and $x_0$ in $S$ with $x_1 P x_0$.  Define $u(x_0) = 0$ and $u(x_1) = 1$.  Now let $x$ be any other element in $S$.  There are five possibilities to consider:

a) $x I x_0$
b) $x I x_1$
c) $x_1 P x$ and $x P x_0$
d) $x P x_1$
e) $x_0 P x$

We show how to define $u(x)$ in each of these cases.  See Fig. 8.2.

*Case (a)*    If $x I x_0$, let $u(x) = u(x_0) = 0$.

*Case (b)*    If $x I x_1$, let $u(x) = u(x_1) = 1$.

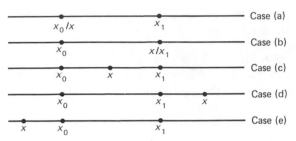

**Fig. 8.2**  Schematic representation of the five cases in the Third Representation Theorem.

*Case (c)*    If $x_1 P x$ and $x P x_0$, then there is a unique number $p$, $0 < p < 1$, such that $[px_1 + (1 - p)x_0] I x$. Define $u(x) = p$. Note that $u(x_0) < u(x) < u(x_1)$.

*Case (d)*    If $x P x_1$, then $x_1$ is intermediate between $x_0$ and $x$. There is a unique number $q$, $0 < q < 1$, such that $[qx + (1 - q)x_0] I x_1$. Define $u(x) = 1/q$. Note that $u(x) > 1 = u(x_1)$.

*Case (e)*    If $x_0 P x$, then $x_0$ is intermediate between $x$ and $x_1$ and there is a unique number $r$, $0 < r < 1$, such that $[rx_1 + (1 - \overset{\bullet}{r})x] I x_0$. Define $u(x) = r/(r - 1)$. Note that $u(x) < 0 = u(x_0)$ in this case.

In this manner, we define $u(x)$ for each element $x$ of $S$. It must be shown that this function satisfies conditions (1) and (2) in the statement of the theorem. Toward this end, let $x$ and $y$ be any two elements in $S$. There are actually 25 cases to consider, depending on whether each of the two elements, $x$ and $y$, lies in Cases (a), (b), (c), (d), or (e). In some of the cases, it is immediate that conditions (1) and (2) must hold. This happens, for example, if both elements are indifferent to $x_0$. We will consider in detail a typical nontrivial case: the one in which both $x$ and $y$ belong to Case (c).

Suppose, then, that $u(x) = p_1$ and $u(y) = p_2$. Let $A$ be the gamble $p_1x_1 + (1 - p_1)x_0$ and let $B$ be the gamble $p_2x_1 + (1 - p_2)x_0$. By definition of the function $u$, we have $A I x$ and $B I y$.

If $p_1 = p_2$, $A$ and $B$ are the same gamble, so that $A I x$ and $A I y$. Since $I$ is a symmetric and transitive relation, we have $x I y$.

If $p_1 > p_2$, then Theorem 2 (with $p = p_1, q = p_2, x = x_1, y = x_0$) gives $A P B$. Axioms 4 and 5 then imply that $x P y$.

Similarly, should $p_1$ be less than $p_2$, the application of Theorem 2 and Axioms 4 and 5 yields $y P x$.

This establishes condition (1).

To prove that condition (2) is true, let $p$ be any real number between 0 and 1. Strictly speaking, we have not yet defined the utility measure of the gamble $px + (1 - p)y$. On the other hand, since $x_1 P x P x_0$ and $x_1 P y P x_0$, Axiom 4 gives $x_1 P [px + (1 - p)y] P x_0$. The same definition of $u$ as above can be used if there is a number $p^*$ such that $[px + (1 - p)y] I [p^*x_1 + (1 - p^*)x_0]$. This is easy to find:

Since $A\,I\,x$ and $B\,I\,y$, Axiom 5 yields $[px + (1 - p)y]\,I\,[pA + (1 - p)B]$ but

$$[pA + (1 - p)B]\,I\,[p\{p_1x_1 + (1 - p_1)x_0\} + (1 - p)\{p_2x_1 + (1 - p_2)x_0\}]$$
$$I\,\{pp_1 + (1 - p)p_2\}x_1 \qquad + \{p(1 - p_1) + (1 - p)(1 - p_2)\}x_0$$
$$I\,\{pp_1 + (1 - p)p_2\}x_1 \qquad + \{1 - (pp_1 + (1 - p)p_2)\}x_0$$

so that $p^* = pp_1 + (1 - p)p_2$ and $u(px + (1 - p)y) = p^* = pu(x) + (1 - p)u(y)$.

The proofs that conditions (1) and (2) hold in the remaining cases are quite similar and are left to the reader. $\square$

## B. Uniqueness of Utility

How much freedom is there in the choice of scale values for the utility function? Recall that scale value for a measure on a binary relational system $\langle S, R \rangle$ was unique up to an order–preserving transformation. For a utility function, there is less freedom. The scale is unique up to changes by a positive linear transformation.

**DEFINITION   A real-valued function $L$ defined on a set $T$ of real numbers is a positive linear transformation if there are constants $\alpha$ and $\beta$ where $\alpha > 0$ such that $L(t) = \alpha t + \beta$ for every $t$ in $T$.**

As an example, let $T$ be the set of numbers between 0 and 100 and consider the positive linear transformation $L(t) = (9/5)t + 32$. Then $L(0) = 32$, $L(40) = 104$ and $L(100) = 212$. This linear transformation may be familiar to you as the one which converts Celsius temperatures to Fahrenheit temperatures.

■ *THEOREM 5*   If $u$ is a utility function in the sense of Theorem 4 and $L$ is a positive linear transformation, then $u^* = L \circ u$ is also a utility function.

*Proof of Theorem 5*   Suppose $L(t) = \alpha t + \beta$ so that $u^*(x) = L(u(x)) = \alpha u(x) + \beta$. Then the inequality

$$u^*(x) > u^*(y)$$

is the same as

$$\alpha u(x) + \beta > \alpha u(y) + \beta$$

or

$$\alpha u(x) > \alpha u(y).$$

Since $\alpha$ is positive, we have $u^*(x) > u^*(y)$ exactly when $u(x) > u(y)$; that is, exactly when $x\,P\,y$.

Similarly,

$$pu^*(x) + (1 - p)u^*(y) = p(\alpha u(x) + \beta) + (1 - p)(\alpha u(y) + \beta)$$
$$= \alpha pu(x) + \alpha(1 - p)u(y) + (p + 1 - p)\beta$$
$$= \alpha[pu(x) + (1 - p)u(y)] + \beta$$
$$= \alpha[u(px + (1 - p)y)] + \beta$$
$$= u^*(px + (1 - p)y),$$

the next to the last equality holding since $u$ satisfies condition (2) of Theorem 4. Thus the function $u^*$ also satisfies condition (2). This completes the proof that $u^*$ is a utility function. $\square$

■ *THEOREM 6*   If $u$ and $v$ are utility functions in the sense of Theorem 4, then there is positive linear transformation $L$ so that $v = L \circ u$.

*Proof of Theorem 6*   Since $x_1 \, P \, x_0$, we must have $v(x_1) > v(x_0)$ so that $v(x_1) - v(x_0) > 0$. Define the positive linear transformation $L(t) = \alpha t + \beta$ by $\beta = v(x_0)$ and $\alpha = v(x_1) - v(x_0)$.

Now let $x$ be any element of $S$. There are five cases to be considered, depending on which of the possibilities (a)–(e) of Theorem 4 is true. We give the proof in two cases:

*Case (c)*   Here $x_1 \, P \, x \, P \, x_0$.

If $u(x) = p$, then $x \, I \, [px_1 + (1 - p)x_0]$ so that $v(x) = v(px_1 + (1 - p)x_0)$ since $v$ preserves $I$. Now the right-hand side can be written as

$$pv(x_1) + (1 - p)v(x_0)$$

since $v$ satisfies condition (2) of Theorem 4. Thus

$$v(x) = pv(x_1) + (1 - p)v(x_0)$$
$$= p(\alpha + \beta) + (1 - p)\beta = p\alpha + \beta = \alpha u(x) + \beta = L(u(x)).$$

*Case (e)*   Here $x \, P \, x_1$.

If $u(x) = p$, set $q = 1/p$ so that $x_1 \, I \, [qx + (1 - q)x_0]$. Again we have $v(x_1) = v(qx + (1 - q)x_0) = qv(x) + (1 - q)v(x_0)$ since $v$ preserves $I$ and satisfies condition (2) of a utility function. Solving for $v(x)$, we obtain

$$v(x) = (1/q)[v(x_1) - (1 - q)v(x_0)]$$
$$= p[\alpha + \beta - (1 - q)\beta]$$
$$= p(\alpha + q\beta) = p\alpha + (pq)\beta = p\alpha + \beta \text{ (since } pq = 1)$$
$$= \alpha u(x) + \beta = L(u(x)).$$

The remaining three cases are left for the reader to verify. $\square$

The proof of Theorem 6 indicates that once values $v(x_1)$ and $v(x_0)$ are chosen for any two nonindifferent outcomes $x_1$ and $x_0$, the utility function $v$ is completely determined, not only for the elements of $S$, but for all gambles with outcomes in $S$.


## V. CLASSIFICATION OF SCALES

Scales which are invariant under positive linear transformations are called *interval scales*. Recall that a scale which is invariant under monotone transformations, such as that given in the First Representation Theorem of Chapter 7, was called an ordinal scale. The idea of classifying scales and measurement functions by the types of transformations that preserve the underlying binary relations is due to the American psychologist S. S. Stevens. In his papers, dating from 1946, Stevens isolates five major types of scales: nominal, ordinal, interval, ratio, and absolute. These are listed in order of increasing restrictions on the type of transformation permitted.

*Nominal scales* are invariant under all one-to-one transformations and are used when the basic empirical observation to be measured is the determination of equality; a standard example is the assignment of numbers to the jerseys of football players on a team: two different players wear two different numbers. As we have seen, the *ordinal scale* is employed when the empirical operation is the determination of "greater or less." *Interval scales* reflect the operation of determining ratios of differences. The measurement of temperature is a good example of an interval scale measurement. The Fahrenheit and Celsius scales are positive linear transformations of each other. As we have seen, the transformation $L(t) = (9/5)t + 32$ converts Celsius to Fahrenheit. The transformation $L^*(t) = (5/9)t - (32/9)$ converts Fahrenheit to Celsius. *Ratio scales* are those invariant under similarity transformations; that is, functions of the form $S(t) = \alpha t$ where $\alpha$ is a positive constant. The underlying empirical observation here is the determination of ratios and is exemplified by the measurement of length, weight, density, loudness, and pitch. Thus, it makes sense to say that one rod is twice as long as another, while it does not make sense to assert that one body of water is twice as hot as another. In the *absolute scale*, only the trivial identity transformation is permitted. Counting, interpreted as an act of measurement, is an example of an absolute scale.

Of the three Representation Theorems, the final one, involving the idea of a utility function and an interval scale, gives the most information about how a subject assesses a set of objects for the degree to which a certain attribute is present. To find out if the student prefers course $x$ to course $y$, it is only necessary to compare the numbers $u(x)$ and $u(y)$. Furthermore, the utility function predicts how the student would rate the differences between pairs of courses.

To see how this is done, suppose the student's ordering of courses is $x, y, z, w$ so that $u(x) < u(y) < u(z) < u(w)$. Offer the student two gambles

$$.5x + .5w \qquad \text{and} \qquad .5y + .5z.$$

If the preference is the first gamble to the second, then

$$u(.5x + .5w) > u(.5y + .5z)$$

so that

$$.5u(x) + .5u(w) > .5u(y) + .5u(z)$$

or

$$u(x) + u(w) > u(y) + u(z),$$

implying that

$$u(w) - u(z) > u(y) - u(x).$$

Thus, the student perceives the difference between $z$ and $w$ to be greater than the difference between $x$ and $y$. Should the student prefer the second gamble to the first, we can make the opposite conclusion.

## VI. INTERPERSONAL COMPARISON OF UTILITY

Suppose the approach of utility theory is used to formulate the Registrar's Problem of Chapter 7. Determine for each student numerical scale values which measure that student's satisfaction with the courses being offered. One further refinement is necessary before we try to solve the Registrar's Problem.

Examine a very simple example. Suppose every student except Bob and Fred has been assigned to some course. There are two enrollment slots left, one in a course on Soviet Literature and one in a class called Presidential Campaigning. Utility values for these students and courses are given in Table 8.1.

Which student should be assigned to which course? There are only two possibilities available. If Bob is assigned to Soviet Literature and Fred to Presidential Campaigning, then adding the corresponding utilities gives $50 + 1.7 = 51.7$ while if Fred is enrolled in the literature course and Bob in the other one, we have $1.6 + 70 = 71.6$.

It seems that the second assignment increases the total satisfaction of the student body more than the first. Recall, however, that the scale values for a utility function are unique only up to a linear transformation. If each of Fred's scale values is multiplied by 300, say, his preferences are still preserved. The resulting scale values are indicated in Table 8.2.

With these values, the first assignment (Bob in Soviet Literature, Fred in Presidential Campaigning) increases satisfaction by $50 + 510 = 560$ while the alternative assignment increases total happiness by only $70 + 480 = 550$. Now the first assignment seems better.

This example shows that the particular choices of scale values affect in a crucial way the solution of the Registrar's Problem. There is no clear, unambiguous solution to the problem because there is as yet no single absolute scale against which to measure the utilities of different individuals. Difficulties arise

**Table 8.1**

|                          | Bob | Fred |
| ------------------------ | --- | ---- |
| Soviet literature        | 50  | 1.6  |
| Presidential campaigning | 70  | 1.7  |

**Table 8.2**

|                          | Bob | Fred |
| ------------------------ | --- | ---- |
| Soviet literature        | 50  | 480  |
| Presidential campaigning | 70  | 510  |

because the given information does not indicate whether Bob's rating a course with 70 is a particularly high or particularly low rating for him. A similar comment holds for Fred's ratings. It makes a great difference in the assignment of courses if Bob's highest rating for a course is a 700 or if it is only a 75. There are, however, several ways of attempting to avoid the indicated difficulty. One way is to construct an absolute scale that forces the interpersonal comparison of utilities.

Suppose that the lowest rating a student gives to any course is $A$ and the highest rating is $B$. Then the linear transformation

$$L(t) = \frac{1}{B-A} t - \frac{A}{B-A}$$

has the property that $L(A) = 0$, $L(B) = 1$ and $0 \leqslant L(t) \leqslant 1$ for all $t$, $A \leqslant t \leqslant B$. Thus if a student's utility function is bounded above and below by numbers $B$ and $A$, respectively, it is possible to rescale his utility measure so that all the scale values lie between 0 and 1. A measure of 70 will be rescaled closer to 1 if the highest rating is a 75 than it will be if the highest rating is a 700.

Continuing with the example, suppose all of Bob's original scale values lie between 0 and 100. Then $A = 0$, $B = 100$ and the required positive linear transformation is $L_B(t) = t/100$. If Fred's original choice of scale values ran between 1 and 2, then the normalizing transformation is

$$L_F(t) = \frac{1}{2-(-1)} t - \frac{-1}{2-(-1)} = \frac{t+1}{3}.$$

These transformations give $L_B(50) = .5$, $L_B(70) = .7$, $L_F(1.6) = .866$, and $L_F(1.7) = .9$. The normalized scale values are also indicated in Table 8.3.

With these values, the first assignment results in an increase of satisfaction of $.5 + .9 = 1.4$ while the second assignment gives $.7 + .866 = 1.566$. The second assignment is preferred to the first if all scales are normalized to lie between 0 and 1. In formulating the Registrar's Problem, we will always choose the numbers $r_{ij}$ to be such normalized utility measurements.

This normalization—which makes possible an interpersonal comparison of utilities—is possible whenever all individuals in the group being studied have original bounded utility functions. Will utility measures necessarily be bounded? The Third Representation Theorem makes no restriction on the size of the set $S$. It may be finite or infinite. If the domain of a utility function is a finite set $S$ (this occurs quite frequently in applications such as the Registrar's Problem), then the scale values will certainly be bounded. Even in the

Table 8.3

|  | Bob | Fred |
|---|---|---|
| Soviet literature | .5 | .866 |
| Presidential campaigning | .7 | .9 |

case that $S$ is finite, however, the set of all gambles with outcomes in $S$ will be infinite. The utility measure has as its domain the infinite set of gambles. There are also many instances when it is necessary or convenient to assume that $S$ is infinite. In such cases, there are no *mathematical* grounds for concluding that the utility function will necessarily be bounded. Sometimes there are empirical considerations for concluding that utility must be bounded.

   Consider, for example, a game with an infinite number of possible outcomes, some desirable and others not. A player in the game wants to construct a utility scale that measures the value to him of each of the outcomes. In his Ph. D. dissertation at Princeton University, John R. Isbell developed a theory of cooperative games that is predicated on the assumption that such a utility scale will always be bounded. "Introspection convinces the present author firmly," he wrote, "that there is no prospect so desirable as to be worth an even bet of his life. He who claims a utility space unbounded above must in principle stand ready to bet his life at any odds provided the price is right."

   To illustrate Isbell's argument more precisely, suppose the utility scale is unbounded above. This means that given any number $M$, then there exists some possible outcome $z$ with $u(z) > M$. Consider, then, the two events

$$x: \text{you win } \$10,000$$

and

$$y: \text{your head is chopped off.}$$

Each of these outcomes is assigned a utility, $u(x)$ and $u(y)$. Let $M$ be the number $10u(x) - 9u(y)$ and let $z$ be an outcome with $u(z) > M$.

   Since $u(z) > 10u(x) - 9u(y)$, we have $u(z) + 9u(y) > 10u(x)$ or $.1u(z) + .9u(y) > u(x)$. This last inequality implies that the gamble $.1z + .9y$ is preferred to the outcome $x$. The conclusion: there is some outcome so good that you are willing to give up a sure chance of winning $10,000 to take a gamble of winning that outcome when there is a 90 percent chance that you will lose the gamble and, with it, your head. Isbell would argue that such an outcome is inconceivable.

   One can construct a similar argument that "proves" that the utility scale is also bounded below. It should be noted that not all utility theorists accept the validity of such arguments.


## VII. HISTORICAL AND BIOGRAPHICAL NOTES

### A. Utility Theory

Utility theory traces its ancestry back to the efforts of economists and mathematicians to develop an applicable theory of how a rational person ought to behave in the face of uncertainty and how, in fact, such a person does act. It was thought for a time that in economic situations people would act to maximize the expected value of money that would accrue to them. Thus the gamble of winning $10 if a fair coin lands heads and winning nothing if it lands tails shows an expected value of

$$\left(\frac{1}{2}\right)(\$10) + \left(\frac{1}{2}\right)(\$0) = \$5.$$

The rational man, under such a theory, should behave toward this gamble as if it were worth $5.

It eventually became apparent that there are many instances when this idea is not applicable. Daniel Bernoulli (1700–1782), a member of the illustrious Swiss family that produced eight mathematicians in three generations, presents one: "Let us suppose a pauper happens to acquire a lottery ticket by which he may with equal probability win either nothing or 20,000 ducats. Will he have to evaluate the worth of the ticket as 10,000 ducats; and would he be acting foolishly, if he sold it for 9,000 ducats?"

In a paper written in 1790, Bernoulli explored the idea that the utility of money—not its actual value—is what people attempt to maximize. He argued that the utility of a fixed amount of money was different for a pauper than for a rich man. A single dollar is more precious to the poor man than to the million-aire; the poor man would feel the loss of a dollar more than the rich man. The difference in the utilities of $10 and $11 is greater, Bernoulli believed, than the difference in the utilities of $1000 and $1001. In general, a fixed increase in cash results in an ever smaller increase in utility as the basic cash wealth to which the increase is applied is made larger. In mathematical terms, this says that the graph of utility as a function of money is concave. See Fig. 8.3.

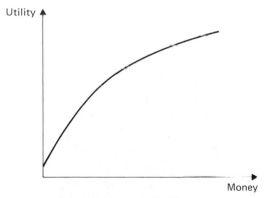

**Fig. 8.3**   A possible graph of utility of money as a function of amount of money. Each increase in money increases utility, so the function is monotonically increasing. Fixed increases in money bring smaller increases in utility as money increases. Thus, the rate of change of utility is negative and the graph of function must be concave down.

Bernoulli's ideas had an important impact on the thinking of economists for a long time, although the formal axiomatization of utility was not developed until this century. The axiomatic approach, introduced by John Von Neumann and Oskar Morgenstern in their book *Theory of Games and Economic Behavior* (1947) has led to a new and deeper interest in this subject in the last 30 years. The treatment of utility in this chapter derives directly from the Von Neumann–Morgenstern formulation. There have been numerous experiments testing the applicability of the utility concept to real-world situations. One of the earliest and most interesting ones is discussed in the paper of Mosteller and Nogee listed in the References.

## B.  John Von Neumann and Oskar Morgenstern

> In John Von Neumann's death on February 8, 1957, the world of mathematics lost a most original, penetrating, and versatile mind. Science suffered the loss of a universal intellect and a unique interpreter of mathematics, who could bring the latest (and develop latent) applications of its methods to bear on problems of physics, astronomy, biology and the new technology.

These are the words of the noted mathematician Stanislaw M. Ulam and they express a judgment of Von Neumann universally shared by mathematicians

John Von Neumann
(right) and Oskar
Morgenstern.

and scientists who know his work. Von Neumann made important contributions to quantum physics, meteorology, the development of the atomic bomb, the theory and applications of high-speed computing machines, and to economics through the theory of games of strategy. He also made a number of outstanding discoveries in pure mathematics in the areas of measure and ergodic theory, continuous geometry, operator theory, topological groups, logic, and set theory.

Von Neumann was born in Budapest, Hungary on December 28, 1903 and was the eldest son of a prosperous banker. His brilliant mind was revealed early. It is said that at the age of 6 he could divide two eight-digit numbers in his head, by age 8 he had mastered calculus, and by age 12 he was reading and understanding advanced books on function theory. His first published paper was written when he was 17, and the definition of ordinal number he created at age 20 is the one that is now universally used by mathematicians.

During the years 1922–1926, Von Neumann was registered as a student of mathematics at the University of Budapest but spent most of his time at the Eidgenossiche Technische Hochschule in Zurich, studying chemistry at the urging of his family who were doubtful of the financial future of a mathematician. Von Neumann was awarded his doctorate in mathematics from Budapest at about the same time he received his diploma in chemical engineering in Zurich.

Von Neumann first came to the United States in 1930 as a visiting lecturer at Princeton University. He became a professor there the next year and served on the faculty until 1933. In that year, the famous Institute for Advanced Study was founded. Among the first six professors given lifetime appointments in the Institute's School of Mathematics were Albert Einstein and John Von Neumann.

For most of the rest of the 1930's, Von Neumann's work was concentrated on pure mathematics. In 1940, however, there was a sharp break in his scientific work. As Paul Halmos describes it, "Until then he was a topflight pure mathematician who understood physics; after that he was an applied mathematician who remembered his pure work."

From 1940 until his death, Von Neumann served as a consultant to the Los Alamos Scientific Laboratory, the Naval Ordinance Laboratory, the Oak Ridge National Laboratory, and other military and civilian agencies. He was appointed to the Scientific Advisory Board of the Air Force and served as a member of the United States Atomic Energy Commission.

The technological development of the last generation which has had the greatest impact on society has been the high-speed electronic computer. Here, too, John Von Neumann played a critical role as a pioneer. He formulated the methods of translating a set of procedures into a language of instructions for a computing machine, made important contributions to the engineering of the first computers, and analyzed the question of whether machines could successfully imitate randomness or become self-reproducing automata.

Game theory as a model for the study of cooperation and competition has as its foundation a paper of Von Neumann written in 1928. His interest in this area was rekindled when the Austrian economist Oskar Morgenstern came to Princeton. Their intensive collaboration in the early years of World War II produced the 600-page *Theory of Games and Economic Behavior*.

Prior to Von Neumann and Morgenstern, mathematical economics had relied heavily on the techniques of mathematical physics and a rather shaky analogy between mechanics and economics. Von Neumann's innovations were to introduce the mathematical tools of axiomatization, convexity, and combinatorics, and the fresh viewpoint of analyzing economic problems as games of strategy. The book also sparked new research into utility theory by mathematicians, economists, and psychologists. In reviewing the book shortly after its publication, A. H. Copeland wrote, "Posterity may regard this book as one of the major scientific achievements of the first half of the twentieth century."

The May 1958 issue of the *Bulletin of the American Mathematical Society* is devoted to a tribute to John Von Neumann and his work. In their essay on his contributions to the theory of games and mathematical economics, H. W. Kuhn and A. W. Tucker conclude,

> By his example and through his accomplishments he opened a broad new channel of two-way communication between mathematics and the social sciences. These sciences were fortunate indeed that one of the most creative mathematicians of the twentieth century concerned himself with some of their fundamental problems and constructed strikingly imaginative and stimulating models with which to attack their problems quantitatively. At the same time, mathematics received a vital infusion of fresh ideas and methods that will continue to be highly productive for many years to come.... There is a great challenge for other mathematicians to follow his lead in grappling with complex systems in many areas of the sciences where mathematics has not yet penetrated deeply.

During the 1930's hundreds of prominent German and Austrian scholars fled their native lands to escape the growing oppression of the Nazi movement. Among this group of exiles—which included Von Neumann, Einstein, and Sigmund Freud—was the economist Oskar Morgenstern.

Morgenstern was born in Goerlitz in the German state of Silesia on January 24, 1902. His roots in Germany were well established; one of his ancestors had been a professor of canon law in Leipzig and published a book of sermons in 1508. Morgenstern's father was a poor businessman and his mother was the illegitimate grand-daughter of Emperor Frederick III of Germany. Morgenstern received his secondary and university education in Vienna, earning a doctorate from the University of Vienna in 1925. He returned to the university as a faculty member four years later after an extended period of study in London, Paris, and Rome, and at Harvard and Columbia Universities in the United States. For nearly a decade, he taught economics in Vienna, edited an academic journal, conducted research, and advised various state agencies. He was the director of the Austrian Institute for Business Cycle Research and served as a consultant to the Austrian National Bank and the Ministry of Commerce. In

1936 he was named a member of the Committee of Statistical Experts of the League of Nations, a position he held until the League was replaced by the United Nations in 1945, and a position from which he helped author a study on *Economic Stability in the Postwar World*.

Morgenstern came to the United States permanently in 1938 when he began a long association with Princeton University. He served on the faculty for 32 years, directed the university's Econometric Research Program and was co-editor of the Princeton Series on Mathematical Economics. He advised the Atomic Energy Commission, the White House, the National Aeronautics and Space Administration, Congress, and the Rand Corporation. Upon retirement from Princeton in 1970, he accepted a position as professor of economics at New York University. Morgenstern died of cancer at his home in Princeton on July 26, 1977.

Although best known for his collaboration with Von Neumann on game theory, Morgenstern also made many contributions to the theory of business cycles, monetary policy, international trade, mathematical economics, econometrics, problems of defense strategy, and statistical decision theory. In addition to numerous technical articles and books, he wrote many essays and reviews for such general circulation magazines as *Fortune*, *Scientific American*, *New York Times Magazine*, and *Encounter*.

In an article published in *Fortune*, Morgenstern issued a warning about the uncritical acceptance of imperfect statistics in business, politics, and economics. This essay is highly recommended reading for mathematical modelers who need to construct and test their models from real-world data. In it, Morgenstern notes,

> Although the natural sciences—sometimes called the "exact" sciences—have been concerned with the accuracy of measurements and observations from their earliest beginnings, they nevertheless suffered a great crisis when it became clear that absolute precision and certainty of important kinds of observations were impossible to achieve in principle. At least all sources of error that occur in the natural sciences also occur in the social sciences: or, in other words, the statistical problems of the social sciences cannot possibly be less serious than those of the natural sciences. But the social sciences pay far less attention to errors than the physical. This is undoubtedly one of the reasons why the social sciences have had a rather uncertain development.*

## EXERCISES

### I. INTRODUCTION

1. Why is it reasonable to conclude that the student sees a greater difference between $x$ and $y$ than between $y$ and $z$ if she prefers $y$ to an even gamble between $x$ and $z$?

---

* Oskar Morgenstern, "Qui numerare incipit errare incipit," *Fortune* (October 1963), pp. 142–144, 173–174, 178–180.

## II. GAMBLES

2.  Show that Theorem 1 implies that $x\,I\,y$ if and only if $u(x) = u(y)$.

3.  Prove Condition (1) of Theorem 1.

4.  Prove Condition (2) of Theorem 1.

5.  Prove Condition (3) of Theorem 1.

6.  Prove Condition (5) of Theorem 1.

7.  Let $p$ and $q$ be numbers between 0 and 1. Show that the compound gamble $px + (1 - p)[(qy + (1 - q)z)]$ is equivalent to the gamble with three outcomes $px + (1 - p)qy + (1 - p)(1 - q)z$.

## III. AXIOMS OF UTILITY THEORY

8.  Do Axioms 1–6 seem reasonable to you? If not, which ones would you modify? How would you test the validity of these axioms experimentally?

9.  Does Axiom 5 follow from Axiom 4 and the other assumptions about gambles?

10.  In the proof of Theorem 2, it is claimed that the gamble $px + (1 - p)y$ is equivalent to the gamble $qx + (1 - q)z$. Why is this true?

11.  Suppose a student prefers $x$ to $y$ and $y$ to $z$ and indicates that her difference in happiness between $x$ and $y$ is the same as the difference between $y$ and $z$. Can you show that she is indifferent between the outcome $y$ and the gamble $.5x + .5z$?

## IV. EXISTENCE AND UNIQUENESS OF UTILITY

12.  If $S$ is a *finite* set of outcomes, show that the proof of Theorem 4 can be considerably simplified.

13.  Suppose $S$ is an infinite set where $x_0$ is the least preferred outcome and $x_1$ the most preferred one. Discuss how the proof of Theorem 4 can be simplified.

14.  Show that the uniqueness of $p$ promised in Theorem 3 is essential to the establishment of a utility function.

15.  Show that conditions (1) and (2) of Theorem 4 hold in each of the following cases:

a)  $x$ and $y$ are in Case (d).

b)  $x$ and $y$ are in Case (e).

c)  $x$ is in Case (d), $y$ is in Case (c).

d)  $x$ is in Case (c), $y$ is in Case (e).

16.  Consider an alternative proof of Theorem 4 that proceeds as follows: Define a utility function $u$ whose domain is $S$ in the same manner as the given proof. Then define the utility of any gamble, $px + (1 - p)y$, with outcomes $x$ and $y$ in $S$, as $u(px + (1 - p)y) = pu(x) + (1 - p)u(y)$. What remains to be proved? Complete the proof.

17.  Let $T$ be the set $T = \{0, 1, 2\}$ and let $L$ be the function $L(0) = -17$, $L(1) = \sqrt{23}$, and $L(2) = 10$. Is $L$ a positive linear transformation?

18.  Suppose $L$ is a positive linear transformation on a set $T$. If $t_1$ and $t_2$ are distinct elements of $T$,

a)  Show that $L(t_1) \neq L(t_2)$.

b)  If $L(t_1) = a_1$ and $L(t_2) = a_2$, determine $\alpha$ and $\beta$.

19. Verify that Theorem 6 is true in Cases (a), (b), and (d).

20. Suppose a student prefers $x$ to $y$ and $y$ to $z$ and that $y I [.3x + .7z]$. Construct a utility function consistent with the given information.

21. Suppose a student prefers $x$ to $y$, $y$ to $z$, and $z$ to $w$. Furthermore, $y I [.4x + .6z]$, $y I [.3x + .7w]$, and $z I [.5y + .5w]$. Can you construct a utility function consistent with these observations?

22. If Alexander's utility measures for tuna fish, hamburger, and peanut butter are 60, 48, and 30, respectively, find the gamble with outcomes of peanut butter and tuna fish that he finds indifferent to hamburger.

## V. CLASSIFICATION OF SCALES

23. In their textbook on mathematical psychology, Coombs, Dawes, and Tversky discuss the problem of measurement on a set when, in addition to stating a preference order, you are also able to order differences between alternatives with respect to preferences. They note that "an admissible transformation in this case must preserve not only the order of the scale values but the order of differences between scale values." They then claim that only positive linear transformations preserve the ordering of intervals for any set of objects. Is this true? Can you prove it?

24. In his work on measurement theory, Campbell (see Chapter 7) claimed that only extensive properties can be measured on an interval scale. Since most psychological and sociological properties are intensive, he believed that interval measurement is not possible in these social sciences. Is this argument valid? Is temperature an extensive property?

## VI. INTERPERSONAL COMPARISON OF UTILITY

25. Solve the Registrar's Problem if there are three students (Ann, Joan, and Kathy), three courses (Plate Tectonics, Computer Methods, and Relativity Theory) and each course is restricted to one student. The original utility scales (not normalized) are given in the following table:

|                   | Ann | Joan | Kathy |
|-------------------|-----|------|-------|
| Plate tectonics   | 3   | 120  | -.6   |
| Computer methods  | 7   | 90   | 1.2   |
| Relativity theory | 2   | 40   | 5.6   |

26. Solve the Registrar's Problem of Exercise 25 if each course is open to two students.

27. What would the details of Isbell's argument look like if he were trying to convince you that there is a lower bound to the nonnormalized utility function?

28. Let $G$ be the set of all gambles with outcomes in the finite set $S$. Prove that any utility function defined on $G$ is necessarily bounded.

## SUGGESTED PROJECTS

1. Is there any explanation, in terms of utility, for why people buy insurance policies and lottery tickets?

2. The St. Petersburg Paradox is often cited as an argument that the utility of money is not directly proportional to the amount of money. The paradox concerns a game in which you toss a coin until it lands tails. If this happens for the first time on the $n$th toss, you receive $\$2^n$. How much money are you willing to pay to enter this game? Show that the expected value of your winnings is infinite. Thus, you should be willing to pay any amount to enter. The "paradox" arises because most people would not pay very much to enter. If you pay $100 to enter the game and flip "tails" on the first toss, you lose $98! The reluctance of people to enter the game if it has a high entrance fee is due, some believe, to the fact that the value of money is not proportional to the money. As one way to resolve the paradox, it has been suggested that the utility of money obeys the relation $u(x) = \sqrt{x}$, where $x$ is the number of dollars. Show that if this is true, then the expected utility of the St. Petersburg gamble is finite. Show, however, that the payoffs in the coin toss can be arranged in such a fashion (say $\$2^{2n}$ instead of $\$2^n$) so that even if $u(x) = \sqrt{x}$, the expected utility is infinite. Does there exist some function $u(x)$ that increases monotonically with $x$ but for which the St. Petersburg game always has finite expected utility, no matter how the payoffs are arranged? Show that the "paradox" disappears if expected utility is finite and we assume that the rational person acts to maximize expected utility. Is this last assumption valid?

3. Not all social scientists have accepted the axioms of utility theory presented in this chapter. M. Allais presents a pair of decision situations each involving two gambles. In situation I, you must choose between

$$\text{Gamble } 1: \$500{,}000 \text{ with probability } 1,$$

and

$$\text{Gamble } 2: \$2{,}500{,}000 \text{ with probability } .1,$$
$$\$500{,}000 \text{ with probability } .89,$$

and

$$\$0 \text{ with probability } .01,$$

In situation II, the choice is between

$$\text{Gamble } 3: \$500{,}000 \text{ with probability } .11, \$0 \text{ with probability } .89,$$

and

$$\text{Gamble } 4: \$2{,}500{,}000 \text{ with probability } .1, \$0 \text{ with probability } .9.$$

Allais argues that most people prefer gamble 1 to gamble 2 and gamble 4 to gamble 3. Show that these preferences, under the axioms of utility theory, lead to the inconsistent inequalities:

a)  $.11u(\$500{,}000) > .1u(\$2{,}500{,}000) + .01u(0),$
and
b)  $.1u(\$2{,}500{,}000) + .01u(0) > .11u(\$500{,}000).$

Do you agree with Allais' preferences? If, after some reflection, you still do, you may wish to read how Savage reacts to them. What other objections could be raised about the relevance of utility theory as a model of the real world?

4. Almost all theories of social justice and many important societal decisions are based on an implict comparison of interpersonal utilities. The suggested normalization of Section VI is an explicit way of constructing such comparisons. What principles of equality and fairness are consistent with such a normalization? What principles are violated? Investigate other ways of determining such comparisons.

## REFERENCES

Allais, M., "Le comportement de l'homme rationnel devant le risque: critique des postulats et axiomes de l'école Americaine," *Econometrica* **21** (1953), 503–546.

Bernoulli, Daniel, "Specimen theoriae novae de mensura sortis," *Commentarii Académiae Scientiarum Imperialis Petropolitanae*, 1730, 1731, 1738; translated by L. Sommer, "Expositions of a new theory of the measurement of risk," *Econometrica* **22** (1954).

Ellsberg, Daniel, "Classic and current notions of measurable utility," *Economic Journal* **64** (1954), 528–556.

Fishburn, Peter, *Utility Theory for Decision Making* (New York: Wiley, 1964).

Herstein, I. N., and J. Milnor, "An axiomatic approach to measurable utility," *Econometrica* **21** (1953), 291–297.

Isbell, J. R., "Absolute games," in A. W. Tucker and R. D. Luce (eds.), *Contributions to the Theory of Games, IV* (Princeton: Princeton University Press, 1959), pp. 357–396.

Luce, R. Duncan, and Patrick Suppes, "Preference, utility and subjective probability," in Luce, Bush, and Galanter, *Handbook of Mathematical Psychology*, Vol. III (New York: Wiley, 1963), Chapter 19.

Mosteller, Frederick, and Philip Nogee, "An experimental measurement of utility," *Journal of Political Economy* **59** (1951), 371–404.

Owen, Guillermo, *Game Theory* (Philadelphia: Saunders, 1969). The proofs of Theorems 4 and 6 are adapted from Chapter 6 of Owen's book.

Savage, Leonard J., *The Foundations of Statistics* (New York: Wiley, 1954), especially Chapter 5, "Utility."

Stevens, S. S., "Mathematics, measurement and psychophysics," *Handbook of Experimental Psychology* (New York: Wiley, 1951), pp. 1–49; and "On the theory of scales of measurement," *Science* **103** (1946), 677–680.

Von Neumann, John, and Oskar Morgenstern, *The Theory of Games and Economic Behavior*, Third edition (New York: Wiley, 1964).

Also see the references to Campbell and to Coombs, Dawes, and Tversky in Chapter 7.

# 9
# Elementary Probability

The most important questions of life are, for the most part, really only questions of probability. Strictly speaking, one may even say that nearly all our knowledge is problematical; and in the small number of things which we are able to know with certainty, even in the mathematical sciences themselves, induction and analogy, the principal means of discovering truth, are based on probabilities, so that the entire system of human knowledge is connected with this theory.

Pierre-Simon de Laplace

## I. THE NEED FOR PROBABILITY MODELS

The deterministic and axiomatic models developed in earlier chapters show that both types of models can serve to give concise and precise descriptions of some real-world situations. Deterministic models have an added feature of being predictive in nature, while the best that axiomatic models seem to do is guarantee the existence or uniqueness of certain kinds of sets or functions.

The usefulness of a model increases if that model gives some new information not yet observed about the situation it is supposed to represent. The predictions of the model can be tested against what actually happens in the real world. Refinements can then be made in the model and better understanding gained of the real-world problem.

The deterministic models of Chapters 1–4 are typical of the type one sees in social-science applications. They consist of systems of differential equations, the mathematical tool that has been most useful in the study of physical systems. Mathematically, differential equations of the type we have examined assert that once the equations and the initial conditions are specified, then the state of the corresponding system at any later moment is completely determined.

The main criticism of the deterministic approach to the study of social problems lies precisely in this feature of the mathematics. Social problems deal with individuals or groups of individuals and we can never completely predict the exact future behavior of any person in a specific situation, no matter how well we understand the situation or the person. People are not particles, this objection concludes, and the equations of physics cannot be used to describe human actions.

There are at least two responses to such objections. First, the mathematical modeler never makes the grandiose claim that his equations *completely* describe the real-world situation. He realizes that he has undoubtedly left out some important variables and that he has simplified the interactions among the variables he has included. At best, he hopes the qualitative nature of his quantitative results will mimic what happens in the real world.

There is a second response to the objection. Accept the premise that determinism is no fit way to describe social phenomena. This does not mean that mathematical social science is inherently any less rigorous than physics. Physicists have come, in this century, to the belief that determinism is also not possible in this most deterministic of all sciences. Nobel Laureate Richard Feynmann emphasizes this realization in his *Lectures on Physics* [1965]:

> We would like to emphasize a very important difference between classical and quantum mechanics. We have been talking about the probability that an electron will arrive in a given circumstance. We have implied that in our experimental arrangement (or even in the best possible one) it would be impossible to predict exactly what would happen. We can only predict the odds! This would mean, if it were true, that physics has given up on the problem of trying to predict exactly what will happen in a definite circumstance. Yes! Physics *has* given up. We do not know how

to predict what would happen in a given circumstance, and we believe that it is impossible—that the only thing that can be predicted is the probability of different events. It must be recognized that this is a retrenchment in our earlier ideal of understanding nature. It may be a backward step, but no one has seen a way to avoid it. . . . We suspect very strongly that it is something that will be with us forever . . . that this is the way nature really *is*.

This chapter begins the study of probabilistic models of human behavior by introducing the basic tools of probability. Before starting, it should be emphasized that while mathematical social scientists believe that the existence of human "free will" implies that the probabilistic approach is the more correct style of modeling, deterministic approaches will still be employed. Most social phenomena are quite complex. Accurate mathematical models must also be complex. A deterministic model based on a given set of axioms may be simpler to analyze than a probabilistic one. In addition, probabilistic models are often analyzed by approximating them with more tractable deterministic ones. A successful modeler cannot dismiss either approach. In Section III and again in Chapters 11 and 13, we will present comparisons of deterministic and probabilistic attacks on the same problems.

## II. WHAT IS PROBABILITY?

### A. Fundamental Definitions
This section (parts A–F) outlines the bare minimum of probability theory on finite sample spaces. Sources for complete treatments are listed in the References at the end of the chapter.

**DEFINITION   Let $E$ be a set with a finite number of elements. A *probability measure on $E$* is defined to be a real-valued function Pr whose domain consists of all subsets of $E$ and which satisfies three rules:**

   **1.** $\Pr(E) = 1$,
   **2.** $\Pr(X) \geqslant 0$ **for every subset $X$ of $E$, and**
   **3.** $\Pr(X \cup Y) = \Pr(X) + \Pr(Y)$ **for every pair of disjoint subsets $X$ and $Y$ of $E$.**

**A finite set $E$ together with a probability measure is called a *sample space*.**

The definitions will be illustrated by several examples.

---

**EXAMPLE 1**    Let $E$ be the set of possible outcomes in an experiment consisting of flipping a coin and noting which side faces up when the coin lands. Then $E$ has two elements, $h$ and $t$, corresponding to "heads" and "tails." Note that $E = \{h, t\}$ and there are four subsets: $E, \emptyset, \{h\}, \{t\}$. An assumption that the coin is fair, that is, there is as much chance of a head as of a tail, may be reflected by the probability measure:

$$\Pr(\emptyset) = 0, \qquad \Pr(E) = 1, \qquad \Pr(\{h\}) = \Pr(\{t\}) = \frac{1}{2}.$$

**EXAMPLE 2**   Suppose that the coin of Example 1 has been weighted so that heads appear twice as often as tails. Then we might assign a different probability measure:

$$\Pr(\emptyset) = 0, \qquad \Pr(E) = 1, \qquad \Pr(\{h\}) = \frac{2}{3}, \qquad \Pr(\{t\}) = \frac{1}{3}.$$

---

Note that Examples 1 and 2 are two different sample spaces with the same underlying set.

---

**EXAMPLE 3**   There is an urn with four marbles. Each marble has a different color: green, blue, red, or white. Reach your hand into the urn and, without looking, remove one marble. If E represents the set of possible outcomes of this experiment, the E consists of four elements, represented by the letters $g, b, r$, and $w$, corresponding to the color of the marble selected. Rather than list the probability measures of all 16 subsets of $E$, define the probability of any subset $X$ by

$$\Pr(X) = \frac{\text{Number of distinct elements in } X}{4}.$$

As an exercise, check that this definition satisfies the three conditions of a probability measure.

**EXAMPLE 4**   The urn of Example 3 is replaced by one holding 4 green marbles, 3 blue ones, 2 red ones, and a single white one. Otherwise the experiment is the same and the set $E$ is the same as in Example 3. Call the outcomes $g, b, r, w$ *elementary events* and assign them weights of $.4, .3, .2$, and $.1$, respectively. Define a probability measure on $E$ by letting $\Pr(X)$ be equal to the sum of the weights of the distinct elementary events in $X$. For example, if $X = \{g, w\}$, then $\Pr(X) = .4 + .1 = .5$. Check that this assignment of probabilities also satisfies Rules (1)–(3).

---

The elementary events in Example 3 were each assigned the same measure, $\frac{1}{4}$. This is an illustration of an *equiprobable measure* which occurs whenever each of the finite number of elements of a set $E$ has the same weight. The probability measure in the equiprobable situation has a very simple form: If $E$ has $n$ distinct elements and $X$ is a subset containing $r$ of these elements, then $\Pr(X) = r/n$.

Note that the equiprobable measure was also used in Example 1, but not in Examples 2 and 4.

It is useful to list here some of the elementary laws of probability implied by the definition of a probability measure. These are gathered together in the following theorem, whose proof is left as an exercise.

■ **THEOREM 1**   If Pr is a probability measure on a finite set $E$, then the following statements are true for all subsets $X, Y, X_1, X_2, \ldots, X_k$ of $E$:

1. If $X \subseteq Y$, then $\Pr(X) \leqslant \Pr(Y)$.

2. $\Pr(\emptyset) = 0$.

3. $\Pr(X \cup Y) = \Pr(X) + \Pr(Y) - \Pr(X \cap Y)$.

4. $\Pr(X^C) = 1 - \Pr(X)$ where $X^C$ is the complement of $X$; that is, $X^C = E - X$.

5. $\Pr(Y) = \Pr(X \cap Y) + \Pr(X^C \cap Y)$.

6. If $X_1, X_2, \ldots, X_k$ are mutually disjoint subsets of $E$, then

$$\Pr(X_1 \cup X_2 \cup \cdots \cup X_k) = \Pr(X_1) + \Pr(X_2) + \cdots + \Pr(X_k)$$
$$= 1 - \Pr(X_1^C \cap X_2^C \cap \cdots \cap X_k^C).$$

## B. Conditional Probability

As you read this section and glance through probability textbooks, you will see many examples having to do with pulling objects out of urns. Probabilists have no particular psychological hangups about urns. Urns simply provide a convenient mechanism for conceptualizing and clarifying many of the important concepts of the subject. Be patient; we will soon be dealing with people and not urns.

Imagine, then, an urn containing six red marbles—numbered 1, 2, 3, 4, 5, 6—and ten green marbles, numbered from 1 to 10. Other than color, the marbles are identical in shape and appearance. As usual, reach into the urn without looking and remove one marble. What is the probability that the selected marble is labeled with a "3"?

A reasonable answer to this question is $\frac{2}{16}$. A reasonable explanation is, "There are 16 marbles and I am no more likely to pick one than another, so assume I am working with the equiprobable measure. Since the set $E$ has 16 elements, each has probability $\frac{1}{16}$. The subset which corresponds to obtaining a marble labeled 3 has exactly two elementary events: the green marble 3 and the red marble 3. Thus the probability is $\frac{1}{16} + \frac{1}{16} = \frac{2}{16}$."

Very good. Nothing new so far. Suppose, however, that you observed that the selected marble was red before you were asked "What is the probability that the selected marble bears a "3" on it?" The reasonable answer to the question is now $\frac{1}{6}$ since there are six red marbles, each equally likely to be chosen, and exactly one of them is labeled "3."

Different answers to the same question are appropriate because different amounts of information were given in each of the situations. Additional information often changes estimates of probabilities. The concept of *conditional probability* makes this precise.

**DEFINITION** **Let Pr be a probability measure defined on a set $E$. If $X$ and $Y$ are any two subsets of $E$ with $\Pr(X) > 0$, then the *conditional probability of Y given X*, denoted $\Pr(Y|X)$ is defined by**

$$\Pr(Y|X) = \frac{\Pr(Y \cap X)}{\Pr(X)}.$$

**If $\Pr(X) = 0$, then the conditional probability of $Y$ given $X$ is not defined.**

To illustrate the definition with the example just given, let $Y$ be the subset corresponding to "The marble is labeled 3" and $X$ the subset corresponding to "The marble is red." Then $\Pr(Y) = \frac{2}{16}$, $\Pr(X) = \frac{6}{16}$ and $\Pr(Y \cap X) = \frac{1}{16}$ since there is exactly one marble which is red and labeled "3." The conditional probability of $Y$ given $X$ is

$$\Pr(Y|X) = \frac{\Pr(Y \cap X)}{\Pr(X)} = \frac{1/16}{6/16} = \frac{1}{6},$$

agreeing with the verbal explanation first given.

In this case, note that the conditional probability of $X$ *given* $Y$ is also defined and is equal to

$$\Pr(X|Y) = \frac{\Pr(X \cap Y)}{\Pr(Y)} = \frac{1/16}{2/16} = \frac{1}{2}.$$

To see that this is a reasonable result, consider that $\Pr(X|Y)$ is the answer to the question, "If you are told that the marble is labeled '3', what is the probability that it is red."

The calculations just given illustrate the critical warning that, in general, $\Pr(Y|X) \neq \Pr(X|Y)$.

---

**EXAMPLE 5**   Two weeks before the state primary to choose a single nominee for election to the United States Senate, there were four candidates. Political experts gave Oppenheim a .4 chance of winning, Bleier had a .3 chance, Neff had .2 chance, and Nye had a .1 chance. Just prior to the election, a grand jury indicts Neff, charging him with accepting illegal campaign contributions. If Neff withdraws from the race, how would this affect the chances of winning of the remaining three candidates?

**Solution**   In the absence of other information, we may assume that we have a set with four elements, Oppenheim, Bleier, Neff, and Nye, with weights of .4, .3, .2, and .1 measuring the probability of each winning. We will compute the chances for Oppenheim winning if Neff withdraws.

By Theorem 1, $\mathrm{Pr}(\text{Neff loses}) = 1 - \mathrm{Pr}(\text{Neff wins}) = 1 - .2 = .8$. To find the conditional probability that Oppenheim wins given that Neff loses, use the definition of conditional probability:

$$\mathrm{Pr}(\text{Oppenheim wins}\,|\,\text{Neff loses}) = \frac{\mathrm{Pr}(\text{Oppenheim wins and Neff loses})}{\mathrm{Pr}(\text{Neff loses})}$$

$$= \mathrm{Pr}(\text{Oppenheim wins})/\mathrm{Pr}(\text{Neff loses})$$

$$= \frac{.4}{.8} = \frac{1}{2}.$$

In this computation, we use condition (5) of Theorem 1 in the form

$$\begin{aligned}\mathrm{Pr}(\text{Oppenheim wins}) &= \mathrm{Pr}(\text{Oppenheim wins and Neff wins}) \\ &\quad + \mathrm{Pr}(\text{Oppenheim wins and Neff loses}) \\ &= 0 + \mathrm{Pr}(\text{Oppenheim wins and Neff loses})\end{aligned}$$

since the subset corresponding to "Oppenheim wins and Neff wins" is empty.

---

## C. Bayes' Theorem

The equation defining conditional probability can be rewritten as

$$\mathrm{Pr}\,(Y \cap X) = \mathrm{Pr}\,(Y\,|\,X)\,\mathrm{Pr}\,(X). \qquad (*)$$

This equation is useful in computing $\mathrm{Pr}(X\,|\,Y)$ in certain instances when the probability $\mathrm{Pr}(Y\,|\,X)$ is given, since

$$\mathrm{Pr}(X\,|\,Y) = \frac{\mathrm{Pr}(X \cap Y)}{\mathrm{Pr}(Y)} = \frac{\mathrm{Pr}(Y \cap X)}{\mathrm{Pr}(Y)} = \frac{\mathrm{Pr}(Y\,|\,X)\,\mathrm{Pr}(X)}{\mathrm{Pr}(Y)}. \qquad (**)$$

---

**EXAMPLE 6**    A multiple-choice exam has four suggested answers to each question, only one of which is correct. A student who has done her homework is certain to identify the correct answer. If a student skips her homework, then she chooses an answer at random. Suppose that two-thirds of the class has done the homework. In grading the test, the teacher observes that Jennifer has the right answer to the first problem. What is the probability that Jennifer did the homework?

**Solution**    Let $X$ denote "Jennifer has done the homework" and $Y$ denote "Jennifer has the right answer." The information given in the problem translates into three probability statements:

$$\mathrm{Pr}(X) = \frac{2}{3}, \qquad \mathrm{Pr}(Y\,|\,X) = 1, \qquad \text{and} \qquad \mathrm{Pr}(Y\,|\,X^c) = \frac{1}{4}.$$

The question asks for the computation of $\Pr(X|Y)$. From Theorem 1, we have $\Pr(Y) = \Pr(Y \cap X) + \Pr(Y \cap X^C)$ and two uses of equation (*) give

$$\Pr(Y \cap X) = \Pr(Y|X)\Pr(X),$$

and

$$\Pr(Y \cap X^C) = \Pr(Y|X^C)\Pr(X^C).$$

Putting this information together with the definition of conditional probability gives the answer:

$$\Pr(X|Y) = \frac{\Pr(X \cap Y)}{\Pr(Y)} = \frac{\Pr(Y|X)\Pr(X)}{\Pr(Y|X)\Pr(X) + \Pr(Y|X^C)\Pr(X^C)}$$

$$= \frac{(1)(2/3)}{(1)(2/3) + (1/4)(1/3)} = \frac{8}{9}$$

The type of calculation used to solved the question of Example 6 occurs in a great many applications. The general rule that underlies it is called Bayes' Theorem and is the content of Theorem 2. It is named after the Reverend Thomas Bayes (1702–1761) and first appeared in print in 1763.

■ **THEOREM 2 (BAYES' THEOREM)**     Let Pr be a probability measure defined on a set $E$ and suppose $Y$ is a subset of $E$ with $\Pr(Y) > 0$. If $X_1, X_2, \ldots, X_k$ is any collection of mutually disjoint subsets of $E$ whose union is all of $E$, and each $X_i$ has positive probability, then

$$\Pr(X_j|Y) = \frac{\Pr(Y|X_j)\Pr(X_j)}{\displaystyle\sum_{i=1}^{k} \Pr(Y|X_i)\Pr(X_i)}.$$

*Proof of Theorem 2*     Write

$$Y = Y \cap E = Y \cap (X_1 \cup X_2 \cup \cdots \cup X_k)$$
$$= (Y \cap X_1) \cup (Y \cap X_2) \cup \cdots \cap (Y \cap X_k)$$

and use Theorem 1 to obtain

$$\Pr(Y) = \sum_{i=1}^{k} \Pr(Y \cap X_i).$$

Use (*) to write $\Pr(Y \cap X_i) = \Pr(Y|X_i)\Pr(X_i)$ so that $\Pr(Y) = \sum_{i=1}^{k} \Pr(Y|X_i)$ $\Pr(x_i)$. An application of equation (**) completes the proof. □

One final example will illustrate the use of Bayes' Theorem.

**EXAMPLE 7**     The President of the United States often seeks recommendations from his Council of Economic Advisers. Suppose there are three advisers

**Table 9.1**

| Adviser | Probabilities of changes in unemployment rate | | |
|---|---|---|---|
| | Decrease(D) | Remain same(S) | Increase(I) |
| $A_1$ | .1 | .1 | .8 |
| $A_2$ | .6 | .2 | .2 |
| $A_3$ | .2 | .6 | .2 |

($A_1, A_2, A_3$ for convenience) with different theories about the economy. The President is considering the adoption of a new policy on wage and price controls and is concerned about the impact of this policy on the unemployment rate. Each adviser gives the President his own predictions about the impact, the predictions being probabilities that the unemployment rate will lessen, remain unchanged, or increase. These are summarized in Table 9.1.

From previous experience with these advisers, the President has formed estimates in his own mind about the chances that each adviser has the correct theory of the economy. Indicate these by $\Pr(A_1) = \frac{1}{6}, \Pr(A_2) = \frac{1}{3}$, and $\Pr(A_3) = \frac{1}{2}$. Suppose the President adopts the proposed policy. One year later, the unemployment rate has increased. How should the President readjust his estimates about the correctness of his advisers' theories?

**Solution**   We are looking for $\Pr(A_1|I)$, $\Pr(A_2|I)$ and $\Pr(A_3|I)$. Compute first the probability of an increase in the unemployment rate:

$$\Pr(I) = \Pr(I|A_1)\Pr(A_1) + \Pr(I|A_2)\Pr(A_2) + \Pr(I|A_3)\Pr(A_3)$$
$$= \left(\frac{8}{10}\right)\left(\frac{1}{6}\right) + \left(\frac{2}{10}\right)\left(\frac{1}{3}\right) + \left(\frac{2}{10}\right)\left(\frac{1}{2}\right) = \frac{3}{10}.$$

Now use Bayes' Theorem:

$$\Pr(A_1|I) = \frac{\Pr(I|A_1)\Pr(A_1)}{\Pr(I)} = \frac{(8/10)(1/6)}{(3/10)} = \frac{4}{9},$$

$$\Pr(A_2|I) = \frac{\Pr(I|A_2)\Pr(A_2)}{\Pr(I)} = \frac{(2/10)(1/3)}{(3/10)} = \frac{2}{9},$$

$$\Pr(A_3|I) = \frac{\Pr(I|A_3)\Pr(A_3)}{\Pr(I)} = \frac{(2/10)(1/2)}{(3/10)} = \frac{1}{3}.$$

Note that $A_1$'s theory seemed least correct before the policy was adopted, but appears to be the most correct one a year later.

## D. Independent Events
Knowledge about some aspects of the outcome of an experiment on a sample space can influence the estimate of the probability of other aspects of the outcome. This influence is measured using conditional probability. Sometimes,

however, the extra knowledge does not influence the estimate. Consider, as an example, an experiment which consists of flipping a coin and rolling a die. The outcome of the experiment consists of two observations: a head or a tail for the coin, and a number between 1 and 6 for the die. The coin in no way affects the die, so the answer to the question "What is the probability that the die shows a 3?" is the same whether or not you know how the coin landed. More exactly, the probability that the die shows a 3 given the coin lands heads is the same as the probability that the die shows a 3 given no information about the coin. A probabilist would say that the coin flip and die roll are *independent* of each other. The general definition looks like this:

**DEFINITION**    Let Pr **be a probability measure on a set** $E$. **If** $X$ **and** $Y$ **are subsets of** $E$ **with** $\Pr(X) > 0$ **and** $\Pr(Y) > 0$, **then** $X$ **and** $Y$ **are** *independent events* **if** $\Pr(Y\,|\,X) = \Pr(Y)$.

If $X$ and $Y$ are independent, then

$$\Pr(X\,|\,Y) = \frac{\Pr(Y\,|\,X)\,\Pr(X)}{\Pr(Y)} = \frac{\Pr(Y)\,\Pr(X)}{\Pr(Y)} = \Pr(X).$$

The definition also gives the very important multiplicative rule for independent events.

■ *THEOREM 3*    Suppose $\Pr(X) > 0$ and $\Pr(Y) > 0$. Then $X$ and $Y$ are independent if and only if $\Pr(X \cap Y) = \Pr(X)\,\Pr(Y)$.

*Proof of Theorem 3*    Recalling equation (*) of Section II.C, we have

$$\Pr(X \cap Y) = \Pr(Y \cap X) = \Pr(Y\,|\,X)\,\Pr(X)$$

so that $\Pr(X \cap Y) = \Pr(Y)\,\Pr(X)$ if and only if $\Pr(Y\,|\,X) = \Pr(Y)$. □

Since the definition of independent events makes use of conditional probabilities, it must be restricted to events with positive probabilities. However, the equation $\Pr(X \cap Y) = \Pr(X)\,\Pr(Y)$ may hold true for events with zero probabilities. For this reason, many probability theorists *define* two events $X$ and $Y$ to be independent if the multiplicative rule is valid.

There is a standard mistake that many students make in thinking about independence. The independence of two events is not determined strictly from the intrinsic nature of the events. Independence is also a function of the probability measure that has been assigned to the original set of outcomes. Two events may be independent under one probability measure, but not independent under another measure. Consider the next two examples.

---

**EXAMPLE 8**    A pyramid is a solid figure with four triangular faces. Suppose the faces are labeled with the letters $a, b, c, d$. Roll the pyramid and observe which triangle faces the ground when the pyramid comes to rest. The set $E$

of outcomes may be denoted by $E = \{a, b, c, d\}$. Let $X$ be the subset $\{a, c\}$ and $Y$ the subset $\{b, c\}$. The $X \cap Y = \{c\}$. If Pr is the equiprobable measure on $E$, then $\Pr(X \cap Y) = \frac{1}{4}$ while $\Pr(X)\ \Pr(Y) = (\frac{2}{4})(\frac{2}{4}) = \frac{1}{4}$. Thus $X$ and $Y$ are independent events in this sample space.

**EXAMPLE 9**   Consider the same situation as Example 8, except that the probability measure is defined by assigning $a, b, c, d$ weights of $.4, .4, .1, .1$, respectively. Then $\Pr(X \cap Y) = .1$ while $\Pr(X)\ \Pr(Y) = (.5)(.5) = .25$. Thus $X$ and $Y$ are not independent in this sample space.

---

By making use of the multiplicative rule, the concept of independence is easily extended to more than two events. Three events $X, Y, Z$ will be called *mutually independent* if each pair of events is independent and

$$\Pr(X \cap Y \cap Z) = \Pr(X)\ \Pr(Y)\ \Pr(Z).$$

More generally, a set of events $X_1, X_2, \ldots, X_n$ in a sample space is *mutually independent* if the probability of the intersection of any $k$ distinct events in the set is equal to the product of the probabilities of the events where $k = 2, 3, \ldots, n$.

Independence is an important idea in discussion of situations in which the same experiment is repeated under identical conditions a number of times. Suppose, for example, that a fair coin is tossed three times. It is reasonable to assume that successive tosses of the coin do not influence each other. The coin has no memory of how it has landed before on earlier tosses. In other words, the sequence of outcomes is a mutually independent set. Let $H_i$ be the subset corresponding to obtaining a head on the $i$th toss, for $i = 1, 2, 3$, then the probability of obtaining heads on all three tosses is $\Pr(H_1 \cap H_2 \cap H_3)$. By the assumption of independence this is equal to $\Pr(H_1)\ \Pr(H_2)\ \Pr(H_3) = (\frac{1}{2})(\frac{1}{2})(\frac{1}{2}) = \frac{1}{8}$.

Modifying the example, suppose the coin has been weighted so the probability of a head on a single toss is $\frac{1}{3}$. If the coin is tossed, what is the probability that it will land heads exactly once? If $A$ is the subset corresponding to obtaining one head in three tosses, then $A$ can be written as the union of three disjoint subsets

$$A = (H_1 \cap T_2 \cap T_3) \cup (T_1 \cap H_2 \cap T_3) \cup (T_1 \cap T_2 \cap H_3)$$

where $T_i$ indicates a tail on toss $i$. By Condition (6) of Theorem 1 and the assumption of independence, we have

$$\Pr(A) = \Pr(H_1)\ \Pr(T_2)\ \Pr(T_3) + \Pr(T_1)\ \Pr(H_2)\ \Pr(T_3) + \Pr(T_1)\ \Pr(T_2)\ \Pr(H_3)$$

$$= \left(\frac{1}{3}\right)\left(\frac{2}{3}\right)\left(\frac{2}{3}\right) + \left(\frac{2}{3}\right)\left(\frac{1}{3}\right)\left(\frac{2}{3}\right) + \left(\frac{2}{3}\right)\left(\frac{2}{3}\right)\left(\frac{1}{3}\right) = \frac{12}{27}.$$

As a significant generalization of this example, consider an experiment with precisely two outcomes with associated probabilities $p$ and $q$, where $p$

and $q$ are nonnegative numbers with $p + q = 1$. Call the outcome with probability $p$ a "success" and the other outcome a "failure." Repeat this experiment a number of times in such a manner that the outcomes of any one experiment in no way affect the outcomes in any other experiment; that is, assume the sequence of outcomes forms a mutually independent set. Let $X_i$ represent the outcome of a success on the $i$th trial of the experiment and $Y_i$ the outcome of a failure on the $i$th trial. Then $\Pr(X_i) = p$ and $\Pr(Y_i) = q = 1 - p$ for each $i$.

Suppose the experiment is repeated four times. The probability that there are successes on the first and fourth trials and failures on the second and third is given by

$$\Pr(X_1 \cap Y_2 \cap Y_3 \cap X_4),$$

which by independence is equal to

$$\Pr(X_1)\Pr(Y_2)\Pr(Y_3)\Pr(X_4) = p\, q\, q\, p = p^2 q^2 = p^2(1 - p)^2.$$

It should be clear that any other prescribed sequence of two successes and two failures in four trials will also have probability $p^2(1 - p)^2$. In general, if the experiment is repeated $n$ times, then the probability of obtaining a prescribed sequence of exactly $k$ successes and $n - k$ failures will be $p^k q^{n-k} = p^k(1 - p)^{n-k}$.

A related question concerns the probability of obtaining exactly $k$ successes in $n$ trials. This probability will be $p^k q^{n-k}$ multiplied by the number of distinct ways one can prescribe a sequence of $k$ successes and $n - k$ failures. This number is equal to

$$\frac{n!}{k!(n-k)!} = \frac{n(n-1)(n-2)\cdots(n-k+1)(n-k)(n-k-1)\cdots(3)(2)(1)}{k(k-1)(k-2)\cdots 1(n-k)(n-k-1)\cdots 1}$$

$$= \frac{n(n-1)(n-2)\cdots(n-k+1)}{k(k-1)(k-2)\cdots 1}.$$

(See Exercises 25–27 for its determination.) Thus, the number of ways of exactly obtaining 3 successes in 7 trials is computed by letting $n = 7$, $k = 3$ so that $n - k + 1 = 5$. The number of ways is then $\dfrac{7 \cdot 6 \cdot 5}{3 \cdot 2 \cdot 1} = 35$. The probability that a fair coin will give 3 heads and 4 tails in 7 tosses is then $35(\frac{1}{2})^3(\frac{1}{2})^4 = \frac{35}{128}$.

## E. Expected Value

The discussion of gambles in the development of utility theory (Chapter 8) presented intuitively an idea of "expected value" or "expectation" of a gamble. This was a number meant to measure the average result of the gamble if it is made many times. In this section the concept will be formally extended to more general probabilistic situations.

**DEFINITION   Let Pr be a probability measure on a finite set $E$. A *random variable* is a real-valued function $R$ defined on $E$. Let $a_1, a_2, \ldots, a_k$ be the set of**

**distinct values taken on by the function** $R$. **Then the** *expected value* **or** *expectation* **of** $R$, **denoted** $EV(R)$, **is the number**

$$EV(R) = \sum_{i=1}^{k} a_i \Pr(R = a_1) = a_1 \Pr(R = a_1) + \cdots + a_k \Pr(R = a_k).$$

The mysteries of this equation will disappear after considering the next few examples.

---

**EXAMPLE 10**  Roll a fair die and let $R$ be equal to the number showing on the top of the die when it comes to rest. Then $R$ takes on the values $1, 2, 3, 4, 5, 6$. The event "$R = 3$" is just the event that the die shows a 3 and thus has probability $\frac{1}{6}$, so that $\Pr(R = 3) = \frac{1}{6}$. Similarly, $R$ takes on each of the other values with probability $\frac{1}{6}$. The expected value of $R$ is given by

$$EV(R) = 1\left(\frac{1}{6}\right) + 2\left(\frac{1}{6}\right) + 3\left(\frac{1}{6}\right) + 4\left(\frac{1}{6}\right) + 5\left(\frac{1}{6}\right) + 6\left(\frac{1}{6}\right) = \frac{21}{6} = \frac{7}{2}.$$

**EXAMPLE 11**  Roll the die of Example 10, but this time let $R$ be the square of the number that appears on top. The function $R$ takes on the values $1, 4, 9, 16, 25,$ and 36, each with probability $\frac{1}{6}$. The expected value of this random variable is $1(1/6) + 4(1/6) + 9(1/6) + 16(1/6) + 25(1/6) + 36(1/6) = 91/6$.

**EXAMPLE 12**  Suppose you win \$3 every time the fair die shows an odd number and lose \$2 each time an even number appears. The set $E$ of outcomes of rolling the die is the same, $E = \{1, 2, 3, 4, 5, 6\}$. Define the random variable $R$ on $E$ by $R(1) = R(3) = R(5) = +3$, and $R(2) = R(4) = R(6) = -2$. Then $\Pr(R = 3) = \Pr(\{1, 3, 5\}) = \frac{1}{6} + \frac{1}{6} + \frac{1}{6} = \frac{1}{2}$, and $\Pr(R = -2)$ is also $\frac{1}{2}$. Then the expected value of $R$ is $3(\frac{1}{2}) + (-2)(\frac{1}{2}) = \frac{1}{2}$. The interpretation of expected value here is that if you roll the die a great many times, you can expect to win, on the average, 50 cents on each roll.

---

Examples 10–12 illustrate the fact that the expected value of a random variable need not be one of the values the random variable actually takes on.

---

**EXAMPLE 13**  Harvey's roommate accidentally knocks Harvey's anthropology term paper into the wastebasket. By the time Harvey discovers what has happened, the janitor has cleaned up the entire dormitory. The contents of the wastebasket have been dumped into one of 9 fully packed garbage cans outside the dorm. Harvey insists that his roommate find the paper. Find the expected value of the number of garbarge cans Harvey's roommate will empty in order to find the term paper.

**Solution**    When the roommate arranges the cans in a line for searching, the position of the can containing the paper is the only critical factor. Let $X_i$ represent the outcome that the paper is in the $i$th can. It is reasonable to assume that each of the nine possible outcomes has probability $\frac{1}{9}$. If the paper is in the $i$th can, then the roommate must empty $i$ cans. Let the random variable $R$ be defined by $R(X_i) = i$. The problem is solved by computing $EV(R)$. Now

$$EV(R) = \sum_{i=1}^{9} i \Pr(R = i)$$

$$= \sum_{i=1}^{9} i \Pr(X_i)$$

$$= \sum_{i=1}^{9} i \left(\frac{1}{9}\right) = \left(\frac{1}{9}\right) \sum_{i=1}^{9} i = \frac{1}{9}(45) = 5.$$

Example 13 shows that there may be many applications of expected value when the random variable is measuring quantities other than money. Example 14 provides another example.

**EXAMPLE 14**    In a study designed to test the efficiency of the postal service, a researcher mailed 1000 letters from Los Angeles to New York on August 1. He kept a careful record of the delivery dates of each letter. The data are summarized in Table 9.2. What is the expected number of days for delivery of a letter?

**Table 9.2**

| Date of delivery | Number of letters delivered |
|------------------|-----------------------------|
| August 4 | 120 |
| August 5 | 200 |
| August 6 | 360 |
| August 7 | 210 |
| August 8 | 110 |

**Solution**    Formulate the question as a probability problem by letting the experiment consist of mailing a letter and observing the date of its delivery. Define the random variable $R$ to be the number of days it takes the letter to be delivered. The problem is to find $EV(R)$.

From the data in Table 9.2, we see that $R$ takes on values $3, 4, 5, 6$, and $7$ with respective probabilities of $.12, .20, .36, .21$ and $.11$. The expected value of $R$ is $3(.12) + 4(.20) + 5(.36) + 6(.21) + 7(.11) = 4.99$. The researcher concluded that, on the average, the postal service takes just under 5 days to deliver a letter.

A final example shows how expected value considerations are used in decision making.

---

**EXAMPLE 15**    A suburban San Francisco construction firm is considering bidding on a contract to build one of two new schools. One possibility is that the firm will submit a bid to construct a high school. The firm estimates that it would make a $50,000 profit on the building, but that it would cost $1,000 to prepare the plans that must be submitted with the bid. (In estimating the profit, all costs, including that of the bid, have been considered.) The second possibility is a bid on a new elementary school. The firm has built several elementary schools in the recent past and estimates that the preparation costs for a bid would be only $500 while the potential profit is $40,000. The construction company has enough resources to submit only one bid. Past experience leads the company to estimate that it has one chance in five of submitting the winning bid for the high school and one chance in four for the winning bid on the elementary school. Which bid should the company prepare and submit?

**Solution**    The relevant data are summarized in Table 9.3.

**Table 9.3**

| Contract | Profit | Bid cost | Probability of winning |
|---|---|---|---|
| High school | $50,000 | $1,000 | .20 |
| Elementary school | $40,000 | $500 | .25 |

If the company submits a winning bid on the high school, its profit is $50,000. If it submits a bid on the high school that is not accepted, then its profit is $-\$1000$. Thus the expected value of submitting a bid on the high school is $50,000)(.20) + (-\$1000)(.8) = \$9200$. The expected value for submitting a bid on the elementary school is $(\$40,000)(.25) + (-\$500)(.75) = \$9625$. This indicates that the firm should submit the bid for constructing the elementary school.

---

## F. Variance and Standard Deviation

The expected value of a random variable $R$ provides information about the "long-term" average value of $R$ when the associated experiment is repeated over and over again. For many purposes, however, an average value may give insufficient or even misleading information.

Consider the distribution of income among a large population. A study shows that the average annual income in the United States is $10,000. Based

**Table 9.4**   Distribution of income
in Ferrisburg

| Income | Number of persons |
|--------|-------------------|
| $5,000 | 10 |
| $8,000 | 20 |
| $10,000 | 40 |
| $12,000 | 20 |
| $15,000 | 10 |

**Table 9.5**

| $i$ | $Pr(R = i)$ | $Pr(S = i)$ |
|-----|-------------|-------------|
| 1 | .3 | 0 |
| 2 | .05 | .05 |
| 3 | .05 | .2 |
| 4 | .2 | .5 |
| 5 | .05 | .2 |
| 6 | .05 | .05 |
| 7 | .3 | 0 |

on this figure, the Congress decides to classify all communities into three categories of income: below average, average, and above average. Communities in which the average income is below $10,000 will be singled out for financial assistance. Three hypothetical communities are of interest here, each having a population of 100 wage earners. In the town of New Haven, every person earns exactly $10,000. In Bristol, 99 persons are unemployed and earn nothing and one person has a trust fund that provides him with $1 million each year. In Ferrisburg, the income distribution is described by Table 9.4.

In each of the three communities, the total community income is $1 million so the average income in each place is $10,000. The town of Bristol would be ineligible for the governmental assistance, even though 99 percent of the population is in a desperate situation! If we want to determine which communities need assistance, more information than average income is required. A measure of "deviation" from the average provides such additional data.

To develop a measure of deviation, consider another example. There are two random variables, $R$ and $S$, defined on the same sample space and each takes on the values $1, 2, 3, 4, 5, 6, 7$, but with different probabilities. These probabilities are given in Table 9.5.

It is easy to calculate that $EV(R) = EV(S) = 4$. Both random variables have an average of 4. Yet it is more likely that the random variable $S$ will take on values closer to the average than that $R$ will. For example, the probability that $R$ lies within 1 unit of the average value of 4 is

$$Pr(R = 3, 4, 5) = .05 + .2 + .05 = .3,$$

while the probability that $S$ lies within one unit of the average is

$$Pr(S = 3, 4, 5) = .2 + .5 + .2 = .9.$$

In only about one time in ten will the values of $S$ differ from the mean by more than one unit, but this will happen about 7 out of 10 times for $R$. The random variable $R$ has more "variability" or "deviation" about its average value than does the random variable $S$.

Suppose that an experiment is carried out using this sample space and the outcome results in the random variable $R$ taking on the value $i$. Then the number

$$i - EV(R)$$

is called the *deviation of i from EV(R)*. The deviation will be positive if $i > EV(R)$ and negative if $i < EV(R)$.

In our example, $EV(R) = 4$, so that the deviations look like:

| $i$ | $i - 4$ |
| --- | --- |
| 1 | $-3$ |
| 2 | $-2$ |
| 3 | $-1$ |
| 4 | $0$ |
| 5 | $1$ |
| 6 | $2$ |
| 7 | $3$ |

The sum of all the deviations is not a good measure of the variation of the random variable, because that sum is 0. We would hope that the variation should be 0 only if the random variable always assumed its expected value, and that the variation would be positive otherwise. We would make the deviations positive in a variety of ways: consider only the absolute values $|i - EV(R)|$ or the square of the differences $(i - EV(R))^2$, for example. It turns out to be more convenient to use the squares of the deviations.

In constructing a measure of variation, then, we might simply add up the squares of the deviations from the expected values. This is not quite satis-factory either, since the sum would be the same, for example, for both random variables $R$ and $S$ in the case. The measure of variation should indicate that $R$ varies more than $S$ from the average values of 4. To obtain such a measure, multiply each particular $(i - EV(R))^2$ by the relative frequency with which it is likely to occur, $\Pr(R = i)$. If this is done for the random variable $R$, the result is

$$(1 - 4)^2 \Pr(R = 1) + (2 - 4)^2 \Pr(R = 2) + \cdots (7 - 4)^2 \Pr(R = 7)$$
$$= 9(.3) + 4(.05) + 1(.05) + 0(.2) + 1(.05) + 4(.05) + 9(.3)$$
$$= 5.09.$$

A similar computation for the random variable $S$ yields

$$(1 - 4)^2 \Pr(S = 1) + \cdots + (7 - 4)^2 \Pr(S = 7)$$
$$= 9(0) + 4(.05) + 1(.2) + 0(.5) + 1(.2) + 4(.05) + 9(0)$$
$$= .8$$

so that the random variable $S$ has a smaller measure of variability then the random variable $R$. Such a measure can be defined for any random variable.

**DEFINITION** Let Pr be a probability measure on a finite set $E$ and suppose $R$ is a random variable taking on values $a_1, a_2, \ldots, a_k$. Then the *variance of R*,

**denoted** $\mathrm{Var}\,(R)$ **is the number**

$$\mathrm{Var}\,(R) = (a_1 - EV(R))^2 \, \mathrm{Pr}\,(R = a_1) + (a_2 - EV(R))^2 \, \mathrm{Pr}\,(R = a_2) + \cdots$$
$$+ (a_k - EV(R))^2 \, \mathrm{Pr}\,(R = a_k)$$

$$= \sum_{i=1}^{k} (a_i - EV(R))^2 \, \mathrm{Pr}\,(R = a_i).$$

---

**EXAMPLE 16**    Let $R$ be the random variable whose values are the number of dots showing on the top of a fair die when it comes to rest after being rolled. As noted earlier, $R$ takes on the values $1, 2, 3, 4, 5, 6$, each with probability $\frac{1}{6}$. The expected value of $R$ is $\frac{7}{2}$ (Example 10). The variation of $R$ is

$$\mathrm{Var}\,(R) = \frac{1}{6}\left[\left(1 - \frac{7}{2}\right)^2 + \left(2 - \frac{7}{2}\right)^2 + \cdots \left(6 - \frac{7}{2}\right)^2\right] = \frac{35}{12}.$$

---

Given a random variable $R$ associated with a sample space, it is possible to define a new random variable $D_R$ which takes on value $(i - EV(R))^2$ whenever $R$ takes on value $i$. Then the variation of $R$ is just the expected value of $D_R$. Another formula for the variation of $R$ is given by the following formula.

■ **THEOREM 4**    $\mathrm{Var}\,(R) = (\sum_{i=1}^{k} a_i^2 \, \mathrm{Pr}\,(R = a_i)) - (EV(R))^2$

**Proof of Theorem 4**    Expand the indicated sum in the definition of variation:

$$\mathrm{Var}\,(R) = \sum_{i=1}^{k} (a_i - EV(R))^2 \, \mathrm{Pr}\,(R = a_i)$$

$$= \sum_{i=1}^{k} (a_i^2 - 2a_i EV(R) + (EV(R))^2) \, \mathrm{Pr}\,(R = a_i)$$

$$= \sum_{i=1}^{k} a_i^2 \, \mathrm{Pr}\,(R = a_i) - 2EV(R) \sum_{i=1}^{k} a_i \, \mathrm{Pr}\,(R = a_i)$$

$$+ (EV(R))^2 \sum_{i=1}^{k} \mathrm{Pr}\,(R = a_i)$$

$$= \sum_{i=1}^{k} a_i^2 \, \mathrm{Pr}\,(R = a_i) - 2EV(R)EV(R) + (EV(R))^2(1)$$

$$= \sum_{i=1}^{k} a_i^2 \, \mathrm{Pr}\,(R = a) - 2(EV(R))^2 + (EV(R))^2. \quad \square$$

The formula of Theorem 4 is easier to use than the definition of variation since the former requires only one subtraction while the latter demands $k$ subtractions. Using the formula to compute the variation of the random variable to Exercise 16, for instance, involves the calculation

$$\text{Var}(R) = \frac{1}{6}[(1^2 + 2^2 + \cdots + 6^2)] - \left(\frac{7}{2}\right)^2 = \frac{91}{6} - \frac{49}{4} = \frac{35}{12}.$$

Since the variance is calculated using squares of the values of the random variable, the units of $\text{Var}(R)$ are the squares of the units of $R$. If the values of $R$ are dollars, then the units of $\text{Var}(R)$ would be "square dollars." In many instances, it is convenient to have a measure of variability about the expected value which is in the same type of units as the random variable itself. This can be accomplished by determining the nonnegative square root of the variance. The resulting number, $\sqrt{\text{Var}(R)}$, is called the *standard deviation* of $R$. It is often denoted by $\text{SD}(R)$.

As a final example, note that the standard deviation of the random variable associated with the throwing of a fair die is $\sqrt{35/12}$ which is approximately 1.71.

## III. A PROBABILISTIC MODEL

Chapter 3 discussed a deterministic model for single species population growth, the so called "pure-birth process." The assumptions of this process are that the population is made up entirely of identical organisms which reproduce independently at a rate that is the same for every individual at all moments. The deterministic model for the pure-birth process is the first-order differential equation $dN/dt = bN$ where $N = N(t)$ is the population at time $t$ and $b$ is the positive constant birth rate for each individual. The solution of the differential equation is $N(t) = Ae^{bt}$ where $A$ is the population at time $t = 0$.

The deterministic model assumes not simply that each individual *may* reproduce but that in actuality it *does* reproduce with absolute certainty. This section outlines a probabilistic model for the pure-birth process. The assumption that makes this a probabilistic model is the assertion that there is a certain probability that a particular individual will reproduce in a given time interval.

More precisely, we assume that the probability of reproduction in a very short time interval is directly proportional to the length of the interval; that is, there is a constant $b$ such that in any small time interval of duration $\Delta t$ the probability of reproduction is $b \Delta t$. Take $\Delta t$ sufficiently small so that no individual can reproduce more than once in the time interval. Thus, during the interval of length $\Delta t$, a given individual either produces one offspring with probability $b \Delta t$ or produces no offspring with probability $1 - b \Delta t$. In a population of $N$ organisms, the probability of a birth during the time interval is then $Nb \Delta t$.

Let $P_N(t + \Delta t)$ denote the probability that the population is of size $N$ at time $t + \Delta t$. This outcome can occur in one of two distinct ways:

a) At time $t$, there were $N - 1$ individuals and one birth occurred in the next $\Delta t$ seconds, or

b) At time $t$, there were $N$ individuals in the population and no births occurred in the next $\Delta t$ seconds.

(By choosing $\Delta t$ sufficiently small, it is safe to assume that not more than one birth takes place. As in any pure-birth process, the assumption is that no individual dies).

For each positive integer $N$ ($N = 1, 2, 3, \ldots$), the fact that (a) and (b) describe disjoint events gives

$$P_N(t + \Delta t) = P_{N-1}(t)b(N - 1)\Delta t + P_N(t)(1 - bN\,\Delta t). \tag{1}$$

Rewrite this equation as

$$P_N(t + \Delta t) - P_N(t) = -bN\,\Delta t P_N(t) + P_{N-1}b(N - 1)\Delta t$$

and divide each side by $\Delta t$ to obtain

$$\frac{P_N(t + \Delta t) - P_N(t)}{\Delta t} = -bN P_N(t) + P_{N-1}(t)b(N - 1). \tag{2}$$

Taking the limit of each side of (2) as $\Delta t$ tends to zero yields a differential equation

$$\frac{dP_N(t)}{dt} = -bN P_N(t) + b(N - 1)P_{N-1}(t). \tag{3}$$

There is such a differential equation for each positive value of $N$. Denote the size of the population at time 0 by $A$ so that $P_A(0) = 1$ and $P_N(0) = 0$ whenever $N \neq A$.

When $N$ is equal to original population $A$, Eq. (3) becomes

$$\frac{dP_A(t)}{dt} = -bA P_A(t) + P_{A-1}(t)b(A - 1). \tag{4}$$

Under the assumption of this simple model that there are only births and no deaths, the population is always at least as large as $A$. The probability that there are ever less than $A$ individuals is 0. In particular, $P_{A-1}(t) = 0$ for all $t$. Equation (4) then simplifies to:

$$\frac{dP_A(t)}{dt} = -bA P_A(t). \tag{5}$$

If we let $y = P_A(t)$, Eq. (5) is of the form $dy/dt = -bAy$ which can be solved by integration to obtain $y = y_0 e^{-bAt}$, where $y_0 = y(0) = P_A(0) = 1$. Thus the model gives

$$P_A(t) = e^{-bAt}. \tag{6}$$

Equation (6) predicts the probability that the population is still at size $A$ at time $t$; that is, the probability that no births have occurred in the interval $[0, t]$. Note that this probability is always positive, but that it decreases as time increases, asymptotically approaching 0 as $t$ increases without bound.

Thus far, the consequences derived from this model are:

$$P_N(t) = \begin{cases} 0 & \text{if } N < A \\ e^{-bAt} & \text{if } N = A. \end{cases}$$

The next step is to calculate $P_{A+1}(t)$, the probability of a population of $A + 1$ individuals at time $t$. Substitute $N = A + 1$ into Eq. (3):

$$\frac{dP_{A+1}(t)}{dt} = -b(A + 1)P_{A+1}(t) + bAP_A(t)$$

and use the result of Eq. (6) to obtain

$$\frac{dP_{A+1}(t)}{dt} + b(A + 1)P_{A+1}(t) = bAe^{-bAt}. \tag{7}$$

Fquation (7) has the form

$$\frac{dx}{dt} + b(A + 1)x = bAe^{-bAt} \tag{8}$$

where $x = P_{A+1}(t)$. Equation (8) is a first-order linear differential equation. It may be solved (see Appendix V) by multiplying through by an integrating factor, $e^{b(A+1)t}$, and then integrating:

$$e^{b(A+1)t}\frac{dx}{dt} + e^{b(A+1)t}(A + 1)bx = bAe^{bt} \tag{9}$$

or

$$\frac{d}{dt}(e^{b(A+1)t}x) = bAe^{bt} \tag{10}$$

which becomes, upon integration,

$$e^{b(A+1)t}x = Ae^{bt} + \text{Constant}; \tag{11}$$

that is,

$$e^{b(A+1)t}P_{A+1}(t) = Ae^{bt} + \text{Constant}. \tag{12}$$

Since $P_{A+1}(0) = 0$, the constant of integration is equal to $-A$ and the solution of the differential equation is

$$P_{A+1}(t) = Ae^{-Abt}(1 - e^{-bt}). \tag{13}$$

Once $P_{A+1}(t)$ is known, it can be used to find $P_{A+2}(t)$ by making use of Eq. (13) and the modeling Eq. (3) with $N = A + 2$:

$$\frac{dP_{A+2}(t)}{dt} = -b(A + 2)P_{A+2}(t) + b(A + 1)P_{A+1}(t) \tag{14}$$

or

$$\frac{dP_{A+2}(t)}{dt} + b(A + 2)P_{A+2}(t) = b(A + 1)Ae^{-Abt}(1 - e^{-bt}). \tag{15}$$

Equation (15) is again a first-order linear differential equation. Multiply each side of the equation by $e^{b(A+2)t}$, integrate, and use the fact that $P_{A+2}(0) = 0$ to obtain the solution

$$P_{A+2}(t) = \frac{(A + 1)A}{2} e^{-Abt}(1 - e^{-bt})^2. \tag{16}$$

Continue in a similar manner to find $P_{A+3}(t), P_{A+4}(t), P_{A+5}(t)$, and so forth. The general formula, which may be checked by induction, is

$$P_N(t) = \binom{N - 1}{A - 1} e^{-Abt}(1 - e^{-bt})^{N-A} \text{ for all } N \geq A, \tag{17}$$

where

$$\binom{N - 1}{A - 1} = \frac{(N - 1)!}{(A - 1)!(N - A)!}$$

(see Exercise 48).

The solution (Eq. 17) of the probabilistic model for a pure-birth process gives the probability distribution of the size of the population at time $t$. While the deterministic model gives a single number as the prediction for the population size at time $t$, the probabilistic model gives much more information; namely, the relative likelihood of each different possible population size at time $t$.

The deterministic model was much simpler to treat mathematically than the probabilistic one. What is the connection between these two models? In what sense is the deterministic model an approximation for the probabilistic one? This relationship becomes clearer if the solution of the probabilistic model is used to compute the expected value of the size of the population at time $t$. This expected value turns out to be $Ae^{bt}$, the number predicted by the deterministic model. The probabilistic model also provides a measure of the variation from this expected value, a measure which is unavailable if a deterministic approach alone is used. The variation is $Ae^{bt}(e^{bt} - 1)$. The calculation of expected value and variance is left to the exercises.

## IV. STOCHASTIC PROCESSES

### A. Definitions

A *stochastic process* is a sequence of experiments in which the outcome of each experiment depends on chance. A stochastic process consisting of a finite number of experiments each having a finite number of possible outcomes is called a *finite stochastic process*. (The Greek word "stochos" means "guess.")

The experiments may or may not be related to each other. The outcomes of one experiment may or may not affect the probabilities of the outcomes of subsequent experiments. Two types of stochastic processes will be emphasized in this book. In the first, the experiments are mutually independent. In the second, called a *Markov chain*, the likelihood of an outcome of one experiment depends only on the outcome of the immediately preceding experiment.

Stochastic processes have been widely used as mathematical models in the study of many diverse social, physical, and biological problems. Researchers have used stochastic processes to investigate problems in economics, genetics, learning theory, educational planning, demography, job mobility, social conformity, evolution, consumer buying behavior, the geographical diffusion of innovations, and in many other fields. In many of these applications a process is studied which may be one of various "states" at each moment. The "states" correspond to the outcomes of the experiments. A sequence of experiments is constructed by examining the process at equally spaced time intervals.

---

**EXAMPLE 17**    The Board of Trustees of a small Vermont college decides to choose a student from one of two dormitories to serve on a housing committee. A dorm will be chosen at random and then a student will be selected at random from that dorm. The dormitories are Starr Hall and Forrest Hall. There are 30 students in Starr; twenty oppose coeducational housing and 10 favor it. Of the 60 students living in Forrest, only 10 favor coed housing and all the others oppose it. What is the probability that the student chosen to serve on the committee will favor coed housing?

**Solution**    Describe the situation in terms of a stochastic process involving two experiments, each with two possible outcomes. In experiment 1, a dorm is chosen. There are two possible outcomes: Starr ($S$) and Forrest ($F$), with probabilities $\Pr(S) = \Pr(F) = \frac{1}{2}$. In experiment 2, a student is chosen. The possible outcomes are: Approves coed housing ($A$) or disapproves coed housing ($D$). The probabilities of $A$ and $D$ depend on which dorm is chosen; that is, they are conditional probabilities. These probabilities are:

$$\Pr(A|S) = \frac{10}{30} = \frac{1}{3}, \qquad \Pr(D|S) = \frac{20}{30} = \frac{2}{3},$$

$$\Pr(A|F) = \frac{10}{60} = \frac{1}{6}, \qquad \Pr(D|F) = \frac{50}{60} = \frac{5}{6}.$$

The problem is to determine $\Pr(A)$. By Theorem 1 and the definition of conditional probability,

$$\Pr(A) = \Pr(A \cap F) + \Pr(A \cap F^c)$$
$$= \Pr(A \cap F) + \Pr(A \cap S)$$
$$= \Pr(A|F)\Pr(F) + \Pr(A|S)\Pr(S)$$
$$= \left(\frac{1}{6}\right)\left(\frac{1}{2}\right) + \left(\frac{1}{3}\right)\left(\frac{1}{2}\right) = \frac{1}{4}.$$

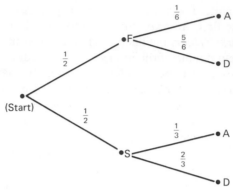

**Fig. 9.1**   Tree diagram corresponding to
Example 17.

## B. Tree Diagrams

A convenient way to study stochastic processes is through the use of tree
diagrams. A tree diagram summarizing the information of Example 17 is shown
in Fig. 9.1.

From the starting point, or *node*, there are two *branches*, corresponding to
the two possible outcomes of the first experiment. The numbers along each
branch give the probabilities of each outcome. From each outcome of the first
experiment there are again a pair of branches representing the two possible
outcomes of the second experiment. The numbers on these branches indicate
the probabilities of the outcomes.

The probability of tracing through any particular path in a tree diagram is
the product of the probabilities along the branches of that path. To find the
probability of selecting a student who approves coed housing, $\Pr(A)$, simply add
up the probabilities of all distinct paths from the start to outcome $A$. In a
similar fashion, the probability of a particular outcome of the final experiment
of a sequence can be computed by summing the probabilities of every path in
the tree diagram which ends at that outcome. The next example gives an additional illustration.

---

**EXAMPLE 18**   The winners of some tennis matches are determined by playing a
best-of-three sets competition. The competitors keep playing until one of them
wins two sets; no set may end in a tie. Figure 9.2 shows a tree diagram illustrating
the possible outcomes for one of the players. Note that the outcomes of certain
sets determine whether or not successive sets are played.

Suppose the player under study has an even chance of winning the first
set, that whenever he wins a set, he has a tendency to relax in the next set so
that his probability of winning drops to $\frac{3}{8}$, and that whenever he loses a set, he
exerts himself to such an extent that his probability of winning the next set
jumps to $\frac{3}{4}$. What is the probability that he will win the match?

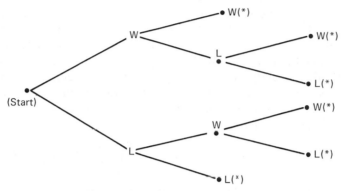

**Fig. 9.2**   Tree diagram for best-of-three tennis competition.
W = Win, L = Lose, and (*) indicates that the match terminates
at the node.

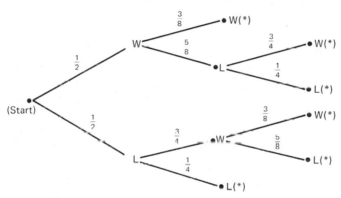

**Figure 9.3**

The probabilities along the branches given by this information are indicated
in Fig. 9.3.

The probability of winning is

$$\Pr(\text{Wins match}) = \Pr(WW) + \Pr(WLW) + \Pr(LWW)$$

$$= \left(\frac{1}{2}\right)\left(\frac{3}{8}\right) + \left(\frac{1}{2}\right)\left(\frac{5}{8}\right)\left(\frac{3}{4}\right) + \left(\frac{1}{2}\right)\left(\frac{3}{4}\right)\left(\frac{3}{8}\right) = \frac{9}{16},$$

where $\Pr(LWW)$ is the probability of losing the first set and then winning the
second and third sets.  The events $WW$ and $WLW$ are similarly defined.

After the first set, the probability of winning a subsequent set depends only
on the result of the previous set.  This probability does not depend, for example,
on the total number of sets he has won previously, or on how many sets have
been played.  The assumptions about this player are those of a Markov chain.

As an alternative possibility, suppose the results of each set are independent of the results of earlier sets. Then the probabilities along each branch might be assigned values of $\frac{1}{2}$. In this, the probability of winning the match is given by $\Pr(WW) + \Pr(WLW) + \Pr(LWW) = (\frac{1}{2})(\frac{1}{2}) + (\frac{1}{2})(\frac{1}{2})(\frac{1}{2}) + (\frac{1}{2})(\frac{1}{2})(\frac{1}{2}) = \frac{1}{2}$.

As a third possibility, suppose the player gets stronger as the match goes on so that his probability of winning each set is twice the probability of winning the previous set. If his probability of winning the first set is $\frac{1}{5}$, then his probability of winning the match is

$$\Pr(WW) + \Pr(WLW) + \Pr(LWW) = \left(\frac{1}{5}\right)\left(\frac{2}{5}\right) + \left(\frac{1}{5}\right)\left(\frac{3}{5}\right)\left(\frac{4}{5}\right) + \left(\frac{4}{5}\right)\left(\frac{2}{5}\right)\left(\frac{4}{5}\right)$$
$$= \frac{54}{125}.$$

The assumptions in this case do not correspond to either a mutually independent sequence of experiments or to a Markov chain.

## C. Examples

This chapter concludes with brief descriptions of a number of stochastic processes in which a single experiment is repeated a number of times. Each repetition of the experiment will be a "step" and the outcomes of the experiment are "states." The viewpoint is one of studying a process that moves in a sequence of steps through a set of states. At each step, there are certain probabilities of being in each of the possible states; these probabilities are the likelihoods of the various outcomes of the experiment.

**EXAMPLE 19**   At each a step a coin is tossed. There are two possible states: heads and tails. The probability of being in the "head" state on each step is $\frac{1}{2}$. It is independent of all previous steps.

**EXAMPLE 20**   Each step is a new day. The states are the hours of the day. We are interested in the time you go to sleep. There is a probability that can be attached to each of the 24 states for today's step. Knowledge of what the probabilities were yesterday will help determine what probabilities to assign for the states today.

**EXAMPLE 21**   Each step is a new month. There are two states, "Flakes No More" and "Head, Neck, and Shoulders," two antidandruff shampoos. We are concerned with the percentage of consumers who use each product. Interpret this as the probability associated with picking a person at random and determining which shampoo she uses. If 60 percent of the consumers use Flakes No More, assume that there is a probability of .6 that a randomly chosen person uses that shampoo.

**EXAMPLE 22**    An investigator for the Equal Opportunity Commission analyzed job mobility for women in Cook County, Illinois. He determined from census data the percentage of women who were professionals, skilled workers, and unskilled workers. He amassed data for six successive generations of women. He then formulated a stochastic process with six steps and three states. Each step corresponded to a new generation. The states were: professional, skilled, and unskilled.

**EXAMPLE 23 (RANDOM WALK)**    A particle is constrained to move along the $x$-axis. It starts at 0 and at each step it may move one unit to the right or one unit to the left. The direction of motion is randomly chosen. To view this motion as a stochastic process, consider that the particle may be in any one of an infinite number of states, corresponding to possible positions it might reach on the $x$-axis $(0, \pm 1, \pm 2, \ldots)$. The study of random walk along a line, in the plane, or in higher dimensional spaces has many applications in modern physics.

**EXAMPLE 24**    A mathematically inclined sports broadcaster applied stochastic processes to study the movement of the puck in a hockey game between the Montreal Canadians and the Philadelphia Flyers. The playing area of the hockey rink can be divided into 5 states: center ice, Montreal territory, Philadelphia territory, Montreal goal, and Philadelphia goal. Each step corresponds to a change of state of the puck. Thus, the puck can not enter the state of "Montreal goal" from the state of "center ice" without first passing through the state of "Montreal territory."

**EXAMPLE 25 (GENETICS)**    The simplest type of inheritance of traits in human beings occurs when a trait is governed by a pair of genes, each of which may be of two types, say $A$ and $B$. An individual may have an $AA$ combination or $AB$ (which is genetically the same as $BA$) or $BB$. Very often, the $AA$ and $AB$ types are indistinguishable in appearance, in which case it is said that $A$ *dominates B*.

An individual is called *dominant* if he has $AA$ genes, *recessive* if he has $BB$, and *hybrid* if he has an $AB$ pairing.

In reproduction, the offspring inherits one gene of the pair from each parent. A basic assumption of genetics is that these genes are selected at random, independently of each other.

Geneticists are interested in the probability of an individual being in one of the three states—dominant, recessive, or hybrid—and in how this probability changes from generation to generation. Each succeeding generation is a new step in this stochastic process.

---

The next chapter is devoted to a detailed study of Markov chains, the type of stochastic process that has been most widely used in model building in social and life sciences.

## EXERCISES

### I. THE NEED FOR PROBABILITY MODELS

1. Can you think of any further objections to the use of deterministic models in the social or life sciences?

2. Are the responses to the objections made against deterministic models adequate to your way of thinking?

3. In what ways can physics be validly described as more "rigorous" than mathematical social science?

### II. WHAT IS PROBABILITY?

#### A. Fundamental Definitions

4. Find a probability measure consistent with the observation that a flipped coin shows tails eight times more frequently than heads.

5. a) Show that the deffnition of $Pr(X)$ in Example 3 establishes a valid probability measure.

   b) Show that the definition of $Pr(X)$ in Example 4 establishes a valid probability measure.

6. Construct an example of a sample space on a set $E$ so that for some nonempty subset $X$ of $E$, $Pr(X) = 0$.

7. Prove Theorem 1.

8. Find $Pr(A \cup B)$ if $Pr(A) = .6$, $Pr(B) = .2$, and $Pr(A \cap B) = .5$.

9. If $Pr(A \cap B) = \frac{1}{5}$, $Pr(A^C) = \frac{1}{4}$, and $Pr(B) = \frac{1}{3}$, find $Pr(A \cup B)$.

10. Prove that $Pr(X \cup Y \cup Z) = Pr(X) + Pr(Y) + Pr(Z) - Pr(X \cap Y) - Pr(X \cap Z) - Pr(Y \cap Z) + Pr(X \cap Y \cap Z)$ for any three subsets $X, Y, Z$ of a sample space.

11. Roll a pair of dice and assume all 36 possible outcomes are equiprobable. Find the probability of each of the following events:

a) The sum of the numbers on the faces is seven.

b) The sum of the numbers is odd.

c) Both numbers are odd.

d) The product of the numbers is greater than 10.

12. The *odds* in favor of an outcome are $r$ to $s$ if the probability of the outcome is $p$ and $r/s = p/(1 - p)$.

a) Show that if the odds in favor of an outcome are $r$ to $s$, then the probability that the outcome will occur is $r/(r + s)$.

b) If you believe the Los Angeles Dodgers have 1 chance in 3 of winning the World Series next year, what odds should you offer in making bets about the series?

13. Probability measures may also be defined on some infinite sets. Let $E$ be the set of all positive integers and let the weight of integer $j$ be equal to $(\frac{1}{2})^j$. The probability, $Pr(X)$, of a subset $X$ of $E$ is defined to be the sum of the weights of the elements of $X$.

a) Show that $\Pr(E) = 1$.

b) Show that Pr, defined in this manner, satisfies the defining properties of a probability measure.

c) What is the probability that an integer chosen from this sample space will be even?

**B. Conditional Probability**

14. Under what conditions does $\Pr(X|Y) = \Pr(Y|X)$?

15. In Example 5, find the probability that Bleier wins given that Neff loses. Which candidate benefits most from Neff's withdrawal? (Note that "best" may be defined in several different ways).

16. There are three chests, each having two drawers. The first chest has a gold coin in each drawer, the second chest has a gold coin in one drawer and a silver coin in the other, and the third chest has a silver coin in each drawer. A chest is chosen at random and a drawer opened. If that drawer contains a gold coin, what is the probability that the other drawer contains a gold coin? Warning: the answer is not $\frac{1}{2}$.

17. If $X$ and $Y$ are events with positive probabilities, show that $\Pr(X|Y)\,\Pr(Y) = \Pr(Y|X)\,\Pr(X)$.

18. Consider the following problem and three proposed solutions. Problem: A census taker is interviewing Mr. Levine who is baby sitting his son. Mr. Levine tells the census taker that he has two children. What is the probability that the other child is a boy?

*Solution 1* There are four possibilities. Mr. Levine has two sons, he has two daughters, he had a son first and then a daughter, or he had a daughter and then a son. In only one of the four cases is the other child also a boy. Thus the probability is $\frac{1}{4}$.

*Solution 2* Since we know that one of the children is a boy, there are only three possibilities: 2 sons, son first and then daughter, daughter first and then son. The probability is $\frac{1}{3}$.

*Solution 3* There are only two possibilities: the other child is either a boy or a girl. The probability is $\frac{1}{2}$.

Which of the three solutions is correct?

**C. Bayes' Theorem**

19. There are three cookie jars in our kitchen containing both chocolate and vanilla cookies. The green jar contains 3 chocolate and 4 vanilla cookies, the blue jar contains 5 chocolate and 2 vanilla, and the red jar contains 2 chocolate and 5 vanilla cookies. While his parents are asleep, Eli sneaks downstairs to the darkened kitchen and steals a cookie. After biting it, he discovers the cookie is a chocolate one. What is the probability that it came from the blue jar?

20. A recently devised self-administered test for pregnancy has been found to have the following reliability. The test detects 75 percent of those who are actually pregnant, but does not detect pregnancy in 25 percent of this group. Among those women who are not pregnant, the test detects 85 percent as not being pregnant, but indicates 15 percent of this group as being pregnant. It is known that in a large sample of college women 2 percent are pregnant. Suppose a coed is chosen at random, given the test, and registers as being pregnant. What is the probability that she actually is?

### D. Independent Events

21. If $X$ and $Y$ are disjoint subsets of $E$, under what conditions are they independent events?

22. An urn contains 8 marbles numbered from 1 to 8. A marble is picked at random and removed from the urn. Then a second marble is picked at random from the remaining seven marbles.

   a) Find the probability that the numbers on the two chosen marbles differ by two or more.

   b) What is the answer to (a) if the first marble is replaced in the urn before the second marble is chosen?

23. *Polya's urn scheme.* An urn originally has $r$ red marbles and $b$ black marbles. A marble is selected at random and removed from the urn. Then that marble and $c$ other marbles of the same color are added to the urn. This procedure is repeated $n - 1$ additional times. Show that the probability of selecting a red ball at any trial is $r/(b + r)$.

24. Suppose $X, Y$, and $Z$ are mutually independent events and $\Pr(X \cap Y) \neq \varnothing$. Show that $\Pr(Z \mid X \cap Y) = \Pr(Z)$.

25. The *factorial* of a positive integer $n$ is denoted $n!$ and is defined to be the product of the integers from 1 to $n$. Thus $3! = 3 \times 2 \times 1 = 6$. For convenience, we define $0! = 1$.

   a) Compute $4!, 5!, 6!$.

   b) Show that $(n + 1)! = (n + 1)n!$ for any positive integer $n$.

26. The symbol $\binom{n}{k}$ where $n$ and $k$ are nonnegative integers and $k \leq n$ is defined to be the number

$$\frac{n!}{k!(n - k)!}.$$

   a) Compute $\binom{6}{k}$ for $k = 0, 1, 2, 3, 4, 5, 6$.

   b) Show that $\binom{n}{k} = \binom{n}{n - k}$.

   c) Prove that $k\binom{n}{k} = n\binom{n - 1}{k - 1}$.

   d) Prove that $\binom{n}{k}$ is always an integer.

27. a) Show that the number of distinct ways of arranging $r$ objects in a straight line is $r!$

   b) Show that the number of distinct ways of choosing $k$ objects from a set of $n$ objects is $\binom{n}{k}$.

   c) An experiment has two possible outcomes: a success with probability $p$ and a failure with probability $1 - p$. Show that the probability of obtaining exactly $k$ successes in $n$ repetitions of the experiment is

$$\binom{n}{k} p^k (1-p)^{n-k}.$$

28. a) Show that $(p+q)^n = \sum_{k=0}^{n} \binom{n}{k} p^k q^{n-k}$ if $n$ is a positive integer.

b) Prove that $\sum_{k=0}^{n} \binom{n}{k} p^k (1-p)^{n-k} = 1$.

### E. Expected Value

29. In Example 15, let $p$ and $q$ be the probabilities of winning the bids for the high school and the elementary school, respectively. For which values of $p$ and $q$ are the expected values of the two bids equal?

30. In the game of "craps" a player rolls a pair of dice. If the sum of the numbers shown is 7 or 11, he wins. If it is 2, 3, or 12, he loses. If it is any other sum, he must continue rolling the dice until he either repeats the same sum (in which case he wins) or he rolls a 7 (in which case he loses). Suppose the outcome of each round is a win or a loss of $5. What is the probability that he will win a round? What is the expected value of shooting craps?

31. A roulette wheel has the numbers $0, 1, 2, \ldots, 36$ marked on 37 equally spaced slots. The numbers from 1 to 36 are evenly divided between red and black. A player may bet on either color. If a player bets on red and a red number turns up after the wheel is spun, she receives twice her stake. If a black number turns up, she loses her stake. If 0 turns up, then the wheel is spun again until it stops on a red or a black. If this is red, the player receives only her original stake and if it is black, she loses her stake. If a player bets $1 on red with each spin, what is her expected value of winning?

32. A new-car dealer receives nine station wagons from the factory for sale. The next day, a telegram from the factory informs him that there is strong reason to believe that the brakes in two of the cars are defective. What is the expected value of the number of cars the dealer will have to test in order to find both defective ones?

33. a) Show that

$$\sum_{k=0}^{n} k \binom{n}{k} p^k (1-p)^{n-k} = n \sum_{k=1}^{n} \binom{n-1}{k-1} p^k (1-p)^{n-k}.$$

b) Show that the sum in (a) is also equal to

$$np \sum_{k=0}^{n-1} \binom{n-1}{k} p^k (1-p)^{n-k-1}.$$

c) Show that the sum in (b) is equal to $np$.

d) Find the expected number of heads in $n$ tosses of a coin if the probability of a head on each toss is $p$.

34. Let $R$ and $S$ be random variables defined on a set $S$. Then the random variable $R + S$ is the function defined on $E$ whose value is $(R+S)(e) = R(e) + S(e)$ for each element $e$ of $E$. Prove that $EV(R+S) = EV(R) + EV(S)$.

35. Let $R$ be a random variable defined on a set $E$. If $c$ is any constant, define the random variable $cR$ and prove that $EV(cR) = cEV(R)$.

36. Let $R$ be a random variable with nonnegative values $a_1, a_2, a_3, \ldots$, defined on the sample space of Exercise 13. The *expected value* of $R$ is defined to be $EV(R) = \sum_{i=1}^{\infty} a_i \Pr(R = a_i)$ provided this infinite series converges.

a) Suppose $R(j) = 3^{-j}$ for each $j$ in $E$. Compute $EV(R)$.

b) Suppose $R(j) = 2^j$ for each $j$ in $E$. Does $R$ have an expected value? Interpret this result in the light of the St. Petersburg paradox.

c) How would you define expected value for a random variable defined on the set of all integers greater than or equal to a fixed positive integer $A$?

### F.  Variance and Standard Deviation

37. Find the variance and standard deviation of income in New Haven, Bristol, and Ferrisburg.

38. A random variable takes on the values $-2, -1, 0, 1, 2$, with probabilities $.2, .3, .3, .1, .1$, respectively. Find the expected value, variance, and standard deviation.

39. Show that the variance of a random variable is zero if and only if the random variable takes on exactly one value with probability 1.

40. Toss a coin 8 times and let $R$ denote the number of heads. Find the expected value, variance, and standard deviation of $R$ if

a) the coin is a fair one,

b) the coin is weighted so that it comes up heads with probability $\frac{3}{5}$.

41. Show that the variance of a random variable can be determined from the formula $\mathrm{Var}(R) = EV(R^2) - (EV(R))^2$.

42. If $R$ is a random variable and $c$ is a constant, show that $\mathrm{Var}(cR) = c^2 \, \mathrm{Var}(R)$.

43. Suppose $R$ is a random variable defined on a set $E$ and $b$ is a constant. Define a new random variable, $R + b$, by $(R + b)(e) = R(e) + b$ for each $e$ in $E$. Show that $\mathrm{Var}(R) = \mathrm{Var}(R + b)$.

44. Find the variance in the number of heads in $n$ tosses of a coin if the probability of a head on each toss is $p$. (See Exercise 33; you should arrive at the number $np(1 - p)$.)

45. Suppose $R$ and $S$ are random variables defined on the same sample space. What is the relation between $\mathrm{Var}(R + S)$, $\mathrm{Var}(R)$, and $\mathrm{Var}(S)$?

### III.  A PROBABILISTIC MODEL

46. Verify the details in the derivation of $P_{A+2}(t)$.

47. Use $P_{A+2}(t)$ and Eq. (3) to compute $P_{A+3}(t)$.

48. Prove, by induction on $N$, that $P_N(t) = \binom{N-1}{A-1} e^{-bAt}(1 - e^{-bt})^{N-A}$ for each $N \geqslant A$.

49. Show that $P_N(t)$ induces a probability measure on the set of all integers greater than or equal to $A$. You must show that $\sum_{N=A}^{\infty} P_N(t) = 1$.

50. Graph $P_N(t)$ as a function of $t$. Show that, for a fixed $N > A$, $P_N(t)$ first increases and then decreases toward 0. For what value of $t$ is the probability greatest?

51. In this problem, you will compute the expected value of the population at time $t$ for the stochastic pure-birth process. For convenience, let $P_N$ denote $P_N(t)$.

a) With this notation, show that Eq. (3) becomes

$$\frac{dP_N}{dt} = -bNP_N + b(N-1)P_{N-1}.$$

b) Use the fact that $P_{A-1}(t) = 0$ for all $t$ to show that

$$\sum_{N=A}^{\infty} (-N^2 P_N + N(N-1)P_{N-1}) = \sum_{N=A}^{\infty} P_N((N+1)N - N^2) = \sum_{N=A}^{\infty} NP_N.$$

c) Let $E = E(t)$ denote the expected value of $P_N = P_N(t)$. Show that $E(0) = A$.

d) Show that $E = \sum_{N=A}^{\infty} NP_N$.

e) Justify each step in the following calculation:

$$\frac{dE}{dt} = \sum_{N=A}^{\infty} N\left(\frac{dP_N}{dt}\right) = \sum_{N-A}^{\infty} N(-bNP_N + b(N-1)P_{N-1})$$

$$= b \sum_{N=A}^{\infty} (-N^2 P_N + N(N-1)P_{N-1}) = b \sum_{N=A}^{\infty} NP_N = bE.$$

f) The expected value $E$ then satisfies the differential equation $dE/dt = bE$ with initial condition $E(0) = A$. Show that the solution of this equation is $E(t) = Ae^{bt}$.

52. Use the approach of Exercise 51 to show that the variance of $P_N(t)$ is given by $Ae^{bt}(e^{bt} - 1)$.

## IV. STOCHASTIC PROCESSES

53. In Example 17, suppose the probability of choosing a dorm is proportional to the number of residents in it.

a) Show that $\Pr(F) = \frac{2}{3}$.

b) Determine $\Pr(A)$.

54. Draw a treee diagram representing the possible outcomes of a baseball World Series. The winner of the series is the first team to win four games.

55. If a baseball team has a probability of .55 of winning each World Series game in which it competes, find

a) the probability that it sweeps the series in four games,

b) the probability that it wins the series after losing the first two games,

c) the probability that it wins the series.

## SUGGESTED PROJECTS

1. The stochastic pure-birth process may be generalized to a birth-and-death process. In addition to the basic assumptions of the pure-birth process, suppose that the probability that an individual will die in a short time interval is directly proportional to the

length of the interval.  Show that this assumption leads to the equation

$$P_N(t + \Delta t) = P_{N-1}(t)b(N-1)\Delta t + P_N(t)(1 - (b+d)N\,\Delta t) + P_{N+1}(t)\,d(N+1)\,\Delta t$$

for some positive constants $b$ and $d$.

Derive a set of differential equations analagous to those of Eq. (3) of the text.  Solve the equations for $P_N(t)$, where $N = A, A \pm 1, A \pm 2, \dots$.

Show that the expected value of the population at time $t$ is $Ae^{(b-d)t}$.  Compare the probabilistic model with the deterministic one.  Find the probability that a population governed by a birth-and-death process will eventually become extinct.

2.  As a different generalization of the pure-birth process, suppose the proportionality factor $b$ is not constant, but is a function of the population $N$.  Show that this leads to a model of the form

$$\frac{dP_N(t)}{dt} = -b_N P_N(t) + b_{N-1}P_{n-1}(t).$$

Investigate such models.

3.  Develop in as much detail as possible a probabilistic model for logistic population growth.

---

## REFERENCES

---

### ELEMENTARY CONCEPTS OF PROBABILITY

Anton, Howard, and Bernard Kolman, *Applied Finite Mathematics*, (New York: Academic Press, 1974), especially Chapters 6 and 7.

Kemeny, John G., J. Laurie Snell, and Gerald L. Thompson, *Introduction to Finite Mathematics*, Third Edition (Englewood Cliffs: Prentice-Hall, 1974), especially Chapter 3.

### MORE ADVANCED AND COMPLETE ACCOUNTS

Feller, William, *An Introduction to Probability Theory and Its Applications* (New York: Wiley, 1957).

Hoel, Paul G., Sidney C. Port, and Charles J. Stone, *Introduction to Probability Theory* (Boston: Houghton-Mifflin, 1971).

### SPECIAL TOPICS

Feynman, Richard P., Robert B. Leighton, and Matthew Sands, *The Feynman Lectures on Physics*, Vol. 3 (Reading, Mass: Addison-Wesley, 1965).

Pollard, J. H., *Mathematical Models for the Growth of Human Populations* (Cambridge: Cambridge University Press, 1973), especially Chapter 5, "Simple birth and death processes."

# 10 Markov Processes

Often do the Spirits
Of great events stride on before
the events,
And in today already walks
tomorrow.

Samuel Taylor Coleridge

## I. MARKOV CHAINS

### A. Definitions

Markov chains have been and continue to be one of the most important and popular tools of mathematical model builders. This chapter presents some of the fundamental ideas of Markov chains and indicates some of their uses. More extended applications are presented in Chapters 11 and 12. The necessary mathematical prerequisites for reading this chapter are the concepts of probability presented in Sections II (A–D) and IV of Chapter 9 and the elementary properties of matrix algebra discussed in Appendix II.

The fundamental principle underlying Markov processes is *the independence of the future from the past if the present is known.* Imagine an experiment which is repeated once each day for many days. If the probabilities of the outcomes of tomorrow's experiment depend only on the outcome of today's experiment and do not depend on the results of any previous experiments, then you are dealing with a Markov process.

In slightly different language, a finite Markov chain is a stochastic process with a finite number of states in which the probability of being in a particular state at the $(n + 1)$st step depends only on the state occupied at the $n$th step; this dependence is the same at all steps. More formally, there is the following definition:

**DEFINITION   An experiment with a finite number of possible outcomes $S_1, S_2, \ldots, S_r$ is repeated a number of times. The sequence of outcomes is a *Markov chain* if there is a set of $r^2$ numbers $\{p_{ij}\}$ such that the conditional probability of outcome $S_j$ on any experiment given outcome $S_i$ on the previous experiment is $p_{ij}$; that is,**

$$p_{ij} = \Pr(S_j \text{ on experiment } n + 1 \,|\, S_i \text{ on experiment } n),\ 1 \leqslant i,j \leqslant r, n = 1, 2, \ldots.$$

**The outcomes $S_1\, S_2, \ldots,\ S_r$ are called *states* and the numbers $p_{ij}$ (which depend only on $i$ and $j$ and not on $n$) are called *transition probabilities*. The transition probabilities may be arranged in a matrix with $r$ rows and $r$ columns,**

$$P = \begin{pmatrix} p_{11} & p_{12} & \cdots & p_{1r} \\ p_{21} & p_{22} & \cdots & p_{2r} \\ \cdots & & & \\ p_{r1} & p_{r2} & \cdots & p_{rr} \end{pmatrix}, \tag{1}$$

**which is called the *transition matrix* for the Markov chain.**

Note that each entry of a transition matrix is nonnegative and that the sum of the numbers in each row of the matrix is 1.

---

**EXAMPLE 1**   A recent study focused on the relationship between the birth weights of English women and the birth weights of their daughters. The weights were split into three categories: low (below 6 pounds), average (between 6 and

8 pounds), and high (above 8 pounds). Among women whose own birth weights were low, 50 percent of the daughters had low birth weights, 45 percent had average weights, and 5 percent had high weights. Women with average birth weights had daughters with average weights half of the time, while the other half was split evenly between low and high categories. Women with high birth weights had female babies with high weights 40 per cent of the time, with low and average weights each occurring 30 per cent of the time.

Example 1 can be considered as a Markov chain with three states (low, average, high), corresponding to an "experiment" of choosing a woman at random and noting her birth weight. The transition matrix, easily derived from the verbal description, looks like this:

$$P = \begin{array}{c} \text{M} \\ \text{o} \\ \text{t} \\ \text{h} \\ \text{e} \\ \text{r} \end{array} \begin{array}{c} \\ \text{Low} \\ \text{Average} \\ \text{High} \end{array} \overset{\displaystyle \begin{array}{c} \text{Daughter} \\ \text{Low} \quad \text{Average} \quad \text{High} \end{array}}{\begin{pmatrix} .5 & .45 & .05 \\ .25 & .5 & .25 \\ .3 & .3 & .4 \end{pmatrix}}. \qquad (2)$$

## B. State Diagrams

Transition probabilities may be conveniently presented in a matrix. They may also be shown in what is called a *transition diagram* or *state diagram*. This is a graph with vertices corresponding to the states and a directed arc from vertex *i* to vertex *j* if the transition probability $p_{ij}$ is positive. The numerical values of the transition probabilities are written alongside the arcs. A transition diagram for Example 1 is shown in Fig. 10.1.

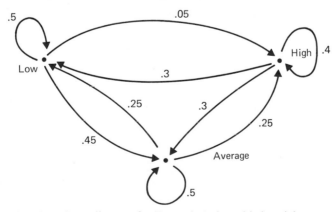

**Fig. 10.1**   State diagram for Example 1 about birth weights.

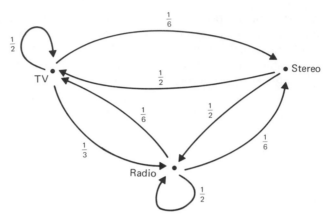

**Fig. 10.2**   State diagram for Example 2 about the Audio-Video Den.

---

**EXAMPLE 2**    The Audi-Video Den, an electronics store in Milwaukee, has
one item on special sale each day; it is either a television, a radio, or a stereo set.
Stereos are never on sale two days in a row; if the store has a stereo as the
special one day, it is equally likely to have a TV or radio on special the next day.
If the special one day is a TV or a radio, there is an even chance of continuing
the item the next day.  If the special item is changed from a TV or radio, only
one-third of the time will a stereo set be the special the next day.

Consider this as an example of Markov chain with states of TV, radio, and
stereo.  The transition matrix is

$$
\begin{array}{c}
\text{Tomorrow's special}\\
\begin{array}{cccc}
 & \text{TV} & \text{Radio} & \text{Stereo}
\end{array}
\end{array}
$$

$$
P = \begin{array}{c}\text{Today's special}\end{array}\begin{array}{c}\text{TV}\\\text{Radio}\\\text{Stereo}\end{array}\begin{pmatrix} 1/2 & 1/3 & 1/6 \\ 1/3 & 1/2 & 1/6 \\ 1/2 & 1/2 & 0 \end{pmatrix} \tag{3}
$$

and the state diagram is shown in Fig. 10.2.

The loops at the TV and radio vertices correspond to the fact that it is
possible for either of these items to be repeated as the specials on consecutive
days.  The absence of a loop at the stereo vertex reflects the store's policy of
never repeating the stereo as a special item on successive days.

---

Although the transition matrix is a powerful tool in analyzing Markov
chains, the state diagram often reveals information about the process not
immediately apparent from the matrix.  For example, Fig. 10.2 indicates that
no matter what item is the special today, it is possible for any one of the three
items to be the special on the day after tomorrow.

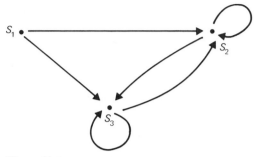

**Figure 10.3**

Figure 10.3 presents a state diagram for another Markov chain. It is evident from this diagram that $S_1$ can be reached, at most, once. If the process is in state $S_1$ at the $n$th step, then it will be in state $S_2$ or $S_3$ at the $(n + 1)$st step. From either of these states it is impossible to return to $S_1$.

The transition matrix for this Markov chain would have the form

$$P = \begin{array}{c} \\ S_1 \\ S_2 \\ S_3 \end{array} \begin{array}{ccc} S_1 & S_2 & S_3 \\ \left(\begin{array}{ccc} 0 & a & 1-a \\ 0 & b & 1-b \\ 0 & c & 1-c \end{array}\right) \end{array} \qquad (4)$$

for some positive numbers $a, b,$ and $c$.

## C. Tree Diagrams

Since Markov chains are particular examples of stochastic processes, they can be analyzed with the help of tree diagrams. For example, if a stereo is the special sale item today, we may be interested in the probability that a stereo will again be the special item three days from now. The tree diagram that enables us to answer this question is drawn in Fig. 10.4. Note that we have omitted the branches corresponding to a zero probability and have used the notation S = Stereo, R = Radio, T = Television.

From the tree diagram, we see that there are four distinct ways the stereo can be the special sale item three days from now: RRS, RTS, TRS, and TTS. Here RRS indicates that radios are the special items for tomorrow and the next day and a stereo the day after that. The desired probability is

$$\text{Pr(RRS)} + \text{Pr(RTS)} + \text{Pr(TRS)} + \text{Pr(TTS)}$$

$$= \left(\frac{1}{2}\right)\left(\frac{1}{2}\right)\left(\frac{1}{6}\right) + \left(\frac{1}{2}\right)\left(\frac{1}{3}\right)\left(\frac{1}{6}\right) + \left(\frac{1}{2}\right)\left(\frac{1}{3}\right)\left(\frac{1}{6}\right) + \left(\frac{1}{2}\right)\left(\frac{1}{2}\right)\left(\frac{1}{6}\right)$$

$$= \frac{1}{24} + \frac{1}{36} + \frac{1}{36} + \frac{1}{24} = \frac{5}{36}.$$

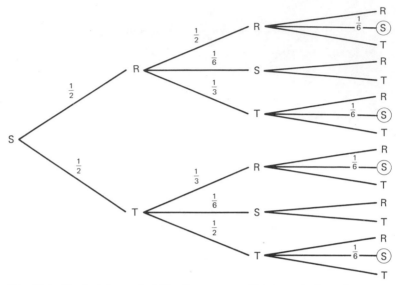

**Fig. 10.4**   To find the probability that a stereo (S) is on sale three days from now, add the probabilities of each of the paths from the starting node S to the circled final S nodes.

In Section II, it will be shown how the same question can be more easily answered by use of the transition matrix and the technique of matrix multiplication.

### D.  Initial Probabilities

In order to describe the way a Markov chain develops, we need, in addition to the transition probabilities, a distribution of *initial probabilities* $(p_1, p_2, \ldots, p_r)$ where $p_k$ is the probability that the outcome of the first experiment is $S_k$. In the study of birth weights for example, the first generation of women investigated had 25 percent of its members of low birth weight, 60 percent of average weight, and 15 percent of high weight. The initial probabilities would then be described by $(p_1, p_2, p_3) = (.25, .6, .15)$.

A Markov chain then operates in the following way.  There is a stochastic process that moves from state to state in a sequence of steps.  By means of the initial probability distribution, the process starts at one of the states $S_k$ with probability $p_k$. If at any step it is in state $S_i$, then it moves to state $S_j$ with probability $p_{ij}$. This probability is found in the distribution of the $i$th row of the transition matrix. The entire process is completely described by the initial probability distribution (a $1 \times r$ vector) and the transition matrix.

### E.  An Absorbing Example

This section concludes with one more example of a Markov process.

**EXAMPLE 3**   The Academic Personnel Committee at Lower Pine Cone College reviews the contracts of all faculty members each year. The rules of the college demand that a professor with tenure must be continued, but all other faculty members can be fired. If a faculty member is not fired, then he may be kept on for another year at the same rank, promoted to a tenured position, or promoted but not given tenure. However, if a professor was promoted and not given tenure the previous year, his next promotion must be to a tenured rank. Life is so pleasant at this college and the job market so dismal that no one leaves the school voluntarily: everyone is either eventually fired or given tenure.

This process may be viewed as a Markov chain. The states are the employment categories of an individual at the end of a particular year: fired $(F)$, promoted to tenure rank $(T)$, promoted but not with tenure $(P)$, and retained at an untenured rank without promotion $(R)$. The transition matrix then has the form

$$\begin{array}{c} \text{Position at end of next year}\\ \begin{array}{cccc} F & T & R & P \end{array}\\ P = \begin{array}{c} \text{Position}\\ \text{at end}\\ \text{of this}\\ \text{year} \end{array} \begin{array}{c} F\\ T\\ R\\ P \end{array} \begin{pmatrix} 1 & 0 & 0 & 0\\ 0 & 1 & 0 & 0\\ a & b & c & d\\ e & f & g & 0 \end{pmatrix} \end{array} \tag{5}$$

where the numbers $a$–$g$ are nonnegative probabilities.

This Markov chain has a feature missing from the others we have examined. There are two states, $F$ and $T$, which may be called *absorbing states*. Once the process enters one of these states, it never leaves.

## II.  MATRIX OPERATIONS AND MARKOV CHAINS

### A.  Stochastic Matrices

If all the entries of a matrix are nonnegative and the sum of the entries in each row is 1, then the matrix is called a *stochastic matrix*. Every transition matrix for a Markov chain is an example of a stochastic matrix. Stochastic matrices have an interesting property: whenever two of them are multiplied, the result is another stochastic matrix.

■ *THEOREM 1*    If $A$ and $B$ are stochastic matrices and the product $AB$ is defined, then $AB$ is a stochastic matrix.

*Proof of Theorem 1*   Suppose $A$ is a $k \times m$ matrix and $B$ is an $m \times n$ matrix. It is clear that all the entries of $AB$ will be nonnegative (review Appendix II if matrix multiplication is not familiar to you). We must show that the sum of the elements in any row of $AB$ is equal to 1. Now the sum of the entries in row *i* of *AB* is given:

$$\sum_{j=1}^{n}(AB)_{ij} = \sum_{j=1}^{n}\left(\sum_{s=1}^{m}A_{is}B_{sj}\right) \quad \text{(definition of matrix multiplication)}$$

$$= \sum_{s=1}^{m}\left(\sum_{j=1}^{n}A_{is}B_{sj}\right) \quad \text{(reversing order of summation)}$$

$$= \sum_{s=1}^{m}\left(A_{is}\sum_{j=1}^{n}B_{sj}\right) \quad \text{(factoring out } A_{is}\text{)}$$

$$= \sum_{s=1}^{m}A_{is}(1) \quad \text{(sum of entries in any row of } B \text{ is 1)}$$

$$= \sum_{s=1}^{m}A_{is} = 1. \quad \text{(sum of entries in any row of } A \text{ is 1).}$$

Since *i* was an arbitrarily chosen row number, the theorem is proved. □

***Corollary*** If *A* is an $r \times r$ stochastic matrix, then so are $A^2$, $A^3$, $A^4$, ....
As an example, consider the $2 \times 2$ stochastic matrix

$$A = \begin{pmatrix} .7 & .3 \\ .4 & .6 \end{pmatrix} \tag{6}$$

that has

$$A^2 = \begin{pmatrix} .61 & .39 \\ .52 & .48 \end{pmatrix}$$

and

$$A^3 = \begin{pmatrix} .583 & .417 \\ .556 & .444 \end{pmatrix}.$$

   As an exercise to be completed before reading any further, interpret the $r \times r$ stochastic matrix as the transition matrix of a Markov chain and prove the corollary directly using probabilistic considerations only.

## B. Probability Distribution After *n* Steps
One of the most important questions about Markov chains is this one: if the process begins in state $S_i$, what is the probability that after *n* steps it will be in state $S_j$? Denote this probability by $p_{ij}^{(n)}$. If we are interested in this problem for all possible starting states $S_i$ and terminating states $S_j$, the probabilities may be represented in a matrix

$$P^{(n)} = \begin{pmatrix} p_{11}^{(n)} & p_{12}^{(n)} & \cdots & p_{1r}^{(n)} \\ p_{21}^{(n)} & p_{22}^{(n)} & \cdots & p_{2r}^{(n)} \\ \cdots & & & \\ p_{r1}^{(n)} & p_{r2}^{(n)} & \cdots & p_{rr}^{(n)} \end{pmatrix} \tag{7}$$

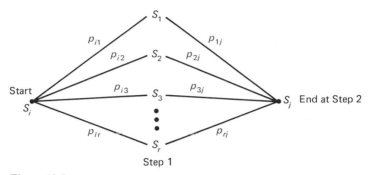

**Figure 10.5**

In Section I.C, we saw how such a problem can be solved through the use of tree diagrams. Tree diagrams are convenient, however, only when $n$ is a relatively small number. If $n$ is large, the number of branches in the corresponding tree diagram is too great to draw easily. In this section, we will see how the question can be answered using matrix multiplication.

If $n = 1$, then $p_{ij}^{(n)} = p_{ij}^{(1)}$ is the probability of moving from state $S_i$ to state $S_j$ in one step. By definition of a Markov process, this is exactly the transition probability $p_{ij}$. Thus $p_{ij}^{(1)} = p_{ij}$ for all $i$ and $j$, and $P^{(1)} = P$.

Determine next $p_{ij}^{(2)}$. The computation is facilitated by examining the relevant portions of the tree diagram in Fig. 10.5.

Note that

$$p_{ij}^{(2)} = p_{i1}p_{1j} + p_{i2}p_{2j} + \cdots + p_{ir}p_{rj} = \sum_{k=1}^{r} p_{ik}p_{kj}$$

The definition of matrix multiplication, however, asserts that this number is just the $ij$th entry of $P^2$. In other words, $p_{ij}^{(2)} = (P^2)_{ij}$ so that $P^{(2)} = P^2$. The matrix which gives the probability distribution after two steps is the square of the transition matrix.

With these first two steps completed, the general result is easy to guess: the matrix of probability distributions after $n$ steps is the $n$th power of the original transition matrix. The proof follows by induction on $n$. For later reference, we list the result as

■ **THEOREM 2**    For a Markov chain, $P^{(n)} = P^n$.

As noted in Section I, a Markov chain is determined by the transition matrix and a distribution of initial probabilities. Suppose the initial states are given by probabilities $p_i^{(0)}$, $i = 1, 2, \ldots, r$. Write the initial probability distribution as a row vector

$$\mathbf{p}^{(0)} = (p_1^{(0)}, \ldots, p_r^{(0)})$$

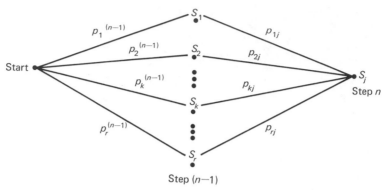

**Fig. 10.6**   Determining $p_j^n$, the probability of being in state $S_j$ after $n$ steps. This depends on the probability of being in each of the states after $(n-1)$ steps and the transition matrix.

If $p_j^{(n)}$ denotes the probability of being in state $S_j$ after $n$ steps, the vector of these probabilities is

$$\mathbf{p}^{(n)} = (p_1^{(n)}, p_2^{(n)}, \dots, p_r^{(n)}).$$

Note that the sum of the entries in each of these vectors is 1; that is, $\mathbf{p}^{(n)}$ is a stochastic matrix of dimension $1 \times r$.

We may now obtain the critical relation between these probability row vectors and the transition matrix. Suppose we wish to compute $p_j^{(n)}$. The tree diagram of Fig. 10.6 tells what to do.

We have

$$p_j^{(n)} = p_1^{(n-1)}p_{1j} + p_2^{(n-1)}p_{2j} + \cdots + p_r^{(n-1)}p_{rj}$$

$$= \sum_{k=1}^{r} p_k^{(n-1)}p_{kj}.$$

Now this last sum is simply the product of the row vector $\mathbf{p}^{(n-1)}$ and the $j$th column of the transition matrix $P$. Thus the components of $\mathbf{p}^{(n)}$ are obtained by multiplying $\mathbf{p}^{(n-1)}$ by the appropriate column of $P$. This gives the important relationship

$$\mathbf{p}^{(n)} = \mathbf{p}^{(n-1)}P. \tag{8}$$

From this relationship, we obtain

$$\mathbf{p}^{(1)} = \mathbf{p}^{(0)}P \tag{9}$$

$$\mathbf{p}^{(2)} = \mathbf{p}^{(1)}P = (\mathbf{p}^{(0)}P)P = \mathbf{p}^{(0)}P^2 \tag{10}$$

$$\mathbf{p}^{(3)} = \mathbf{p}^{(2)}P = (\mathbf{p}^{(0)}P^2)P = \mathbf{p}^{(0)}P^3 \tag{11}$$

A straightforward induction argument establishes the general result stated in the next theorem.

■ **THEOREM 3**    For any Markov chain, $\mathbf{p}^{(n)} = \mathbf{p}^{(0)} P^n$.

---

Review of notation

$p_{ij}$ = probability of moving from state $S_i$ to state $S_j$ in one step.

$P$  = $r \times r$ transition matrix whose entries are $p_{ij}$.

$p_{ij}^{(n)}$ = probability of moving from $S_i$ to $S_j$ in exactly $n$ steps.

$P^{(n)}$ = $r \times r$ matrix whose entries are $p_{ij}^{(n)}$.

$p_j^{(n)}$ = probability of being in state $S_j$ after $n$ steps.

$\mathbf{p}^{(n)}$ = $1 \times r$ vector whose entries are $p_j^{(n)}$.

*Main results:*    1.  $P^{(n)} = P^n$

                        2.  $\mathbf{p}^{(n)} = \mathbf{p}^{(0)} P^n$

---

## C. Applications

The result of Theorem 3 can be used to answer the question about the Audio-Video Den stated in Section I.C. In this Markov chain, $S_1$ = television, $S_2$ = radio, and $S_3$ = stereo. The question concerned the probability that a stereo will be the special sale item three days hence if it is the sale item today. Taking today as the 0th step of the process, we have $\mathbf{p}^{(0)} = (0,0,1)$. By Theorem 3, the probability distribution after three steps is $\mathbf{p}^{(3)} = (0,0,1)P^3$. Now the row vector $(0,0,1)P^3$ will simply be the third row of $P^3$. Carrying out the matrix multiplication gives

$$P^2 = \begin{pmatrix} 16/36 & 15/36 & 5/36 \\ 15/36 & 16/36 & 5/36 \\ 15/36 & 15/36 & 6/36 \end{pmatrix} \tag{12}$$

and

$$P^3 = \begin{pmatrix} 93/216 & 92/216 & 31/216 \\ 92/216 & 93/126 & 31/216 \\ 93/126 & 93/216 & 30/216 \end{pmatrix} \tag{13}$$

so that $\mathbf{p}^{(3)} = (\frac{93}{216}, \frac{93}{216}, \frac{30}{216})$, and the probability of being in state $S_3$ after three steps is the final entry of this vector, $\frac{30}{216} = \frac{5}{36}$.

Once the matrix $P^3$ is determined, any question about the nature of this Markov chain during its first three steps can be answered.

As another illustration of the use of Theorem 3, consider the birth weight model of Example 1. Suppose the initial generation of mothers surveyed contained 25 percent low birth weight women, 60 percent average weight, and 15 percent high weight. What would the distribution look like for the generation of their great-great-granddaughters? Since $S_1$ = low, $S_2$ = average, $S_3$ = high, we have $\mathbf{p}^{(0)} = (.25, .6, .15)$ and we need to find $\mathbf{p}^{(4)} = \mathbf{p}^{(0)} P^4$, where $P$ is the transition matrix (2). In this case, the fourth power of the transition matrix is

$$P^4 = \begin{pmatrix} .347969 & .442762 & .209269 \\ .346813 & .438719 & .214469 \\ .348113 & .438863 & .213025 \end{pmatrix}$$

and the required probability vector is

$$\mathbf{p}^{(4)} = (.347297, .439751, .212952).$$

The conclusion then is that about 35 percent of the great-great-grandaughters will have low birth weights, 44 percent average weights, and 21 percent high weights.

As a final application, consider the tenure model of Example 3. Over the past 10 years, the Academic Personnel Committee has consistently followed a pattern of promotion described by the transition probabilities

$$a = .1, \quad b = .01, \quad c = .67, \quad d = .22, \quad e = .05, \quad f = .45, \quad g = .5$$

so that the transition matrix has the form

$$P = \begin{array}{c} \\ F \\ T \\ R \\ P \end{array} \begin{array}{cccc} F & T & R & P \\ \begin{pmatrix} 1 & 0 & 0 & 0 \\ 0 & 1 & 0 & 0 \\ .1 & .01 & .67 & .22 \\ .05 & .45 & .50 & 0 \end{pmatrix} \end{array}. \tag{14}$$

Suppose there are now 100 members of the faculty, distributed $30, 40, 30$ in the states $T, R, P$, respectively. If the personnel committee continues its past policies for another five years, let us determine the status of this group of professors at the end of that period.

For simplicity, assume that no one on the faculty leaves the system through retirement, death, or some voluntary action. Let $\mathbf{p}^{(0)} = (0, .3, .4, .3)$ represent the initial distribution. We seek $\mathbf{p}^{(5)} = \mathbf{p}^{(0)}P^5$. Matrix multiplication gives

$$P^5 = \begin{pmatrix} 1 & 0 & 0 & 0 \\ 0 & 1 & 0 & 0 \\ .33 & .3 & .29 & .08 \\ .2 & .57 & .18 & .05 \end{pmatrix}$$

where the entries have been rounded off to two decimal places. Thus the distribution after 5 years is

$$\mathbf{p}^{(5)} = (.19, .59, .17, .05).$$

The prediction of this model is that 19 of the untenured faculty members will be fired, 29 will have advanced to tenured rank so that the faculty will have 59 tenured members, 17 will have been retained but without promotion, and 5 will be given promotions without tenure.

Although this model cannot predict what happens to a particular untenured professor during the five years, it is still a quite useful tool for planning and decision making. The personnel committee can use the model to predict the cumulative effects of its past policies if they are continued into the future or to assess the effects of proposed changes in the transition probabilities.

The next two sections, III and IV, present a more detailed mathematical treatment of two particular types of Markov processes: regular chains and absorbing chains.

## III. REGULAR MARKOV CHAINS

### A. Definitions

If you glance back at the matrix $P^3$ of Eq. (13),

$$P^3 = \begin{array}{c} \\ \text{TV} \\ \text{Radio} \\ \text{Stereo} \end{array} \begin{array}{ccc} \text{TV} & \text{Radio} & \text{Stereo} \\ \begin{pmatrix} 93/216 & 92/216 & 31/216 \\ 92/216 & 93/216 & 31/216 \\ 93/216 & 93/216 & 30/216 \end{pmatrix} \end{array} \qquad (13)$$

it may surprise you that the rows of the matrix are almost identical. In the discussion of the Audio-Video Den, for which the matrix was derived, we saw that the probability of being in the "stereo state" after three steps, if the process began in the stereo state, is the third component of the third row of $P^3$; that is, $\frac{30}{216}$. We can also read from the matrix $P^3$ that the probability of being in the stereo state after 3 steps, if the starting state is "TV" or "radio" is practically the same: $\frac{31}{216}$. It appears, then, that the long-range probability that a stereo is the special sale item may, in fact, be independent of what item is the special when the process starts. Inspection of the first and second columns of $P^3$ indicates that this may be true for televisions and radios as well.

As another illustration, consider the distribution of birth weights of great-great-granddaughters for different initial distributions of birth weights of the original generation of mothers. Some of these are presented in Table 10.1.

Note that despite wide variations in the choice of an initial distribution, the probability distribution after 4 steps is always very close to $(.35, .44, .21)$.

The type of behavior shown by these two examples occurs whenever the underlying Markov chain process possesses a regularity property.

**DEFINITION**   **A Markov process is a *regular chain* if some power of the transition matrix has only positive entries.**

Table 10.1

| $p^{(0)}$ | $p^{(4)}$ |
| --- | --- |
| $(.25, .6, .15)$ | $(.347297, .439751, .212952)$ |
| $(\frac{1}{3}, \frac{1}{3}, \frac{1}{3})$ | $(.347631, .440115, .212254)$ |
| $(1, 0, 0)$ | $(.347969, .442762, .209269)$ |
| $(.1, .8, .1)$ | $(.347058, .439138, .213804)$ |
| $(0, 0, 1)$ | $(.348113, .438863, .213025)$ |

In particular, the Markov process is regular if all entries in the transition matrix $P = P^1$ are positive. Thus the birth weight model of Example 1 is a regular chain. The matrix of transition probabilities for the Audio-Video Den illustration (Example 2) contains a 0 entry, but its second power, $P^2$, has all entries positive (Eq. 12). Thus this is a regular chain also.

If the transition matrix of a Markov process is an identity matrix, then so is every power of that matrix and the underlying chain is not regular. The tenure model (Example 3) is not a regular chain either; every power of the transition matrix will have its first two rows identical to the first two rows of $P$ and hence will contain entries equal to 0.

A Markov process is a regular one if there is some positive integer $n$, so that the process may be in any one of the possible states $n$ steps after starting, regardless of the initial state. The smallest $n$ for which this is possible is the smallest positive integer $n$ for which $P^n$ has no zero entries.

If $P$ is the transition matrix of a regular Markov chain, then it turns out that the powers of $P$ approach a matrix $W$, all of whose rows are the same. If $\mathbf{w}$ denotes the row vector formed from any of the rows of $W$, then it also happens that $\mathbf{w}P = \mathbf{w}$. There results will be formalized, proved, and applied in the next few pages.

**DEFINITION**    **A vector w is a *fixed point vector* of the matrix $P$ if $\mathbf{w}P = \mathbf{w}$. A Markov chain is said to be in *equilibrium* if the probability distribution at some step is given by a fixed point vector of the transition matrix.**

Note that if $\mathbf{w}P = \mathbf{w}$, then $\mathbf{w}P^2 = (\mathbf{w}P)P = \mathbf{w}P = \mathbf{w}$, and, in general, $\mathbf{w}P^n = \mathbf{w}$.

---

**EXAMPLE 4**    The zero vector $\mathbf{0} = (0,0,\dots,0)$ is a fixed point vector of every transition matrix.

**EXAMPLE 5**    If $P$ is the transition matrix

$$P = \begin{pmatrix} .7 & .3 \\ .4 & .6 \end{pmatrix}$$

and $\mathbf{w}$ is the vector $\mathbf{w} = (\frac{4}{7}, \frac{3}{7})$, it is easy to check that $\mathbf{w}P = \mathbf{w}$.

**EXAMPLE 6**    If $P$ is any $2 \times 2$ matrix,

$$P = \begin{pmatrix} a & b \\ c & d \end{pmatrix} \text{ with } b + c \neq 0, \tag{15}$$

then the vector

$$\mathbf{w} = \left( \frac{c}{b+c}, \frac{b}{b+c} \right)$$

is a fixed point vector of $P$.

---

## B.  First Basic Theorem

■ *THEOREM 4 (FIRST BASIC THEOREM FOR REGULAR MARKOV CHAINS)*
If $P$ is the transition matrix for a regular Markov chain, then

a)  the powers $P^n$ approach a stochastic matrix $W$;

b)  each row of $W$ is the same vector $\mathbf{w} = (w_1, w_2, \ldots, w_r)$;

and

c)  the components of $\mathbf{w}$ are positive.

In order to prove this theorem, we first establish a helpful lemma.

*LEMMA*   Suppose $P$ is an $r \times r$ transition matrix having no zero entries and
let $q$ be the smallest entry of $P$. Let $\mathbf{x}$ be an $r \times 1$ column vector, having largest
component $M_0$ and smallest component $m_0$. Let $M_1$ and $m_1$ be the largest
and smallest components of the vector $P\mathbf{x}$.  Then

a)  $M_1 \leqslant M_0$,

b)  $m_1 \geqslant m_0$, and

c)  $M_1 - m_1 \leqslant (1 - 2q)(M_0 - m_0)$.

---

**EXAMPLE 7**   If $P$ is the transition matrix (2) of the birth weight model, that is,

$$P = \begin{pmatrix} .5 & .45 & .05 \\ .25 & .5 & .25 \\ .3 & .3 & .4 \end{pmatrix} \tag{2}$$

then we have $q = .05$. If $\mathbf{x}$ is the vector

$$\mathbf{x} = \begin{pmatrix} .2 \\ .3 \\ .5 \end{pmatrix},$$

then $M_0 = .5$ and $m_0 = .2$.

According to the lemma, the largest component of $P\mathbf{x}$ will be at most .5,
the smallest component will be at least .2, and the difference between these
components, $M_1 - m_1$ will be at most

$$(1 - 2[.05])(.5 - .2) = (.9)(.3) = .27.$$

This claim may be checked by carrying out the indicated matrix multiplication.  We obtain

$$P\mathbf{x} = \begin{pmatrix} .26 \\ .325 \\ .35 \end{pmatrix}$$

so that $M_1 = .35 < .5 = M_0$ and $m_1 = .26 > .2 = m_0$. The difference satisfies

$$M_1 - m_1 = .35 - .26 = .09 < .27.$$

---

Before proceeding to a proof of the lemma, note that if all entries of a transition matrix $P$ are positive, then we must have $0 < q \leqslant \frac{1}{2}$ since the sum of the entries in each row is 1. Thus $0 \leqslant 1 - 2q < 1$. In particular, the lemma asserts that $(M_1 - m_1) < (M_0 - m_0)$. The effect of applying the matrix $P$ to the vector $\mathbf{x}$ is to produce a vector $P\mathbf{x}$ whose components are more nearly equal than the components of $\mathbf{x}$.

**Proof of the lemma**   The $i$th component of $P\mathbf{x}$ is the product of the $i$th row of the matrix $P$ and the vector $\mathbf{x}$; that is,

$$(P\mathbf{x})_i = (p_{i1}, p_{i2}, \ldots, p_{ir}) \begin{pmatrix} x_1 \\ x_2 \\ \vdots \\ x_r \end{pmatrix} = p_{i1}x_1 + p_{i2}x_2 + \cdots + p_{ir}x_r. \tag{16}$$

Since $p_{i1} + p_{i2} + \cdots + p_{ir} = 1$, the $i$th component of $P\mathbf{x}$ may be regarded as the expected value of a gamble whose outcomes are the components of $\mathbf{x}$ which occur with probabilities given by the entries of the $i$th row of $P$. Considering each of the rows of $P$ as a different gamble, the number $M_1$ measures the expected value of the most favorable gamble. We shall concentrate on this particular gamble.

If the outcomes of the gamble are changed so that one of them is $m_0$ and all the rest are $M_0$, then the new gamble will have an expected value at least as large as the original gamble. Now the largest possible expected value for such a gamble occurs if the smallest outcome, $m_0$, occurs with the smallest probability, $q$. In this case, the expected value is $qm_0 + (1 - q)M_0$. Thus we have

$$M_1 \leqslant qm_0 + (1 - q)M_0 \leqslant qM_0 + (1 - q)M_0 = M_0, \tag{17}$$

establishing the inequality $M_1 \leqslant M_0$.

A similar argument, based on considering the least favorable gamble, shows that

$$m_1 \geqslant qM_0 + (1 - q)m_0 \geqslant qm_0 + (1 - q)m_0 = m_0 \tag{18}$$

so that $m_1 \geqslant m_0$.

Multiply the first inequality of (18) by $(-1)$ and add to the first inequality of (17) to obtain

$$M_1 - m_1 \leqslant q(m_0 - M_0) + (1 - q)(M_0 - m_0) = (1 - 2q)(M_0 - m_0),$$

completing the proof of the lemma.  $\square$

***Proof of Theorem***    We deal first with the case when all entries of $P$ are positive. Suppose $\mathbf{x}$ is a column vector. Let $q$ be the smallest entry in $P$ and let $M_n$ and $m_n$ denote the largest and smallest components of $P^n\mathbf{x}$.

Since $P^n\mathbf{x} = P(P^{n-1}\mathbf{x})$, repeated applications of the lemma give

$$M_1 \geqslant M_2 \geqslant M_3 \geqslant \cdots, \tag{19}$$

$$m_1 \leqslant m_2 \leqslant m_3 \leqslant \cdots, \tag{20}$$

and

$$M_n - m_n \leqslant (1 - 2q)(M_{n-1} - m_{n-1}), \tag{21}$$

so that

$$M_n - m_n \leqslant (1 - 2q)^n(M_0 - m_0). \tag{22}$$

Since $1 - 2q$ is less than 1, $(1 - 2q)^n$ tends to 0 as $n$ gets large. Thus the difference $M_n - m_n$ also goes to zero. This implies that $M_n$ and $m_n$ approach a common limit and $P^n\mathbf{x}$ tends to a vector all of whose components are the same.

This common value will lie between $m_n$ and $M_n$, for all $n$. Since $0 < m_0 \leqslant M_0 < 1$, the common value is a strictly positive number less than 1.

Now let $\mathbf{x}$ be the column vector with $k$th component equal to 1 and all other components 0. Then $P^n\mathbf{x}$ is simply the $k$th column of $P^n$. We have shown that the $k$th column of $P^n$ tends to a vector with all components equal. Denote the common value of the components by $w_k$. Thus $P^n$ tends to a matrix $W$ with all rows the same vector $\mathbf{w} = (w_1, w_2, \ldots, w_r)$.

Since the sum of the entries in each row of $P^n$ is always 1, regardless of $n$, the same must be true of the limit $W$ (because the limit of a sum is the sum of the limits). Thus $W$ is a stochastic matrix. This establishes the theorem in the case that all entries of $P$ are positive.

In the general case of a regular Markov chain, the transition matrix $P$ may have some zero entries. Since the Markov chain is regular, some power $P^N$ of $P$ has all positive entries. If $q^*$ is the smallest entry of $P^N$, then the first part of the proof shows that

$$(M_{N+1} - n_{N+1}) \leqslant (1 - 2q^*)(M_N - m_N).$$

The sequence $\{d_n\}$ where $d_n = M_n - m_n$ is then a nondecreasing sequence with a subsequence $\{d_{n+N}\}$ tending to 0. This forces the entire sequence $\{d_n\}$ to have limit 0. The rest of the proof is the same as the proof of the special case. $\square$

## C.  Second Basic Theorem

The next important theorem shows an easy way to find the limiting matrix $W$ of a regular Markov chain.

■ ***THEOREM 5 (SECOND BASIC THEOREM FOR REGULAR MARKOV CHAINS)***
If $P$ is the transition matrix for a regular Markov chain and $W$ and $\mathbf{w}$ are the

matrix and vector promised by Theorem 4, then

a) for any stochastic row vector $\mathbf{p}$,   $\mathbf{p}P^n$ approaches $\mathbf{w}$; and
b) the vector $\mathbf{w}$ is the unique fixed point stochastic vector of $P$.

***Proof of Theorem 5***   Since $P^n \to W$, we have $\mathbf{p}P^n \to \mathbf{p}W$. Every entry in the $k$th column of $W$ is $w_k$ so the $k$th component of $\mathbf{p}W$ is equal to $w_k$ multiplied by the sum of the entries of $\mathbf{p}$. Since $\mathbf{p}$ is a stochastic vector, that sum is 1. Thus the $k$th component of $\mathbf{p}W$ is $w_k$. In other words, $\mathbf{p}W = \mathbf{w}$. This proves (a).

To prove (b), note that the powers of $P$ approach $W$ so that $P^{n+1} = P^nP$ approaches $W$ also. But $P^nP$ also approaches $WP$. Thus $W = WP$.

Each row of the matrix equation $W = WP$ simply asserts that $\mathbf{w} = \mathbf{w}P$ so that $\mathbf{w}$ is a fixed point vector of $P$. By Theorem 4, $\mathbf{w}$ is a stochastic vector. All that is left to show is the uniqueness of $\mathbf{w}$. Accordingly, suppose $\mathbf{v}$ is any stochastic fixed point vector of $P$. The $\mathbf{v}P^n$ approaches $\mathbf{w}$. But $\mathbf{v}$ is a fixed point vector for $P$, so that $\mathbf{v}P^n = \mathbf{v}$ for all $n$. Thus $\mathbf{v}$ approaches $\mathbf{w}$. But $\mathbf{v}$ is a constant vector. Hence $\mathbf{v} = \mathbf{w}$. This completes the proof of Theorem 5. $\square$

If $P$ is the transition matrix of a regular Markov chain and $\mathbf{p}^{(0)}$ is the initial probability distribution, then Theorem 5 implies that $\mathbf{p}^{(0)}P^n$ approaches $\mathbf{w}$, the unique fixed point stochastic vector of $P$, regardless of the particular numerical values of the entries of $\mathbf{p}^{(0)}$. We have already shown, however, that $\mathbf{p}^{(0)}P^n = \mathbf{p}^{(n)}$, the probability distribution after $n$ steps. Thus $\mathbf{p}^{(n)}$ approaches $\mathbf{w}$. In other words, no matter what the initial probabilities are for a regular Markov chain, after a large number of steps the probability that the process is in a particular state $S_k$ will be very nearly $w_k$: a regular Markov chain approaches equilibrium.

To illustrate the approach to equilibrium, consider the transition matrix of Example 5:

$$P = \begin{pmatrix} .7 & .3 \\ .4 & .6 \end{pmatrix}$$

A fixed point vector $\mathbf{w} = (w_1, w_2)$ for $P$ must satisfy $\mathbf{w}P = \mathbf{w}$; that is,

$$(w_1, w_2)P = (w_1, w_2), \tag{23}$$

which is equivalent to

$$.7w_1 + .4w_2 = w_1$$
$$.3w_1 + .6w_2 = w_2 \tag{24}$$

or

$$-.3w_1 + .4w_2 = 0$$
$$.3w_1 - .4w_2 = 0 \tag{25}$$

and this system is satisfied by any pair of numbers, $w_1$ and $w_2$, such that $w_2 = \frac{3}{4}w_1$. Since a stochastic vector must have $w_1 + w_2 = 1$, we have

$$w_1 + \left(\frac{3}{4}\right)w_1 = 1.$$

This gives $w_1 = \frac{4}{7}$ and $w_2 = \frac{3}{7}$. The unique fixed-point stochastic vector for the transition matrix $P$ is

$$\mathbf{w} = (\tfrac{4}{7}, \tfrac{3}{7}) = (.571428, .428572).$$

The first few powers of $P$ are given by

$$P^2 = \begin{pmatrix} .61 & .39 \\ .52 & .48 \end{pmatrix} \qquad P^3 = \begin{pmatrix} .583 & .417 \\ .556 & .444 \end{pmatrix}$$

$$P^4 = \begin{pmatrix} .5749 & .4251 \\ .5668 & .4332 \end{pmatrix} \qquad P^5 = \begin{pmatrix} .57247 & .42753 \\ .57004 & .42996 \end{pmatrix}$$

$$P^6 = \begin{pmatrix} .57141 & .428259 \\ .57102 & .428988 \end{pmatrix} \qquad P^7 = \begin{pmatrix} .571522 & .428478 \\ .571304 & .428696 \end{pmatrix}$$

$$P^8 = \begin{pmatrix} .571457 & .428543 \\ .571391 & .428609 \end{pmatrix} \qquad P^9 = \begin{pmatrix} .571437 & .428563 \\ .571417 & .428583 \end{pmatrix}$$

and we see that $P^n$ does approach $W$. If the Markov chain starts with initial probability vector $\mathbf{p}^{(0)} = (.9, .1)$, then the distributions after the first 10 steps are:

$$
\begin{aligned}
\mathbf{p}^{(1)} &= (.67, .33) \\
\mathbf{p}^{(2)} &= (.601, .399) \\
\mathbf{p}^{(3)} &= (.5803, .4197) \\
\mathbf{p}^{(4)} &= (.57409, .42591) \\
\mathbf{p}^{(5)} &= (.572227, .427773) \\
\mathbf{p}^{(6)} &= (.571668, .428332) \\
\mathbf{p}^{(7)} &= (.571668, .428332) \\
\mathbf{p}^{(8)} &= (.57145, .42855) \\
\mathbf{p}^{(9)} &= (.571435, .428565) \\
\mathbf{p}^{(10)} &= (.571431, .428569).
\end{aligned}
$$

## D. Applications

This section on regular Markov chains concludes with some illustrations of how Theorems 4 and 5 can be applied to certain mathematical models.

---

**EXAMPLE 8**   A study of "brand loyalty" in the antidandruff shampoo market showed that 70 percent of consumers who bought Flakes No More would buy it again when it was time to repurchase shampoo, and 30 percent would switch to the other available brand, Head, Neck, and Shoulders. The study also showed that 40 per cent of Head, Neck, and Shoulders users would switch to Flakes No More while 60 percent would continue with the brand. In the long run, how much of the market can Flakes No More capture?

**Solution**    This is a regular Markov chain with two states, customer chooses Flakes No More (F) or Head, Neck, and Shoulders (H). The transition matrix is

$$\begin{array}{c}\text{Next purchase}\\ \begin{array}{cc} F & H \end{array}\\ P = \begin{array}{c}\text{This}\\ \text{purchase}\end{array} \begin{array}{c} F \\ H \end{array}\begin{pmatrix} .7 & .3 \\ .4 & .6 \end{pmatrix}\end{array}$$

Since the unique fixed point stochastic vector for $P$ is $\mathbf{w} = (\frac{4}{7}, \frac{3}{7})$, in the long run $\frac{4}{7}$ of the population will be using Flakes No More and $\frac{3}{7}$ will use Head, Neck, and Shoulders.

---

**EXAMPLE 9**    According to the birthrate model of Example 1, what are the long term distributions of birth weights among female babies?

**Solution**    We need to compute the fixed point stochastic vector for the transition matrix $P$ of Eq. (2). This leads to the matrix equation

$$(w_1, w_2, w_3)\begin{pmatrix} .5 & .45 & .05 \\ .25 & .5 & .25 \\ .3 & .3 & .4 \end{pmatrix} = (w_1, w_2, w_3)$$

which becomes the system

$$.5w_1 + .25w_2 + .3w_3 = w_1$$
$$.45w_1 + .5w_2 + .3w_3 = w_2$$
$$.05w_1 + .25w_2 + .4w_3 = w_3$$

and this is equivalent to the homogeneous system

$$-.5w_1 + .25w_2 + .3w_3 = 0$$
$$.45w_1 - .5w_2 + .3w_3 = 0$$
$$.05w_1 + .25w_2 - .6w_3 = 0.$$

A solution to this system is any triple of numbers $w_1, w_2, w_3$ such that $w_1 = \frac{90}{55}w_3$ and $w_2 = \frac{114}{55}w_3$. To find a stochastic vector, impose the extra condition that $w_1 + w_2 + w_3 = 1$. This gives $w_3 = \frac{55}{259}$ so that the fixed point stochastic vector is

$$\mathbf{w} = (90/259, \quad 114/259, \quad 55/259) = (.34749, \quad .440155, \quad .212355).$$

Hence about 35 percent of the births will be in the low range, 44 percent in the average range, and 21 percent in the high range.

---

Chapter 11, which you may wish to read at this time, gives an extended discussion of a mathematical model in anthropology which makes critical use of a regular Markov chain to investigate certain questions about cultural stability.

## IV. ABSORBING MARKOV CHAINS

This section offers a detailed look at another important class of Markov chains frequently used in mathematical models of social and biological phenomena.

### A. Definitions and Questions

A state $S_k$ in a Markov chain is called an *absorbing state* if it is impossible to leave it; that is, the transition probabilities satisfy

$$\begin{cases} p_{kk} - 1 \\ p_{kj} = 0 \quad \text{if } j \neq k. \end{cases}$$

A Markov chain is an *absorbing chain* if it has at least one absorbing state and from every state it is possible to reach some absorbing state in a finite number of steps. If a state is not an absorbing state, it is called a *transient state*.

The Markov chain describing the personnel policies of Lower Pine Cone College (Example 3) is an absorbing chain with two absorbing states ($F$ and $T$) and two transient states ($R$ and $P$). It is possible to reach either of the absorbing states from either of the transient states in a single step.

The state diagram of Fig. 10.7 represents an absorbing Markov with the absorbing states ($S_1$, $S_4$, and $S_6$). From state $S_2$, the process can move to $S_4$ in two steps. From state $S_3$, the process may move to $S_4$ in one step. From state $S_5$, the process can move to $S_4$ (two steps) or $S_6$ (one step).

Some of the important questions about absorbing Markov chains are the following:

1. Will the process eventually reach an absorbing state?

2. What is the average number of times we can expect the process to be in one transient state if it starts in another (or the same) transient state?

3. What is the average number of steps before the process enters an absorbing state?

4. What is the probability that the process will be absorbed in a particular state if it starts in a given transient state?

Our procedure in this section will be to introduce first the notation by which the answers to these questions may be presented, state the answers to the

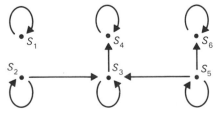

**Fig. 10.7**   State diagram illustrating a Markov Chain with three absorbing states ($S_1$, $S_4$, $S_6$).

questions, illustrate with a few examples, and then give the proofs of the relevant theorems.

## B. Notation and Answers

There is a standard way of representing the transition matrix of an absorbing chain: list the absorbing states first and then the transient states. For the Lower Pine Cone College example, the transition matrix is already in standard form:

$$
P = \begin{array}{c} \\ F \\ T \\ R \\ P \end{array}
\begin{array}{c} \begin{array}{cccc} F & T & R & P \end{array} \\
\left(\begin{array}{cc|cc}
1 & 0 & 0 & 0 \\
0 & 1 & 0 & 0 \\
\hline
a & b & c & d \\
e & f & g & 0
\end{array}\right)
\end{array}. \tag{26}
$$

A standard form for the transition matrix of the chain whose state diagram is given by Fig. 10.7 is

$$
P = \begin{array}{c} \\ S_1 \\ S_4 \\ S_6 \\ S_2 \\ S_3 \\ S_5 \end{array}
\begin{array}{c} \begin{array}{cccccc} S_1 & S_4 & S_6 & S_2 & S_3 & S_5 \end{array} \\
\left(\begin{array}{ccc|ccc}
1 & 0 & 0 & 0 & 0 & 0 \\
0 & 1 & 0 & 0 & 0 & 0 \\
0 & 0 & 1 & 0 & 0 & 0 \\
\hline
0 & 0 & 0 & a & 1-a & 0 \\
0 & b & 0 & 0 & 1-b & 0 \\
0 & 0 & c & 0 & d & 1-c-d
\end{array}\right)
\end{array}. \tag{27}
$$

If an absorbing Markov process with $r$ states has $k$ absorbing states, then the transition matrix has the standard form:

$$
\begin{array}{c} \\ \text{Absorbing states} \\ \text{Transient states} \end{array}
\begin{array}{c} \begin{array}{cc} \text{Absorbing} & \text{Transient} \\ \text{states} & \text{states} \end{array} \\
\left(\begin{array}{c|c}
I & 0 \\
\hline
R & Q
\end{array}\right)
\end{array}
$$

where

$I$ is the $k \times k$ identity matrix;

$0$ is the $k \times (r - k)$ zero matrix;

$R$ is a $(r - k) \times k$ matrix, and

$Q$ is a $(r - k) \times (r - k)$ matrix.

If $I$ is the $(r - k) \times (r - k)$ identity matrix, then it turns out that the square matrix $I - Q$ is always invertible. The matrix $N = (I - Q)^{-1}$ is called the *fundamental matrix* of the Markov chain. Let $N_{ij}$ represent the $ij$th element of $N$, $T_i$ the sum of the entries in row $i$ of $N$, and $b_{ij}$ the $ij$th entry of the matrix $B = NR$.

We can now state the answers to the four important questions about absorbing Markov chains:

1. Every absorbing Markov process eventually reaches some absorbing state.

2. The number $N_{ij}$ is the average number of times the process is in the $j$th transient state if it starts in the $i$th transient state.

3. The number $T_i$ is the average number of steps before the process enters an absorbing state if it starts in the $i$th transient state.

4. The number $B_{ij}$ is the probability of eventually entering the $j$th absorbing state if the process starts in the $i$th transient state.

These results are easier to remember if you keep track of the sizes of the matrices. The matrix $N$ is $(r - k)$ by $(r - k)$ and its rows and columns correspond to transient states. The matrix $B = NR$ has size $(r - k) \times k$; the rows correspond to transient states and the columns to absorbing states.

***An Application***   Consider the personnel policies of Lower Pine Cone College (Example 3) with the transition probabilities given in Section II.C:

$$a = .1, \quad b = .01, \quad c = .67, \quad d = .22, \quad e = .05, \quad f = .45, \quad g = 5.$$

The matrices $R$ and $Q$ are given by

$$R = \begin{pmatrix} .1 & .01 \\ .05 & .45 \end{pmatrix} \qquad Q = \begin{pmatrix} .67 & .22 \\ .5 & 0 \end{pmatrix}$$

and we have

$$I - Q = \begin{pmatrix} 1 - .67 & 0 - .22 \\ 0 - .5 & 1 - 0 \end{pmatrix} = \begin{pmatrix} .33 & -.22 \\ -.5 & 1 \end{pmatrix}$$

so that

$$N = (I - Q)^{-1} = \begin{pmatrix} 4.54545 & 1 \\ 2.27273 & 1.5 \end{pmatrix}$$

and

$$B = NR = \begin{matrix} & F & T \\ R & \\ P & \end{matrix}\begin{pmatrix} .504545 & .495455 \\ .302273 & .697727 \end{pmatrix}.$$

Here are some conclusions we may make about this absorbing Markov process:

a) Every nontenured faculty member will eventually be promoted to a tenure rank or he will be fired;

b) A faculty member who has just been promoted but not given tenure (initial state $P$) will eventually be given tenure with a probability of .697727 ($B_{22}$) or be fired with probability .302273 ($B_{21}$). He should expect to wait, on the average, 3.77273 years ($T_2 = N_{21} + N_{22}$) before the decision is made.

c) A professor who was retained at her present rank by the committee this year (initial state $R$) faces a probability of .495455 of eventually gaining tenure and probability of .504545 that she eventually will be fired. Her expected waiting time for a decision is 5.54545 years ($T_1 = N_{11} + N_{12}$).

More extended discussions of particular absorbing Markov chains will be found in the mathematical model of learning presented in Chapter 12 and the sports examples of Section IV.C below.

### C.  Sports Examples

Imagine two teams, A and B, playing a championship series of three games. The first team to win two games is declared the winner of the series. Let $p$ represent the probability that team A will win any one particular game and let $q = 1 - p$. Let $m - n$ denote the state that the series stands at $m$ wins for team A and $n$ wins for team B. The initial state is then 0–0 while 2–0 denotes a clean sweep for A, and 1–1 means the series is even after 2 games. There are eight possible states: 0–0, 1–0, 0–1, 1–1, 2–0, 2–1, 1–2, 0–2. The absorbing states are 2–0, 2–1, 1–2, and 0–2 since the series ends as soon as one team has won two games. A state diagram for this Markov process appears in Fig. 10.8.

From the state diagram, a standard form for the transition diagram can be constructed:

$$P = \begin{array}{c} \\ 2\text{--}0 \\ 2\text{--}1 \\ 1\text{--}2 \\ 0\text{--}2 \\ 0\text{--}0 \\ 1\text{--}0 \\ 0\text{--}1 \\ 1\text{--}1 \end{array} \begin{array}{c} \begin{array}{cccc} 2\text{--}0 & 2\text{--}1 & 1\text{--}2 & 0\text{--}2 \end{array} \quad \begin{array}{cccc} 0\text{--}0 & 1\text{--}0 & 0\text{--}1 & 1\text{--}1 \end{array} \\ \left( \begin{array}{cccc|cccc} 1 & 0 & 0 & 0 & 0 & 0 & 0 & 0 \\ 0 & 1 & 0 & 0 & 0 & 0 & 0 & 0 \\ 0 & 0 & 1 & 0 & 0 & 0 & 0 & 0 \\ 0 & 0 & 0 & 1 & 0 & 0 & 0 & 0 \\ \hline 0 & 0 & 0 & 0 & 0 & p & q & 0 \\ p & 0 & 0 & 0 & 0 & 0 & 0 & q \\ 0 & 0 & 0 & q & 0 & 0 & 0 & p \\ 0 & p & q & 0 & 0 & 0 & 0 & 0 \end{array} \right) \end{array}.$$

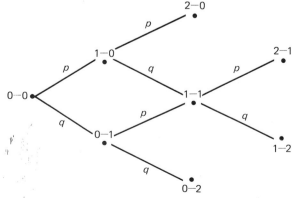

**Fig. 10.8**   State diagram for a three-game series.

The matrix $I - Q$ has the form

$$
I - Q = \begin{array}{c}
\\
0\text{--}0 \\
1\text{--}0 \\
0\text{--}1 \\
1\text{--}1
\end{array}
\begin{array}{cccc}
0\text{--}0 & 1\text{--}0 & 0\text{--}1 & 1\text{--}1 \\
\left(\begin{array}{cccc}
1 & -p & -q & 0 \\
0 & 1 & 0 & -q \\
0 & 0 & 1 & -p \\
0 & 0 & 0 & 1
\end{array}\right)
\end{array}
$$

and the fundamental matrix $N = (I - Q)^{-1}$ is

$$
N = \begin{array}{c}
\\
0\text{--}0 \\
1\text{--}0 \\
0\text{--}1 \\
1\text{--}1
\end{array}
\begin{array}{cccc}
0\text{--}0 & 1\text{--}0 & 0\text{--}1 & 1\text{--}1 \\
\left(\begin{array}{cccc}
1 & p & q & 2pq \\
0 & 1 & 0 & q \\
0 & 0 & 1 & p \\
0 & 0 & 0 & 1
\end{array}\right)
\end{array}
$$

so that the matrix $B = NR$ is given by

$$
B = \begin{array}{c}
\\
0\ 0 \\
1\text{--}0 \\
0\text{--}1 \\
1\text{--}1
\end{array}
\begin{array}{cccc}
2\text{--}0 & 2\text{--}1 & 1\text{--}2 & 0\text{--}2 \\
\left(\begin{array}{cccc}
p^2 & 2p^2 q & 2pq^2 & q^2 \\
p & pq & q^2 & 0 \\
0 & p^2 & pq & q \\
0 & p & q & 0
\end{array}\right)
\end{array}
$$

Since the series begins in state 0–0, examine the first rows of $N$ and $B$. Team A wins the series if the absorbing state is 2–0 or 2–1. Thus the probability that A wins the series is the sum of the first two entries of the first row of $B$:

$$\Pr(\text{Team A wins series}) = p^2 + 2p^2 q. \tag{28}$$

The series lasts two games if the absorbing state is 2–0 or 0–2 and it lasts three games if the absorbing state is 2–1 or 1–2. From the first row of $B$, we obtain

$$\Pr(\text{Series lasts two games}) = p^2 + q^2 \tag{29}$$

$$\Pr(\text{Series lasts three games}) = 2p^2 q + 2pq^2 = 2pq(p + q) = 2pq(1) = 2pq. \tag{30}$$

The expected length of the series is the sum of entries in the first row of $N$:

$$1 + p + q + 2pq = 1 + p + (1 - p) + 2p(1 - p) = 2(1 + p - p^2). \tag{31}$$

Now the function $f(p) = 2(1 + p - p^2)$ achieves its maximum (2.5) at $p = .5$ and decreases monotonically to 2 as $p$ increases to 1. Thus we can determine $p$ from the average length of a large number of series.

As an example, the United States Lawn Tennis Association's *Official Encyclopedia of Tennis* lists the results of 112 men's tennis tournaments in which the winner was determined by a three-set series. Of these matches, 67 were concluded after two sets and 45 lasted three sets, for an average length of 2.401 sets. From Eq. (31), this corresponds to a probability $p = .72486$ of a player winning a single given set.

With this value of $p$, Eqs. (29) and (30) predict that in 112 matches 67.22 would last two sets and 44.78 would last three sets.

Turn now to the situation of players A and B engaged in a five-set championship series. The first player to win 3 sets is the winner. As before, $p$ denotes the probability that player A will win any one particular set and $q = 1 - p$.

Treating this series as a Markov process, there are 15 states:

Six absorbing states   $3-0, 3-1, 3-2, 2-3, 1-3, 0-3,$

and

Nine transient states: $0-0, 1-0, 0-1, 2-0, 1-1, 0-2, 2-1, 1-2, 2-2.$

The model of this competition is an absorbing Markov chain with matrices $Q$ and $R$ given by

|       | 0–0 | 1–0 | 0–1 | 2–0 | 1–1 | 0–2 | 2–1 | 1–2 | 2–2 |
|-------|-----|-----|-----|-----|-----|-----|-----|-----|-----|
| 0–0   | 0   | $p$ | $q$ | 0   | 0   | 0   | 0   | 0   | 0   |
| 1–0   | 0   | 0   | 0   | $p$ | $q$ | 0   | 0   | 0   | 0   |
| 0–1   | 0   | 0   | 0   | 0   | $p$ | $q$ | 0   | 0   | 0   |
| 2–0   | 0   | 0   | 0   | 0   | 0   | 0   | $q$ | 0   | 0   |
| $Q =$ 1–1 | 0 | 0 | 0 | 0 | 0 | 0 | $p$ | $q$ | 0 |
| 0–2   | 0   | 0   | 0   | 0   | 0   | 0   | 0   | $p$ | 0   |
| 2–1   | 0   | 0   | 0   | 0   | 0   | 0   | 0   | 0   | $q$ |
| 1–2   | 0   | 0   | 0   | 0   | 0   | 0   | 0   | 0   | $p$ |
| 2–2   | 0   | 0   | 0   | 0   | 0   | 0   | 0   | 0   | 0   |

and

|       | 3–0 | 3–1 | 3–2 | 2–3 | 1–3 | 0–3 |
|-------|-----|-----|-----|-----|-----|-----|
| 0–0   | 0   | 0   | 0   | 0   | 0   | 0   |
| 1–0   | 0   | 0   | 0   | 0   | 0   | 0   |
| 0–1   | 0   | 0   | 0   | 0   | 0   | 0   |
| 2–0   | $p$ | 0   | 0   | 0   | 0   | 0   |
| $R =$ 1–1 | 0 | 0 | 0 | 0 | 0 | 0 |
| 0–2   | 0   | 0   | 0   | 0   | 0   | $q$ |
| 2–1   | 0   | $p$ | 0   | 0   | 0   | 0   |
| 1–2   | 0   | 0   | 0   | 0   | $q$ | 0   |
| 2–2   | 0   | 0   | $p$ | $q$ | 0   | 0   |

.

The fundamental matrix $N$ is

$$
N = \begin{array}{c|ccccccccc}
 & 0\text{--}0 & 1\text{--}0 & 0\text{--}1 & 2\text{--}0 & 1\text{--}1 & 0\text{--}2 & 2\text{--}1 & 1\text{--}2 & 2\text{--}2 \\
\hline
0\text{--}0 & 1 & p & q & p^2 & 2pq & q^2 & 3p^2q & 3pq^2 & 6p^2q^2 \\
1\text{--}0 & 0 & 1 & 0 & p & q & 0 & 2pq & q^2 & 3pq^2 \\
0\text{--}1 & 0 & 0 & 1 & & p & q & p^2 & 2pq & 3p^2q \\
2\text{--}0 & 0 & 0 & 0 & 1 & 0 & 0 & q & 0 & q^2 \\
1\text{--}1 & 0 & 0 & 0 & 0 & 1 & 0 & p & q & 2pq \\
0\text{--}2 & 0 & 0 & 0 & 0 & 0 & 1 & 0 & p & p^2 \\
2\text{--}1 & 0 & 0 & 0 & 0 & 0 & 0 & 1 & 0 & q \\
1\text{--}2 & 0 & 0 & 0 & 0 & 0 & 0 & 0 & 1 & p \\
2\text{--}2 & 0 & 0 & 0 & 0 & 0 & 0 & 0 & 0 & 1 \\
\end{array}
$$

and the matrix $B = NR$ is

$$
B = \begin{array}{c|cccccc}
 & 3\text{--}0 & 3\text{--}1 & 3\text{--}2 & 2\text{--}3 & 1\text{--}3 & 0\text{--}3 \\
\hline
0\text{--}0 & p^3 & 3p^3q & 6p^3q^2 & 6p^2q^3 & 3pq^3 & q^3 \\
1\text{--}0 & p^2 & 2p^2q & 3p^2q^2 & 3pq^3 & q^3 & 0 \\
0\text{--}1 & 0 & p^3 & 3p^3q & 3p^2q^2 & 2pq^2 & q^2 \\
2\text{--}0 & p & pq & pq^2 & q^3 & 0 & 0 \\
1\text{--}1 & 0 & p^2 & 2p^2q & 2pq^2 & q^2 & 0 \\
0\text{--}2 & 0 & 0 & p^3 & p^2q & pq & q \\
2\text{--}1 & 0 & p & pq & q^2 & 0 & 0 \\
1\text{--}2 & 0 & 0 & p^2 & pq & q & 0 \\
2\text{--}0 & 0 & 0 & p & q & 0 & 0 \\
\end{array}
$$

The sum of the entries in the first row of $N$ gives the expected number of sets in the series:

$$1 + p + q + p^2 + 2pq + q^2 + 3p^2q + 3pq^2 + 6p^2q^2. \tag{32}$$

The sum $B_{11} + B_{12} + B_{13}$ gives the probability that player A wins the series:

$$\Pr(\text{A wins series}) = p^3 + 3p^3q + 6p^3q^2. \tag{33}$$

To determine the probability distribution for the length of the series, we have:

$$\Pr(\text{Series ends in 3 sets}) = B_{11} + B_{16} = p^3 + q^3, \tag{34}$$
$$\Pr(\text{Series ends in 4 sets}) = B_{12} + B_{15} = 3p^3q + 3pq^3, \tag{35}$$
$$\Pr(\text{Series ends in 5 sets}) = B_{13} + B_{14} = 6p^3q^2 + 6p^2q^3. \tag{36}$$

To test this model of tennis competition, suppose that the probability $p = .72486$, based on our earlier observations, holds in general competition. Then the expected length of a best-of-five-sets series becomes, using (32),

$$\text{Predicted expected length} = 3.83697 \text{ sets.} \tag{37}$$

The national men's singles champion of the USLTA is determined each year in a tournament which climaxes in a best-of-five-sets series between the two finalists. In the 89 championships decided between 1881 and 1969, there were

38   three-set matches,

28   four-set matches, and

23   five-set matches,

which gives

$$\text{Observed average length} = 3.8314 \text{ sets.} \tag{38}$$

The predicted and observed average lengths are remarkably close. Furthermore, Eqs. (34)–(36) predict

35.75   three-set matches,

32.01   four-set matches, and

21.24   five-set matches

in a group of 89 matches.

A standard statistical test (the chi-squared) shows that the observed and predicted distributions are significantly close together to lend weight to the assumption that tennis competition does follow the behavior of a Markov process.

Of course, the other rows of $N$ and $B$ also make predictions about the course of the tennis competition. The entry $B_{32} = p^3$, for example, predicts the probability of a player A winning the match if he loses the first set. We can compare this prediction to the observed value for the USLTA championships as a further test of the model. The model predicts this would occur 8.23 times in a group of 89 matches. In actual fact, this has happened 9 times in the USLTA championships.

It is interesting to note that for a fixed probability $p$ of winning any given set, the probability of winning a match increases with the number of required victories. Some representative figures are given in Table 10.2.

In their book on finite Markov chains, John Kemeny and J. Laurie Snell [1960] investigate tennis competition from a slightly different point of view. As we have noted, a match is decided by the winner of a three-set or a five-set series. A player wins a set by being the first to win 6 or more games and have a lead of at least 2 games over his opponent. Thus possible final scores in a set are $6-0, 6-1, \ldots, 6-4, 7-5, 8-6, \ldots$ where the numbers represent games won. An

**Table 10.2**

| Probability of winning a given set | .51 | .6 | .72846 |
|---|---|---|---|
| Probability of winning 3 set match | .515 | .648 | .815 |
| Probability of winning 5 set match | .519 | .683 | .868 |
| Probability of winning 7 set match | .522 | .710 | .904 |

individual game is won by the first player to amass four or more points, provided he leads by at least two points.

Kemeny and Snell compute the probability of winning a game, a set, and a match if a player has probability $p$ of winning each *point*. They show, for example, that if $p = .51$, then the likelihood of winning the match is .635 while if $p = .6$, then the probability of winning the match rises to .9996. If there is a significant difference (.2 or more) in the abilities of the players, as measured by $p - (1 - p)$, then the better player is almost certain to win. Even if the difference is small ($p = .51, 1 - p = .49$), the better player still wins more than 63 per cent of the time.

## D. Theorems

This section contains statements of and outlines of proofs for the major results about absorbing Markov chains already discussed and illustrated. Detailed, rigorous proofs may be found in Kemeny and Snell's book on Markov chains.

■ *THEOREM 6*    In an absorbing Markov chain, the probability that the process will eventually enter an absorbing state is 1.

*Sketch of Proof of Theorem 6*    Let $S_i$ be a transient state of the Markov process. It is possible to reach at least one of the absorbing states in a finite number of steps, if the process begins in $S_i$. Let $r_i$ denote the minimum number of steps necessary to reach some absorbing state from $S_i$. Let $p_i$ denote the probability that the process does *not* reach any absorbing state in $r_i$ steps if it starts in $S_i$. Then $p_i$ is strictly less than 1.

Let $r$ denote the largest of the numbers $r_i$ and $p$ the largest of the probabilities $p_i$, where $i$ ranges over the index numbers of the transient states. Then the probability of not reaching an absorbing state in $r$ steps is less than $p$. Similarly the probability of not reaching an absorbing state in $2r$ steps is less than $p^2$. In general, the probability of not reaching an absorbing state in $nr$ steps is less than $p^n$. Since $p < 1$, the probabilities $p^n$ tend to 0 as $n$ gets large. Thus the probability of eventually reaching some absorbing state must tend to 1. □

■ *THEOREM 7*    Let $P$ be the transition matrix of an absorbing Markov chain in standard form

$$P = \begin{array}{c} \\ k \text{ absorbing states} \\ r - k \text{ transient states} \end{array} \begin{array}{cc} \text{Absorbing states} & \text{Transient states} \\ \left( \dfrac{I}{R} \right. & \left. \dfrac{0}{Q} \right) \end{array}.$$

Then $P^n$ has the form

$$P^n = \left( \begin{array}{c|c} I & 0 \\ \hline R_n & Q^n \end{array} \right)$$

where $Q^n$ is the $n$th power of $Q$ and $R_n$ is a $(r - k) \times k$ matrix.

**Proof of Theorem 7**    The states have been numbered so that $S_1, S_2, \ldots, S_k$ are the absorbing states and $S_{k+1}, S_{k+2}, \ldots, S_r$ are the transient states. The matrix $Q$ has the form

$$Q = \begin{pmatrix} q_{k+1, k+1} & q_{k+1, k+2} & \cdots & q_{k+1, r} \\ \cdots & & & \\ q_{r, k+1} & q_{r, k+2} & \cdots & q_{r, r} \end{pmatrix}$$

where $q_{k+i, k+j}$ is the transition probability of moving from the $i$th transient state to the $j$th transient state in one step.

Consider the matrix $P^2$. The probability of moving from the $i$th transient state to the $j$th transient state in 2 steps is the $(k+i, k+j)$-th entry of $P^2$. This number is the matrix product of the $(k+i)$-th row of $P$,

$$(r_{k+i, 1}, r_{k+i, 2}, \ldots, r_{k+i, k}, q_{k+i, k+1}, \ldots, q_{k+i, r})$$

and the $j$th column of $P$,

$$\left. \begin{pmatrix} 0 \\ 0 \\ \vdots \\ 0 \\ q_{k+1, k+j} \\ q_{k+2, k+j} \\ \vdots \\ q_{r, k+j} \end{pmatrix} \right\} k \text{ zeroes.}$$

This product is equal to $\sum_{s=1}^{r-k} q_{k+i, k+s} q_{k+s, k+j}$ and that number is simply the product of the $i$th row and $j$th column of $Q$; that is, the $ij$th entry of $Q^2$. Thus the lower right hand corner of $P^2$ is $Q^2$. The corresponding result for $P^n$ follows by induction on $n$. $\square$

This theorem says that the probability of moving from the $i$th transient state to the $j$th transient state in $n$ steps is the $ij$th entry of $Q^n$. From the proof of Theorem 6, however, we know that this probability tends to zero. Thus we have

**Corollary**    The powers of the matrix $Q$ tend to 0; that is, $\lim_{n \to \infty} Q^n = 0$.

■ **THEOREM 8**    The matrix $I - Q$ has an inverse.

**Sketch of Proof of Theorem 8**    For $n = 1, 2, 3, \ldots$, let $C_n$ be the matrix defined by

$$C_n = I + Q + Q^2 + \cdots + Q^{n-2} + Q^{n-1}.$$

Then

$$QC_n = Q + Q^2 + Q^3 + \cdots + Q^{n-1} + Q^n$$

and

$$(I - Q)C_n = C_n - QC_n = I - Q^n. \tag{39}$$

Now let $n$ increase on both sides of Eq. (39). Letting $N = \lim_{n \to \infty} C_n$ and using the fact that $\lim_{n \to \infty} Q^n = 0$, we have

$$(I - Q)N = I - 0 = I \tag{40}$$

so that $N$ is the inverse of $I - Q$. $\square$

Admittedly, the derivation of Eq. (40) from (39) is highly nonrigorous, but the reader is assured that everything can be fully justified with epsilons and deltas.

■ **THEOREM 9**    Let $n_{ij}$ be the expected number of times that an absorbing Markov chain is in the $j$th transient state $S_{k+j}$ if it starts in the $i$th transient state $S_{k+i}$. If $N$ is the matrix whose entries are given by $n_{ij}$, then $N$ is the inverse of $I - Q$.

***Proof of Theorem 9***    If $i = j$, then $n_{ij}$ is at least one. Using the fact that the expected value of a sum is the sum of the expected values, we have the relation

$$n_{ij} = d_{ij} + (p_{k+i, k+1}n_{1j} + p_{k+i, k+2}n_{2j} + \cdots + p_{k+i, r}n_{rj}) \tag{41}$$

where $d_{ij} = 1$ if $i = j$ and 0 if $i \neq j$. The transition probabilities $p_{k+i, k+j}$ are obtained from the transition matrix. The relation (41) follows since we must consider all possible moves to other transient states at the first step. Note that the transition probabilities entering the equation are exactly the entries of $Q$. The matrix form of Eq. (41) then is

$$N = I + QN, \tag{42}$$

which gives $IN = I + QN$ or $I = IN - QN = (I - Q)N$. Since $(I - Q)N = I$, $N$ is the inverse of $I - Q$. $\square$

***Corollary***    The sum of the entries in any row of $N$ is the expected number of times the process is in some transient state for a given starting transient state; that is, the expected number of steps before the process enters an absorbing state.

■ **THEOREM 10**    Let $P$ be the transition matrix of an absorbing Markov chain in standard form and let $N = (I - Q)^{-1}$. Let $b_{ij}$ be the probability that the process will enter the $j$th absorbing state if it starts in the $i$th transient state. Then $b_{ij}$ is the $ij$th entry of the matrix $B = NR$.

***Proof of Theorem 10***    The process could enter the absorbing state at the first step with probability $p_{k+i, j}$ or it could first move to some other transient state and then eventually move into the $j$th absorbing state. Thus we have the relation

$$b_{ij} = p_{k+i, j} + \sum_{s=1}^{r} p_{k+i, k+s}b_{sj} \tag{43}$$

where the summation runs over all the transient states. Note that the transition probability $p_{k+i, j}$ is an entry of $R$ and the transition probabilities $p_{k+i, k+s}$ are entries of $Q$. Hence the matrix form of Eq. (43) is

$$B = R + QB, \tag{44}$$

so that

$$R = B - QB = (I - Q)B. \tag{45}$$

Multiply each side of Eq. (45) by $N = (I - Q)^{-1}$ to obtain

$$NR = (I - Q)^{-1}(I - Q)B = B. \quad \square \tag{46}$$

## V.  BIOGRAPHICAL AND HISTORICAL NOTES

### A.  A. A. Markov

Markov processes are named after the man who first studied them, the Russian mathematician Andrei Andreevich Markov.  Markov was born in Ryazan,

Andrei Andreevich Markov.  Novosti from Sovfoto.

Russia on June 14, 1856 and was the son of a member of the gentry who managed a large private estate.

The young Markov suffered from poor health and needed crutches until he was ten years old. His talent for mathematics was spotted early and he received a gold medal for his undergraduate thesis at St. Petersburg University (1878) entitled "On the integration of differential equations by means of continued fractions." He completed his doctoral dissertation on continued fractions and the problem of moments six years later. In 1883, Markov married Maria Ivanovna Valvatyeva whom he had known since childhood as she was the daughter of the proprietress of the estate managed by his father.

Markov combined an active research program with his teaching at St. Petersburg University for 25 years. He made important contributions to number theory, continued fractions, approximate quadrature formulas, function theory, integration in elementary functions, differential equations, and probability theory. He retired in 1905 to make room on the faculty for younger mathematicians, although he continued to present the course on probability. Markov's lectures and papers were noted for an irreproachable strictness of argument and a rather peremptory manner of stating opinions on the work of others. One biographer, Alexander Youschkevitch, described Markov as having "a mathematical cast of mind that takes nothing for granted" and reported that he was extremely exacting with his students and associates. It is said that during his lectures, Markov bothered little about the order of equations on the blackboard and even less about his personal appearance.

Markov was actively concerned with the politics of his time. He participated in the liberal movement in Russia at the beginning of the twentieth Century. He protested the Tsar's overruling of the election of Maxim Gorky to the St. Petersburg Academy of Sciences and repudiated his own membership in the electorate after the illegal dissolution of the Second State Duma (parliament) by the government in 1907. In 1913, when the government celebrated the 300th anniversary of rule by the Romanov family, Markov organized a countercelebration of the 200th anniversary of Bernoulli's discovery of the law of large numbers.

In September 1917, Markov asked to be sent to the interior of Russia. He spent the famine winter in the little country town of Zaraisk, teaching mathematics without pay. He died in St. Petersburg on May 20, 1922.

Although he worked in a number of different areas of mathematics, Markov's contributions to probability theory produced the greatest effect on the development of science. The work on the law of large numbers and the central limit theorem by Chebyshev (Markov's teacher), Lyapunov, and Markov created the basis for the modernization of probability theory.

Markov initiated the study of stochastic processes that would later bear his name in a 1906 paper "Rasprostranenie zakona bolshikh chisel na velichiny, zavi syaschchie drug ot druga" ("The extension of the law of large numbers on mutually dependent variables"). Markov arrived at his chains by starting from the internal needs of probability theory and not from applications to the physical or social sciences. He did study the application of his theory to the distribution of vowels and consonants in Pushkin's *Eugene Onegin*; this work is often cited as the first modern paper on mathematical linguistics.

## B. Further Applications

The English biologist-mathematician Sir Francis Galton (1822–1911) became interested in the survival and extinction of family names. The mathematical model he formulated in 1889 was one which involved the fundamental assumptions of Markov processes.

Paul and Tatyana Ehrenfast investigated a Markov chain model for diffusion in a 1907 paper about the same time that Einstein and Smoluchowski were using Markov processes to study Brownian motion.

Since these early studies, there have been many applications of Markov processes to the modeling of phenomena in the physical, life, and social sciences. Physicists have employed them to the theory of cascade processes, radioactive transformation, nuclear fission detectors, and the theory of tracks in nuclear research emulsions. Astronomers have studied fluctuations in the brightness of the Milky Way and the spatial distribution of galaxies using Markov chains. Chemists use stochastic models to understand chemical reaction kinetics and the statistical theory of polymer chains.

Mathematically inclined biologists have employed Markov chains and more general stochastic processes to learn more about population growth, structure of biological populations, taxis and kinesis, embryogenesis, evolution, molecular genetics, pharmacology, tumor growth, and epidemics.

Some of the areas of investigation in the social sciences that have been pursued through the use of Markov chains include voting behavior, geographical mobility within a country, the spread of ghettos in urban areas, growth and decline of towns, competition in the brewing industry, the size of economic firms, the spread of the use of intrauterine devices in Taiwan, prediction of enrollments in colleges and universities, the epidemiology of mental diseases, changes in personal attitudes, and the deliberations of a trial jury.

---

## EXERCISES

### I. MARKOV CHAINS

1. Two competing companies, Pollution Products and Environmental Hazards, simultaneously introduce new enzyme laundry detergents. Market tests indicate that during a year, Pollution keeps 60 per cent of its customers and loses 40 per cent of its customers to Environmental. On the other hand, Environmental keeps half of its customers and loses the other half to Pollution. Set up this process as a Markov chain. Determine the transition matrix and sketch a state diagram.

2. Abigail spends her entire weekly allowance on either candy or toys. If she buys candy one week, she is 60 percent sure to buy toys the next week. The probability that she buys toys in two successive weeks is $\frac{1}{5}$. Set up this process as a Markov chain. Determine the transition matrix and sketch a state diagram.

3. A political scientist in Canada discovered that of the sons of Conservatives, 80 percent vote Conservative and the rest vote Labor, of the sons of Labor supporters, 60 percent vote Labor, 20 percent vote Conservative and 20 percent vote for the New Democratic Party (NDP), and of the sons of NDP followers, 75 vote NDP, 15 per cent vote Labor and 10 percent vote Conservative.

a) What is the probability that the grandson of a Conservative will vote for the NDP?

b) Set up this process as a Markov chain, with steps corresponding to successive generations. Determine the transition matrix and sketch the state diagram.

4. A secret Defense Department report gives the following analysis of the arms race between the United States and the Soviet Union: There are four possible states: War, Total Disarmament, Escalating Arms Race and Deescalating Arms Race. It is not possible to change the situation if War or Total Disarmament is occurring this year. If there is an Escalating Arms Race this year, the probability of continued escalation next year is .6, of Deescalation next year is .2, and of War next year is .2. If there is a Deescalating Arms Race this year, the probability of continued deescalation next year is .7, of escalation next year is .1, and of total disarmament next year is .2.

Set up this process as a Markov chain. Determine the transition matrix and sketch the state diagram.

5. The National League and American League alternate as hosts for the opening game of each year's World Series. Show that this process can be set up as a Markov process with transition matrix

$$P = \begin{pmatrix} 0 & 1 \\ 1 & 0 \end{pmatrix}.$$

6. A particle moves along a line from an initial position 2 feet to the right of the origin. Each minute it moves one foot to the right with probability $\frac{1}{2}$ or one foot to the left. There are barriers at the origin and 4 feet to the right of the origin; if the particle hits a barrier, it remains there. Show that this process can be set up as a Markov process with five states. Determine the transition matrix and draw the state diagram.

7. The random walk of Exercise 6 is modified so that if the particle reaches the barrier at the origin, it must move one foot to the right in the next minute, while if it hits the other barrier, it must move one foot to the left in the next minute. Determine the transition matrix for the associated Markov chain.

8. Find the probability that a women whose birth weight was average has a granddaughter with an average birth weight.

9. Sketch the state diagram for the Lower Pine Cone College example.

10. Can accurate weather predictions be made from a Markov model of climate which uses only today's weather to forecast tomorrow's?

## II. MATRIX OPERATIONS AND MARKOV CHAINS

11. Using probabilistic considerations only, show that the square of a stochastic matrix is also a stochastic matrix.

12. A stochastic matrix is *doubly stochastic* if the sum of the entries in each column is 1. If $A$ and $B$ are doubly stochastic square matrices, is $A^2$ doubly stochastic? Is $AB$?

13. Write out inductive proofs for Theorems 2 and 3.

14. Use matrix multiplication to solve Exercise 8.

15. Abigail bought a toy with her allowance this week (see Exercise 2). Find the probability that she will buy a toy four weeks from now.

16. Find the distribution of birth weights (Example 1) after one generation if the initial probability distribution is $(.4, .3, .3)$.

17. Suppose the distribution of birth weights of a generation of daughters is $\mathbf{p}^{(1)} = (.31, .45, .24)$. Can you find the distribution of birth weights of the mothers?

18. Use the state diagram in Fig. 10.3 to find the probability that the process reaches state $S_3$ in two steps if it starts in state $S_1$.

19. Let $P$ be the transition matrix of Eq. (4). Compute $P^2$. What can you say about the first column of $P^3$? $P^n$?

20. Consider the transition matrix of Eq. (16). Can you determine whether it is more likely that a newly hired professor will eventually be given tenure or be fired?

## III. REGULAR MARKOV CHAINS

21. The matrices determined in Exercises 1–7 are all transition matrices for Markov processes. Which ones are regular?

22. Find, if possible, a fixed point vector for each of the transition matrices of Exercises 1–7.

23. Does a matrix of the form $A = \begin{pmatrix} a & b \\ -b & d \end{pmatrix}$ have a fixed point vector?

24. How often, in the long run, will a stereo be the special sale item at the Audio-Visual Den (Example 2)?

25. Analyze the long range prospects for the competition model described in Exercise 1.

26. How often, on the average, does Abigail spend her allowance on candy (Exercise 2)?

27. What are the long term predictions for the male vote in Canada according to the data of Exercise 3?

28. Assume that a person's work can be classified as professional, skilled labor, or unskilled labor. Assume that of the children of professionals, 80 percent are professional, 10 percent are skilled laborers, and 10 percent are unskilled laborers. In the case of children of skilled laborers, 60 percent are skilled laborers, 20 percent are professionals, and 20 percent are unskilled laborers. Finally, in the case of unskilled laborers, 50 percent of the children are unskilled laborers, and 25 percent each are in the other two categories. Assume that every person has a child and form a Markov chain by following a given family through several generations. In commenting on the society described, the famed sociologist Harry Perlstadt has written, "No matter what the initial distribution of the labor force is, in the long run the majority of the workers will be professionals." Is he correct? Why?

29. Suppose $P$ is the transition matrix of a regular Markov chain and let $W$ be the matrix given by Theorem 4. Prove that the matrix $I - (P - W)$ is invertible. Compute this matrix and its inverse if $P$ is the matrix of Example 5.

30. Let $N = (I - (P - W)^{-1}$ be the inverse of the matrix of Exercise 29. Here $N$ is called the *fundamental matrix* of a regular Markov process. Show that each of the following statements is true (a) if $P$ is the matrix of Example 5 and (b) $P$ is the transition matrix of any regular Markov process:

  i) $NP = PN$.

  ii) $\mathbf{w}N = \mathbf{w}$, where $\mathbf{w}$ is the fixed point stochastic vector of $P$.

  iii) $I - N = W - PN$.

  iv) $N$ is a stochastic matrix.

31. Let $\mathbf{u}$ be a given stochastic vector. Is it always possible to find a regular transition matrix $P$ such that $\mathbf{u}$ is a fixed point vector of $P$?

## IV. ABSORBING MARKOV CHAINS

32. Which of the transition matrices of Exercises 1–7 represent absorbing Markov processes?

33. What is the likelihood that the arms race described in Exercise 4 will end in a war? If there is an escalating arms race this year, what is the expected number of years before the arms race resolves itself into war or disarmament?

34. What predictions can you make about the random walk models of Exercises 6 and 7 using the theorems about regular and absorbing Markov processes?

35. Let $N$ be the fundamental matrix of an absorbing Markov chain. Show that $N$ is invertible and prove that $NQ = N - I$.

36. Let $S_i$ and $S_j$ be two transient states in a Markov process. Show that there are positive numbers $b$ and $c$, with $c$ less than 1, so that $p_{ij}^{(n)} \leqslant bc^n$. [*Hint*: Examine the proof of Theorem 6.]

37. Let $P$ be the transition matrix of an absorbing Markov chain with $r$ states. Let $B^*$ be the $r \times r$ matrix whose $ij$th entry is the probability of being absorbed in state $S_j$ if the process starts in state $S_i$. Prove that $PB^* = B^*$.

38. Supply a rigorous proof for Theorem 8.

39. A trio of nineteenth century Russian noblemen fight a three-way duel. The three men are of different abilities in pistol shooting. They have respective probabilities of $\frac{1}{2}$, $\frac{1}{3}$, and $\frac{1}{6}$ of hitting and killing the target at which they aim. In each round of the duel, the men shoot simultaneously and each one aims at the best marksman not yet killed. Treat this duel as a Markov chain by taking as the states the men who survive any one round. Find $N$ and $B$ and interpret the results.

40. *Gambler's Ruin.* Iris has \$3 and Ron has \$2. They flip a fair coin. If it is a head, Iris pays Ron \$1. Otherwise, Ron pays Iris \$1. How long will it take for one of the players to go broke or win all the money?

## V. FURTHER APPLICATIONS

For the remaining problems, see the last section of Chapter 9.

41. Each individual belongs to one of three possible genotypes: $AA$ (dominant), $AB$ (hybrid), or $BB$ (recessive). In a laboratory experiment, an individual of unknown genotype

is mated with a hybrid. Show that the probabilities for the genotypes $AA$, $AB$, and $BB$ of the offspring are given by vectors:

a) $(.5, .5, 0)$ if the unknown parent is dominant;

b) $(.25, .5, .25)$ if the unknown parent is hybrid; and

c) $(0, .5, .5)$ if the unknown parent is recessive.

42. Suppose the experiment of Exercise 41 is repeated a large number of generations; that is, in each generation an offspring is chosen at random and mated with a hybrid. Set up this process as a Markov chain, show that it is regular, and find the unique fixed point stochastic vector. Interpret the result.

43. Consider a large population in which mating is completely random, half the offspring are female, and the proportion of genotypes is the same for both males and females. Let $\mathbf{p}^{(0)}$ be the probability vector for the genotypes of an initial generation of parents and let $\mathbf{p}^{(k)}$ be the probability vector of genotypes of the $k$th generation of offspring.

a) Find the transition matrix $P$ of this Markov process so that $\mathbf{p}^{(k)} = \mathbf{p}^{(0)}P^k$.

b) Show that $\mathbf{p}^{(1)}$ is a fixed point vector for $P$.

   The conclusion of (b) is that the distribution of the genotypes is stable after only one generation. This result is called the *Hardy-Weinberg equilibrium principle* and was discovered independently in 1908 by G. H. Hardy and W. Weinberg.

44. Show that the Hardy-Weinberg principle may not be valid if parents of one genotype have, on the average, more offspring than parents of another genotype. How can the principle be modified in such a case?

---

**SUGGESTED PROJECTS**

---

1. Analyze World Series competition in the spirit of the tennis examples as an absorbing Markov chain. Let $p$ be the probability of winning any particular game. Determine the transition matrix $P$ and associated matrices $Q$, $N$, and $B$. Show that for $.5 \leqslant p \leqslant 1$, the expected length of a World Series is a monotonically decreasing function $p$. Thus $p$ can be determined from the observed average length of World Series competition. Does this value of $p$ predict closely the number of 4, 5, 6, and 7 game series that have occurred? Is there some way of estimating $p$ without relying on World Series information? Here are some possibilities:

a) Let $A$ be the average number of runs scored in the season by the American League pennant winner and let $L$ be the similar number for the National League counterpart. Let $p$, the probability that the American League champion wins a given game, be $A/(A + L)$.

b) Instead of using runs scored, use the difference between runs scored and runs allowed.

c) Instead of using runs scored, use the number of games won.

2. An *egordic* Markov process is one in which it is possible to go from any given state to any other one in a finite number of steps, but the number may depend on which states are chosen. For example, certain states may only be reached in an odd number of steps, while others require an even number. Show that every regular Markov process is an ergodic one. Find some examples of ergodic chains which are not regular. Many of the

important theorems about regular chains are also true for ergodic ones, although of necessity, the proofs are different. Which theorems are these? What real-world processes can be modeled with ergodic Markov chains?

3. Markov models have been used in many studies of learning theory and social conformity in which the states correspond to certain "states of mind" which may not be directly observable: the subject may be limited to a certain number of observable responses, for example, but the same response can occur if the subject is in any of several different states. Can the transition matrix be reconstructed from the observed behavior? Assuming that the initial state can be determined, note that the entries of the matrix $B$ can be observed. Is this enough to find $Q$ and $R$?

4. It may happen that a stochastic process operates in such a fashion that the probability of being in a particular state at any step depends on the states occupied in the *two* immediately preceding steps. Strictly speaking, this is not a Markov process. Show that it can be made into a Markov process by doubling the number of states. One area where this idea can be applied is to the study of the outcomes of political elections where the winners come from one of several parties. Would a model assuming that the results of an election depend on the two preceding elections necessarily be a more accurate one than a model taking into account only the most previous election? Use such a model to study the results of Congressional elections in a single district during the twentieth century.

5. Consider a Markov chain with transition matrix $P$. Suppose that before making a transition from state $S_i$ to state $S_j$, the process spends a time $t_{ij}$ in state $S_i$. These "holding times," $t_{ij}$, may be given by a probability distribution. Such a process is called a *semi-Markov process*. It has been used as a model to study the movement of coronary patients within different care units of a hospital (the absorbing states are death and discharge from hospital). Let $t_0$ be the time the process spends in state $S_i$ for each transition into that state. Find the expected value of $t_i$, the expected total amount of time the process will spend in state $S_j$ if it has just arrived in state $S_i$, and the expected amount of time the process will spend in transient states.

6. Investigate how the following two questions could be answered for a regular or an absorbing Markov process:

If $S_i$, $S_j$, and $S_k$ are any three states,

a) What is the expected number of steps for the process to move from $S_i$ to $S_j$ for the time?

b) If the process starts in $S_i$, what is the probability that it will reach $S_j$ before $S_k$?

## REFERENCES

### GENERAL

Bharucha-Reid, A. T., *Elements of the Theory of Markov Processes and Their Applications* (New York: McGraw-Hill, 1960). A particularly good source for applications in the physical sciences.

Kemeny, John G., and J. Laurie Snell, *Finite Markov Chains* (New York: Van Nostrand, 1960). The basic theory and many applications to the social sciences. I have followed the notation and terminology of this book, so it will be easy for you to read.

## MORE SPECIFIC APPLICATIONS

Bartholomew, David, *Stochastic Models for Social Processes* (New York: Wiley, 1967).

Bartlett, M. S., *Stochastic Population Models in Ecology and Epidemiology* (London: Methuen, 1960).

Blumen, I., M. Kogan, and P. J. McCarthy, *The Industrial Mobility of Labor as a Probability Process* (Ithaca: Cornell Studies of Industrial and Labor Relations, 1955, Volume 6.

Bush, R. R., and C. F. Mosteller, *Stochastic Models for Learning* (New York: Wiley, 1955).

Cohen, Bernard P., *Conflict and Conformity: A Probability Model and its Applications* (Cambridge: MIT Press, 1963).

Kao, Edward P. C., "Modeling the movement of coronary patients within a hospital by semi-Markov processes," *Operations Research* **22** (1974), 683–699.

# 11
# Two Models of Cultural Stability

Anthropology needs mathematics, not because mathematics is glamorous these days, but because mathematics can help anthropologists solve the kinds of problems anthropologists want to solve.

Paul Kay

## I. INTRODUCTION

Communities of people cannot long survive unless the basic needs of the inhabitants are met. In a rudimentary "society" each individual might take care only of his own requirements. He would find food, gather and prepare it, build his own shelter, and provide his own entertainment, medical care, and transportation. In most societies, however, people are dependent on one another for various goods and services. There is a division of labor among the residents. One person or group of persons specializes in constructing houses while another harvests the crops. Certain members debate and modify the laws while others insure that violators are apprehended and punished.

Furthermore, the obligations and the privileges of a single member of the society are different at different stages of the person's life. The social and economic contributions to the community of a 7-year-old, for example, vary from that of a 47-year-old. These in turn are not the same as those of a person of age 77.

Other factors besides age are often important in determining what is expected of an individual or what he is allowed to do. The person's sex, race, religion, and perhaps even height and weight, can control what occupations he will pursue and the extent of his power or influence in the society. The continued cultural viability of a community may depend quite crucially on the factors that are used to structure the division of privilege and responsibility among the members.


## II. THE GALLA SYSTEM

In this chapter, we will examine a system for the division of labor that has been used by some of the Galla tribes in Ethiopia. We shall consider only a simplified version of the actual system, so that we may focus on some important questions. In the Galla system, the critical functions of the tribe are structured through five age grades, called the Dabella, Folle, Kondala, Luba, and Yuba.

Each male in the society moves through the age-grade system, spending a period of eight consecutive years in each grade. Since there are five grades, it takes an individual 40 years to pass through the system. The key feature of this age-grade system is that a man enters the lowest grade at the moment his father retires from the highest grade. In other words, a son enters the system exactly 40 years after his father enters.

To illustrate this scheme, suppose your father enters the lowest grade when he is 13 years old and that you are born when he is 30 years old. Then your father retires from the system when he is 53 (40 + 13) years old. At that time, you will enter the system. Your age will be 53 − 30 = 23.

To continue this example, suppose that you have two sons, one who is born when you are 35 and the other when you are 45. You will leave the system at age 63. Your two sons will enter the system at the same time, although their ages will be different. The elder will be 28 years old and the younger will be

18 years old. They will move through the system together, entering the successive grades at the same time, and retiring in the same year.

The calendar years of entrance into the Galla system of all the male descendents of a man is then determined once we know the year the man himself entered. If a man enters the lowest grade in the year 1900, all his sons enter in the year 1940, even if the man dies before the date of his retirement. It is also possible that a son may enter the system before he is born! To see how this may happen, suppose that the man who entered the system in 1900 was very young. Then it is quite conceivable that he has a son who is born in 1950. In such a case, it is assumed that the son entered the lowest (Dabella) grade in 1940. At his birth then, the son is considered to be a member of the Folle grade and will advance to the Konda grade in 1956. This son would retire from the grade system in 1980 at the age of 30.

This age-grade system, as we have described it so far, poses no essential problems for the Galla society. What makes the system interesting to study is that the roles of a male in the tribe depend entirely on which of the five grades he is occupying and not on his age, wisdom, or strength. Two members of the Luba grade, for example, have the same rights and responsibilities, even if one is 7 years old and the other 47.

What are the particular roles assigned to the males in each grade? The anthropologist George Peter Murdock [1959] gives a concise description:

> During the first grade . . . males are forbidden to have sex relations and they wander about begging food, which is always termed "milk" from married women. This is strongly suggestive of the behavior of infants. During the second grade they become initiated into sexual life but without forming stable relationships, and they engage in masked processions and behave generally in an irresponsible manner suggestive of adolescence. In the third grade they serve as warriors and are permitted to marry. Military valor is encouraged in some tribes . . . by requiring the taking of the genitals of a slain enemy as a trophy to qualify for full participation in the activities of the next, or ruling, grade. When an age-set enters the fourth, or Luba, grade, its members take over all important administrative, judicial, and priestly offices in the tribe and run its affairs for eight years . . . . The chief of the age-set, elected when it occupied the second grade, now becomes the high chief of the tribe. Another man becomes speaker of the general assembly. Others assume various administrative and judicial offices—chief priest, finance minister, and so on. During the last, or Yuba, grade, these men relinquish their posts and become "guardians," serving the new officials in a purely advisory capacity.

Murdock's description indicates that the system may have been based, in its origin, on the maturity levels and abilities that corresponded with chronological age; that is, when the age-grade system began, the lower grade was made up entirely of children, while the highest grade was composed of the tribe's elders. As we have seen from our examples, however, in succeeding generations, the relationship between a man's age and the grade he occupies may be very complex.

Since the rules of the age-grade system permit a young man to occupy a high grade, while an older man may be restricted to the activities allowed to members of a lower grade, tensions can easily arise in the tribe. Another anthropologist, Hans Hoffmann [1965], studied this system with the use of mathematical models. He raised the fundamental problem:

> It is evident that the stability of Galla communities is threatened by the arbitrary interval of 40 years that is interposed between generations. Since this interval is often greater than the actual chronological difference between generations, the ages of some of the people in the grades may become progressively greater. This can result in humiliation and incongruity. An old man, entering the first grade, would be required to abstain from sexual activity and to wander around with its youthful members begging food. Further, if he should die before attaining the higher grades, important governmental offices may go unfilled.

The fact that it is possible for a man to "enter" the age-grade system before his actual birth leads to a similar kind of difficulty. He may reach the middle grades of the system at too early a chronological age. He may not be equipped to fulfill the military or ruling functions with any competence. By the time he has the physical strength, talents, and experience to occupy these roles with distinction, he has graduated to the highest grade, where his services are no longer available to the tribe.

Thus, the society may be seriously weakened because it does not have access to the skills of its members at the time it needs them.

"It is curious fact," writes A. H. J. Prins [1953], "peculiar to the Galla institution, that the physical age of those who occupy simultaneously one and the same grade varies so widely, even from young children to fairly old men. . . . Viewed from the institutional angle, what it comes to is that most members of any grade fail to accomplish what is socially expected of them. The grade is supposed to exist because of the expected execution of a delegated task which regards more or less the real ages of the participants, but owing to factual circumstances widely differing from those reflected in the implicit charter, the grades, especially the lower ones, seem to have become an institutional (or even 'functional') failure. This failure has to be attributed to the composition of the personnel."

If there is too high a proportion of males in the society who are "out of phase" with the roles of the age-grade system, it will be difficult to maintain both a strong community and the age-grade system.

Since every community must place a high premium on its own survival, we may well ask if the age-grade system can continue unchanged over a period of many generations. Does the system possess stability as a component of the culture? Must it change to relieve the tensions we have described? Or will the differences between the 40-year intervals and the gaps between successive generations somehow "smooth out" over the years so that these tensions are essentially absent?

Hoffmann developed two models to study these questions. The first [1965] is a relatively simple deterministic model, while the second [1971] is a more sophisticated probabilistic one that makes use of Markov chains.

## III. A DETERMINISTIC MODEL

To formulate a mathematical model, we must make some careful definitions and assumptions about the phenomena we hope to study. To investigate whether the age-grade system possesses stability, Hoffmann [1965] first had to make precise the idea of a stable system. He proposed the following:

**DEFINITION    A *stable* system is one which tends to maintain a realistic relationship between age and role behavior.**

For his deterministic model, Hoffmann investigated an axiom about sufficient conditions for a system to be stable.

**AXIOM 1    A realistic relationship between age and role behavior can be maintained if, between any arbitrary number of generations, the ages at which an ancestor and his distant offspring entered the first grade are equal.**

This axiom provides the means for translating our verbal discussions about stability into mathematics. Note that the condition for stability is an equality between numbers. We can make this more transparent by introducing some notation.

For the $i$th generation, we let $A_i$ denote the age at which a man enters the first grade. Thus, $A_1$ gives the age of the first man of interest when he enters the lowest grade, $A_2$ the age of his son, $A_3$ the age of his grandson, and so on. For simplicity, we will assume that each man has exactly one son.

By $P_i$, we will denote the age of the man in the $i$th generation when his son is born.

In terms of this notation, we have two ways of writing the age of the man in the first generation at his retirement from the age-grade system. On the one hand, since he enters the system at age $A_1$ and remains in it for 40 years, he retires at age $A_1 + 40$. On the other hand, since his son enters at the time the father retires, the father's age at retirement is also given by $P_1 + A_2$. Thus, we have the basic relationship,

$$A_1 + 40 = P_1 + A_2, \tag{1}$$

which we may rewrite as

$$A_2 = A_1 + 40 - P_1. \tag{2}$$

If we require that a man and his son enter the age-grade system at the same age, then we are insisting that $A_1 = A_2$. Substituting this equality into Eq. (2) yields

$$40 - P_1 = 0$$

or

$$P_1 = 40.$$

The basic relationship stated in Eq. (2) holds for every pair of father and son; thus we have,

$$A_{i+1} = A_i + 40 - P_i. \tag{3}$$

In particular, this gives us

$$\begin{aligned}
A_3 &= A_2 + 40 - P_2 \\
&= (A_1 + 40 - P_1) + 40 - P_2 \\
&= A_1 + 2(40) - (P_1 + P_2)
\end{aligned}$$ (4)

and

$$\begin{aligned}
A_4 &= A_3 + 40 - P_3 \\
&= A_1 + 2(40) - (P_1 + P_2) + 40 - P_3 \\
&= A_1 + 3(40) - (P_1 + P_2 + P_3).
\end{aligned}$$ (5)

A simple induction argument shows that

$$A_{n+1} = A_1 + n(40) - (P_1 + P_2 + \cdots + P_n).$$ (6)

We have seen that a man and his son will enter the age-grade system at the same age exactly if the son is born when his father is 40 years old. From Eq. (4), we may conclude that a man and his grandson will enter the age-grade system at the same age, that is, $A_3 = A_1$, exactly if

$$P_1 + P_2 = 80,$$ (7)

or

$$\frac{P_1 + P_2}{2} = 40.$$ (8)

This last equation asserts that the average age of parenthood of the first two generations must be 40 if the man and his grandson are to enter the system at the same age.

Now, Axiom 1 asserts that stability is maintained if the ages of entry of a man and his distant descendant are the same. If $n$ denotes a large, arbitrary number of generations, then this condition is expressed by the equality

$$A_{n+1} = A_1.$$ (9)

Substituting this equality into Eq. (6) gives

$$A_1 = A_1 + 40n - (P_1 + P_2 + \cdots + P_n),$$ (10)

or

$$40n = P_1 + P_2 + \cdots + P_n,$$ (11)

so that

$$40 = \frac{P_1 + P_2 + \cdots + P_n}{n}.$$ (12)

Now the number on the right-hand side of Eq. (12) is simply the average of the numbers $P_1, P_2, \ldots, P_n$. We may then conclude from this deterministic model that the age-grade system of the Gallas will be stable if, over a large number of generations, the average age at which a man becomes a father is 40.

This deterministic model has the advantage that the predicted condition for stability—average age of 40 for parenthood—can be readily checked by examining accurate census data for the tribe.

This model has a number of important limitations, however. It deals only with one-dimensional father-son links and ignores the branching of descent lines representing siblings. In other words, the model assumes that a man has only one son when, in fact, many men have several sons. Of course, some men have no sons, and this shows another weakness of the model. The model transforms every given family into points of future time when it may, in fact, no longer exist.

Other aspects of this model and possible refinements and improvements of it will be presented in the exercises. In the next section, we will examine Hoffmann's probabilistic model for the question of cultural stability of the age-grade system.

## IV. A PROBABILISTIC MODEL

The stability of the Galla age-grade system is threatened by the possibilities of disparities between chronological ages and assigned cultural roles. To promote stability, it is desirable that the lower grades consist largely of adolescents. What is crucial is not the absolute number of members of different ages in a particular grade, but the relative numbers. If most candidates for initiation into the lower grades are youthful, then there will be little tension in the system and we may expect it to continue to function largely unchanged for a number of generations. We can predict the level of tension that is likely to arise in the future if we know the ages of the males at the time they enter the age-grade system.

For computational simplicity, we will consider three age categories, or states, for the age at the time of initiation into the lowest grade:

$$S_1: \text{ages } 13-19,$$
$$S_2: \text{ages } 20-29,$$
$$S_3: \text{ages } 30 \text{ or over.}$$

The vector $(x_1, x_2, x_3)$ will represent the proportion of males in each state. For example, if there are 100 men about to be initiated into the age-grade system with 25 in $S_1$, 55 in $S_2$, and 20 in $S_3$, we will represent this by the vector

$$(25/100, \quad 55/100, \quad 20/100) = (.25, \quad .55, \quad .20). \tag{13}$$

If the Galla system is to survive, the set of males about to enter the grade system should consist largely of younger men. The state $S_1$ should contain a relatively large proportion of the set while $S_3$ should include a relatively smaller fraction. As new generations enter the system, there should not be a significant drift from $S_1$ to $S_3$.

To determine the shifts from one state $S_i$ to another $S_j$ in successive generations, we determine for each male about to enter the system, the age of his father when the father entered the system.

Using Hoffmann's example, suppose that we examine a set of 240 males and record for each his state and his father's state at the time of initiation. The data are conveniently displayed in a matrix in which the rows correspond to the father's state and the columns to the son's state:

$$
\begin{array}{c}
\text{Son's state at time of initiation} \\
\begin{array}{ccc}
S_1 & S_2 & S_3
\end{array}
\end{array}
$$

$$
\begin{array}{ll}
\text{Father's} & S_1 \\
\text{state at time} & S_2 \\
\text{of initiation} & S_3
\end{array}
\begin{pmatrix}
10 & 25 & 30 \\
55 & 60 & 35 \\
5 & 15 & 5
\end{pmatrix}
$$

We see from this matrix that the largest group (60) were in their 20's when they were initiated and so were their fathers. There were only 5 males who were initiated after the age of 30, but whose sons were initiated in their teens.

As noted above, our concern is not so much with absolute numbers, but with proportions. If we examine the 65 fathers who were initiated into the age-grade system as teenagers, we see that $\frac{10}{65}$ of them had sons who were initiated as teenagers, $\frac{25}{65}$ had sons initiated in their twenties, and $\frac{30}{65}$ had sons initiated after the age of 30. We compute similar fractions for the fathers in states $S_2$ and $S_3$ and obtain the matrix

$$
\begin{array}{ccc}
S_1 & S_2 & S_3
\end{array}
\qquad\qquad
\begin{array}{ccc}
S_1 & S_2 & S_3
\end{array}
$$

$$
\begin{array}{l}
S_1 \\
S_2 \\
S_3
\end{array}
\begin{pmatrix}
10/65 & 25/65 & 30/65 \\
55/150 & 60/150 & 35/150 \\
5/25 & 15/25 & 5/25
\end{pmatrix}
=
\begin{array}{l}
S_1 \\
S_2 \\
S_3
\end{array}
\begin{pmatrix}
2/13 & 5/13 & 6/13 \\
11/30 & 12/30 & 7/30 \\
1/5 & 3/5 & 1/5
\end{pmatrix}
$$

or, in decimal notation,

$$
\begin{array}{ccc}
& S_1 & S_2 & S_3
\end{array}
$$

$$
P =
\begin{array}{l}
S_1 \\
S_2 \\
S_3
\end{array}
\begin{pmatrix}
.154 & .384 & .462 \\
.367 & .4 & .233 \\
.2 & .6 & .2
\end{pmatrix}
$$

Now it is possible to regard the entries in the matrix as probabilities. Thus the probability that a father in state $S_2$ has a son in state $S_3$ is given as .233. Hoffmann considers this matrix as a transition matrix from one generation to the next and notices that if we assume that this matrix remains constant, then we can study the Galla age-grade system using the tools of Markov chain analysis.

For example, if our initial distribution of states is given by the vector

$$
\mathbf{p}^{(0)} = (.25, .55, .20),
$$

then the distribution of states after one generation is

$$
\mathbf{p}^{(1)}P = (.28, .44, .28).
$$

After a single generation, there will be a slightly higher proportion of sons in $S_3$ than there were sons a generation ago. If this trend continues, the stability of the age-grade system is threatened.

Let's see what happens to the distribution after two generations. It will be given by the vector $\mathbf{p}^{(2)}$ where

$$\mathbf{p}^{(2)} = \mathbf{p}^{(1)}P = (\mathbf{p}^{(0)}P)P = \mathbf{p}^{(0)}P^2 = (.27, .46, .27).$$

It is easy to see that the drift from $S_1$ to $S_3$ evidenced after one generation has not continued.

In a similar fashion, we can compute the distribution of states after 3 generations, 4 generations, and so on. It is more interesting at this point, however, to determine the long range behavior of the distribution vector. All of the entries of the transition matrix $P$ are positive, so we are dealing with a regular Markov process. The long-term distribution of states is then given by the unique fixed-point stochastic vector $\mathbf{w}$ of $P$. This is the vector $\mathbf{w} = (w_1, w_2, w_3)$ with the properties that $\mathbf{w} = \mathbf{w}P$ and $w_1 + w_2 + w_3 = 1$. Using the methods of Chapter 10 and Appendix II, we find that the components of $\mathbf{w}$ are

$$w_1 = \frac{663}{2518} = .263,$$

$$w_2 = \frac{1140}{2518} = .453,$$

$$w_3 = \frac{715}{2518} = .284.$$

If our process is a Markov chain, then the proportion of males in the three states will tend toward $S_1 = .263$, $S_2 = .453$, $S_3 = .284$. Hoffmann notes that these values are not radically different from the initial vector $(.25, .55, .20)$ so that the system may be considered stable.

## V. CRITICISMS OF THE MODELS

In what sense is Hoffmann correct in claiming that the mathematical model predicts that the Galla age-grade system is stable? In the first place, the long-term behavior of the distribution is close to the distribution of the initial vector. If the society was able to tolerate the distribution of states when the system began, it will be able to tolerate distributions just as well in later generations. Even if the initial distribution vector was quite different from $\mathbf{w}$, there is still reason to conclude the system is stable. The age-grade system is most threatened if the proportion of older men in the lower grades continues to increase. The calculation of the limiting vector $\mathbf{w}$ shows that this proportion will remain, in the long run, under 30 percent. Whether or not the society can tolerate that high a proportion in the lowest age group is a question that can be decided only by more careful observation of the Gallas.

The discussion of the particular numbers obtained in Hoffmann's example is not central to a criticism of his approach. It should be pointed out that the data he used were not obtained by an actual observation or census of the Gallas, but were chosen arbitrarily. Hoffmann wished to demonstrate how Markov chains could be used to study a problem of cultural stability. The entries of the transition matrix were chosen to represent a not unreasonable situation for which no bias toward or away from stability was immediately apparent.

The critical assumption in Hoffmann's model is that the process is a Markov one; that is, that the transition matrix remains constant from generation to generation over many years. How reasonable is this assumption? Are the transition probabilities going to be the same for a generation of fathers that suffered through a drought or were decimated by illness or war as they are for a generation that has known plentiful harvest, good health, and peace? If one generation produces a set of males most of whom enter the lowest grade at an advanced age, will the next generation try to adjust its birth rates to compensate for this condition?

Hoffmann's response to these criticisms is that there is value in the Markov chain approach even if there is no reason to believe that the transition matrix is constant [1971]: "If we are unwilling to postulate the invariance of the transition matrix, it is still possible to use the model as a decision procedure. The limiting vector of an observed transition matrix is readily calculated. Then one can state: 'This pattern of transitions is/is not compatible with the stability of the . . . system.'"

If we are willing, on the other hand, to postulate that the transition matrix remains constant, we can ask some important questions about Hoffmann's Markov chain model. In our early discussions about the age-grade system, we noted that it is quite conceivable that many males will enter the lowest grade before adolescence. This group is omitted entirely from Hoffmann's model. For completeness, he could have included a state $S_0$ corresponding to those who were initiated before the age of 13. If this state is included, then the transition matrix becomes a $4 \times 4$ array. If it is a regular matrix, then the theory of Chapter 10 still holds and a limiting vector $\mathbf{w}$ can be computed, although the calculations are more tedious.

In the exercises and suggested projects, you will be asked to explore further some possible modifications of this probabilistic model.

## VI. HANS HOFFMANN

Hans Hoffmann's work in anthropology has ranged from field studies of Eskimo hunters and the cultures of the Amazon River basin to new theoretical developments in mathematical anthropology. He has also conducted ethnographic research among a mental hospital population receiving new psychiatric drugs, and he has served as a consultant on a project attempting a mathematical analysis of children's games.

Hoffmann was born in Koblenz, Germany in 1929, but received his professional education in the United States. He did his undergraduate work at Cornell University where he was a mathematics major who devoted substantial

Hans Hoffmann and two of his children.

time also to the fields of physics, astronomy, anthropology, and Chinese literature. He received his doctorate in anthropology from Yale University in 1957 for a thesis on cultural homogeneity among the Attawapsikat Cree. The field data for this study, which was supervised by an anthropologist and a psychologist, were gathered by Hoffmann and his wife Betty in James Bay, Canada.

Interest in the hunters of the northern forest led Hoffmann to the field work among the Eskimos and Crees in the mid-1950's. Among the unpublished material Hoffmann collected are reminiscences and ethnographic comments by his Cree informant gathered while Hoffmann observed his life in camp and accompanied him on hunting expeditions.

The Amazon River basin has also held a long-term fascination for Hoffmann. "So far," he writes, "this has led to three field trips to the Shipibo of the Ucayali river in Eastern Peru. I am particularly interested in contemporary changes in technology and their effects on the continuity of Amazonian cultures. This research is illuminated by an independent interest in lowland archeology. Several of my studies in mathematical anthropology are based on my Amazonian data. Conversely, mathematical culture theory has supplied an analytical framework for making field observations."

Much of Hoffmann's recent work has been devoted to mathematical models in theoretical anthropology. He has published papers on deterministic, stochastic, and game theory models of cultural systems, material culture in a four dimensional world, linear programming approaches to "cultural intensity," and an extensive survey of mathematical systems and their possible application to anthropological problems.

In a chapter for the *Biennial Review of Anthropology*, Hoffmann [1969] describes the role of mathematical models:

> Although human imagination is unbounded, our unaided ability to experience it is limited. Experiencing requires tools, and as these become developed, wider realms of imagination can be made one's own. We can imagine differences in the length of objects, but need a tool—the natural numbers—to experience them. We can imagine an infinity of numbers beyond the integers and their inverses, but need a tool—Cantor's diagonal proof—to experience their existence. For this reason, tools are the essence of culture; whether physical or mental, they permit man to experience wider ranges of his universe ... Mathematics is a tool that enables man to understand and control an immense number of events and processes in the physical world. Mathematics, in particular, is a tool that penetrates realms of imagination hopelessly beyond the experience of a toolless mind. Moreover, once mathematical tools have been developed, they often reverse their effect and enlarge not only one's experience but also one's imagination.

Hoffmann has taught at the University of Oklahoma, University of Arkansas, Cornell, and the State University of New York at Binghamton, where he is now Professor of Anthropology. "From a long-range point of view," he says, "I do expect to return to empirical investigations when the mathematical issues that have intrigued me have been at least looked into. While mathematics is an exhilarating world to explore, it cannot really compete with the Amazon. Most likely I will combine a long standing interest in the construction and sailing of small boats with that in the life of Indian traders on the Amazon tributaries. ... I look forward to returning to the Amazon when the ages of my children make extensive field work feasible once more."

---

## EXERCISES

---

### II. THE GALLA SYSTEM

1. Meyer entered the age-grade system at the age of 15 and his son Frank was born when Meyer was 35 years old. Frank became the father of Michael at age 39. Michael's sons Eli and Alexander were born when he was aged 25 and 31, respectively. How old will Eli and Alexander be when they retire from the system?

2. Is it possible for a man to be born directly into the highest grade? Is it possible for him to be born after his "retirement" from the age-grade system?

### III. A DETERMINISTIC MODEL

3. Prove Eq. (6) by mathematical induction.

4. What is the relation of $A_{n+1}$ and $A_1$ if the average age of parenthood of the intervening $n$ generations is less than 40 years? greater than 40 years?

5. How do the results of the deterministic model change if the length of time of an individual in the age-grade system is $k$ years, instead of 40 years?

6. What would you estimate the life expectancy of an Ethiopian tribesman to have been in the eighteenth and nineteenth centuries? Is it likely that the average of parenthood could have been 40?

7. Note that the rules of the age-grades do not allow a man to marry until he has been in the system for at least 16 years. What effect does this have on the average age of parenthood?

8. How would you modify the deterministic model to allow for the fact that some men have no sons, while others have more than one?

9. If the society is undergoing exponential or logistic population growth, will this affect the stability of the age-grade system?

10. Prins argued that "the functioning of the system of age-grades of the Galla ... requires birth regulation as one of its basic institutional elements."

a) Show that the results of Hoffmann's deterministic model indicate that this is *not* a necessary condition for stability.

b) Prins claimed that restricting procreation to a man's last 12 years in the system would be the ideal way to achieve stability. In what sense, if any, is this true?

## IV. A PROBABILISTIC MODEL

11. Using Hoffmann's transition matrix $P$, calculate $\mathbf{p}^{(1)}, \mathbf{p}^{(2)}$, and $\mathbf{p}^{(3)}$ if

a) $\mathbf{p}^{(0)} = (1, 0, 0)$

b) $\mathbf{p}^{(0)} = (\frac{1}{3}, \frac{1}{3}, \frac{1}{3})$

c) $\mathbf{p}^{(0)} = (0, \frac{3}{4}, \frac{1}{4})$

d) $\mathbf{p}^{(0)} = (p, q, 1 - p - q)$

12. Repeat Exercise 11 with the transition matrix

$$
M = \begin{array}{c} \\ S_1 \\ S_2 \\ S_3 \end{array}
\begin{array}{ccc}
S_1 & S_2 & S_3 \\
\left(\begin{array}{ccc}
.6 & .3 & .1 \\
.1 & .8 & .1 \\
.1 & .2 & .7
\end{array}\right)
\end{array}
$$

13. Repeat Exercise 11 if every entry in the transition matrix is $\frac{1}{3}$.

14. Find the unique fixed point stochastic vector for

a) the matrix $M$ of Exercise 12,

b) the matrix of Exercise 13.

Are these stable systems?

15. Add a fourth state $S_0$ for those who entered the system before age 13, assume that $\mathbf{p}^{(0)} = (.1, .2, .3, .4)$ and that the transition matrix is

$$
\begin{array}{c} \\ S_1 \\ S_2 \\ S_3 \\ S_4 \end{array}
\begin{array}{cccc}
S_1 & S_2 & S_3 & S_4 \\
\left(\begin{array}{cccc}
.5 & .3 & .15 & .05 \\
.2 & .6 & .15 & .05 \\
0 & .2 & .7 & .1 \\
0 & .05 & .15 & .8
\end{array}\right)
\end{array}
$$

a) Compute $\mathbf{p}^{(1)}$ and $\mathbf{p}^{(2)}$

b) Is the transition matrix regular? If so, find its unique fixed-point stochastic vector. Does it give rise to a stable system?

16. Is it conceivable that the transition matrix might not be regular? What are the consequences of this for the model?

## SUGGESTED PROJECTS

1. What are the effects on the stability of the age-grade system if one or more of the following modifications are made?

a) A son enters the system at his father's death if his father dies before retirement;

b) The eldest son enters exactly 40 years after his father does, but younger sons must wait until they are the same age as their older brother was when he was initiated;

c) A son enters 40 years after his father does or at the age of 10, whichever event takes place later; thus, no one enters before the age of 10.

Can the deterministic and probabilistic models of this chapter be changed to incorporate these variations? Are new models necessary?

2. Discuss the practical problems of determining the entries of the transition matrix from observations and census data. Can you determine, in the absence of such information, bounds for the sizes of the entries of the transition matrix? Are all transition matrices whose entries satisfy these bounds necessarily regular?

3. Prins discusses age-grade systems among the Kipsigis and Kikuyus of Kenya as well as the Gallas of Ethiopia. Develop mathematical models for these age-grade systems. Do these systems have problems of stability?

## REFERENCES

Hoffmann, Hans, "Formal versus informal estimates of cultural stability," *American Anthropologist* **67** (1965), 110–115. Used with permission.

Hoffmann, Hans, "Markov chains in Ethiopia," in Paul Kay, ed., *Explorations in Mathematical Anthropology* (Cambridge: MIT Press, 1971), pp. 181–190. Used with permission.

Hoffmann, Hans, "Mathematical Anthropology," in Bernard J. Siegel, ed., *Biennial Review of Anthropology* (Stanford, Calif.: Stanford University Press, 1969).

Legesse, Asmarom, *Gada: Three Approaches to the Study of African Society* (New York: Free Press, 1973).

Murdock, George Peter, *Africa: Its Peoples and Their Cultural History* (New York: McGraw-Hill, 1959), pp. 323–327.

Prins, Adriaan Hendrik Johan, *East African Age-Class Systems* (Groningen, Djakarta: Wolters, 1953).

# 12 Paired-Associate Learning

The mind is slow to unlearn what it has been long in learning.

Seneca

## I. THE LEARNING PROBLEM

The study of learning has been a basic concern of psychology for more than a century and there is a vast literature of books and articles developing different theories or presenting the results of learning experiments involving human and animal subjects. In this chapter, I will discuss briefly a very simple model of a particular kind of learning situation. The model was developed by Gordon Bower (and independently by R. R. Bush and F. A. Mosteller) around 1960 in the early days of mathematical learning theory. Mathematical model building for learning processes has had a rich and varied history during the past twenty years and the current "state of the art" has advanced quite far beyond the material we will study. Bower's work is worth examining for us because it shows how a number of predictions can be deduced from a simple model and because it illustrates an actual use of the absorbing Markov chains studied in Chapter 10.

The learning problem Bower examined is exemplified by a task familar to most students. Suppose you are studying for a vocabulary test in your Swahili course. You must be able to translate into Swahili a prescribed list of 25 English words. This learning situation demands that

1.  You must learn the Swahili words. This includes proper pronounciation and spelling.

2.  You must learn to match the correct Swahili word to the appropriate English word.

Bower's model of "paired-associate" (PAL) learning is concerned with the second task, the associative "hook-up" of the relevant responses to their appropriate stimulus members.

To describe the learning situation more carefully, suppose that the experimenter determines a set of ordered pairs $(s, r)$ where $s$ is chosen from a finite set $S$, called the *stimulus set*, and $r$ is selected from a finite collection $R$, labeled the *response set*. An element $s$ is shown to a subject and she tries to give the corresponding $r$. The subject, in other words, is trying to find the appropriate value $f(x)$ of a function when she is told the domain value $x$.

In the example of the foreign language word list, the set $S$ consists of 25 English words and the set $R$ of 25 Swahili words. The function $f$ for this example is one-to-one, but it need not have this property in general.

When the subject is first presented with a stimulus, she can only guess what the appropriate response is supposed to be. After she guesses, the experimenter tells her what the correct response should have been. This is the first point in the experiment at which learning may occur.

If there are $K$ elements in the set $S$, then a *trial* is defined as one cycle of presentation of each of the $K$ items, the order of appearance of the items being randomized over successive trials. After the first trial, the subject may either guess again or give the correct response because she has learned it from the result of a previous trial.

Each subject in the experiment responds to each element of $S$ on the first trial. The order of presentation of the stimulus elements is scrambled, and the subject is asked again. This procedure is repeated until the subject responds correctly to all elements of $S$ on two consecutive trials. It is then assumed that the subject has completed the learning task. In theory, the experiment for a single subject could last infinitely many trials, but in practice, the learning task is chosen so that it is completed by all subjects by the twentieth trial.

Data is collected from the experiment by recording each correct response by an 0 and each incorrect response by a 1. If we fix our attention on a single element of $S$, then the subject generates a sequence

$$x_1, x_2, \ldots, x_n, \ldots$$

of 0's and 1's. To repeat, the number $x_i$ is 0 if the subject made the correct response to the particular stimulus $s$ when presented with it on the $i$th trial, and it is a 1 if there was an incorrect response on the $i$th trial.

"Stripped to its barest essentials," Bower [1961] explains, "the job for a theory of PAL is to describe and account for the general characteristics of these sequences. The best job of description, of course, would be to reproduce the original sequences. Theories, as economic abstractions, do not perform this task but they can provide general descriptions (e.g., the trial number of the second success) about a sample of sequences allegedly generated under the same process laws. Obviously, models that deliver predictions about many different aspects of such sequences are preferable to less tractable models, since each prediction provides an opportunity to test the adequacy of the model. In turn, the number of predictions derivable in closed form from a model reflects to a large extent the simplicity of the assumptions used to represent the process under consideration. The assumptions of the model to be presented appear to achieve almost maximal simplicity for a model about learning; accordingly, it is possible to derive in closed form an extensive number of predictions (theorems) referring to properties of the response sequences obtained from the learning subject."

## II. THE MODEL

### A. Axioms of the Model

Bower's model assumes at the start that each stimulus item in the list of paired associates may be represented by exactly one element from a set $S$ and that the correct response to that stimulus item becomes associated in an all-or-none fashion. He also assumes that the subject knows the elements of the response set before the experiment begins; thus, the model can concentrate on the second associative aspect of the learning problem as discussed in Section I.

The process of associating elements in $S$ with elements in $R$ is governed, according to the model, by five basic axioms:

**AXIOM 1    On each presentation of an item from the set $S$, only two states, $C$ and $U$, are possible for the subject with respect to this item.  If the subject is in state $C$ for that item, then she knows the correct response and will give it.  If the subject is in state $U$ for that item, then she does not know the proper response and she guesses an element from the permitted set of responses.**

If the subject knows the proper response, we say she is in the *conditioned state $C$*; otherwise, she is in the *unconditioned state $U$*.

**AXIOM 2    At the beginning of the experiment, the subject is in state $U$ for each item in $S$.**

**AXIOM 3    The state $C$ is an absorbing state; if an item has become conditioned, then continued study of the same correct response will insure that the item remains conditioned.**

**AXIOM 4    If the subject is in state $U$ immediately preceding any trial, then the transition probability of moving from $U$ to $C$ on the next trial is a positive constant $c$, which is the same for each trial, each item, and each subject.**

**AXIOM 5    If the subject is in state $U$, then the probability that she guesses the correct response is $1/N$ where $N$ is the number of elements in the set $R$.**

These axioms contain a number of simplifying assumptions about how humans learn, some of which may seem startlingly naive to you.  Does it indeed seem reasonable to assume that there is a transition probability $c$ that does not vary from person to person?  Even for a single subject, is it not likely that the chances of becoming conditioned to an item would depend on the nature of the item?

The assumption (Axiom 5) that a subject in state $U$ chooses from the response set with equiprobability also seems suspect.  While she may not have learned, for example, to associate the Swahili word *twiga* with the English word *giraffe*, the subject may know that the correct response is one of three or four Swahili words from the total list of 25.  In other words, she may be guessing at random not from the set $R$, but from some smaller subset $R'$.  Also, if she has become conditioned to associate, say, the Swahili *simba* with the English *lion*, then she will not respond with *simba* when asked to translate *giraffe*.  Thus, as more items become conditioned, the probability of a correct guess should increase.

Several responses to these criticisms of the axioms are possible. We shall see how Bower designed a specific learning situation in which some of these objections cannot arise. More importantly, however, every mathematical model contains simplifying assumptions. Whether these simplifications are reasonable ones to make can only be judged after the predictions of the model are compared with observations of the real-world system that is being modeled. In Section III, we will make these comparisons. Let's examine now what can be deduced from the set of axioms.

The words "state" and "transition probabilities" are used in the statements of the axioms deliberately. They indicate that we mean to use Markov chains to study the paired-associate learning situation. Axioms 1, 3, and 4 assert that the learning process is an absorbing Markov chain. From these axioms, we can construct the transition matrix which describes the movement from state to state in successive trials for a given item.

The transition matrix has the form

$$P = \begin{matrix} & C & U \\ C & \\ U & \end{matrix} \begin{pmatrix} 1 & 0 \\ c & 1-c \end{pmatrix}$$

where the rows give the state prior to the start of one trial and the columns give the state prior to the start of the next trial.

From Axiom 2, the initial probability vector is

$$\mathbf{p}^{(0)} = (0, 1),$$

because the subject does not know at the outset how the items have been associated.

The model has a single parameter, $c$, which is the likelihood that an unconditioned item will become conditioned as the result of a reinforced trial (evoking the correct response). The effect of successive reinforced trials is to provide repeated opportunities for the item to become conditioned.

From a subject's response to the stimulus on a particular trial, we cannot always assert which state is being occupied. A correct response is certain if the subject is in state $C$ but it is also possible that the subject was in state $U$ and made a lucky guess. If, however, the subject makes an incorrect response on the trial, then the subject must have been in the unconditioned case. This fact makes it possible to prove a number of theorems about the model.

## B. Predictions of the Model

Bower derives a large number of predictions about the learning process from his Markov chain model. We will list some of them here and give proofs of a few.

It is possible to deduce from the model:

(A)  The average number of trials before learning the item;

(B)  The probability, $q_n$, of an error on the $n$th trial. In fact, this is really an infinite number of predictions: $q_1, q_2, \ldots$ ;

(C)  The average number, $u_1$, of errors before learning an item;

(D)  The probability of a run of $k$ consecutive errors ($k = 1, 2, 3, \ldots$) that start on the $n$th trial ($n = 1, 2, 3, \ldots$);

(E)  The expected value of $r_k$ where $r_k$ represents the number of error runs of length $k$;

(F)  The expected value of $R$ where $R = r_1 + r_2 + \cdots$, the total number of error runs;

(G)  The probability distribution of $T$, the total number of errors on each item; that is, we deduce $\Pr(T = k)$ for $k = 0, 1, 2, \ldots$ (note that $E(T) = u_1$);

(H)  The expected value of $c_{k,n}$, where $c_{k,n}$ is the number of times that an error on trial $n$ is followed by an error $k$ trials later;

(I)  The expected values $c_k$ of the "autocorrelations" of $x_n$ and $x_{n+k}$ over all trials $n$ of the experiment; that is,

$$c_k = \mathrm{EV}\left[\sum_{n=1}^{\infty} x_n x_{n+k}\right] = \sum_{n=1}^{\infty} \mathrm{EV}\,(c_{k,n}).$$

For instance, $c_2$ is the average number of times errors occur two trials apart;

(J)  The average number of alternations of successes and failures;

(K)  The average number of errors before the $k$th success, $k = 1, 2, \ldots$ ;

(L)  The proportion of items for which there are no errors following the $k$th success for $k = 0, 1, 2, \ldots$ ;

(M)  The probability distribution for the number of errors between the $k$th and the $(k + m)$th success, for all positive integers $k$ and $m$; and

(N)  The probability distribution of the number of successes between adjacent errors.

## C.  Deriving the Predictions

In this section, we will show how some of the predictions (A)–(N) may be deduced from the model.

We begin by writing the transition matrix $P$ in the standard form (Chapter 10, IV):

|                  | Absorbing states | Transient states |
|------------------|:----------------:|:----------------:|
| Absorbing states | $I$              | $0$              |
| Transient states | $R$              | $Q$              |

In this case, we obtain

$$P = \begin{array}{cc} & \begin{array}{cc} C & \qquad\quad U \end{array} \\ \begin{array}{c} C \\ U \end{array} & \left( \begin{array}{c|c} 1 & 0 \\ c & 1-c \end{array} \right) \end{array}$$

so that $Q$ is the $1 \times 1$ matrix $(1 - c)$. Thus $I - Q = 1 - (1 - c) = c$. Hence the fundamental matrix is

$$N = (I - Q)^{-1} = \frac{1}{c}.$$

The following conclusions are immediate:

1. Since every such Markov process eventually reaches an absorbing state, every subject will eventually learn every item;

2. The average number of trials per item that a subject is in the unconditioned state is $1/c$.

In this way, we have derived prediction (A):

■ **THEOREM 1**   The average number of trials before learning the item will be $1/c$.

Our next task will be to show that the probability $q_n$ of an error on the $n$th trial of an item is given by

$$q_n = (1 - c)^{n-1} \left( 1 - \frac{1}{N} \right).$$

This result is true essentially for two reasons. First, the subject must fail to be conditioned on each of the first $n - 1$ trials. On each trial, this happens with probability $1 - c$. Second, the subject must guess incorrectly on the $n$th trial; according to Axiom 5, this happens with probability $(1 - (1/N))$.

In order to give a more rigorous proof, we need to introduce a little extra notation.

We define $C_n$ to be the event that the subject is in state $C$ immediately prior to the response on the $n$th trial and $U_n$ the event that she is in state $U$ at that time. These are mutually exclusive events, so we have

$$\Pr(C_n) + \Pr(U_n) = 1.$$

Axiom 3 gives us the result that $\Pr(C_1) = 0$ and $\Pr(U_1) = 1$. The axioms of the model also give us

$$\Pr(x_n = 1 | C_n) = 0 \qquad \text{and} \qquad \Pr(x_n = 1 | U_n) = 1 - \frac{1}{N}. \tag{1}$$

In the notation of Markov Chains, we have

$$\mathbf{p}^{(0)} = (\Pr(C_1), \Pr(U_1)),$$
$$\mathbf{p}^{(1)} = (\Pr(C_2), \Pr(U_2)) = \mathbf{p}^{(0)}P$$

. . .

$$\mathbf{p}^{(n-1)} = (\Pr(C_n), \Pr(U_n)) = \mathbf{p}^{(0)}P^{n-1}$$
$$\mathbf{p}^{(n)} = (\Pr(C_{n+1}), \Pr(U_{n+1})) = \mathbf{p}^{(0)}P^n$$

. . .

Ordinary matrix multiplication and simplification shows that

$$P^2 = \begin{pmatrix} 1 & 0 \\ c & 1-c \end{pmatrix} \begin{pmatrix} 1 & 0 \\ c & 1-c \end{pmatrix} = \begin{pmatrix} 1 & 0 \\ c + c(1-c) & (1-c)^2 \end{pmatrix}$$
$$= \begin{pmatrix} 1 & 0 \\ 1 - (1-c)^2 & (1-c)^2 \end{pmatrix}$$

A simple induction argument then leads to the conclusion that

$$P^k = \begin{pmatrix} 1 & 0 \\ 1 - (1-c)^k & (1-c)^k \end{pmatrix} \qquad k = 1, 2, 3, \ldots. \tag{2}$$

With $k$ set equal to $n-1$, we obtain

$$(\Pr(C_n), \Pr(U_n)) = \mathbf{p}^{(0)}P^{n-1} = (0, 1)P^{n-1} = (1 - (1-c)^{n-1}, (1-c)^{n-1}) \tag{3}$$

so that

$$\Pr(C_n) = 1 - (1-c)^{n-1} \qquad \text{and} \qquad \Pr(U_n) = (1-c)^{n-1}. \tag{4}$$

We have enough machinery now to establish prediction (B).

■ *THEOREM 2*    The probability of an error on the $n$th trial is given by

$$(1-c)^{n-1}\left(1 - \frac{1}{N}\right).$$

*Proof of Theorem 2*    The probability of an error on the $n$th trial can be represented as $\Pr(x_n = 1)$. Since the subject was in one of the mutually exclusive states $C$ or $U$ before the $n$th trial began, we have

$$\Pr(x_n = 1) = \Pr(X_n = 1 \cap U_n) + \Pr(x_n = 1 \cap C_n)$$
$$= \Pr(x_n = 1 \mid U_n) \Pr(U_n) + \Pr(x_n = 1 \mid U_n) \Pr(C_n)$$

where the second equality comes from elementary results about conditional probabilities (Chapter 9, II).

Now we make use of Eqs. (1) and (4) to write

$$\Pr(x_n = 1) = \left(1 - \frac{1}{N}\right)(1 - c)^{n-1} + 0(1 - (1 - c)^{n-1})$$

$$= \left(1 - \frac{1}{N}\right)(1 - c)^{n-1},$$

the desired result.  $\square$

Our next deduction from the axioms gives a result which is useful in determining the value of the parameter $c$ in experimental situations.

■ *THEOREM 3*    The expected total number of errors, $u_1$, before learning an item is

$$\frac{\left(1 - \frac{1}{N}\right)}{c}.$$

To obtain this result, we first introduce a new random variable. Let $T_M$ denote the total number of errors made by a subject on a particular item in the first $M$ trials. Since $x_n = 1$ if the subject makes an error on the $n$th trial and is 0 otherwise, we have

$$T_M = x_1 + x_2 + \cdots + x_M;$$

in other words, $T_M$ is itself the sum of $M$ random variables. We want to compute the expected value of $T_M$. It is clear that the expected value of $T_M$ will be related to the expected values of the $x_i$'s. It turns out that this relationship is a particularly simple one.

*LEMMA*    Let $R_1$ and $R_2$ be two random variables defined on the same finite set $E$ which has probability measure Pr. Then $EV(R_1 + R_2) = EV(R_1) + EV(R_2)$.

**Proof of Lemma**    $EV(R_1 + R_2) = \sum_{x \text{ in } E} (R_1 + R_2)(x) \Pr(x)$

$$= \sum_{x \text{ in } E} (R_1(x) + R_2(x)) \Pr(x)$$

$$= \sum_{x \text{ in } E} [R_1(x) \Pr(x) + R_2(x) \Pr(x)]$$

$$= \sum_{x \text{ in } E} R_1(x) \Pr(x) + \sum_{x \text{ in } E} R_2(x) \Pr(x)$$

$$= EV(R_1) + EV(R_2).$$

An easy induction argument establishes the corollary:

**Corollary**    The expected value of a finite sum of random variables is the sum of their expected values.

We can use the corollary to begin to compute the expected value of $T_M$:

$$EV(T_M) = EV(x_1 + x_2 + \cdots + x_M)$$
$$= EV(x_1) + EV(x_2) + \cdots + EV(x_M).$$

The computation of the expected value of an $x_i$ is easy:

$$EV(x_i) = 1\,Pr(x_i = 1) + 0\,Pr(x_i = 0)$$
$$= Pr(x_i = 1)$$
$$= \left(1 - \frac{1}{N}\right)(1 - c)^{i-1}, \text{ by Theorem 2.}$$

Putting these results together, we have

$$EV(T_M) = \left(1 - \frac{1}{N}\right)(1 - c)^0 + \left(1 - \frac{1}{N}\right)(1 - c)^1 + \cdots + \left(1 - \frac{1}{N}\right)(1 - c)^{M-1}$$
$$= \left(1 - \frac{1}{N}\right)[(1 - c)^0 + (1 - c)^1 + (1 - c)^2 x + \cdots + (1 - c)^{M-1}].$$

Now the expression in square brackets is the sum of the first $M$ terms of a geometric progression with first term 1 and common ratio $(1 - c)$.

Thus

$$EV(T_M) = \left(1 - \frac{1}{N}\right)\left[\frac{1 - (1 - c)^M}{1 - (1 - c)}\right] = \left(1 - \frac{1}{N}\right)\left[\frac{1 - (1 - c)^M}{c}\right]. \qquad (5)$$

We find the expected number of total errors that will be made before an item is learned by letting $M \to \infty$ in Eq. (5). This establishes the statement of Theorem 3.

Finally, we will derive some results on the extent to which an error on a given trial tends to be followed by an error some number of trials later. Let $c_{k,n}$ denote the product

$$c_{k,n} = x_n \cdot x_{n+k}.$$

This product has value 1 exactly when the subject makes errors on the $n$th trial and on the $(n + k)$th trial; otherwise it is 0. The expected value of $c_{k,n}$ is then given by

$$EV(c_{k,n}) = Pr(x_{n+k} = 1 \cap x_n = 1)$$
$$= Pr(x_{n+k} = 1 \mid x_n = 1)\,Pr(x_n = 1)$$
$$= Pr(x_{n+k} = 1 \mid x_n = 1)\left(1 - \frac{1}{N}\right)(1 - c)^{n-1}.$$

To find the conditional probability in this equation, we note how an error occurs on the $(n + k)$th trial. It must be the case that conditioning fails during each of the $k$ trials after the $n$th one and also that the subject guesses incorrectly on the $(n + k)$th trial. Thus we have

$$\Pr(x_{n+k} = 1 \mid x_n = 1) = (1 - c)^k \left(1 - \frac{1}{N}\right).$$

We find then that

$$EV(c_{k,n}) = \left(1 - \frac{1}{N}\right)(1 - c)^k \left(1 - \frac{1}{N}\right)(1 - c)^{n-1}.$$

The average value of the "autocorrelation" of $x_n$ and $x_{n+k}$ over all trials is

$$c_k = EV\left(\sum_{n=1}^{\infty} x_n x_{n+k}\right) = \sum_{n=1}^{\infty} EV(c_{k,n}) = \sum_{n=1}^{\infty} \left(1 - \frac{1}{N}\right)^2 (1 - c)^k (1 - c)^{n-1},$$

so that

$$c_k = \left(1 - \frac{1}{N}\right)^2 (1 - c)^k \sum_{n=1}^{\infty} (1 - c)^{n-1}.$$

This last sum is an infinite geometric progression with initial term 1 and common ratio $(1 - c)$. The sum equals $1/(1 - (1 - c)) = 1/c$. Hence we have

$$c_k = \frac{\left(1 - \frac{1}{N}\right)^2 (1 - c)^k}{c}.$$

This gives us the predictions (H) and (I) promised in the preceding section. In this derivation, we have used infinite sums rather recklessly. The arguments can be made rigorous by restricting ourselves first to finite sums and then employing a limiting process. The procedure is much the same as in the proof of Theorem 3. The reader is encouraged to supply the details.

By arguments similar to the ones of this section (some easier, others more complex), we can deduce formulas for the other predictions (A)–(N) of the model. You will do this in the Exercises.

Now that we have a good number of predictions of how subjects would behave in a paired-associate learning situation if the axioms are correct, we can turn to the task of comparing them with real-world observations.

## III. TESTING THE MODEL
Bower compared the predictions of his model with the results obtained in an experiment involving 29 subjects. He presented each subject with a list of 10 pairs of consonant letters; these pairs constituted the stimuli. The subject had to learn to associate each pair with either the integer 1 or the integer 2. For each

subject, five of the pairs were selected at random to be associated with 1; the correct response for the other five pairs then was 2. The experiment continued until the subject was able to complete two consecutive cycles of all 10 pairs. The letters were written on cards and the cards were shuffled between trials to randomize the order of presentation of the stimuli.

Since "1" is the correct response to five different stimuli, the subject cannot discard any element in the response set even after becoming conditioned to some of the stimulus items. Also, as there are only two possible responses, the subject has to guess—when guessing is necessary—from the full response set. Note how the design of the experiment deals with some of the objections we raised earlier about the simplicity of the axioms.

Bower observed that the average number of errors per item made by his subjects was 1.45. Since $N = 2$ in this experiment, Theorem 2 gives a predicted average of $1/(2c)$ errors. Equating the predicted value with observed one gives $c = 1/2.9 = .345$. This estimate of $c$ will be fixed throughout the remaining discussion of the data.

A major feature of interest to psychologists in experiments like Bower's is the "learning curve." This is a graph of the percentage of incorrect responses as a function of the number of trials. To obtain the observed learning curve we plot the proportion of wrong responses versus the number of trials and then connect these points with a smooth curve. The theoretical learning curve is derived from the model and is the graph of $q_n$ as a function of $n$.

Figure 12.1 is from Bower's paper [1961] and it shows how closely the predicted learning curve fits the observed one.

Another graphic example of how well the model fits the observed data is provided by the distribution of $T$, the total number of errors per item. Bower's

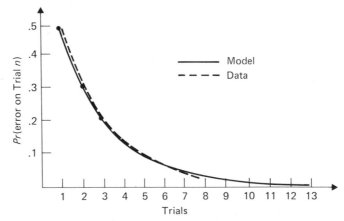

**Fig. 12.1**   The probability of an incorrect response over successive trials of the experiment. Taken from Bower [1961], with permission.

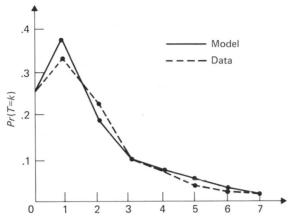

**Fig. 12.2**  Distribution of $T$, the total number of errors per item.

Markov chain model predicts that

$$\Pr(T=k) = \begin{cases} b/N & \text{for } k=0 \\ \dfrac{b(1-b)^k}{1-c} & \text{for } k \geqslant 1 \end{cases}$$

where $b$ is the constant

$$b = \frac{c}{1 - \dfrac{1-c}{N}}$$

For $c = .345$ and $N = 2$, we have $b = .513$, so the model predicts

$$\Pr(T=k) = \begin{cases} .256 & \text{for } k=0, \\ \dfrac{.513(.487)^k}{.655} & \text{for } k \geqslant 1. \end{cases}$$

The graphs of predicted and observed distributions of $T$ are shown in Fig. 12.2.

Bower made a number of other comparisons of the data collected from his actual experiment with the predictions of his model. Some of these are collected in Table 12.1.

Since the observed value of the average number of errors per item was used to calculate $c$, we automatically get perfect agreement for the first statistic. It is rather remarkable that the other 21 pairs of numbers are so close together in value.

One final comparison of Bower's model with experimentally observed data may be of interest. According to the axioms of the model, if the subject makes a

**Table 12.1**  Comparison of model's prediction and observed data

| Statistic | Prediction of model | Observed data |
|---|---|---|
| 1. Average number of errors/item | 1.45 | 1.45 |
| 2. Standard deviation (SD) of (1) | 1.44 | 1.37 |
| 3. Average number of errors before first success | .749 | .785 |
| 4. SD of (3) | .98 | 1.08 |
| 5. Average number of errors between first and second success | .361 | .350 |
| 6. SD of (5) | .76 | .72 |
| 7. Average number of errors before second success | 1.11 | 1.13 |
| 8. SD of (7) | 1.10 | 1.01 |
| 9. Average number of successes between errors | .488 | .540 |
| 10. SD of (9) | .72 | .83 |
| 11. Average trial of last error | 2.18 | 2.33 |
| 12. SD of (11) | 2.40 | 2.47 |
| 13. Total error runs | .973 | .966 |
| 14. Error runs of length 1 | .655 | .645 |
| 15. Error runs of length 2 | .215 | .221 |
| 16. Error runs of length 3 | .070 | .058 |
| 17. Error runs of length 4 | .023 | .024 |
| Autocorrelation of errors: | | |
| 18. one trial apart ($c_1$) | .479 | .486 |
| 19. two trials apart ($c_2$) | .310 | .292 |
| 20. three trials apart ($c_3$) | .201 | .187 |
| 21. Alternations of success and failure | 1.45 | 1.143 |
| 22. Probability of a success following an error | .672 | .666 |

mistake on the $n$th trial, then the item was not conditioned prior to the start of that trial. The subject was in state $U$ when the $n$th trial began just as when the first trial started. The model asserts that the degree of the subject's associative connection with that item and the correct response has not effectively changed since the experiment started. In terms of predicting the subject's future behavior on this item, we get the same results whether or not we neglect the first $n - 1$ trials.

In particular, we may consider the average number of errors that follow an error on trial $n$. According to Bower's model, this number is the constant $u_1(1 - c) = (1 - c)(1 - 1/N)/c$, which is independent of $n$. This prediction is in sharp contrast to the prediction of the "linear model" of learning. The linear model predicts that the number of errors expected following an error on trial $n$ should be a decreasing function of $n$, since associative strength is assumed to increase steadily with the number of preceding reinforced trials.

To test which, if either, prediction was correct. Bower used the data from the 29 subjects of the experiment we have described along with data from 47 other subjects involved in similar learning experiments. The results, shown in Fig. 12.3, show that Bower's model is much closer to the observed data.

In summary, then, a simple model seems to predict quite well the results of learning in a simple paired-associated task. As Bower [1961] concludes, "The fact that the . . . model gives an adequate quantitative account of these paired-associate data satisfies one important requisite of a scientific theory, that of being close to the data. If, in addition, the theory is mathematically tractable in that numerous consequences are easily derived in closed form, then indeed we are in a fortunate position. The main task of this paper has been to show that the . . . model is mathematically tractable . . . This property of the model is due to the extreme simplicity of its assumptions about the association process. One might effectively argue that the present model nearly achieves the absolute minimum in assumptions for a workable theory of learning.

"Once one has demonstrated the predictive validity of a model for a limited class of experimental situations, there remains the task of characterizing more generally those experimental arrangements to which the model may be expected to apply . . . We explicitly restricted the model to the $S$-$R$ association process and have used simplified experimental situations in which response learning was precluded. Within this restricted domain of paired-associate learning, the model has proved extremely useful in investigating the effects on learning of variations in the number of response alternatives and in the reinforcement conditions prevailing during learning . . . Ultimately, one would like to have a set of

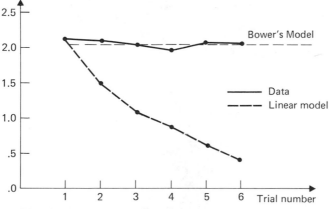

**Fig. 12.3**   Average number of errors following an error on trial $n$.

combination axioms whereby the assumptions about $S$-$R$ association and response learning may be combined for predicting results in those experimental situations involving the concurrent operation of these two processes."

## IV.  GORDON H. BOWER

Gordon Howard Bower is an experimental psychologist on the faculty of Stanford University.  He was born in the small town of Scio, Ohio during the Depression year of 1932.  As a young man, he helped out in his father's general store and worked on several local farms.  A talented baseball and basketball player, Bower received an athletic scholarship to attend Western Reserve University.  He gave up the opportunity for a professional baseball career so that he could pursue his interest in psychology.

After graduating from Western Reserve in 1954, Bower spent a year at the University of Minnesota studying the philosophy of science under a Woodrow Wilson Fellowship.  He left the Midwest to continue his graduate program at Yale University where he was awarded his doctorate in psychology in 1959.

Gordon Bower.

Bower's research and teaching interests have centered on conditioning, learning, human memory, mathematical models, and computer simulation of memory processes. He has written more than 100 technical articles and four books.

The quality and significance of Bower's research has been recognized by many honors, including elections to the prestigious National Academy of Sciences and the American Academy of Arts and Sciences.

## EXERCISES

1. Let $S_M = 1 + r + r^2 + \cdots + r^{M-1}$ where $r$ is a real number and $M$ is a positive integer.

a) Show that $S_M - rS_M = 1 - r^M$ so that $S_M = (1 - r^M)/(1 - r)$, if $r \neq 1$.

b) If $|r| < 1$, show that $S = \lim_{M \to \infty} S_M = 1/(1 - r)$. In this case, we say $S = 1 + r + r^2 + \cdots$.

c) Find the value of $a + ar + ar^2 + \cdots$ where $|r| < 1$ and $a$ is a constant.

d) What happens to these sums in the cases

i) $|r| > 1$?

ii) $r - 1$?

iii) $r = -1$?

2. What are the predictions of Bower's model if

a) $c = 0$?

b) $c = 1$?

Do either of these cases have relevance for human learning?

3. Investigate the consequence of Bower's model if the initial vector is $\mathbf{p}^{(p)} = (\frac{1}{2}, \frac{1}{2})$. How might this initial vector occur in an experimental situation?

4. Prove, by induction on $k$, that the $k$th power of the transition matrix of the Bower model can be written in the form

$$P^k = \begin{pmatrix} 1 & 0 \\ 1 - (1 - c)^k & (1 - c)^k \end{pmatrix}$$

for all $k = 1, 2, 23, \ldots$. [Hint: It is sufficient to check only the entries in the second column; why?]

5. Prove the corollary to the Lemma of Section II.

6. A mathematically rigorous derivation of the formula for $c_k$ can be given. Define

$$c_k^{(m)} = \text{EV} \left( \sum_{n=1}^{m} x_n x_{n+k} \right) \quad \text{and} \quad c_k = \lim_{m \to \infty} c_k^{(m)}.$$

a) Show that $c_k^{(m)} = \left(1 - \frac{1}{N}\right)^2 (1 - c)^k \left[\frac{1 - (1 - c)^m}{1 - c}\right]$.

b) Compute $\lim_{m \to \infty} c_k^{(m)}$.

7. Show that $EV\left(\sum_{n=1}^{\infty} n x_n\right) = u_1/c$.

8. Show that $EV\left(\sum_{n=1}^{\infty} x_n/n\right) = \dfrac{1-(1/N)}{1-c} \log \dfrac{1}{c}$.

9. a) Prove that the formula for $Pr(T = k)$ in Section III is correct.

   b) Show that $EV(T) = u_1$.

   c) Show that $Var(T) = u_1 + (1 - 2c)u_1^2$.

10. Define $u_j$ by $u_j = \sum_{n=1}^{\infty} x_n x_{n+1} \cdots x_{n+j-1}$ for $j = 1,2,\ldots$. Under what conditions is $x_n x_{n+1} \cdots x_{n+j-1}$ nonzero?

11. For the sequence of labeled responses 1111100110001101000 . . . (all the rest zeros) show that

a) $u_1 = 10$,                                b) $u_2 = 6$,

c) $u_3 = 3$,                                 d) $u_4 = 2$,

e) $u_5 = 1$,                                 f) $r_1 = 1$,

g) $r_2 = 2$,                                 h) $r_3 = r_4 = 0$,

i) $r_5 = 1$,                                 j) $R = 4$.

12. Show that the following relations hold true for the example of Exercise 11:

a) $r_j = u_j - 2u_{j+1} + u_{j+2}$

b) $R = u_1 - u_2$.

13. Prove that the relations of Exercise 12 hold true for all sequences of labeled responses.

14. a) Prove that

$$Pr(x_{n+i} = 1 | x_n = 1, x_{n+1} = 1, \ldots, x_{n+i-1} = 1)$$
$$= Pr(x_{n+i} = 1 | x_{n+i-1} = 1).$$

   b) Show that $Pr(x_{n+1} = 1 | x_n = 1) = (1 - c)[1 - (1/N)]$.

15. Let $\alpha = (1 - c)\left(1 - \dfrac{1}{N}\right)$. Show that

a) $EV(u_j) = u_1 \alpha^{j-1}$.

b) $EV(R) = u_1(1 - \alpha)$

c) $EV(r_j) = R(1 - \alpha)\alpha^{j-1}$

16. Let $A_n$ be the random variable $A_n = (1 - x_n)x_{n+1} + x_n(1 - x_{n+1})$.

a) Show that $A_n = 1$, if $x_n = 1$ and $x_{n+1} = 0$.

b) Show that $A_n = 1$, if $x_n = 0$ and $x_{n+1} = 1$.

c) Show that $A_n = 0$, if $x_n = x_{n+1}$.

17. Let $A = \sum_{n=1}^{\infty} A_n$, where $A_n$ is as defined in Exercise 16.

a) Show that $A$ counts the number of alternations of successes and failures.

b) Evaluate the expected value of $A$ and show that $EV(A) = u_1[c + (2(1 - c)/N]$.

c) What is $EV(A)$ if $N = 2$? Does the result make any intuitive sense to you?

18. Show that $g$, the probability that the first success occurs by guessing, is given by

$$g = \frac{1}{N} + \left(1 - \frac{1}{N}\right)(1-c)\frac{1}{N} + \left(1 - \frac{1}{N}\right)^2 (1-c)^2 \frac{1}{N} + \cdots = \frac{1}{N(1-\alpha)}$$

19. Let $J$ be the random variable which is the number of errors before the first success. Show that

$$\Pr(J = i) = \begin{cases} 1/N & \text{for } i = 0, \\ [1 - (1/N)(1-\alpha)\alpha^{i-1}] & \text{for } i \geqslant 1. \end{cases}$$

20. Show that the quantity $b$ in the formula for $\Pr(T = k)$ is the probability that no errors occur following a correct guess.

21. If $p_1$ denotes the probability that no error follows the first correct response, show that $p_1 = 1 - (1-b)/N$.

22. Let $W$ be the random variable which is the number of the trial on which the last error occurs.

a) Show that $\Pr(W = k) = \begin{cases} b/N & \text{for } k = 0, \\ b[1 - (1/N)](1-c)^{k-1} & \text{for } k \geqslant 1. \end{cases}$

b) Show that $EV(W) = bu_1/c$.

23. Some authors define the learning curve to be the graph of the proportion of *correct* responses as a function of the number of trials. Using this definition, sketch the learning curve predicted by the Bower model, using $c = .345$.

24. Does the design of Bower's experiment answer all the objections about the simplicity of the axioms? Which objections do you believe are most significant?

25. Compute $EV(x_n x_{n+k} x_{n+2k})$.

26. Compute $\Pr(x_n = 0 \,|\, x_{n+k} = 1)$.

27. Find the probability that the subject is in state $C$ by trial $n + k$ given that the last error occurred on trial $n$.

## SUGGESTED PROJECTS

1. In the text and exercises, formulas for some—but not all—of the predictions (A)–(N) of the Bower model are given. Discover and prove formulas for the remaining predictions.

2. Formulate and analyze a mathematical model for the following paired-associate learning situation. The experiment will be exactly the same as Bower's except that whenever a subject gives a response, the experimenter tells her only if the response is correct or incorrect. He does not tell her what the correct response is if she gives an incorrect one. Thus there is much less frequent reinforcement of the connection between a stimulus element and its correct response. Which axioms of Bower's model would you retain? Which ones need modification? Compare the predictions of your model with those of Bower's.

3. The "linear model" for PAL is briefly mentioned in Section III. Find out what the assumptions and conclusions of this model are. Which predictions agree with those of the Bower model? In what learning situations would it be a more relevant model? Begin

with the paper of Robert Bush and Saul Sternberg [1959] (see References) or the early chapters of Frank Restle and James G. Greeno [1970].

4. At the beginning of this chapter, we divided the paired-associate learning task into two steps. Bower's model is concerned with the second part of the learning problem. Formulate a model for the learning process corresponding to the first step. Do Markov chains seem an appropriate modeling tool for this problem?

## REFERENCES

Bower, Gordon H., "Application of a model to paired-associate learning," *Psychometrika* **26** (1961), 255–280. Used with permission.

Bush, Robert R., and Frederick A. Mosteller, "A comparison of eight models," in R. R. Bush and W. K. Estes, eds., *Studies in Mathematical Learning Theory* (Stanford: Stanford University Press, 1959), 293–307.

Bush, Robert R., and Saul Sternberg, "A single-operator model," in R. R. Bush and W. K. Estes, eds., *Studies in Mathematical Learning Theory* (Stanford: Stanford University Press, 1959) 204–214.

Krantz, David, ed., *Contemporary Developments in Mathematical Psychology* (San Francisco: Freeman, 1974).

Restle, Frank, and James G. Greeno, *Introduction to Mathematical Psychology* (Reading, Mass: Addison-Wesley, 1970).

# 13
# Epidemics

Swords and lances, arrows, machine guns, and even high explosives have had far less power over the fate of nations than the typhus louse, the plague flea, and the yellow-fever mosquito.

Hans Zinsser

## I. INTRODUCTION

### A. Epidemics and History

The period of Greek history from the end of the Persian Wars to the death of Alexander the Great (roughly 480 to 325 B.C.) was critical to the development of Western civilization. The creative achievements of the Greeks of this time in art, literature, philosophy, science, mathematics, and political science exerted an influence on Western cultural history unequaled by any other people.

Foremost among the Greek communities of 2500 years ago was the city-state of Athens. No other state rivaled Athens in its extent of empire, wealth, power, and intellectual and cultural activity, and none possessed so pure a democracy. The "Golden Age" of Athens coincided closely with the reign of Pericles, the most dominating personality of his time, who rose to power in 469 B.C. while still in his early 30's. The Golden Age began to tarnish, however, with the outbreak of the Peloponnesian War in 431 B.C. The war, which lasted a quarter of a century, was essentially a series of military struggles between Athens and Sparta, the other predominant city-state. Athens was primarily a sea power with a strong navy, but it had a weak army compared to the Spartans who had a strong army and no major fleet of ships. Pericles' strategy was to withdraw the population of the surrounding area into Athens, to make his state invulnerable to land attack, and to raid the coasts of his enemy.

The strategy worked well during the first year of the war and it seemed inevitable that Sparta would be defeated quickly. The Athenian plan of bringing large numbers of people into the fortified city area, however, had a disastrous and unforeseen consequence. Overcrowding and unsanitary conditions provided an ideal setting for the spread of disease. In 430 B.C., an epidemic devastated Athens. The disease, whose exact nature is still unknown, was virulent and highly contagious. Between 30 and 60 percent of the Athenians died within six to eight days of contracting the illness. Many of those who survived the high fevers, violent coughs, and distressing vomiting of the disease fell victim to other medical complications. Even those who lived on were often scarred by the epidemic and left with blindness, deformed arms or legs, and amnesia.

The contemporary Greek historian Thucydides, whose *History of the Peloponnesian War* is a classic of Western literature, provides a vivid account of the illness and its after effects. "Physicians, in ignorance of the nature of the disease," he wrote, "sought to apply remedies, but it was in vain, and they themselves were among the first victims, because they often came into contact with it. No human art was of any avail, and as to supplications in temples, inquiries of oracles and the like, they were utterly useless, and at last men were overpowered by the calamity and gave them all up.... The general character of the malady no words can describe, and the fury with which it fastened upon each sufferer was too much for human nature to endure." Many of the dead were left unburied and birds and animals that preyed on the corpses became infected and spread the disease even further. Many Athenians committed suicide to escape the pain and suffering of the infection.

When it appeared that the epidemic had at last ended, Pericles sent his fleet to capture the Spartan-held stronghold at Potidaea. The ships had barely reached the sea when the plague broke out among the crews with such ferocity that they were forced to return to Athens. There were fresh outbreaks in 429 and 428 B.C. and Pericles himself fell victim. After his death, Athens never again found a leader of his stature and wisdom.

The plague of Athens was instrumental to the disintegration of the Athenian empire. The destruction of the fighting power of the navy and the disastrous reduction in population at home prevented Athens from achieving a swift victory over Sparta. The war dragged on for years, with eventual defeat for the Athenians.

Perhaps worse than the loss of life was the demoralization of the city-state that the plague brought in its wake. The descent of a highly civilized state into the depths of cruelty and desperation is one of the major themes of Thucydides' history. He records [1942] the lawlessness which swept through Athens:

> Men who had hitherto concealed what they took pleasure in, now grew bolder. For seeing the sudden change—how the rich died in a moment, and those who had nothing immediately inherited their property—they reflected that life and riches were alike transitory, and they resolved to enjoy themselves while they could, and to think only of pleasure. Who would be willing to sacrifice himself to the law of honor when he knew not whether he would ever live to be held in honor? The pleasure of the moment and any sort of thing which conduced to it took the place both of honor and of expediency. No fear of Gods or law of man deterred a criminal. Those who saw all perishing alike, thought that the worship or neglect of the Gods made no difference. For offences against human law no punishment was to be feared; no one would live long enough to be called to account. Already a far heavier sentence had been passed and was hanging over a man's head; before that fell, why should he not take a little pleasure?

The Athenian plague is perhaps the earliest for which we have a detailed account of the influence of epidemics upon historical events. It is, however, but one of many disastrous situations. In the fourteenth century, there were an estimated 25 million deaths in a population of 100 million Europeans attributed to an epidemic of bubonic plague. In 1520 the Aztecs suffered an epidemic of smallpox that resulted in the death of half their population of 3.5 million. When measles first came to the Fiji Islands in 1875 as a result of a trip to Australia by the King of Fiji and his son, it caused the death of 40,000 people in a population of 150,000. In the three-year period from 1918 to 1921, there were an estimated 25 million cases of typhus in the Soviet Union and about one in ten victims died from the disease. In a world-wide epidemic of influenza in 1919, more than 20 million persons perished from the illness and subsequent attacks of pneumonia. The possibility that a similar strain of influenza virus might attack the United States in 1976 led the government to plan for the vaccination of the entire nation of more than 200 million people.

These examples, and hundreds of others which could be cited, indicate clearly that epidemics are major public health problems which require careful study and prompt action to protect the citizenry. In this chapter, we will present some simple mathematical models of the spread of infectious diseases. These models will serve as an introduction to the rapidly growing field of mathematical epidemiology where mathematicians and biologists are working together to gain a better understanding of the spread and control of epidemics. "The real stimulus," writes Norman Bailey [1975], an internationally reknowned leader in this field, "comes from the need to be able to influence in a rational way public health decision-making on the control of serious diseases that affect many hundreds of millions of people in the world today. When mathematical modeling is directed towards theoretical problems, which if solved would have practical implications for the control or eradication of disease, then it can be both intellectually satisfying and socially valuable."

In the following sections of this chapter, we will present some of the features of infectious diseases that ought to be incorporated into realistic mathematical models, develop two deterministic models and a stochastic model and discuss their relationships, and conclude with a brief sketch of the development of mathematical epidemiology.

## B.  Some Features of Epidemics

The spread of an infectious disease among a population can be a complicated process with many possible variations. Consider first a single individual who may be infected by some contagious pathogenic agent. The organism may enter his body through the bite of a flea (as in bubonic plague), or a mosquito (yellow fever), through intimate personal contact with another infected person (syphilis), by air-borne agents spread by coughing or sneezing (pneumonia), or by drinking contaminated water (typhoid fever).

After initial infection, there may follow a *latent period* during which the individual exhibits no symptoms of the disease and cannot transmit it to others. The latent period is followed by an *infectious period* when he can pass on the illness. These two periods may be overlapped by an *incubation period* which is defined as the time between initial infection and first appearance of physical symptoms. Thus, an individual may be transmitting a disease to others during a period when he and others are unaware that he is sick. This is characteristic of some diseases, such as chicken pox and measles, now common mainly among younger children.

Once the symptoms appear, the affected individual may continue to be an active transmitter, especially if the disease is a mild one such as a cold or minor respiratory infection. On the other hand, the individual may be withdrawn from the general population temporarily (by quarantine or hospitalization, for example) or permanently, through death. The chances of recovery or death vary from day to day during the various stages of the illness as do the chances that the individual will convey the infection to previously unaffected people.

If the individual recovers from the disease, there are still many options. A permanent *immunity* to the disease may be acquired so that there is never again susceptibility to the symptoms even if there is reinfection. The immunity may be of such a nature that the individual can no longer even transmit the disease to others, or, on the other hand, he may become a *carrier*, a person who can spread the illness but is otherwise unaffected by it. The immunity may be temporary so that there is no susceptibility to the disease again for many months or years (tetanus), or there may be no immunity at all: the so-called "English sweating sickness" which ravaged Western Europe in the late fifteenth and early sixteenth centuries attacked some individuals two or more times in brief succession after they had recovered from an initial bout of the disease's associated tremors, fever, cardiac pain, vomiting, severe headache, and stupor.

As an epidemic spreads through a local community, city, nation, or continent, the number of unaffected members becomes reduced. In due course of time, the epidemic may appear to end, as no new cases of the disease are observed. In an early paper in the history of mathematical models of epidemics, two Edinburgh researchers, W. O. Kermack and A. G. McKendrick [1927], posed the fundamental goal of such models. "One of the most important problems in epidemiology," they wrote, "is to ascertain whether this termination occurs only when no susceptible individuals are left, or whether the interplay of the various factors on infectivity, recovery and mortality, may result in termination, whilst many susceptible individuals are still present in the unaffected population."

If it can be shown that a particular epidemic will end when only a small proportion of the potentially susceptible members of the community have been affected, then there may be little cause for panic or widespread emergency public-health measures. Conversely, it is important to know early in the growth of an epidemic of a disease with a high mortality rate that large numbers of the population may become victims.

Even when a number of simplifying assumptions are made, mathematical models of epidemics tend to be quite complex and require advanced analytic and probabilistic techniques to solve. Even some of the simpler models give rise to mathematical problems which have yet to be solved. While waiting for the mathematicians to solve these problems, modelers must resort to approximate results or computer simulations (see Chapter 14) to derive their predictions. Because of the technical mathematical difficulties posed by many models, this chapter will concentrate only on some very simple models of epidemics. Even though the models are simple, they do yield qualitative results which are consistent with observations and are helpful to biologists and public health officials.

## II. DETERMINISTIC MODELS

### A. Basic Assumptions

In studying a community subject to a possible epidemic, it is convenient to partition the population into four mutually exclusive subgroups:

1. The *susceptibles* (S), those persons who are currently uninfected, but may become infected;

2. The *latently infected* (L), those who are currently infected, but not yet capable of transmitting the disease to others;

3. The *infectives* (I), those who are currently infected and capable of spreading the infection; and

4. The *removeds* (R), those persons who have had the disease and are dead, or have recovered and are permanently immune, or are isolated until death, recovery, or permanent immunity occur.

The numbers of persons, S, L, I, and R, in each category change with time. The mathematical models that will be studied attempt to discover how these numbers fluctuate with respect to time, denoted as usual by t, and with respect to each other.

Since the course of most epidemics is usually short (a few weeks or months) compared to the normal life span of an individual, a reasonable simplifying assumption is that the population of the community remains constant, except, of course, as it is lowered by deaths due to the epidemic disease itself. Suppose, then, that there are no births, no deaths from other causes, and no immigration or emigration during the course of the epidemic. This initial assumption is stated mathematically as the following axiom.

**AXIOM 1    There is positive constant $N$ such that**

$$S(t) + L(t) + I(t) + R(t) = N \qquad \text{for all } t.$$

**For the simplification of some formulas, this equation is frequently written as**

$$S + L + I + R = N. \tag{1}$$

The second assumption is also one that is basic to almost all mathematical models of epidemics: the rate of change of the susceptible population is proportional to the rate of contact between susceptibles and infectives. If the amount of human interaction is great, the epidemic spreads more rapidly. History records the rapid spread of many diseases in crowded cities or army camps, while showing that epidemics move more slowly through isolated rural areas with lower population densities. For simple models, it is usually assumed that the rate of contact is directly proportional to the population of susceptibles and infectives. In mathematical terms, the second basic assumption is the following:

**AXIOM 2    There is a positive constant $\beta$ such that**

$$\frac{dS}{dt} = S'(t) = -\beta I(t)S(t) \qquad \textbf{for all } t. \qquad (2)$$

The constant $\beta$ is called the *infection rate*. Note that $S'(t)$ is always negative (or possibly zero), since the number of persons who have not yet caught the disease $(S)$, can only decrease with time.

There is one final assumption that is common to the models to be presented in this chapter. We suppose that the disease being investigated has a latency period which is negligibly short; that is, an individual can transmit the disease essentially as soon as he is infected. Typhus fever presents such a possibility. Typhus is often spread from person to person through the bite of a hair louse. A louse carrying the disease may leave the body of a person it has just bitten and move on to a nearby person at any moment. In the language of the variables of the deterministic models, we have this axiom:

**AXIOM 3    $L(t) = 0$    for all $t$.**

## B.  A Simple Epidemic Model

This section investigates a deterministic model of a simple epidemic. In addition to Axioms 1–3, one further simplification is made. We assume that there is no removal from the population; the population of removeds remains at 0. In a human population, such an assumption might be justified for an illness such as a mild cold epidemic in a college dormitory. None of the affected students dies, acquires permanent immunity, or is sick enough to be isolated. The assumption is commonly valid also in many cases of disease in animal or plant population, where dead or diseased members in a natural environment are not removed. Formally stated, the assumption is

**AXIOM 4    $R(t) = 0$    for all $t$.**

A mathematical model for an epidemic satisfying Axioms 1–4 is easily analyzed using the tools of elementary calculus. Axioms 1, 3, and 4 give the basic relation between susceptibles and infectives:

$$S + I = N. \qquad (3)$$

For convenience, assume the epidemic starts at time $t = 0$ with a single infected person, so the initial conditions are

$$I(0) = I_0 = 1 \qquad \text{and} \qquad S(0) = S_0 = N - 1. \qquad (4)$$

The analysis of this simple epidemic begins by using Eq. (3) to rewrite Axiom 2 as the differential equation

$$\frac{dI}{dt} = \frac{d(N-S)}{dt} = -\frac{dS}{dt} = \beta I S = \beta I (N - I), \tag{5}$$

so that the number of infectives is governed by the differential equation

$$\frac{dI}{dt} = \beta I (N - I), \qquad I(0) = 1. \tag{6}$$

Equation (6) is a differential equation for logistic growth. Such equations were studied extensively in Chapter 3. They are solved by separating the variables ($I$ and $t$ in this case) and integrating, using a partial fraction decomposition:

$$\int \frac{dI}{I(N-I)} = \int \beta \, dt,$$

or

$$\int \left( \frac{1}{I} + \frac{1}{N-I} \right) dI = \int \beta N \, dt,$$

so that

$$\log I - \log (N - I) = \beta N t + \text{constant},$$

which may be written in the equivalent form

$$\frac{I}{N - I} = K e^{\beta N t} \tag{7}$$

where the constant $K$ is found, using Eq. (4) to be $1/(N-1)$. Equation (7) may then be rewritten as

$$I(t) = \frac{N}{1 + (N - 1)e^{-\beta N t}}. \tag{8}$$

Since $\beta$ is positive, it is apparent from Eq. (8) that

$$\lim_{t \to \infty} I(t) = N. \tag{9}$$

Thus the model predicts that everyone in the population will eventually contract the disease. Since $S + I = N$, we have $S = N - I$, or

$$S(t) = N - I(t) = \frac{N(N - 1)}{e^{\beta N t} + (N - 1)} = \frac{N}{1 + e^{\beta N t}/(N - 1)}. \tag{10}$$

The graphs of $S$ and $I$ as functions of $t$ are given in Figs. 13.1 and 13.2 for the case $N = 1001$ and $\beta = .003$. According to this model, if a single infective person enters a community of 1,000 susceptibles, then at the end of 4 time units, only about 6 healthy people are left. The decline in the number of susceptibles is also represented in Table 13.1.

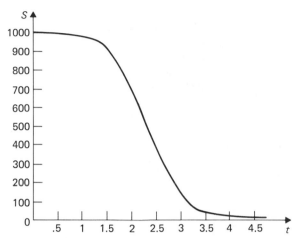

**Fig. 13.1**    The graph of $S(t)$ as a function of $t$ for the simple deterministic model, with $N = 1001$ and $\beta = .003$.

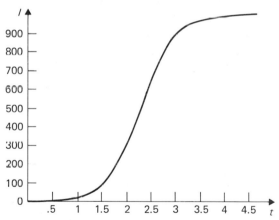

**Fig. 13.2**    The graph of $I(t)$ as a function of $t$ for the simple deterministic model, with $N = 1001$ and $\beta = .003$.

The data collected in an epidemic often consists in the number of new cases of the disease reported each day or each week. The *rate* at which new cases arise is the derivative of $I$ with respect to time $t$. From Eq. (8), this rate can be computed explicitly as a function of $t$:

$$I'(t) = \frac{dI}{dt} = \frac{N^2(N - 1)\beta e^{-\beta N t}}{(1 + (N - 1)e^{-\beta N t})^2}. \qquad (11)$$

**Table 13.1**   Decline in the number of susceptibles for selected times in the simple epidemic with $N = 1001$ and $\beta = .003$. The number $S(t)$ is computed from Eq. (10).

| Time $t$ | Susceptibles $S(t)$ |
| --- | --- |
| 0 | 1000 |
| .5 | 996.5 |
| 1 | 981 |
| 1.5 | 917 |
| 2 | 712 |
| 2.5 | 355 |
| 3 | 109 |
| 3.5 | 26.6 |
| 4 | 6 |
| 4.5 | 1.4 |

The graph of $I'(t)$ as a function of $t$ is called the *epidemic curve*. The epidemic curve for $N = 1001$ and $\beta = .003$ is shown in Fig. 13.3. At the start of the epidemic ($t = 0$), the derivative has value

$$I'(0) = \frac{N^2(N-1)\beta}{(1+(N-1))^2} = \beta(N-1). \tag{12}$$

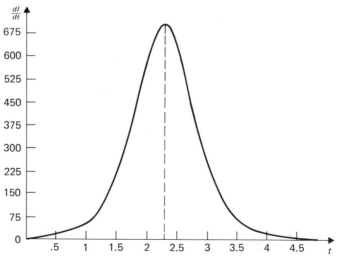

**Fig. 13.3**   The epidemic curve for the simple deterministic model with $N = 1001$ and $\beta = .003$.

**Table 13.2** Fluctuations in the rate of
new cases as measured by $I'(t)$, using
Eq. (11) with $N = 1001$ and $\beta = .003$.
The values of $I'(t)$ have been rounded
off to the nearest integer.

| Time $t$ | Rate of New Cases, $I'(t)$ |
|---|---|
| 0 | 3 |
| .5 | 13 |
| 1 | 58 |
| 1.5 | 229 |
| 2 | 617 |
| 2.5 | 688 |
| 3 | 292 |
| 3.5 | 78 |
| 4 | 18 |
| 4.5 | 4 |

Assuming that $\beta$ has been computed using time measured in weekly units, the particular epidemic of Fig. 13.3 would begin with about 3 cases per week. Table 13.2 shows additional numerical data on the values of $I'(t)$.

The maximum value for the rate of new cases occurs at the maximum height of the epidemic curve. The time at which this maximum occurs represents a critical moment in the history of the epidemic: it is spreading most rapidly at this instant and the consequent demand for medical services and personnel may be at its peak. To find the maximum value of $I'(t)$, consider its derivative

$$I''(t) = \left[\frac{(N-1)N^3\beta^2 e^{-\beta Nt}}{(1+(N-1)e^{-\beta Nt})^3}\right][(N-1)e^{-N\beta t}-1]. \tag{13}$$

Now the factor inside the first square brackets in Eq. (13) remains positive for all values of $t$. Thus the sign of $I''(t)$ depends on the sign of the remaining factor

$$\frac{N-1}{e^{\beta Nt}} - 1. \tag{14}$$

This factor is positive when $t = 0$ and it tends to $-1$ as $t$ gets large (Why?). This implies that the epidemic curve reaches its maximum height when this factor is zero. This occurs when

$$e^{\beta Nt} = (N-1), \tag{15}$$

that is

$$t_{max} = \frac{\log(N-1)}{\beta N}. \tag{16}$$

At this moment, the rate of new infections is

$$I'(t_{max}) = \frac{N^2\beta}{4} \tag{17}$$

and the number of infected individuals is

$$I(t_{\max}) = \frac{N}{2}.$$

(18)

The graph of the epidemic curve of Fig. 13.3 appears to be symmetric about the vertical line through $t_{\max}$. The apparent symmetry is real and holds in general for the simple epidemic model; see Exercise 6.

Note finally from Eq. (16) that the smaller the value of $\beta$ is, the longer it takes the epidemic curve to reach its peak. Thus the model shows that the more densely crowded a population is, the faster will an epidemic spread through the community.

Although this simple model has a number of interesting results consistent with real-world observations, it makes one prediction that rarely is correct in actual epidemics. The model asserts that before the epidemic runs its course everyone will contract the illness. In real epidemics, the epidemic ends—in the sense that no new infectives are seen—while there are still many susceptibles in the population. We turn next to a model that is consistent with this observation.

## C.  A More General Epidemic Model

**Description of model**    The simple epidemic model just studied assumed that once an individual became an infective, he remained one from then on. Thus the population of infectives could only increase. In this section, we examine a model in which the subgroup of infectives is *increased* by the introduction of formerly susceptible persons and is *decreased* by the removal of some individuals who either die from the disease, recover from it and acquire permanent immunity, or are isolated from the remaining population during the course of their illness. In place of Axiom 4, this more general model assumes that individuals are removed from the infective class at a rate which is proportional to the number of infectives; that is, there is a constant removal rate per person. In mathematical terms, the new axiom is as follows:

**AXIOM 4\***    **There is a positive constant $r$ such that $R'(t) = dR/dt = rI(t)$ for all $t$.**

The constant r is called the *removal rate* and the ratio $p = r/\beta$ is the *relative removal rate*.

For a model satisfying Axioms 1, 2, 3, and 4\*, we have

$$I = N - S - R,$$

(19)

so that

$$\frac{dI}{dt} = 0 - \frac{dS}{dt} - \frac{dR}{dt} = \beta IS - rI.$$

(20)

Assuming that the epidemic starts in a community of $N$ persons with a positive number $I_0$ of infectives and with $S_0 = N - I_0$ susceptibles, the mathematical model is the system of differential equations

$$\frac{dS}{dt} = -\beta SI, \beta > 0 \tag{21.1}$$

$$\frac{dI}{dt} = \beta SI - rI, r > 0 \tag{21.2}$$

$$\frac{dR}{dt} = rI \tag{21.3}$$

with initial conditions

$$S(0) = S_0, \qquad I(0) = I_0 > 0, \qquad R(0) = R_0 = 0,$$

and the relation

$$S(t) + I(t) + R(t) = N \qquad \text{for all } t \geqslant 0.$$

In the remainder of this section, we shall explore the many conclusions that can be derived from this model.

**Qualitative behavior of $R$, $S$, and $I$**    Since $r$ is positive and $I$ is nonnegative, $dR/dt = rI$ is always nonnegative, so $R$ is a monotonic nondecreasing function of $t$. In fact, $R$ is a strictly increasing function except at the time the number of infectives drops to zero.

Since $\beta > 0$ and $S$ and $I$ are nonnegative, we have $dS/dt \leqslant 0$ for all $t$. Thus the number of susceptibles is a monotonic nonincreasing function: the population of susceptibles can only decrease as time goes on.

Write the rate of change of infectives as $dI/dt = I(\beta S - r)$. The sign of this rate then depends on the sign of $(\beta S - r)$. The number of infectives can increase only at times that $dI/dt$ is positive; that is, at times when

$$S > \frac{r}{\beta} = p. \tag{22}$$

In particular, if the initial population level of susceptibles, $S_0$, is below the relative removal rate $p$, then there is no epidemic. The number of infectives is always less than the original number ($I_0$) and decreases as time goes on. The disease dies out as infected individuals are being removed (by recovery or death) at a faster rate than they are becoming sources of further infection. This is what epidemiologists term a *threshold phenomenon*. There is a critical value which the initial susceptible population must exceed for there to be an epidemic. For example, if a sufficiently high percentage of the population has been sucessfully vaccinated against the disease, then there will be no epidemic. Alternatively, holding the susceptible population fixed, infection can spread only if the relative removal rate is sufficiently small: an epidemic can be halted by increasing the relative removal rate $p$.

**Limits of R, S, and I**  The numbers of removeds, susceptibles, and infectives must always lie between 0 and $N$, the total size of the community. The function $R(t)$ is bounded above by $N$ and is monotonically nondecreasing, so the number of removeds reaches a limit as time goes on; that is, $\lim_{t \to \infty} R(t)$ exists. Denote this number by $R_\infty$. Thus,

$$\lim_{t \to \infty} R(t) = R_\infty \leqslant N. \qquad (23)$$

Similarly $S(t)$ is a nonincreasing function of $t$ that must remain greater than or equal to 0, so it has a limit also as $t$ increases. There is a nonnegative number $S_\infty$ such that

$$\lim_{t \to \infty} S(t) = S_\infty \geqslant 0. \qquad (24)$$

Consider the limiting value for the number of infectives. From Eq. (19),

$$\lim_{t \to \infty} I(t) = \lim_{t \to \infty} (N - S(t) - R(t))$$

$$= \lim_{t \to \infty} N - \lim_{t \to \infty} S(t) - \lim_{t \to \infty} R(t) \qquad (25)$$

$$= N - S_\infty - R_\infty.$$

Let $I_\infty$ denote this limiting value.

Note that the number $R_\infty/N$ is the proportion of the population which eventually has the disease. It provides a convenient measure of the intensity of the epidemic.

**Relation of R and S**  The relationship between the number of susceptibles and number of removeds during the course of the epidemic becomes more apparent if we use equations (21.1) and (21.3) to write

$$\frac{dS}{dR} = \frac{-\beta SI}{rI} = \frac{-\beta}{r} S = \frac{-1}{p} S, \qquad (26)$$

a relation which holds whenever there are still infectives in the population. The differential equation (26) is easily solved to obtain

$$S = S_0 e^{(-1/p)R}. \qquad (27)$$

Since $R(t) \leqslant R_\infty \leqslant N$ for all $t$, we have $e^{(-1/p)R} \geqslant e^{(-1/p)N}$ so that

$$S(t) \geqslant S_0 e^{(-1/p)N}, \qquad \text{for all } t. \qquad (28)$$

Since the right-hand side of Eq. (28) is a strictly positive number, we have

$$S_\infty = \lim_{t \to \infty} S(t) > 0. \qquad (29)$$

Here is a crucial prediction of this model: there will always be some people ($S_\infty$ of them) in the community who escape the disease. The epidemic will die out, but not because there aren't susceptible individuals left.

**Relation of S and I**   Examine next the relationship between the number of susceptibles and the number of infectives during the epidemic. Equations (21.1) and (21.2) define an autonomous system of differential equations (see Chapter 4) for which the only critical points lie on the line $I = 0$. We are interested in orbits of the system which lie in the first quadrant of the $(S,I)$-plane.

From the two equations, we have

$$\frac{dI}{dS} = \frac{I(\beta S - r)}{-\beta S I} = -1 + \frac{r}{\beta S} = -1 + \frac{p}{S}, \tag{30}$$

whenever $I \neq 0$.

Separating the variables in the differential equation (30) and integrating yields

$$\int 1 \, dI = \int \left(-1 + \frac{p}{S}\right) dS, \tag{31}$$

so that

$$I = -S + p \log S + C, \tag{32}$$

where $C$ is a constant. At time $t = 0$, there are $I_0$ infectives and $S_0$ susceptibles so that

$$C = I_0 + S_0 - p \log S_0 = N - p \log S_0. \tag{33}$$

This gives

$$I = N - S + p \log \left(\frac{S}{S_0}\right). \tag{34}$$

Thus the orbits for solutions of the autonomous system lie along the curve $I = g(S) = N - S + p \log(S/S_0)$. Since $g(S_0) = I_0 > 0$ and $\lim_{S \to 0^+} g(S) = -\infty$, the curve crosses the line $I = 0$ at some positive value of $S$ less than $S_0$. Since the only critical points for the system lie on the line $I = 0$, the orbit must approach $(S_\infty, 0)$ as $t$ increases. Thus $I_\infty = 0$.

The orbit is traced out from right to left as $t$ increases since $S$ is a non-increasing function of time. From Eq. (30), we have

$$g''(S) = \frac{d^2 I}{dS^2} = -p/S^2 \tag{35}$$

which is always negative. Thus the graph of $I$ as a function of $S$ is concave down and reaches its maximum when $dI/dS = 0$. From Eq. (30), this happens when $S = p$. The relation between $I$ and $S$ is shown in Fig. 13.4. The initial state of the population is represented by the point $(S_0, I_0)$ on this curve. If this point falls to the left of the line $S = p$, then no epidemic occurs: $I(t)$ shrinks monotonically toward zero. On the other hand, if $S_0 > p$, then the number of infectives increases initially until $S$ passes below $p$ after which the number of infectives again falls toward zero.

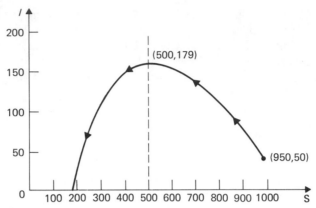

**Fig. 13.4**   The graph of $I = N - S + p \log(S/S_0)$ with $N = 1000$, $p = 500$, $S_0 = 950$. Here $S_\infty$ is about 186 and the maximum value of $I$ is about 179.

**Finding S**    To locate $S_\infty$ more precisely, note that Eq. (25) gives $S_\infty = N - R_\infty - I_\infty$, but we have just seen that $I_\infty = 0$ so that

$$S_\infty = N - R_\infty. \tag{36}$$

The relation between $S$ and $R$ given by Eq. (27) is

$$S(t) = S_0 e^{(-1/p)R(t)}, \tag{27}$$

and if we let $t \to \infty$ in Eq. (27), we have

$$S_\infty = S_0 e^{(-1/p)R_\infty}. \tag{37}$$

Combining this relationship with Eq. (36) produces

$$S_\infty = S_0 e^{(-1/p)(N - S_\infty)}, \tag{38}$$

so that $S_\infty$ is a solution of the equation

$$S_0 e^{(-1/p)(N-x)} - x = 0. \tag{39}$$

Unfortunately, we cannot solve this equation analytically for $x$ as an explicit function of $S_0, p,$ and $N$, but we can show that there is a unique positive solution and we can approximate its value to any desired accuracy. Toward these ends, define the function

$$f(x) = S_0 e^{(-1/p)(N-x)} - x \qquad \text{for } x \geqslant 0.$$

Note that

$$f(0) = S_0 e^{(-1/p)N} > 0,$$

while

$$f(N) = S_0 - N < 0.$$

Since $f$ is a continuous function of $x$, the Intermediate Value Theorem of elementary calculus asserts that there is at least one number $x^*$ between 0 and $N$ for which $f(x^*) = 0$. Hence there is at least one positive root of the equation.

Consider next the derivative of $f$:

$$f'(x) = \left(\frac{S_0}{p}\right)e^{(-1/p)(N-x)} - 1 = \frac{(f(x) + x)}{p} - 1,$$

so that

$$f'(x^*) = \frac{(f(x^*) + x^*)}{p} - 1 = \frac{(0 + x^*)}{p} - 1 = \frac{x^*}{p} - 1.$$

Since $x^* = S_\infty < p$, $f'(x^*) < 0$. If there are two or more roots, then Rolle's Theorem guarantees there is a point between the roots at which the derivative is 0. But the derivative is negative at both roots and the second derivative $f''(x) = S_0(1/p)^2 e^{(-1/p)(N-x)}$ is always positive, so the derivative must always be negative between the roots. This contradiction shows that there cannot be more than one root.

The preceding discussion establishes the fundamental theorem for this general epidemic model:

■ **THEOREM (THRESHOLD THEOREM OF EPIDEMIOLOGY)**    If $S_0 < r/\beta$, then $I(t)$ goes monotonically to zero. If $S_0 > r/\beta$, then the number of infectives increases as $t$ increases and then tends monotonically to zero. The limit of $S(t)$ as $t \to \infty$ exists and is the unique positive root of the equation

$$S_0 e^{(-\beta/r)(N-x)} - x = 0.$$

**Approximation of $S_\infty$**    This last equation cannot be solved for $x$ in closed form, but various methods are available to approximate its value. A particularly simple one, based on the Intermediate Value Theorem, will be discussed here.

Suppose we have a continuous function defined on the closed interval $[0, N]$ with the property that $f(0) > 0$ and $f(N) < 0$. By the Intermediate Value Theorem, there is a root of the equation $f(x) = 0$ somewhere on this interval of length of $N$. Split this interval into two equal parts, subintervals $[0, N/2]$ and $[N/2, N]$. If $f(N/2) < 0$, then there is a root between 0 and $N/2$ while if $f(N/2) > 0$, there is a root between $N/2$ and $N$. In either case, we have narrowed the search for a root to an interval of length $N/2$. By examining the midpoint of this interval, we can narrow the search down to an interval of length $N/2^2$. Continuing this process $k$ times produces an interval of length $N/2^k$ which contains a root of $f(x) = 0$. By choosing $k$ sufficiently large, we can find a numerical value for the root to a desired degree of accuracy.

As an example, consider a population of 1001 individuals with a single infective at time 0. With $\beta = .001$ and $r = .9$, this "bisection" process requires 10 steps to obtain a value of $S_\infty$ equal to 799 which is accurate to the nearest integer. In such an epidemic, about 80 percent of the population would not be affected by the disease.

**Relation between R and t**   Note that we have not derived explicit solutions of the differential equations of (21.1)–(21.3) in the form of functions of time. In this section, we will find an approximate solution for $R(t)$. We concentrate on the number of removeds, since it is frequently not possible to determine when an individual is first infected, but it is usually easier to observe when he has been removed.

Rewrite equation (21.3), $dR/dt = rI$ as

$$\frac{dR}{dt} = r(N - S - R), \tag{40}$$

which, by Eq. (27), can be represented as

$$\frac{dR}{dt} = r(N - R - S_0 e^{(-1/p)R}). \tag{41}$$

This is a single differential equation in the variables $R$ and $t$, with initial condition $R(0) = 0$. Although an exact solution of this equation is possible, at least in parametric terms, the necessary work is rather complicated. We shall illustrate an approximate approach which yields a number of interesting properties and is typical of the way some analytic models are studied.

A Taylor series approximation for the exponential function $e^x$ is given by choosing an initial string of terms from the series

$$e^x = 1 + x + \frac{x^2}{2} + \frac{x^3}{3!} + \cdots + \frac{x^k}{k!} + \cdots.$$

Approximating the function with the first three terms gives

$$e^x \sim 1 + x + \frac{x^2}{2}$$

and with $x = (-1/p)R$, this yields in place of Eq. (41),

$$\frac{dR}{dt} \sim r\left(N - R - S_0\left(1 - \frac{R}{p} + \frac{R^2}{2p^2}\right)\right) \tag{42}$$

Ultimately when the epidemic ends, $dR/dt = 0$. If the original infective population is very small, so that the number of initial susceptibles is close to the total population, we have $S_0 \sim N$, so that $dR/dt = 0$ and $R = R_\infty$ and

$$r\left(S_0 - R_\infty - S_0 + \frac{S_0 R_\infty}{p} - \frac{S_0 R_\infty^2}{2p^2}\right) \sim 0,$$

which occurs when

$$R_\infty \sim 2p\left(1 - \frac{p}{S_0}\right). \tag{43}$$

This gives an approximate measure of the total number of people who have contracted the disease. Since an epidemic occurs only if $S_0 > p$, let $v$ be the positive number $S_0 - p$ so that $S_0 = p + v$. Then Eq. (43) can be written

$$R_\infty \sim \frac{2pv}{p + v}. \tag{44}$$

If $v$ is small in comparison to $p$, then $p/(p + v)$ is nearly 1 and $R_\infty \sim 2v$. In other words, the total size of the epidemic is about $2v$ cases. The initial population of susceptibles, $p + v$, is thus reduced to $p + v - 2v = p - v$. The susceptible population is eventually about as far below the threshold as it was originally above it.

This last observation, as well as the Threshold Theorem, was discovered by Kermack and McKendrick in 1927. A more precise version of this threshold result is possible by an exact solution of the differential equation (41), but the epidemiological implications are quite similar. In addition to the results presented here, Kermack and McKendrick compared their predicted results to an actual epidemic, an outbreak of plague in Bombay in 1905–06. This comparison is shown in Fig. 13.5. The vertical axis represents the number of deaths per week and the horizontal units of measure is time in weeks. Since almost all cases terminated fatally, the vertical component is approximately $dR/dt$.

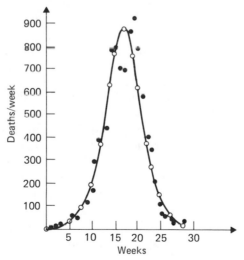

**Fig. 13.5** Kermack and McKendrick's comparison of the predicted curve of $dR/dt$ as a function of $t$ and data on the number of deaths from plague (solid dots) in Bombay over the period of December 17, 1905 to July 21, 1906. The calculated curve conforms roughly to observed figures.

## III. A PROBABILISTIC APPROACH

### A. A Stochastic Model of Simple Epidemics

In earlier chapters, there were several discussions of the weaknesses of the deterministic approach in models involving social or life sciences and the consequent need for probabilistic models. In addition to those general arguments, there are several that are particularly appropriate for models of epidemics. One of the fundamental assumptions of the deterministic models presented in Section II concerned the rate at which the susceptible population is reduced as an infectious disease spreads through a community. We assumed that the rate of change was proportional to the number of contacts between the susceptible and infective subpopulations and, further, that this number was proportional to the sizes of these two subgroups. In mathematical terms, we had the equation $dS/dt = -\beta S(t)I(t)$. This axiom presumes that there is a homogeneous mixing of the members of the community. This is not a realistic presumption if the community is large enough to contain significant subgroups of different ages, interests, occupations, and geographical locations. The axiom is more likely to be accurate for a small group, such as recruits in an army camp or students living in a dormitory. But the smaller the group size, the less reasonable is a deterministic approach, since this approach is based on the hope that statistical fluctuations in behavior "smooth out" for large groups. These fluctuations are important in the study of small groups. The element of probability is of considerable importance here and should be incorporated into the mathematical model.

Even if our interest in the model is focused on the average number or expected value of susceptibles or infectives, a probabilistic approach is required. For, although with some population processes (such as the pure birth model of Chapter 9) the expected value was identical to the corresponding deterministic prediction, this is not always true of epidemic processes.

In this section we will develop a probabilistic version of the simple epidemic model of Section II.B. In the simple model, $R(t) = 0$ and $S(t) = N - I(t)$ for all $t$, so it is sufficient to investigate the function $I(t)$. The probabilistic model does not predict a precise value for $I(t)$ for each time $t$. Instead the model gives a set of probability distributions for $I(t)$; that is, the model yields for each $t$ and each nonnegative integer $m$, a probability—denoted $p_m(t)$—that there are exactly $m$ infectives at time $t$:

$$p_m(t) = \Pr(I(t) = m). \tag{45}$$

Note first that the number of infectives cannot exceed the total population $N$ of the community at any time so that

$$p_m(t) = 0 \qquad \text{for all } t \qquad \text{if } m \geqslant N + 1. \tag{46}$$

The function $I(t)$ can then be thought of as a random variable which takes on possible values $0, 1, 2, \ldots, N$. The simple epidemic model assumes that 1 of the

$N$ persons in the community is an infective when the epidemic begins at time 0. Thus

$$p_m(0) = \begin{cases} 1 & \text{if } m = 1, \\ 0 & \text{if } m \neq 1. \end{cases} \qquad (47)$$

The probabilistic model of a simple epidemic is developed in the same spirit as the model for a pure-birth process presented in Chapter 9. The particular assumptions are these:

*Assumption 1*    A susceptible individual is infected when he comes into contact with an infective person.

*Assumption 2*    Once an individual is infected, he remains an infective for the remaining time.

*Assumption 3*    The probability that there is exactly one contact between a susceptible and an infective in a particular very short period of time is proportional to the number of susceptibles, the number of infectives, and the length of the time interval.  In other terms, there is a positive constant $\beta$ such that

$$\text{Pr}(\text{Exactly one contact in time interval } (t, t + \Delta t)) = \beta I(t)S(t)\,\Delta t$$
$$= \beta I(t)(N - I(t))\,\Delta t$$

since there are no removeds in the simple model.

*Assumption 4*    The probability of more than one contact between susceptibles and infectives in a very short time period is negligibly small.
These assumptions are used to determine the probability of $m$ infectives at time $t + \Delta t$, the number $p_m(t + \Delta t)$.  There are three distinct and mutually exclusive ways that the community can have precisely $m$ infectives at such a moment:

Event (A)  There were exactly $m$ infectives at time $t$ and there was no contact between susceptibles and infectives during the period $(t, t + \Delta t)$;

Event (B)  There were exactly $(m - 1)$ infectives at time $t$ and there was precisely one susceptible-infective contact in $(t, t + \Delta t)$; and

Event (C)  There were less than $(m - 1)$ infectives at time $t$ and there was more than one infective-susceptible contact in $(t, t + \Delta t)$.

By Assumption 4, the event (C) has negligible probability and can be ignored if $\Delta t$ is very small.  Thus

$$p_m(t + \Delta t) = \text{Pr}(A) + \text{Pr}(B). \qquad (48)$$

Now

$$Pr(B) = Pr(1 \text{ contact and } I(t) = m - 1)$$
$$= Pr(1 \text{ contact} | I(t) = m - 1) Pr(I(t) = m - 1)$$
$$= \beta(m - 1)(N - (m - 1))\Delta t \, p_{m-1}(t)$$

by Assumption 3.

The probability of event (A) is computed similarly:

$$Pr(A) = (0 \text{ contacts and } I(t) = m)$$
$$= (0 \text{ contacts} | I(t) = m) Pr(I(t) = m)$$
$$= (1 - Pr(1 \text{ contact} | I(t) = m)) Pr(I(t) = m)$$
$$= (1 - \beta m(N - m) \Delta t) \, p_m(t).$$

These equations yield the basic relationship

$$p_m(t + \Delta t) = (1 - \beta m(N - m) \Delta t)p_m(t) + \beta(m - 1)(N - m + 1)\Delta t \, p_{m-1}(t) \quad (49)$$

which may be rewritten as

$$\frac{p_m(t + \Delta t) - p_m(t)}{\Delta t} = -\beta m(N - m)p_m(t) + \beta(m - 1)(N - m + 1)p_{m-1}(t). \quad (50)$$

Now let $\Delta t \to 0$ in Eq. (50) obtain, as a limit, the differential equation

$$\frac{dp_m(t)}{dt} = -\beta m(N - m)p_m(t) + \beta(m - 1)(N - m + 1)p_{m-1}(t). \quad (51)$$

The probabilistic model consists of this collection of differential equations, one each for $m = 1, 2, \ldots, N$ together with the initial conditions of Eq. (47).

## B. Deductions from the Model

Examine the differential equation (51) first in the case $m = 1$. The equation takes the form

$$\frac{dp_1(t)}{dt} = -\beta(1)(N - 1)p_1(t) + \beta(0)(N + 1)p_0(t) = -\beta(N - 1)p_1(t). \quad (52)$$

which has solution

$$p_1(t) = e^{-\beta(N-1)t}. \quad (53)$$

The first prediction of this model is that there is always a positive probability that the epidemic does not spread beyond the original infective person, but that this probability decreases exponentially toward zero as time continues. This prediction follows from the fact that $\beta(N - 1)$ is a positive constant and from knowledge of the exponential function $e^{-\beta(N-1)t}$.

Next consider the case $m = 2$. The differential equation (51) then has the form

$$\frac{dp_2}{dt} = -\beta(2)(N-2)p_2(t) + \beta(1)(N-2+1)p_1(t) \tag{54}$$

$$= -2\beta(N-2)p_2(t) + (N-1)\beta e^{-\beta(N-1)t}$$

so that

$$\frac{dp_2}{dt} + 2\beta(N-2)p_2(t) = \beta(N-1)e^{-\beta(N-1)t}. \tag{55}$$

Equation (55) is a first-order linear differential equation. It can be solved directly (see Appendix V) by making use of an integrating factor. In this case, the factor is $e^{2\beta(N-2)t}$ and the solution is found to be, using $p_2(0) = 0$, to be

$$p_2(t) = \frac{N-1}{N-3}[1 - e^{-\beta(N-3)t}]e^{-\beta(N-1)t}. \tag{56}$$

This procedure can be continued to find $p_3(t)$ as the solution of the differential equation obtained by setting $m = 3$ in Eq. (51) and making use of the explicit form of $p_2(t)$ together with the initial condition $p_3(0) = 0$. The corresponding differential equation is

$$\frac{dp_3(t)}{dt} = -3\beta(N-3)p_3(t) + 2\beta(N-2)\frac{(N-1)}{(N-3)}[1 - e^{-\beta(N-3)t}]e^{-\beta(N-1)t} \tag{57}$$

and the solution is

$$p_3(t) = \frac{(N-1)(N-2)}{(N-3)(N-4)(N-5)} \frac{(N-5) - 2(N-4)e^{-\beta(N-3)t} + (N-3)e^{-2\beta(N-4)t}}{e^{\beta(N-1)t}}. \tag{58}$$

In theory, we could continue in this fashion to obtain $p_4(t), p_5(t), \ldots, p_N(t)$ as explicit functions of $t$. The computations become formidable very quickly, however, and this is not an efficient procedure if $N$ is moderately large. A more sophisticated mathematical technique permits a direct computation of the complex formula for $p_m(t)$ where $m$ is any integer between 1 and $N$; the details can be found in Chapter 5 of Norman Bailey's *The Mathematical Theory of Epidemics* (see References).

## C. A Comparison of Deterministic and Probabilistic Models

In the discussion of the pure-birth process given in Chapter 9, it was noted that the expected value of the population as given by the probabilistic model coincided exactly with the predicted value from the deterministic model. For models of epidemics, the expected values are, in general, different from the solutions of the corresponding deterministic differential equations. We shall illustrate this for the models of a simple epidemic.

For each time $t$, the number of infectives is a random variable taking on values $1, 2, \ldots, N$ with probabilities given by $p_m(t)$, $m = 1, 2, \ldots, N$. The expected value of the number of infectives is

$$\varphi(t) = \sum_{m=1}^{N} m p_m(t). \tag{59}$$

The deterministic model predicts that the number of infectives at time $t$ is given by the formula

$$I(t) = \frac{N}{1 + (N - 1)e^{-\beta N t}}. \tag{8}$$

In this section we will show that the two functions $\varphi(t)$ and $I(t)$ are not identical. There are a number of ways of doing this. One method would be to calculate $p_m(t)$ as an explicit function of $t$ for each $m$ and then use these to obtain an analytical description of $\varphi(t)$. As already noted, this approach leads to considerable computational difficulties. An alternative approach is to find some time $t$ at which $\varphi$ and $I$ exhibit different properties. We will adopt this approach and show in particular that $\varphi''(0)$ and $I''(0)$ are different numbers.

Note first that the deterministic model gives

$$I'(t) = \beta I(t)(N - I(t))$$

so that

$$I''(t) = \beta[I'(t)(N - I(t)) + I(t)(-I'(t))]$$
$$= \beta I'(t)(N - 2I(t)).$$

These equations give

$$I(0) = 1,$$
$$I'(0) = \beta(N - 1),$$

and

$$I''(0) = \beta\beta(N - 1)(N - 2) = \beta^2(N - 1)(N - 2).$$

Since $p_m(0) = 0$ if $m \neq 1$ and $p_1(0) = 1$, we have $\varphi(0) = 1$. Thus $\varphi(0) = I(0)$. Examining the fundamental differential equation for the probabilistic model of a simple epidemic

$$\frac{dp_m(t)}{dt} = -\beta m(N - m)p_m(t) + \beta(m - 1)(N - m + 1)p_{m-1}(t), \tag{51}$$

we find that

$$p_1'(0) = -\beta(1)(N - 1)p_1(0) + \beta(0)(N - 1 + 1)p_0(0) = -\beta(N - 1), \tag{60}$$

while

$$p_2'(0) = -\beta(2)(N - 2)p_2(0) + \beta(1)(N - 2 + 1)p_1(0) = \beta(N - 1) \tag{61}$$

and

$$p_m'(0) = 0 \qquad \text{for all } m \geqslant 3. \tag{62}$$

Now we can calculate the derivative of the expected value:

$$\varphi'(t) = \frac{d\varphi}{dt} = \frac{d}{dt}\left(\sum_{m=1}^{N} mp_m(t)\right)$$

$$= \sum_{m=1}^{N} \frac{d}{dt}(mp_m(t)) \tag{63}$$

$$= \sum_{m=1}^{N} mp_m'(t)$$

$$= p_1'(t) + 2p_2'(t) + 3p'(t) + \cdots + Np_N'(t).$$

Evaluation of the derivative at time $t = 0$ gives

$$\varphi'(0) = p_1'(0) + 2p_2'(0) + 3p_3'(0) + \cdots + Np_N'(0)$$
$$= -\beta(N-1) + 2\beta(N-1) + 3(0) + 4(0) + \cdots + N(0) \tag{64}$$
$$= \beta(N-1).$$

So far we have succeeded in showing that $\varphi$ and $I$ agree to the extent that $\varphi(0) = I(0)$ and $\varphi'(0) = I'(0)$. Finally, we evaluate $\varphi''(0)$. First, compute the expression for $\varphi''(t)$:

$$\varphi''(t) = \frac{d\varphi'(t)}{dt} = \sum_{m=1}^{N} mp_m''(t). \tag{65}$$

Now

$$p_m''(t) = \frac{dp_m'(t)}{dt} = \frac{d}{dt}(-\beta m(N-m)p_m(t) + \beta(m-1)(N-m+1)p_{m-1}(t)) \tag{66}$$

$$= -\beta m(N-m)p_m'(t) + \beta(m-1)(N-m+1)p_{m-1}'(t).$$

In evaluating $\varphi''(0)$ there will be precisely four nonzero terms in the sum of the right-hand side of Eq. (65). These will occur when the index $m$ is 1, 2, and 3:

$$\varphi''(0) = 1(-\beta)(1)(N-1)p_1'(0) + 2(-\beta(2)(N-2)p_2'(0))$$
$$\quad + 2\beta(1)(N-2+1)p_1'(0) + 3(\beta(3-1)(N-3+1)p_2'(0))$$
$$= -\beta(N-1)(-\beta(N-1)) + 2[-2\beta(N-2)\beta(N-1)] \tag{67}$$
$$\quad + \beta(N-1)(-\beta(N-1)) + 3[2\beta(N-2)\beta(N-1)]$$
$$= \beta^2(N-1)(N-3).$$

Thus we have $I''(0) = \beta^2(N-1)(N-2)$ while $\varphi''(0) = \beta^2(N-1)(N-3)$ so that the functions $I(t)$ and $\varphi(t)$ are not identical.

Note that the ratio $I''(0)/\varphi''(0) = (N-2)/(N-3)$ is greater than one, so that the function $I'(t)$ is initially growing at a faster rate that $\varphi'(t)$. In fact, it can be shown that for all $t > 0$, $I(t)$ is always greater than $\varphi(t)$. Note also that for large values of $N$, the ratio is close to 1, so that the graphs of the functions $I(t)$

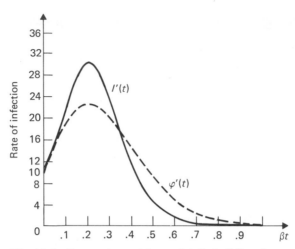

Fig. 13.6   Comparison of deterministic (solid) and probabilistic (broken line) epidemic curves for a simple epidemic with $S_0 = 10$.

and $\varphi(t)$ as functions of $t$ will be similar, at least close to $t = 0$. The graph of $\varphi(t)$ does not exhibit the same symmetry as the graph of $I(t)$, but the times at which both curves reach their maximum values are close together. The graphs of these functions for $N = 11$ are shown in Fig. 13.6.

The deterministic model of a simple epidemic offered a direct solution with no great mathematical difficulty. The probabilistic model of the same simple epidemic involves considerably greater complication. The development of a probabilistic model for the general epidemic as discussed in Section II.C is beyond the scope of the mathematics introduced in this text, as are models which are even more realistic in their assumptions.

## IV. THE DEVELOPMENT OF MATHEMATICAL EPIDEMIOLOGY

In an historical sketch of epidemics written in the early nineteenth century, a Vermont country doctor, Joseph A. Gallup [1815] noted that

> Epidemic diseases, and their sequelae, occupy a very large portion of the catalogue of human maladies. No section of the globe is exempt from their ravages, and no society of individuals has been excused from weeds of mourning by the devastation of these scourges of man. They follow wherever the footsteps of man lead the way, and his traces are bestrewed with monumental inscriptions of human frailty.

Records of epidemics appear in the literature of the ancient Greeks and the Bible reports epidemics occurring among the Egyptians several thousand years earlier. Statistical information on the incidence and locality of cases of infectious diseases was first collected by two Englishmen, the statistician John Graunt

(1620–1674) and the political economist and physician Sir William Petty (1623–1687) during the seventeenth century.

In 1840, William Farr (1807–1883), another English statistician and commissioner of the census, published some of his studies on statistical information which he hoped would lead to the discovery of empirical laws on the growth and decline of epidemics. By a detailed examination of the spatial and temporal pattern of outbreaks of cholera, the English physician John Snow (1813–1858) demonstrated in 1855 that the disease was being spread by the contamination of water supplies. (Snow is also remembered as the man who introduced into English surgical practice the use of ether as an anesthetic.) In 1873, William Budd (1811–1880), established a similar manner for proving the spread of typhoid. Budd, another English physician, advocated disinfection as a method of preventing the spread of contagious diseases and recommended measures that stamped out Asiatic cholera and rinderpest in his country.

A coherent, predictive theory of epidemics requires both the development of sufficiently powerful mathematical techniques and the formation of sufficiently precise hypotheses about the spread of diseases that are suitable for expression in mathematical terms. The research achievements of biological scientists, especially those of Louis Pasteur and Robert Koch in the second half of the nineteenth century, established the physical bases for the cause of infectious disease and made possible both the mathematical modeling of epidemics and, more importantly, the public health measures that have lessened the chances of widespread epidemics.

Pasteur (1822–1895), the famous French chemist, is known for his discovery that bacteria were the cause of anthrax, for his development of successful vaccines against anthrax and cholera, and for his pioneering treatment of hydrophobia in man and rabies in dogs. Pasteur also isolated the bacilii causing two distinct diseases of silkworms and found a method of preventing the spread of these diseases, thereby saving the French silk industry.

A German physician and bacteriologist, Koch (1843–1910), was the first person to isolate and obtain a pure culture of the anthrax bacillus, to isolate tubercle bacillus, and to identify the comma bacillus as the cause of Asiatic cholera. He traveled to South America to study rinderpest, to India to study bubonic plague and cholera, and to Africa to learn more about malaria and sleeping sickness. Koch was awarded the 1905 Nobel prize in physiology and medicine.

The first deterministic model of epidemics appeared in the English medical journal *Lancet* in 1906. This model, created by W. H. Hamer, stressed the fundamental assumptions that the continuing spread of an epidemic depends on the number of susceptibles and the rate of contact between susceptibles and infectives. Hamer's mathematical assumptions, in one modified form or another, appear in almost all deterministic and probabilistic models of epidemics.

Beginning in 1911, Sir Ronald Ross published a series of books and papers developing a detailed deterministic model of malaria. A British physician born in India in 1857, Ross began his research into malaria in 1892 and after five years of patient work was able to piece together the life history of the malarial parasite in mosquitoes. Ross' work earned him the 1902 Nobel prize for physiology and medicine. In addition to his medical and mathematical writings, Ross published a novel, was a professor of tropical sanitation, and was director-in-chief of the Ross Institute and Hospital for Tropical Diseases in London. He died in 1932.

More elaborate deterministic models were developed by Kermack and McKendrick in a succession of papers published between 1927 and 1939. Perhaps their most important discovery was the Threshold Theorem discussed here in Section II.C. This result helped researchers account for the absence or occurrence of outbreaks of many epidemic diseases. Although McKendrick is best known for his work on deterministic models, he was also the first person to publish (in 1926) a probabilistic account of an epidemic process. Other pioneers in the use of probabilistic models were M. Greenwood in England and Lowell J. Reed and Wade Hampton Frost in the United States.

There were a number of important advances in mathematical epidemiology in the 1940's and 1950's, including Norman T. J. Bailey's complete solution of the probabilistic model for a simple epidemic (1950). In 1957, Bailey published the first textbook giving a systematic treatment of the whole field of mathematical modeling of epidemics. In a survey article ten years later, Klaus Dietz noted that since Bailey's book appeared, "the contributions to this subject have themselves behaved like an epidemic." Bailey has recently written a subsequent edition, under the title *The Mathematical Theory of Infectious Diseases*, which provides a modern survey of this fast-growing discipline.

## EXERCISES

### DETERMINISTIC MODEL OF SIMPLE EPIDEMIC

1. Use the relation $dI/dt = \beta I(N - I)$ to sketch a graph of $dI/dt$ as a function of $I$. Can you draw any conclusions about the model from this graph?

2. Derive Eq. (8) from Eq. (7).

3. Show that Eq. (6) gives $I''(t) = \beta^2 I(N - I)(N - 2I)$. Does this result imply that the maximum value of $I'(t)$ necessarily occurs when $I = N/2$?

4. Show that Eq. (11) can be derived from Eq. (8) and the relation $dI/dt = \beta I(N - I)$ without further differentiation.

5. Discuss how you would obtain a numerical value for $\beta$ from observed information concerning the number of infectives and susceptibles at various times.

6. Show that $I'(t_{max} + \alpha) = I'(t_{max} - \alpha)$ for all $\alpha$; that is, verify the claim that the epidemic curve is symmetric about the vertical line through $t_{max}$.

7. Show that $S(t)$ drops below 1 as soon as $t$ exceeds $2t_{max}$. In what sense does this observation justify the claim that "the simple epidemic is over by time $2t_{max}$"?

8. Generalize the simple model by allowing $\beta$ to be a continuous function, $\beta(t)$, of time $t$, rather than a simple constant. In particular, discuss the consequences of the model in each of the following cases:

a) $\beta(t)$ is an increasing function; for example, $\beta(t) = t$.

b) $\beta(t)$ is a decreasing function; for example, $\beta(t) = e^{-t}$.

c) $\beta(t)$ is a periodic function; for example, $\beta(t) = \cos t$.

9. Generalize the simple model to situations in which the size of the total community changes during the course of the epidemic because of births or from deaths due to causes other than the infectious disease. In particular, investigate the simple model if $N(t)$ is growing

a) exponentially;                                        b) logistically.

10. Investigate the simple model if $I(0) = I_0$ is greater than 1. Find analogues of Eq. (8) and (11) in particular.

11. Sketch the epidemic curve if $N = 1000$, $I_0 = 100$ and $\beta = .003$. Use the results of Exercise 10.

12. When the early stages of an epidemic are observed, steps are often taken to prevent its spread. Suppose, for example, that public health officials administer vaccines at a constant rate of $\alpha$ innoculations per time unit. Suppose this program continues until the entire population is either vaccinated or infected. The mathematical model in this situation might take the form

$$\frac{dI}{dt} = \beta I(t)(N - \alpha t - I(t))$$

since $N - \alpha t - I(t)$ represents the number of susceptibles.

a) Why is this a reasonable model?

b) Show that an epidemic described by this model ends when $t = N/\alpha$.

c) What predictions can you make from this model without solving the differential equation explicitly?

d) Can you solve the differential equation?

## DETERMINISTIC MODEL OF GENERAL EPIDEMIC

13. A simpler model than the one discussed in the text is based on the equations

$$\frac{dS}{dt} = -\beta S_0 I,$$

$$\frac{dI}{dt} = \beta S_0 I - rI,$$

$$\frac{dR}{dt} = rI,$$

where $\beta$ and $r$ are again positive constants measuring the rates at which susceptibles become infected and infective individuals are removed.

a) Determine $S, I$, and $R$ as explicit functions of $t$ if initial numbers are $S_0, I_0$, and $R_0 = N - S_0 - I_0$.

b) Prove that if $\beta S_0 < r$, the disease will not produce an epidemic.

c) Discuss what happens in the case $\beta S_0 > r$.

14. In discussing the limiting behavior of $R, S$, and $I$ we made use of a theorem which states that if $f(t) \leqslant N$ for all $t$ and if $f$ is monotonically nondecreasing, then there exists a number $L \leqslant N$ such that $\lim_{t \to \infty} f(t) = L$. Find a proof of this theorem.

15. Use Eq. (27) to sketch a graph showing the relation between $S$ and $R$.

16. Apply the bisection technique to the function $f(x) = x^2 - 2$ to find an approximation of $\sqrt{2}$ accurate to two decimal places.

17. Apply the bisection technique to Eq. (39) with $S_0 = 1000$, $N = 1001$, $r = .9$, and $\beta = .002$ to estimate $S_\infty$ to the nearest integer.

18. Newton's method is a technique for finding roots of the equation $f(x) = 0$ when $f$ is a differentiable function. It often is a more efficient technique than the bisection method. Most calculus texts will contain some discussion of Newton's method. Investigate how you might apply Newton's method to calculate $S_\infty$.

19. Equation (34) defines $I$ as a continuous function of $S$,

$$I = g(S) = N - S + p \log\left(\frac{S}{S_0}\right).$$

Show that $g(S_0) > 0$ and that $g(S_0/e^{p^N}) < 0$.

20. Find the exact solution to Eq. (41). See Bailey's text if you get stuck.

21. Solve Eq. (41) if a Taylor series approximation for $e^x$ is used when the series is terminated after

a) One term;

b) Two terms;

c) Four terms.

22. Show that the epidemic curve is not symmetric about any vertical line.

23. Use Eqs. (43) and (44) and the approximation $R_\infty \sim 2v$ to obtain various estimates for $R_\infty$ in the case $\beta = .001$, $r = .9$, $N = 1001$, $I_0 = 1$. Compare results with the number obtained by using the bisection technique.

24. Repeat Exercise 23 using the data from Exercise 17.

## PROBABILISTIC MODEL FOR SIMPLE EPIDEMIC

25. Graph $p_2(t)$ as a function of $t$. For what value of $t$ does it reach a maximum?

26. Carry out the details of determining $p_3(t)$ and graph the function.

27. Determine $p_4(t)$ and sketch its graph.

28. Show that Eq. (51) is valid for $m = 1$ although the derivation given for Eq. (51) does not quite work.

29. Prove that $p_0(t) = 0$ for all $t$ for the given model.

30. Work out some details of the model if the initial population of infectives, $I_0$, is greater than 1.

31. Can $\varphi(t)$ be computed using the technique of Exercise 51 of Chapter 9?

32. What conclusions can you make about the variance of the number of infectives for the probabilistic model with $I_0 = 1$?

33. Investigate Bailey's explicit solution of the probabilistic model.

## SUGGESTED PROJECTS

1. Modify the deterministic model to allow for a constant, nonzero infectious period; that is, assume that a constant number of days must pass between the time a person becomes infective and the time he can transmit the disease to others. Analyze such a model and interpret the mathematical conclusions.

2. Generalize the deterministic model of Section II.C to allow for a nonconstant population, $N(t)$. In particular, investigate the model if the population is growing exponentially or logistically.

3. Formulate a probabilistic version of the deterministic model of Section II.C and analyze it in the spirit of Section III.

4. Soper proposed a mathematical model for the spread of measles that he believed adequately explained the recurrence of measles epidemics. Study his model and some of the corrections and extensions that have been made.

5. How would you modify the assumptions of the epidemic models to build a model about the spread of rumors or of technological innovations?

## REFERENCES

### EPIDEMICS AND HISTORY

Cartwright, Frederick F., *Disease and History* (New York: Crowell, 1972).

Defoe, Daniel, *A Journal of the Plague Year* (London: Oxford University Press, 1969).

Gallup, Joseph A., *Sketches of Epidemic Disease in the State of Vermont* (Boston: Wait and Sons, 1815).

McNeill, William H., *Plagues and Peoples* (Garden City, New York: Doubleday, 1976).

Thucydides, *History of the Peloponnesian War*, translated by B. Jowett in F. R. B. Godolphin, ed., *Greek Historians*, Volume I (New York: Random House, 1942).

Zinsser, Hans, *Rats, Lice and History*, Fourth Edition (London: Routledge, 1942).

### PAPERS OF HISTORICAL INTEREST

Bailey, Norman T. J., "A simple stochastic epidemic," *Biometrika* **37** (1950), 193–202.

Kermack, W. D., and A. G. McKendrick, "A contribution to the mathematical theory of epidemics," *Journal of the Royal Statistical Society* **115** (1927), 700–721.

Hamer, W. H., "Epidemic disease in England," *Lancet* **1** (1906), 723–739.

McKendrick, A. G., "Applications of mathematics to medical problems," *Proceedings of the Edinburgh Mathematical Society* **44** (1926), 98–130.

Ross, R., *The Prevention of Malaria*, Second Edition (London: Murray, 1911).

Soper, H. E., "Interpretation of periodicity in disease-prevalence," *Journal of Royal Statistical Society* **92** (1929), 34–73.

## TEXTS AND SURVEY ARTICLES

Bailey, Norman T. J., "Approaches to the control of infectious disease," in J. Gani, ed., *Perspectives in Probability and Statistics* (London: Applied Probability Trust, 1975).

———, *The Mathematical Theory of Epidemics* (London: Griffin, 1957).

———, *The Mathematical Theory of Infectious Diseases* (London: Griffin, 1975).

Bartlett, Maurice S., *Stochastic Population Models in Ecology and Epidemiology* (London: Methuen, 1960).

Dietz, K., "Epidemics and Rumours: A Survey," *Journal of Royal Statistical Society* **130** (1967), 505–528.

Poole, Robert W., "Epidemics and disease," in *Introduction to Quantitative Ecology* (New York: McGraw-Hill, 1974) Chapter 8. Good discussion of how models must be modified for epidemics in nonhuman populations.

Waltman, Paul, *Deterministic Threshold Models in the Theory of Epidemics* (New York: Springer-Verlag, 1974).

# 14

# Roulette Wheels and Hospital Beds:

A Computer Simulation of Operating and Recovery Room Usage

We are more than half what we are by imitation. The great point is to choose good models and to study them with care.

Philip Dormer Stanhope, Earl of Chesterfield

## I. INTRODUCTION

### A. The Need for Simulation

In previous chapters we have seen that a wide variety of problems can be successfully attacked by modeling their essential features with mathematical concepts and then using the analytical tools of the mathematician to make predictions about a system's behavior. There are many problems in the social and physical sciences, however, which do not appear to be amenable to solution by currently available analytic methods.

The mathematical modeling approach can break down in two essentially different ways. If we re-examine the basic diagram for model building (Fig. 14.1), we note where the difficulties may arise.

In the first place, we must translate the important features of the real-world phenomenon into mathematics. But which branch of mathematics do we choose? For some problems, there seem to exist several different classes of techniques from which we can choose. A deterministic approach using differential equations may suggest itself, or perhaps a probabilistic scheme using Markov chains seems useful. The history of scientific thought reveals many instances when a branch of pure mathematics was seized upon as the proper vehicle for a study of real-world phenomena. To develop his theory of general relativity, for example, Albert Einstein made use of non-Euclidean geometries, a subject previously considered by many to be frivolous and entirely lacking in applicable content. For some real-world systems, however, the complexity and variety of the interactions among the important variables—as we understand them—do not seem to fit any existing part of mathematics. In such an instance, the modeler may have to create new mathematical tools. There is much evidence that many important parts of mathematics were developed to provide models for problems in the physical sciences; the same process is beginning to occur in the social sciences as well.

A second kind of difficulty occurs in taking the step from mathematical model to mathematical conclusions. The modeler may believe, for example, that the problem he is interested in can best be formulated as a question in geometric topology. It may turn out, however, that the topological question has not yet been settled, but is an unsolved research problem in mathematics. The work of Isaac Newton provides an example of this sort of difficulty. In the

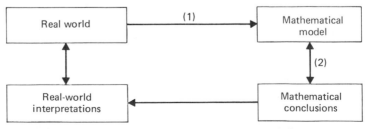

**Fig. 14.1**   The schematic diagram illustrating the modeling process.

seventeenth century, Newton used his celebrated laws of motion and gravitational attraction to formulate a mathematical model for the relative motion of two bodies. The model was a differential equation which required 12 integrations to solve explicitly. These were worked out by Newton and, taking the bodies to be the sun and a planet in the solar system, it was shown that the model's predicted behavior of planetary orbits was in precise agreement with the laws of planetary motion that had been empirically determined by Johann Kepler. This achievement was one of the great milestones in the history of thought. When Newton turned to the analysis of the interactions of three bodies (for example, the interaction of gravitational attractions of the earth, moon, and sun), his laws led to another differential equation. An explicit solution for this equation required 18 successive integrations. Newton was unable to carry out the integrations completely. Neither was any other mathematician, physicist, or astronomer during the next 200 years. Finally, in the late nineteenth Century, Henri Poincaré showed that it was impossible to get an exact solution for Newton's equation; further progress on the problem could only be made by approximation techniques.

Thus the mathematical modeler may have to wait until new branches of mathematics are created or unsolved problems in existing branches are resolved before he can obtain a valid and useful model. In many real-world situations, however, there is a demand that a "solution" to the problem be found immediately.

In such situations, the modeler will often abandon theoretical formulations for simulation models. Simulation is a dynamic act of imitation of one or more essential features of a system. In a simulation we try to copy the behavior of a process where the possible causes and outcomes are fairly well understood while the relationships among them may be quite complex and incapable of simple analytic description.

It is easier to grasp the concept of simulation by examining several examples than by attempting to present additional definitions.

## B.  Examples of Simulation

A company that had been manufacturing elevators for many years decided to produce electric buses to be used for public transportation. After some preliminary testing, the company built a prototype electric bus and offered it to the city of San Francisco for a free trial demonstration. Mass transit officials in the city wanted to know how well the electric bus would perform on a heavily traveled route that climbs a steep hill. They discussed replacing the gasoline-powered bus that normally serviced that route with the electric bus for a day so they might assess how well the new bus would climb or fail to climb the hill when it was filled with passengers.

The city's safety officer objected that if the electric bus failed and slid down the hill out of control, many people could be injured. He suggested that the transit officials simulate an actual ascent of the hill by loading the electric bus with sandbags whose total weight and distribution inside the bus would resemble a busload of people. A test run could then be made with the sandbags. If the bus failed, the social costs of the accident would then be far less than if the bus were crammed with people.

The suggested test run is a simulation of an actual one. Most of the important features of an actual run are present in the simulated one. If the bus loaded with sandbags should fail, then it is likely that the same bus with an equal weight of humans aboard would also fail. But what if the bus succeeds in making it to the top of the hill and back down again without incident during the simulation? Is this a guarantee that it will do as well with living cargo? After all, the people may move around inside the bus while it is moving and may even take it into their heads to begin rocking the vehicle. The sandbags cannot imitate this behavior. Even if we feel that the motion of the passengers is not a critical factor, there is still a question of how many simulated runs we should try before declaring the bus safe. We shall return to these kinds of objections later in the chapter.

As a second example of simulation, consider the engineer who first proposed designing a giant jet aircraft with the engines mounted on the tail of the plane instead of under the front wings. The cost of building a prototype plane of the actual size to be marketed would cost millions of dollars, all of which would be wasted if the plane couldn't get off the ground or crashed shortly after takeoff on a test flight. The engineer has the problem of testing his design without actually building the plane.

A possible solution for him is to construct a small, scaled-down version of the plane and to test this model in a wind tunnel. The stability of the model aircraft can be tested in a variety of wind conditions approximating those the full-sized plane might encounter in the air. If the model plane cracks up every time it is subjected to the equivalent of a 25-knot wind, perhaps there is something fundamentally wrong in its design. On the other hand, if the model performs well in the wind-tunnel experiments, the engineer has increased faith that his idea is a good one. In the experiment, the model plane simulates a real plane and the wind tunnel simulates actual wind conditions. The experiment has the advantage of being relatively inexpensive to perform, but it has drawbacks too. The tunnel may not provide a sufficiently realistic imitation of atmospheric conditions. The model plane is, of course, of a different size and made of different materials than the plane it is meant to simulate. The full-sized plane may not necessarily behave in the same fashion as its scaled-down version. Still, simulation may be the only reasonable, safe, quick, and inexpensive way to test the plane's design.

In this chapter, we will examine, in some detail, an example of a computer simulation. By now you are familiar with the use of the computer as a tool in the analysis of a theoretical model, principally as a source of high-speed numerical computation. In simulation experiments, the computer is employed as a substitute for a theoretical model. We define a set of numerical-valued variables which are to represent the principal features of the system to be simulated. Then we formulate a computer program as a set of instructions, representing the decision rules or laws that determine how the system's features are to be modified as time goes on. In principle, this sort of computation can be carried out by hand, using pencil and paper, but the computer gives us the enormous advantages of speed, tirelessness, and the lack of forgetting intermediate results. The details of a particular computer simulation will be presented in Part V. First, we need to explain the problems we hope to solve by a simulation.

## II. THE PROBLEMS OF INTEREST

The diagnosis and treatment of many medical disorders require that a patient be hospitalized for one or more days. One of the major constraints on the service which a hospital can render to the surrounding community is, then, the number of hospital beds it has. If often happens that a person with a non-emergency medical problem may have to wait several days to be admitted to the hospital because all its beds are filled.

When this kind of problem begins to affect too many patients of too many of the doctors on its staff, the hospital administration may plan to construct new hospital facilities to provide an increase in the number of its beds. If the hospital decides to expand its bed complement, then it must also consider the increased demands that will be made on other aspects of its operations. It must determine whether its current medical and nonmedical facilities are adequate to provide for the larger number of patients who will be in the hospital each day. The hospital must decide, for example, how many new nurses to hire, how much new equipment to order, whether to expand the pathology and pharmacy departments, and so on.

In this chapter, we will examine how simulation techniques can help assess the increased need for operating-room (OR) and recovery-room (RR) facilities that an expanded bed complement will produce. This was the problem studied by Homer H. Schmitz of the Deaconess Hospital in St. Louis, Missouri and N. K. Kwak of St. Louis University. Deaconess Hospital was planning to add 144 medical-surgical beds to its currently existing facilities in the early 1970's. Schmitz and Kwak formulated three primary questions:

1. How many more surgical procedures will Deaconess Hospital perform because of the increased bed capacity?

2. How much operating-room time and space will the surgical procedures require?

3. How much recovery-room time and space will the surgical procedures require?

The first question was answered by a relatively simple extrapolation technique, while insight into the other problems was gained through a computer simulation.

Homer H. Schmitz,
Vice President and
Director of Management
Services at Deaconess
Hospital in St. Louis,
Missouri. Schmitz has
administrative
responsibility for
14 departments of the
hospital, serves on the
faculty of St. Louis
University in both the
College of Business
Administration and the
School of Nursing and
Allied Health, and is the
author of more than
25 articles in the health-
care field.

N. K. Kwak, Professor of
Management Sciences at
St. Louis University.
Professor Kwak received his
Ph.D. degree in economics
from the University of
Southern California. He is
the author of a text on
mathematical programming,
two research monographs,
and numerous articles and
reviews in professional
journals.

## III. PROJECTING THE NUMBER OF SURGICAL PROCEDURES

Schmitz and Kwak [1972] began their study by collecting information on hospital procedures in effect during the period when the expanded bed complement was still in its planning stages. An analysis of the hospital's records for 1970 indicated that 42 percent of medical-surgical (M/S) patients actually had surgery. Assuming that the relative proportions of medical and surgical patients would not be affected by an increase in bed complement, it is a simple matter to project that if 144 M/S beds are added, then approximately 60 of them (144 × .42) will be utilized by patients who have surgery.

A critical factor in estimating the number of surgical procedures that would be performed is the length of stay in the hospital for each patient. This, of course, would depend on the nature of the surgery. For example, in 1970, 4.5 percent of the total number of surgical procedures performed at the Deaconess Hospital were ophthalmology cases. The average length of stay for these cases was 7.4 days. Of the 60 new beds that will be used by surgical patients, we can estimate that about .045 × 60 = 2.7 beds will be used by ophthalmology patients. Imagine that a particular bed is set aside for ophthalmology patients. An average patient will occupy that bed for 7.4 days. Thus, during the year 49 patients (365/7.4 = 49) will be able to be treated for each ophthalmology bed. Since there will be 2.7 new ophthalmology beds, during the year there will be 132 (2.7 × 49) new ophthalmology surgical procedures.

Using the assumptions of full-bed utilization and the same patient mix in the future as was experienced in the past, Schmitz and Kwak estimated the increases in surgical procedures for six other major types of surgery in the same way as for the ophthalmology cases. Their results are presented in Table 14.1.

These extrapolations were based on an actual count of 6293 surgical procedures performed in 1970. Adding the projected total of 3376 new procedures, we arrive at an estimate of 9669 projected surgical procedures when the new bed complement is fully utilized.

The daily surgical load is then determined by dividing the annual number of surgical procedures by the number of days in the year. Thus, the hospital

**Table 14.1**   Increase in surgical cases based on increased bed count

| Type of surgery | Increase in number of cases per year |
|---|---|
| Ophthalmology | 132 |
| Gynecology | 282 |
| Urology | 264 |
| Orthopedic | 202 |
| Ear-nose-throat (ENT) | 1098 |
| Dental surgery | 715 |
| Other major surgery | 683 |
| Total projected increase | 3376 |

can expect to have 9669/365 surgical procedures on an average day.  For the simulation procedure, this number is rounded off to the next integer, 27.

## IV. ESTIMATING OPERATING-ROOM DEMANDS

### A.  Length of Stay in Operating Room

How many operating rooms will be necessary to perform 27 surgical procedures each day?  This will depend on several factors, such as the time of day of the first operation, the length of time necessary to prepare an operating room for a new patient after an old one has left, and the number of hours per day that surgeons are willing to work.  A principal factor will be the length of time each operation requires.

Let us illustrate with some crude estimates.  Suppose each operation (including make-ready time for the next patient) takes exactly one hour.  Suppose also that the surgeons will work only during the period between 8 o'clock

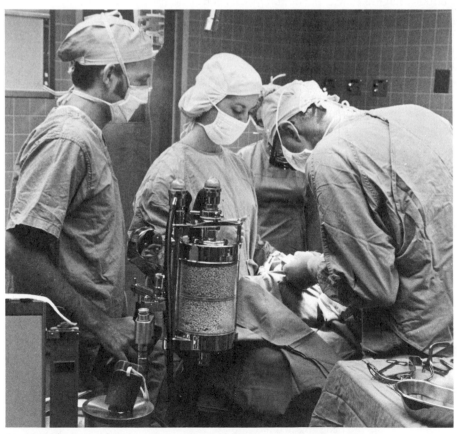

An operating room in use at Deaconess Hospital.

in the morning and 5 o'clock in the afternoon. Then each operating room can be used for 9 hours each day, so 9 surgical procedures can be completed in each room. It would then take 3 operating rooms to accomodate the expected 27 daily procedures.

Of course, in actual practice not every operation takes one hour. A tonsillectomy requires much less time than a heart transplant, for example. We might argue, however, that our crude estimate of 3 operating rooms would hold up if the *average* length of an operation is one hour. As we saw in our study of expected value in Chapter 9, there are difficulties that arise if we look only at average values. There can be quite a variation in the lengths of operations that still produce an average of one hour. Also, although the average length for the 9669 procedures may well be close to an hour, this may not be the case for a randomly selected group of 27 of them.

Why do we say "randomly selected"? Although the hospital can estimate fairly accurately the total number of different types of surgical procedures to be performed over a 12-month period, it cannot predict the order in which the patients will present themselves for treatment. On some days, there may be a relatively large number of patients who need operations that will last more than two hours, while on other days almost all the procedures will be relatively minor ones. The hospital must be ready to handle these deviations from the average.

It is necessary, then, to examine more carefully the lengths of stays in the operating room. Schmitz and Kwak did this by collecting a sample of 445 surgical patients treated in 1970 at Deaconess Hospital. Data was collected on the type of surgery performed, the length of time spent in the operating room, and the number of days the patient was hospitalized. The percentages of the various types of surgery and the average length of stay for the total population of patients in the hospital were inferred from this sample data; in Section III, we saw how these numbers were used.

In Table 14.2, the actual and relative frequencies for length of stay in the operating room for the 445 patients of the sample are presented.

**Table 14.2**   Length of stay in the operating room

| Length of stay in hours | Frequency | Relative frequency |
|---|---|---|
| 0.01–0.50 | 181 | 40.7 |
| 0.51–1.00 | 103 | 23.2 |
| 1.01  1.50 | 64 | 14.4 |
| 1.51–2.00 | 42 | 9.4 |
| 2.01–2.50 | 22 | 4.9 |
| 2.51–3.00 | 13 | 2.9 |
| 3.01–3.50 | 8 | 1.8 |
| 3.51–4.00 | 5 | 1.1 |
| More than 4.00 | 7 | 1.6 |
| Total | 445 | 100.0 |

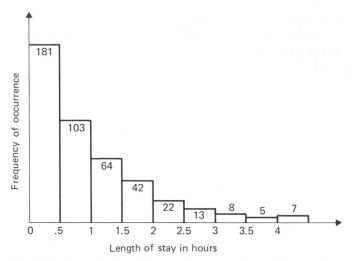

**Fig. 14.2**   Length of stay in operating room observed in sample of 445 patients.

In Table 14.2 and in all subsequent discussion, time segments are given in hundredths of an hour rather than in minutes, because this simplifies the mathematical calculations.  From Table 2, for example, we note that 2.9 percent of all operations lasted between two and one-half hours and three hours.

The data in Table 2 show that the frequency of length of stay tends to decrease as the length of stay increases.  This trend is indicated more sharply in Fig. 14.2 where the frequency is plotted against the length of stay; this kind of graph is called a *histogram.*

Whenever a scientist sees data that shows one variable rapidly diminishing (or increasing) as another variable increases uniformly, he suspects that the two variables are related in an exponential fashion.  A statistical analysis of the data of Table 2 shows that the distribution of times of surgical procedures closely follows a curve given by what probability theorists would call a *negative-exponential distribution* with respect to time.  This is a curve of the form $y = \mu e^{-\mu t}$ where $\mu$ is a positive constant representing the reciprocal of the average length of stay in the operating room.

For such a distribution, the probability that an operation lasts at most $t$ hours is given by

$$P(t) = 1 - e^{-\mu t}.$$

Thus the probability that an operation lasts between $a$ hours and $b$ hours can be computed as $P(b) - P(a)$.  For more details of these kinds of probability distribution, the reader may consult Drake [1967] or any other standard probability text.

Schmitz and Kwak assumed that the length of stay in the operating room would be given accurately by a negative exponential distribution with constant $\mu$ obtained by taking the observed average length of stay (1.03 hours) in their sample of 445 surgical cases. This distribution predicts, for example, that 9.0 percent of the operations will last between $1\frac{1}{2}$ and 2 hours. This compares well with the observed frequency of 9.4 percent in the sample.

## B.  Random Selection of Patients

We come now to the key step in the simulation process. We are not going to perform any actual operations. Rather, we will select "patients" at random and keep track of how long the patient's operation should last. Our patients will be the 1000 integers between 000 and 999, inclusive. Since 2 percent of the patients need operations lasting more than 4 hours (this is determined from the negative-exponential distribution), we must reserve a bloc of 20 of the integers to represent these cases. Let us say that we reserve the bloc from 980 to 999. If the number we select at random falls between these limits, then we pretend to perform an operation lasting more than four hours. If the number selected falls outside these limits, then it belongs to a bloc of numbers representing patients who require an operation for a different length of time.

In Table 14.3, we list the type of surgery, associated length of time, frequency of length of time, and the bloc of numbers reserved for it.

One problem remains. Once we determine that a patient is to be in the operating room for a time, say, between 1.51 and 2.00 hours, how long do we actually keep him there? Evidence shows that the average length of an operation requiring less than one-half hour is .47 hours; we will round this number off to .5 for the simulation. For the other categories, we will take as the average length of time the midpoint of the time interval. Thus we arrive at the simulated

**Table 14.3**  Assignment of random numbers

| Type of surgery | Time interval | Relative frequency | Random number bloc |
|---|---|---|---|
| ENT | | 15.8 | 000–157 |
| Urology (to RR) | | 08.4 | 158–241 |
| Urology (no RR) | 0.01–0.50 | 08.5 | 242–326 |
| Ophthalmology (no RR) | | 05.8 | 327–384 |
| All other surgery | 0.51–1.00 | 23.6 | 385–620 |
| " " " | 1.01–1.50 | 14.6 | 621–766 |
| " " " | 1.51–2.00 | 09.0 | 767–856 |
| " " " | 2.01–2.50 | 05.5 | 857–911 |
| " " " | 2.51–3.00 | 03.4 | 912–945 |
| " " " | 3.01–3.50 | 02.1 | 946–966 |
| " " " | 3.51–4.00 | 01.3 | 967–979 |
| " " " | More than 4.00 | 02.0 | 980–999 |

**Table 14.4**  Simulated length of operations

| Random number | Simulated time in OR (in hours) |
|---|---|
| 000–384 | .5 |
| 385–620 | .75 |
| 621–766 | 1.25 |
| 767–856 | 1.75 |
| 857–911 | 2.25 |
| 912–945 | 2.75 |
| 946–966 | 3.25 |
| 967–979 | 3.75 |
| 980–999 | 4.15 |

lengths of operating-room time listed in Table 14.4. Schmitz and Kwak actually used a more sophisticated approach, based on the negative exponential distribution, to arrive at the average length of operation for each time interval, but their numbers are not significantly different from ours.

How are the random numbers generated? We wish to insure that each of the 1,000 numbers 000 to 999 has the same probability of selection. Tables of 1,000,000 or more random integers have been published and these tables are often used for such simulations. Another method of choosing the numbers would be to build a balanced roulette wheel with a thousand numbered slots on it evenly distributed about the circumference. A random number is then determined by spinning the roulette wheel. Because the roulette wheel is a familiar device for generating random events, the type of model we are using is often called a *Monte Carlo simulation* in honor of the famous European gambling casino. Many computer languages have subroutines that produce numbers sufficiently uniformly distributed to be used in simulation experiments; these subroutines are, in fact, simulations of a roulette wheel.

In addition to operating room demands, Schmitz and Kwak were concerned with needs for recovery-room beds. After a surgical procedure in which a general anesthetic is administered, patients are taken to a recovery room in which nurses are constantly present to monitor their vital signs for some period before the patients are taken back to their hospital rooms. The method by which recovery room demands are handled in the simulation is explained in the next section, where we describe in detail the rules of the simulation.

## V. THE SIMULATION MODEL

### A. Rules of the Simulation

In carrying out the simulation of the length of stay in the operating room and the recovery room, a set of rules was formulated by Schmitz and Kwak to reflect the medical policies of the hospital. The rules were these:

1. Twenty-seven cases were simulated based on the increased bed complement.

2. The random numbers used to select patients were generated independently for each simulated day.

3. All ENT, urology, and ophthalmology surgical cases have an average length of stay in the operating room of .5 hours.

4. Fifty percent of the urology surgical cases do not go to the recovery room because they are performed under a local anesthetic. Whether or not the urology case goes to the recovery room is governed by the random number chosen; see Table 3.

5. All ENT surgical cases go to the recovery room.

6. None of the ophthalmology cases go to the recovery room. The few ophthalmology cases that actually go to the recovery room in practice are balanced out by the few ENT cases that do not go to the recovery room.

7. Any operation lasting more than .5 hours is considered major surgery and the patient spends 3 hours in the recovery room. Otherwise, if a patient goes to the recovery room, he stays there for $1\frac{1}{2}$ hours.

8. The starting time for the beginning of the surgical schedule is 7.50; that is, 7:30 a.m.

9. The necessary "make-ready" time from the moment that one surgical case leaves the operating room until it is ready to receive the next case is .25 hours.

10. It takes .08 hours to transport a patient from the operating room to the recovery room.

11. The necessary "make-ready" time from the moment that a patient leaves the recovery room until his bed is ready for the next occupant is .25 hours.

12. The first operating room to be vacated is the first one to be put back into use when the need arises.

13. The first recovery-room bed to be vacated is the first one to be put back into use when the need arises.

14. If there is no previously vacated recovery-room bed when the patient arrives from surgery, a new bed is created.

The only missing piece of information that is necessary to begin the simulation is the number of available operating rooms. Since this is one of the factors to be determined, the simulation may be run for many hypothetical days with different numbers of operating rooms.

## B. Results of the Simulation

We illustrate the results of a single simulation with five operating rooms. Table 14.5 contains the necessary information for one simulated day.

**Table 14.5**  An example of the simulation

| Schedule number | Random number | Length of operation | Time operation begins | Time operation ends |
|---|---|---|---|---|
| 1  | 889 | 2.25 | 7.50  | 9.75  |
| 2  | 396 | 0.75 | 7.50  | 8.25  |
| 3  | 358 | 0.50 | 7.50  | 8.00  |
| 4  | 715 | 1.25 | 7.50  | 8.75  |
| 5  | 502 | 0.75 | 7.50  | 8.25  |
| 6  | 068 | 0.50 | 8.25  | 8.75  |
| 7  | 604 | 0.75 | 8.50  | 9.25  |
| 8  | 270 | 0.50 | 8.50  | 9.00  |
| 9  | 228 | 0.50 | 9.00  | 9.50  |
| 10 | 782 | 1.75 | 9.00  | 10.75 |
| 11 | 379 | 0.50 | 9.25  | 9.75  |
| 12 | 093 | 0.50 | 9.50  | 10.00 |
| 13 | 011 | 0.50 | 9.75  | 10.25 |
| 14 | 648 | 1.25 | 10.00 | 11.25 |
| 15 | 527 | 0.75 | 10.00 | 10.75 |
| 16 | 987 | 4.15 | 10.25 | 14.40 |
| 17 | 214 | 0.50 | 10.50 | 11.00 |
| 18 | 474 | 0.75 | 11.00 | 11.75 |
| 19 | 238 | 0.50 | 11.00 | 11.50 |
| 20 | 045 | 0.50 | 11.25 | 11.75 |
| 21 | 408 | 0.75 | 11.50 | 12.25 |
| 22 | 116 | 0.50 | 11.75 | 12.25 |
| 23 | 209 | 0.50 | 12.00 | 12.50 |
| 24 | 048 | 0.50 | 12.00 | 12.50 |
| 25 | 393 | 0.75 | 12.50 | 13.25 |
| 26 | 550 | 0.75 | 12.50 | 13.25 |
| 27 | 306 | 0.75 | 12.75 | 13.50 |

We can easily trace through the first steps in constructing Table 14.5.

1.  The first random number selected is 889.  From Table 14.4, we see that this patient will have an operation lasting 2.25 hours, because 889 belongs to to bloc of numbers 857–911.

2.  Adding the simulated length of the operation to the starting time of the operation (7.50), we find that the operation ends at 9.75.  Operating room 1 will then be ready for a new patient at 9.75 + .25 = 10.00 hours.

3.  We add .08 to the ending time of the operation to determine that the patient arrives at the recovery room at 9.83.

4.  Since this patient underwent major surgery, he will remain in the recovery room for three hours, leaving it at 12.83.

5.  The recovery-room bed he occupied will be ready for another patient at 12.83 + .25 = 13.08.

6.  Since there are five operating rooms in this simulation, the first five pa-

| Operating room number | Recovery room Yes | Recovery room No | Time recovery begins | Time recovery ends | RR bed no. | Time RR bed available |
|---|---|---|---|---|---|---|
| 1 | X | | 9.83 | 12.83 | 7 | 13.08 |
| 2 | X | | 8.33 | 11.33 | 1 | 11.58 |
| 3 | | X | — | — | — | — |
| 4 | X | | 8.83 | 11.83 | 3 | 12.08 |
| 5 | X | | 8.33 | 11.33 | 2 | 11.58 |
| 3 | X | | 8.83 | 10.33 | 4 | 10.58 |
| 2 | X | | 9.33 | 12.33 | 5 | 12.58 |
| 5 | | X | — | — | — | — |
| 4 | X | | 9.58 | 11.08 | 6 | 11.33 |
| 3 | X | | 10.83 | 13.83 | 4 | 14.08 |
| 5 | | X | — | — | — | — |
| 2 | X | | 10.08 | 11.58 | 5 | 11.83 |
| 4 | X | | 10.33 | 11.83 | 9 | 12.08 |
| 1 | X | | 11.33 | 14.33 | 6 | 14.58 |
| 5 | X | | 10.83 | 13.83 | 10 | 14.08 |
| 2 | X | | 14.48 | 17.48 | 5 | 17.73 |
| 4 | X | | 11.08 | 12.58 | 11 | 12.83 |
| 3 | X | | 11.83 | 14.83 | 2 | 15.08 |
| 5 | X | | 11.58 | 13.08 | 1 | 13.33 |
| 4 | X | | 11.83 | 13.33 | 5 | 13.58 |
| 1 | X | | 12.33 | 15.33 | 3 | 15.58 |
| 5 | X | | 12.33 | 13.83 | 9 | 14.08 |
| 3 | X | | 12.58 | 14.08 | 5 | 14.33 |
| 4 | X | | 12.58 | 14.08 | 12 | 14.33 |
| 1 | X | | 13.33 | 16.33 | 11 | 16.58 |
| 5 | X | | 13.33 | 16.33 | 7 | 16.58 |
| 3 | | X | — | — | — | — |

tients will start surgery at the same time, 7.50. The second patient on the schedule, represented by random number 396, is the first patient to reach the recovery room, so he is assigned RR bed 1. The first patient of the day on the schedule (random number 889) is actually the seventh patient to reach the recovery room. That explains why he is assigned RR bed 7.

7. Note also from this simulation that when operating room 1 is ready for its second procedure, it receives the fourteenth patient (random number 648) on the schedule. Surgery for the patients higher on the schedule takes place in the other operating rooms.

8. The third scheduled operation was performed on random number 358. From Table 3, we note that this patient is an ophthalmology case and will not go to the recovery room.

9. Random number 214 represents the seventeenth scheduled operation of the day. Table 3 indicates that this patient will receive a urology operation requiring 1.5 hours in the recovery room (since 214 belongs to the bloc 158–241).

For this simulated day, using five operating rooms, we discover that the surgical schedule is completed at 14.40 (about 2:24 p.m.), the last departure from the recovery room occurs at 17.73 (about 5:44 p.m.), and that 12 recovery-room beds were needed.

## C. Conclusions

In their paper, Schmitz and Kwak present the results of four simulated days. On three of the days, 11 recovery-room beds were needed and on the fourth, there was a demand for 12 beds. On all four days, the surgical schedule was completed by 5:30 p.m. The latest departure from the recovery room was about 8:36 p.m. These simulations all assumed that there were five operating rooms available.

The simulation of a daily surgical schedule that we have described can be carried out by hand in less than an hour. On a high-speed electronic computer, the simulation can be completed in a small fraction of this time, so that it is possible to repeat the simulation a great many times at a very modest cost.

It should be apparent from our description that it is a simple matter to vary the number of surgical cases for the day as well as the number of operating rooms. If there are only four operating rooms, then we can see that the surgical schedule of 27 procedures will not be completed until the evening hours, while if we increase to six operating rooms, some will stand empty for a good part of the afternoon. To obtain more precise estimates of time, of course, we need only run through the simulation process with these constraints.

Schmitz and Kwak conducted the simulation using 3, 4, 5, and 6 operating rooms. Based on 27 surgical procedures per day, they discovered that the

Table 14.6    Validating the simulation

| Schedule number | Random number | Length of operation | Time operation begins | Time operation ends |
|---|---|---|---|---|
| 1 | 889 | 2.25 | 7.50 | 9.75 |
| 2 | 396 | 0.75 | 7.50 | 8.25 |
| 3 | 358 | 0.50 | 7.50 | 8.00 |
| 4 | 715 | 1.25 | 8.25 | 9.50 |
| 5 | 502 | 0.75 | 8.50 | 9.25 |
| 6 | 068 | 0.50 | 9.50 | 10.00 |
| 7 | 604 | 0.75 | 9.75 | 10.50 |
| 8 | 270 | 0.50 | 10.00 | 10.50 |
| 9 | 228 | 0.50 | 10.25 | 10.75 |
| 10 | 782 | 1.75 | 10.75 | 12.50 |
| 11 | 379 | 0.50 | 10.75 | 11.25 |
| 12 | 093 | 0.50 | 11.00 | 11.50 |
| 13 | 011 | 0.50 | 11.50 | 12.00 |
| 14 | 648 | 1.25 | 11.75 | 13.00 |
| 15 | 527 | 0.75 | 12.25 | 13.00 |
| 16 | 987 | 4.15 | 12.75 | 16.90 |
| 17 | 214 | 0.50 | 13.25 | 13.75 |

optimum number of operating rooms was found to be 5 and that there would consistently be a need for at least 12 recovery-room beds. They also concluded that it was not necessary to staff the recovery room beyond 9 or 10 p.m. each day.

### D. Validation

The effectiveness of any model is measured by how closely its predictions match those actions of the system which are observed in the real world. One way to test our Monte Carlo simulation of operating-and recovery-room usage would be to expand the operating-room capacity to 5 rooms when the bed complement is increased by 144 and then simply observe if the daily surgical schedule works out as well as the simulation says it should. Unfortunately, this could be a very costly testing procedure, both in terms of construction dollars and patient well-being, especially if the assumptions underlying the simulation are poor ones, or if important factors have been omitted from it.

Fortunately, there is an alternative validation procedure. We can determine how well the model simulates a situation for which observed data already exists. In our case, we know how the hospital system functioned in 1970 before the addition of new M/S beds. We may then perform our simulation for the daily surgical schedule of 1970. We will be testing the validity of the simulation to predict the future by determining how well it simulates the past or present.

Since there were 6293 procedures in the year 1970, our simulation would call for 17 (6293/365) procedures per day. Suppose that there were 3 operating rooms available in 1970, but that all the other rules of the simulation were the same. The results of this simulation, using the random numbers of the first 17 patients of Table 14.5, are shown in Table 14.6.

| Operating room number | Recovery room Yes | No | Time recovery begins | Time recovery ends | RR bed no. | Time RR bed free |
|---|---|---|---|---|---|---|
| 1 | X | | 9.83 | 12.83 | 4 | 13.08 |
| 2 | X | | 8.33 | 11.33 | 1 | 11.58 |
| 3 | | X | — | — | — | — |
| 3 | X | | 9.58 | 12.58 | 3 | 12.83 |
| 2 | X | | 9.33 | 12.33 | 2 | 12.58 |
| 2 | X | | 10.08 | 11.58 | 5 | 11.83 |
| 3 | X | | 10.58 | 13.58 | 6 | 13.83 |
| 1 | | X | — | — | — | — |
| 2 | X | | 10.83 | 12.33 | 7 | 12.58 |
| 1 | X | | 12.58 | 15.58 | 2 | 15.83 |
| 3 | | X | — | — | — | — |
| 2 | X | | 11.58 | 13.08 | 1 | 13.33 |
| 3 | X | | 12.08 | 13.58 | 5 | 13.83 |
| 2 | X | | 13.08 | 16.08 | 7 | 16.33 |
| 3 | X | | 13.08 | 16.08 | 3 | 16.33 |
| 1 | X | | 16.98 | 19.98 | 4 | 20.23 |
| 2 | X | | 13.83 | 15.33 | 6 | 15.58 |

With a simulated daily surgical schedule of 17 cases and three operating rooms, note that all operations have been completed by 16.90 (4:54 p.m.), that there is a need for 7 recovery-room beds, and that the latest time that a patient leaves the recovery room is 19.98 (about 8 p.m.). If these values are close to those observed for a typical day in 1970, this would reinforce the belief that the method of simulation chosen is a valid one. It is interesting to note here that the average length of the 17 operations on this simulated surgical schedule is 1.04 hours, compared with an observed figure of 1.03 for the sample of 445 cases in 1970.

### E. Possible Refinements

There are several ways that we could increase the sophistication of this simulation to imitate better the actual operating-and recovery-room usages. Instead of using 30-minute time intervals for our surgical categories, we could have used 10-minute or even 5-minute intervals. This would give a more precise and accurate distribution of lengths of time in the operating room. The determination of recovery-room usage was based on the simplifying assumption that a patient who arrived in the recovery room would spend either 1.5 or 3 hours there, depending on the length of his operation. In fact, the length of time in the recovery room does not take on only these two values. The nature of the surgery performed, the length of time it took, and the age and general state of health of the patient will all be factors in establishing how many hours he will be kept in the recovery room.

The sample data of the 445 patients could have been used to determine a probability distribution for length of time in the recovery room. This distribution then could have been incorporated into the simulation in much the same way that the negative-exponential distribution for length of stay in the operating room was.

This method of simulation is thus seen to be extremely flexible as it allows for various levels of sophistication. As Schmitz and Kwak [1972] point out,

> In general, this method gives a close approximation to reality under conditions when it is not possible to ascertain by observation the operation of a department. It was found to be extremely accurate when it did become possible to observe the operation of the department. The uses of the method are limited only by the imagination and ingenuity of the user.

### F. How Many Days to Simulate?

In the models we first studied in this book—deterministic, axiomatic, and probabilistic—conclusions about the behavior of a real-world system were *deduced* from a mathematical model by the standard techniques of proving theorems and solving equations. When simulation is used to study an actual system, the conclusions we reach can only be *inferred* from the outcome of sample runs of the simulation.

Since chance plays such a basic role in a Monte Carlo simulation, repeating the simulation a second time—with exactly the same rules—will produce different results, because different random numbers will be generated. We cannot be content with running our simulation for one daily surgical schedule and making predictions on the basis of the outcomes we see. We need to repeat the simulation many times to assess the effect of chance on the differences in outcomes that will be produced. But how many times is a sufficient number? Consider a prediction, for example, that 12 recovery-room beds will be sufficient for 5 operating rooms. How does the degree of confidence in this prediction grow with the number of simulated days on which no more than 12 beds are demanded? The proper answer to questions like this and for the general evaluation of simulation experiments may require quite sophisticated statistical techniques. Some problems have been solved (see Chapter 8 of John Smith, *Computer Simulation Models*), but many thorny difficulties remain. Mathematicians are actively developing a theory of simulation that will enable this powerful technique to be used more widely and knowledgeably.

## VI. OTHER EXAMPLES OF SIMULATION

The Monte Carlo method was first used to solve problems in nuclear physics where more traditional mathematical techniques failed to give the needed numerical results.

As a very elementary example, suppose you wish to evaluate a particular definite integral

$$\int_a^b f(x)\, dx$$

where $f$ is a continuous function on the interval $[a, b]$. From the Fundamental Theorem of Calculus, this is a trivial problem provided you can find an anti-derivative of $f$; that is, a function $F$ such that $F'(x) = f(x)$ for all $x$ in $[a, b]$. Then the value of the definite integral is given as the difference $F(b) - F(a)$.

In many instances, the function $F$ cannot be found so easily. In fact, for most functions $f$ (examples are $f(x) = (\sin x)/x$ and $f(x) = e^{-x^2}$), it is impossible to find $F$ in closed form as a rational combination of the standard functions of calculus.

There are various approximation techniques in such cases for finding the numerical value of the definite integral. The Monte Carlo method is one such technique.

For convenience, suppose that the function $f$ takes on only nonnegative values and that it is bounded on the interval $[a, b]$ by the positive number $M$. Then the graph of $f$ over the interval is entirely contained in a rectangle of dimensions $(b - a)$ by $M$. (See Fig. 14.3.)

The value of the definite integral $\int_a^b f(x)\, dx$ is the measure of the shaded area $A$ in the rectangle which is below the graph of the curve $y = f(x)$. The

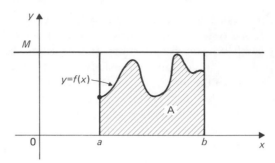

**Fig. 14.3**   The shaded region has area
$A = \int_a^b f(x)\,dx.$

relative area,

$$p = \frac{A}{(b-a)M} \qquad (1)$$

is then a number between 0 and 1. This number can be interpreted as a probability. If a point is picked completely at random from the points of the rectangular region, then the probability that the point lies in the shaded area under
the curve is precisely the number $p$ of Eq. (1).

If there is some other independent way of finding the probability $p$, then
the value of the definite integral can be found simply as

$$\int_a^b f(x)\,dx = A = p(b-a)M.$$

The Monte Carlo method provides a way of obtaining the probability $p$
directly. We need to recall the *relative frequency* interpretation of probability
introduced in Chapter 9. Imagine the experiment of choosing a point at random
from the rectangular region and noting whether or not it lies in $A$. If this experiment is repeated a large number $N$ of times, then $p$ is approximately the frequency of selecting points in $A$; that is,

$$p \sim \frac{\text{Number of times point chosen lies in } A}{N} \qquad (2)$$

Our understanding of probabilities is that the approximation in Eq. (2)
improves as $N$ increases. If we conduct the experiment 10,000 times, then we
should get an accurate estimate of $p$, and hence an accurate estimate of $\int_a^b f(x)\,dx$.

A point can be chosen at random from the rectangular region by first
choosing its $x$-coordinate at random and then its $y$-coordinate at random. The
$x$-coordinate must lie between the numbers $a$ and $b$ and the $y$-coordinate
between 0 and $M$. If we have a random number generator that produces num-

bers between 000 and 999 with an equiprobable distribution, then we may start by generating two random numbers, $r$ and $s$. We then determine a point in the desired region with coordinates $(x_0, y_0)$ where

$$x_0 = a + \frac{r(b-a)}{999}$$

and

$$y_0 = \frac{sM}{999}.$$

To decide if the randomly chosen point $(x_0, y_0)$ belongs to $A$, we need only compute $f(x_0)$ and determine whether the inequality

$$y_0 < f(x_0) \tag{3}$$

is valid. If it is, then the point belongs to $A$; otherwise, it does not.

To obtain our approximation for $p$, we generate $N$ points in the rectangular region in the manner just described and keep track of what proportion of times the coordinates of the point satisfy the inequality (3).

The real value of the Monte Carlo method comes in situations where other techniques to obtain approximate numerical answers either do not exist or are much less efficient. The development of the electronic computer in the 1940's led to the widespread use of the Monte Carlo method and Monte Carlo simulation in physics, engineering, and chemistry.

Not all simulations use the Monte Carlo device, only those in which probabilistic considerations play an important role in the operation of the system that is being studied. "Deterministic" simulation has been used very successfully in studying the path of a spaceship, for example. If a rocket is sent on a lunar landing expedition, the system consists of four bodies exerting gravitational attractions on each other: sun, earth, moon, and spaceship. Newton's laws give the deterministic differential equation controlling the path of flight of the ship. We can simulate the solution curve of the equation by using a sophisticated version of the Euler method discussed in Chapter 2.

Although simulation was initially used in the physical sciences, by the mid-1950's social scientists were beginning to apply it also to a variety of problems. Simulation has been used as a tool for research, teaching, decision making, and historical reconstruction. Social scientists have used simulation to study specific topics such as the spread of urban ghettoes, the outbreak of World War I, the behavior of the stock market, the introduction of a new product in a competitive market, and neurotic processes in psychopathology. Disciplines as diverse as geography, political science, cognitive and social psychology, medicine, international relations, anthropology, education, sociology, and business administration have all been affected to some extent by the results of simulation studies.

For a more complete introduction to this active and growing subject, you may wish to examine the book by Guetzkow and others [1972] which contains essays on the advantages and limitations of simulation as well as a number of particular case studies.

## EXERCISES

1. The projected daily surgical schedule of 27 procedures was based on the assumption that operations would be performed every day. Find the length of the schedule if no operations are done on Sunday.

2. Of the 6293 surgical procedures performed in 1970, approximately how many were ophthalmology cases?

3. Find the annual total number of ophthalmology surgical procedures projected for the expanded bed complement.

4. Find the percentage of the projected 9669 procedures that will be ophthalmology cases.

5. Compare the percentage obtained in Exercise 4 with the 4.5 percent experienced in 1970. Are the percentages the same? Should they be the same?

6. Suppose that 6 percent of the surgical procedures in 1970 were gynecology cases and that the average stay in the hospital for such a case was 4.7 days. Show that this would yield a projected increase of 279 gynecological procedures for the expanded bed complement.

7. If a projected increase of 312 beds is estimated for a surgical category that represented 7.1 percent of all procedures in 1970, what was the average length of stay per patient in this category?

8. Schmitz and Kwak report that the projected 9669 annual procedures would represent an increase of 53.6 percent over the 1970 totals. Does this give you enough information to determine the number of M/S beds in the hospital in 1970? To determine the average length of stay of a surgical patient? What other data would you need in order to answer these questions?

*Exercises 9–16 refer to the simulation of Table 14.5.*

9. In which operating room was the largest number of procedures performed? The smallest number? What was the average number of procedures per operating room?

10. Which operating room was used for the longest period of time? What was the average length of time of usage per operating room?

11. Using the random numbers of Table 14.5, trace through the effects on the number of required recovery-room beds of

  a) shortening the "make-ready" time in the recovery room to .20 hours;

  b) lengthening the recovery-room time to 4 hours for major surgery and 2 hours for minor surgery.

12. Using the random numbers from Table 14.5, work through the simulation with the original rules, but with only 3 operating rooms. Determine the following:

a) Time of completion of surgical schedule,

b) Number of recovery-room beds required, and

c) Latest time a patient leaves the recovery room.

13. Repeat Exercise 12 with

a) 6 operating rooms,

b) 4 operating rooms instead of 5.

14. Trace through a simulated surgical schedule using the original rules and the random numbers of Table 14.5, except that whenever a random number $R$ occurs, choose the patient represented by the random number $999 - R$.

15. Generate your own random number sequence and go through a simulated day.

16. What refinements in the model would you suggest that would make the simulation more realistic? For some hints, see Fetter and Thompson [1965].

## SUGGESTED PROJECTS

1. Investigate the negative-exponential distribution. Show, in particular, that the simulated length of stay in the operating room can be determined by drawing a number from a list of random exponential numbers of mean 1 and then multiplying it by an appropriate interarrival mean. See Schmitz and Kwak's paper and Drake's book (References).

2. (For those with background in statistics). Suppose the simulation we have described is repeated $N$ times and it is observed that the largest number of recovery-room beds ever needed is 12 and that the latest time an operation was completed was 6 p.m. How large should $N$ be so that we can assert that the probability of needing more than 12 recovery-room beds or that an operation would continue past 6 p.m. is less than .05? (See Chapter 8 of John Smith, *Computer Simulation Models*.)

3. Write a computer program to carry out the Monte Carlo simulation of operating- and recovery-room usage described in this chapter. Carry out the simulation for a 30-day period and analyze the results.

4. Show that the data usually collected in a major league baseball game to determine players' batting, pitching, and fielding averages gives sufficient information to construct a Monte Carlo simulation that provides estimates on a team's run production as a function of the particular batting order chosen. Discuss the relative difficulty of modeling some particular aspect of football, basketball, or hockey by simulation. What information would be required? Is it readily available?

5. Suppose you are the manager of a supermarket. You must decide what is the largest number of items to allow a customer on the express lane. You wish to select the number that will minimize the average length of time all customers must wait in line before being checked out. What data would you need? How would you construct the simulation?

6. Write a computer program to evaluate definite integrals using the Monte Carlo technique. Test the program on functions whose integrals can be computed exactly by Fundamental Theorem of Calculus. How many points need to be chosen to obtain a good approximation? How does the Monte Carlo method compare in efficiency to other techniques, such as Simpson's Rule?

## REFERENCES

Drake, Alvin W., *Fundamentals of Applied Probability Theory* (New York: McGraw-Hill, 1967).

Fetter, R. B., and J. D. Thompson, "The simulation of hospital systems," *Operations Research* **13** (1965), 689–711.

Guetzkow, Harold, Philip Kotler, and Randall L. Schultz, eds., *Simulation in Social and Administrative Science* (Englewood Cliffs, N.J.: Prentice-Hall, 1972).

Schmitz, Homer H., and N. K. Kwak, "Monte Carlo simulation of operating-room and recovery-room usage," *Operations Research* **20** (1972), 1171–1180. Used with permission of the Operations Research Society of America and the authors.

Smith, John, *Computer Simulation Models* (New York: Hafner, 1968).

# Appendix I: Sets

By a *set* we mean a well-defined collection of objects, called the *elements* or (members) of the set. Some examples of sets are:

1. The set $A$ of real numbers less than 21;
2. The set $B$ of college sophomores in Texas universities;
3. The set $C$ of negative integers;
4. The set $D$ of three-headed residents of Muskegon, Michigan;
5. The set $E$ of solutions of the equation $\tan x - \log x = x^3$; and
6. The set $F$ of integers strictly between 3 and 10.

We use the notation "$x \in X$" to represent the statement that "The element $x$ is a member of the set $X$." If $x$ is not an element of $X$, denote this by $x \notin X$. In our examples, $4 \in A$ and $24 \notin A$.

Sets may be described in terms of some common property shared by the elements. A set may also be given by listing all its members; when this is done, the elements are typically written within braces. Here are some further examples:

7. $G = \{\text{single, double, triple, home run}\}$
8. $H = \{4, 5, 6, 7, 8, 9\}$
9. $I = \{1, 2, 3, \ldots\}$
10. $J = \{\text{Washington, Adams, Jefferson}, \ldots, \text{Nixon, Ford, Carter}\}$

Some sets occur so frequently in applications that special symbols have been invented for them. The set of real numbers, for examples, is commonly denoted by $\mathbb{R}$ and the set of integers by $\mathbb{Z}$.

A third way of describing a set is by a special notation easily understood by an example. The set of integers strictly between 3 and 10 would be written

$$\{x \in \mathbb{Z} : 3 < x < 10\}$$

where the colon ":" is read "such that."

Note that the descriptions of the sets $F$ and $H$ in these examples specify the same collection of numbers. So does the description $K = \{9, 8, 7, 6, 5, 4\}$. It is reasonable to call these sets equal by the following definitions.

**DEFINITION**    **If $X$ and $Y$ are sets, then $X$ and $Y$ are *equal*, denoted $X = Y$, precisely if the sets contain exactly the same elements.**

The sets $F$ and $A$ of the examples are not equal, since 17 is an element of $A$ but not of $F$. However, every element of $F$ is an element of $A$, so $F$ is a sub-subcollection, or "subset," of $A$.

**DEFINITION**    **If $X$ and $Y$ are sets and every element of $X$ is also an element of $Y$, then we say $X$ is a *subset* of $Y$. This is denoted by $X \subseteq Y$.**

Observe that although sets $A$ and $I$ have some common elements, neither is a subset of the other. We might denote this by $A \nsubseteq I$ and $I \nsubseteq A$.

***Proposition 1***    $X = Y$ if and only if $X \subseteq Y$ and $Y \subseteq X$.

The set containing no elements is called the *empty set* and is denoted $\emptyset$. Observe that the set $D$ in the examples is the empty set. If $X$ is any set, then $\emptyset \subseteq X$ (proof: try to find some element of $\emptyset$ which is not an element of $X$). Also note that every set is a subset of itself.

If $X$ is any set, we may consider the collection of all subsets of $X$. This set is called the *power set* of $X$. As an example, the set $X = \{x, y, z\}$ has eight distinct subsets:

$$\emptyset, \{x\}, \{y\}, \{z\}, \{x, y\}, \{x, z\}, \{y, z\}, X.$$

A set $X$ is *finite* if it contains exactly $n$ distinct elements for some non-negative integer $n$. The sets $B, D, E, F, G, H$, and $J$ of the examples are finite sets.

***Proposition 2***    If $X$ is a finite set with precisely $n$ distinct elements, then the power set of $X$ contains $2^n$ distinct elements.

**DEFINITION**    **If $S$ is a set and $X$ is a subset of $S$, then the set of elements of $S$ which are not in $X$ is called the *complement of $X$ in $S$*. It is denoted $S - X$ or sometimes by $X^c$ (if there is no ambiguity about $S$).**

As an example, if $S = \{1, 2, 3, 4, 5\}$ and $X = \{3, 4\}$, then $S - X = \{1, 2, 5\}$.

*Exercise*  Show that $S - (S - X) = X$.

By definition, the sets $X$ and $S - X$ have no elements in common. This is also true of the sets $A$ and $B$ of the examples and for many other pairs of sets. Such sets are said to be *pairwise disjoint*. Other pairs of sets do share common elements and there is a special notation for this set of common elements.

**DEFINITION**  **If $X$ and $Y$ are sets, then the set $X \cap Y$ is the set of all elements that are in both $X$ and $Y$. The set $X \cap Y$ is called the *intersection* of $X$ and $Y$.**

In the examples,

$A \cap I = \{x: x \in A \text{ and } x \in I\}$

$\quad = \{x: x \text{ is a real number less than 21 and } x \text{ is a positive integer}\}$

$\quad = \{x: x \text{ is a positive integer less than 21}\}$

$\quad = \{1, 2, \ldots, 20\}.$

If $X$ and $Y$ are pairwise disjoint, then we have $X \cap Y = \emptyset$.

There is another important operation of combining sets which consists in forming the collection of all elements that belong to either set.

**DEFINITION**  **If $S$ is a set and $X$ and $Y$ are subsets of $S$, then the *union* of $X$ and $Y$, denoted $X \cup Y$, is the set of elements in $X$ or $Y$ or both. In our notation,**

$$X \cup Y = \{z: z \in X \text{ or } z \in Y\}$$

As an example, suppose $X = \{1, 2, 3, 5\}$ and $Y = \{3, 4, 5, 6, 7\}$. Then the union is $X \cup Y = \{1, 2, 3, 4, 5, 6, 7\}$.

To study relations and functions, it is necessary to introduce the concept of a Cartesian product of two sets.

**DEFINITION**  **If $X$ and $Y$ are any two sets, then the *Cartesian product* of $X$ and $Y$, denoted $X \times Y$, is the set of all ordered pairs $(x, y)$ where $x$ is a member of $X$ and $Y$ is a member of $Y$. In terms of our notation,**

$$X \times Y = \{(x, y): x \in X \text{ and } y \in Y\}.$$

The next example should clarify this definition. If $X = \{1, 2, 3\}$ and $Y = \{3, 4\}$, then we have

$$X \times Y = \{(1, 3), (1, 4), (2, 3), (2, 4), (3, 3), (3, 4)\},$$
$$Y \times X = \{(3, 1), (3, 2), (3, 3), (4, 1), (4, 2), (4, 3)\},$$

and

$$Y \times Y = \{(3, 3), (3, 4), (4, 3), (4, 4)\}.$$

What is $X \times X$?

The principle of mathematical induction, which is used in a number of proofs in this text, can be formulated in terms of sets. Let $N$ be the set of positive integers and suppose $X$ is a subset of $N$. The *axiom of mathematical induction* asserts:

IF: (i) $1 \in X$ and (ii) whenever $n \in X$, then $n + 1 \in X$,

THEN: $X = N$.

An equivalent axiom, easier to remember, but sometimes more cumbersome to use, is: Every nonempty set of positive integers has a least element.

---

**EXAMPLE**   Show that $1 + 2 + 3 + \cdots + k = k(k + 1)/2$ for every positive integer $k$.

**Solution I**   Let $X$ be the subset of $N$ for which the equation is valid. Then $1 \in X$ since $1 = 1(1 + 1)/2$; thus (i) is satisfied. To show (ii) is true, suppose $n \in X$. Then $1 + 2 + \cdots + n = n(n + 1)/2$. Adding $n + 1$ to each side of this equation produces

$$1 + 2 + \cdots + n + (n + 1) = (1 + 2 + \cdots + n) + (n + 1)$$

$$= \frac{n(n + 1)}{2} + (n + 1)$$

$$= \frac{(n + 1)(n + 2)}{2}$$

which is just the statement that $n + 1 \in X$. Since (i) and (ii) are true, the principle of mathematical induction asserts that $X = N$; that is, the equation is true for every positive integer.

**Solution II**   Let $A$ be the set of all positive integers for which the equation is not true. If $A$ is nonempty, then it has a smallest element $k$. But then we have

a) $k \neq 1$,

b) $1 + 2 + \cdots + k \neq k(k + 1)/2$

c) $1 + 2 + \cdots + (k - 1) = (k - 1)k/2$

Condition (c) is true because $k - 1$ is smaller than $k$ and the equation is true for all positive integers less than $k$. Now (a), (b) and (c) are inconsistent. We have a contradiction to the assumption that $A$ is nonempty. Thus $A$ must be empty and the equation is valid for every positive integer.

---

**EXERCISES**

---

1. Use mathematical induction to prove Proposition 2.

2. Show that $X \cup Y = Y \cup X$ and $X \cap Y = Y \cap X$ for all sets $X$ and $Y$, but that, in general, $X \times Y \neq Y \times X$.

3. Show that $(X \cup Y) \cup Z = X \cup (Y \cup Z)$ and $(X \cap Y) \cap Z = X \cap (Y \cap Z)$ for all sets $X, Y, Z$ so that the expressions $X \cup Y \cup Z$ and $X \cap Y \cap Z$ are well-defined. What can you say about $(X \times Y) \times Z$ and $X \times (Y \times Z)$?

# Appendix II: Matrices

By a matrix, we simply mean a rectangular array of numbers. Examples of matrices are

$$A = \begin{pmatrix} 3 & 2 & 1 \\ -1 & 0 & 7 \end{pmatrix},$$

$$B = \begin{pmatrix} 1 & 2 \\ 3 & 4 \end{pmatrix},$$

$$C = (.2, .3, .5, .4),$$

$$D = \begin{pmatrix} 1.5 \\ -6 \\ 9.9 \\ 0 \\ 22 \end{pmatrix}.$$

Matrices are classified according to their size and shape by specifying the number of rows and columns. An $m \times n$ *matrix* is a matrix with $m$ rows and $n$ columns. Thus $A$ is a $2 \times 3$ matrix, $B$ is a $2 \times 2$ matrix, $C$ is a $1 \times 4$ matrix and $D$ is a $5 \times 1$ matrix. Any $1 \times n$ matrix is called a *row vector* while an $m \times 1$ matrix is said to be a *column vector*. The individual numbers in vectors are called *components* of the vector. If $m = n$, the matrix is said to be *square* and to have an *order* equal to the number of rows. Thus $B$ is a square matrix of order 2. Two matrices have the same *size* if they have the same number of rows and columns. The four matrices $A, B, C,$ and $D$, it should be noted, are of different sizes.

The general $m \times n$ matrix $M$ has the form

$$M = \begin{pmatrix} a_{11} & a_{12} & \cdots & a_{1n} \\ a_{21} & a_{22} & \cdots & a_{2n} \\ \cdots & & & \\ a_{m1} & a_{m2} & \cdots & a_{mn} \end{pmatrix}.$$

The number in the $i$th row and $j$th column of a matrix is called the $ij$th *entry* of the matrix, and may be denoted $M_{ij}$. Thus $A_{23} = 7$.

Two matrices are said to be *equal* matrices if they are of the same size and the corresponding entries are all equal. We write $A = B$ to denote that two matrices $A$ and $B$ are equal. For example, if we consider the six matrices

$$U = (1, 2), \quad V = \begin{pmatrix} 1 \\ 2 \end{pmatrix}, \quad W = (1, 2), \quad X = (2, 1), \quad Y = (1, 0), \quad Z = (1, 2, 0),$$

only the matrices $U$ and $W$ are equal.

Matrix addition is defined for matrices of the same size by the addition of the corresponding entries. Thus the $ij$th entry of the sum of two matrices is the sum of their $ij$th entries; in symbols,

$$(A + B)_{ij} = A_{ij} + B_{ij}.$$

As an example, if the matrices $A$ and $B$ are given by

$$A = \begin{pmatrix} 3 & 2 & 1 \\ -1 & 0 & 7 \end{pmatrix}, \quad B = \begin{pmatrix} 5 & 4 & -6 \\ 2 & 1 & 0 \end{pmatrix}, \tag{1}$$

then the sum, $A + B$, is given by

$$A + B = \begin{pmatrix} 3+5 & 2+4 & 1-6 \\ -1+2 & 0+1 & 7+0 \end{pmatrix} = \begin{pmatrix} 8 & 6 & -5 \\ 1 & 1 & 7 \end{pmatrix}.$$

The matrices $A$ and $C$, given by

$$A = \begin{pmatrix} 3 & 2 & 1 \\ -1 & 0 & 7 \end{pmatrix}, \quad C = \begin{pmatrix} 4 & 5 \\ 2 & 0 \\ -1 & -1 \end{pmatrix},$$

cannot be added, even though they have the same number of entries.

A matrix, all of whose entries are 0, is called a *zero matrix* and we denote the $m \times n$ zero matrix by $0^{mn}$ or sometimes simply by 0 if the size of the matrix is clear from the context.

If $A$ is a matrix and $c$ is a constant, then we can define the *scalar multiple* $cA$ to be the matrix obtained by multiplying each entry of $A$ by the constant $c$. In symbols, this is $(cA)_{ij} = c(A_{ij})$; that is, the $ij$th entry of $cA$ is $c$ times the $ij$th entry of $A$.

If $A$ is the matrix of (1), then the matrices $2A$ and $-1A$ are given by

$$2A = \begin{pmatrix} 6 & 4 & 2 \\ -2 & 0 & 14 \end{pmatrix}, \qquad -1A = \begin{pmatrix} -3 & -2 & -1 \\ 1 & 0 & -7 \end{pmatrix}.$$

We will denote the matrix $-1A$ simply by $-A$. If $A$ and $B$ are matrices of the same size, then the expression $B + -A$ is well defined as a matrix addition. We will write such an expression as $B - A$ and call the operation *matrix subtraction*. What this boils down to is that subtraction of matrices is defined by subtraction of corresponding entries.

Our first theorem lists the basic properties of matrix addition and scalar multiplication. These properties follow easily from analogous properties of the addition and multiplication of ordinary numbers.

■ **THEOREM 1**    Let $A$, $B$, and $C$ be any $m \times n$ matrices and let $c$ and $d$ be any real numbers. Then

1. $A + B$ is an $m \times n$ matrix.
2. $A + B = B + A$.
3. $A + (B + C) = (A + B) + C$.
4. $A + 0 = A$.
5. For each matrix $A$, there is a matrix, $-A$, such that $A + (-A) = 0$.
6. $cA$ is an $m \times n$ matrix.
7. $c(A + B) = cA + cB$.
8. $(c + d)A = cA + dA$.
9. $c(dA) = (cd)A$.
10. $1A = A$.

*Proof of Theorem 1*    We will prove (2); the other properties follow by similar reasoning and are left as exercises for the reader. By definition of matrix addition, the $ij$th entry of $A + B$ is $A_{ij} + B_{ij}$. But $A_{ij}$ and $B_{ij}$ are numbers, so we have $A_{ij} + B_{ij} = B_{ij} + A_{ij}$. Now $B_{ij} + A_{ij}$ is the $ij$th entry of $B + A$. Since the corresponding entries of $A + B$ and $B + A$ are equal, the matrices are equal. □

Knowledge of Properties 1–10 of Theorem 1 is essential for working with matrices. You will have little difficulty remembering them as they are so similar to the operations involving real numbers. Matrix multiplication, which we introduce next, is a different story.

**Matrix multiplication**    One might define the product of two matrices to be the matrix obtained by multiplying corresponding entries. Such a definition would have a number of applications; you will be invited to explore the consequences of such a definition in the exercises. When a mathematician speaks of matrix multiplication, he has a different operation in mind, an operation that was invented to handle many very useful applied problems.

To explain this operation, we will begin with the example of a cashier at the checkout counter of the campus bookstore. Suppose that you purchase 6 pencils, 4 notebooks, 2 packs of index cards, 36 paper clips, and 1 sweatshirt at the store. How does the cashier determine what to charge you?

The cashier makes the following calculation:

Total Cost = (Total cost of pencils) + (total cost of notebooks)
 + (total cost of index cards) + (total cost of paper clips)
 + (total cost of sweatshirts)

 = (Number of pencils)(cost per pencil) + (number of notebooks)(cost per notebook) + (number of packs of index cards)(cost per pack) + (number of paper clips)(cost per clip) + (number of sweatshirts)(cost per shirt).

Let us represent the purchases by a row vector

$A$ = (6 pencils, 4 notebooks, 2 packs of cards, 36 clips, 1 sweatshirt)
 = (6, 4, 2, 36, 1)

and represent the unit cost of each item by a column vector

$$B = \begin{pmatrix} 5 \\ 75 \\ 30 \\ 2 \\ 398 \end{pmatrix} \begin{array}{l} \text{cents per pencil} \\ \text{cents per notebook} \\ \text{cents per pack of index cards} \\ \text{cents per paper clip} \\ \text{cents per sweatshirt.} \end{array}$$

Then the total cost is given by

Total cost = (6)(5) + (4)(75) + (2)(30) + 36(2) + 1(398)
 = 30 + 300 + 60 + 72 + 398
 = 860 cents or $8.60

Matrix multiplication will be defined so that the total cost is the product of the purchase vector and the cost vector.

As a second example, consider a gamble with three possible outcomes: +$5, −$2, and +$25 with respective probabilities of .25, .7, and .05. Then the expected value of the gamble (see Chapter 9) is (5)(.25) + (−2)(.7) + (25)(.05) = $1.10. If we denote the outcomes of the gamble by the row vector $A = (5, -2, 25)$ and the probabilities by the column vector

$$B = \begin{pmatrix} .25 \\ .7 \\ .05 \end{pmatrix},$$

then the expected value is given by the product of these two matrices.

With these two examples in mind, we are ready to make our first formal definition about matrix multiplication.

**DEFINITION**   If $A$ is $1 \times m$ **row vector and** $B$ **is a** $m \times 1$ **column vector, then the**
*product* $AB$ **is defined to be the number given by**

$$AB = \sum_{k=1}^{m} a_{1k}b_{k1} = a_{11}b_{11} + a_{12}b_{21} + \cdots + a_{1m}b_{m1}$$

**where** $A = (a_{11}, a_{12}, \ldots, a_{1m})$ **and**

$$B = \begin{pmatrix} b_{11} \\ b_{21} \\ \vdots \\ b_{m1} \end{pmatrix}.$$

Note that a row vector and a column vector may be multiplied by this
definition only if the number of components in each vector is the same.

Now suppose that $A$ is a $1 \times m$ vector and $B$ is an $m \times n$ matrix. According
to the definition given above, it is possible to multiply the row vector $A$ by each
column of the matrix $B$ simply by treating that column as a column vector. This
gives us a natural way to define the product of a vector and a matrix.

**DEFINITION**   If $A$ **is a** $1 \times m$ **row vector and** $B$ **is a** $m \times n$ **matrix, then the product**
$AB$ **is defined to be the** $1 \times n$ **matrix whose** $j$th **component is the product of the**
**vector** $A$ **and the** $j$th **column of** $B$.

---

**EXAMPLE**   Suppose $A = (3, 2, -1)$ and

$$B = \begin{pmatrix} 5 & 4 \\ -2 & 0 \\ 1 & 9 \end{pmatrix}.$$

Then the product $AB$ is a $1 \times 2$ matrix. The first component is the product of
the vector $(3, 2, -1)$ and the vector

$$\begin{pmatrix} 5 \\ -2 \\ 1 \end{pmatrix}$$

which is $(3)(5) + (2)(-2) + (-1)(1) = 10$. The second component is the product
of $A$ and the second column of $B$. The value of this second component is
$(3)(4) + (2)(0) + (-1)(9) = 3$. Thus the product $AB$ is the matrix $(10, 3)$.

---

Finally, suppose that $A$ is a $k \times m$ matrix and $B$ is an $m \times n$ matrix. Then it
is possible to multiply each row of $A$ by the matrix $B$ by using the definition we
have just given. Each such multiplication yields a $1 \times n$ row vector. Fitting
these $k$ row vectors together in a natural fashion gives a $k \times n$ matrix.

**DEFINITION**  If $A$ is a $k \times m$ matrix and $B$ is an $m \times n$ matrix, then the *product* $AB$ is defined to be the $k \times n$ matrix whose $ij$th entry is the product of the $i$th row of $A$ and the $j$th column of $B$. Thus $(AB)_{ij} = \sum_{r=1}^{m} a_{ir} b_{rj}$.

---

**EXAMPLE**  Consider the following four matrices:

$$A = \begin{pmatrix} 1 & 2 & 7 \\ -3 & 0 & 8 \end{pmatrix}, \quad B = \begin{pmatrix} 9 & -6 \\ -2 & 1 \\ 4 & 1 \end{pmatrix}, \quad C = \begin{pmatrix} 3 & 6 \\ 2 & 4 \end{pmatrix}, \quad D = \begin{pmatrix} 2 & 8 \\ 6 & 9 \end{pmatrix}.$$

Then we have the following products

$$AB = \begin{pmatrix} 33 & 3 \\ 5 & 26 \end{pmatrix}, \qquad BA = \begin{pmatrix} 27 & 18 & 15 \\ -5 & -4 & -6 \\ 1 & 8 & 36 \end{pmatrix},$$

$$BD = \begin{pmatrix} -18 & 18 \\ 2 & -7 \\ 14 & 41 \end{pmatrix}, \qquad DB \text{ is not defined,}$$

$$CD = \begin{pmatrix} 42 & 78 \\ 28 & 52 \end{pmatrix}, \qquad DC = \begin{pmatrix} 22 & 44 \\ 36 & 72 \end{pmatrix},$$

$$CC = \begin{pmatrix} 21 & 42 \\ 14 & 28 \end{pmatrix}, \qquad C(CC) = (CC)C = \begin{pmatrix} 147 & 294 \\ 98 & 196 \end{pmatrix}.$$

---

Note that the product $BD$ is defined, but not the product $DB$. The products $AB$ and $BA$ are both defined, but they are not of the same size. The products $CD$ and $DC$ are of the same size, but are not equal.

Besides checking the details of computation in this example, you should not continue reading until you are impressed with two facts about matrix multiplication:

1. The product $AB$ of two matrices is defined only when the number of columns of $A$ is equal to the number of rows of $B$. The product has the same number of rows as $A$ and the same number of columns as $B$.

2. Matrix multiplication is not commutative. Even if the products $AB$ and $BA$ are both defined and are both the same size, the matrices $AB$ and $BA$ are not necessarily equal.

The fact that, in general, $AB \neq BA$ is the first significant difference between matrix arithmetic and ordinary arithmetic. There are other surprising results in store. We know that if the product of two numbers is zero, at least one of the factors must be zero. This is not true for matrices. The next example illustrates what can happen.

**EXAMPLE**   Let

$$A = \begin{pmatrix} 4 & 2 \\ -2 & -1 \end{pmatrix} \qquad \text{and} \qquad B = \begin{pmatrix} 3 & 2.5 \\ -6 & -5 \end{pmatrix}.$$

Then the product $AB$ is the zero matrix,

$$AB = \begin{pmatrix} 0 & 0 \\ 0 & 0 \end{pmatrix},$$

although no entry of either factor is a zero.

Before you give up in despair, it is well to point out that a number of properties of ordinary arithmetic continue to hold true for matrix multiplication. Some of these are listed in the next theorem. For convenience, the theorem is stated for square matrices although some of the results hold more generally.

■ **THEOREM 2**    Let $A, B,$ and $C$ be any $n \times n$ matrices and let $c$ be any constant. Then the following properties are all true:

1.  $AB$ is an $n \times n$ matrix
2.  $A(BC) = (AB)C$
3.  $A(B + C) = AB + AC$
4.  $(B + C)A = BA + CA$
5.  $c(AB) = (cA)B = A(cB)$
6.  There is a unique $n \times n$ matrix $I$ such that $AI = IA = A$ for every $n \times n$ matrix $A$.

*Note*    The matrix $I$ of Property (5) is called the *identity matrix* and is defined by the condition:

$$I_{ij} = \begin{cases} 1 & \text{if } i = j, \\ 0 & \text{if } i \neq j. \end{cases}$$

That is, the identity matrix has the form

$$I = \begin{pmatrix} 1 & 0 & 0 & \cdots & 0 \\ 0 & 1 & 0 & \cdots & 0 \\ 0 & 0 & 1 & \cdots & 0 \\ & & & \cdots & \\ 0 & 0 & 0 & \cdots & 1 \end{pmatrix}.$$

In particular the $2 \times 2$ and $3 \times 3$ identity matrices have the form

$$\begin{pmatrix} 1 & 0 \\ 0 & 1 \end{pmatrix} \qquad \text{and} \qquad \begin{pmatrix} 1 & 0 & 0 \\ 0 & 1 & 0 \\ 0 & 0 & 1 \end{pmatrix}, \qquad \text{respectively.}$$

***Proof of Theorem 2***   The hardest result to establish is (2). The others are substantially easier and will be left, as is the custom, as exercises.

We let $D$ represent the matrix $BC$ and let $E = AB$. We need to show that the $ij$th entry of $[A(BC)]$ is the same as the $ij$th entry of $[(AB)C]$. Now we have

$$[A(BC)]_{ij} = (AD)_{ij} = \sum_{k=1}^{n} a_{ik}d_{kj},$$

where

$$d_{kj} = (BC)_{kj} = \sum_{r=1}^{n} b_{kr}c_{rj},$$

so that

$$[A(BC)]_{ij} = \sum_{k=1}^{n} a_{ik} \sum_{r=1}^{n} b_{kr}c_{rj},$$

but since ordinary arithmetic of real numbers is commutative and associative, we write this double sum as

$$\sum_{k=1}^{n} \sum_{r=1}^{n} a_{ik}(b_{kr}c_{rj}) = \sum_{k=1}^{n} \sum_{r=1}^{n} a_{ik}b_{kr}c_{rj}$$

$$= \sum_{r=1}^{n} \sum_{k=1}^{n} a_{ik}b_{kr}c_{rj} = \sum_{r=1}^{n} \sum_{k=1}^{n} (a_{ik}b_{kr})c_{rj}$$

$$= \sum_{r=1}^{n} e_{ir}c_{rj} = (EC)_{ij} = [(AB)C]_{ij}$$

where

$$e_{ir} = E_{ir} = (AB)_{ir} = \sum_{k=1}^{n} a_{ik}b_{kr}. \quad \square$$

The fact that the matrices $(AB)C$ and $A(BC)$ are identical means that we can ignore the parentheses and write $ABC$ to represent the product. It also means that we may define, unambiguously, positive integral powers of a square matrix. That is, if $A$ is an $n \times n$ matrix, then $A^2 = AA$, $A^3 = AAA$, $A^4 = AAAA$, and so on.

**Inverses**   In your first studies of algebra, you learned to solve equations of the form

$$ax + c = d$$

where $a, c$, and $d$ were given numbers, and $x$ was an unknown number.

We can form analogous algebraic questions for matrices. Suppose for example that $A, C$, and $D$ are given $n \times n$ matrices. Does there exist an $n \times n$ matrix $X$ such that

$$AX + C = D? \tag{2}$$

If so, how do we compute $X$?

Since matrices of the same size can be subtracted, Eq. (2) is equivalent to

$$AX = D - C. \qquad (3)$$

Now suppose there is an $n \times n$ matrix $B$ so that $BA = I$ where $I$ is the $n \times n$ identity matrix. If we multiply each side of Eq. (3) on the left by $B$, we obtain

$$B(D - C) = B(AX) = (BA)X = IX = X.$$

The question of solving the matrix equation (2) reduces then to finding a matrix $B$ with the stated property.

**DEFINITION** **Let $A$ be an $n \times n$ matrix. Any $n \times n$ matrix $B$ such that $AB = BA = I$ is called an *inverse* of $A$.**

*Corollary of the Definition* If $B$ is an inverse of $A$, then $A$ is an inverse of $B$.

---

**EXAMPLE** The matrix

$$B = \begin{pmatrix} 3 & -4 \\ -5 & 7 \end{pmatrix}$$

is an inverse of the matrix

$$A = \begin{pmatrix} 7 & 4 \\ 5 & 3 \end{pmatrix}.$$

This is verified by computing the products $AB$ and $BA$.

---

The definition of an inverse does not rule out the possibility that a matrix may have more than one inverse. Our first theorem about inverses shows that this cannot happen; if a matrix has an inverse, then it has a unique one.

■ *THEOREM 3* If $B$ and $B'$ are inverses of the matrix $A$, then $B = B'$.

*Proof of Theorem 3* The proof is a clever, one line affair:

$$B = BI = B(AB') = (BA)B' = IB' = B'. \quad \square$$

According to Theorem 3, we may speak of *the* inverse of a matrix. Since the identity matrix $I$ plays the same role in matrix multiplication as the number 1 in the multiplication of numbers, the inverse of a matrix plays the role of the reciprocal. For this reason, the inverse of the matrix $A$ is denoted by $A^{-1}$.

As an application of the inverse of a matrix, consider the following example.

---

**EXAMPLE** If a Holstein cow is fed $x$ units of grain and $y$ units of hay per day, then she will produce $7x + 4y$ pounds of skim milk and $5x + 3y$ pounds of butterfat per week. How much would you have to feed her to get 41 pounds of milk and 30 pounds of butter fat?

**Solution**   Let $A$ be the matrix

$$\begin{pmatrix} 7 & 4 \\ 5 & 3 \end{pmatrix}$$

and let $X$ be a $2 \times 1$ matrix whose components are units of grain and hay, respectively. Then $AX$ is a $2 \times 1$ matrix whose components represent the pounds of skim milk and butterfat, respectively. Let $D$ be the column vector of desired output,

$$D = \begin{pmatrix} 41 \\ 30 \end{pmatrix}.$$

Then we are trying to find a vector $X$ such that $AX = D$. Multiplying each side of this equation on the left by $A^{-1}$ gives the answer: $X = A^{-1}D$. Since $A^{-1}$ is

$$\begin{pmatrix} 3 & -4 \\ -5 & 7 \end{pmatrix},$$

we have

$$X = \begin{pmatrix} 3 & -4 \\ -5 & 7 \end{pmatrix}\begin{pmatrix} 41 \\ 30 \end{pmatrix} = \begin{pmatrix} 3 \\ 4 \end{pmatrix}.$$

The farmer should feed the cow 3 units of grain and 4 units of hay.

---

***Existence of Inverses***   It is not true that every square matrix has an inverse. Consider, for example, the matrix

$$A = \begin{pmatrix} 1 & 0 \\ 0 & 0 \end{pmatrix}.$$

If $B$ is any $2 \times 2$ matrix,

$$B = \begin{pmatrix} a & b \\ c & d \end{pmatrix},$$

then the product $AB$ has the form

$$AB = \begin{pmatrix} a & 0 \\ c & 0 \end{pmatrix},$$

and no choice of $a$ and $c$ will make this the identity matrix. Thus $A$ has no inverse.

Clearly, the presence of so many zeros as entries of $A$ has something to do with the lack of an inverse. However, less suspicious-looking matrices may also fail to possess inverses.

---

**EXAMPLE**   The matrix $C$, given by

$$C = \begin{pmatrix} 3 & 6 \\ 2 & 4 \end{pmatrix}$$

does not have an inverse.

Suppose, to the contrary, that there was a matrix $B$ such that $CB = I$. Now the product of $C$ and the first column of the matrix $B$ must give the first column of the identity matrix. If the first column of $B$ looks like

$$\binom{a}{c}$$

then we must have the two equations

$$3a + 6c = 1,$$

$$2a + 4c = 0.$$

But if $2a + 4c = 0$, then $a + 2c = 0$ so that $3a + 6c = 0$ and cannot equal 1.

---

The existence of an inverse for a square matrix hinges, then, on the question of whether a certain system of linear algebraic equations has a solution.

The problem of determining whether an inverse exists and, if it does, of computing it is somewhat simplified by the following theorem.

■ **THEOREM 4** If $A$ and $B$ are square matrices of order $n$ and $AB = I$, then $BA$ also is the identity.

Because the proof of this theorem is not elementary, we will not present it. Any standard linear algebra text will contain the proof. For example, see Paul C. Shields, *Elementary Linear Algebra* (New York: Worth, 1968), Appendix 2.

Suppose, then, that we are given a $2 \times 2$ matrix $A$,

$$A = \begin{pmatrix} a & b \\ c & d \end{pmatrix}.$$

According to Theorem 4, $A$ will have an inverse exactly if there is a matrix $B$,

$$B = \begin{pmatrix} w & x \\ y & z \end{pmatrix},$$

such that

$$AB = I = \begin{pmatrix} 1 & 0 \\ 0 & 1 \end{pmatrix}.$$

The matrix equality $AB = I$ translates into a system of four linear equations in four unknowns:

$$\begin{aligned} aw + by &= 1, \\ ax + bz &= 0, \\ cw + dy &= 0, \\ cx + dz &= 1. \end{aligned} \tag{4}$$

The existence of an inverse for a given $3 \times 3$ matrix reduces similarly to the existence of a solution of a system of nine linear equations in nine unknowns.

The system of Eq. (4) splits quite naturally into two systems, each containing two linear equations in two unknowns:

$$aw + by = 1,$$
$$cw + dy = 0,$$

and

$$ax + bz = 0,$$
$$cx + dx = 1.$$

Note that the coefficients of the unknown terms on the left-hand sides of these two systems are the same. The systems correspond to the matrix problem of finding column vectors $X_1$ and $X_2$ so that $AX_1$ and $AX_2$ are the first and second columns of the $2 \times 2$ identity matrix.

In general, if $A$ is an $n \times n$ matrix, then $A$ has an inverse if and only if there are column vectors $X_1, X_2, \ldots, X_n$ so that $AX_i$ is the $i$th column of the $n \times n$ identity matrix, $i = 1, 2, \ldots, n$. Thus the problem of finding the inverse or determining its nonexistence reduces to an algebraic problem: determine the nature or nonexistence of solutions to $n$ systems of linear equations, where each system contains $n$ equations in $n$ unknowns. The coefficients of the unknowns in all the systems are the same, only the constants on the right-hand side change. There is a systematic method for solving this problem—the Gauss-Jordan elimination process. It is discussed in detail in Appendix III.

---

### EXERCISES

---

1. Consider the three row vectors, $\mathbf{u} = (4, 2, 3)$, $\mathbf{v} = (-2, 3, 0)$ and $\mathbf{w} = (-1, 1, 1)$. Compute:

a) $2\mathbf{u}$,                    b) $-\mathbf{v}$,                    c) $3\mathbf{u} - 2\mathbf{v}$,

d) $\mathbf{u} + \mathbf{w}$,        e) $\mathbf{u} - \mathbf{v} + \mathbf{w}$,        f) $4\mathbf{u} - 3\mathbf{v} + 2\mathbf{w}$.

2. If $3\mathbf{v} - 2\mathbf{w} = 0$ for a pair of vectors $\mathbf{v}$ and $\mathbf{w}$, what is the relationship between the components of $\mathbf{v}$ and $\mathbf{w}$?

3. Suppose $4\mathbf{u} - 2\mathbf{v} + 3\mathbf{w} = 0$ for three vectors $\mathbf{u}, \mathbf{v}, \mathbf{w}$. What is the relationship among the components of these vectors?

4. If $A$ is a matrix, then we say $A \geqslant 0$ if every entry of $A$ is nonnegative.

a) Define $A \leqslant 0$ analagously.

b) Prove that if $A \geqslant 0$, then $-A \leqslant 0$.

5. If $A$ and $B$ are matrices of the same size, define $A \geqslant B$ to mean $A - B \geqslant 0$. Show that if $A \geqslant B$ and $B \geqslant C$, then $A \geqslant C$.

6. Suppose $A, B, C,$ and $D$ are matrices whose sizes are $3 \times 4$, $5 \times 4$, $4 \times 4$, and $4 \times 3$, respectively. Find the size of each of the following:

a) $AC$,                    b) $CB$,                    c) $DA$,

d) $ADC$,                   e) $BCDA$.

7. Let matrices $A, B,$ and $C$ be given by

$$A = \begin{pmatrix} 2 & 0 & -3 \\ 1 & -1 & 4 \\ 3 & 2 & 1 \end{pmatrix}, \qquad B = \begin{pmatrix} 5 & 6 \\ -7 & 0 \\ 8 & 2 \end{pmatrix}, \qquad C = \begin{pmatrix} 0 & 0 \\ 2 & -3 \\ 4 & 1 \end{pmatrix}.$$

Compute:

a) $B + C$,    b) $B - 2C$,    c) $A(B + C)$,    d) $A^2$.

8. Let 0 be a zero matrix and suppose $A0$ is defined. Show that $A0$ is also a zero matrix.

9. Prove Theorem 1.

10. Prove Theorem 2.

11. Show that the system of equations

$$2x - 3y = 46$$
$$9x + 7y = 27$$

can be represented in matrix form $Au = v$ for a suitably chosen $2 \times 2$ matrix $A$ and vectors $u$ and $v$.

12. Show that any system of linear equations can be written in the form $Au = v$ where $A$ is a suitably chosen matrix and $u$ and $v$ are vectors.

13. A matrix is *invertible* if it has an inverse. Suppose $A$ and $B$ are $n \times n$ invertible matrices.

a) Show that $AB$ is invertible and $(AB)^{-1} = B^{-1}A^{-1}$.

b) Is $A + B$ necessarily invertible?

14. Let $A$ be an $m \times n$ matrix and $B$ an $n \times m$ matrix. Then both products $AB$ and $BA$ are square matrices.

a) If $m > n$, show that $AB$ has no inverse.

b) If $m > n$, can $BA$ have an inverse?

15. Suppose $A$ is an invertible $n \times n$ matrix with inverse $B$. Find, where possible, inverses of the following matrices:

a) $A^2$,                   b) $A^3$,                   c) $2A$,

d) $-A^7$,                  e) $(A^{-1})^2$,            f) $ABA$.

16. Let $A$ and $B$ be matrices of the same size and define an operation $A * B$ by $(A * B)_{ij} = A_{ij}B_{ij}$; that is, multiply together corresponding entries. Show that this operation is commutative and associative. Is there an "identity" element? Which matrices have "inverses" under this operation? Can you find any applications for this operation?

# Appendix III: Solving Systems of Equations

The equation

$$7x_1 + 2x_2 = 5 \tag{1}$$

is an example of a *linear equation in two unknowns* $x_1$ and $x_2$. This equation is true for some values of the unknowns (for example, $x_1 = 1$, $x_2 = -1$), but false for other values (for example, $x_1 = 2$, $x_2 = 1$). The set of all vectors

$$\mathbf{X} = \begin{pmatrix} x_1 \\ x_2 \end{pmatrix}$$

for which the equation is true is called the *solution set* of the equation. Any element of this set is called a *solution* of the equation. It is easy to check that every solution of Eq. (1) is a vector of the form

$$\begin{pmatrix} \alpha \\ (5 - 7\alpha)/2 \end{pmatrix}$$

where $\alpha$ can be any real number. Conversely, every vector of this form is a solution of Eq. (1).

The general linear equation in two unknowns has the form

$$a_1 x_1 + a_2 x_2 = b \tag{2}$$

where $a_1, a_2$, and $b$ are given constants, and $a_1$ and $a_2$ are not both zero.

The general *linear equation in n unknowns* $x_1, x_2, \ldots, x_n$ is an equation of the form

$$a_1 x_1 + a_2 x_2 + \cdots + a_n x_n = b \tag{3}$$

where the $a_1, a_2, \ldots, a_n$ and $b$ are given constants and at least one of the $a_i$'s is nonzero. The set of all vectors

$$\mathbf{X} = \begin{pmatrix} x_1 \\ x_2 \\ \vdots \\ x_n \end{pmatrix} \tag{4}$$

for which Eq. (3) is true is called the *solution set* of (3).

Since a linear equation in 2 unknowns is the equation of a straight line in the plane, a vector

$$\mathbf{X} = \begin{pmatrix} x_1 \\ x_2 \end{pmatrix}$$

is a solution if and only if the point $(x_1, x_2)$ lies on the line.

A *system of m linear equations in n unknowns* is a collection of linear equations

$$\begin{aligned}
a_{11} x_1 + a_{12} x_2 + \cdots + a_{1n} x_n &= b_1 \\
a_{21} x_1 + a_{22} x_2 + \cdots + a_{2n} x_n &= b_2 \\
&\vdots \\
a_{m1} x_1 + a_{m2} x_2 + \cdots + a_{mn} x_n &= b_m
\end{aligned} \tag{5}$$

where the constants $a_{ij}$ and $b_i$ are given. Note that $a_{ij}$ is the coefficient of $x_j$ in the $i$th equation.

The *solution set of a system* is defined to be the intersection of the solution sets of the individual equations; that is, a vector

$$\mathbf{X} = \begin{pmatrix} x_1 \\ x_2 \\ \vdots \\ x_n \end{pmatrix}$$

is a solution of the system (5) if and only if it is a solution of each equation.

In the case of two equations in two unknowns,

$$\begin{aligned}
a_{11} x_1 + a_{12} x_2 &= b_1 \\
a_{21} x_1 + a_{22} x_2 &= b_2,
\end{aligned} \tag{6}$$

each equation represents a straight line in the plane, so the solution set corresponds to the set of all points lying on both lines. There are three possibilities for the intersection of two lines in the plane: the lines intersect in a single point, the lines are parallel and do not intersect at all, or the lines are coincident.

These three cases are illustrated, respectively, by the examples

$$7x_1 + 2x_2 = 5$$
$$4x_1 - 3x_2 = 7, \tag{7}$$

$$7x_1 + 2x_2 = 5$$
$$14x_1 + 4x_2 = 7, \tag{8}$$

$$7x_1 + 2x_2 = 5$$
$$14x_1 + 4x_2 = 10. \tag{9}$$

The solution set of system (7) consists of the single vector

$$\begin{pmatrix} 1 \\ -1 \end{pmatrix}.$$

The solution set of system (8) is empty, and the solution of system (9) is again any vector of the form

$$\mathbf{X} = \begin{pmatrix} x_1 \\ x_2 \end{pmatrix} = \begin{pmatrix} \alpha \\ (5 - 7\alpha)/2 \end{pmatrix}, \alpha \text{ is arbitrary.}$$

The equations of a general linear system are the equations of "hyperplanes" in $n$-dimensional space and the solution sets correspond to the points lying on the intersection of these hyperplanes. Although these intersections may take many forms, there are essentially the same three possibilities as for the system of two equations in two unknowns:

i) exactly one solution;

ii) no solutions; or

iii) infinitely many solutions.

The main purpose of this appendix is to describe a systematic procedure for obtaining the solution set of a system of linear equations. The basic idea is to replace the original system by a sequence of equivalent, progressively simpler systems.

**DEFINITION**   Two systems of equations are called *equivalent* if they have the same solution set; that is, every solution of either one is a solution of the other.

---

**EXAMPLE**   The systems

$$7x_1 + 2x_2 = 5$$
$$4x_1 - 3x_2 = 7 \tag{7}$$

and

$$13x_1 + 9x_2 = 4$$
$$-4x_1 + 7x_2 = -11 \tag{10}$$

are equivalent systems.

---

■ **THEOREM 1**    If the positions of any two equations in a system are interchanged to form a new system, then the new system is equivalent to the original system.

**EXAMPLE**    The systems

$$11x_1 + 12x_2 - 7x_3 = 8$$
$$3x_1 + 2x_2 + 9x_3 = 7 \qquad (11)$$
$$x_1 - x_2 + x_3 = 4$$

and

$$x_1 - x_2 + x_3 = 4$$
$$3x_1 + 2x_2 + 9x_3 = 7 \qquad (12)$$
$$11x_1 + 12x_2 - 7x_3 = 8$$

are equivalent.

***Proof of Theorem 1***    Let $X_i$ be the solution set of the $i$th equation of the original system. Suppose equations $j$ and $k$ are interchanged. Then the solution set of the original system is

$$X_1 \cap X_2 \cap \cdots X_{j-1} \cap X_j \cap X_{j+1} \cap \cdots \cap X_k \cap X_k \cap X_{k+1} \cap \cdots \cap X_n$$

and the solution set of the system after interchanging is

$$X_1 \cap X_2 \cap \cdots \cap X_{j-1} \cap X_k \cap X_{j+1} \cdots \cap X_{k-1} \cap X_j \cap X_{k+1} \cap \cdots \cap X_n.$$

Since intersection of sets is a commutative operation, the two solution sets are the same. □

■ **THEOREM 2**    If an equation of a given linear system is replaced by a nonzero multiple of itself plus a multiple of another equation of the system to obtain a new system, then the new system is equivalent to the original system.

**EXAMPLE**    Suppose the second equation of system (11) is replaced by $(-1)$ times the second equation plus 3 times the first equation:

$$3x_1 + 2x_2 + 9x_3 = 7$$

is replaced by

$$(-3x_1 - 2x_2 - 9x_3 = -7) + (3x_1 - 3x_2 + 3x_3 = 12) = -5x_2 - 6x_3 = 5.$$

The new system is

$$11x_1 + 12x_2 - 7x_3 = 8$$
$$3x_1 + 2x_2 + 9x_3 = 7 \qquad (13)$$
$$- 5x_2 - 6x_3 = 5.$$

By Theorem 2, Eqs. (11) and (13) are equivalent. Note that system (13) is "simpler" in the sense that we have eliminated one of the unknowns in one of the equations.

*Proof of Theorem 2*   If the $i$th equation of the original system (5) is replaced by $c$ times the $i$th equation plus $d$ times the $j$th equation, then the new system is

$$a_{11}x_1 + a_{12}x_2 + \cdots + a_{1n}x_n = b_1$$
$$\cdots$$
$$c(a_{i1}x_1 + \cdots + a_{in}x_n) + d(a_{j1}x_1 + \cdots + a_{jn}x_n) = cb_i + db_j \qquad (14)$$
$$\cdots$$
$$a_{m1}x_1 + a_{m2}x_2 + \cdots + a_{mn}x_n = b_m.$$

Now, every vector **X** which satisfies the equations of (5) will also satisfy the equations of (14). On the other hand, system (5) can be obtained from system (14) by a similar operation: replace the $i$th equation of (14) by $(1/c)$ times the $i$th equation plus $(-d/c)$ times the $j$th equation. Thus every vector satisfying the equations of (14) will also satisfy the equations of (5). We have seen that the solution set of each system is a subset of the other. Hence, the solution sets are equal. □

The method of solution we shall describe is called the Gauss-Jordan elimination procedure. It consists of a sequence of operations using Theorem 1 and Theorem 2 to obtain new, equivalent systems which eliminate, at each step, at least one unknown in one of the equations. To be more precise, we use Theorem 2 to eliminate $x_1$ from every equation except the first, then use Theorem 2 to eliminate $x_2$ from every equation except the second, and so on. Eventually, we obtain a system whose solution set can be determined by inspection. We shall illustrate the procedure with several examples.

**EXAMPLE**   Consider system (7)

$$7x_1 + 2x_2 = 5$$
$$4x_1 - 3x_2 = 7 \qquad (7)$$

*Step 1.* Replace the first equation by $(\frac{1}{7})$ times the first equation. We obtain:

$$x_1 + \frac{2}{7}x_2 = \frac{5}{7}$$
$$4x_1 - 3x_2 = 7. \qquad (15)$$

*Step 2.* In system (15), replace the second equation by the second equation plus $(-4)$ times the first equation. The result is:

$$x_1 + \frac{2}{7}x_2 = \frac{5}{7}$$
$$-\frac{29}{7}x_2 = \frac{29}{7}. \qquad (16)$$

*Step 3.* Replace the second equation by $(-\frac{7}{29})$ times itself:

$$x_1 + \frac{2}{7}x_2 = \frac{5}{7}$$

$$x_2 = -1.$$

(17)

*Step 4.* Replace the first equation by the first equation plus $(-\frac{2}{7})$ times the second equation:

$$x_1 \quad = 1$$

$$x_2 = -1.$$

(18)

Now the solution set can be read off from the equations of system (18). It consists of the unique vector

$$\mathbf{X} = \begin{pmatrix} 1 \\ -1 \end{pmatrix}.$$

As a second example, consider the system:

$$x_2 - 2x_3 = 0$$

$$2x_1 + x_2 - 4x_3 = 6$$

$$x_1 + x_2 + x_3 = 3.$$

(19)

*Step 1.* Interchange the first and third equations:

$$x_1 + x_2 + x_3 = 3$$

$$2x_1 + x_2 + 4x_3 = 6$$

$$x_2 - 2x_3 = 0.$$

(20)

*Step 2.* Use the first equation to eliminate $x_1$ in the other equations. Since $x_1$ is already missing in the third equation, we only have to work on the second equation. Replace it by the second equation plus $(-2)$ times the first equation:

$$x_1 + x_2 + x_3 = 3$$

$$-x_2 + 2x_3 = 0$$

$$x_2 - 2x_3 = 0.$$

(21)

*Step 3.* Use the second equation to eliminate $x_2$ from the other equations:

a) Replace second equation by $(-1)$ times second.

b) Replace first equation by first equation plus $(-1)$ times second.

c) Replace third equation by third plus $(-1)$ times second.

The result is:

$$x_1 + 3x_3 = 3$$

$$x_2 - 2x_3 = 0$$

$$0 = 0.$$

(22)

From Eqs. (22), we see that we can assign any value to $x_3$ and then compute $x_1$ and $x_2$ from the first two equations. For example, if $x_3 = 0$, then $x_1 = 3$ and $x_2 = 0$; if $x_3 = 1$, then $x_1 = 0$ and $x_2 = 2$. Thus the vectors

$$\mathbf{X}_1 = \begin{pmatrix} 3 \\ 0 \\ 0 \end{pmatrix} \quad \text{and} \quad \mathbf{X}_2 = \begin{pmatrix} 0 \\ 2 \\ 1 \end{pmatrix}$$

are solutions to the original system. The general solution can be described by letting $x_3$ take on any arbitrary value $\alpha$. Then $x_1 = 3 - 3\alpha$ and $x_2 = 2\alpha$. Thus the solution set is the set of all vectors of the form

$$X = \begin{pmatrix} 3 - 3\alpha \\ 2\alpha \\ \alpha \end{pmatrix}, \quad \alpha \text{ arbitrary.}$$

---

If the right-hand side of Eqs. (19) had been replaced by the constant vector

$$b = \begin{pmatrix} 1 \\ 2 \\ 3 \end{pmatrix}$$

then we would have obtained the system

$$\begin{aligned} x_2 - 2x_3 &= 1 \\ 2x_1 + x_2 + 4x_3 &= 2 \\ x_1 + x_2 + x_3 &= 3 \end{aligned} \tag{19'}$$

The procedure to solve this system is the same as that for system (19); the operations we use in the Gauss-Jordan process are dictated only by the coefficients of the unknowns $x_1, x_2, \ldots, x_n$ and are independent of the constants on the right-hand sides of the equations.

After completing Steps 1, 2 and 3, we would arrive at

$$\begin{aligned} x_1 + 3x_3 &= -1 \\ x_2 - 2x_3 &= 4 \\ 0 &= -3. \end{aligned} \tag{22'}$$

The system (22') has no solution, since the third equation is not true for any choice of $x_1, x_2$, and $x_3$. Thus the equivalent system (19') has no solution. Geometrically, the equations of (19') represent three planes in 3-dimensional space which have no common point. The three planes of system (19) intersect along a line.

The Gauss-Jordan elimination procedure can be somewhat simplified by adopting matrix notation. The original system of linear equations (5) can be represented by the matrix equation

$$AX = B$$

where $A$ is the $m \times n$ matrix of coefficients

$$A = \begin{pmatrix} a_{11} & a_{12} & \cdots & a_{1n} \\ a_{21} & a_{22} & \cdots & a_{2n} \\ \vdots & & & \\ a_{m1} & a_{m2} & \cdots & a_{mn} \end{pmatrix}$$

and $\mathbf{X}$ and $\mathbf{B}$ are the column vectors

$$\mathbf{X} = \begin{pmatrix} x_1 \\ x_2 \\ \vdots \\ x_n \end{pmatrix}, \mathbf{B} = \begin{pmatrix} b_1 \\ b_2 \\ \vdots \\ b_m \end{pmatrix}.$$

In the Gauss-Jordan process, the entries of $A$ and $\mathbf{B}$ will change after each operation. We can keep track of these changes by considering an $m \times (n + 1)$ *augmented matrix*

$$(A | B) = \begin{pmatrix} a_{11} & a_{12} & \cdots & a_{1n} & b_1 \\ a_{21} & a_{22} & \cdots & a_{2n} & b_2 \\ \cdots & & & & \\ a_{m1} & a_{m2} & \cdots & a_{mn} & b_m \end{pmatrix}$$

Then the operations of Theorems 1 and 2 can be interpreted as operations on the rows of the augmented matrix:

a) interchange two rows of $(A | \mathbf{B})$;
b) replace one row of $(A | \mathbf{B})$ by the sum of a nonzero multiple of that row and a multiple of another row.

---

**EXAMPLE**   The system

$$2x_1 + 10x_2 + 6x_3 = 14$$
$$4x_1 + 22x_2 - 8x_3 = 12$$

has augmented matrix

$$\begin{pmatrix} 2 & 10 & 6 & | & 14 \\ 4 & 22 & -8 & | & 12 \end{pmatrix}.$$

To solve the system, we carry out the operations of the Gauss-Jordan procedure on the rows of the augmented matrix.

*Step 1.* Replace the first row by $(\frac{1}{2})$ the first row. The result is

$$\begin{pmatrix} 1 & 5 & 3 & | & 7 \\ 4 & 22 & -8 & | & 12 \end{pmatrix}.$$

*Step* 2. Replace the second row by the second row plus ($-4$) times the first row. The result is

$$\begin{pmatrix} 1 & 4 & 3 & \Big| & 7 \\ 0 & 2 & -20 & \Big| & -16 \end{pmatrix}.$$

*Step* 3. Replace the second row by ($\frac{1}{2}$) times the second row:

$$\begin{pmatrix} 1 & 5 & 3 & \Big| & 7 \\ 0 & 1 & -10 & \Big| & -8 \end{pmatrix}.$$

*Step* 4. Replace the first row by the first row plus ($-5$) times the second row:

$$\begin{pmatrix} 1 & 0 & 53 & \Big| & 47 \\ 0 & 1 & -10 & \Big| & -8 \end{pmatrix}.$$

This augmented matrix represents the system

$$x_1 + 53x_3 = 47$$
$$x_2 - 10x_3 = -8$$

which has as its solution set, the set of vectors of the form

$$\mathbf{X} = \begin{pmatrix} 47 - 53\alpha \\ -8 + 10\alpha \end{pmatrix}, \alpha \text{ arbitrary.}$$

---

With these examples in mind, we may describe the Gauss-Jordan procedure more explicitly:

1. Interchange equations (or rows of the augmented matrix) so that the first equation has a nonzero coefficient of $x_1$.

2. Replace the first equation by the first equation multiplied by the reciprocal of the coefficient of $x_1$.

3. Use the new first equation to eliminate $x_1$ in every other equation. The $i$th equation is replaced by the $i$th equation plus ($-a_{i1}$) times first equation ($i = 2, 3, \ldots, m$).

4. Let $j$ be the smallest number such that $x_j$ occurs with some nonzero coefficient in some equation other than the first. Interchange equations so that the new second equation has a nonzero coefficient of $x_j$.

5. Replace the second equation by the second equation multiplied by the reciprocal of the coefficient of $x_j$.

6. Use the new second equation to eliminate $x_j$ in all equations (including the first equation) except the second. Follow the procedure of the third step to do this.

7. Let $k$ be the smallest number so that $x_k$ appears with a nonzero coefficient in some equation other than the first two. Make this the new third equation and use it to eliminate $x_k$ in every equation except the third.

8. Continue in this manner until further simplification is not possible. Read off the solution set from the resulting system.

## Computing the Inverse of a Square Matrix

The Gauss-Jordan procedure can be used for any system of $m$ linear equations in $n$ unknowns. In this section, we apply the procedure to the problem of determining the inverse of a square matrix.

Suppose we wish to find the inverse of the matrix

$$A = \begin{pmatrix} 7 & 4 \\ 5 & 3 \end{pmatrix}.$$

The discussion in Appendix II shows that we need to find vectors $\mathbf{X}_1$ and $\mathbf{X}_2$ so that

$$A\mathbf{X}_1 = \begin{pmatrix} 1 \\ 0 \end{pmatrix} \quad \text{and} \quad A\mathbf{X}_2 = \begin{pmatrix} 0 \\ 1 \end{pmatrix},$$

that is, we need to solve the systems

$$\begin{aligned} 7x_1 \div 4x_2 &= 1 \\ 5x_1 + 3x_2 &= 0 \end{aligned} \quad \text{and} \quad \begin{aligned} 7x_1 + 4x_2 &= 0 \\ 5x_1 + 3x_2 &= 1. \end{aligned}$$

There are two approaches we may take:

**Approach I**  Solve the more general system

$$\begin{aligned} 7x_1 + 4x_2 &= a \\ 5x_1 + 3x_2 &= b \end{aligned}$$

and then find $\mathbf{X}_1$ by letting $a = 1$, $b = 0$ and find $\mathbf{X}_2$ by letting $a = 0$ and $b = 1$. The augmented matrix is

$$\left( \begin{array}{cc|c} 7 & 4 & a \\ 5 & 3 & b \end{array} \right).$$

The steps in the Gauss-Jordan procedure are:

*Step 1.* Divide row 1 by 7:

$$\left( \begin{array}{cc|c} 1 & 4/7 & a/7 \\ 5 & 3 & b \end{array} \right).$$

*Step 2.* Replace row 2 by row 2 $- 5$ (row 1):

$$\left( \begin{array}{cc|c} 1 & 4/7 & a/7 \\ 0 & 1/7 & (7b - 5a)/7 \end{array} \right).$$

*Step 3.* Replace row 2 by 7 (row 2):

$$\left( \begin{array}{cc|c} 1 & 4/7 & a/7 \\ 0 & 1 & 7b - 5a \end{array} \right).$$

*Step 4.* Replace row 1 by row 1 $- (4/7)$(row 2):

$$\left( \begin{array}{cc|c} 1 & 0 & 3a - 4b \\ 0 & 1 & 7b - 5a \end{array} \right).$$

Letting $a = 1$, $b = 0$, we obtain

$$\mathbf{X}_1 = \begin{pmatrix} 3 \\ -5 \end{pmatrix}$$

and letting $a = 0$, $b = 1$ produces

$$\mathbf{X}_2 = \begin{pmatrix} -4 \\ 7 \end{pmatrix}.$$

Thus the reverse of $A$ is

$$A^{-1} = (\mathbf{X}_1, \mathbf{X}_2) = \begin{pmatrix} 3 & -4 \\ -5 & 7 \end{pmatrix}.$$

**Approach II**   Solve the two systems simultaneously by using a doubly augmented matrix

$$\left( \begin{array}{cc|cc} 7 & 4 & 1 & 0 \\ 5 & 3 & 0 & 1 \end{array} \right).$$

Since the steps for solution are the same, we merely note the augmented matrices:

After Step 1: $\left( \begin{array}{cc|cc} 1 & 4/7 & 1/7 & 0 \\ 5 & 3 & 0 & 1 \end{array} \right).$

After Step 2: $\left( \begin{array}{cc|cc} 1 & 4/7 & 1/7 & 0 \\ 0 & 1/7 & -5/7 & 1 \end{array} \right).$

After Step 3: $\left( \begin{array}{cc|cc} 1 & 4/7 & 1/7 & 0 \\ 0 & 1 & -5 & 7 \end{array} \right).$

After Step 4: $\left( \begin{array}{cc|cc} 1 & 0 & 3 & -4 \\ 0 & 1 & -5 & 7 \end{array} \right).$

Note that in this approach, we begin with $(A|I)$ and end up with $(I|A^{-1})$.

No matter which approach is used, it is important that the operation which is used at each step is applied to *all* the coefficients in the indicated row of the augmented matrix.

---

**A FINAL EXAMPLE**   Consider the system

$$
\begin{aligned}
x_1 + x_2 + x_3 &= a \\
2x_1 - 4x_2 + 7x_3 &= b \\
-x_1 + 5x_2 - 6x_3 &= c
\end{aligned}
$$

which has augmented matrix

$$\left(\begin{array}{ccc|c} 1 & 1 & 1 & a \\ 2 & -4 & 7 & b \\ -1 & 5 & -6 & c \end{array}\right)$$

The reader should verify that the following steps, taken in the indicated order,

1. Replace row 2 by row 2 − 2 row 1;
   replace row 3 by row 3 + row 1;
2. Replace row 2 by $(-\frac{1}{6})$ row 2;
   replace row 1 by row 1 + (−1) row 2;
   replace row 3 by row 3 − 6 (row 2);

yields the augmented matrix

$$\left(\begin{array}{ccc|c} 1 & 0 & 11/6 & (8a - b)/6 \\ 0 & 1 & -5/6 & 2a - b \\ 0 & 0 & 0 & -a + b + c \end{array}\right).$$

The corresponding system of equations has a solution if and only if $-a + b + c = 0$. In particular, if $a = 1$, $b = 0$, $c = 0$, then $-a + b + c = -1 \neq 0$. Thus if $A$ is the matrix,

$$A = \left(\begin{array}{ccc} 1 & 1 & 1 \\ 2 & -4 & 7 \\ -1 & 5 & -6 \end{array}\right).$$

Then it is impossible to find a vector $\mathbf{X}$ such that

$$A\mathbf{X}_1 = \left(\begin{array}{c} 1 \\ 0 \\ 0 \end{array}\right).$$

Hence the matrix $A$ does not have an inverse.

**EXERCISES**

1. Solve the system
$$x_1 + 4x_2 + 3x_3 = 1$$
$$-3x_2 - 2x_3 = 2$$
$$-7x_2 - 5x_3 = 4.$$

2. Solve the system

$$x_1 - 2x_2 - 3x_3 = 2$$
$$x_1 - 4x_2 - 13x_3 = 14$$
$$-3x_1 + 5x_2 + 4x_3 = 0.$$

3. Solve the system

$$x + 2y + z = 3$$
$$3x + 6y + 11z = 8$$
$$-2x - 4y + 4z = 9.$$

4. Solve the system

$$8x - 8y + 2u + 4v + 2w = -14$$
$$4x + 2y - 2u - v + 7w = 29$$
$$x + 4y + 3u + 5v + 7w = 2$$

for $x, y, v$ in terms of $u$ and $w$. (No promises that the arithmetic is simple).

5. The Gauss-Jordan procedure works even if the number of equations equals or exceeds the number of unknowns. Solve the following system for $w$ and $x$ in terms of $y$ and $z$:

$$w + 2x + 3y + 4z = 10$$
$$2w - x + y - z = 1$$
$$3w + x + 4y + 3z = 11$$
$$-2w + 6x + 4y + 10z = 18.$$

6. The system

$$x + y + z + w = 8$$
$$x - 2y + 4z = -1$$
$$2x - y + 5z + w = 6$$

is inconsistent; that is, it has no solutions (add the first two equations together and compare the result with the third equation). Try to solve for $x$ in terms of $y, z, w$, using the Gauss-Jordan procedure, and discuss what happens.

7. Construct a flow chart for the Gauss-Jordan procedure.

8. Show that when the Gauss-Jordan procedure is used to find an inverse of a square matrix, the result is either that there is no inverse or there is a unique inverse; that is, show why there cannot be infinitely many solutions of the corresponding system of linear equations.

9. Let $\mathbf{X}_1$ and $\mathbf{X}_2$ be any two solutions of the matrix equation $A\mathbf{X} = 0$ where 0 is a zero matrix.

a) Show that $\mathbf{X}_1 + \mathbf{X}_2$ is also a solution.

b) Show that $c\mathbf{X}_1$ is a solution where $c$ is any constant.

c) Show that $A\mathbf{X} = 0$ always has at least one solution, and that if it has two distinct solutions, then it must have infinitely many distinct solutions.

10. Let $X^*$ be any solution of $AX = B$ where $A$ and $B$ are given matrices, and let $X_0$ be a solution of $AX = 0$.

a) Show that $X^* + X_0$ is a solution of $AX = B$.

b) Show that every solution of $AX = B$ can be written in the form $X = X^* + X_1$ where $X_1$ is some solution of $AX = 0$.

11. Find, if possible, inverses of the following matrices:

$$A = \begin{pmatrix} 3 & 1 \\ 11 & 4 \end{pmatrix}, \qquad B = \begin{pmatrix} 5 & 6 \\ 4 & 5 \end{pmatrix}, \qquad C = \begin{pmatrix} 8 & 4 \\ 6 & 3 \end{pmatrix},$$

$$D = \begin{pmatrix} 0 & 1 \\ 1 & 0 \end{pmatrix}, \qquad E = \begin{pmatrix} 1 & 2 & 3 \\ 4 & 5 & 6 \\ 7 & 8 & 9 \end{pmatrix}, \qquad F = \begin{pmatrix} 0 & 0 & 1 \\ 1 & 0 & 0 \\ 0 & 1 & 0 \end{pmatrix}$$

12. Let $A$ be the $2 \times 2$ matrix

$$A = \begin{pmatrix} a & b \\ c & d \end{pmatrix}$$

a) Show that $A$ has an inverse if and only if $ad - bc \neq 0$.

b) Determine $A^{-1}$ if $ad - bc \neq 0$.

13. Let $B$ be an arbitrary $3 \times 3$ matrix. Find necessary and sufficient conditions on the entries of $B$ for the matrix to have an inverse.

14. The Otter Creek Manufacturing Company produces two kinds of skis, "Premium" and "Quality." From $x$ pounds of wood and $y$ pounds of plastic, it can produce $7x + 4y$ pairs of Premium skis and $5x + 3y$ pairs of Quality skis. If there is a demand for 5600 pairs of Premiums and 4100 pairs of Quality skis, how much wood and plastic should the company order?

# Appendix IV: Functions of Two Variables

Let $S$ be a subset of the $(x,y)$-plane. A relationship which assigns a unique number to each point of $S$ is called a *real-valued function of two variables*. The domain of such a function is a set of ordered pairs $(x, y)$ of real numbers and the range is a subset of the reals. We may denote such a function by the letters customarily reserved for functions: $f, g, h, F, G, H, \varphi, \theta, \ldots$.

We write

$$z = f(x, y)$$

to denote the fact that $f$ assigns the number $z$ to the ordered pair $(x, y)$.

---

**EXAMPLE 1**  Consider the function $f(x, y) = x^2 + y^4$. We then have $f(9,2) = 9^2 + 2^4 = 81 + 16 = 97$, $f(-9, 2) = 97$, and $f(-7,0) = 49$. This function is defined for all values of $x$ and $y$ so its domain is the entire plane. Since $x^2 + y^2$ is the sum of two nonnegative numbers, no negative numbers can be in the range. On the other hand, if $z$ is any nonnegative real number, then $f(z^{1/2}, 0) = z$. Thus the range of $f$ is the set of all nonnegative real numbers. Since $f(9, 2) = f(-9,2) = f(9, -2) = f(-9, -2)$, the function is not one-to-one.

**EXAMPLE 2**  Let $f$ be the function given by $f(x, y) = 1/(y\sqrt{x})$. Then we have $f(4, 3) = \frac{1}{6}$, $f(9, -\frac{1}{3}) = -1$, while $f(-5,2)$ and $f(2,0)$ are undefined. Now $f$ is defined whenever $x$ is positive and $y$ is nonzero. Thus the domain of $f$ is the open right half-plane excluding the $x$-axis; that is $S = \{(x, y): x > 0, \ y \neq 0\}$. The range of $f$ consists of all real numbers except 0, for if $z \neq 0$, then $f(1, 1/z) = z$.

---

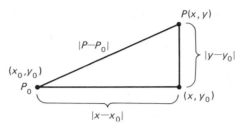

**Fig. IV.1**    The distance $|P - P_0|$ from $P_0$ to $P$ is the length of the hypotenuse of a right triangle with sides of length $|x - x_0|$ and $|y - y_0|$.

**CONTINUITY**    The definition of continuity for a function of two variables is much the same as that for a function of one variable. The basic idea is exactly the same: small changes in domain values yield relatively small changes in range values. We obtain a more precise definition by using the $\varepsilon$-$\delta$ approach.

**DEFINITION**    **A function $f$ of one variable is *continuous* at $x_0$ if for every positive number $e$, there is a positive number $d$ such that $|f(x) - f(x_0)| < \varepsilon$ whenever $|x - x_0| < \delta$.**

**DEFINITION**    **A function $f$ of two variables is *continuous* at $P_0 = (x_0, y_0)$ if for every positive number $\varepsilon$, there is a positive number $\delta$ such that $f(P) - f(P_0) < \varepsilon$ whenever $|P - P_0| < \delta$. Here $P$ is a point $(x, y)$ in the plane and $|P - P_0|$ is the Euclidean distance $((x - x_0)^2 + (y - y_0)^2)^{1/2}$ between points in the plane, derived from the Pythagorean Theorem (see Fig. IV.1).**

**Partial derivatives**    Recall that a derivative of a function of one variable $y = f(x)$ is a measure of the rate of change of the "dependent" variable $y$ with respect to changes in the "independent" variable $x$. For a function of two variables, $f(x, y) = z$, we have a dependent variable $z$, and two independent variables, $x$ and $y$. We can measure rates of change of $z$ with respect to $x$ and with respect to $y$.

Computationally, partial derivatives are easy to find. The partial derivative of $f$ with respect to $x$ is denoted by $\partial f/x$ or $\partial z/x$ or $f_x$. To compute $f_x$, simply pretend that $y$ is a constant and carry out ordinary differentiation with respect to $x$ on the formula for $f(x, y)$. The partial derivative of $f$ with respect to $y$, denoted by $\partial f/\partial y$ or $\partial z/\partial y$ or $f_y$, is computed in an analagous fashion. Some examples are provided in Table IV.1.

**Table IV.I**

| $f(x, y)$ | $f_x(x, y)$ | $f_y(x, y)$ | $f_x(9, 2)$ | $f_y(9, 2)$ | $f_x(-9, 2)$ | $f_y(-9, 2)$ |
|---|---|---|---|---|---|---|
| $x^2 + y^4$ | $2x$ | $4y^3$ | $18$ | $32$ | $-18$ | $32$ |
| $x^2 y$ | $2xy$ | $x^2$ | $36$ | $81$ | $-36$ | $81$ |
| $1/y\sqrt{x}$ | $-\frac{1}{2}x^{-3/2}y^{-1}$ | $-y^2 x^{-1/2}$ | $-\frac{1}{108}$ | $-\frac{1}{12}$ | undefined | undefined |

The formal definitions of the partial derivatives look like this:

$$f_x(x_0, y_0) = \lim_{h \to 0} \frac{f(x_0 + h, y_0) - f(x_0, y_0)}{h},$$

if the limit exists, and

$$f_y(x_0, y_0) = \lim_{k \to 0} \frac{f(x_0, y_0 + k) - f(x_0, y_0)}{k},$$

if the limit exists.

**Higher order derivatives**    Since $f_x$ and $f_y$ are also functions of two variables, we can compute the partial derivatives of each of these. This leads to four *second order partial derivatives*: $f_{xx}, f_{xy}, f_{yx}, f_{yy}$.

For the example $f(x, y) = x^2 + y^4$, we have

$$f_{xx}(x, y) = 2, \qquad f_{xy}(x, y) = 0 = f_{yx}(x, y), \qquad f_{yy}(x, y) = 12y^2.$$

There is nothing to stop us now from computing partial derivatives of higher and higher orders. For instance, the expression $f_{xyxx}$ would denote the function of two variables obtained by differentiating $f$ first with respect to $x$, then with respect to $y$, and then twice more with respect to $x$.

This process might break down, however, for example, the function $f(x, y) = x^{3/2}y$ is defined and continuous everywhere and so are the functions

$$f_x(x, y) = \frac{3}{2}x^{1/2}y, \qquad f_y(x, y) = x^{3/2}$$

$$f_{xy}(x, y) = f_{yx}(x, y) = \frac{3}{2}x^{1/2}$$

but the second order partial derivative $f_{xx}$ is undefined whenever $x = 0$.

The *graph* of a function of two variables with domain $S$ is the set

$$G_f = \{(x, y, z): (x, y) \text{ is in } S \text{ and } z = f(x, y)\}.$$

The set $G_f$ represents a two-dimensional surface in three-dimensional space. The higher the order of partial derivatives that exist for $f$, the "smoother" this surface will be.

It is a remarkable result that if $f_{xy}$ and $f_{yx}$ are both continuous functions, then they are equal. Check this for the functions in Table IV.I.

---

**EXERCISES**

---

1.  Determine $f_x$ and $f_y$ where $f(x, y)$ is given by

a)  $\sin x \cos y$,                         b)  $x^2 + x \sin (x + y)$,

c)  $e^{x + 2y}$,                               d)  $\log (x - y^2)$.

2. Check whether $f_{xy} = f_{yx}$ where $f$ is given by

a) $x^2y + y^2x + xy$,                                         b) $\cos(x^2 - y^2)$,

c) $(x + y)^{-1}$.

3. Compute $f_{xx} + f_{yy}$ for

a) $f(x, y) = x^3 - 3xy^2$,                              b) $f(x, y) = \log(x^2 + y^2)$.

4. Find the domain and range of each function of two variables given in the appendix and the exercises.

# Appendix V: Differential Equations

In this text we deal with a number of differential equations of a fairly simple type. The following paragraphs will serve as an introduction for those who have not studied this topic before.

By a *first-order differential equation*, we will mean an equation of the form

$$\frac{dy}{dx} = F(x, y), \tag{1}$$

where $F$ is a given function of two variables defined on some region $R$ of the $(x,y)$-plane. Equation (1) asserts that $y$ is a differentiable function of $x$ over some interval $[a, b]$ and that the derivative satisfies (1) for all values of $x$ in that interval. A more precise statement would be that there is a function $y = f(x)$ such that

A) $f$ is a differentiable function of $x$ on $[a, b]$;

B) the graph $\{(x, y): y = f(x), a \leqslant x \leqslant b\}$ is contained in $R$; and

C) $f'(x^*) = F(x^*, f(x^*))$ for all $x^*$ in $[a, b]$.

---

**EXAMPLE 1** Consider the differential equation

$$\frac{dy}{dx} = 3x^2 y + \frac{y}{2\sqrt{x}}. \tag{2}$$

Here the function $F(x, y)$ is given by $F(x, y) = 3x^2 y + y/(2\sqrt{x})$. This function is defined everywhere on the region $R$ of the plane consisting of all points with positive first coordinate, the "open right half-plane." If $a$ and $b$ are any two positive numbers with $a < b$, then the function

$$y = f(x) = 8e^{x^3 + \sqrt{x}} \tag{3}$$

satisfies (A), (B), and (C). You should verify this (immediately).

Note that the function

$$f(x) = e^{x^3 + \sqrt{x} - 7} \tag{4}$$

also satisfies (A), (B), and (C).

---

Any function which fulfills the conditions of (A), (B), and (C) is called a *solution* of the differential equation (1). Thus the functions described in Eqs. (3) and (4) are two different solutions of the differential equation (2).

It should be pointed out at once that not every differential equation has a solution. Some continuity properties about $F$ and its partial derivatives usually need to be satisfied to guarantee that a solution exists. Example 1 illustrates the fact that a differential equation may have more than one solution. In fact, the differential equation (2) has infinitely many solutions (list some). There is a uniqueness result, however. If the function $F$ satisfies certain continuity properties and $(x_0, y_0)$ is any point in $R$, then there is a unique solution of the differential equation $dy/dx = F(x, y)$ whose graph passes through $(x_0, y_0)$.

---

**EXAMPLE 1 (continued)**  The function $f(x) = 8e^{x^3 + \sqrt{x}}$ is the unique solution of Eq. (2) whose graph goes through the point $(4, 8e^{66})$.

---

The exact statement of the basic existence and uniqueness theorem for first-order differential equations follows. Its proof can be found in most standard textbooks on differential equations; two of these are listed at the end of this appendix.

■ **THEOREM**    Suppose the functions $F$ and $F_y$ are continuous at all points of the region $R$ of the $(x,y)$-plane. Let $(x_0, y_0)$ be any point of $R$. Then there is an interval $I$ of real numbers containing $x_0$ and

1. There is a unique function $y = f(x)$ which is a solution of the differential equation $dy/dx = F(x, y)$ for which $f(x_0) = y_0$;
2. The solution exists for all values of $x$ for which the points $(x, f(x))$ lie in $R$; and
3. The solution $f$ varies continuously with the choice of $x, x_0$, and $y_0$.

In this appendix, we shall discuss techniques for discovering solutions to differential equations when the function $F(x, y)$ takes on one of three very special forms.

*Case 1 (Classic Integration)*    Suppose $F(x, y) = g(x)$; that is, $F$ is a function only of $x$.

In this case, the differential equation has the form

$$\frac{dy}{dx} = g(x). \tag{5}$$

To solve this equation we need only to find a function whose derivative is $g(x)$. This is the classic integration problem of elementary calculus. The solution of (5) has the form

$$y = \int g(x)\, dx. \tag{6}$$

When the indefinite integration of (6) is carried out, we are left with a constant of integration. If an initial point $(x_0, y_0)$ is specified, we can find the value of the constant.

---

**EXAMPLE 2**    Find the unique solution of the differential equation

$$\frac{dy}{dx} = 2x + 3\sqrt{x}$$

whose graph passes through $(4, 26)$.

**Solution**    We have $y = \int 2x + 3\sqrt{x}\, dx$ so that

$$y = x^2 + 2x^{3/2} + C,$$

where $C$ is an arbitrary constant. To find the solution through $(4, 26)$, let $x = 4$ and $y = 26$ in the last equation:

$$26 = 4^2 + 2(4)^{3/2} + C = 16 + 16 + C = 32 + C$$

so that $C = 26 - 32 = -6$. Thus the function we seek is $y = f(x) = x^2 + 2x^{3/2} - 6$.

---

An alternative way to obtain Eq. (6) from Eq. (5) is to rewrite Eq. (5) as an equivalent integral equation

$$\int dy = \int g(x)\, dx. \tag{7}$$

We then integrate the left-hand side of (7) with respect to $y$ and the right-hand side with respect to $x$. This yields

$$y + C = \int g(x)\, dx,$$

which is clearly equivalent to (6).

This particular device leads to the solution for our second type of first-order differential equation.

*Case 2 (**Variables Separate**)*   Suppose $F(x, y) = g(x)h(y)$; that is, $F$ can be written as the product of a function of $x$ and a function of $y$. In this case, we say the variables separate.

When the variables separate, the differential equation $dy/dx = F(x, y)$ can be written as

$$\frac{dy}{dx} = g(x)h(y). \tag{8}$$

To solve the equation, we write down the corresponding integral equation

$$\int \frac{1}{h(y)} \, dy - \int g(x) \, dx \tag{9}$$

and carry out the indicated integrations.

---

**EXAMPLE 3**   Solve the differential equation of Example 1:

$$\frac{dy}{dx} = 3x^2 y + \frac{y}{2\sqrt{x}} = y\left(3x^2 + \frac{1}{2\sqrt{x}}\right). \tag{2}$$

**Solution**   We write the integral equation

$$\int \frac{1}{y} \, dy = \int 3x^2 + \frac{1}{2\sqrt{x}} \, dx.$$

The next step is to carry out the integrations indicated:

$$\log y + C_1 = x^3 + \sqrt{x} + C_2.$$

A better form for this equation is

$$\log y = x^3 + \sqrt{x} + C.$$

Note that we have not yet found $y$ as an explicit function of $x$, but we have "solved" the differential equation to the extent that we have found a relationship between $y$ and $x$ which contains no derivatives. In this particular case, we may go further by exponentiating each side of this last equation. We obtain

$$e^{\log y} = y = e^{[x^3 + \sqrt{x} + C_3]} = e^{[x^3 + \sqrt{x}]}e^{C_3}$$

or, more simply, $y = Ce^{[x^3 + \sqrt{x}]}$.

In carrying out the details of this solution, we have assumed that $y$ is strictly positive. A similar result is obtained if $y$ is negative. What happens if $y$ is zero?

---

*Case 3 (**The Linear Equation**)*   Suppose $F(x, y) = q(x) - yp(x)$ where $q$ and $p$ are continuous functions of $x$. Since $y$ occurs only to the first power, this is called a *linear* differential equation. The expression for $F(x, y)$ is linear in $y$, though not necessarily linear in $x$.

---

**EXAMPLE 4**  Consider the differential equation

$$\frac{dy}{dx} + 2xy = 2x \sin x + \cos x. \tag{10}$$

This equation is rewritten as

$$\frac{dy}{dx} = (2x \sin x + \cos x) - 2xy$$

from which we see that it is a linear differential equation with

$$q(x) = 2x \sin x + \cos x \quad \text{and} \quad p(x) = 2x.$$

I will now show you how to solve this particular linear equation before tackling the general case. What we do may seem strange and terribly un-motivated, but it has the advantage of working: (Motivation can be given, but we want this section to be reasonably short.)

Multiply each side of Eq. (10) by $e^{x^2}$. Since $e^{r(x)}$ is positive for all values of $x$ for any function $r(x)$, we obtain an equivalent equation:

$$e^{x^2}\frac{dy}{dx} + 2xe^{x^2}y = 2xe^{x^2} \sin x + e^{x^2} \cos x. \tag{11}$$

At first appearance, we have not improved the situation. It's the second look that counts: the left-hand side of Eq. (11) is precisely a derivative; in fact,

$$e^{x^2}\frac{dy}{dx} + 2xe^{x^2}y = \frac{d}{dx}(e^{x^2}y)$$

and so Eq. (11) may be rewritten as

$$\frac{d}{dx}(e^{x^2}y) = 2xe^{x^2} \sin x + e^{x^2} \cos x. \tag{12}$$

Now we may integrate each side of Eq. (12) with respect to $x$. The result is

$$e^{x^2}y = \int (2xe^{x^2} \sin x + e^{x^2} \cos x) \, dx \tag{13}$$

or

$$e^{x^2}y = e^{x^2} \sin x + C.$$

Simplifying, we obtain

$$y = \sin x + Ce^{-x^2}. \tag{14}$$

If we were asked to find the solution of Eq. (10) passing through $(0, -2)$, we simply set $x = 0$ and $y = -2$ in Eq. (14) in order to compute $C$:

$$-2 = 0 + C = C.$$

The unique solution of the differential equation passing through $(0, -2)$ is

$$y = \sin x - 2e^{-x^2}.$$

We are now ready to handle the general first-order linear differential equation

$$\frac{dy}{dx} + p(x)y = q(x).\tag{15}$$

The first step is to multiply each side of Eq. (15) by the *integrating factor* $e^{\int p(x)}$. Then the left-hand side of the resulting equation is an exact derivative and the differential equation can be written in the form

$$\frac{d}{dx}(e^{\int p(x)}y) = e^{\int p(x)}q(x).\tag{16}$$

Integration with respect to $x$ yields the solution:

$$e^{p(x)}y = \int e^{\int p(x)}q(x)\,dx.\tag{17}$$

It would be helpful to examine one final example of a linear differential equation:

**EXAMPLE 5**   Find the solution of the differential equation $dy/dx = x + y$ passing through $(0, 4)$.

**Solution**   Rewrite the differential equation in the form

$$\frac{dy}{dx} - 1y = x$$

from which we recognize that $p(x) = -1$ and $q(x) = x$. The integrating factor is $e^{\int -1\,dx} = e^{-x}$. Multiplication of the rewritten differential equation by $e^{-x}$ gives

$$e^{-x}\frac{dy}{dx} - e^{-x}y = xe^{-x},$$

which may be reorganized as

$$\frac{d}{dx}(e^{-x}y) = xe^{-x}.$$

Integration of each side with respect to $x$ gives

$$e^{-x}y = -e^{-x}(1 + x) + C$$

so that

$$y = Ce^{x} - (1 + x).$$

Since we are given that $y = 4$ when $x = 0$, we have $4 = C - (1 + 0)$; thus $C = 5$. Hence the unique solution of $dy/dx = x + y$ through $(0, 4)$ is $y = 5e^{x} - (1 + x)$.

**Implicit solutions**    In all of the examples presented here, the solution techniques described led to an explicit formula for $y$ in terms of $x$. This is not always possible and, even when possible, is not necessarily desirable. Consider, for example, the differential equation $dy/dx = -2x/y$. This is an example of an equation in which the variables separate. Integration and simple rearrangement yields

$$y^2 = C - 2x^2.$$

The solution to the original differential equation is either $y = (C - 2x^2)^{1/2}$ or $y = -(C - 2x^2)^{1/2}$ depending on the sign of the second coordinate of the initial point. In this example, it is more useful to consider the implicit relation between $x$ and $y$:

$$2x^2 + y^2 = C,$$

from which we see immediately that the points on the solution curve lie on an ellipse centered about the origin.

**Other differential equations**    We have presented solution techniques for only three particular types of first-order differential equations of the form $dy/dx = F(x, y)$. There are other large classes of functions $F(x, y)$ for which exact solutions can be obtained; some of these are discussed in the book by Bear listed in the References.

The type of differential equation we have discussed is called a *first-degree* equation because the derivative $dy/dx$ appears only to the first power. Higher-degree differential equations can also be studied. The equation

$$\left(\frac{dy}{dx}\right)^3 + \sin x \left(\frac{dy}{dx}\right) - \log x = e^{-x^2}$$

is an example of a third-degree equation.

Another way differential equations are classified is according to the highest order of differentiation that occurs. For example, the differential equation

$$\cos x \frac{d^2 y}{dx^2} + \tan^{-1} x \frac{dy}{dx} + \frac{1}{1 + x^2} = 0$$

is a second-order differential equation.

Three of the major areas studied in differential equations are

1. techniques for solving various special types of equations;
2. approximation methods to obtain numerical solutions to equations which cannot otherwise be solved; and
3. theoretical results on the existence, uniqueness, and qualitative behavior of solutions.

This appendix deals with the first topic; an example of the second topic is given in Chapter 2, while Chapter 4 illustrates what can be done in the third area.

## EXERCISES

Find the unique solution of each of the following differential equations of the form $dy/dx = F(x, y)$ passing through the point $(x_0, y_0)$.   The function $F$ is stated first, followed by the initial point.

1.  $x; (2, -3)$

2.  $\cos x; (0, 1)$

3.  $1/(1 + x^2); (1, 0)$

4.  $2y; (0, 2)$

5.  $2xy; (0, 2)$

6.  $x/y^2; (1, 0)$

7.  $y/x; (1, 1)$

8.  $xy + x; (0, 0)$

9.  $x^2 - (y/x); (1, 0)$

10.  $\sin x - y; (0, 2)$

## REFERENCES

Bear, H. S., *Differential Equations* (Reading, Mass.: Addison-Wesley, 1962).

Bellman, Richard, and Kenneth Cooke, *Modern Elementary Differential Equations* (Reading, Mass.: Addison-Wesley, 1971).

# Bibliography

There is quite a large literature on mathematical models in the social and life sciences. In addition to the references at the end of each chapter in the text, we list here a few titles in each of a dozen important areas.

## *General*

Blalock, H. M., Jr., *Theory Construction: From Verbal to Mathematical Formulations*, (Englewood Cliffs, N.J.: Prentice-Hall, 1969).

Charlesworth, J. C., ed., *Mathematics and the Social Sciences* (symposium sponsored by American Academy of Political and Social Sciences, Philadelphia, 1963).

Freudenthal, H., ed., *The Concept and the Role of the Model in Mathematics and Natural and Social Sciences* (New York: Gordon-Breach, 1961).

Lazarsfield, Paul F., ed., *Mathematical Thinking in the Social Sciences* (Chicago: Free Press, 1954).

———, ed., *Readings in Mathematical Social Science* (Cambridge: M.I.T. Press, 1966).

Roberts, Fred S., *Discrete Mathematical Models with Applications to Social, Biological, and Environmental Problems* (Englewood Cliffs, N.J.: Prentice-Hall, 1976)

## *Anthropology*

Banton, M., *The Relevance of Models for Social Anthropology* (New York: Praeger, 1965).

Key, Paul, ed., *Explorations in Mathematical Anthropology* (Cambridge: M.I.T. Press, 1971).

White, D. R., "Mathematical anthropology," in J. J. Honigmann, ed., *Handbook of Social and Cultural Anthropology* (Chicago: Rand-McNally, 1972).

White, Harrison C., *An Anatomy of Kinship: Mathematical Models for Structures of Cumulated Roles* (Englewood Cliffs, N.J.: Prentice-Hall, 1963).

### Biology
Iosifescu, M., and P. Tautu, *Stochastic Processes and Applications in Biology and Medicine* (New York: Springer-Verlag, 1973).

Lotka, A., *Elements of Mathematical Biology* (New York: Dover, 1956).

Moorhead, Paul S., and Martin M. Kaplan, eds., *Mathematical Challenges to the Neo-Darwinian Interpretation of Evolution* (Philadelphia: Wistar Institute Press, 1967).

Smith, J. Maynard, *Mathematical Ideas in Biology* (Cambridge: Cambridge University Press, 1971).

———, *Models in Ecology* (Cambridge: Cambridge University Press; 1974).

Thom, Rene, *Structural Stability and Morphogenesis* (Reading, Mass.: Benjamin, 1975).

### Economics
Allen, R. G. D., *Mathematical Economics* (London: Macmillan, 1956).

Arrow, Kenneth J., and Tibor Scitovsky, *Readings in Welfare Economics* (Homewood, Ill.: Irwin, 1969).

Henderson, J., and R. Quandt, *Microeconomic Theory* (New York: McGraw-Hill, 1958).

Leontieff, W., *Input-Output Economics* (New York: Oxford University Press, 1966).

Puckett, Richard H., *Introduction to Mathematical Economics* (Lexington, Mass: Heath, 1971).

Hadar, Josef, *Mathematical Theory of Economic Behavior* (Reading, Mass.: Addison-Wesley, 1971).

### Geography
Chorley, R. J., and P. Haggett, eds., *Models in Geography* (London: Methuen, 1967).

Cole, J. P., and C. A. M. King, *Quantitative Geography* (London: Wiley, 1968).

King, Cuchlaine A. M., "Mathematics in geography," *International Journal of Mathematics Education, Science, and Technology* 1 (1970), 185–205.

### History
Rashevsky, N., *Looking at History Through Mathematics* (Cambridge: M.I.T. Press, 1968).

Swierenga, Robert P., ed., *Quantification in American History* (New York: Atheneum, 1970).

### Language and Linguistics
Brainerd, B., *Introduction to the Mathematics of Language Study* (New York: American Elsevier, 1971).

Gross, Maurice, *Mathematical Models in Linguistics* (Englewood Cliffs, N.J.: Prentice-Hall, 1972).

Harris, Z. S., *Mathematical Structure of Language* (New York: Wiley, 1968).

Wall, Robert, *Introduction to Mathematical Linguistics* (Englewood Cliffs, N.J.: Prentice-Hall, 1972).

## Law

Finkelstein, Michael O., and William B. Fairley, "A Bayesian approach to identification evidence," *Harvard Law Review* **83** (1970), 489–517.

Schubert, Glendon A., *Quantitative Analysis of Judicial Behavior* (Glencoe: Free Press, 1959).

Tribe, Laurence H., "Trial by mathematics," *Harvard Law Review* **84** (1971), 1329–1393.

## Learning Theory

Atkinson, R. C.; G. H. Bower; and E. J. Crothers, *An Introduction to Mathematical Learning Theory* (New York: Wiley, 1965).

Bush, R. R., and W. K. Estes, eds., *Studies in Mathematical Learning Theory* (Stanford: Stanford University Press, 1959).

Bush, R. R., and C. F. Mosteller, *Stochastic Models for Learning* (New York: Wiley, 1955).

## Management

Gaver, Donald P., and Gerald L. Thompson, *Programming and Probability Models in Operations Research* (Monterey, Calif.: Brooks/Cole, 1973).

Hillier, Frederick S., and Gerald L. J. Lieberman, *Introduction to Operations Research* (San Francisco: Holden-Day, 1967).

Masser, Ian, *Analytical Models for Urban and Regional Planning* (New York: Wiley, 1972).

Massy, William F.; David D. Montgomery; and Donald G. Morison, *Stochastic Models of Buying Behavior* (Cambridge: M.I.T. Press, 1970).

## Political Science

Alker, H. R.; K. Deutsch; and A. H. Stoetzel, *Mathematical Approaches to Politics* (San Francisco: Jossey, Bass, 1973).

Bernd, Joseph L., ed., *Mathematical Applications in Political Science II* (Dallas: Southern Methodist University Press, 1966).

Bernd, Joseph L., and James F. Herndon, eds., *Mathematical Applications in Political Science*, III, IV, V, VI (Charlottesville: University of Virginia Press, 1967, 1969, 1971, 1972).

Claund, J. M., ed., *Mathematical Applications in Political Science*, I (Dallas: Arnold Foundation Monographs, Southern Methodist University Press, 1965).

Howard, Nigel, *Paradoxes of Rationality: Theory of Metagames and Political Behavior* (Cambridge: M.I.T. Press, 1971).

## Psychology

Atkinson, R. C., ed., *Studies in Mathematical Psychology* (Stanford: Stanford University Press, 1964).

Coombs, Clyde H.; Robyn M. Dawes; and Amos Tversky, *Mathematical Psychology, an Elementary Introduction* (Englewood Cliffs, N.J.: Prentice-Hall, 1970).

Krantz, David H.; Richard C. Atkinson; R. Duncan Luce; and Patrick Suppes, eds., *Contemporary Developments in Mathematical Psychology*, 2 vols. (San Francisco: Freeman, 1974).

Luce, R. Duncan; R. R. Bush; and Eugene Galanter, eds., *Handbook of Mathematical Psychology*, I, II, III (New York: Wiley, 1963, 1963, 1965).

_____, *Readings in Mathematical Psychology* (New York: Wiley, 1963).

Restle, Frank, and James G. Greeno, *Introduction to Mathematical Psychology* (Reading, Mass.: Addison-Wesley, 1970).

### Sociology

Bartholomew, David, *Stochastic Models for Social Processes* (New York: Wiley, 1967).

Boudon, Raymond, *Mathematical Structures of Social Mobility* (San Francisco: Jossey-Bass, 1973).

Coleman, James S., *Introduction to Mathematical Sociology* (New York: Free Press, 1964).

Fararo, Thomas J., *Mathematical Sociology: An Introduction to Fundamentals* (New York: Wiley, 1973).

Halmos, Paul, ed., "Stochastic processes in sociology," *Sociological Review Monograph*, 1974.

## JOURNALS OF INTEREST

The journals listed below, readily available in most college and university libraries, regularly publish articles employing mathematical models in the social and life sciences.

*Acta Sociologica*
*American Economic Review*
*American Journal of Psychology*
*American Journal of Sociology*
*American Political Science Review*
*Annals of Economic and Social Measurement*

*Behavioral Science*
*Bell Journal of Economics and Management Science*
*Biometrics*
*Biometrika*
*Biotechnology and Bioengineering*
*British Journal of Mathematical and Statistical Psychology*
*Brookings Papers on Economic Activity*
*Bulletin of Mathematical Biology*
*Bulletin of Mathematical Biophysics*

*Canadian Journal of Economics and Political Science*

*Decision Sciences*
*Demography*

*Ecology*
*Econometrica*
*Economica*
*Economic Geography*
*Economic Journal*

*General Systems*
*Geographical Analysis*

*Human Relations*

*Indian Economic Journal*
*Information and Control*
*Interfaces*
*International Economic Review*
*International Journal of Game Theory*

*Journal of American Statistical Association*
*Journal of Applied Probability*
*Journal of Conflict Resolution*
*Journal of Economic Behavior*
*Journal of Economic Theory*
*Journal of Experimental Psychology*
*Journal of Finance*
*Journal of Mathematical Biology*
*Journal of Mathematical Economics*
*Journal of Mathematical Psychology*
*Journal of Mathematical Sociology*
*Journal of Peace Research*
*Journal of Political Economy*
*Journal of Royal Statistical Society*
*Journal of Theoretical Biology*

*Management Science*
*Mathematical Biosciences*
*Metroeconomica*

*Naval Research Logistics Quarterly*
*Networks*

*Operational Research Quarterly*
*Operations Research*
*Oxford Economic Papers*

*Peace Research Society (International) Papers*
*Population*
*Population Studies*
*Psychological Review*
*Psychometrika*

*Quality and Quantity*
*Quarterly Review of Economics*

*Review of Economic Studies*

*Sankhya*
*Selected Rand Abstracts*
*SIAM: Journal of Applied Mathematics*
*Simulation*
*Sociological Methodology*
*Sociology*

*Sociometry*

*Synthese*

*Theoretical Population Biology*

*Transportation Research*

*Transportation Science*

# Answers to Selected Exercises

## CHAPTER 1

12. a) $t_F = \sqrt{-2y_0/g}$

    b) $g = -2y_0/t_F^2$ and $y_0$, $t_F$ are measurable from observations.

13. $t_F = \dfrac{v_0 \pm \sqrt{v_0^2 + 64y_0}}{32}$         14. $-\sqrt{v_0^2 + 64y_0}$

15. a) 4 feet.   b) $\frac{1}{2}$ second.   c) $\frac{3}{4}$ second.   d) $-16$ feet/second.   e) 16 feet/second.

16. No. Wonder Woman reaches the ground about 9.59 seconds after the man falls. He hits the ground after 8 seconds.

18. $c^2 < 16R^2/(16 + R)$          19. $-2R < y_0 < 4 - R$

20. $x = 88t$, $y = -16t^2 + H$, where $x$ and $y$ are measured in feet and $H$ is the height of the cliff.

21. The bomb takes 50 seconds to reach the earth. The airplane can fly $8\frac{1}{3}$ miles during this time.

## CHAPTER 2

3. b) $C = 2$, $D = 1$

9. b) $m_1 = \sqrt{ab}$, $m_2 = -\sqrt{ab}$

f) $C = (ay_0 + \sqrt{ab}x_0)/(2\sqrt{ab})$, $D = (x_0\sqrt{ab} - ay_0)/(2\sqrt{ab})$

h) $\infty$

10. $g(t) = \dfrac{(\sqrt{ab}y_0 + bx_0)e^{\sqrt{ab}t} + (\sqrt{ab}y_0 - bx_0)e^{-\sqrt{ab}t}}{2\sqrt{ab}}$

11. $A = (1/7)(-1 + 3x_0 + 4y_0)$, $B = (1/7)[x_0 - y_0 + (19/6)]$

14. The lines are parallel if and only if $mn = ab$. There is a runaway arms race if the $y$-intercept of $L'$ is greater than the $y$-intercept of $L$. If the $y$-intercept of $L'$ is smaller than that of $L$, mutual disarmament results.

20. a) At $t = .59$, both $dx/dt$ and $dy/dt$ become positive.

21. a)2.5   b) 2.47368

22. With $\Delta t = .1$, both $dx/dt$ and $dy/dt$ become negative at $t = .8$. With $\Delta t = 1$, the signs of the derivatives change with each increment of $t$.

25. b) $A = 2 - \sqrt{6}$, $B = 2 + \sqrt{6}$

## CHAPTER 3

1. $1000(3/2)^{24}$ which is approximately 16,834,112.

2. Rate of growth is $(\log 3)/20$ which is approximately .055.

3. No. If population doubles in 50 years, it will quadruple in 100 years.

4. $a = (1/t_1) \log(P_1/P_0)$

6. $45(\log 3/\log 2)$ or approximately 71.32 years.

7. a) $P = 100{,}000e^{(1/10)t \log 5}$   b) 2.5 million   c) $t_1 = 10 \log 2/\log 5$

8. 34.7 years.

12. $dP/dt = \alpha P^k$ gives $P = [(1 - k)\alpha t + P_0^{1-k}]^{1/(1-k)}$.

13. $\dfrac{4 - \sqrt{2}}{4}$      15. About 7400 years ago.

16. 10 log 10,000, or approximately 92.1 years.

18. a) $P(t) = P_0 + at$   b) $P(t) = (1/b)[(a + P_0b)e^{bt} - a]$

d) $P(t) = (a/b)[\cos c - \cos(bt + c)] + P_0$

21. Point of inflection occurs when population is at $a/2b$, one-half of the carrying capacity. This occurs at $t = d/a = (-1/a)\log(bK)$.

23. Using census data from 1790, 1850, and 1910 to determine the constants, the rate of population growth begins to slow down sometime in 1915.

25. With 1870, 1920, and 1970 census figures, $d \approx 1.962$, $a = .0258$, and the carrying capacity, $k$, is 312.86 million.

26. With 1790, 1880, and 1970 census figures, $d = 4.164$, $a = .0305$, and the carrying capacity, $k$, is 256.76 million.

27. a) $P(t) = (100{,}000)/(1 + e^{d-at})$ where $d = 6.907$ and $a = .1825$.   b) 54 years.

30. b) $x(t) = N/(1 + Ce^{-Nkt})$ where $C$ is a constant of integration.   d) $N$

## CHAPTER 4

|  | $F$ | $G$ | $F_x$ | $F_y$ | $G_x$ | $G_y$ |
|---|---|---|---|---|---|---|
| 7. a) | $ay - mx + r$ | $bx - ny + s$ | $-m$ | $a$ | $b$ | $-n$ |
| b) | $ax - byx$ | $mxy - ny$ | $a - by$ | $-bx$ | $my$ | $mx - n$ |
| c) | $ax - byx$ | $my - nxy$ | $a - by$ | $-bx$ | $-ny$ | $m - nx$ |

9. See Exercise 15 of Chapter 2.

15. $x = Ce^{-t}$, $y = De^{-t}$ for any constants $C$ and $D$ are solutions.

17. a) $f(1 + h, 2 + k) \approx 2 - 2h + k$    b) $f(0 + h, 0 + k) \approx 0 + 0h + 0k$
    c) $f(4 + h, 1 + k) \approx 1 + \log 4 + h/4 + k/2$

20. a) When $x > 0$, both factors, $x^m$ and $e^{-nx}$ are positive.
    d) $f'(x) = x^{m-1}e^{-nx}(m - nx)$
    e) $f''(x) = x^{m-2}e^{-nx}(n^2x^2 - 2mnx + m^2 - m)$. Points of inflection occur when $x = (m/n) \pm (\sqrt{m}/n)$. Curve is concave down for all $x$ such that $|x - (m/n)| < \sqrt{m}/n$.

## CHAPTER 5

1. c) $(100, 200)$

2. a) $\{(x, y): 5x + 2y = 1000, 140 \leqslant x \leqslant 200\}$   b) $M = 2000 - 5.5x$   c) $(140, 150)$

4. a) $(200, 0)$   b) $(140, 150)$   c) $(100, 200)$   d) $(0, 250)$

5. $(100, 200)$                    6. $M = 1300$

8. Vertices are $(0, 0)$, $(200, 0)$, $(140, 150)$, $(120, 175)$, $(80, 210)$, $(0, 250)$. Maximum revenue is $1423.50 and occurs at $(120, 175)$.

9. 136 packages of Aristocrat mixture and 120 packages of Regency assortment.

10. Let $x, y, z, w$ be the number of packages of Fancy, Deluxe, Aristocrat, and Regency mixtures to be prepared. The problem is to maximize $4.5x + 4y + 4.1z + 4.9w$ subject to restrictions:

$$30x + 12y + 25z + 10z \leqslant 6000$$
$$10x + 8y + 5z + 16z \leqslant 2600$$
$$4x + 8y + 10z + 5\tfrac{1}{3}x \leqslant 2000$$
$$x \geqslant 0, y \geqslant 0, z \geqslant, x \geqslant 0$$

15. b) Maximize $3x + 2y$ subject to $x \leqslant 4$, $x + y \leqslant 9$, $-x + y \leqslant 5$, $x \geqslant 0$, $y \geqslant 0$.

17. 100 variables, 45 constraints.

18. $A$: Dogoff, $B$: Josephs, $C$: Cragdodge, $D$: Reapingwillst

22. If $x$ is the number of males and $y$ the number of females, the problem is to find nonnegative values for $x$ and $y$ such that $2400x + 2000y$ is minimized, subject to restrictions:

$$8000x + 3000y \geqslant 2{,}500{,}000$$
$$200x + 100y \leqslant 85{,}000$$
$$1200x + 1300y \geqslant 1250 \quad (x + y)$$

25. If $x, y, z$ represent the number of photographs, reprints, and original essays, respectively, then we need

$$x + y + z = 40$$
$$x \geqslant 12$$
$$z \geqslant y$$
$$y \leqslant 10$$
$$z \leqslant 20.$$

27. $\mathbf{c} = (3,4)$, $\mathbf{b} = \begin{pmatrix} 3 \\ 2 \\ 8 \end{pmatrix}$, and $A = \begin{pmatrix} 1 & 2 \\ 1 & 1 \\ 0 & 1 \end{pmatrix}$

29. $\mathbf{x} = \begin{pmatrix} 2.4 \\ .4 \end{pmatrix}$                    30. Unbounded solution.

46. a) Yes.   b) Yes.   c) No.

59. $x = -4 + 5u - 23v$                    61. 2 iterations are necessary.
    $y = -3.5 + 4.5u - 21v$
    $w = 3 - 4u + 15v$

64. $x - 116\frac{2}{3}, y = 166\frac{2}{3}, z = 20$                    65. Unbounded solution.

66. Optimal mixture in all three cases is 20 photographs, 20 original essays, 0 reprints.

67. $x = 1, y - 1, M = 7$                    70. Make 2700 Atlantic pins.

71. $x = 13/15, y = 32/45$                    73. $x_1 = 0, x_2 = 2, x_3 = 1, m = 19$

74. $x_1 = 0, x_2 = 4$                    75. Unbounded solution

76. $x = 10, y = 0$                    77. $x_1 = 5/3, x_2 = x_3 = x_4 = 0$

78. $\mathbf{x} = (10/9, 20/9, 5/9)$                    79. $x_1 = 80/11, x_2 = 0, x_3 = 70/11, x_4 = 0$

## CHAPTER 6

4. No. A defeats B and B defeats C, but C defeats A.

10. $x:12, z:9, y:7, w:5$.

## CHAPTER 7

2. $A * B$ and $B * A$

5. 
| Example | Reflexive | Symmetric | Transitive | Connected |
|---------|-----------|-----------|------------|-----------|
| 1 | No | No | Yes | No |
| 2 | Yes | Yes | Yes | No |
| 3 | Yes | No | Yes | Yes |
| 7 | No | No | Yes | No |
| 8 | No | No | Yes | Yes |
| 11 | No | No | No | Yes |
| 12 | No | No | Yes | Yes |

6. Transitive, but not connected.

10. Strong orders: $>$, $<$                         13.  5 equivalence classes.
    Weak orders: $\geqslant$, $\leqslant$
    Equivalence relation: $=$

20. b) $m(y) = 0$, $m(z) = 1$, $m(x) = 2$, $m(w) = 3$

34. a) $S =$ integers and $x \triangle y = x - y$

## CHAPTER 8

17. No.

18. b) $\alpha = (a_2 - a_1)/(t_2 - t_1)$, $\beta = (a_1 t_2 - a_2 t_1)/(t_2 - t_1)$

20. $u(x) = 1$, $u(y) = .3$, $u(z) = 0$                         22.  Hamburger $I$ .6 tuna + .4 peanut butter.

25. Ann in Computer Methods, Joan in Plate Tectonics, Kathy in Relativity Theory.

26. Same solution as in Exercise 25.

## CHAPTER 9

4. $\text{Pr}(\text{head}) = 8/9$                 8.  3/10                             9.  53/60

11. a) 1/6   b) 1/2   c) 1/4   d) 17/36

12. b) 1 to 2                         13.  c) 1/3                         16.  2/3

18. Solution 2.                       19.  1/2                           20.  5/51

21. $\text{Pr}(X) = 0$ or $\text{Pr}(Y) = 0$                 22.  a) 3/4   b) 21/32

25. a) $4! = 24$, $5! = 120$, $6! = 720$

26. a) $1, 6, 15, 20, 15, 6, 1$                         29.  $102p - 81q = 1$.

30. Probability of winning a round is 244/495.  Expected value is $-7/9$ dollars.

31. $-1.35$ cents.                         33.  d) $np$

37. Variances: New Haven (0), Bristol ($9.9 \times 10^9$), Ferrisburg ($6.6 \times 10^6$)

38. Expected value: $-.4$, Variance: 1.44, Standard deviation: 1.2

40. a) Expected value: 4, Variance: 2, Standard deviation: $\sqrt{2}$
    b) Expected value: 24/5, Variance: 48/25, Standard deviation: $(4/5)\sqrt{3}$

47. $P_{A+3}(t) = \dfrac{(A + 2)(A + 1)A}{6} e^{-bAt}(1 - e^{-bt})^3$

50. $t = (1/b) \log(N/A)$                         53.  b) 2/9

55. a) .0915   b) .2562   c) .6083

## CHAPTER 10

1. Transition matrix is:

$$
\begin{array}{cc}
 & \begin{array}{cc} \text{PP} & \text{EH} \end{array} \\
\begin{array}{c} \text{PP} \\ \text{EH} \end{array} & \begin{pmatrix} .6 & .4 \\ .5 & .5 \end{pmatrix}
\end{array}
$$

2. Transition matrix is:

$$
\begin{array}{c}
 & \begin{array}{cc} \text{Candy} & \text{Toys} \end{array} \\
\begin{array}{c} \text{Candy} \\ \text{Toys} \end{array} &
\left( \begin{array}{cc}
.4 & .6 \\
.8 & .2
\end{array} \right)
\end{array}
$$

3. Transition matrix is:

$$
\begin{array}{c}
 & \begin{array}{ccc} \text{Conservative} & \text{Labor} & \text{NDP} \end{array} \\
\begin{array}{c} \text{Conservative} \\ \text{Labor} \\ \text{NDP} \end{array} &
\left( \begin{array}{ccc}
.8 & .2 & 0 \\
.2 & .6 & .2 \\
.1 & .15 & .75
\end{array} \right)
\end{array}
$$

4. The transition matrix is:

$$
\begin{array}{c}
 & \begin{array}{cccc} \text{War} & \text{Disarmament} & \text{Escalation} & \text{De-escalation} \end{array} \\
\begin{array}{c} \text{War} \\ \text{Total disarmament} \\ \text{Escalation} \\ \text{De-escalation} \end{array} &
\left( \begin{array}{cccc}
1 & 0 & 0 & 0 \\
0 & 1 & 0 & 0 \\
.2 & 0 & .6 & .2 \\
0 & .2 & .1 & .7
\end{array} \right)
\end{array}
$$

6. Transition matrix has the form:

|   | 0 | 1 | 2 | 3 | 4 |
|---|---|---|---|---|---|
| 0 | 1 | 0 | 0 | 0 | 0 |
| 1 | .5 | 0 | .5 | 0 | 0 |
| 2 | 0 | .5 | 0 | .5 | 0 |
| 3 | 0 | 0 | .5 | 0 | .5 |
| 4 | 0 | 0 | 0 | 0 | 1 |

7. Transition matrix has the form:

|   | 0 | 1 | 2 | 3 | 4 |
|---|---|---|---|---|---|
| 0 | 0 | 1 | 0 | 0 | 0 |
| 1 | .5 | 0 | .5 | 0 | 0 |
| 2 | 0 | .5 | 0 | .5 | 0 |
| 3 | 0 | 0 | .5 | 0 | .5 |
| 4 | 0 | 0 | 0 | 1 | 0 |

15. .4432

16. $(.365, .42, .215)$

17. Distribution of mothers' birthweights is given by $(.2, .6, .2)$.

18. $a(1 - b) + (1 - a)(1 - c)$

19. $P^2 = \begin{pmatrix} 0 & ab + (1 - a)c & a(1 - b) + (1 - a)(1 - c) \\ 0 & b^2 + (1 - b)c & b(1 - b) + (1 - b)(1 - c) \\ 0 & bc + (1 - c)c & c(1 - b) + (1 - c)^2 \end{pmatrix}$

21. Exercises 1–3 are examples of regular Markov processes.

24. One day a week.

25. Pollution Products captures 5/9 of the market.

26. Abby spends her allowance on candy 4/7 of the time.

27. Conservatives get 7/16 of vote, Labor gets 5/16, and NDP gets 4/16.

28. The long range distribution of professionals, skilled, and unskilled laborers is given by (30/57, 15/57, 12/57).

29. $I - (P - W) = \begin{pmatrix} 61/70 & 9/70 \\ 12/70 & 58/70 \end{pmatrix}$

and its inverse is $\begin{pmatrix} 406/343 & -63/343 \\ -84/343 & 427/343 \end{pmatrix}$.

32. Exercises 4 and 6 give examples of absorbing Markov processes.

33. The probability of a war if the initial state is escalation is .6. The probability of war if initial state is de-escalation is .2. If there is an escalating arms race this year, then the average number of years before absorption is 5.

39. Let $x, y, z$ denote duelists with probabilities of 1/2, 1/3, and 1/6 of killing the opponent at which each aims. The transition matrix has the form:

|          | None | x    | y    | z    | x, z | y, z  | x, y, z |
|----------|------|------|------|------|------|-------|---------|
| None     | 1    | 0    | 0    | 0    | 0    | 0     | 0       |
| x        | 0    | 1    | 0    | 0    | 0    | 0     | 0       |
| y        | 0    | 0    | 1    | 0    | 0    | 0     | 0       |
| z        | 0    | 0    | 0    | 1    | 0    | 0     | 0       |
| x, z     | 1/12 | 5/12 | 0    | 1/12 | 5/12 | 0     | 0       |
| y, z     | 1/18 | 0    | 5/18 | 2/18 | 0    | 10/18 | 0       |
| x, y, z  | 0    | 0    | 0    | 4/18 | 5/18 | 4/18  | 5/18    |

Then $N = \begin{pmatrix} 12/7 & 0 & 0 \\ 0 & 9/4 & 0 \\ 60/91 & 9/13 & 18/13 \end{pmatrix}$

and $B = \begin{pmatrix} 1/7 & 5/7 & 0 & 1/7 \\ 1/8 & 0 & 5/8 & 1/4 \\ 17/182 & 40/91 & 5/26 & 25/91 \end{pmatrix}$.

Thus the probability that all three will be killed is 17/182. Note that when the duel begins, $x$ fires at $y$, while $y$ and $z$ fire at $x$.

40. On the average, it takes 6 plays of the game. The probability that Ron wins all $5 if he begins with $2 is .4.

42. Fixed point stochastic vector is (.25, .5, .25).

## CHAPTER 11

1. Eli will be 76 and Alexander 70.        2. Yes; Yes.

11. a) $\mathbf{p}^{(1)} = (.154, .384, .462)$, $\mathbf{p}^{(2)} = (.257, .49, .253)$, $\mathbf{p}^{(3)} = (.27, .446, .284)$

    b) $\mathbf{p}^{(1)} = (.24, .461, .298)$, $\mathbf{p}^{(2)} = (.266, .456, .278)$, $\mathbf{p}^{(3)} = (.264, .451, .285)$

    c) $\mathbf{p}^{(1)} = (.325, .45, .225)$, $\mathbf{p}^{(2)} = (.26, .44, .3)$, $\mathbf{p}^{(3)} = (.261, .456, .283)$

12. a) $\mathbf{p}^{(1)} = (.6, .3, .1)$, $\mathbf{p}^{(2)} = (.4, .44, .16)$, $\mathbf{p}^{(3)} = (.3, .504, .196)$

    b) $\mathbf{p}^{(1)} = (.267, .433, .3)$, $\mathbf{p}^{(2)} = (.233, .487, .28)$, $\mathbf{p}^{(3)} = (.217, .515, .268)$

    c) $\mathbf{p}^{(1)} = (.1, .65, .25)$, $\mathbf{p}^{(2)} = (.15, .6, .25)$, $\mathbf{p}^{(3)} = (.175, .575, .25)$

13. Each vector is (1/3, 1/3, 1/3).

14. a) $(.2, .55, .25)$   b) $(1/3, 1/3, 1/3)$
15. a) $\mathbf{p}^{(1)} = (.09, .23, .315, .365)$, $\mathbf{p}^{(2)} = (.091, .246, .323, .34)$
    b) Markov process is regular since each entry of $P^2$ is positive. The fixed point stochastic vector is $(4/35, 2/7, 1/3, 4/15)$.

## CHAPTER 12

1. c) $a/(1 - r)$   d) Diverges in all three cases.
3. $\mathbf{p}^{(k)} = (1/2)(2 - (1 - c)^k, (1 - c)^k)$            17. c) $EV(A) = u_1$

## CHAPTER 13

13. a) $I = I_0 e^{(\beta S_0 - r)t}$, $R = r\left(R_0 + \dfrac{I_0}{\beta S_0 - r}[e^{(\beta S_0 - r)t} - 1]\right)$
16. 1.41                                    17. 151
21. a) $R = N - S_0 - (N - S_0 - R_0)e^{-rt}$
23. $R_\infty \sim 2pv/(p + v)$ gives 180, $R_\infty \sim 2v$ gives 200.
24. $R_\infty \sim 2pv/(p + v)$ gives 495, $R_\infty \sim 2v$ gives 1100.

## CHAPTER 14

1. 31    2. 283    3. 415    4. 4.3 percent.    7. 4.98 days
9. Room 5 had 7 procedures, rooms 3 and 4 had 6 each, and rooms 1 and 2 had 4 each. Average number was 5.4 procedures.
10. Operating room 2 was used for longest period. Each room was used an average of 5.88 hours.

## APPENDIX II

1. a) $(8, 4, 6)$   b) $(2, -3, 0)$   c) $(16, 0, 9)$   d) $(3, 3, 4)$   e) $(5, 0, 4)$   f) $(20, 1, 14)$
2. a) $3 \times 4$   b) Undefined.   c) $4 \times 4$   d) Undefined.   e) $5 \times 4$

7. a) $\begin{pmatrix} 5 & 6 \\ -5 & -3 \\ 12 & 3 \end{pmatrix}$   b) $\begin{pmatrix} 5 & 6 \\ -11 & 6 \\ 0 & 0 \end{pmatrix}$   c) $\begin{pmatrix} -26 & 3 \\ 58 & 21 \\ 17 & 15 \end{pmatrix}$   d) $\begin{pmatrix} -5 & -6 & -9 \\ 13 & 9 & -3 \\ 11 & 0 & 0 \end{pmatrix}$

11. $A = \begin{pmatrix} 2 & -3 \\ 9 & 7 \end{pmatrix}$, $u = \begin{pmatrix} x \\ y \end{pmatrix}$, $v = \begin{pmatrix} 46 \\ 27 \end{pmatrix}$

13. b) No.                                    14. b) Yes.
15. a) $B^2$   b) $B^3$   c) $(\frac{1}{2})B$   d) $-B^7$   e) $A^2$   f) $B$

## APPENDIX III

1. $x_1 = 3$, $x_2 = -2$, $x_3 = 2$
2. $x_1 = -10 - 7x_3$, $x_2 = -6 - 5x_3$, $x_3$ is arbitrary.

3. $x = -10.5$, $y = 5.5$, $z = 2.5$

4. $x = (1/4)(17 + u - 5w)$, $y = (1/8)(33 + u - 9w)$, $z = (1/4)(-15 - 3u - 1w)$

5. $w = 2.4 - y - .4z$, $x = 3.8 - y - 1.8z$

11. $A^{-1} = \begin{pmatrix} 4 & -1 \\ -11 & 3 \end{pmatrix}$, $B^{-1} = \begin{pmatrix} 5 & -6 \\ -4 & 5 \end{pmatrix}$, $C$ has no inverse;

$D^{-1} = \begin{pmatrix} 0 & 1 \\ 1 & 0 \end{pmatrix}$, $E$ has no inverse, $F^{-1} = \begin{pmatrix} 0 & 1 & 0 \\ 0 & 0 & 1 \\ 1 & 0 & 0 \end{pmatrix}$.

14. 400 pounds of wood, 700 pounds of plastic.

## APPENDIX IV

1. a) $f_x(x, y) = \sin x \cos y$, $f_y(x, y) = -\sin x \sin y$

   b) $f_x(x, y) = 2x + x \cos(x + y) + \sin(x + y)$, $f_y(x, y) = x \cos(x + y)$

   c) $f_x(x, y) = e^{x + 2y}$, $f_y(x, y) = 2e^{x + 2y}$

   d) $f_x = 1/(x - y^2)$, $f_y(x, y) = (-2y)/(x - y^2)$

3. a) 0   b) 0

## APPENDIX V

1. $y = (1/2)(x^2 - 10)$

2. $y = 1 + \sin x$

3. $y = \arctan x - (\pi/4)$

4. $y = 2e^{2x}$

5. $y = 2e^{x^2}$

6. $y = [(3/2)(x^2 - 1)]^{1/3}$

7. $y = x$

8. $y = e^{x^2/2} - 1$

9. $y = (1/4)\left(3x^2 + \dfrac{1}{x^2}\right)$

10. $y = (1/2)(\sin x - \cos x + 5e^{-x})$

# Index

WESTMAR COLLEGE LIBRARY